# A LATIN READER FOR THE STUDY OF EARLY ENGLISH LAW

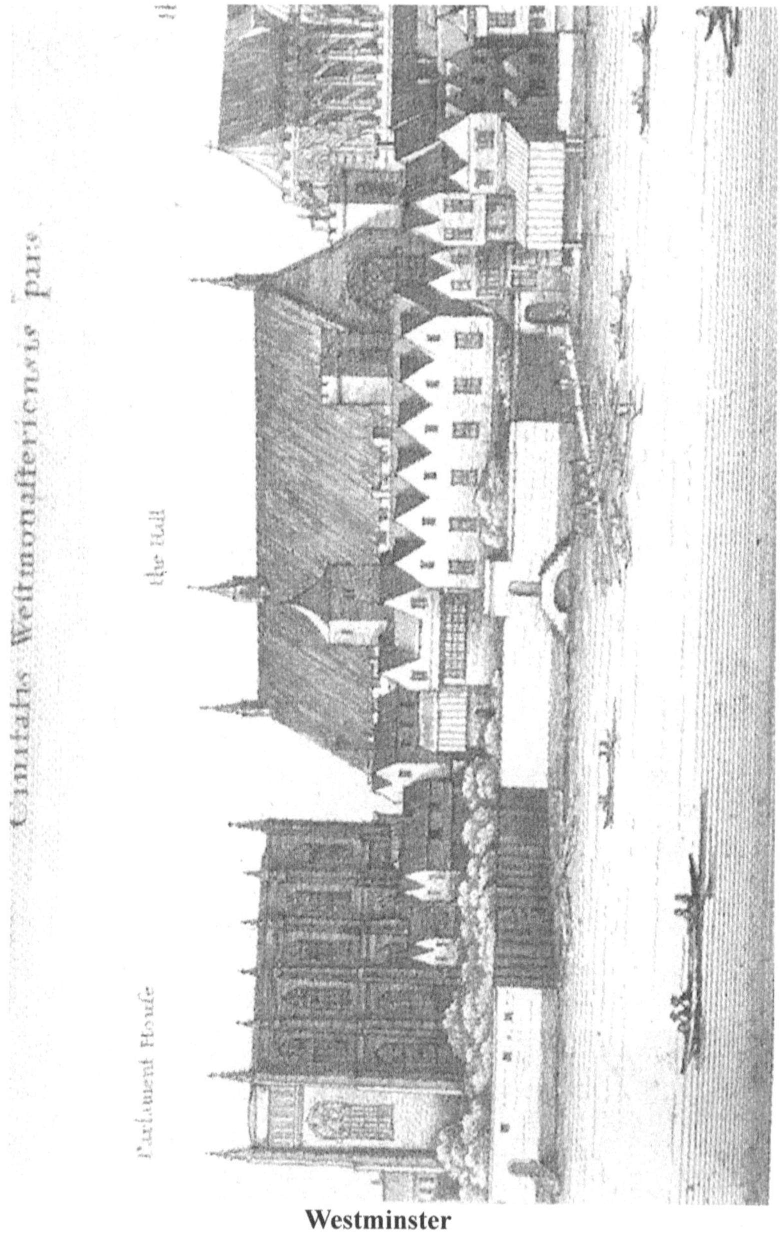


**Westminster**

# A Latin Reader for the Study of Early English Law:

*With Introductions, Selections, Translations, Notes, & Glossary*

By

Robert J. Meindl

&

Mark T. Riley

SOPHRON EDITOR
2018

ISBN 13: 978-0-9991401-5-4

ISBN 10: 09991401-59

**Illustrations:**



## Acknowledgements

Of the many friends and colleagues who gave freely of their time and knowledge toward the creation of this book, the authors are particularly grateful to: Dr. Gabriela Kompatscher Gufler of the University of Innsbruck, Prof. Conrad van Dyk of Concordia University, and Prof. R. F. Yeager of the University of West Florida.

Design by Sophron Editor

# CONTENTS

# INTRODUCTION

The history of English law is indissolubly linked to Latin, the language in which it first acquired the status of a discipline. Beginning in customary Old English legal formulations prior to the Conquest, the law in England undertook a grand new phase of its development under the Norman kings and their successors, who initially employed Latin as the language of the law before it yielded to French and English in their turn. The customary law of the Anglo-Saxons gradually gave way, grudgingly, to the law common to the king's courts and subjects, the common law, which was initially shaped in the prestigious classical language by the conclusions of various royal assemblies that were issued as ordinances, statutes, assizes, constitutions, establishments and other titles from the array of words used to designate legislation in the middle ages.[1] Under England's new kings, a coherent body of royal law began to shape, and replace over time, the Germanic *mores et consuetudines* (ways and customs) that had come into existence under Anglo-Saxon rulers. Soon these laws were addressing one another, as in the Statute of Westminster II (1285), chapter 11, where *sicut in aliis statutis continentur* (just as they are contained in other statutes) was subsequently interpreted by Justice Bereford as a reference to the Statute of Marlborough (1267), chapter 23.[2]

At the same time that royal assemblies were grappling with legislative solutions to the legal problems of society, a new royal judiciary was also bringing a national legal system into being. The task of the justices was to put into practice the new legal maxims of the crown in a new court setting, separate from and superior to the seignorial, hundredal, and county courts that initially administered the customary law. The new royal courts, at first the general eyres and then the district assizes

1 For a full discussion of the terminological complexities attendant upon the growth of legislation, see Richardson and Sayles 1934 201-3, 540-71.

2 See the discussion in Plucknett 1922/2010 45.

that succeeded them, gradually replaced the seignorial and subordinated the hundredal and county courts, extending thereby the scope of the central courts in Westminster and bringing a consistent set of legal principles, and royal authority, to bear in a uniform way upon an entire nation. Royal judges, especially those of King's Bench and Common Pleas, were soon engaged in the business of refining legislative efforts that proved in the event not to have provided the degree of exactness they had intended and issuing judgments that soon became guides to others in like cases. Chapter 24 of Westminster II directs attention to writs *in consimili casu* (in a similar case) and royal justices were quick to apply the concept in a general sense. The tandem efforts of constituent assemblies and decision-making justices created over time the framework of a national legal system.

While the business of the courts was for the most part conducted in Law French, its rolls were kept in Latin in a new legal script (anglicana) designed to be easier to read and write than the more decorative literary hand (textura) found in general use. In the interests of efficiency, it also developed an abbreviated style that is extremely difficult for today's uninitiated reader to process. While all the following texts are extant in the standard abbreviated form in both manuscript and printed versions, we present them in normalized versions.

In addition to the legislative and judicial contributions to the developing common law, a third body of materials developed, at first largely in Latin, to record, discuss, and teach the body of materials that was accruing. Late Anglo-Saxon and early Norman compilations had been attempts to write down, in little discernible order, the rules that had been put in place for determining legal issues. Soon, however, lawyerly minds were at work setting forth the law in clearly organized presentations intended to explain how it was meant to function and, accordingly, how its elements should be employed to greatest effect.

Since the royal court system developed first the fiscal court known as the Exchequer, we have included generous selections from the *Dialogus de Scaccario*, which explains in great detail the workings of the royal financial procedures. After the Exchequer, the royal court spun off first Common Pleas and then King's Bench, which in their turn generated first the general eyres and then the district assizes. Although they will prove to be unsuccessful in the end, some theoretical efforts were made as well to channel the various streams of the law existent in England and provide a theoretical legal basis that could accommodate diverse influences. The greatest of these is the text now known simply as *Bracton*, an accumulation by several hands over several generations that attempted to use the civil law to guide the emergent English common law. In addition, manuals intended for use by lawyers in need of specific guidance in specific situations soon became common as the legal profession developed and eventually institutionalized the mechanisms for teaching its neophytes and guiding its practicing members. A major contribution to such efforts was the text known as *Glanvill*, but there were many other less important works, which we represent by the previously untranslated manual titled *Modus Componendi Brevia.*

We have attempted to provide a reasonable and manageable selection of Latin materials from among the large body of available texts, and no doubt readers will note the absence of materials, in particular statutes and cases, that could as well have been included. In some cases important legislation, even in the early years, was in French and so fell outside our scope. In other cases we were inhibited by the constraints of size, for clearly not all the relevant documents could be accommodated in one volume. Our hope is that we have included an adequate sampling of the Latin that was employed in the business of the law from the early years of Norman rule to the late fourteenth century, by which time the use of legal Latin was reserved largely for the records of courts and parliaments, written on vellum membranes that were then stitched together and rolled for storage in the famous *rotuli.* We attempt in the introductions to individual texts to provide a basic account of historical context and significance, especially for subsequent ages. Our translations seek to be as literal as intelligibly possible in order to ease the readers' movements back and forth across the linguistic boundary between medieval Latin and modern English.

Perhaps the most obvious hurdle the student faces when approaching early legal Latin is the terminology, which can be daunting at first. Accordingly, we provide explanatory footnotes and a glossary of terms to guide the reader through the specialized vocabulary. A well-known story is told about a witticism of Thomas More's on just this topic. While in Flanders on a mission for the king, More met a scholar who boasted that he would answer any question that might be put to him in Latin. More accordingly inquired, "*An averia capta in withernamia sunt irreplegibilia?*" The scholar had no idea what this might mean, for *averia* (farm animals), *withernamia* (distraints), and *irreplegebilia* (not subject to replevin) are words peculiar to the common law. The sentence, which means, "Are cattle seized in withernams subject to replevin," is hardly intelligible to anyone who does not know that a withernam is a writ allowing the sheriff to seize cattle of value equal to those which had been stolen if he could not find the stolen cattle themselves, and that replevin is a procedure by which recovered goods can be provisionally restored to an owner pending settlement of an action to determine ownership.

California State University, Sacramento
[June 1 2018]

# LEGISLATION

**Court of Common Pleas**

## Constitutions of Clarendon

The Constitutions of Clarendon play a key role in the dispute between Henry II and Thomas Becket, his chancellor and archbishop of Canterbury, over the respective authorities of crown and crozier. While the contention began with an unrelated issue (a disagreement over the payment of the sheriff's aid) that was debated at the council of Woodstock in July of 1163, by the time the council of Westminster met in October of that same year the focus had shifted to the issue of royal jurisdiction over the clergy. This discussion carried over to the council held at Clarendon in January of 1164, where the issue opened up into the overall relationship of the spiritual to the temporal authority. The council held at Northampton later that same year in October took up the matter once again, but relations between Henry and Becket had deteriorated to such an extent that the chancellor went into exile immediately upon its conclusion.

The sixteen articles promulgated at Clarendon are a largely successful attempt to come to a compromise with the church on the jurisdictional rights of royal over church law. Becket came into the council under considerable pressure from the pope and the bishops to accede to the royal position and demonstrably signed off on the king's demands that the practices of the past be recognized and agreed to by all present. However, Becket's murder in 1170 opened the matter up again and cost Henry the right to judge "criminous clerics" in the royal courts, leaving their fates in the ecclesiastical courts where they had customarily been protected from the king's justice. An essential prerequisite to the establishment of a national legal system in England, the curtailment of ecclesiastical jurisdiction, a process already underway by the time the Constitutions were written (1164), was accordingly not to be completed for some time and jurisdictional disputes with the church were commonplace. The working solution to the problem of jurisdiction, however, turned out to be the writ of prohibition, obtainable by any defendant in an ecclesiastical court, which ordered the plaintiff and the judge to desist from proceeding. The writ could be contested, but nevertheless it put the common law courts in charge of deciding the scope of ecclesiastical authority.

We take our text from Stubbs, *Select Charters*, 163-67. The translation is our own.

Anno ab Incarnatione Domini MCLXIV, papatus Alexandri anno Ivto, illustrissimi regis Anglorum Henrici secundi anno decimo, in praesentia ejusdem regis, facta est ista recordatio vel recognitio cujusdam partis consuetudinum et libertatum et dignitatum antecessorum suorum, videlicet regis Henrici avi sui, et aliorum quae observari et teneri debent in regno. Et propter dissensiones et discordias quae emerserant inter clerum et Justitias domini regis et barones regni de consuetudinibus et dignitatibus, facta est ista recognitio coram archiepiscopis et episcopis et clero et comitibus et baronibus et proceribus regni. Et easdem consuetudines recognitas per archiepiscopos et episcopos et comites et barones et per nobiliores et antiquiores regni, Thomas Cantuariensis archiepiscopus, et Rogerus Eboracensis archiepiscopus, et Gillebertus Londoniensis episcopus, et Henricus Wintoniensis episcopus, et Nigellus Eliensis episcopus, et Willelmus Norwicensis episcopus, et Robertus Lincolniensis episcopus, et Hilarius Cicestrensis episcopus, et Jocelinus Sarisberiensis episcopus, et Ricardus Cestrensis episcopus, et Bartholomaeus Exoniensis episcopus, et Robertus Herefordensis episcopus, et David Menevensis episcopus, et Rogerus Wigornensis electus, concesserunt, et in Verbo Veritatis viva voce firmiter promiserunt tenendas et observandas, domino regi et haeredibus suis, bona fide et absque malo ingenio, praesentibus istis: Roberto comite Leghestriae, Reginaldo comite Cornubiae, Conano comite Britanniae, Johanne comite de Augo, Rogero comite de Clara, comite Gaufredo de Mandevilla, Hugone comite Cestriae, Willelmo comite de Arundel, comite Patricio, Willelmo comite de Ferrariis, Ricardo de Luci, Reginaldo de Sancto Walerico, Rogero Bigot, Reginaldo de Warennia, Richero de Aquila, Willelmo de Braiosa, Ricardo de Camvilla, Nigello de Moubrai, Simone de Bello Campo, Humfrido de Boun, Matthaeo de Herefordis, Waltero de

Meduana, Manassero Biseth dapifero, Willelmo Malet, Willelmo de Curci, Roberto de Dunestanvilla, Jocelino de Baillolio, Willelmo de Lanvalis, Willelmo de Caisneto, Gaufrido de Ver, Willelmo de Hastinges, Hugone de Morevilla, Alano de Nevilla, Simone filio Petri, Willelmo Malduit camerario, Johanne Malduit, Johanne Mariscallo, Petro de Mara, et multis aliis proceribus et nobilibus regni, tam clericis quam laicis.

Consuetudinum vero et dignitatum regni recognitarum quaedam pars praesenti scripto continetur. Cujus partis capitula haec sunt;

**Cap. i.** De advocatione et praesentatione ecclesiarum si controversia emerserit inter laicos, vel into laicos et clericos, vel inter clericos, in curia domini regis tractetur vel terminetur.

**Cap. ii.** Ecclesiae de feudo domini regis non possunt in perpetuum dari absque assensu et concessione ipsius.

**Cap. iii.** Clerici rectati et accusati de quacunque re, summoniti a Justitia regis venient in curiam ipsius, responsuri ibidem de hoc unde videbitur curiae regis quod ibidem sit respondendum; et in curia ecclesiastica, unde videbitur quod ibidem sit respondendum; ita quod Justitia regis mittet in curiam sanctae ecclesiae ad videndum qua ratione res ibi tractabitur. Et si clericus convictus vel confessus fuerit, non debet de cetero eum ecclesia tueri.

**Cap. iv.** Archiepiscopis, episcopis, et personis regni, non licet exire de regno absque licentia domini regis. Et si exierint, si domino regi placuerit, assecurabunt, quod nec in eundo, nec in moram faciendo, nec in redeundo, perquirent malum vel damnum regi vel regno.

**Cap. v.** Excommunicati non debent dare vadium ad remanens, nec praestare juramentum, sed tantum vadium et plegium standi judicio ecclesiae ut absolvantur.

**Cap. vi.** Laici non debent accusari nisi per certos et legales accusatores et testes in praesentia episcopi, ita quod archidiaconus non perdat jus suum, nec quicquam quod inde habere debeat. Et si tales fuerint qui culpantur, quod non velit vel non audeat aliquis eos accusare, vicecomes requisitus ab episcopo faciet jurare duodecim legales homines de vicineto, seu de villa, coram episcopo, quod inde veritatem secundum conscientiam suam manifestabunt.

**Cap. vii.** Nullus qui de rege tenet in capite, nec aliquis dominicorum ministrorum ejus, excommunicetur, nec terrae alicujus illorum sub interdicto ponantur, nisi prius dominus rex, si in terra fuerit, conveniatur, vel Justitia ejus, si fuerit extra regnum, ut rectum de ipso faciat: et ita ut quod pertinebit ad curiam regiam ibidem terminetur, et de eo quod spectabit ad ecclesiasticam curiam, ad eandem mittatur ut ibidem tractetur.

**Cap. viii.** De appellationibus si emerserint, ab archidiacono debent procedere ad episcopum, ab episcopo ad archiepiscopum. Et si archiepiscopus defecerit in justitia exhibenda, ad dominum regem perveniendum est postremo, ut praecepto ipsius in curia archiepiscopi controversia terminetur, ita quod non debet ulterius procedere absque assensu domini regis.

**Cap. ix.** Si calumnia emerserit inter clericum et laicum, vel inter laicum et clericum, de ullo tenemento quod clericus ad eleemonsinam velit attrahere, laicus vero ad laicum feudum, recognitione duodecim legalium hominum, per capitalis Justitiae regis considerationem terminabitur, utrum tenementum sit pertinens ad eleemosinam sive ad laicum feudum, coram ipso Justitia regis. Et si recognitum fuerit ad eleemosinam pertinere, placitum erit in curia ecclesiastica, si vero ad laicum feudum, nisi ambo de eodem episcopo vel barone advocaverint, erit placitum in curia regia. Sed si uterque advocaverit de feudo illo ante eundem episcopum vel baronem, erit placitum in curia ipsius; ita quod propter factam recognitionem seisinam non amittat, qui prior seisitus fuerat, donec per placitum dirationatum fuerit.

**Cap. x.** Qui de civitate, vel castello, vel burgo, vel dominico manerio domini regis fuerit, si ab archidiacono vel episcopo super aliquo delicto citatus fuerit, unde debeat eisdem respondere et ad citationes eorum satisfacere noluerit, bene licet eum sub interdicto ponere, sed non debet excommunicari priusquam capitalis minister domini regis villae illius conveniatur, ut justiciet eum ad satisfactionem venire. Et si minister regis inde defecerit, ipse erit in misericordia domini regis, et exinde poterit episcopus ipsum accusatum ecclesiastica justitia cohibere.

**Cap. xi.** Archiepiscopi, episcopi, et universae personae regni, qui de rege tenent in capite, habent possessiones suas de domino rege sicut baroniam, et inde respondent Justitiis et ministris regis, et sequuntur et faciunt omnes rectitudines et consuetudines regias, et sicut barones ceteri, debent interesse judiciis curiae domini regis cum baronibus, usque dum perveniatur in judicio ad diminutionem membrorum vel mortem.

**Cap. xii.** Cum vacaverit archiepiscopatus, vel episcopatus, vel abbatia, vel prioratus de dominio regis, debet esse in manu ipsius, et inde percipiet omnes reditus et exitus sicut dominicos. Et cum ventum fuerit ad consulendum ecclesiae, debet dominus rex mandare potiores personas ecclesiae, et in capella ipsius domini regis debet fieri elctio assensu domini regis et consilio personarum regni, quas ad hoc faciendum vocaverit. Et ibidem faciet electus homagium et fidelitatem domino regi sicut ligio domino, de vita sua et de membris et de honor e suo terreno, salvo ordine suo, priusquam sit consecratus.

**Cap. xiii.** Si quisquam de proceribus regni defortiaverit archiepiscopo, vel episcopo, vel archidiacono, de se vel de suis justitiam exhibere, dominus rex debet eos justiciare. Et si forte aliquis defortiaverit domino regi rectitudinem suam, archiepiscopi et episcopi et archidiaconi debent eum justiciare ut domino regi satisfaciat.

**Cap. xiv.** Catalla eorum qui sunt in forisfacto regis non detineat ecclesia vel cimiterium contra justitiam regis, quia ipsius regis sunt, sive in ecclesiis sive extra fuerint inventa.

**Cap. xv.** Placita de debitis, quae fide interposita debentur, vel absque interpositione fidei, sint in justitia regis.

**Cap. xvi.** Filii rusticorum non debent ordinari absque assensu domini de cujus terra nati dignoscuntur.

Facta est autem praedictarum consuetudinum et dignitatum recordatio regiarum a praefatis archiepiscopis et episcopis et comitibus et baronibus, et nobilioribus, et antiquioribus regni, apud Clarendonam quarto die ante Purificationem Beatae Mariae perpetuae Virginis, domino Henrico cum patre suo domino rege ibidem praesente. Sunt autem et aliae multae et magnae consuetudines et dignitates sanctae matris ecclesiae et domini regis et baronum regni, quae in hoc scripto non continentur. Quae salvae sint sanctae ecclesiae et domino regi et haeredibus suis et baronibus regni, et in perpetuum inviolabiliter observentur.

### Translation

In the year from the incarnation of the Lord 1164, in the fourth year of Alexander's papacy,[1] in the tenth year of the most illustrious king of the English Henry the second, in the presence of that same king, was made this record or recognition[2] of some part of the customs and liberties and dignities of his ancestors, namely of king Henry his grandfather and others, which ought to be heeded and held in the realm. And because of the dissensions and discords that had arisen between the clergy and the lord king's justices and the barons of the realm concerning customs and dignities, this recognition was made before the archbishops and bishops and clergy and earls and barons and leading figures of the realm. And these same customs, having been recognized by the archbishops and bishops and earls and barons and by the more noble and elder of the realm, archbishop Thomas of London, and archbishop Roger of York, and bishop Gilbert of London, and bishop Henry of Winchester, and bishop Nicholas of Ely, and bishop William of Norwich, and bishop Robert of Lincoln, and bishop Hilary of Chichester, and bishop Jocelyn of Salisbury, and bishop Richard of Chester, and bishop Bartholemew of Oxford, and bishop Robert of Herford, and bishop David of Mans, and bishop-elect Roger of Worcester have granted and on the word of truth

1 Alexander III, pope from 1159-1181.

2 A recognition can be an inquest by jury or an explanatory statement issued by such an inquest. Accordingly, something that has been recognized has been investigated.

firmly promised the lord king and his heirs in an oral statement that they shall keep and observe, in good faith and absent wicked intent, in the presence of these men: earl Robert of Leicester, earl Reginald of Cornwall, count Conan of Brittany, count John of Eu, earl Robert of Clare, earl Geoffrey of Mandeville, earl Hugo of Chester, earl William of Arundel, earl Patrick, earl William of Ferrières, Richard of Luce, Reginald of Saint-Valery, Roger Bigot, Reginald de Warrene, Richer of Laigle, William of Briouze, Richard de Camville, Nigel de Moubrai, Simon de Beauchamp, Humphrey de Bohun, Matthew of Hereford, Walter of Mayenne, steward Manasser Bissett, William Malet, William of Courcy, Robert of Dunstaville, Jocelyn de Balliol, William de Lanvalis, William de Chesney, Geoffrey de Ver, William of Hastings, Hugh of Morville, Alan de Neville, Simon fitz Peter, chamberlain William Maudit, John Maudit, John the Marshall, Peter de Mara, and many other leading figures and nobles of the realm, as well religious as lay.

A certain part, indeed, of the realm's customs and dignities that were recognized are contained in the present writing, of which part these are the chapters.

**Chapter 1:** Concerning advowson and presentation of churches, if a controversy has arisen between laymen, or between laymen and clergy, or among clergy, let it be dealt with and ended in the court of the lord king.

**Chapter 2:** Churches of the lord king's fee cannot be given in perpetuity without the same's assent and concession.

**Chapter 3:** Clerics charged and accused of whatsoever matter, summoned by the king's Justice, shall come into his court, in that very place to answer concerning that whereupon it will seem to the king's court should be answered in that very place; and in the ecclesiastical court when it will seem that it should be answered in that very place, and concerning that which will belong to the ecclesiastical court, let it be sent to the same so that it be handled in that very place.

**Chapter 8:** Concerning appeals, if they should arise, let them proceed from archdeacon to bishop, from bishop to archbishop. And if the archbishop fails to furnish justice, he should be reported finally to the lord king, so that the dispute be decided by his decree in the archbishop's court, so that it should not proceed further without the consent of the lord king.

**Chapter 9:** If a dispute has arisen between a cleric and a lay person, or between a lay person and a cleric, about any tenement that the cleric wishes to claim as frank-almoign[1] but the lay person as a lay fee, it shall be determined before the king's Justice himself, by a recognition of twelve law-worthy men, through a decision of the king's chief Justice, whether the tenement belongs to frank-almoign or a lay fee. And if it has been recognized to belong to frank-almoign, it should be pleaded in the ecclesiastical court, but if to a lay fee, it shall be pleaded in the royal court unless both claim from the same bishop or baron. But if either has made a claim about that fee before that same bishop or baron, it shall be pleaded in his court, so that he who had been seised before does not lose seisin because of that recognition until it has been deraigned by a plea.[2]

**Chapter 10:** Whoever has been from a city, or castle, or burgh, or demesne manor of the lord king, if he has been summoned upon some transgression by an archdeacon or bishop, whereby he should answer them and he has not wished to accept their summons, it is perfectly acceptable to place him under interdict, but he should not be excommunicated before the king's chief official of that vill is agreed, so that he might compel him judicially to come to acceptance. And if the king's minister should fail thereby, he himself will be in the mercy[3] of the lord king, and thenceforth the bishop can restrain the accused person with ecclesiastical justice.

---

1 A "tenure in free alms," a property acquired by the church in perpetuity in exchange for perpetual prayers.
2 Until a title has been established.
3 Subject to royal amercement.

**Chapter 11:** Archbishops, bishops, and all persons of the realm who hold from the king in capite shall have their properties from the lord king just like land held in baronial tenure, and thereby let them answer to the king's Justices and ministers and follow and perform all the royal rights and customs, and just like the other barons they should be present with the barons at the judgments of the lord king's courts, up to the point when it may come in a judgment to the loss of members or death.

**Chapter 12:** When an archbishopric has been vacated, or a bishopric, or an abbacy, or a priorship of the lord king's, it should be in his hand, and, just like his demesne manors, he should take all the returns and profits. And when it has come time to provide for the vacant benefice of a church, the lord king should summon powerful parsons[1] of the church, and in the lord king's own chapel election should be made with the assent of the lord king and by a counsel of the realm's parsons whom he has called in order to take care of the matter. And in that very place let the electee do homage and fealty to the lord king, just as to his liege lord, concerning his life and members and earthly honor, saving his order, before he is consecrated.

**Chapter 13:** If any of the nobles of the realm has deforced[2] an archbishop, or bishop, or archdeacon to do justice for himself or his men, the lord king should bring them to justice. And if perhaps someone has deforced the lord king his right, the archbishops and bishops and archdeacons ought to bring him to justice in a way that is satisfactory to the lord king.

**Chapter 14:** Let a church or cemetery[3] not distrain against the king's justice the chattels of those who are in the king's forfeiture, because they are the king's own whether they have been found in churches or without.

**Chapter 15:** Let pleas of debt that are owed by an imposed pledge or without a pledge having been imposed be in the king's jurisdiction.

1 Beneficed priests.
2 Prevented from occupying or ejected from an estate or office.
3 A church property (not necessarily a graveyard).

**Chapter 16:** Sons of villeins should not be ordained without the assent of the lord on whose land they are known to have been born.

And the record of the aforesaid royal customs and privileges has been made by the before-mentioned archbishops and bishops and earls and barons and nobles and elders of the realm at Clarendon on the fourth day before the purification of the blessed Mary the perpetual virgin, the lord Henry being present in that very place with his father the lord king. And there are also many other and great customs and privileges of holy mother the church and the lord king and his barons that are not contained in this deed. Which are reserved to holy church and the lord king and his heirs and barons of the realm and should be observed inviolate in perpetuity.

## The Assize[1] of Clarendon

The Assize of Clarendon, the first of Henry II's great legislative accomplishments, detailed judicial procedures for the repression of felonies such as robbery, murder, theft in excess of five shillings' value, and the harboring of those who had committed them after 1154, the end of Stephen's reign and the beginning of Henry's. The marking of a temporal boundary beyond which prosecution is declined suggests as well the kernel of the idea of recent dispossession (*novel disseisin*), the action for which was devised about the same time and presumably issued in an assize of disseisin that has not survived but which is mentioned in the Pipe Roll for 1166. An article concerning unjust dispossession occurs in the Assize of Northampton, a restatement and enhancement of Clarendon issued in 1176,[2] but the actions upon "disseisin against the assize" which begin in 1166 establish a strong connection to Clarendon,

1 In this sense, an assize is a legislative decree. The word is also used to designate the assembly at which such a decree is promulgated, the judicial sessions of certain royal courts, particular actions brought before them, and, sometimes, their determinations.

2 Van Caenegem 1988 42-3.

the main concern of which was general lawlessness in the realm following the reign of Stephen.

The procedures established at Clarendon are historic. Perhaps most importantly, sheriffs will now appoint juries of presentment, the ancestor of the grand jury, from the hundreds and vills. Their twelve members will make their presentment to sheriffs at their bi-annual tourns (sheriffs' courts) or to justices in eyre (itinerant judges) in order to determine the identity of known or suspected robbers, murderers, thieves, or those who have harbored them. Those taken by this inquest who are tenants at whatever level on a seigneurial feoffment may be released if their feudal superiors or their representatives provide suitable surety within three days of arrest. Others will be held in local gaols or such will be constructed to hold them. If no eyre justice is at hand, the sheriffs will send word to the nearest eyre court and request instructions for the disposition of their prisoners, who will be transported when specified. Those arrested will at some point undergo the ordeal by water to determine guilt or innocence.

In order to facilitate the inquest, the Assize specifically denies all exemptions from jury service and grants sheriffs free entry into all estates and boroughs in order to inspect the men under the frankpledge who are suitable candidates, that is, those whose law-worthy character has already been established, and subsequently to arrest those then named by the jury after it has been constituted and indictments have been issued. The group targeted for criminal prosecution is expanded in articles 11 and 12 to include outlaws, probably specifically those who have sought refuge from the Assize in wilderness areas, and those who have received property from those who have fled the Assize. Those who manage to clear their names before the justices, but whose reputations are held nevertheless to be suspect, will be given eight days to go into foreign exile. Those who seek to avoid prosecution or exile by moving from place to place are to be considered vagrants and denied lodging except in a town and then not beyond the extent of a day. Those who flee the jurisdiction of one sheriff to that of another shall be arrested by the sheriff into whose county they have removed and their lands and properties confiscated on the king's behalf. Religious orders are specifically forbidden to take refugees from the Assize into their communities and, in an afterthought to the document's main intent, anyone harboring those recently declared heretic at Oxford shall have his house burned. As a final condition, the Assize asserts the king's right to pursue indefinitely those who have been designated. Everything about this Assize marks it is a component of Henry II's efforts to consolidate his personal hold over his realm by extending the scope of royal power.

The Assize of Clarendon contains the seeds of habeas corpus in articles three, four, and seven, but its lasting contribution to English law is the shift it marks away from legal procedure by an individual appeal of felony to a jury conclusion functioning as a public accusation.

> We take our text from Stubbs, *Select Charters*, pp. 170-75.[1] The translation is our own.

Incipit Assisa de Clarenduna facta a rege Henrico, scilicet secondo, de assensu archiepiscoporum, episcoporum, abbatum, comitum, baronum, totius Angliae.

**1.** Inprimis statuit praedictus rex Henricus de consilio omnium baronum suorum, pro pace servanda et justitia tenenda, quod per singulos comitatus inquiratur, et per singulos hundredos, per xii. legaliores homines de hundredo, et per iv. legaliores homines de qualibet villata, per sacramentum quod illi verum dicent: si in hundredo suo vel villata sua sit aliquis homo qui sit rettatus vel publicatus quod ipse sit robator vel murdrator vel latro vel aliquis qui sit receptor robatorum vel murdratorum vel latronum, postquam dominus rex fuit rex. Et hoc inquirant Justitiae coram se, et vicecomites coram se.

---

1 The text in Stubb's *Select Charters* has been questioned by Richardson and Sayles in *The Governance of Mediaeval England* 198-9 and 238-44, which argues that arson and falsifying (which includes counterfeiting and forgery) were in the 1166 text and not added ten years later at Northampton.

**2.** Et qui invenietur per sacramentum praedictorum rettatus vel publicatus quod fuerit robator vel murdrator vel latro vel receptor eorum, postquam dominus rex fuit rex, capiatur et est ad juisam aquae, et juret quod ipse non fuit robator vel murdrator vel latro vel receptor eorum postquam dominus rex fuit rex, de valentia v. solidorum quod sciat.

**3.** Et si dominus ejus qui captus fuerit vel dapifer ejus vel homines ejus requisierint eum per plegium infra tertium diem postquam captus fuerit, replegiatur ipse et catalla ejus donec ipse faciat legem suam.

**4.** Et quando robator vel murdrator vel latro vel receptores eorum capti fuerint per praedictum sacramentum, si Justitiae non fuerint tam cito venturae in illum comitatum ubi capti fuerint, vicecomites mandent propinquiori Justitiae per aliquem intelligentem hominem, quod tales homines ceperint; et Justitiae remandabunt vicecomitibus ubi voluerint quod illi ducantur ante illos: et vicecomites illos ducant ante Justitias; et cum illis ducant de hundredo et de villata ubi capti fuerint, duos legales homines ad portandum recordationem comitatus et hundredi, quare recapti fuerint, et ibi ante Justitiam facient legem suam.

**5.** Et de illis qui capti fuerint per pradedictum sacramentum hujus Assisae, nullus habeat curiam vel justitiam nec catalla, nisi dominus rex in curia sua coram Justitiis ejus, et dominus rex habebit omnis catalla eorum. De illis vero qui capti fuerint aliter quam per hoc sacramentum, sit sicut esse solet et debet.

**6.** Et vicecomites qui eos ceperint ducant eos ante Justitiam sine alia summonitione quam inde habeant. Et cum robatores vel murdratores vel latrones et receptores eorum, qui capti fuerint per sacramentum vel aliter, tradantur vicecomitibus, et ipsi recipiant eos statim sine dilatione.

**7.** Et in singulis comitatibus ubi non sunt gaiolae, fiant in burgo vel aliquo castello regis de denariis regis et bosco ejus si prope fuerit, vel de alio bosco propinquo, per visum servientium regis, ad hoc ut vicecomites in illis possint illos qui capti fuerint per ministros qui hoc facere solent et per servientes suos, custodire.

**8.** Vult etiam dominus rex quod omnes veniant ad comitatus ad hoc sacramentum faciendum, ita quod nullus remaneat pro libertate aliqua quam habeat, vel curia vel soca quam habuerit, quin veniant ad hoc sacramentum faciendum.

**9.** Et non sit aliquis infra castellum vel extra castellum, nec etiam in honor e de Walingeford, qui vetet vicecomites intrare in curiam vel terram suam ad videndos francos plegios, et quod omnes sint sub plegiis: et ante vicecomites mittantur sub libero plegio.

**10.** Et in civitatibus vel burgis nullus habeat homines vel recipiat in domo sua vel terra sua vel soca sua, quos non in manu capiat quod eos habebit coram Justitia si requisiti fuerint, vel sint sub francoplegio.

**11.** Et nulli sint in civitate vel burgo vel castello vel extra, nec in honor e etiam de Walingeford, qui vetent vicecomites intrare in terram suam vel socam suam, ad capiendum illos qui rettati fuerint vel publicati quod sint robatores vel murdratores vel latrones vel receptores eorum, vel utlagati vel rettati deforesta; sed praecipit quod juvent illos ad capiendum eos.

**12.** Et si aliquis fuerit captus qui fuerit saisiatus de roberia vel latrocinio, si ipse fuerit diffamatus et habeat malum testimonium de publicamento, et non habeat warantum, non habeat legem. Et si non fuerit publicatus, pro saisina quam habet, eat ad aquam.

**13.** Et si aliquis fuerit recognoscens coram legalibus hominibus vel hundredis de roberia vel murdro vel latrocinio vel de receptione eorum, et postea negare voluerit, non habeat legem.

**14.** Vult etiam dominus rex quod ipsi qui facient legem suam et mundi erunt per legem, si ipsi fuerint de pessimo testimonio, et publice et turpiter diffamati testimonio multorum et legalium hominum, foras jurent terras regis, ita quod infra viii. dies mare transibunt, nisi aura eos detinuerit; et cum prima aura quam habebunt postea mare transibunt, et ultra in Angliam non revertentur nisi per misericordiam domini regis: et ibi sint utlagati; et si redierint capiantur sicut utlagati.

**15.** Et prohibit dominus rex ne aliquis vaivus, id est vagus vel ignotus, hospitetur alicubi nisi in burgo, et ibi non hospitetur nisi una nocte, nisi ibi infirmetur, vel equus ejus, ita quod monstrare possit monstrabile essonium.

**16.** Et si ibi fuerit plusquam una nocte, capiatur ille et teneatur donec dominus ejus venerit ad eum plegiandum, vel donec ipse habeat salvos plegios; et ille similiter capiatur qui hospitatus fuerit.

**17.** Et si aliquis vicecomes mandaverit alii vicecomiti quod homines fugerint de comitatu suo in alium comitatum pro roberia vel pro murdro vel latrocinio vel receptione eorum, vel pro utlagia vel pro retta forestae regis, ille capiat eos: et etiam si per se vel per alios sciat quod tales homines fugerint in comitatum suum, capiat eos et custodiat donec de eis habeat salvos plegios.

**18.** Et omnes vicecomites faciant inbreviari omnes fugitivos, qui fugerint de suis comitatibus; et hoc faciant coram comitatibus, et illorum nomina scripta portabunt ante Justitias cum primo ad illos venerint, ut illi quaerantur per totam Angliam, et eorum catalla capiantur ad opus regis.

**19.** Et vult dominus rex quod ex quo vicecomites susceperint summonitiones Justitiarum errantium, ut ipsi cum comitatibus suis sint ante illos, ipsi congregabunt comitatus suos et inquirent omnes qui de novo venerint in suos comitatus post hanc assisam; et illos mittent per plegios, quod erunt coram Justitias, vel illos custodient, donec Justitiae ad eos venerint, et tunc habebunt coram Justitias.

**20.** Prohibet etiam dominus rex ne monachi vel canonici vel aliqua domus religionum recipiant aliquem de populo minuto in monachum vel canonicum vel fratrem, donec sciatur de quali testimonio ipse fuerit, nisi ipse fuerit infirmus ad mortem.

**21.** Prohibet etiam dominus rex, quod nullus in tota Anglia receptet in terra sua vel soca sua vel domo sub se, aliquem de secta illorum renegatorum qui excommunicati et signati fuerunt apud Oxeneforde. Et si quis eos receperit, ipse erit in misericordia domini regis; et domus, in qua illi fuerint, portetur et comburatur. Et hoc jurabit unusquisque vicecomes quod hoc tenebit, et hoc jurare faciet omnes ministros suos, et dapiferos baronum, et omnes milites et franco-tenentes de comitatibus.

**22.** Et vult dominus rex quod haec assisa teneatur in regno suo quamdiu ei placuerit.

## Translation

Here begins the Assize of Clarendon, made in the reign of Henry, that is, the second, by the assent of the archbishops, bishops, abbots, counts, [and] barons of all England.

**1.** To begin with, by the counsel of all his barons the aforesaid King Henry has resolved, in order to preserve the peace and observe justice, that it shall be determined in every county and hundred, through [the agency of] twelve upright men from each hundred and four from each vill, under oath that they shall speak the truth, if in their hundred or vill there is any man who has been charged or proclaimed to be a robber or murderer or thief, or been the harborer of robbers, murderers, or thieves, since the lord king became king. And let the Justices investigate this personally, and let the sheriffs [investigate] personally.

**2.** And whoever shall be found by the oath of the aforesaid men to have been charged or proclaimed to be a robber or murderer or thief or their harborer, since the lord king became king, let him be seized and let him go to the ordeal by water and swear that he has not been a robber or murderer or thief, or a harborer of them to the value of five shillings that he knows, since the lord king became king.

**3.** And if the master of one who has been seized, or his steward or his men, should request his release on bail within three days after he has been seized, let him give himself and his chattels as surety until he shall have undergone his trial.

**4.** And when a robber or murderer or thief or those who have been their harborers have been taken by the aforesaid inquiry, if Justices will not be coming very soon into that county where they have been taken, let the sheriffs send word to a nearby Justice by some trustworthy man that they have taken such men; and the Justices will send word back to the sheriffs [informing them] when they wish that those should be brought before them; and the sheriffs shall bring them before the Justices; and with them they shall bring two law-worthy men from the hundreds and vills where they have been taken, for the purpose of bearing the county's and hundred's account of why they were taken, and there before a Justice let them be tried.

**5.** And concerning those who have been taken by the aforesaid inquiry of this Assize, let no man have the jurisdiction or sentencing or chattels save the lord king in his own court before his own Justices, and the lord king will have all their chattels. But concerning those who have been taken otherwise than through this inquiry, let it be just as it is customary and ought to be.

**6.** And let the sheriffs who have taken them lead them before a Justice without any summons other than they had hitherto. And when the robbers or murderers or thieves and their harborers, who were arrested in this inquiry or elsewhere, are handed over to the sheriffs, let them take them into custody without delay.

**7.** And in each county where there are no gaols, let them be made in a borough or some castle of the king from the king's money or his timber if it is nearby, or from other nearby timber, under the supervision of the king's servants, to the end that the sheriffs will be able to keep in them those who have been taken by the officials and their servants who are accustomed to do this.

**8.** The lord king also wishes that all should come to the county for the purpose of performing this inquiry, that no one thus should default on account of some liberty that he might have, or some court or exemption that he might have, so that they do not come for the purpose of performing this inquiry.

**9.** And let there be no one within or without his castle, not even in the honor of Wallingford, who forbids the sheriffs to enter into his court or land to inspect the frankpledge, and that all be under frankpledge, and let those under frankpledge be sent before the sheriffs.

**10.** And in the cities or boroughs let no man have or receive men in his house or his land or his jurisdiction whom he will not on his own responsibility bring before the Justice if they have been summoned, or be under frankpledge.

**11.** And let there be no one in the city or borough or castle or without, not even in the honor of Wallingford, who denies the sheriff's entry into his land or his jurisdiction in order to take those who have been charged or proclaimed to be robbers or murderers or thieves or their harborers, or outlawed or charged with forest offenses, but he [the king] commands that they aid them [the sheriffs] for the purpose of taking them [the suspects].

**12.** And if someone has been taken who has been seised by robbery or theft, if he has been defamed and has had unfavorable testimony by denunciation, and he has no warrant, let him not be tried. And if he has not been denounced for the seisin that he has, let him go to the water.

**13.** And if someone has admitted robbery or murder or theft or harboring in the presence of lawful men or the hundreds, and afterwards he wishes to deny it, let him not have law.

**14.** The lord king also wishes that those who undergo the ordeal and are cleared of guilt by the ordeal, if they have been publicly and shamefully denounced by the most damning testimony of both many men and lawful men, shall abjure the king's lands so that they cross the sea within eight days, unless the wind detain them; and with the first wind that they afterwards have they shall cross the sea, and let them not return again into England unless by the king's mercy; and there [i.e. in England] let them be outlaws; and if they should return let them be taken just like outlaws.[1]

**15.** And the lord king forbids that any vagrant, that is, a wandering or unknown person, be lodged anywhere except in a borough, and he will

---

1 "So much for Henry II's belief in the efficacy of miracles as proof of innocence," remarks Van Caenegem 1988 70.

not be lodged there but for one night unless he or his horse becomes ill there, so that he can show a demonstrable reason for delay (essoin).

**16.** And if he will have been there more than one night, let him be taken and held until his lord will come to his pledge, or until he himself offers reliable pledges; and likewise let him be taken who has been his host.

**17** And if any sheriff has sent word to another sheriff that men have fled from his county into another county for robbery or for murder or theft or for harboring such men, or for outlawry or for charged offenses against the king's forest, let him take them; and also if he should know by himself or from others that such men have fled into his county, he shall take and hold them until he shall have reliable pledges for them.

**18.** And let all the sheriffs cause all fugitives who have fled from their counties to be registered, and let this be done before officials, and let their names be taken before the Justices as soon as they have arrived, so that they might be sought throughout all England, and let their chattels be seized for the king's benefit.

**19.** And the lord king wishes that, from the time when the sheriffs receive the summons of the Justices in eyre that they should be before them with their subordinates, they will gather their companions and ask after all those who have recently come into their counties after this assize; and they should put them under pledge that they will go before the Justices, or they should take custody of them until the Justices have come to them, and then bring them before the Justices.

**20.** The lord king also forbids that monks or canons or whoever of a religious establishment should accept any common person as monk or canon or brother until it is known in what repute he has lived, unless he is mortally ill.

**21.** The lord king also forbids that anyone in all England should receive in his land or jurisdiction or home under him anyone from that sect of heretics who were excommunicated and branded at Oxford. And if someone should receive them, he himself shall be at the mercy of the king; and let the house, in which they were, be taken outside the vill and burned. And each sheriff shall swear that he will observe this, and he shall have all his subordinates swear this, and the stewards of the barons, and all the knights and freeholders of the counties.

**22.** And the lord king wishes that this assize be maintained in his realm as long as it please him.

## The Assize of Northampton

The Assize of Northampton, according to one modern commentator,[1] was likely a component of the organization of the general eyre since it was issued as a set of instructions to the eyre justices of the initial six districts established to administer the royal law throughout England. It was as well a restatement of the Assize of Clarendon that increased the penalties of the former legislation and extended the authority of justices at the expense of sheriffs. However, it also established the possessory action of *mort d'ancestor* and is the first official document to make mention of an assize for recent dispossession, which in the Pipe Roll for 1181 will be called *novel disseisin* for the first time.[2] *Novel disseisin* and *mort d'ancestor* are the two most important of the four petty assizes created in the reign of Henry II and, as their titles indicate, are actions to determine issues of inheritance and disseisin, albeit only disseisin from the beginning of Henry II's reign (1154). The significance of *mort d'ancestor,* according to Plucknett, is that it "strengthened the claims of an heir to land against the feudal lord."[3] The other two petty assizes, *utrum* and *darrein presentment*, concern ecclesiastical issues: *utrum* establishes whether land is ecclesiastical or secular and *darrein presentment* determines who has the right to present a benefice. They are called petty assizes to distinguish them from the Grand Assize, initiated by the writ of right (available no later than 1158), that allowed an alternative to trial by combat, i.e. a judicial duel that presumably would reflect divine wishes for the outcome. The Grand Assize, also known as

1 Rothwell 1975 411.
2 Van Caenegem 1988 44.
3 Plucknett 1956/2010 19.

the Assize of Windsor, is first mentioned in *Glanvill* (c. 1189). Northampton also claims for the king the right to take to the royal courts some cases involving one of the feudal incidents, a payment due a lord upon the occasion of a tenant's death, there to be resolved by sworn inquest.

We take out text from Stubbs, *Select Charters,* 179-82. The translation is our own.

Hae sunt Assisae factae apud Clarendune, et postea recordatae apud Northamtoniam.

**1.** Si quis retatus fuerit coram justitiariis domini regis de murdro vel latrocinio, vel roberia, vel receptatione hominum talia facientium, vel de falsoneria vel iniqua combustione, per sacramentum duodecim militum de hundredo, et si milites non adfuerint, per sacramentum duodecim liberorum legalium hominum, et per sacramentum quatuor hominum de unaquaque villa hundredi, eat ad judicium aquae, et si perierit alterum pedem amittat. Et apud Northamtoniam additum est pro regore justitiae quod dexterum similiter pugnum cum pede amittat, et regnum abjuret, et infra quadraginta dies a regno exulet. Et si ad aquam mundus fuerit, inveniat plegios et remaneat in regno, nisi retatus fuerit de murdro vel alia turpi felonia per commune comitatus et legalium militum patriae, de quo si praedicto modo retatus fuerit, quamvis ad aquam salvus fuerit, nihilominus intra quadraginta dies a regno exeat, et catalla sua secum asportet, salvo jure dominorum suorum, et regnum abjuret in misericordia domini regis. Haec autem assisa atenebit a tempore quo assisa facta fuit apud Clarendonam, continue usque ad hoc tempus; et amodo quamdiu domino regi placuerit, in murdro, et proditione, et iniqua combustione, et in omnibus praedictis capitulis nisi in minutis furtis et roberiis, quae facta fuerunt tempore guerrae, sicut de equis et bobus et minoribus rebus.

**2.** Item nulii liceat neque in burgo neque in villa hospitari aliquem extraneum, ultra unam noctem, in domo sua, quem ad rectum habere noluerit, nisi hospitatus ille essonium rationabile habuerit, quod hospes domus monstret vicinis suis. Et cum recesserit, coram vicinis recedat et per diem.

**3.** Si quis saisitus fuerit de murdro vel latrocinio vel roberia vel falsoneris, et inde sit cognoscens, vel de aliqua alia felonia quam fecerit, coram praeposito hundredi vel burgi, et coram legalibus hominibus; id postea coram Justitiis negare non poterit. Et si idem sine saisina coram eis aliquid hujusmodi recognoverit hoc similiter coram Justitiis negare non poterit.

**4.** Item si quis obierit francus-tenens, haeredes ipsius remaneant in tali saisina qualem pater suus habuit die qua fuit vivus et mortuus, de feodo suo; et catalla sua habeant unde faciant divisam defuncti: et dominum suum postea requirant, et ei faciant de relevio et aliis quae ei facere debent de feodo suo. Et si haeres fuerit infra aetatem, dominus feodi recipiat homagium suum et habeat in custodia illum quamdiu debuerit. Alii domini, si plures fuerint, homagium ejus recipiant, et ipse faciat eis quod facere debuerit. Et uxor defuncti habeat dotem suam et partem de catallis ejus quae eam contingit. Et si dominus feodi negat haeredibus defuncti saisinam ejusdem defuncti quam exigunt, Justitiae domini regis faciant inde fieri percognitionem per duodecim legales homines, qualem saisinam defunctus inde habuit die qua fuit vivus et mortuus: et sicut recognitum fuerit, ita haeredibus ejus restituant. Et si quis contra hoc fecerit et inde attaintus fuerit, remaneat in misericordia regis.

**5.** Item Justitiae domini regis faciant fieri recognitionem de dissaisinis factis super Assisam, a tempore quo dominus rex venit in Angliam, proximo post pacem factam inter ipsum et regem filium suum.

**6.** Item Justitiae capiant domini regis fidelitates infra clausum Pascha, et ad ultimum infra clausum Pentecosten, ab omnibus, scilicet comitibus, baronibus, militibus et libere tenentibus, et etiam rusticis, qui in regno manere voluerint. Et qui facere noluerit fidelitatem, tanquam inimicus domini regis capiatur. Habent etiam Justitiae praecipere, quod omnes illi qui nondum fecerunt homagium et ligantiam domino regi, quod ad terminum quem eis nominabunt veniant et faciant regi homagium et ligantiam sicut ligio domino.

**7.** Item Justitiae faciant omnes justitias et rectitudines spectantes ad dominum regem et ad coronam suam, per breve domini regis, vel illorum qui in loco ejus erunt, de feodo dimidii militis et infra, nisi tam grandis sit querela quod non possit deduci sine domino rege, vel talis quam Justitiae ei reportent pro dubitatione sua, vel ad illos qui in loco ejus erunt. Intendant tamen pro posse suo ad commodum domini regis faciendam. Faciant etiam assisam de latronibus iniquis et malefactoribus terrae; quae assisa est per consilium regis filii sui et hominum suorum, per quos ituri sunt comitatus.

**8.** Item Justitiae provideant quod castella diruta prorsus diruantur et diruenda bene prosternantur. Et nisi hoc fecerint, dominus rex judicium curiae suae de eis habere voluerit sicut de contemptoribus praecepti sui.

**9.** Item Justitiae inquirant de excaetis, de ecclesiis, de terris, de feminis quae sunt de donatione domini regis.

**10.** Item baillivi domini regis respondeant ad scaccarium, tam de assiso redditu, quam de omnibus perquisitionibus suis, quas faciunt in bailliis suis; exceptis illis quas pertinent ad vicecomitatum.

**11.** Item Justitiae inquirant de custodiis castellorum, et qui, et quantum, et ubi eas debeant, et postea mandent domino regi.

**12.** Item latro, ex quo capitur, vicecomiti tradatur ad custodiendum. Et si vicecomes absens fuerit, ducatur ad proximum castellanum, et ipse illum custodiat donec illum liberet vicecomiti.

**13.** Item Justitiae faciant quaerere per consuetudinem terrae illos qui a regno recesserunt; et nisi redire voluerint infra terminum nominatum, et stare ad rectum in curia domini regis, postea utlagentur; et nomina utlagorum afferant at Pascha, et ad festum Sancti Michaelis, ad scaccarium, et exinde mittantur domino regi.

## Translation

These are the assizes made at Clarendon, and later reconsidered at Northampton.

**1.** If someone has been taken before the justices of the lord king for murder or theft or robbery, or the harboring of men doing such things, or for forgery or arson, by the oath of twelve knights of the hundred, and, if knights are not present, by the oath of twelve law-worthy free men and by the oath of four men from each vill of the hundred, let him go to the ordeal by water, and if he fails let him lose one foot. And at Northampton was added by rule of justice that he should likewise lose his right fist with the foot and abjure the realm, and within forty days be exiled from the realm. And if he has gone pure to the water, let him find pledges and remain in the realm, unless he has been taken for murder or another shameful felony by the common report of the county and the community of law-worthy knights, by whom if he has been taken in the aforesaid manner, although he has been saved at the water, nonetheless let him be banished from the realm within forty days, and remove his chattels with him, saving the rights of his lords, and abjure the realm in the mercy of the lord king. Moreover, this assize shall be maintained from the time when the assize was made at Clarendon, continuously up to this time, and henceforth as long as it please the king, in murder, and treason, and arson, and in all the abovesaid articles except in petty theft and robbery which have been done in time of war, such as concerning horses and oxen and more insignificant things.

**2.** Also, it is permitted to no one, neither in borough nor in vill, to harbor any stranger beyond one night in his house whom he does not wish to have to right,[1] unless reasonably that lodger has an essoin, which let the host of the house show to his neighbors. And when he departs, let him depart in the presence of the neighbors and by day.

---

1 Meaning "to produce for trial," i.e. to be legally responsible for. See Latham, *Revised Medieval Latin Word List*, s.v. *rectum*.

**3.** If someone has been seised[1] by murder or theft or robbery or forgery, or from some other felony that he has committed, he should afterwards confess, both before the reeve of the hundred or the borough and in the presence of law-worthy men, that afterwards he will not be able to deny it before the Justices. And if he has acknowledged before them something of this sort without seisin, likewise he will not be able to deny it before the Justices.

**4.** Also, if someone has fulfilled frankpledge,[2] let his heirs remain in such seisin of his fee as their father had on the day when he was living and dead, and let them have his chattels, whence let them make the devise of the dead man[3]; and afterward let them seek his lord, and let them do him *relevium*[4] and the other things which they are obliged to do him concerning his fee. And if the heirs are not of age, let the lord of the fee receive their homage and have them in his custody as long as he ought. Other lords, if there were several, shall take their homage, and let each do for them what he is obliged to do. And the wife of the dead man shall have her dower and the part of his chattels which pertain to her. And if the lord of the fee denies his dead man's heirs the seisin of the dead man that they claim, let the Justices of the lord king cause then an inquest to be made by twelve law-worthy men what seisin the dead man then had on the day when he was living and dead; and just as the recognition[5] will have gone, thus let them re-establish his heirs. And if someone has done contrary to this and thence has been attainted, let him remain in the king's mercy.

**5.** Also, let the Justices of the lord king cause a recognition to take place for disseisin made upon the assize, from the time when the lord king

1 That is, acquired possession or tenure of a fee.
2 A way of saying the man is a freeholder.
3 That is, divide up his non-real property.
4 The feudal relief, the payment to the overlord by the heir upon succession.
5 *Percognito*, a variation on *recognitio*, an investigation, here the inquest.

came into England immediately after the peace made between himself and the king his son.[1]

**6.** Also, the Justices shall take the lord king's pledges before *Pascha clausum*[2] and at the latest before *Pentecosten clausum*,[3] by all, that is earls, barons, knights and freeholders, and even peasants, who wish to remain in the realm. And he who does not wish to make pledge shall be taken as an enemy of the lord king. The Justices shall also order that all those who have not yet made homage and allegiance to the lord king shall at the time appointed them come and make homage and allegiance to the king as their liege lord.

**7.** Also, let the Justices determine all suits and rights pertaining to the lord king and to his crown by the writ of the lord king or of those who shall be in his place, concerning the fee of a half knight and below, unless the complaint is so great that it is not possible to be brought to trial without the lord king, or is such as the Justices should report to him because of their doubts, or to those who are in his place. Let them strive nevertheless to their utmost to bring about the profit of the lord king. Let them also make the assize for godless thieves and the land's evildoers, which assize is by the counsel of the king's own son and men, on whose behalf they [the Justices] are going to travel the counties.

**8.** Also, let the Justices see to it that demolished castles are utterly demolished and having been demolished are well strewn. And unless they have done this, the lord king will wish to have the judgment of his court upon them just as for those contemptuous of his command.

**9.** Also, let the Justices inquire about escheats, about churches, about lands, about women who are given in marriage by the lord king.

1 Henry, heir to the throne and called the young king to distinguish him from his father, was crowned at age 15, after what was then the French manner, while his father was still alive. He fought an unsuccessful civil war in 1173-74 that ended with the signing of peace on 30 September 1374. He died in 1180 of dysentery while campaigning once more against his father.

2 Whitsunday, i.e. the day of Pentecost. See Manley 1892 1, 88-108.

3 The Sunday after Pentecost.

**10.** Also, let the bailiffs of the lord king answer to the Exchequer, as much about the rendering of accounts from the assize as about all his perquisites, which they make in their bailiwicks, with the exception of those things that pertain to the sheriff.

**11.** Also, let the Justices inquire about the keeping of castles, both who owes service for them and how much and where, and afterward let them send word to the lord king.

**12.** Also, let a thief be handed over by the one who takes him to the sheriff for keeping. And if the sheriff is away, let him be led to the nearest castellan [governor of a castle], and he shall keep him until he delivers him up to the sheriff.

**13.** Also, let the Justices conduct an inquest, according to the custom of the land, into those who have fled from the realm, lest they have wished to return before the time specified, and bring [them] to justice in the court of the lord king and let them afterwards be outlawed; and let them report the names of the outlaws, at Easter and at the Feast of St Michael, to the Exchequer,[1] and thereafter let them be sent to the lord king.

## Lateran Council IV, Canon 18[2]

The separation of canon and customary law can hardly be said to have begun in 1215 when the Fourth Lateran Council was convened by Pope Innocent III, one of the most influential popes in church history, but its actions did impel a giant step forward in the development of modern secular legal procedure when it forbade clergy members to play any role in the trials by ordeal that characterized medieval legal procedures and

1 The sessions of the Exchequer, at which sheriffs made an accounting of their farms [tax receipts – see glossary], initially convened at Easter and Michaelmas. Two more sessions were ultimately added at the feast days of St Hilary and the Trinity. The four terms of the courts during the year were accordingly Hilary, Easter, Trinity, and Michaelmas.

2 The Fourth Lateran Council, comprised of over a thousand church dignitaries, patriarchs, bishops, and abbots, was convoked at Rome by Pope Innocent III in November 1215.

reasserted a prohibition against judicial trials by combat. It is important to note that the Council did not abolish such actions, the authority for which it patently lacked, and that ordeals by fire and water as well as judicial combats continued for some time. It only prohibited clerical participation in them. Within a generation, however, jury trials became the standard method of resolving charges, although certainly not in the forms and manners we would clearly recognize in modern procedures. Initially the Grand Assize provided an alternative to judicial combat, but since a defendant could still choose the older solution and a jury trial was not inevitably the outcome of this procedure, the petty assizes grew quickly in popularity and became the normal manner of pursuing many suits. Henry III issued a temporary instruction to the justices in eyre in 1219, ordering them to use their discretion and order imprisonment for the most serious crimes, exile for those lesser, and the use of pledges for the least serious "since the trial by fire and water has been prohibited by the Roman church."[1]

While Henry's remark would seem to place the responsibility for the prohibition squarely upon the church, in fact widespread dissatisfaction played a role in the Council's decision. R. C. Van Caenegem shows how "this hallowed system of proof [...] was fatally attacked from many quarters and in many countries [...]. The underlying reason was presumably a fairly general crisis of faith in its efficiency and justification. The same ordeals which the Church had blessed and administered for centuries were now exposed as diabolical practices by theologians, who said that it was 'tempting God' to demand constant miracles, even for the sake of saving innocent suspects. They fought these *tentamenta diabolica* vigorously and decided that they had to be 'exterminated' by Holy Church. They quoted the words of St Augustine 'Nemo debet tentare Deum, quando habet ex humana ratione quid faciat' and the Scriptures 'Thou shalt not tempt the Lord thy God.' Peter the Chanter, a famous figure in the Parisian schools of the late twelfth century, could only see tricks and cheating in them: he knew a man who,

1 Rothwell 1975 340.

before he had to undergo the water ordeal, learnt through patient exercise how to control his breathing so as to succeed in the trial. And as far as the ordeal of hot iron was concerned, it was clear that 'innocence was too closely connected with calluses.' The canonists wavered and hesitated all through the twelfth century, until the Fourth Lateran Council gave a clear and authoritative judgment."[1]

> We take our text from Schroeder; *Disciplinary Decrees*, 569. Our translation is based, with some changes, on Schroeder, 258.

Sententiam sanguinis nullus clericus dictet aut proferat, sed nec sanguinis vindictam exerceat, aut ubi exercetur intersit. Si quis autem hujusmodi occasione statuti ecclesiis vel personis ecclesiasticis aliquod praesumpserit inferre dispendium, per censuram ecclesiasticam compescatur. Nec quisquam clericus litteras scribat, aut dictet pro vindicta sanguinis destinendas. Unde in curiis principum haec solicitudo non clericis sed laicis committatur. Nullus quoque clericus rottariis[2] aut balistariis, aut hujusmodi viris sanguinum praeponatur, nec illa chirugiae partem subdiaconus, diaconus, vel sacerdos exerceant, quae ad ustionem vel incisionem inducit. Nec quisquam purgationi aquae serventis vel frigidae, seu ferri candentis, ritum cujuslibet benedictionis aut conscrationis impendat, salvis nihilominus prohibitionibus de monomachiis sive duellis antea promulgatis.

## Translation

Let no cleric pronounce a sentence of death, or execute such a sentence, or be present at its execution. If anyone in consequence of this prohibition should presume to inflict damage on churches or injury on ecclesiastical persons, let him be restrained by ecclesiastical censure. Nor shall any cleric write or dictate letters destined for the execution of such a sentence. Wherefore, in the chanceries of the princes let this matter be committed to laymen and not to clerics. Neither may a cleric be in charge

1 Van Caenegem 1988 68-9.

2 Presumably from *ruptarius* or *ruptuarius,* "mercenary" or "highwayman" (Fr. *routier*).

of mercenaries, crossbowmen, or other men of such kind devoted to the shedding of blood. Let no subdeacon, deacon, or priest practice that part of surgery involving burning and cutting. Neither shall anyone bestow any blessing on judicial tests or ordeals by hot or cold water or hot iron; the earlier prohibitions in regard to trial by combat remain in force.

## Magna Carta: The Great Charter

The Great Charter of Liberties, to give its full title, is still widely regarded as the foundation of individual rights and protection against arbitrary justice imposed rather than systematic justice adjudicated by legal methods and principles. Such a view is, however, as much myth as reality given that the original meanings of key passages on the subject of judicial procedure have been much re-interpreted over time to give them meanings not intended by the document's framers. The right to a jury trial, for instance, is still derived from the Charter's insistence that defendants be tried by their peers, even though the intention of the framers was more likely to protect the barons against trial by their social inferiors. The three principles embodied in the document that have endured are due process, proportional punishment, and judicial administration divorced from revenue raising.

The first version of the Charter, that sealed by King John in an attempt to still the opposition aroused by his reckless oppression during the Great Interdict,[1] was law for only a few weeks before it was amended in a second version in 1216. The elaborate provisions concerning the king's forests were extracted and put into a separate document called the Charter of the Forests, and several of the more extreme provisions were annulled, most importantly the last, which had erected a commission of barons with the authority to enforce the Charter. A third version, further

1 A period of contention between Pope Innocent III and King John that began when the pope refused to accept John's candidate for Archbishop of Canterbury, insisting instead upon Stephen Langton, who was in the end appointed. It ended with John's capitulation to the pope in 1213, but its effects and consequences continued until the king's death.

modified in favor of the Crown, was almost immediately re-issued in the name of Henry III, John's infant successor, when the king died in 1216. When Henry came of age in 1225, he issued the fourth edition of the Great Charter, which differed only slightly from the third. Plucknett calls it "a sober, practical, and highly technical document," and notes that "this is the document which is still law (except in so far as it has been repealed)."[1] It is cited sometimes as 9 Henry III.

The present text, the fifth version, was confirmed by King Edward I in the twenty-fifth year of his reign (1297), at which time it was placed on the Statute Rolls. It differs from the fourth version that it copies in only one word ("pounds" vice "marks" in Chapter 2), and is occasionally cited as the *Confirmatio Cartarum* of 25 Edward I. The sixty provisions of the original Great Charter are reduced in it to thirty-seven.

We take our text from Luders, *Statutes of the Realm*, I, 1-15. The translation is our own.

Edwardus Dei gratia Rex Anglie Dominus Hibernie & Dux Aquitanie Omnibus ad quos presentes littere pervenerint salutem. Inspeximus Magnam Cartam domini H. quondam regis Anglie patris nostri de Libertatibus Anglie in haec verba. HENRICUS Dei gratia Rex Anglie Dominus Hibernie Dux Normanie Aquitanie & Comes Andegavie Archiepiscopis Episcopis Abbatibus Prioribus Comitibus Baronibus Vicecomitibus Prepositis Ministris & omnibus ballivis & fidelibus suis presentem cartam inspecturis salutem. Sciatis quod nos intuitu Dei & pro salute anime nostre & animarum antecessorum & successorum nostrorum ad exaltationem sancte ecclesie & emendationem regni nostri spontanea & bona voluntate nostra dedimus & concessimus Archiepiscopis Episcopis Abbatibus Prioribus Comitibus Baronibus & omnibus de regno nostro has libertates subscriptas tenendas in regno nostro Anglie imperpetuum.

**Cap. I:** In primis concessimus Deo & hac presenti carta nostra confirmavimus pro nobis & heredibus nostris imperpetuum quod ecclesia

1 Plucknett 1956/2010 23.

Anglicana libera sit & habeat omnia jura sua integra & libertates suas illesas. Concessimus etiam & dedimus omnibus liberis hominibus regni nostri pro nobis & heredibus nostris imperpetuum has libertates subscriptas habendas & tenendas eis & heredibus suis de nobis & heredibus nostris imperpetuum.

**Cap. II:** Si quis Comitum vel Baronum nostrorum sive aliorum tenentium de nobis in capite per servitium militare mortuus fuerit & cum decesserit heres ejus plene etatis fuerit & relevium debeat habeat hereditatem suam per antiquum relevium scilicet heres vel heredes Comitis de Comitatu integro per centum libras heres vel heredes Baronis de Baronia integra per Centum marcas heres vel heredes militis de feodo Militis integro per Centum solidos ad plus & qui minus habuerit minus det secundum antiquam consuetudinem feodorum.

**Cap. III:** Si autem heres alicujus talium infra etatem fuerit dominus ejus non habeat custodiam ejus nec terre sue antequam homagium ejus ceperit & postquam talis heres fuerit in custodia cum ad etatem pervenerit scilicet viginti & unius anni habeat hereditatem suam sine relevio & sine ita tamen quod si ipse dum infra etatem fuerit fiat miles nichilominus terra remaneat in custodia dominorum suorum usque ad terminum predictum.

**Cap. IV:** Custos terre hujusmodi heredis qui infra etatem fuerit non capiat de terra heredis nisi rationabiles exitus & rationabiles consuetudines & rationabilia servicia & hoc sine destructione & vasto hominum & rerum. Et si nos commiserimus custodiam alicujus talis terre vicecomiti vel alicui alii qui de exitibus terre illius nobis debeat respondere & ille de custodia destructionem vel vastum fecerit nos ab eo capiemus emendam & terra committatur duobus legalibus & discretis hominibus de feodo illo qui de exitibus terre illius nobis respondeant vel illi cui illos assignaverimus. Et si dederimus vel vendiderimus alicui custodiam alicujus talis terre & ille inde destructionem fecerit vel vastum amittat illam custodiam & tradatur duobus legalibus & discretis hominibus de feodo illo qui similiter nobis respondeant sicut predictum est.

**Cap. V:** Custos autem quamdiu custodiam terre hujusmodi habuerit sustentet domos parcos vivaria stagna molendina & cetera ad terram illam pertinentia de exitibus terre ejusdem & reddat heredi cum ad plenam etatem pervenerit terram suam totam instauratam de carucis & de omnibus aliis rebus ad minus sicut illam recepit. Hec omnia observentur de custodiis Archiepiscopatuum Episcopatuum Abbathiarum Prioratuum ecclesiarum & dignitatum vacantium que ad nos pertinent excepto quod custodie hujusmodi vendi non debent.

**Cap. VI:** Heredes maritentur absque disparagatione.

**Cap. VII:** Vidua post mortem mariti sui statim & sine difficultate aliqua habeat maritagium suum & hereditatem suam nec aliquid det pro dote sua nec pro maritagio suo vel pro hereditate sua quam hereditatem maritus suus & ipsa tenuerunt simul die obitus ipsius mariti sui & maneat in capitali mesuagio mariti sui per quadraginta dies post obitum mariti sui infra quos dies assignetur ei dos sua nisi prius fuerit ei assignata vel nisi domus illa sit castrum & si de castro recesserit domus ei competens statim provideatur in qua possit honeste morari quousque dos sua ei assignetur secundum quod predictum est & habeat rationabile estoverium suum interim de communi. Assignetur autem ei pro dote sua tertia pars totius terre mariti sui que sua fuit in vita sua nisi de minori fuerit dotata ad hostium ecclesie. Nulla vidua distringatur ad se maritandam dum voluerit vivere sine marito. Ita tamen quod securitatem faciat quod se non maritabit sine assensu nostro si de nobis tenuerit vel sine assensu domini sui si de alio tenuerit.

**Cap. VIII:** Nos vero vel Ballivi nostri non seisiemus terram aliquam vel redditum pro debito aliquo quamdiu catalla debitoris presentia sufficiunt ad debitum reddendum & ipse debitor paratus sit inde satisfacere. Nec plegii ipsius debitoris distringantur quamdiu ipse capitalis debitor sufficiat ad solutionem ipsius debiti & si capitalis debitor defecerit in solutione debiti non habens unde reddat aut reddere nolit cum possit plegii de debito respondeant & si voluerint habeant terras & redditus debitoris quousque sit eis satisfactum de debito quod ante pro eo solverunt nisi capitalis debitor monstraverit se inde esse quietum versus eosdem plegios.

**Cap. IX:** Civitas Londonii habeat omnes libertates suas antiquas & consuetudines suas. Preterea volumus & concedimus quod omnes civitates alie & burgi & ville & barones de quinque portubus & omnes portus habeant omnes libertates & liberas consuetudines suas.

**Cap. X:** Nullus distringatur ad faciendum majus servitium de feodo militis nec de alio libero tenemento quam inde debetur.

**Cap. XI:** Communia placita non sequantur Curiam nostrum set teneantur in aliquo loco certo.

**Cap. XII:** Recognitiones de nova disseisina & de morte antecessoris non capiantur nisi in suis comitatibus & hoc modo: Nos, vel si extra regnum fuerimus capitalis Justiciarius noster, mittemus Justiciarios nostros per unumquemque Comitatum semel in anno qui cum militibus comitatuum capiant in comitatibus assisas predictas & illa que in illo adventu suo in comitatus per Justiciarios nostros predictos ad dictas assisas capiendas missos terminari non possunt per eosdem terminentur alibi in itinere suo & ea que per eosdem propter difficultatem aliquorum articulorum terminari non possunt referantur ad Justiciarios nostros de Banco & ibi terminentur.

**Cap. XIII:** Assise de ultima presentatione semper capiantur coram Justiciarios de Banco & ibi terminentur.

**Cap. XIV:** Liber homo non amercietur pro parvo delicto nisi secundum modum ipsius delicti & pro magno delicto secundum magnitudinem delicti salvo contenemento suo & mercator eodem modo salva mercandisa sua & villanus alterius quam noster eodem modo amercietur salvo wanagio suo si inciderit in manum nostrum. Et nulla predictarum misericordiarum ponatur nisi per sacramentum proborum & legalium hominum de visneto. Comites & barones non amercientur nisi per pares suos & non nisi secundum modum delicti. Nulla ecclesiastica persona amercietur secundum quantitatem beneficii sui ecclesiastici set secundum laicum tenementum suum & secundum quantitatem delicti.

**Cap. XV:** Nec villa nec liber homo distringatur facere pontes ad riparias nisi qui ab antiquo & de jure facere debent.

**Cap. XVI:** Nulle riparie defendantur de cetero nisi ille que fuerunt in defenso tempore Henrici Regis Avi nostri per eadem loca & eosdem terminos sicut esse consueverunt tempore suo.

**Cap. XVII:** Nullus vicecomes constabularius coronator vel alii ballivi nostri teneant placita corone nostre.

**Cap. XVIII:** Si aliquis tenens de nobis laicum feodum moriatur & vicecomes vel ballivus noster ostendat litteras nostras patentes de summonitione nostra de debito quod defunctus nobis debuit liceat vicecomiti vel ballivo nostro attachiare & imbreviare omnia bona & catalla defuncti inventa in laico feodo ad valentiam illius debiti per visum legalium hominum. Ita tamen quod nichil inde amoveatur donec persolvatur nobis debitum quod clarum fuerit & residuum relinquatur executoribus ad faciendum testamentum defuncti & si nichil nobis debeatur ab ipso omnia catalla cedant defuncto salvis uxori ejus & pueris ipsius rationabilibus partibus suis.

**Cap. XIX:** Nullus constabularies vel ejus ballivus capiat blada vel alia catalla alicujus qui non sit de villa ubi castrum situm est nisi statim reddat denarios inde aut respectum inde habere possit de voluntate venditoris. Si autem de ipsa villa fuerit infra quadraginta dies precium reddat.

**Cap. XX:** Nullus constabularius distringat aliquem militem ad dandum denarios pro custodia castri si ipse eam facere voluerit in propria persona sua vel per alium probum hominem facere si ipse eam facere non possit propter rationabilem causam. Et si nos adduxerimus vel miserimus eum in exercitum sit quietus de custodia secundum quantitatem temporis quo per nos fuerit in exercitu de feodo pro quo fecit servicium in exercitu.

**Cap. XXI:** Nullus vicecomes vel ballivus noster vel aliquis alius capiat equos vel carettas alicujus pro cariagio faciendo nisi reddat liberationem antiquitus statutam scilicet pro una caretta ad duos equos decem denarios per diem & pro caretta ad tres equos quatuordecim denarios per diem. Nulla caretta dominica alicujus ecclesiastice persone vel militis vel alicujus domini per ballivos nostros capiatur. Nec nos nec ballivi nostri nec alii capiemus boscum alienum ad castra vel ad alia agenda nostra nisi per voluntatem illius cujus boscus ille fuerit.

**Cap. XXII:** Nos non tenebimus terras illorum qui convicti fuerint de felonia nisi per unum annum & unum diem & tunc reddantur terre ille dominis feodorum.

**Cap. XXIII:** Omnes kidelli deponantur de cetero penitus per Tamisiam & Medweyam & per totam Angliam nisi per costeram maris.

**Cap. XXIV:** Breve quod vocatur *Praecipe* de cetero non fiat alicui de aliquo libero tenemento unde liber homo perdat curiam suam.

**Cap. XXV:** Una mensura vini sit per totum regnum nostrum & una mensura cervisie & una mensura bladi scilicet quarterium Londoniense & una latitudo pannorum tinctorum russettorum & haubergettorum, scilicet due ulne infra listas. De ponderibus vero sit sicut de mensuris.

**Cap. XXVI:** Nichil de cetero detur pro brevi inquisitionis ab eo qui inquisitionem petit de vita vel de membris set gratis concedatur & non negetur.

**Cap. XXVII:** Si aliqui teneant de nobis per feodi-firmam vel per socagium vel burgagium & de alio teneant terram per servicium militare nos non habebimus custodiam heredis nec terre sue que est de feodo alterius occasione illius feodi-firme vel socagii vel burgagii nec habebimus custodiam illius feodi-firme vel socagii vel burgagii nisi ipsa feodi-firme debeat servicium militare. Nos non habebimus custodiam heredis vel alicujus terre quam tenet de aliquo alio per servicium militare occasione alicujus parve serjantie quam tenet de nobis per servicium reddendi nobis cultellos vel sagittas vel hujusmodi.

**Cap. XXVIII:** Nullus ballivus de cetero ponat aliquem ad legem manifestam nec ad juramentum simplici loquela sua sine testibus fidelibus ad hoc inductis.

**Cap. XXIX:** Nullus liber homo capiatur vel imprisonetur aut disseisiatur de libero tenemento suo vel libertatibus vel liberis consuetudinibus suis aut utlagetur aut exulet aut aliquo modo destruatur nec super eum ibimus nec super eum mittemus nisi per legale judicium parium suorum vel per legem terre. Nulli vendemus nulli negabimus aut differemus rectum vel justitiam.

**Cap. XXX:** Omnes mercatores nisi publice antea prohibiti fuerint habeant salvum & securum conductum exire de Anglia & venire in Angliam & morari & ire per Angliam tam per terram quam per aquam ad emendum & vendendum sine omnibus toltis malis per antiquas & rectas consuetudines preterquam in tempore guerre & si sint de terra contra nos guerrina & tales inveniantur in terra nostra in principio guerre attachientur sine dampno corporum vel rerum donec sciatur a nobis vel a capitali Justiciario nostro quomodo mercatores terre nostre tractentur qui tunc inveniuntur in terra illa contra nos guerrina & si nostri salvi sint ibi alii salvi sint in terra nostra.

**Cap. XXXI:** Si quis tenuerit de aliqua escaeta sicut de honor e Wallingfordie Bolonie Nottingham Lancastrie vel aliis escaetis que sunt in manu nostra & sint baronie & obierit heres ejus non det aliud relevium nec faciat nobis aliud servicium quam faceret baroni si illa esset in manu baronis & nos eodem modo eam tenebimus quo baro eam tenuit. Nec nos occasione talis baronie vel escaete habebimus aliquam escaetam vel custodiam aliquorum nostrorum hominum nisi de nobis alibi tenuerit in capite ille qui tenuit baroniam vel escaetam.

**Cap. XXXII:** Nullus liber homo det de cetero amplius alicui vel vendat de terra sua quam ut de residuo terre sue sufficienter possit fieri domino feodi servitium ei debitum quod pertinet ad feodum illud.

**Cap. XXXIII:** Omnes patroni abbathiarum qui habent cartas regum Anglie de advocatione vel antiquam tenuram vel possessionem habeant earum custodiam cum vacaverint sicut habere debent & sicut superius declaratum est.

**Cap. XXXIV:** Nullus capiatur aut imprisonetur propter appellum femine de morte alterius quam viri sui.

**Cap. XXXV:** Nullus comitatus de cetero teneatur nisi de mense in mensem & ubi major terminus esse solebat major sit. Nec aliquis vicecomes vel ballivus suus faciat turnum suum per hundredum nisi bis in anno & non nisi in loco debito & consueto videlicet semel post Pascham & iterum post festum Sancti Michaelis. Et visus de franco plegio tunc fiat ad illum terminum sancti Michaelis sine occasione. Ita scilicet quod quilibet habeat libertates suas quas habuit vel habere consuevit tempore Henrici Regis avi nostri vel quas postea perquisivit. Fiat autem visus de franco plegio sic videlicet quod pax nostra teneatur & quod theothinga teneatur integra sicut esse consuevit & quod vicecomes non querat occasiones & quod contentus sit de eo quod vicecomes habere consuevit de visu suo faciendo tempore Henrici Regis avi nostri.

**Cap. XXXVI:** Nec liceat de cetero alicui dare terram suam domui religiose ita quod illam resumat de eadem domo tenendam. Nec liceat alicui domui religiose terram alicujus sic accipere quod tradat illam illi a quo eam recepit tenendam. Si quis autem de cetero terram suam alicui domui religiose sic dederit & super hoc convincatur donum suum penitus cassetur & terra illa domino illius feodi incurratur.

**Cap. XXXVII:** Scutagium de cetero capiatur sicut capi consuevit tempore Henrici Regis avi nostri. Et salve sint archiepiscopis episcopis abbatibus prioribus Templaribus Hospitelaribus comitibus baronibus & omnibus aliis tam ecclesiasticis personis quam secularibus omnes libertates & libere consuetudines quas prius habuerunt. Omnes autem consuetudines & libertates predictas quas concessimus in regno nostro tenendas quantum ad nos pertinent erga nostros. Omnes de regno nostro tam clerici quam laici observent quantum ad se pertinent erga suos. Pro hac autem donatione & concessione libertatum istarum & aliarum contentarum in carta nostra de libertatibus foreste archiepiscopi episcopi abbates priores comites barones milites libere tenentes & omnes de regno nostro dederunt nobis quintamdecimam partem omnium mobilium suorum. Concessimus etiam eisdem pro nobis & heredibus nostris quod nec nos nec heredes nostri aliquid perquiremus per quod libertates in hac carta contente infringantur vel infirmentur. Et si ab aliquo contra hoc aliquid perquisitum fuerit nichil valeat & pro nullo habeatur. Hiis testibus domino S. Cantuariensi Archiepiscopo, E. Londoniensi Episcopo, J. Bathoniensi Episcopo, P. Wyntonio, H. Lincoln'iensi, R. Sarum, W. Roffensi, W. Wygorniensi, J. Eliensi, H. Herefordensi, R. Cicestrensi, W. Exoniensi Episcopis; Abbate sancti Edmundi, Abbate sancti Albani, Abbate de Bello, Abbate Sancti Augustini Cantuariensis, Abbate de Evesham, Abbate de Westmonasterio, Abbate de Burgo Sancti Petri, Abbate de Reding, Abbate de Abyndonia, Abbate de Malmsburio, Abbate de Wynchecumbe, Abbbate de Hida, Abbate de Certeseye, Abbate de Shirburna, Abbate de Cerne, Abbate de Abbotebira, Abbate de Middletonio, Abbate de Seleby, Abbate de Cirencestrensi; H. de Burgo Justiciario, H. Comite Cestrie & Lincolnie, W. Comite Sarum, W. Comite Warrenia, G. de Clare Comite Gloucestrensis & Hertfordia, W. de Ferrars Comite Derbentio, W. de Mandevill Comite Essexie, H. de Bigod Comite Norffolcie, W. Comite Albemarlie, H. Comite Herefordie; J. Constabularius Cestrie, R. de Ros, R. Filio Walteri, R. de Veteri Ponte, W. de Bruere, R. de Muntefichet, P. Filio Herberti, W. de Aubeny, F. Gresly, F. de Breuse, J. de Monemue, J. Filio Alani, H. de Mortuo Mari, W. de Bello Campo, W. de Sancto Johanne, P. de Malo Lacu, Briano de Insula, Thomas de Multon, R. de Argentein, G. de Nevill, W. Mauduit, J. de Balun, & aliis. Data apud Westmonasterium, xi. Die Februario anno regni nostri nono.

Nos autem donationes & concessiones predictas ratas habentes & gratas eas pro nobis & heredibus nostris concedimus & confirmamus easque tenore presentium innovamus volentes & concedentes pro nobis & heredibus nostris quod carta predicta in omnibus & singulis suis articulis imperpetuum firmiter & inviolabiliter observetur etiam si aliqui articuli in eadem carta contenti hucusque forsitan non fuerint observati. In cujus rei testimonium has litteras nostras fieri fecimus patentes. T. Edwardo filio nostro apud Westmonasterium duodecimo die Octobri anno regni nostri vicesimo quinto.

### Translation

Edward, by the grace of God King of England, Lord of Ireland, and Duke of Aquitania, to all those to whom present these words have arrived, greeting. We have looked at the Great Charter of the Lord Henry, formerly King of England, our father, concerning the liberties of England in these words: Henry, by the grace of God King of England, Lord of Ireland, Duke of Normandy and Aquitania and Count of Anjou, to the archbishops, bishops, abbots, priors, earls, barons, sheriffs, provosts, ministers, and all bailiffs and to the faithful who shall see the present Charter, greeting. Know that we by the intention of God and for the salvation of our soul and of the souls of our predecessors and of our successors, to the exaltation of Holy Church and the amendment of our realm, freely and by our good will give and concede to our archbishops, bishops, abbots, priors, earls, barons, and all of our realm these liberties written below, that they be kept in our realm of England in perpetuity.

**Chapter 1: A confirmation of liberties.**

First, we have conceded to God and by this our present Charter have confirmed for us and our heirs in perpetuity that the English Church shall be free and have all its rights and liberties whole and inviolable. We have also conceded and we grant to all freemen of our realm for us and our heirs in perpetuity these below-written liberties to them and their heirs for their having and holding of us and our heirs in perpetuity.

**Chapter 2: The relief of the King's tenant of full age.**

If any of our earls or barons or any other of those holding from us in chief by a knight's service should die and his heir when he is deceased is of full age and owes relief, he shall have his inheritance by the old relief, that is, the heir or heirs of an earl of an entire earldom for one hundred marks, or the heirs of a baron of an entire barony for one hundred marks, or the heirs of a knight of an entire knight's fee for one hundred shillings at the most, and who has less will give less according to the old custom of the fees.

**Chapter 3: The wardship of an heir within full age. The heir a knight.**

If, however, the heir of any such be under age, his lord shall not have custody of him nor of his land before he has received his homage, and after such an heir is in his custody until he has come to his age, that is, twenty-one years, he shall have his inheritance without relief, and even if nevertheless he is made a knight while under age notwithstanding, his land shall remain in the custody of his lord until the above-stated termination.

**Chapter 4: No waste shall be made by a lord within an heir's lands.**

The guardian of the land of such an heir who is under age shall not take from the land of the heir except reasonable revenues and reasonable customary dues and reasonable services and that without destruction and waste of men and property. And if we commit the custody of such a one's land to the sheriff or to anyone else who ought to answer to us for the customary dues of that same land and he make destruction or waste from the things in custody, we will seize from him amends and the land shall be entrusted to two lawful and discrete men of that fee who shall answer to us for the revenues of that land or to those whom we will assign. And if we grant or sell to anyone the custody of any such land and he there shall cause destruction or waste, let him lose that custody and let it be given to two lawful and discrete men from that fee who likewise shall answer to us just as is said above.

**Chapter 5: Guardians shall maintain the inheritance of their lords and of bishoprics, etc.**

A guardian, moreover, as long as he has custody of land in such a way shall maintain the houses, parks, fish ponds and moats, mills and the other things pertaining to that land from the customary dues of his land and return to the heir when he come to full age all his land equipped with ploughs and all the other things at least just as he received it. All these things shall be observed from the custodianships of archbishops, bishops, abbots, priors, churches, and vacant dignities which pertain to us, except that custody of this manner ought not be sold.

**Chapter 6: Heirs shall be married without disparagement.**

**Chapter 7: A widow shall have her marriage, inheritance, and quarantine. The king's widow, etc.**

A widow, after the death of her husband, at once and without impediment, shall have her marriage portion and her inheritance, nor shall she give anything for her dower nor for her marriage portion nor for her inheritance which her husband and she held together on the day of her husband's death, and she shall remain in the chief messuage[1] of her husband for forty days after the death of her husband, within which days her dower shall be assigned her unless it were already assigned her or unless that house is a castle, and if she should depart from the castle let at once a suitable house be provided her in which she may honestly remain until her dower is assigned to her as it is said above, and let her have reasonable provisions from the common property. Moreover, let her be assigned for her dower a third part of all her husband's land which was his in his life unless she was given less at the church's door. No widow shall be forced to marry when she wishes to live without a husband. Nevertheless, let surety be made that she will not marry without our assent if she holds from us or without the assent of her lord if she holds from another.

**Chapter 8: How sureties shall be charged to the king.**

But we or our bailiffs shall not seize any land or revenue for any debt as long as the present chattels of the debtor suffice to repaying the debt, and the debtor himself is prepared to make satisfaction there. Nor shall the debtor's pledges themselves be distrained as long as the principal debtor himself satisfies the settlement of the debt, and if the principal debtor

1 A residential structure together with its outbuildings and associated land.

defaults on the payment of the debt, not having wherewithal with which he might pay or he does not wish to pay when he is able, let the pledges answer for the debt, and if they wish let them have the debtor's lands and revenues until satisfaction is made to them for the debt that they paid for him before, unless the principal debtor shows that he is quit against those same pledges.

**Chapter 9: The Liberties of London and other cities and towns confirmed.**

Let the city of London have all its ancient liberties and customs. Moreover, we wish and concede that all other cities and boroughs and vills and the barons of the Cinque Ports and all other ports shall have all their liberties and free customs.

**Chapter 10: None shall distrain for more service than is due.**

Let no man be distrained to do more service for a knight's fee nor for any other freehold than is thence owed.

**Chapter 11: Common pleas shall not follow the king's court.**

Let Common Pleas not follow our court, but let them be held in some fixed place.

**Chapter 12: Where and before whom assizes shall be taken. Adjournment for difficulty.**

Actions for *novel disseisin* and *mort d'ancestor* shall not be held except in their own counties and in this manner: If we are outside the realm let our chief Justice send our Justices through each county once a year, who with the knights of the counties shall hold the aforesaid assizes in the counties, and those things which upon the arrival in the counties by our aforesaid Justices sent to hold the said assizes cannot be determined shall be determined by them somewhere else on their eyre and those things which by them cannot be determined on account of the difficulty of some articles shall be referred to our Justices of the Bench and there determined.

**Chapter 13: Assizes of *darrein presentment.***

Assizes of *darrein presentment*[1] shall always be held before the Justices of the Bench and there determined.

**Chapter 14: How men of all sorts shall be amerced, and by whom.**

A freeman shall not be amerced for a minor delict except according to the manner of the delict and for a major delict according to the magnitude of the delict, saving the maintenance of his status, and a merchant according to the same manner, saving his merchandise, and another villain than ours shall be amerced in the same manner, saving his means of cultivation, if he should fall into our hands. And none of the aforesaid amercements shall be imposed except by the oath of honest and lawful men of the venue. Earls and barons shall not be amerced except by their peers and only according to the manner of the delict. No ecclesiastical individual shall be amerced according to the size of his ecclesiastical benefice but according to his lay holding and the gravity of his delict.

**Chapter 15: Making of bridges and banks.**

No vill or freeman shall be distrained to make bridges on riverbanks except those obligated to make them from long ago and by right.

**Chapter 16: Defending of banks.**

No riverbanks shall be defended [reinforced] from henceforth except those that were in defense in the time of King Henry our grandfather by the same places and the same periods of time as they were accustomed to be in his time.

**Chapter 17: Holding pleas of the crown.**

1 Resolving issues of who had the right to present a benefice, that is, name a replacement priest to an endowed church, typically began by establishing the landholder who had presented the benefice most recently (in Anglo-Norman the "last presentation" is *darrein presentment*) and then determining which of the contenders was that bestower's legal successor.

No sheriff, constable, coroner nor any other bailiffs of ours shall hold pleas of our crown.

**Chapter 18: The king's debtor dying, the king shall be first paid.**

If anyone holding a lay fee from us dies, and our sheriff or bailiff presents our letters patent for our summons for the debt that the dead man owed us, it shall be permitted our sheriff or bailiff to attach and register all the goods and chattels of the dead man found in the lay fee to the valuation of that debt in the view of lawful men, in such a way, however, that nothing shall be moved from thence until it shall be clear that the debt to us is resolved, and the remnant shall be left to the executors in order to execute the testament of the dead man, and if nothing is owed to us all the chattels shall cease for the dead man, saving to his wife and children their reasonable shares.

**Chapter 19: Purveyance for a castle.**

No warden of a castle nor his bailiff shall take grain or any other chattels of anyone who is not from the vill where the castle is situated except he pays in shillings, unless he is able to have a postponement by the will of the seller. If, however, he is from the same vill he shall pay the price within forty days.

**Chapter 20: Doing of castle-ward.**

No warden of a castle shall compel any knight by distraint[1] to give money for the keeping of his castle if he himself wishes to do it in his proper person or do it through another honest man if he himself is unable to do it on account of reasonable cause. And if we take or send him in an army let him be quit from castle-ward according to the length of time when he is with us in the army for the fee for which he does service in an army.

**Chapter 21: Taking of horses, carts, and wood.**

1 The seizure of chattels to ensure compliance.

No sheriff nor bailiff of ours or of any other shall take the horses or carts of anyone in order to make carriages unless he pays the allowance of the old statute, that is, for a two-horse cart ten pence per day, and for a three-horse cart fourteen pence per day. No demesne cart of any ecclesiastical individual or knight or any other lord shall be taken by our bailiffs. Nor shall we nor the bailiffs of us take another's wood for our castles or for any other uses of ours unless by the will of him whose wood it is.

**Chapter 22: How long felons' lands shall be holden by the king.**

We will not hold the lands of those who have been convicted of felony except for one year and one day and then those lands shall be given back to the lords of the fees.

**Chapter 23: In what places weirs shall be put down.**

Let all weirs from henceforth be removed along the Thames and Medway and throughout England only along the coast of the sea.

**Chapter 24: In what case a *praecipe in capite*[1] is not grantable.**

The writ that is called *praecipe* shall not from henceforth be issued to anyone from any freehold whereby a free man may lose his house.

**Chapter 25: There shall be but one measure throughout the realm.**

Let there be one measure of wine through our entire realm and one measure of ale and one measure of grain, that is, the Quarter of London, and one width of the measures of dyed russet cloth and haubergett[2] cloth, that is, two ells within the edges. And let it be for weights as it is for measures.

**Chapter 26: Inquisition of life and member.**

1 A chancery writ used to recover lands held directly from the king.
2 A coarse, thick desirable cloth. Russet is a thinner fabric of less value.

Let nothing from henceforth be given for a writ of inquisition by him who seeks inquisition concerning life or members, but let it be granted freely and not denied.[3]

**Chapter 27: Tenure of the king in socage, and of another by knight's service. Petit Serjeanty.**

If any persons should hold from us by fee-farm or by socage or burgage and hold land from another by knight's service, we will not have the custody of his heir nor of his land which is by the fee of another by the occasion of that fee-farm or socage or burgage, nor will we have custody of that fee-farm or socage or burgage unless that same fee-farm owes knight's service. We will not have custody of the heir of any land that he holds from any other by knight's service or by the occasion of any Petit Serjeanty[2] that he holds of us by service for the purpose of paying us knives or arrows or such like.

**Chapter 28: Wager of law shall not be without witness.**

Let no bailiff henceforth put anyone to manifest law nor to an oath by his mere statement without faithful witnesses having been brought forward for the purpose.

**Chapter 29: None shall be condemned without trial. Justice shall not be sold or deferred.**

Let no freeman be taken or imprisoned or disseised of his freehold or liberties or his free customs or outlawed or exiled or in any way destroyed, nor will we go upon him nor will we send upon him except by the legal judgment of his peers or by the law of the land. We will sell to no man or deny to no man right or justice.

**Chapter 30: Merchants coming into this realm shall be well used.**

---

3 A precursor to the writ of habeas corpus, this provision required that an inquiry be held in cases in which a defendant might be punished by deprivation of life or limb.

2 Impersonal services to the king such as the annual presentation of implements of war.

All merchants, unless previously they have been publicly prohibited, shall have safe and secure conduct to depart from England and to come into England and to remain and to go through England by land as well as by water for the purpose of buying and selling without all evil tolts[1] according to the ancient and rightful customs, except in wartime, and if they be from a land warring against us and are found in our land in the beginning of the war, they shall be attached without trespass of their bodies or things until it is known by us or by our Chief Justice how the merchants of our land shall be treated who are found there in that land warring against us, and if ours are safe there let the others be safe in our land.

**Chapter 31: Tenure of a barony coming into the King's hands by escheat.**

If anyone should hold escheat from another, as from the honor of Wallingford, Boulogne, Nottingham, Lancaster or other escheats which are in our hands and are baronies, and he dies, let his heir not pay relief nor do to us any other service than he would do to the baron if it should be in the baron's hands, and we will hold it in the same manner in which the baron held it. Nor shall we have by occasion of such barony or escheat any escheat or custody of any of our other men unless he who held the barony or escheat held elsewhere in capite.

**Chapter 32: Lands shall not be alienated to the prejudice of the lord's service.**

Let no freeman henceforth give or sell from his land any more than that he will be able from the remnant of his land to perform sufficiently to the lord of the fee the service owed to him that pertains to that fee.

**Chapter 33: Patrons of abbeys shall have the custody of them in the time of vacancy.**

---

1 Tolts or maltolts are unjust taxes or exactions. Tolt also is the name of the writ and process that takes a case from a seignorial to a county court.

All patrons of abbeys who have the charter of England's kings for advowson[1] or have ancient tenure or possession of the same shall have the custody of them when they have been vacated just as they ought and just as it was aforesaid stated.

**Chapter 34: In what case alone a woman shall have an appeal of death.**

Let no man be taken or imprisoned on account of a woman's appeal concerning the death of anyone other than her husband.

**Chapter 35: At what time shall be kept a county court, sheriff's tourn, and a leet.**

Let no county court be held henceforth except from month to month, and, where a greater time is customary, let it be greater. Nor let any sheriff or bailiff hold his tourn through the hundred except twice a year, and not except in the obligated place and as customary, that is, once after Easter and again after the feast of Saint Michael. And let the view of frankpledge then be made at that term of Saint Michael without occasion[2], namely so that everyone may have his liberties which he had or used to have in the time of King Henry our grandfather, or which afterward he purchased; moreover, let the view of frankpledge be made so that our peace be kept and that the tithing is kept whole just as it was used to be, and that the sheriff not seek occasions and that he be content with that which the sheriff used to have for the purpose of making his view in the time of King Henry our grandfather.

**Chapter 36: No land shall be given in mortmain.[3]**

It shall not be allowed henceforth to anyone to give his land to a religious house and take again that same holding from the same house. Nor shall it be allowed to any religious house to accept the land of anyone so that it

1 The right to present an appointee to a benefice.
2 Without cause or reason for holding it at some other time.
3 The "dead hand" of the church, so-called because land held by the church would no longer descend hereditarily and accordingly would not continue to yield feudal incidents to a demesne lord.

hand it over to him from whom it received the holding. If anyone henceforth, moreover, gives his land to some religious house and is convicted of this, let that gift be annulled and that land accrue to the lord of that fee.

**Chapter 37: A subsidy in respect of this Charter, and the Charter of the Forest, granted to the King.**

Let scutage[1] henceforth be taken just as it used to be in the time of King Henry our grandfather. And let be saved to archbishops, bishops, abbots, priors, Templars, Hospitallers, earls, barons, and all other ecclesiastical as well as secular persons all the liberties and free customs which they earlier have had. Moreover, let all the aforesaid customs and liberties which we have granted to be held in our realm, as far as they pertain to us, be granted to our men. Let all from our realm, religious as well as lay, observe what pertains to them as to their own men. Moreover, for this gift and grant of these liberties and of the other contents in our Charter of the Liberties of the Forest the archbishops, bishops, abbots, priors, earls, barons, knights, freeholders and others of our realm have given us the fifteenth part of all their movables. Likewise, we have granted to them for us and our heirs that neither we nor our heirs shall request anything by which the liberties contained in this Charter shall be infringed or weakened. And if something is procured by someone contrary to this, let it not avail and be held for nothing. Witnessed by S. the Lord Archbishop of Canterbury, E. the Bishop of London, J. the Bishop of Bath, P. of Winchester, H. of Lincoln, R. of Salisbury, W. of Rochester, W. of Worcester, J. of Ely, H. of Hereford, R. of Chichester, W. of Exeter, bishops; by the Abbot of St. Edmunds, the Abbot of St. Albans, the Abbot of Bello, the Abbot of St. Augustines in Canterbury, the Abbot of Evesham, the Abbot of Westminster, the Abbot of Bourgh St. Peter, the Abbot of Reading, the Abbot of Abingdon, the Abbot of Malmesbury, the Abbot of Winchcomb, the Abbot of Hyde, the Abbot of Certesey, the Abbot of Sherburn, the Abbot of Cerne, the Abbot of Abbotebir, the

1 Payment in lieu of providing armed men of various sorts for military service.

Abbot of Middleton, the Abbot of Seleby, the Abbot of Cirencester; by H. the Justiciarius of Burg, by H. Earl of Chester and Lincoln, W. Earl of Salisbury, W. Earl of Warren, G. de Clare Earl of Gloucester and Hereford, W. de Ferrars Earl of Derby, W. de Mandeville Earl of Essex, H. de Bygod Earl of Norfolk, W. Earl of Albemarle, H. Earl of Hereford; by J. the Constable of Chester, by R. de Ros, R. Fitzwalter, R. de Vyponte, W. de Bruer, R. de Montefichet, P. Fitzherbert, W. de Aubenie, F. Gresly, F. de Breus, J. de Monemue, J. Fitzallen, H. de Mortimer, W. de Beuchamp, W. de St. John, P. de Mauli, Brian de Lisle, Thomas de Multon, R. de Argenteyn, G. de Nevil, W. de Mauduit, J. de Balun, and by others. Given at Westminster the 11th day of February the 9th year of our reign.

We, moreover, having approved the aforesaid gifts and grants for us and our heirs, grant and confirm them and by the tenor of these presents we renew them, willing and granting for us and our heirs that the aforesaid Charter in each and every one of its articles in perpetuity shall be firmly and inviolably observed, even if some articles contained in this Charter perchance have not been observed. In witness of this matter we have caused our Letters Patents to be made. Witnessed by Edward our son at Westminster the 12th day of October in the 25th year of our reign.

## Statute Concerning the Jews

An early instance of the effort to exclude Jews from western Europe. There is, however, no evidence to suggest that this particular piece of legislation was enforced or had much effect. Tallies continued to be used instead of the specified chirographs and no expulsion of Jews followed. The provision concerning chirographs[1] was subsequently amended to require that the sealed copy be deposited in the *archae*, chests used as archives, and the foot, the third copy, go to the Jew, as indicated in mandates to sheriffs in 1240 and 1241. Although the text was never

1 Contracts executed in triplicate. Normally the first two copies went to the parties and the third, the "foot," was placed in safe-keeping. This third copy prevented the signatories from altering their copies to their advantage.

entered on the rolls, there seems to be no reason to doubt the authenticity of this legislation. Other countries will pass similar laws, the most famous of which will be enacted in Spain after the Reconquest. For a general discussion, see Joe and Caroline Hillaby 2013 26.

We take out text from Richardson, *Law Quarterly Review* 54 (1938) 393. The translation is our own.

**1.** Anno regni regis Henrici filii Iohannis xvijo, iiijo die Aprilis in crastino Pasce, statutum fuit ab eodem rege apud Cantuariam quod nullum mutuum de cetero trahatur cum Iudeis per talliam set per cyrograffum, cuius alteram partem Iudeus habeat, cum signo Christiani mutuum contrahentis appenso, et alteram partem habeat Christianus mutuum contrahens. Tercia vero pars que vocatur pes reponatur in archa saluo custodienda per cirograffarios Christianos et Iudeos, et cirograffum cuius pes non fuerit inuentus in archa, sicut predictum est, nullum habeat vigorem.

**2.** Nullus Iudeus aliquid det mutuo per penam, set de libra capiat duos denarios per ebdomodam de lucro et non plus, ita quod nichil ponatur in sortem nisi primum mutuum.

**3.** Nullus Iudeus remaneat in regno nostro nisi talis sit quod regi possit servire et bonos plegios inueniat de fidelitate. Alii vero Iudei, qui nichil habent vnde regi serviant, exeant de regno infra instans festum sancti Michaelis anno regni regis predicti xvijo: quod si vlterius moram fecerunt detrudantur in carcerem et non deliberentur sine speciali mandato regis.

**4.** Nullus Iudeus de cetero aliquid mutuum det super vasa ecclesiastica aut super pannos sanguinolentes aut madidos aut quasi vi confunctos.[1]

---

1 Rothwell 1975 350 emends *confunctus* to *conpunctus* and translates as "holed." In either case, the sense is that the cloth has been ruined and just like material rendered imperfect in other ways should not be marketed.

### Translation

**1.** In the seventeenth year of the reign of king Henry the son of John, on the fourth day of April on the day after Easter, a statute was made by that same king at Canterbury that no loan from henceforth should be made with Jews by tally but by chirograph, whose one part the Jew should have, with the seal of the Christian contracting the loan appended, and the other part the Christian contracting the loan should have. A third part that is called the foot should be placed in a chest in the safe keeping of the chirographers, Christians and Jews, and the chirograph whose foot has not been found in the chest, just as aforesaid, shall have no force.

**2.** No Jew shall grant something as a loan as punishment, but he may take in profit two pence per week for a pound and not more, so that nothing is put in jeopardy but the initial loan.

**3.** Let no Jew remain in our reign unless he be such that can serve the king and find good pledges of his fidelity. Other Jews, who have nothing whereby they might serve the king, shall depart from the kingdom before the approaching feast of St. Michael in the year of the reign of the aforesaid king the eighteenth: but if they make further delay let [them] be cast into prison and not released without the king's special mandate.

**4.** No Jew from henceforth shall grant any loan upon church vessels or upon cloth goods that have been ruined by blood or moisture or by forceful handling.

## The Provisions, or so-called Statute, of Merton

The conclusions reached by Henry III and his assembled prelates and nobles, gathered at Merton upon the occasion of Queen Eleanor's coronation, dealt with a miscellany of issues pertaining to legitimacy, enclosure of common pasture, and dower. Like Magna Carta, it is a component of the struggle between the king and his barons over rights. Maitland calls it "the first set of laws which in later days usually bears the name of statute."[1] To signify its importance, its conclusions were later

1 Pollock and Maitland 1898 1,179.

repeated for the most part in the Provisions of Marlborough. It is printed as the first document in *The Statutes of the Realm.*

> We take out text from Luders, *Statutes of the Realm*, I, 1-14. As Plucknett points out, the text is taken from a private source (MS Claudius D. II) and the official contemporary versions are "consigned to footnotes."[1] The translation is our own.

Provisum est in curia domini Regis, die mercurii in crastino sancti Vincencii, anno regni Regis Henrici filii Regis Johannis vicesimo, apud Merton, coram archiepiscopo Cantuariensi, & episcopis suffraganeis, coram majori parte comitum & baronum Anglie ibidem existentium, pro coronatione ipsius domini Regis & Alianore Regine, pro qua omnes vocati fuerunt; cum tractatum esset de communi utilitate regni super articulis subscriptis: ita provisum fuit, & concessum, tam a predictis archiepeiscopis, episcopis, comitibus, baronibus, quam ab ipso Rege & aliis.

**1.** De viduis vero que post mortem virorum suorum expelluntur de dotibus suis & dotes suas, vel quarentenam habere non possunt sine placito, videlicet quod quicunque deforciaverit eis dotes suas vel quarentenam suam de tenementis de quibus viri sui obierunt seisiti & ipse vidue postea per placitum recuperaverint ipsi qui de injusto deforciamento convicti fuerint reddant eisdem viduis dampna sua videlicet valorem totius dotis eis contingentis a tempore mortis virorum suorum usque ad diem quo ipse vidue per judicium curie seisinam suam inde recuperaverint: et nichilominus ipsi deforciatores sint in misericordia domini regis.

**2.** Item, omnes vidue de cetero possunt legare blada sua de terra sua, tam de dotibus suis, quam de aliis terris & tenementis suis, salvis servitiis dominorum, que de dotibus & aliis tenementis suis debentur.

**3.** Item, si quis fuerit disseisitus de libero tenemento suo, & coram justiciariis itinerantibus seisinam suam recuperaverit per assisam nove disseisine, vel per recognitionem eorum qui fecerint disseisinam, & ipse

1 Plucknett 1922/2010 13.

disseisitus per vicecomitem seisinam suam habuerit, Si iidem disseisiatores postea, post iter justiciariorum, de eodem tenemento iterum eundem conquerentem disseisiverint & inde convicti fuerint, statim capiantur & in prisona domini Regis detineantur, quousque per dominum Regem, per redemptionem, vel aliquo alio modo, deliberentur. [Et hec est forma qualiter tales convicti puniri debeant, videlicet cum conquerentes ad curiam venerint, habeant breve domini Regis vicecomiti directum, in quo contineatur eorum narratio de disseisina facta super disseisinam. Et ideo mandetur vicecomiti, quod assumptis secum custodibus placitorum corone, & aliis legalibus militibus, in propria persona sua accedat ad tenementum illud vel pasturam illam de quibus facta fuerit querela & coram eis per primos juratores, & per alios vicinos & legales homines, diligentem inde faciat inquisitionem, & si ipsum iterum invenerit disseisitum, sicut predictum est, faciat tunc secundum provisionem predictam; sin autem, tunc sit conquerens in misericordia domini regis & alius quietus recedat. Nec debet vicecomes, sine speciali precepto domini Regis, hujusmodi loquelam prosequi.

Eodem modo fiat de illis, qui seisinam recuperaverint per assisam mortis antecessoris et de omnibus terris et tenementis recuperatis per juratas in curia domini Regis, si postea disseisiti fuerint a prioribus deforciatoribus, versus quos recuperaverint per juratam quoquo modo.

**4.** Item, quia multi magnates Anglie, qui feoffaverint milites & libere tenentes suos de parvis tenementis in magnis maneriis suis, questi fuerunt quod commodum suum facere non potuerunt de residuo maneriorum suorum, sicut de vastis, boscis, & pasturis, cum ipsi feoffati habeant sufficientem pasturam, quantum pertinet ad tenementa sua, ita provisum est & concessum, quod quicunque hujusmodi feoffati assisam nove disseisine deferant de communa pasture sue, et coram justiciariis recognitum fuerit, quod tantam pasturam habeant quantum sufficerit ad tenementa sua, & quod habeant liberum ingressum & egressum de tenementis suis usque ad pasturam suam, tunc inde sint contenti; & illi, de quibus conquesti fuerint, recedant quieti de hoc quod commodum suum de terris, vastis, boscis, & pasturis fecerint. Si autem dixerint quod sufficientem pasturam non habeant, vel sufficientem ingressum vel egressum, quantum pertinet ad tenementa sua, tunc inquiratur veritas per assisam, et si per assisam recognitum fuerit per eosdem, quod in aliquo fuerit impeditus eorum ingressus vel egressus, vel quod non habeant sufficientem pasturam, & sufficientem ingressum & egressum, sicut predictum est, tunc recuperent seisinam suam per visum juratorum: ita quod per discretionem & sacramentum eorum habeant conquerentes sufficientem pasturam, & sufficientem ingressum & egressum, in forma predicta; et disseisitores sint in misericordia domini Regis, & dampna reddant, sicut reddi debent ante provisionem istam. Si autem recognitum fuerit per assisam, quod conquerentes sufficientem habent pasturam, cum libero & sufficienti ingressu & egressu, ut predictum est, tunc licite faciant alii commodum suum de residuo, & recedant de illa assisa quieti.

**5.** Similiter provisum est, & concessum a domino Rege, quod de cetero non currant usure contra allquem infra etatem existentem, a tempore mortis antecessoris sui, cujus heres ipse est, usque ad legitimam etatem suam; ita tamen quod propter hoc non remaneat solucio debiti principalis, simul cum usura ante mortem antecessoris sui, cujus heres ipse est.

**6.** De heredibus per parentes, vel per alios, vi abductis, vel detentis, ita provisum est, quod quicunque laicus inde convictus fuerit, quod puerum sic [detinuerit, abduxerit, vel][1] maritaverit, reddat perdenti valorem maritagii, et pro delicto corpus ejus capiatur & imprisonetur, donec perdenti emendaverit delictum si puer maritetur et preterea donec domino Regi satisfecerit pro transgressione et hoc fiat de herede infra quatuordecim annos existente. De herede autem, [qui] cum sit quatuordecim annorum, vel ultra, usque ad plenam etatem, si se maritaverit sine licencia domini sui, ut ei auferat maritagium suum, & dominus offerat ei rationabile maritagium, ubi non disparagetur, dominus suus tunc teneat terram ejus ultra terminum etatis sue, scilicet viginti & unius anni per tantum tempus, quod possit inde duplicem valorem maritagii recipere, secundum estimationem legalium hominum, vel

1 The insertion is from MSS Rot. Bodl., Harl. 493A, and Cott. XVI. See Plucknett 1922/2010 13-14.

secundum quod ei pro eodem maritagio prius fuerit oblatum sine fraude & malicia, & secundum quod probari poterit in curia domini Regis. De dominis qui maritaverint illos quos habent in custodia [sua] villanis, vel aliis, sicut burgensibus, ubi disparagentur; [tunc] si talis heres fuerit infra quatuordecim annos, & talis etatis, quod consentire non possit, tunc si parentes conquerantur, dominus ille amittat custodiam usque ad legitimam etatem heredis & omne commodum, quod inde perceptum fuerit, convertatur in commodum ipsius qui infra etatem est, secundum disposicionem & provisionem parentum contra dedecus ei factum; si autem fuerit quatuordecim annorum, & ultra, quod consentire poterit, & tali maritagio consenserit, nulla sequatur pena.

**7.** Si quis heres, cujuscunque fuerit etatis, pro domino suo se noluerit maritare, non compellatur hoc facere, sed cum ad etatem pervenerit, det domino suo, & satisfaciat ei de tanto quantum percipere posset ab aliquo pro maritagio, antequam terram suam recipiat, & hoc sive voluerit se maritare, sive non; quia maritagium ejus qui infra etatem est, mero jure pertinet ad dominum feodi.

**8.** De narracione descensus in brevi de recto ab antecessore a tempore H. Regis senioris, anno & die, provisum est quod de cetero non fiat mencio de tam longinquo tempore set a tempore H. Regis avi nostri, & locum habeat ista provisio ad Pentecosten, anno vicesimo primo & non ante; brevia prius impetrata procedant: brevia mortis antecessoris, de nativis, & de ingressu non excedant ultimum reditum domini Regis Johannis in Angliam. Brevia nove disseisine non excedant primam transfretactionem domini Regis, qui nunc est in Vasconiam. Et locum habeat ista provisio a tempore predicto, & brevia prius impetrata procedant.

**9.** Ad breve [domini] R. de bastardia, utrum aliquis natus ante matrimonium habere poterit hereditatem, sicut ille qui natus est post, responderunt omnes episcopi quod nolunt nec possunt ad istud respondere, quia hoc esset contra communem formam ecclesie. Ac rogaverunt omnes episcopi magnates ut consentirent quod nati ante matrimonium essent legitimi, sicut illi qui nati sunt post matrimonium, quantum ad successionem hereditariam, quia ecclesia tales habet pro legitimis. Et omnes comites & barones una voce responderunt, quod nolunt leges Anglie mutare, que usitate sunt & approbate.

**10.** Provisum est insuper, quod quilibet liber homo, qui sectam debet ad comitatum, [trithingum,] hundredum, & wapentachium, vel ad curiam domini sui, libere possit facere attornatum suum, ad sectas illas pro eo faciende.

**11.** De malefactoribus in parcis & vivariis non est discussum, quia magnates petierunt propriam prisonam suam de illis quos ceperant in parcis & vivariis suis, quod quidem dominus Rex contradixit & ideo differtur.

### Translation

It was provided in the court of the lord King, on Wednesday the morrow of [the feast of] St Vincent, in the twentieth year of the reign of king Henry the son of king John, at Merton, in the presence of the archbishop of Canterbury and the suffragan bishops, in the presence of the greater part of the earls and barons of England being there for the coronation of the same lord king and queen Eleanor, for which all had been summoned, when there had been a discussion of the common utility of the realm upon the below written articles, it was in this manner provided and granted as well by the aforesaid archbishops, bishops, earls, barons, as by the king himself and the others.

**1.** For widows who after the death of their husbands are driven out of their dowers and cannot have their dowers or free bench[1] without a plea, namely because someone deforced them their dowers or their free bench of tenements of which their husbands died seised and the widows themselves have recovered afterward by a plea, let those who have been

1 The practice whereby a widow could retain her late husband's tenement until she remarried. *Quarentena* is from *quadraginta*, the forty day period after the husband's death within which the widow must make her claim. It came to be called "free bench" because some widows, as tenants of the manor, sat on the bench of the *pares curiae* (peers of court).

convicted of the unjust deforcement return to those same widows their damages, namely the value of all the dower belonging to them from the time of the death of their husbands up to the day when the same widows by judgment of the court recovered then their own seisin; and nonetheless the deforcers themselves shall be in the mercy[1] of the lord king.

**2.** Likewise, any widows from henceforth can bequeath their grain from their land, whether from their dowers or from their other lands and tenements, the services of the lords excepted, which are owed from dower and any other tenements of theirs.

**3.** Likewise, if someone is disseised of his freehold, and if, before the justices in eyre, he has recovered his seisin by the assize of *novel disseisin* or by the examination of those who made the disseisin, and the person disseised has had his seisin by the sheriff, if those same disseisors afterward, after the eyre of the Justices, again disseise the same petitioner of the same tenement, and thence have been convicted, let [them] be seized at once and detained in the prison of the lord King until they are delivered by the lord King, through a fine or in some other manner. [And this is the form how such having been convicted should be punished, namely, when the plaintiffs come to court, let them have the writ of the lord King directed to the sheriff, in which let be contained their plea of disseisin made upon disseisin. And therefore it shall be commanded to the sheriff that, taking with him the crown's keepers of pleas and other lawful knights, in his own person he shall go to that tenement or that pasture concerning which the complaint has been made, and by other neighbors and lawful men he shall there hold a diligent judicial inquest, and if he finds the same man again disseised, just as it is aforesaid, then let him act according to the aforesaid provision, but if otherwise, then the plaintiff shall be in the mercy of the lord King, and the other shall depart quit. Nor should the sheriff, without a special order of the lord King,

1 To be subject to amercement.

prosecute a claim of this sort.][1] Let it be done in the same manner for those who have recovered seisin by the assize of *mort d'ancestor* and for all lands and tenements recovered by juries in the court of the lord King, if afterwards they have been disseised by the original deforcers, against whom they recovered by a jury in any way.

**4.** Likewise, because many magnates of England who have feoffed their knights and freeholders by small tenements on their great manors have caused inquests to be made because they have been unable to make their profit from the rest of their manors, such as waste, woods, and pastures, when the feoffees themselves have sufficient pasture as much as pertains to their tenements, thus it is provided and conceded that whatsoever feoffees of this sort should bring an assize of *novel disseisin* for their common of pasture and it has been shown before the justices that they have as much pasture as suffices to their tenements and that they have free ingress and egress from their tenements to the pasture, then let them be content, and those of whom they have complained let go quit that they have made their profit from the lands, wastes, woods, and pastures. If, however, they shall say that they do not have sufficient pasture or sufficient ingress or egress, as much as pertains to their tenements, then let the truth be sought by the assize, and should it be shown by the assize that it was by those same men that their ingress or egress was impeded in some way, or that they did not have sufficient pasture and sufficient ingress and egress just as it was aforesaid, then let them recover their seisin by view of those having been sworn, so that by their decision and oath the plaintiffs shall have sufficient pasture and sufficient ingress and egress in the aforesaid form. And let the disseisors be in the mercy of the lord King, and let them return damages just as they were obligated to be returned before this provision. However, if it was recognized by the assize that the plaintiffs have sufficient pasture with free and sufficient ingress and egress as aforesaid, then let the others lawfully make their profit, and depart quit from that assize.

1 The bracketed lines are included in some versions of the provisions but omitted in others.

**5.** Likewise it is provided and granted by the lord King that from henceforth usuries shall not run against anyone being under age, from the time of his ancestor's death whose heir he himself is, until his lawful age; however, let the payment of the principal debt not be stayed on account of this, together with the usury before the death of his ancestor whose heir he himself is.

**6.** For heirs abducted by force or detained by parents or others, it is thus provided: that whatever layman convicted thereof that he has so married off a child shall return the value of the maritagium[1] to the one who has lost it and for the transgression let his body be taken and imprisoned until he has made the transgression right with the one who has lost his maritagium if the child is married, and moreover until he has satisfied the lord King for trespass and let this be done for an heir being under fourteen years. However, for an heir who is fourteen years or more, up to full age, if he marries himself without license of his lord so that he deprive him his maritagium, and his lord offers him a reasonable marriage where he is not disparaged, then let his lord hold his land beyond the *terminus* of his age, namely [beyond] twenty-one years, for so long a time that he can then receive the double value of the maritagium according to the estimate of lawful men, or according to what was before offered him for the same maritagium without fraud and malice and according to what can be proved in the court of the lord King. For lords who have married those whom they have in their custody to villains or others, such as burgesses, whereby they are disparaged, if such an heir is less than fourteen years and of such age that he is unable to consent, then if the parents complain let the lord lose custody until the legal age of the heir and let all profit he would have received be converted to the profit of the one who is under age, according to the disposition and provision of the parents, against the disgrace caused him;

1 *Maritagium* signifies (1) a marriage, (2) the payment due a demesne lord for his permission to wed, and (3) a wedding gift made to a bride by a husband at the church door. Here it is used in the first two senses. We have left it untranslated in the second meaning.

however, if he is fourteen years and above, that he can consent, and if he has consented to such a marriage, let no penalty ensue.

**7.** If a certain heir, of whatever age he should be, will not wed himself for his lord, let him not be compelled to do so, but when he has come of age, let him, before he may receive his land, give his lord and satisfy him for as much as he could receive from anyone for a maritagium, and that whether he wishes to wed himself or not, because the maritagium of him who is under age belongs by unadulterated right to the lord of the fee.

**8.** For a count[1] of descent in a writ of right from an ancestor from the time of King Henry the Elder, for the year and day, it is provided that henceforth let mention not be made of a time so long ago but from the time of King Henry our grandfather, and this provision shall lie[2] at Pentecost in the twenty-first year [of our reign] and not before; writs sued out before shall proceed: writs of *mort d'ancestor*, neifty, and entry shall not go beyond the last return of the lord King John into England. Writs of *novel disseisin* shall not exceed the first voyage of the lord King, who is now in Normandy. And this provision shall lie from the aforesaid time and writs sued out before shall proceed.

**9.** To the lord King's writ of bastardy, whether someone born before matrimony can have an inheritance just as he who was born afterwards, all the bishops answered that they did not wish to nor could they respond to that, because it was against a common principle of the church. But all the bishops asked the magnates if they would agree that those born before matrimony were as legitimate as those who were born after matrimony as regards hereditary succession, because the church holds such for legitimate. And all the earls and barons answered with one voice

1 The *narratio* was a narrative account of the plea in a writ or given before a court. Its OF equivalent is *conte*, which was Englished to "count." Pleaders accordingly were known as counters.

2 "To lie," in the sense of to apply or pertain, is the technical English term used to translate *locum habere* and *iacere* (sometimes *peto* and *competo*) in Latin legal documents. A *writ of neifty* (a few lines below) is a writ by which a lord claimed someone as his serf.

that they did not wish to change the laws of England that were used and approved.

**10**. It is provided moreover that any free man who owes suit to the county, tithing, hundred and wapentake, or to his lord's court, can freely pay his attorney to handle those suits for him.

**11.** There was no discussion of malefactors in parks and fish ponds, because the magnates wanted their own prison for those whom they had seized in their parks and fish ponds, which indeed the lord King spoke against and therefore it was deferred.

## Statute of Marlborough

This act is most important for its concern with suit of court. It seeks both to enforce the lord's right to summon his tenants into his court when they fail to fulfil their obligations and to restrict that right to its lawful use. Plucknett puts the statute clearly in historical context: "The statute of Marlborough of 1267, coming immediately after the war,[1] is naturally much concerned with distress. Chapter 1 forbids distresses 'between neighbor and neighbor'; these are the acts of political duress, and sometimes simply spoliation, which often took place during the wars, at times cloaked under the excuse of self-help for real or imaginary injuries received. Here, as elsewhere in the statute, there is an endeavor to restrict distress to situations where the parties were feudally lord and tenant. Thus Chapter 2 forbids distraining men to do suit of court unless they are tenants, or unless the lord has hundredal jurisdiction over them; nor may he distrain out of his fee or bailiwick—an old common-law principle which evidently needed reiteration. By Chapter 3 it is an offense to refuse to allow distresses to be replevied, and by Chapter 4 it is an offense to take unreasonable distresses or to drive them out of the county. Chapter 15 forbids distresses (save by royal officers) upon a royal highway or common street. These provisions were implemented by the

1 The Second Baron's War (1264-67), a civil war led by Henry III and his eldest son Edward against a force of barons led by Simon de Montfort.

creation of new forms of writs of 'trespass upon the statute' for use against offenders."[1]

The seignorial courts will survive for some time, but freeholders of a demesne lord are learning it is generally to their advantage to remove their suits to county courts by the process of tolt and thence, if necessary, to the royal courts by a writ of *praecipe*. The manor court, or hallmoot, which dealt with matters pertaining to villeins, will endure until the end of serfdom.

This statute is also notable for its prohibition of fraudulent trusts concocted in order to avoid the feudal obligations attendant upon the transfer of feoffs from a deceased landholder to his heir.

> We take our text from Pickering, *The Statutes at Large*, I, 55-74. The translation is partially our own and partially by Rothwell, *English Historical Documents*, 384-92.

Anno gratie Millesimo Ducentesimo Sexagesimo septimo, regni autem domini H. Regis, filii Regis Johannis quinquagesimo secundo, in Octabris Sancti Martini, providente ipso domino Rege ad regni sui Anglie melioracionem & exhibicionem justicie, prout regalis officii exposcit utilitas, pleniorem, convocatis discretioribus ejusdem regni, tam majoribus quam minoribus, provisum est & statutum ac concordatum & ordinatum, ut cum regnum Anglie multis tribulationibus & dissensionum incommodis, nuper depressum, in reformacione legum & jurium, quibus pax & tranquilitas incolarum conservari indigeat, ad quod remedium salubre per ipsum Regem et suos fideles oportuit adhiberi, provisiones, ordinationes, & statuta subscripta ab omnibus regni ipsius incolis, tam Majoribus quam minoribus, firmiter ac inviolabiliter temporibus perpetuis statuit observari.

**1.** Cum autem tempore turbationis nuper in regno suborte, & deinceps, multi Magnates & alii justiciam non dignati fuerint recipere per dominum Regem & Curiam suam, prout debuerunt & consueverunt temporibus predecessorum ipsius domini Regis, & etiam tempore suo;

1 Plucknett 1949/1962 58-9.

sed de vicinis suis & aliis per seipsos graves ultiones fecerunt, & districtiones, quousque redempciones receperint, ad voluntatem suam. Et preterea quidam eorum se per Ministros domini Regis justiciari non permittunt, nec sustineant quod per ipsos liberentur districtiones, quas auctoritate propria fecerint ad voluntatem suam: Provisum est, & concorditer concessum, quod tam majores, quam minores, justiciam habeant & recipiant in Curia domini Regis; Et nullus de cetero ultiones aut districtiones faciat per [propriam] voluntatem suam, absque consideracione Curie domini Regis, [et] si forte dampnum vel injuria sibi fiat, unde emendas habere voluerit de vicino suo, sive majore vel minore. Super autem articulo supradicto provisum est & concessum, ut si quis de cetero ultionem hujusmodi capiat per voluntatem suam propriam absque consideractione Curie domini Regis, ut predictum est, & inde convincatur, puniatur per redemcionem & hoc secundum quantitatem delicti. Et similiter si super vicinum suum faciat districcionem sine consideracione Curie domini Regis, per quod dampnum habeat, puniatur eodem modo, & hoc secundum quantitatem delicti. Et nichilominus fiant emende plene & sufficientes eisdem qui dampnum sustinuerunt per hujusmodi districciones.

**2.** Nullus insuper major vel minor distringat aliquem ad veniendum ad Curiam suam, qui non fit de feodo suo, aut super ipsum non habeat jurisdiccionem per Hundredum vel [per] Ballivam suam; nec districciones faciat extra feodum suum, seu locum, ubi ballivam habeat, vel jurisdiccionem; & qui contra hoc statutum venerit, puniatur eodem modo, & hoc secundum delicti quantitatem.

**3.** Si quis autem major vel minor permittere noluerit liberari per ministros domini Regis, & secundum legem & consuetudinem regni, districciones quas fecerit; aut etiam sustinere noluerit summoniciones & attachiamenta, seu executiones judiciorum Curie domini Regis fieri, puniatur modo predicto, tanquam se justiciari non permittens. Quod si quis major vel minor districciones faciat super tenentem suum pro servitiis & consuetudinibus, que sibi deberi dicat, vel pro re altera, unde ad dominum feodi pertineat facere districciones, & postea convincatur, quod tenens ejus ea sibi non debeat; non ideo puniatur dominus per redemptionem, ut in supradictis casibus, si permittat districciones liberari secundum legem & consuetudinem regni; sed amercietur velut hactenus consuetum est, & tenens dampna sua recuperet versus eum.

**4.** Nullus de cetero faciat ducere districciones, quas fecerat, extra Comitatum in quo fuerit; Et si vicinus hoc fecerit super vicinum suum, & per voluntatem suam, & sine judicio, puniatur per redemptionem, ut supra, veluti de re contra pacem. Verumtamen si dominus hoc super tenentem suum fecerit castigetur per gravem misericordiam. Districciones insuper sint rationabilies, & non nimis graves. Et qui districciones fecerint irrationabiles, & indebitas, graviter amercientur propter excessum districcionum ipsarum.

**5.** Magna Carta in singulis suis articulis teneatur, tam in hiis que ad Regem pertinent, quam ad alios; & hoc coram Justiciariis itinerantibus, in suis itineribus & vicecomitibus in Comitat' suis, cum opus fuerit, demandetur, & brevia versus eos, qui contravenerint, gratis concedantur coram Rege, vel coram Justiciariis de Banco, vel coram Justiciariis itinerantibus, cum in partes illas venerint.

Similiter Carta de Foresta, [in singulis suis articulis usque teneatur, et contravenientes per ipsum dominum Regem cum inde convicti fuerint puniuntur.]

**6.** De hiis autem, qui primogenitos & heredes suos infra etatem existentes, feoffare solent de hereditate sua, ut per hoc ammitterent domini feodorum custodias suas; provisum est, & concorditer concessum, quod occasione hujussmodi falsi feoffamenti nullus Capitalis dominus amittat custodiam suam.

De hiis insuper, qui de terris suis, quas tradere voluerint ad terminum confingunt feoffamenta, annorum, ut domini feodorum amittant custodias suas, falsa continentia quod eis satisfactum est de summa servicii in illis contenti usque ad terminum aliquem; ita quod post terminum solvere teneantur hujusmodi feoffati summam aliquam, valorem terrarum illarum in multo excedentem, ut sic post terminum illum terra eorum revertatur ad ipsos, eo quod nemo eas [sic] pro tanto tenere curaret: provisum est, & concorditer concessum, ut per hujusmodi fraudem nullus Capitalis dominus amittat custodiam suam. Verumptamen non licebit eis hujusmodi feoffatos sine judicio disseisire; set breve habeant de hujusmodi custodia sibi reddenda, & per testes in cartis in hujusmodi feoffamentis contentos una cum aliis liberis & legalibus de patria, & per quantitatem & valorem tenementi, & per quantitatem summe que inde reddi debet post terminum predictum, attingatur utrum hujusmodi feoffamenta bona fide facta sint, aut in fraudem ad auferendum Capitalibus dominis feodi custodiam suam.

Si vero Capitales domini per judicium Curie recuperent in hujusmodi casibus custodiam suam, salva fit nichilominus hujusmodi feoffatis actio sua, quam ad terminum, seu ad feodum recuperandum inde habuerint, cum heredes ad legitimam etatem pervenerint.

Quod si aliqui Capitales domini feoffatos aliquos malitiose implacitaverint, fingentes casum istum, maxime ubi feoffamenta legitime & bona fide facta fuerint, tunc adjudicentur feoffatis dampna sua, & mise sue quas fecerint occasione placiti predicti, & ipsi actores per misericordiam puniantur.

**7.** In placito communi de custodiis, si ad magnam districcionem non venerint deforciatores, tunc bis vel ter iteretur breve predictum ad terminos quibus fieri poterit, infra medietatem anni sequentis, ita quod singulis vicibus legatur breve in pleno Comitatu, ubi prius inventus fuerit deforciator: et ibi publice denuncietur, ut veniat ad diem sibi prefixum: quod si se subtraxerit, ita tamen quod infra medietatem anni responsurus non venerit, nec vicecomes eum invenire possit, per quod corpus suum habere possit coram Justiciariis, ad respondendum secundum legem & consuetudinem regni, tunc, tanquam rebellis, et se justiciari non permittens, amittat seisinam hujusmodi custodie, salva sibi alias actione sua, si forte jus habeat ad eandem.

In casibus autem, ubi custodie pertinent ad custodias heredum infra etatem existentium, & ubi custodes petunt custodias que accidunt heredibus, vel tanquam pertinentes ad eorum hereditatem, non amittant hujusmodi heredes infra etatem existentes per necligenciam vel rebellionem suorum custodum, sicut in casu predicto; sed currat lex communis eodem modo quo prius consuevit.

**8.** Illi vero qui pro iterata disseisina capti fuerint et detenti, non deliberentur sine speciali precepto domini Regis, et hoc per finem cum domino Rege faciendum pro hujusmodi transgressione sua; et si compertum fuerit, quod Vicecomes aliter eos deliberaverit, graviter propter hoc amercietur; et nichilominus illi, qui per Vicecomitem sine precepto domini Regis sic liberentur, pro sua transgressione puniantur.

**9.** De sectis quidem faciendis ad Curiam Magnatum, et aliorum dominorum ipsarum Curiarum, de cetero sic observandum est, quod nullus, qui per cartam feoffatus est, distringatur de cetero ad sectam faciendam ad Curiam domini sui, nisi per formam carte sue specialiter teneatur ad sectam illam faciendam; hiis autem exceptis, quorum antecessores, vel ipsimet, hujusmodi sectam facere consueverunt ante primam transfretationem predicti domini Regis in Britanniam, a tempore cujus transfretationis elapsi sunt triginta et novem anni et medietas unius armi, a tempore quo hujusmodi constituciones fuerint constitute. [Et] similiter nullus feoffatus de cetero since [sine] carta a tempore conquestus, vel aliquo alio antiquo feoffamento, distringatur ad hujusmodi sectam faciendam, nisi ipsemet vel antecessores sui eam facere consueverunt ante primam transfretationem predictam. Qui autem per cartam pro certo servicio, veluti pro libero servicio tot solidorum annuatim pro omni servicio solvendorum, feoffati sunt, ad sectam, vel ad aliud, ultra forman sui feoffamenti, non teneantur. Et si hereditas aliqua, de qua tantum unica secta debeatur, ad plures heredes, participes ejusdem hereditatis, devolvatur; ille qui habet eineciam [exneciam] hereditatis illius, unicam faciat sectam pro se et particibus suis, et alii participes sui pro portione sua contribuant ad sectam illam faciendam. Si plures feoffati fuerint de hereditate aliqua, de qua unica secta debeatur, dominus illius feodi unicam sectam inde habeat, nec possit de hereditate illa nisi unicam sectam exigere, sicut prius fieri consuevit. Et si autem contingat, quod domini Curiam tenentes suos contra hanc constitucionem pro hujusmodi secta distringant, tunc ad querimeniam tenentium illorum attachientur, quod ad Curiam domini Regis veniant ad brevem diem, inde responsuri, et unicum habeant essonium, si fuerint in regno; et incontinenti deliberentur conquerenti averia sua, sive alie districciones hac occasione facte, et deliberate remaneant, donec placitum inde inter eos terminetur. Et si domini Curiarum, qui hujusmodi districciones fecerint, ad diem, ad quem attachiati fuerint, non venerint, vel diem per essonium suum sibi datum non observaverint, tunc mandetur Vicecomiti, quod eos ad alium diem venire faciat, ad quem diem si non venerint, mandetur Vicecomiti, quod distringantur per omnia que habent in balliva sua, ita quod Vicecomes respondeat domino Regi de exitibus, et quod habeat corpora eorum ad certum diem prefigendum: ita quod si ad illum diem non venerint, eat pars conquerens inde sine die, et averia sua sive districciones alie deliberate remaneant, donec sectam illam domini recuperaverint per consideracionem Curie domini Regis; et cessent interim districciones hujusmodi, salvo dominis curiarum jure suo, de sectis illis perquirendis, in forma juris, cum inde loqui voluerint: et cum domini Curiarum venerint responsuri conquerentibus de hujusmodi transgressionibus, si super hoc convincantur, tunc per consideracionem Curie domini regis recuperent versus [eos] conquerentes dampna sua, que sustinuerunt occasione districcionis predicte.

Simili modo si tenentes post hanc constitucionem subtrahant dominis feodi sectas, quas facere debeant, et quas ante tempus predicte transfretacionis et hactenus facere consueverunt, tunc per eandem justitiam et celeritatem, quoad dies prefigendos, et districciones admittendas, consequantur domini Cur' justiciam de sectis illis, una cum dampnis suis, quemadmodum tenentes dampna sua recuperant; et hoc scilicet de dampnis recuperandis intelligatur de subtraccionibus sibi factis, et non de subtraccionibus factis predecessoribus suis. Verumptamen domini Curiarum seisinam de hujusmodi sectis recuperare non poterunt per defaltam, sicut hactenus fieri consuevit. De sectis autem, que ante tempus supradictum subtracte fuerunt, currat lex communis sicut prius consuevit.

**10.** De turnis Vicecomitum provisum est, ut, necesse non habeant ibi venire Archiepiscopi, Episcopi, Abbates, Priores, Comites, Barones, nec aliqui viri religiosi, nec mulieres, nisi eorum presentia ob aliquam causam specialiter exigatur; set teneatur turnus sicut temporibus predecessorum domini Regis teneri consuevit. Et si qui in Hundredis diversis habeant tenementa [sua], non habeant necesse venire ad hujusmodi turnos, nisi in ballivis ubi fuerint conversantes, et teneantur turni secundum forman magne carte Regis, et sicut temporibus Regis Ricardi et Johannis teneri consueverunt.

**11.** Provisum est eciam, quod nec in itinere Justiciariis, nec in Comitatibus, Hendredis, nec in Curia Baronum, de cetero capiantur fines ab aliquibus pro pulcre placitando, nec per sic quod non occasionentur.

Et sciendum, quod per istam constitutionem non tolluntur fines certi, seu presentationes [prestationes] arentate a tempore quo dominus Rex primo transfretavit in Britanniam usque nunc.

**12.** In placito vero dotis [de dote] quod vocatur unde nichil habet, dentur de cetero quatuor dies per annum ad minus, et plures si commode fieri possit, ita quod habeant quinque vel sex per annum ad minus. In assisis autem ultime presentacionis, et in placito quare impedit de ecclesiis vacantibus, dentur dies de quindena in quindenam, vel de tribus septimanis in tres septimanas, prout locus propinquus fuerit, vel remotus. In placito vero quare impedit, si ad primum diem, ad quem summonitus fuerit, non venerit nec essonium miserit impeditor, attachietur ad alium diem, quo die si non venerit, nec essonium miserit, distringatur per magnam districcionem superius dictam; et si tunc non venerit, per ejus defaltam scribatur Episcopo loci, quod reclamatio impeditoris illa vice conquerenti non obsistat, salvo impeditori alias jure suo, cum inde loqui voluerit. Eadem lex de attachiamentis faciendis de omnibus brevibus, ubi attachiamenta jacent, quoad districciones, faciendas firmiter observetur;

Ita tamen, quod secundum attachiamentum fiat per meliores plegios, et postmodum ultima districcio.

**13.** Et sciendum, quod postquam aliquis posuerit se in inquisicionem aliquam, que emerserit, vel emergere possit in hujusmodi brevibus, non habeat nisi unicum essonium, et [vel] unicam defaltam; ita scilicet, quod si ad diem sibi datum per essonium suum non venerit, aut si secundo die defaltam fecerit, tunc inquisicio illa per defaltam ipsius capiatur, et tunc secundum inquisicionem per defaltam ipsius ad judicium procedatur. Et si inquisicio illa capta fuerit in Comitatu per Vicecomitem, vel per Coronatorem, ad Justiciarios domini Regis ad certum diem remittenda; et si pars rea non venerit ad illum diem, tunc per defaltam ipsius assignetur ei alius dies secundum discrecionem Justiciariorum; et mandetur Vicecomiti, quod ad diem illum faciat ipsum venire ad audiendum judicium suum, si velit, secundum inquisicionem illam; ad quem diem si non venerit, propter defaltam suam procedatur ad judicium. Eodem modo fiat, si non veniat ad diem sibi datum per essonium suum.

**14.** De [in] cartis vero exemptionnis et libertatis, ne ponantur impetrantes in assisis, juratis, vel recognitionibus aliquibus; provisum est, quod si adeo necessarium fit eorum juramentum, quod fine eis justicia exhiberi non poterit [possit] veluti in magna assisa, et in perambulationibus, et in cartis vel scriptis convencionum, ubi fuerint testes nominati, aut in attinctis, aut in aliis casibus consimilibus, jurare cogantur; salva sibi alias libertate et exemptione sua supradictis.

**15.** Nulli de cetero liceat districciones facere ex quacunque causa extra feodum suum, nec in regia via, aut communi strata, nisi domino Regi aut Ministris suis.

**16.** Si heres aliquis post mortem sui antecessoris infra etatem extiterit, et dominus suus custodiam terrarum suarum habuerit, si dominus ille dicto heredi, cum ad legitimam etatem pervenerit, terram suam sine placito reddere noluerit, heres ille terram suam per assisam mortis antecessoris sui recuperabit, una cum dampnis que sustinuerit propter detencionem illam, a tempore quo fuerit legitime etatis. Quod si heres alicujus in morte antecessoris sui plene etatis fuerit, et heres ille apparens, et pro herede cognitus, inventus fit in hereditate illa, capitalis dominus cum non eiciat [ejiciat] nec aliquid ibi capiat nec amoveat, set tantum simplicem seisinam inde faciat pro recognitione dominii sui. Et si Capitales domini hujusmodi heredem extra seisinam suam maliciose teneant, per quod breve mortis antecessoris ipsum oportet impetrare [placitare] tunc dampna sua recuperet sicut in Actione nove disseisine.

De hereditatibus autem que de domino Rege tenentur in capito sic observandum est, quod dominus Rex liberam inde seisinam habeat, sicut prius fieri consuevit; nec heres nec aliquis alius in hereditatem illam se intrudat, priusquam illam de manibus domini Regis recipiat, prout hujusmodi hereditates de manibus Antecessorum suorum recipi consueverunt, et hoc intelligatur de terris et feodis, que ratione servicii militaris, vel serjantie, seu jure patronatus, in manu domini Regis esse consueverunt.

**17.** Provisum est eciam, quod si terra, que tenetur in socagio, fit in custodia parentum heredum eo quod [ille dum] heres infra etatem extiterit, custodes illi [illius] vastum facere non possunt, vel vendicionem, vel aliquam destruccionem de hereditate illa; sed salvo eam custodiant ad opus dicti heredis, Ita quod cum ad legitimam etatem pervenerit, sibi respondeant de exitibus dicte hereditatis, per legitimam computationem, salvis ipsis custodibus rationabilibus misis suis. Nec eciam possunt dicti custodes dicti heredis maritagium dare vel vendere, nisi ad commodum dicti heredis: set si parentis dicti heredis propinquiores qui hujusmodi custodias habuerint, de toto tempore illo, a quo brevia placitandi non conceduntur, hujusmodi custodias habeant ad commodum heredis, ut predictum est, sine vasto, vel exilio, vel destruccionibus faciendis.

**18.** Nullus autem escaetor, vel inquisitor, vel Justiciarius ad assisas capiendas specialiter assignatus, vel ad querelas audiendas et determinandas, de cetero potestatem habeat amerciandi aliquem pro defalta communis summonicionis, nisi Capitales Justiciarii in itineribus suis. [Provisum est insuper, quod nullus religiosus feoda alicujus ingrediatur sine assensu nostro, & capitalis domini, de quo feoda illa immediate tenentur.]

**19.** De essoinis autem provisum est, quod in Comitatu, Hendredo, aut in Curia Baronum, aut aliis Curiis, nullus habeat necesse jurare pro essonio suo warrantizando.

**20.** Nullus de cetero (excepto domino Rege) placitum teneat de falso judicio facto in Curia tenentium suorum; quia hujusmodi placita specialiter spectant ad coronam et dignitatem domini Regis.

**21.** Provisum est, quod si averia aliqua injuste capiantur, et detineantur, Vicecomes post querimoniam inde sibi factam, ea sine impedimento vel contradiccione ejus qui dicta averia cepit, deliberare possit, si extra libertates capta fuerint. Si infra libertates capta fuerint, et ballivi libertatis ea liberare noluerint, tunc vicecomes per defaltam eorum [ipsorum] ea faciat deliberari.

**22.** Nullus de cetero possit distringere libere tenentes suos ad respondendum de libero tenemento suo, nec de aliquibus ad liberum tenementum suum spectantibus; nec jurare faciat libere tenentes suos contra voluntatem suam; desicut hoc nullus facere possit sine [speciali] precepto domini Regis.

**23.** Provisum est eciam, quod si Ballivi, qui dominis suis compotum reddere tenentur, se subtraxerint, et terras et tenementa non habuerint, per que distringi possint; tunc per eorum corpora attachientur, ita quod Vicecomes, in cujus balliva inveniantur, eos venire faciat ad compotum suum reddendum.

Firmarii tempore firmarum suarum vastum vel exilium non faciant de boscis, domibus, vel hominibus, nec de aliquibus ad tenementa que habent ad firmam spectantibus, nisi specialem inde habuerint concessionem, sive convencionis mentionem, adeo quod hoc facere possint. Et si fecerint, et super hoc convincantur, dampna plene refundant, et graviter per misericordiam puniantur.

**24.** Justiciarii itinerantes de cetero non amercient villatas in itinere suo, eo quod singuli duodecim annorum non venerint coram Vicecomitibus et Coronatoribus, ad inquisitiones de roberiis, et incendiis, et aliis ad Coronam spectantibus faciendam; dum tamen de villatis illis venerint sufficientes, per quos hujusmodi inquisiciones plene fieri possint: exceptis inquisicionibus de morte hominis faciendam, ubi omnes duodecim annorum venire debent, nisi rationabilem habeant causam absentie sue.

**25.** Murdrum de cetero non adjudicetur coram Justiciariis, ubi infortunium [fertunium] tantummodo adjudicatum est, sed locum habeat murdrum in interfectis per feloniam, et non aliter.

**26.** Provisum est insuper, quod nullus, qui coram Justiciariis itinerantibus vocatur ad Warantum de placito terre vel tenementi, amercietur de cetero, pro eo quod presens non fuerit, quando vocabatur ad Warantum (excepto primo die adventus Justiciariorum ipsorum) set si Warantus ille fit inffra Comitatum, tunc injungatur Vicecomiti, quod ipsum infra tercium diem, vel quartum, secundum locorum distanciam, faciat venire, sicut in itinere Justiciar' fieri consuevit. Et si extra Comitatum maneat, tunc rationabilem habeat summonicionem quindecim dierum ad minus, secundum discrecionem Justiciaii, et legem communem.

**27.** Si clericus aliquis pro crimine aliquo, vel recto [retto] Quod ad Coronam pertineat, arettatus [arestatus] fuerit, et postmodum per preceptum Regis in ballium traditus fuerit, vel replegiatus, ita quod hii, quibus traditus fuerit in ballium, eum habeant coram Justiciariis; non amercientur, illi de cetero quibus traditus fuerit in ballium, vel alii plegii sui, si corpus suum habeant coram Justiciariis, licet coram eis propter privilegium clericale respondere noluerit, vel non possit.

**28.** Provisum est eciam, quod si depredactiones vel rapine alique fiant Abbatibus, Prioribus, vel aliis prelatis ecclesiasticis, et ipsi jus suum de hujusmodi depredactionibus prosequentes morte preveniantur, antequam justiciam inde fuerint affecuti; successores eorum habeant accionem ad bona ecclesie sue de manibus hujusmodi transgressorum repetend'.

Similem [similiter] insuper habeant accionem successores de hiis, que domui et ecclesie sue recenter [retenta] ante obitum predecessorum suorum [&] per hujusmodi violenciam fuerint subtracta, licet predicti predecessores sui jus suum prosecuti non fuerint in vita sua. Si autem in terris et [vel] tenementis hujusmodi religioforum, de quibus eorum prelati obierint seisiti, ut de jure ecclesie sue, aliqui se intrudant tempore vacationis, eorum successores breve habeant ad recuperandam seisinam suam; et adjudicentur eis dampna sua, sicut in nova disseisina adjudicari consuevit.

**29.** Provisum est eciam, quod si alienationes ille, de quibus brev de ingressu dari consuevit, per tot gradus fiant, quod breve illud in forma prius usitata habere [haberi] non possit, habeat conquerens breve de recuperanda seisina, sine mencione graduum, ad cujuscunque manus per hujusmodi alienaciones res illa devenerit, per brevia originalis per consilium domini Regis providenda.

### Translation

In the year of grace one thousand two hundred sixty-seven, and also the fifty-second of the lord king Henry [III], the son of king John, on the octave of Saint Martin, having been provided by the lord king himself to the betterment of his realm of England and the fuller display of justice, just as the usage of royal office urges, the more discerning men of his same realm having been called together, as well the greater as the lesser, it was provided and established and agreed and ordained that the kingdom of England, lately oppressed with the many tribulations and troubles of dissensions—to the end that it is necessary a salubrious remedy be applied by the same king and his faithful men in a reformation of the laws and rights by which the peace and tranquility of its inhabitants are to be preserved—resolves that the below-written provisions, ordinances, and statutes be observed by all the inhabitants of the same kingdom, as well the greater as the lesser, firmly and inviolably for all time.

**1.** Since, however, in the time of turbulence lately arisen in the realm and afterwards, many magnates and others have not deigned to receive justice from the lord king and his court, just as they ought and have been accustomed in the times of the same lord king's predecessors, and even in his time, but by themselves have made grave revenges and distraints of their neighbors and others until they have received fines according to their own will, and, besides, some of them do not allow themselves to be justiced by the ministers of the lord king, nor do they suffer that distraints be released by them that they have made by their own authority to their own will, it is provided and unanimously granted that as well the greater as the lesser shall have and receive justice in the lord king's court, and no one henceforth shall make revenges or distraints by his own will without a decision of the lord king's court, even if perhaps damage or injury is done to him whereby he wishes to have amends of his neighbor, either greater or lesser. Moreover, upon the aforesaid article it is provided and granted that, if someone henceforth should take revenge of some sort by his own will without regard to the court of the lord king, as it is aforesaid, and afterwards should be convicted, let him be punished by a fine and this according to the size of the delict.[1] And likewise, if he should make a distraint upon his neighbor, without a decision of the lord king's court, by which he [the neighbor] may have damage, let him be punished in the same manner [i.e. by a fine], and this according to the size of the delict. And nevertheless, let full and sufficient amends be made to those who have sustained damage by distraints of this sort.

**2.** Moreover, let no one greater or lesser distrain someone to come to his own court who is not of his fee or over whom he does not have jurisdiction by the hundred [court] or by his own bailiwick, nor shall he make distraints outside his own fee or the place where he has bailiwick or jurisdiction, and he who goes against this statute shall be punished in the same manner and this according to the size of the delict.

---

1 Used in the general sense of transgression. In Roman law the word designates the equivalent of a tort.

**3.** Moreover, if someone greater or lesser will not allow the distraints he has made to be discharged by the lord king's ministers and according to the law and custom of the realm, or also does not wish to uphold summonses and attachments or executions of the judgments of the lord king's court to be made, he shall be punished in the aforesaid manner, as though not allowing himself to be justiced. But if someone greater or lesser shall make distraints upon his tenant for services and customs that he says are owed him, or for other matters where it pertains to the lord of the fee to make distraints, and afterwards is convicted because his tenant does not owe them to him, let the lord therefore not be punished by a fine as in the aforesaid cases if he allows the distraints to be released according to the law and custom of the realm, but let him be amerced as much as it is the custom and let the tenant recover his damages against him.

**4.** Let no one henceforth cause distraints that he has made to be taken outside the county in which he is. And if a neighbor has done this upon his neighbor and by his own will and without a judgment, let him be punished by a fine, as above, just as for an action against the peace. Nevertheless, if a lord has done this upon his tenant, let him be reproved with a heavy fine. Distraints, moreover, shall be reasonable and not unduly heavy. And they who make unreasonable distraints and undue, let them be heavily fined on account of the excess of the distraints.

**5.** Magna Carta shall be kept in each of its articles, as well in those which pertain to the king as to others, and let this be demanded before eyre justices in their circuits and sheriffs in their counties when there is a need, and writs against those who have opposed shall be granted freely before the king or before the justices of the bench or before the eyre justices when they have come into those parts.

Likewise the Charter of the Forest [shall be kept in each one of its articles everywhere, and transgressors, when they have been thereof convicted, shall be punished by the lord king himself.]

**6.** For those, moreover, who while alive are accustomed to enfeoff their first-born sons and minor heirs of their inheritance, so that by this the lords might lose their wardships of the fees, it is provided and unanimously granted that no capital lord shall lose his wardship on account of a false enfeoffment.

In addition, for those who concoct false feoffments for their lands that they wish to demise for a term of years so that the lords of the fees might lose their wardships—specifying that the total of the services contained in them has been satisfied up to some fixed date, so that after that date feofees of this sort are required to pay some amount exceeding by a great deal the value of those lands, to the extent that after that date their land might revert to themselves because no one would care to hold them [sic] for so much—it is provided and unanimously granted that no capital lord shall lose his wardship through fraud of this sort. Nevertheless, it shall not be permitted them to disseise feofees of this sort without a judgment, but let them have a writ for returning wardship of this sort to themselves, and by the witnesses contained in the charters in feoffments of this sort together with other freemen and law-worthy men of the community, and from the size and value of the tenement, and by the size of the amount which then ought to be returned after the aforesaid date, let it be determined whether feoffments of this sort have been made in good faith or in fraud in order to deprive chief lords their wardship. But if chief lords recovered their wardship in such cases by a court judgment, let the action of such feofees be preserved notwithstanding, either for recovering their term or thereafter the fee they will have when heirs have arrived at a legal age.

But if some chief lords have sued any feofees maliciously, contriving such a case especially when the feoffments have been made legally and in good faith, then let the damages of the feofee be adjudged, and the expenditures they have incurred on the occasion of the aforesaid plea, and let those who brought the legal action be punished by amercement.[1]

1 From this point we follow, with occasional variation, the translation by Rothwell 1975 384-92.

**7.** In the common plea of wardships, if the deforciants do not appear at the grand distress, then the said writ shall be repeated two or three times at the terms when it can be done during the following half-year, so that each time the writ shall be read in full county unless the deforciant is found previously, and it shall there be publicly proclaimed that he should appear on a day prescribed for him. But if he withdraws so that he does not appear to answer within the said half-year and the sheriff is unable to find him so as to be able to produce him before the justices to answer according to the law and custom of the realm, then as a rebel and one not letting himself be brought to justice he shall lose seisin of such wardship, saving to him his action at another time if perchance he has a right to it. But in cases where wardships belong to the guardians of heirs under age and wardships which fall to those heirs as belonging to their inheritance are claimed from those guardians, such heirs under age shall not lose by the negligence or rebellion of their guardian, as in the case above-mentioned, but thc law shall run in thc way it did before.

**8.** They who are taken and imprisoned for repeated disseisin shall not be delivered without the king's special command and this by making fine with the lord king for their trespass of this kind. And if it is found that the sheriff has delivered them otherwise he shall be heavily amerced on account of this, and those delivered by the sheriff without the king's command shall be punished for their trespass nonetheless.

**9.** Regarding doing suit to the courts of magnates and other lords of courts, the observance henceforth shall be thus, namely, that no one who is enfeoffed by charter shall be distrained in future to do such suit to his lord's court unless he is specifically bound by the terms of his charter to do that suit, except those whose ancestors used to or who have themselves been used to do such suit before the lord king's first crossing to Brittany, from the time of which crossing thirty-nine and a half years[1] have elapsed at the time these constitutions were decreed. And likewise no one enfeoffed without charter from the time of the Conquest or by

1 A scribal error for twenty-nine and one-half. The year of the referenced crossing was 1230.

other ancient enfeoffment shall be distrained in future to do such suit unless he and his ancestors used to do it before the above-mentioned crossing of the lord king. Those, however, who are enfeoffed by charter in return for a certain service, for example, free service of so many shillings to be paid annually in lieu of all service, shall not be bound to do suit or anything else beyond the terms of their enfeoffment. And if any inheritance from which one suit only is due descends to a number of heirs as coparceners of that inheritance, he who has the rights of the eldest-born of the inheritance shall do the one suit for himself and his coparceners and his other coparceners for their shares shall contribute to the doing of that suit.

But if it happens that lords of courts distrain their tenants for such suits contrary to this provision, then on complaint of those tenants they shall be attached to appear in the lord king's court at an early date to answer thereto and have but a single essoin if they are in the realm, and the beasts or other distresses levied in this connection shall be released to the plaintiff immediately and stay released until the plea thereon between them is determined. And if lords of courts who levied such distresses do not appear on the day for which they were attached or keep the day given them by essoin, then word shall be sent to the sheriff to cause them to come for another day, and if on that day they do not appear, the sheriff shall be ordered to distrain them by all they have in his bailiwick, so that he, the sheriff, shall be responsible to the lord king for the issues and for producing their persons on a definite, prearranged day to the end that, if they do not appear on that day either, the plaintiff may go away *sine die*[1] and the beasts or other distresses shall stay released until those lords recover the suit by award of the lord king's court: and such distraints shall cease meanwhile, saving to lords of courts their right to sue for those suits by process of law, when they wish to plead thereon. And when lords of courts appear to answer those who complain of this sort of distress and are convicted of it, then by judgment of the court the

1 Without a day having been set for the court to reconvene, in effect an indefinite adjournment.

plaintiff shall recover from them the damages they have sustained by reason of the aforesaid distress.

In similar fashion, if after this constitution tenants withdraw from their lords' suits which they ought to do and which from before the time of the aforesaid crossing until now they have been accustomed to do, lords of courts shall obtain justice concerning the suits, together with their damages, by the same procedure and with the same dispatch in prearranging days and awarding distresses that tenants recover their damages. And this, namely this matter of recovering damages, is to be understood as relating to withdrawings of suit from themselves and not of withdrawings from their predecessors. Lords of courts shall not, for all that, be able to recover from their tenants seisin of such suits by default, as that has not been the custom hitherto. As regards suits withdrawn before the time aforesaid, the common law shall apply as it used to apply before.

**10.** On sheriff's tourns, it is provided that archbishops, bishops, abbots, priors, earls, barons shall not be bound to attend, nor any men of religion or women, unless their presence is especially required, but the tourn shall be held as it used to be in the days of the lord king's predecessors. And if they have tenements in various hundreds, they are not bound to attend such tourns save in the bailiwicks they ordinarily live in. And tourns shall be held in accordance with the terms of the king's great charter and as they used to be held in the days of king Richard and king John.

**11.** It is provided also that neither in the eyre of justices nor in county court, hundred court, or court baron shall fines be taken in future for beaupleader[1] or on condition that they be not troubled. And be it known that fines certain or payments commuted to a yearly rent between the time the king first crossed into Brittany and now are not abolished by this constitution.

---

1 Fines for not pleading aptly or fairly.

**12.** In the plea of dower which is called *unde nihil habet* at least four days shall be given in the year in future, and more if it can conveniently be done, in order that six days or at least five a year may be managed.

In the assize of *darrein presentment* and in the plea *quare impedit* in connection with vacant churches, day shall be given every fortnight or every three weeks according as the place is near or far. And in the plea of *quare impedit* if the defendant neither appears nor sends an essoin on the first day for which he was summoned, then he shall be attached for another day, and if on that day he does not appear or send an essoin he shall be distrained by the aforesaid grand distress. And if then he does not appear, word shall be sent because of his default to the bishop [concerned] that the claim of the defendant shall not that time hinder the plaintiff, saving to the defendant his right another time when he wishes to sue therefor.

The same law as to the making of attachments in all writs where attachments lie shall henceforth be firmly observed in the making of distresses. So, however, that the second attachment shall be by better pledges and afterwards the last distress.

**13.** And be it known that after anyone has put himself on any inquest which has arisen or can arise in writs of this sort, he shall have but one essoin or one default, so namely, that if he does not appear on the day given him by his essoin or makes a second default, then by his default the inquest shall be taken and in accordance with the inquest the court shall proceed to judgment. If however the inquest is taken in the county before the coroners or the king's justices for return on a certain day and the defendant does not appear on that day, then because of his default another day shall be assigned to him at the justices' discretion and word sent to the sheriff to cause him to appear on that day to hear, if he wishes, his judgment in accordance with the inquest; and if on that day he does not appear, the court shall proceed to judgment because of his default. Let it be done in the same way if he does not appear on the day given him by his essoin.

**14.** Concerning charters of exemption and liberty that those who acquire them shall not be put on assizes, juries, or recognitions, it is provided that if their oath is so necessary that without it justice cannot be done, for example in the grand assize and in perambulations and when in charters or deeds of covenant they are named as witnesses, or in attaints or other like cases, they shall be compelled to serve, saving to them their aforesaid liberty and exemption at other times.

**15.** Save only for the lord king and his officers, it shall be lawful henceforth for no one for whatever cause to levy distresses outside his fee or on the king's highway or a public way.

**16.** If any heir after the death of his ancestor is under age and his lord has the wardship of his lands and will not give them back to the said heir when he comes of age without being sued, the heir shall recover his land by reason of the death of his ancestor together with the damages he has sustained by the detention from the time when he came of age. Now if an heir is of full age on the death of his ancestor, is the heir apparent, and is acknowledged as heir and is found in the inheritance, his chief lord shall not eject him nor take or remove anything there, but shall take only simple seisin thereof as a recognition of his lordship. And if the chief lord maliciously withholds seisin so that it is necessary for the heir to sue by an action of *mort d'ancestor* or *cosinage*, then he shall recover his damages as in the action of *novel disseisin*.

As regards inheritances which are held in chief of the lord king, however, the observance shall be this: that the lord king shall have the first seisin thereof as he previously used to; nor shall the heir or anyone else enter forcibly into the inheritance before receiving it from the hands of the lord king in the way inheritances of this sort used to be received from his or his ancestors' hands. And this shall be understood of lands and fees which used to be in the king's hands by reason of knight-service or serjeanty or right of patronage.

**17.** It is provided also that if land held in socage is in the wardship of kinsmen of an heir because the heir is under age, those guardians shall have no power to do waste or sale or any destruction in the inheritance, but shall keep it safely for the use of the said heir, so that when he comes of age they shall answer to him by proper accounting for the issues of the said inheritance, saving to those guardians their reasonable costs. Neither can the said guardians sell or give the marriage of the said heir except for the benefit of the said heir. But next of kin who have had this sort of wardship ever since the time when writs of impleading were not granted may keep such wardships for the benefit of the heir as before stated without committing waste, exile or destruction.

**18.** No escheator, anyone empowered to hold enquiries, or justice assigned to take any assizes or to hear and determine any plaints shall henceforth have power to amerce anyone for defaulting on the common summons, save the chief justice or justices in eyre in their circuits.

**19.** Concerning essoins it is provided that in county court, hundred court, court baron or other courts, no one shall be bound to swear to warrant his essoin.

**20.** Henceforth no one except the lord king shall hold a plea in his court about a false judgment given in the court of his tenants, because such pleas pertain especially to the crown and dignity of the lord king.

**21.** It is provided also that, if anyone's beasts are taken and unjustly detained, the sheriff upon complaint made to him thereof can release them without hindrance or contradiction from him who took the said beasts if they were taken outside liberties. And if such beasts are taken within liberties and the bailiffs of the liberties will not release them, then because of the default of those bailiffs the sheriff shall have them released.

**22.** No one henceforth can distrain his free tenants to answer for their freehold nor for any matters touching their freehold, nor shall he put his freeholders to the oath against their will, inasmuch as no one can do this without a precept of the lord king.

**23.** It is provided also that if bailiffs who are bound to render account to their lords take themselves off and have no lands or tenements by which they can be distrained, then they shall be attached by their bodies so that the sheriffs in whose bailiwicks they are found can make them appear to render their account.

Also farmers during the term of their farms shall not commit waste, sale or exile[1] in respect of houses, woods, men, or anything belonging to the tenements they have at farm, unless they have a special concession in writing or mention in the deed of covenant that they can. And if they do this and are convicted of it, they shall restore damages in full and be heavily amerced.

**24.** Also, justices in eyre shall not henceforth amerce townships in their eyre because not everyone twelve years old appeared before the sheriff and coroners for the holding of inquests into robberies and arsons or other things pertaining to the crown, provided that sufficient come from those vills to enable juries for such inquests to be made up in full, except inquests concerning a man's death, when all who are twelve ought to appear unless they have reasonable cause of absence.

**25.** Murdrum[2] shall not henceforth be adjudged before justices when [death by] misadventure only has been adjudged, but shall be imposed in cases of death by felony and not otherwise.

**26.** It is moreover provided that no one vouched to warranty before justices in eyre in a plea of land or tenement shall henceforth be amerced because he is not present when he is vouched to warranty, except on the first day of the coming of the justices; instead, if he is within the shire, the sheriff shall then be commanded to have him appear within the third day, or the fourth, according to the distance of the places, as used to be done in the eyre of the justices. And if he lives outside the shire, then he shall have a reasonable summons of at least a fortnight according to the discretion of the justices and the common law.

**27.** If any clerk is arrested for any crime or charge pertaining to the crown and afterwards by the king's command delivered on bail or

1 Exile in this sense means unjust ejection from a freehold.
2 Here the fine levied upon the district, not the act of killing.

replevied on condition that they to whom he was delivered on bail have him before the justices, they to whom he was delivered on bail or his other pledges shall not henceforth be amerced if they have his body before the justices, even if he will not or cannot answer before them because of benefit of clergy.

**28.** It is also provided that if any acts of plundering and pillaging are committed against abbots or other prelates of the church, and they started legal proceedings over such depredations but were forestalled by death before they obtained justice therein, their successors shall have the right to take proceedings to reclaim from the hands of such transgressors the goods of their church recently removed by such violence before the death of their predecessors. The successors shall have like right of action, moreover, over those things recently removed from their house and church by such violence before the death of their predecessors, even if their said predecessors had not started legal proceedings while they were living.

And if any intrude themselves into the lands or tenements of such religious (of which their prelates died seised as by right of their church) during a vacancy, their successors shall have letters[1] to recover their seisin, and their damages shall be awarded to them, as has customarily been done in *novel disseisin.*

**29.** It is provided also that if the alienations for which a writ of entry used to be given are made through so many degrees that that writ cannot be had in the form previously used, the plaintiff shall have a writ for recovering seisin without mention of the degrees, into whosesoever hands the matter shall have come through such alienations, by original writs to be provided for the purpose by the king's council.

## Officium Coronatoris

The office of coroner, established in 1194, generally becomes the second most powerful post in the county after the sheriff, who is henceforth

1 That is, a writ.

relieved of or given assistance in a variety of tasks that become associated with the new office because coroners typically performed them when directed to do so. The "crown pleas" that belonged to the office, however, and were automatically performed by the coroner, "consisted of holding inquests upon dead bodies, receiving abjurations of the realm made by felons in sanctuary, hearing appeals, confessions of felons and appeals of approvers [informers], and attending and sometimes organizing exactions and outlawries promulgated in the county court."[1] The text known as *Officium Coronatoris*, at one time considered to have statutory force, provides an overview of responsibilities undertaken at various times by coroners but is in no way an official portrayal of the office. It is, in fact, extracted from *Bracton* and reflects that text's understanding of the early thirteenth century plea rolls upon which it is based.

We take out text from Luders, *Statutes of the Realm*, I, 40-41. The translation is our own.

## Statutes of the Realm

Hec sunt inquirenda a coronatoribus domini regis. In primis quum coronatores domini regis habent mandatum, a ballivis domini regis, vel a probis hominibus patrie, quod accedant ad occisos, vel subito mortuos, vel vulneratos, vel domorum fractores, vel ad locum ubi dicitur thesaurum esse inventum, statim accedere debent, & statim mandare debent quatuor villatis vicinis, vel quinque, vel sex, quod sint coram ipsis in tali loco: Et cum venerint ibi coronatores per sacramentum illorum debent facere inquisitionem in hac forma; scilicet si fuerit de homine occiso, primo est inquirendum ubi occisus fuerit; scilicet an in campo, an in domo, an ad luctam, an ad tabernam, an ad congregacionem: et si quis vel qui ibidem fuerint: similiter est inquirendum qui vel quales culpabiles fuerint, sive de facto, sive de forcia, & quis fuerit in curia, et qui ibidem fuerint homines vel femine, cujuscunque fuerint etatis, dum tamen loqui sciant et habeant discrecionem aliquam: et quot inventi fuerint culpabiles

1 Hunnisett 1961 1.

per inquisitionem aliquorum predictorum modorum, capientur & liberentur vicecomiti, et ponantur in gaiolam: & quot inventi fuerint qui non sunt culpabiles, attachientur usque adventum justiciarii, et nomina eorum omnium in rotulis coronatoris scribentur. Si quis autem talium occisus fuerit in campis, vel in boscis, et inveniatur, primo videndum est si utrum ibi occisus fuerit vt non, si forte ibi deferetur, sequantur vestigia, si sciri potest eorum qui corpus ibi detulerunt vel equi qui duxerint vel caretta, si forte caretta deferatur vel equo: Inquiratur etiam si interfectus notus fuerit vel ignotus, et ubi nocte illa precedente fuerit hospitatus: Si autem hujus occisi fuerint, de quibus dicitur quod sint culpabilies, statim accedant coronatores ad domum illorum, et inquirent que catalla habuerunt, vel que blada in grangia; et si liber fuerit, quam terram habeat et quid valeat per annum, sive que blada habeat in terra: et cum ita adquisierint de omnibus, appreciari facient terram bladum, et catalla, sicut statim vendi possunt, & liberentur tot villatis proximis ad respondendum de praedictis coram justiciariis: similiter de terra libera, quantum valeat per annum, salvo servicio dominorum feodi, & teneant terram in manu domini Regis, quousque domini feodi pro ea finem fecerint. Hiis inquisitis statim sepeliantur corpora mortuorum vel occisorum.

Similiter inquirendum est de submersis vel subito mortuis: et postea videndum est, de talibus corporibus, utrum sic submersi fuerint, vt occisi, vel jugulati, per signum colli vel per signum aliorum membrorum, vel per aliquam lesuram in corpore inventam: et sic procedendum est in forma predicta: si non fuerint occisi tunc debet coronator attachiare inventores et omnes alios in societate. De thesauro invento, debet coronator inquirere qui sciunt inventores, et similiter qui inde rettati sunt; et hoc scire potest, si quis solito ad tabernam accesserit et diutius sic se habuerit; pro tali suspecatione attachiare debentur per quatuor vel sex pleggios, vel per plures, si invenire possint. Si autem aliquis fuerit appellatus de raptu, appellatus attaciare debet, si appellum recens fuerit, et videant signum veritatis, per ampnum sanguinolentum, vel hutesium levatum, et tales attachiari debet per quatuor plegios, vel sex, si inveniri possint; si autem appellum fuerit sine hutesio, & sine signo manifesto, tunc sufficiunt plegii duo. De appello vero de plaga et hujusmodi, si plaga fuerit mortalis statim capientur appellati, et teneantur, donec sciatur si poterit convalescere lesus vel non, quod si moriatur teneantur rei, scilicet culpabiles; si vero convaluerit, attachiantur per quatuor plegios, vel sex, secundum quod plaga fuerit; et de mahemio attachientur per plures quam per quatuor; et de simplici autem vulnere sine mahemio duo plegii sufficiunt; item de omnibus plagis videndum est que sit longitudo, latitudo, et profunditas, et quibus armis lesus fuit vulneratus et in quo loco corporis: et si plures inde sint culpabiles, et si plura sint vulnera, et quis qualem plagam fecit: et sic debent omnia irrotulari in rotulo coronatoris. Si vero aliqui appellati fuerint, appellatus de facto capiatur, et appellati de forcia attachiantur salvo, quousque appellati de facto convincantur. De equis, batellis, carettis, per que aliquis sit interfectus, que proprie dicuntur vavi, apprecientur et tradentur villatis.

De wrecco maris ubicunque inveniatur, si quis manus imponat attachietur per bonos plegios et salvos, et precium wreccionis apprecietur, & liberetur villatis. Si autem aliquis rettatus fuerit de morte alicujus, capietur & inprisonetur ut supra; similiter de omnibus homicidiis et burgatoribus levetur hutesium, sicut alibi est consuetudo in Anglia; et omnes sequentur hutesium et vestigia, si fieri potest, et qui non fecerint, et super hoc convincti fuerint quod noluerint, attachientur quod sint coram Justiciariis.

### Translation

## The Office of the Coroner

These are the matters that should be investigated by the lord king's coroners. In the first place, when coroners receive a message from the lord king's bailiffs or from the upright people of a community that they should go to slayings or the unexpectedly dead or injured, or burglaries, or to a place where treasure is said to have been found, they should go at once and forthwith order four or five or six of those from the neighboring vills that they should be before them in such a place. And when they have come, the coroners should make an inquest upon their oath in this form, namely, if it was about a manslaughter, first let it be investigated where the slaying was, and if in field or house, or bed or tavern, or in a gathering, and if anyone, and who, were in the same place. Likewise it should be investigated who and what sort were blameworthy, whether in fact or by force, and who were in the house and who were the men and women in that same place of whatever estate, provided however that they know how to speak and have some discernment. And however many are found guilty by an inquest of any of the aforesaid manners, let them be taken and delivered to the sheriff and put in gaol. And however many were found who are not blameworthy, let them be attached until the arrival of the justices in eyre and their names written in the coroner's roll. And if someone of any sort was slain in fields or woods and has been found there, first let it be asked whether he was killed there or not, and if perhaps he was brought there, if it is possible, let the trails be followed of those who brought the body there or who led the horse or cart if perhaps he was brought by horse or cart. Let it also be asked if the slain was known or unknown and where he was lodged on the preceding night. And if they were slain by those of whom it is said that they are guilty, let the coroners go forthwith to their house and inquire what chattels they have and what grain in the granary, and if they are freedmen how much land they have and how much it is worth per year and what grain they have in the fields. And when they have inquired about everything, let them cause the chattels and grain to be appraised and the land valued, just as if they could be sold instantly, and let them be handed over to so many in the neighboring vills to answer for the aforesaid before the justices; and likewise for a freehold, how much it is valued per year, saving the service to the fee of lords, and let them hold the land in the lord king's hand until the lords of the fee have made the fine for it. When these matters have been investigated, let the bodies of the dead or slain be buried.

In like manner it should be investigated concerning the drowned or the suddenly dead, and afterwards, by the marking of the neck or by the marking of other members or by some other injury found on the body, [it should be investigated] whether they were so drowned or slain or strangled, whereupon the proceeding must be in the aforesaid form. If they were not slain, then the coroner should attach the finders and all the others in their company. For found treasure, the coroner ought to inquire who the finders were and likewise who are reputed thereof, and he can know this if someone has gone to a tavern regularly and has done so for a long time. For such suspicion let them be attached by four or six pledges, or by more if they can be found. And if someone is appealed of rape, the accused should be arrested if the accusation is recent and they should see the mark of truth by a stream of bleeding, or the hue and cry raised, and such men should be attached by four pledges or six, if they can be found. If, however, he has been arrested without the hue and cry, and without an obvious mark, then two pledges suffice. And for the accusation of wound and suchlike, if the wound was mortal let the accused be seized forthwith and held until it is known if the injured person can recover or not, but if he should die of the matter let the culprits be taken, that is, those culpable, but if he has survived, let them be attached by four pledges, or six, according to what the wound was. And for mayhem [maiming], let them be attached by as many as four, but for a simple injury, however, without mayhem, two pledges suffice; likewise for all wounds should be viewed what is the length, width, and depth, and by which arms the injury was inflicted and in which part of the body, and if many there are culpable, and if many are wounded, and who made what manner wound; and thus should everything be enrolled in the coroner's roll. And if others have been accused, let the one accused of the deed be seized, and let those accused of force be attached by surety until those accused by deed are fettered. For horses, boats, carts by which someone was slain, which are properly called deodands,[1] let them be valued and handed over to the vills.

For wreck of the sea found anywhere, if anyone should lay hands on it, let him be attached by good pledges and secure, and let the price of the wreck be valued and let it be delivered to the vills. And if someone has been reputed of someone's death, let him be taken and imprisoned as above, and for all homicides and burglaries let the hue and cry be raised, just as elsewhere it is the custom in England, and let everybody follow the hue and cry and the trail, if it can be done, and those who do not and are convicted of it because they did not want to, let them be attached that they be before the justices.

## Statute of Mortmain

There are two enactments commonly called the Statutes of Mortmain, our present text being the first of them and the Statute of Westminster III (*Quia Emptores*) of 1290 the second. The first forbids the transference of estates to the church, which took land effectively out of the king's fiscal control, and the second prohibits subinfeudation, thereby preventing the practice of frankalmoin by which land had found its way to the church, and reaffirms the prohibition against the transfer of lands and tenements to the church.

We take our text from Pickering, *The Statutes at Large*, I, 133-35. The translation is our own.

Rex Justiciis suis de Banco salutem. Cum dudum provisum fuisset quod viri religiosi feoda aliquorum non ingrederentur sine licentia & voluntate capitalium dominorum de quibus feoda illa immediate tenentur & viri religiosi postmodum nichilominus tam feoda sua propria quam aliorum hactenus ingressi sint ea sibi appropriando & emendo & aliquando ex dono aliorum recipiendo per quod servicia que ex hujusmodi feodis debentur & que ad defensionem regni ab initio provisa fuerunt indebita

1 An object forfeited when it occasioned or was the instrument of someone's death.

subtrahuntur & domini capitales escaetas suas inde amittunt. Nos super hoc pro utilitate regni congruum remedium provideri volentes de consilio Prelatorum Comitum & aliorum fidelium regni nostri de consilio nostro existentium providibus statuimus & ordinavimus quod nullus religiosus aut alius quicumque terras aut tenementa aliqua emere vel vendere aut sub colore donationis aut termini vel alterius tituli cujuscumque ab aliquo recipere aut alio quovis modo arte vel ingenio sibi appropriare presumat sub forisfactura eorumdem per quod ad manum mortuam terre & tenementa hujusmodi deveniant quoque modo. Providimus etiam quod si quis religiosus aut alius contra presens statutum aliquo modo arte vel ingenio venire presumpserit liceat nobis & aliis immediatis capitalibus dominis feodi taliter alienati illud infra annum a tempore alienationis hujusmodi ingredi & tenere in feodo & hereditate. Et si capitalus dominus immediatus negligens fuerit & feodem hujusmodi ingredi noluerit infra annum tunc liceat proximo capitali domino mediato feodi illius infra dimidium annum sequentem feodum illud ingredi & tenere sicut predictum est & sic quilibet dominus mediatus faciat si propinquior dominus in ingrediendo hujusmodi feodi negligens fuerit ut predictum est. Et si omnes hujusmodi capitales domini hujusmodi feodi qui plene fuerint etatis & infra quatuor maria & extra prisonam per unum annum negligentes vel remissi fuerint in hac parte nos statim post annum completum a tempore quo hujusmodi emptiones donationes aut alias appropriationes fieri contigerit terras & tenementa' hujusmodi capiemus in manum nostram & alios inde feoffabimus per certa servicia nobis inde ad defensionem regni nostri facienda salvis capitalibus dominis feodorum illorum wardis escaetis & aliis ad ipsos pertinentibus ac serviciis inde debitis & consuetis. Et ideo vobis mandamus quod statutum predictum coram vobis legi & decetero firmiter teneri & observari faciatis. T, Rex apud Westmonasterium xv. die Novembris anno &c. septimo.

## Translation

The king to his justices in bench, greeting. Since it was once provided that men of religion should not enter into possession of someone's fees without the permission and will of the chief lords of whom those fees are immediately held, and men of religion have nevertheless afterward until now entered into possession as well of their own fees as of others, appropriating them to themselves and buying them and receiving them as gifts from others, by which the services owed from such fees, and which to the defense of the realm from the beginning were provided, are unduly withheld and chief lords lose thereby their escheats. We, wishing for this a suitable remedy to be provided for the utility of the realm, by the advice having been provided of the prelates, earls, and other faithful subjects of our realm being of our counsel, have established and ordained that no religious or whatsoever other person should presume to buy or sell, or under colour of donation or fixed term, or to receive from someone by title of any sort, or by any means or scheme appropriate to himself lands or any tenements, under penalty of their forfeiture, through which lands and tenements of any sort come in any way into the possession of the dead hand. We have also provided that if some religious or other presumes to go against the present statute by some manner, art or scheme, it shall be permitted us and other immediate chief lords of the fee alienated in such a way to enter it within a year from the time of such alienation and hold it in fee and heritably. And if an immediate chief lord has been negligent and did not wish to enter a fee of such a sort within a year, then let it be permitted the next chief lord mediate of that fee[1] to enter that fee within the following half year and hold it just as was aforesaid and thus let whatsoever mediate lord do if the nearer lord has been negligent in entering a fee of this sort as was aforesaid. And if all such chief lords of such a fee who are of full age and within the four seas and out of prison have been negligent or remiss for one year in this regard, we will take into our hand immediately after a completed year

1 That is, the next higher chief lord.

from the time when such sales, grants, or other appropriations happen to be made and we will then enfeoff others for fixed services to be made us thence to the defense of our realm, reserving to the chief lords of those fees the wards, escheats, and other matters pertaining to them and the services and customs thence due. And so we command you that you make the aforesaid statute to be read before you and henceforth to be firmly held and observed. Witness the king at Westminster on the fifteenth day of November in the seventh year, etc.

## Statute of Westminster II

A landmark work of legislation, the Statute of Westminster II deals with a wide range of important subjects, ranging from the lengthy and difficult discussion of *maritagium* at its outset through replevin, mesne, wardship, *novel disseisin*, mortmain, rape and ravishment, to common land and its enclosure at its end. Its author, or at least one of them, is thought to be Chief Justice Ralph Hengham, who once advised someone not to gloss the statute, since "we know it better than you, for we made it."[1] For several centuries, from Blackstone to the twentieth century, it was thought by many to be the basis for the development of action on the case until Plucknett demonstrated otherwise.[2] The statute's lasting contribution would seem to be its condemnation of sheriffs who used false charges to extort money from persons who had not been properly charged. Accordingly, it provided that an action for false imprisonment could be brought against a sheriff who arrested and extorted money from a person who had not been lawfully indicted by a jury of twelve.[3]

1 Plucknett 1949/1962 73.
2 Plucknett 1931 778-99.
3 Such is the conclusion reached in a widely-used modern textbook. See Langbein *et al*. 2009 217.

We take our text from Luders, *Statutes of the Realm*, I: 71-95. The translation is by Rothwell, *English Historical Documents* 1975, 428-57.

Cum nuper Dominus Rex in quindena sancti Johannis Baptiste anno regni sui sexto, convocatis prelatis Comitibus, Baronibus & consilio suo apud Gloucestriam, quia multi de regno suo exheredationem patiebantur eo quod in multis casibus ubi remedium apponi debuit prius non fuit per predecessores suos aut ipsum remedium provisum, quedam statua populo suo valde necessaria & utilia edidit, per que populus suus Anglicanus & Hibernicus sub suo regimine gubernatus celeriorem justitiam quam prius in suis oppressionibus consecutus est, ac quidam casus in quibus lex deficiebat remanserunt non determinati, quedam enim ad reprimendum oppressionem populi remanserunt statuenda, Dominus Rex in parleamento suo post Pascha anno regni sui tertiodecimo apud Westmonisterium, multas oppressiones & legum defectus, ad supplecionem predictorum statutorum apud Gloucestrem editorum, recitari fecit & statuta edidit ut patebit in sequenti.

**1.** In primis, de tenementis que multociens dantur sub conditione, videlicet cum aliquis dat terram suam alicui viro & ejus uxori & heredibus de ipsis viro & muliere procreatis, adjecta conditione expressa tali quod si hujusmodi vir & mulier sine herede de ipsis viro & muliere procreato obissent, terra sic data ad donatorem vel ad ejus heredem revertatur. In casu etiam cum quis dat tenementum in liberum maritagium quod donum habet conditionem annexam, licet non exprimatur in carta doni, que talis est, quod si vir & mulier sine herede de ipsis procreato obierint tenementum sic datum ad donatorem vel ad ejus heredem revertatur. In casu etiam cum quis dat tenementum alicui & heredibus de corpore suo exeuntibus, durum videbatur & adhuc videtur hujusmodi donatoribus & heredibus donatorum quod voluntas ipsorum in donis suis expressa non fuerit prius nec adhuc est observata. In omnibus enim predictis casibus post prolem suscitatam & exeuntem ab ipsis quibus tenementum sic fuit datum conditionaliter, hucusque habuerunt hujusmodi feoffati potestatem alienandi tenementum sic datum &

exheredandi de tenemento exitum ipsorum contra voluntatem donatorum & formam de dono expressam. Et preterea cum deficiente exitu de hujusmodi feoffatis tenementum sic datum ad donatorum vel ad ejus heredem reverti debuit per formam in carta de dono expressam, licet exitus si quis fuerit obisset, per factum & feoffamentum ipsorum quibus tenementum sic fuit datum sub conditione exclusi fuerunt hucusque, de reversione eorundem tenementorum quod manifeste fuit contra forman doni sui. Propter quod dominus Rex, perpendens quod necessarium & utile est in predictis casibus apponere remedium, statuit quod voluntas donatoris secundum formam in carta doni sui manifeste expressam de cetero observetur, ita quod non habeant illi, quibus tenementum sic fuit datum sub conditione, potestatem alienandi tenementum sic datum quo minus ad exitum illorum quibus tenementum sic fuerit datum remaneat post eorum obitum, vel ad donatorem vel ad ejus heredem, si exitus deficiat per hoc quod nullus sit exitus omnino, vel si aliquis exitus fuerit, per mortem deficiet, herede hujusmodi exitus deficiente. Nec habeat de cetero secundus vir hujusmodi mulieris aliquid in tenemento sic dato per conditionem post mortem uxoris ejus per Legem Anglie, nec exitus de secundo viro & muliere successionem hereditariam, set statim post mortem viri & mulieris quibus tenementum sic fuit datum post eorum obitum vel ad eorum exitum vel ad donatorem vel ad ejus heredem ut predictum est revertatur. Et quia in novo casu novum remedium est apponendum fiat impetranti tale breve: Precipe A. quod juste, &c. reddat B. tale manerium cum pertinentiis quod C. dedit tali viro & tali mulieri & heredibus de ipsis viro & muliere exeuntibus. Vel, Quod C. dedit tali viro in liberum maritagium cum tali muliere, & quod post mortem predictorum viri & mulieris predicto B. filio predictorum viri & mulieris descendere debet per formam donationis predicte ut dicit. Vel, Quod C. dedit tali & heredibus de corpore suo exeuntibus & quod post mortem ipsius talis predicto B. filio predicti talis descendere debet per formam, &c. Breve per quod donator habet recuperare suum deficiente exitu satis est in usu in cancellaria Et sciendum quod hoc statutum quoad alienationem tenementi contra forman doni imposterum faciendam locum habet, & ad dona prius facta non extenditur. Et si finis super hujusmodi tenemento imposterum levetur, ipso jure sit nullus, nec habeant heredes aut illi ad quos spectat reversio, licet plene sint etatis in Anglia & extra prisonam, necesse apponere clamium suum.

**2.** Quia domini feodorum distringentes tenentes suos per serviciis sibi debitis multotiens gravantur per hoc quod cum tenentes sui districtionem suam per breve vel sine brevi replegiaverint, ac ipsi domini cum ad querimoniam tenentium suorum ad comitatum vel ad aliam curiam habentem potestatem placitandi placita de vetito namio, per attachiamentum venerint, & rationabilem & justam districtionem advocaverint, per hoc quod tenentes deadvocant nichil tenere nec clamant tenere de eo qui districtionem fecit & advocavit, remansit qui distrinxit in misericordia & tenentes sui quieti, quibus pro illa deadvocatione per recordum comitatus sive aliarum curiarum que recordum non habent pena infligi non potest. De cetero provisum est & statutum quod cum hujusmodi domini in comitatu vel hujusmodi curia justitiam de hujusmodi tenentibus suis consequi non possint quam cito attachiati fuerunt ad sectam tenentium suorum, concedatur eis breve ad ponendum loquelam illam coram Justiciariis, coram quibus & non alibi justitia hujusmodi dominis exhiberi poterit. Et inseratur causa in brevi quia talis distrinxit in feodo suo pro serviciis & consuetudinibus sibi debitis. Nec per istud statutum derogatur legi communi usitate que non permisit placitum aliquod poni coram Justiciam ad petitionem defendentis. Quia licet prima facie videbatur tenens actor & dominus defendens habito tamen respectu ad hoc quod dominus distringit & sequitur pro serviciis & consuetudinibus sibi a retro existentibus, realiter potius apparebit actor sive querens quam defendens. Et ut in certo sint Justiciarii de qua recenti seisina potuerunt domini advocare rationabilem districtionem super tenentes suos, de cetero concordatum est quod rationabilis districtio advocari poterit de seisina antecessorum suorum vel predecessorum a temporem quo breve nove disseisine currit. Et quia aliquando contingit quod cum tenens postquam replegiaverit averia sua averia illa vendit vel elongat quominus returnum fieri possit domino distringenti si adjudicetum. Provisum est quod vicecomites aut ballivi de cetero non recipiant a conquerentibus solummodo plegios de prosequendo antequam deliberationem faciant de averiis, set etiam de averiis retornandis si adjudicetur returnum. Et si quis alio modo plegios receperit respondeat ipse de pretio averiorum & habeat dominus distringens recuperare per breve quod reddat ei tot averia vel tot catalla, & si non habeat ballivus unde reddat, reddat superior suus. Et quia aliquando contingit quod postquam adjudicatum fuerit distringenti returnum averiorum, & sic districtus, postquam averia sic retornata iterum replegiaverit, cum viderit distringentem comparentem in curia paratum sibi respondere, defaltam fecerit, ob quam iterum adjudicabitur distringenti returnum averiorum & sic bis, tertio & in infinitum, replegiabuntur averia, nec habebunt judicia curie Regis in hoc casu effectum, super quo non fuit prius remedium provisum, ordinatus est in hoc casu talis processus quod quam cito adjudicatum fuerit distringenti returnum averiorum per breve de judicio mandetur vicecomiti quod returnum habere faciat distringenti de averiis, in quo brevi inseratur quod vicecomes ea non deliberet sine brevi in quo fiat mentio de judicio per Justiciarias reddito, quod fieri non poterit nisi per breve quod exeat de rotulis Justiciariorum coram quibus deducta fuerit loquela. Cum igitur adierit Justicia & petierit averia sua iterum replegiari, fiat ei hoc breve de judicio, quod vicecomes capta securitate de prosequendo, & etiam de averiis vel catallis retornandis vel eorum pretio si adjudicetur returnum, deliberet ei averia vel catalla prius retornata & attachietur qui distrinxit ad veniendum ad certum diem coram Justiciariis coram quibus placitum deducatur in presentia partium. Et si iterato ille qui replegiaverit fecerit defaltam vel alia occasione adjudicetur returnum districtionis jam bis replegiate, remaneat districtio illa imperpetuum irreplegiabilis, set si de novo & de nova causa fiat districtio de nova districtione servetur processus supradictus.

**3.** In casu quando vir amisit per defaltam tenementum quod fuit jus uxoris sue durum fuit quod uxor post mortem viri sui non habuit aliud recuperare quam per breve de Recto, propter quod Dominus Rex statuit quod mulier post mortem viri sui habeat recuperare per breve de ingressu cui ipsa in vita sua contradicere non potuit, quod in forma predicta[1] erit placitanda. Si contra petitionem mulieris tenens excipiat quod habuit ingressum per judicium & comperto quod per defaltam, ad quod tenens necesse habet respondere si ab eo queratur, tunc necesse habet ulterius ostendere jus suum secundum formam brevis quod prius impetravit super virum & uxorem. Et si verificare poterit quod jus habet in tenemento petito nichil capiat mulier per breve suum, quod si ostendere non poterit recuperet mulier tenementum petitum, hoc observato quod si vir absentaverit se & noluerit jus uxoris sue defendere, vel invita uxore reddere voluerit, si uxor ante judicium venerit parata petenti respondere & jus suum defendere, admittatur uxor. Eodem modo si tenens in dotum, per Legem Anglie, vel aliter ad terminum vite vel per donum in quo reservatur reversio fecerit defaltam, vel reddere voluerit, admittantur heredes & illi ad quos spectat reversio ad responsionem si venerint ante judicium; & si per defaltam aut redditionem reddatur judicium tunc habeant heredes & illi ad quos spectat reversio post mortem hujusmodi tenentium recuperare per breve de ingresu, in quo servetur idem processus sicut dictum est supra in casu ubi vir amittit tenementum uxoris; & sic in casibus predictis due concurrunt actiones una inter petentem & tenentem & alia inter tenentem jus suum ostendantem & petentem.

**4.** In casu quando vir implacitatus de tenemento reddit tenementum petitum suo adversario de plano post mortem viri Justiciarii adjudicant mulieri dotem suam si per breve queratur; set in casu quando vir amittit tenementum petitum per defaltam, si mulier post mortem viri sui petat dotem, compertum est quod per aliquos Justiciarios adjudicata fuerit dos mulieri petenti non obstante defalta quam vir suus fecit, aliis Justiciariis in contraria oppinione existentibus & contrarium judicantibus: ut de cetero amputetur hujusmodi ambiguitas, sic in certo ordinatum est, quod in utroque casu audiatur mulier que dotem petit. Et si excipiatur contra ipsam quod vir ipsum tenementum unde dos petita est amisit per judicium per quod dotem habere non debet; et si queratur per quod

1 Rothwell emends to *subscripta*.

judicium, & compertum fuerit quod per defaltam, ad quod tenens necesse habet respondere tunc oportet tenentem ulterius respondere & ostendere quod ipse tenens jus habuit & habet in predicto tenemento, secundum formam brevis quod prius super virum impetravit. Et si ostendere poterit quod vir mulieris non habuit jus in tenemento, nec aliquis alius quam ipse qui tenet, recedat quietus & uxor nichil capiat de dote; quod si ostendere non poterit, recuperet mulier dotem suam. Et sic in casibus istis, & in quibusdam casibus subsequentibus, scilicet quando uxor dotata amittit dotem per defaltam, & tenentes in maritagium per Legem Anglie, vel ad terminum vite vel per feodum talliatum, concurrunt plures actiones; quia hususmodi tenentes cum oporteat eos petere tenementa sua per defaltam amissa, & ad hoc perventum fuerit, quod tenens necesse habet ostendere jus suum, non possunt ipsi sine hiis ad quos spectat reversio de jure respondere. Et ideo conceditur eis quod vocent ad warantum, ac si essent tenentes, si warantum habeant. Et cum warantus warantizaverit procedat placitum inter illum qui seiesitus est & warrantum, secundum tenorem brevis quod tenens prius impetravit & per quod recuperavit per defaltam, & sic ex pluribus actionibus ad ultimum perveniatur ad unum judicium, videlicet ad hoc quod hujusmodi petentes recuperant petitionem suam, vel quod tenentes eant quieti. Et si actio hujusmodi tenentis qui necesse habet ostendere jus suum mota fuerit per breve de Recto, licet magna assisa vel duellum jungi non possint per verba consueta, jungi tamen possunt per verba satis apta; quia cum tenens in hoc quod ostendit jus suum quod ei competit per breve quod prius impetravit sit loco actoris, bene poterit warantus defendere jus tenentis, qui loco petentis ut dictum est habetur, & seisinam antecessoris sui offerre defendere per corpus liberi hominis sui, vel ponere se in magnam assisam & petere recognitionem fieri, utrum ipse majus jus habeat in tenemento petito an predictus talis; vel alio modo jungi poterit magna assisa sic; talis defendit jus, &c. et cognoscit seisinam antecessoris sui & ponit se in magnam assisam, &c. & petit recognitionem fieri utrum ipse majus jus habeat in predicto tenemento ut in illo de quo feoffavit talem, vel quod talis remisit & quietum clamavit, &c. an predictus talis.

Cum aliquando contingat quod mulier non habens jus petendi dotem, herede alicujus infra etatem existente, impetret breve de dote super custodem & custos per favorem mulieris dotem reddiderit vel defaltam fecerit vel placitum ita ficte per collusionem defenderit per quod dos hujusmodi mulieri in prejudicium heredis adjudicata fuerit, provisum est quod heres cum ad etatem pervenerit habeat actionem petendi seisinam antecessoris sui versus hujusmodi mulierem, qualem haberet versus alium quemcumque deforiatorem; Ita tamen quod salva sit mulieri versus petentem exceptio ostendendi quod jus habet in dote sua, quod si ostendere poterit recedat quieta & dotem suam retineat & sit heres in misericordia & amercietur graviter secundum discretionem Justicie, sin autem recuperet heres petitionam suam.

Eodem modo subveniatur mulieri si heres vel alius eam implacitaverit de dote sua si dotem suam per defaltam amiserit, in quo casu sua defalta non sit ei ita prejudicialis quin dotem suam si jus habeat recuperare possit, & fiat ei tale breve: Precipe A. quod juste, &c. reddat tali que fuit uxor talis tantam terram cum pertinentiis in N. quam clamat esse rationabilem dotem suam, vel de rationabili dote sua, & quam talis ei deforceat. Et ad istud breve habeat tenens exceptionem suam ad ostendendum quod mulier jus non habet in dote, quod si verificare poterit recedat quietus; alioquin recuperet mulier tenementum quod prius tenuit in dotem.

Et cum temporibus retroactis aliquis terram suam amisisset per defaltam non habuit aliud recuperare quam per breve de recto, quod eis competere non poterit qui de mero jure loqui non potuerunt, veluti tenentes ad terminum vite, vel per liberum maritagium vel per feodum talliatum, in quibus casibus salvatur reversio; provisum est decetero quod eorum defalta non sit eis ita prejudicialis quin statum suum, si jus habeant, recuperare possint per aliud breve quam per breve de Recto. De maritagio amisso per defaltam fiat tale breve: Precipe A. quod juste, &c. reddat B. tale manerium de C. cum pertinentiis quod clamat esse jus &

maritagium suum & quod A. ei injuste deforceat. Eodem modo de tenemento tento ad terminum vite per defaltam amisso fiat breve: Precipe A. quod juste & sine dilatione reddat B. manerium de C., cum pertinentiis quod clamat esse jus & maritagium suum & quod predictus A. ei injuste deforceat; vel, quod clamat tenere ad terminum vite sue, vel, quod clamat tenere sibi & heredibus suis de corpore suo exeuntibus, & quod predictus A. ei injuste deforceat.

**5.** Cum de advocationibus ecclesiarum non sint nisi tria brevia originalia, videlicet breve de Recto & duo de possessionibus scilicet Ultime presentationis & Quare Impedit, & hucusque usitatum fuerit in regno quod cum aliquis jus non habens presentandi presentaverit ad aliquam ecclesiam cujus presentatus sit admissus ipse qui verus est patronus per nullum aliud breve recuperare poterit advocationem suam quam per breve de Recto quod habet terminari per duellum vel per magnam assisam, per quod heredes infra etatem existentes per fraudem & negligentiam custodum, heredes etiam sive majores sive minores per negligentiam vel fraudem tenentium in dotem per Legen Anglie, vel mulierum tenentium in dotem, vel alio modo ad terminum vite vel annorum vel foedum talliatum multotiens exheredationem patiebantur de avocationibus suis, vel ad minus quod melius eis fuit ponebantur ad breve de Recto, & in casu omnino exheredati fuerunt hucusque; statutum est quod hujusmodi presentationes non sint hujusmodi rectis heredibus aut illis ad quos post mortem aliquorum hujusmodi advocationes reverti debent prejudiciales, quia quotienscumque aliquis jus non habens tempore hujusmodi custodarium presentaverit, vel tempore tenentium in dotem per Legem Anglie vel alio modo ad terminum vite vel annorum vel per feodum talliatum, in proxima vacatione postquam heres ad etatem pervenerit vel advocatio post mortem in forma predicta tenentium ad heredem plene etatis existentem revertitur habeat eandem actionem & exceptionem per breve de advocatione possessorium qualem haberet ultimus antecessor hujusmodi heredis plenam habens etatem in ultima vacatione tempore suo accidente ante mortem suam vel antequam dimissio facta fuerit ad terminum vel ad feodum talliatum ut predictum est. Hoc idem observetur de presentationibus factis ad ecclesias de hereditate uxorum tempore quo fuerunt sub potestate virorum suorum, quibus per istud statutum subveniatur per remedium supradictum. Viris etiam religiosis Episcopis Archiepiscopis Rectoribus ecclesiarum & aliis personis ecclesiasticis per istud idem statutum subveniatur, Si quis jus presentandi non habens presentaverit ad ecclesias, domibus suis prelatie dignitati aut personatui spectantes, tempore quo vacaverint prelatie dignitates aut personatus hujusmodi.

Nec tamen ita large intelligatur istud statutum quod persone ad quarum remedium istud statutum est editum habeant recuperare supradictum dicentes quod custodes, tenentes in dotem per Legem Anglie, vel aliter ad terminum vite vel annorum, vel viri, ficte defenderunt placitum per ipsos vel contra ipsos motum; Quia judicia in curia Regis reddita per istud statutum non adnichilentur set stet judicium in suo robore quousque per judicium curie Regis tanquam erronium, si error inveniatur, adnulletur; vel assisa Ultime presentationis vel inquisitio per breve Quare impedit si transierit per attinctam vel per certificationem adnulletur que gratis concedatur. Et de cetero una forma placitandi in brevibus Ultime presentationis & quare impedit inter Justiciis observetur, quoad hoc, si pars rea excipiat de plenitudine ecclesie per suam propriam presentationem, non propter plenitudinem illam remaneat loquela, dummodo breve infra tempus semestre impetretur quamquam infra tempus semestre presentationem suam recuperare non possit. Et cum aliquando inter plures clamantes advocationem alicujus ecclesie pax fuerit formata inter partes & irrotulata coram Justicias in rotulo vel in fine sub hac forma, quod unus primo presentet & in sequente vacatione alius & in tertia tertius, et sic de pluribus si plures sint. Et cum unus presentaverit & habuerit suam presentationem quam habere debet per formam illius conventionis, & in proxima vacatione impediatur ille ad quem sequens spectat presentatio per aliquem qui fuit pars illius conventionis vel loco ejus, statutum est quod de cetero non habeant hujusmodi impediti necesse perquirere breve Quare impedit, set habeat recursum ad rotulum vel ad finem; Et si in rotulo vel in fine comperta fuerit predicta pax vel conventio, mandetur vicecomiti quod scire faciat parti impedienti quod sit ad aliquem brevem diem continentem spatium quindecim dierum vel trium septimanarum, secundum quod locus est propinquus vel remotus, ostensurus si quid sciat dicere quare sic impeditus talem presentationem suam habere non debeat. Et si non venerit vel forte venerit & nichil sciat dicere quare sic impeditus presentationem suam habere non debeat ratione alicujus facti post pacem irrotulatam vel cirographatam, recuperet presentationem suam cum dampnis suis. Et cum contingat quod post mortem antecessorum suorum quis ad ecclesiam presentaverit, assignata fuerit illa advocatio in dotem alicujus mulieris, vel teneatur per Legem Anglie, et tenentes in dotem vel per legem Anglie presentaverint & verus heres post mortem hujusmodi tenentium per legem Anglie, vel in dotem impediatur presentare cum ecclesia vacaverit, provisum est quod de cetero sit in electione impediti utrum perquirere velit per breve Quare impedit, vel Ultime presentationis. Hoc etiam observetur de advocationibus dimissis ad terminum vite vel annorum vel ad feodum talliatum. Et de cetero in brevibus Ultime presentationis & Quare impedit adjudicentur dampna videlicet si tempus semestre transierit per impedimentum alicujus ita quod si Episcopus ecclesiam conferat & verus patronus ea vice presentationem suam amittat adjudicentur dampna ad valorem medietatis ecclesie per annum. Et si impeditor nichil habeat unde restituere possit dampna in casu quando Episcopus confert per lapum temporis puniatur per prisonam duorum annorum Et si advocatio disrationetur infra tempus semestre puniatur tamen impeditor per prisonam dimidii anni. Et de cetero concedantur brevia de Capellis, prebendis, vicariis, Hospitalibus, Abbatiis, Prioratibus & aliis domibus que sunt de advocationibus aliquorum que prius concedi non consueverunt. Et cum per breve Indicavit impediatur rector alicujus ecclesie ad petendum decimas in vicina parochia, habeat patronus rectoris sic impediti breve ad petendum advocationem dicimarum petitarum. Et cum disrationaverit procedat postmodum placitum in curia Christianitatis, quatenus disrationatum fuerit in curia Regis. Cum advocatio descendit participibus licet unus bis presentet & usurpet super coheredem, non propter hoc exclusus sit ille in toto qui fuit negligens, set alias habeat turnum suum presentandi cum acciderit.

**6.** Cum quis petat tenementum versus alium & implacitatus vocaverit ad warantum & warantus dedicat warantiam & die pendeat placitum inter tenentem & warantum, cum ad ultimum convincatur quod vocatus ad warantum warantizare tenetur, per legem & consuetudinem hactenus usitatam non fuit aliqua pena inflicta vocato, qui warantizare dedixit nisi tantum quod warantizaret & esset in misericorda quia prius non warantizavit, quod durum fuit petenti qui multotiens per collusionem inter tenentem & warantum magnas sustinuit dilationes. Propter quod statuit dominus rex, quod sicut tenens amitteret tenementum petitum si vocasset ad warantum & warantus se posset devolvere de warantia, eodem modo amittat warantus si warantiam dedicat & convincatur quod warantizare debeat. Et si inquisitio pendeat inter tenentem & warantum & petens petat breve ad faciendum venire juratam concedatur ei.

**7.** Custodi de cetero concedatur breve de Amensuratione dotis, nec per sectam custodis si ficte & per collusionem sequatur versus mulierem tenentem in dotem precludatur heres cum ad etatem pervenerit ad dotem amensurandum secundum quod per legem Anglie fuerit amensuranda. Et tam in brevi isto quam in brevi de Amensuratione pasture celerior quam prius de cetero fit processus, Ita quod cum perventum fuerit ad magnam districtionem dentur dies infra quos duo comitatus teneantur ad quos publica fiat proclamatio quod defendens veniat ad diem in brevi contentum querenti responsurus; ad quem diem si venerit procedat placitum inter eos. Et si non venerit & proclamatio supradicto modo per vicecomitem testificata fuerit, procedatur per defaltam ad amensurationem faciendam.

**8.** Cum per placitum motum per breve de Amensuratione pasture pastura fuerit amensurata, aliquando coram justiciis aliquando in comitatu coram vicecomite, multotiens contingit quod post hujusmodi amensurationem factam iterum ponit ille qui primo superoneravit pasturam plura animalia quam ad ipsum pertinet habenda nec hucusque provisum esset remedium; statutum est quod de secunda superoneratione fiat remedium querenti sub hac forma, quod conquerens habeat breve de judicio, si coram Justiciis amensurata fuerit pastura, quod vicecomes in presentia partium premunitarum si interesse voluerint, inquirat de secunda superoneratione, que si inventa fuerit mandetur Justicia sub sigillo vicecomitis & sigillis juratorum, & Justiciarii adjudicent dampna conquerenti, & ponant in extractis valorem animalium que superonerans post amensurationem factam posuit in pasturam ultra quod debuit, & extractas liberent Baronibus de Scaccario ut inde respondeant domino regi. Si in comitatu facta fuerit amensuratio tunc ad instantiam querentis exeat breve de cancellaria, quod vicecomes inquirat super hujusmodi superoneratione. Et de averiis positis in pastura ultra debitum numerum vel de pretio, et domino regi ad scaccarium suum respondeant. Et ne vicecomites fraudem faciant domino Regi in isto casu, concordatum est quod omnia hujusmodi brevia de secunda superoneratione que exeunt de cancellaria irrotulentur, & in fine anni mittatur transcriptum ad Scaccarium, sub sigillo Cancellarii, ut videant Thesaurarius & Barones de Scaccario qualiter vicecomites respondeant de exitibus hujusmodi brevium. Eodem modo irrotulentur brevia de redisseisina & mittantur ad Scaccarium in fine anni.

9. Cum capitales domini distringant feodum suum pro serviciis & consuetudinibus sibi debitis, & medius fit qui tenentem acquietare debet cum non jaceat in ore tenentis postquam districtionem replegiaverit dedicere demandam capitalis domini qui advocat in curia domini regis justam districtionem fieri super tenentem suum videlicet super medium, multi per hujusmodi districtiones hucusque gravati extiterunt per hoc quod medius licet haberet per quod distringi posset magnas fecerit dilationes antequam ad curiam venerit ad respondendum hujusmodi tenentibus suis ad breve de medio, per hoc etiam quod durius fuit in casu quando medius nichil habuit; In casu etiam quando si tenens paratus esset facere capitali domino servicia & consuetudines exactas, & capitalis dominus servicia & consuetudines sibi debitas renuebat percipere per

manus alterius, quam proximi tenentis sui, & sic amiserunt hujusmodi tenentes in dominico prosicuum terrarum suarum, aliquando ad tempus aliquando toto tempore suo, nec fuit antea aliquod remedium in hoc casu provisum; Ordinatum est & provisum in hoc casu remedium imposterum sub hac forma, quod quam cito hujusmodi tenens in dominico habens medium inter ipsum & capitalem dominum distringitur, statim perquirat sibi tenens breve de Medio, & si medius habens terram in eodem comitatu defugerit usque ad magnam districtionem, detur querenti in brevi suo de magna districtione talis dies, ante cujus adventum duo comitatus teneantur, & precipiatur vicecomiti quod distringat medium per magnam districtionem prout in brevi continetur, et nichilominus vicecomes in duobus plenis comitatibus solempniter proclamari faciat, quod hujusmodi medius veniat ad diem in brevi contentum responsurus tenenti suo; ad quem diem si venerit procedat placitum inter eos modo consueto, et si non venerit, amittat hujusmodi medius servicium tenentis sui, & amodo non respondeat ei tenens in aliquo; set, omisso illo medio, respondeat capitali domino de eisdem serviciis & consuetudinibus que prius facere debuit predicto medio, nec habeat capitalis dominus potestatem distringendi, dum predictus tenens offerat ei servicia debita & consueta. Et si capitalis dominus exegerit plusquam medius ei facere deberet, habeat tenens in hoc casu exceptionem quam haberet medius. Si vero medius nichil habuerit in potestate Regis, nichilominus perquirat tenens breve suum de medio, ad vicecomitem illius comitatus in quo distringitur. Et si vicecomes mandaverit quod nichil habet ubi potest summoneri nichilominus sequatur breve de attachiamento. Et si vicecomes mandaverit quod nichil habet per quod potest attachiari, nichilominus sequatur breve de magna districtione & fiat proclamatio in forma predicta. Si vero medius non habeat terram in comitatu in quo fit districtio, set habeat terram in alio comitatu, tunc exeat breve originale ad summonendum medium ad vicecomitem illius comitatus in quo fit districtio, et cum testificatum fuerit per illum vicecomitem quod nichil habeat in comitatu suo, exeat breve de judicio ad summonendum medium, ad vicecomitem illius comitatus in quo testificatum fuerit quod habet tenementa, et fiat secta in illo comitatu, quousque perveniatur ad magnam districtionem et proclamationem sicut dictum est supra de medio habente terram in eodem comitatu in quo fit districtio, et nichilominus fiat secta in comitatu in quo nichil habet sicut dictum est supra de medio nichil habente, quousque perveniatur ad magnam districtionem et proclamationem, et sic post proclamationem in utroque comitatu factam, abjudicetur medius a feodo et servicio suo. Cum aliquando contingat quod tenens in dominico feoffatus est ad tenendum per minus servicium quam medius facere debuit capitali domino & cum post hujusmodi proclamationem, attornatus sit tenens capitali domino, medio omisso, necesse habebit tenens respondere capitali domino de serviciis et consuetudinibus que medius ei prius facere debuit. Et postquam venerit medius in curia, et cognoverit quod acquietare debeat tenentem suum, vel adjudicetur ad acquietandum, si post hujusmodi cognitionem vel judicium querimonia perveniat quod medius non acquietavit tenentem suum, tunc cxcat brcvc dc judicio, quod vicecomes distringat medium ad acquietandum tenentem suum et ad essendum coram Justiciariis ad certum diem ad ostendendum quare prius non acquietavit; Et cum per districtionem venerit, audiatur querens, et si querens verificare poterit quod ipsum non acquietavit, satisfaciet de dampnis, et per judicium tenens recedat quietus de suo medio et attornetur capitali domino. Et si ad primam districtionem non venerit exeat breve de alia districtione, et fiat proclamatio. Et postquam testificata fuerit procedatur ad judicium sicut superius dictum est. Et sciendum quod per hoc statutum non excluduntur tenentes quin habeant warantiam, si de tenementis suis implacitentur super medios suos & eorum heredes sicut prius habuerunt. Nec etiam excluduntur tenentes, quin sequi possint versus medios suos secundum consuetudinem prius usitatam, si viderint quod processus eorum plus valeat per antiquam consuetudinem, quam per istud statutum. Et sciendum, quod per istud statutum non providetur remedium quibuscumque mediis set solummodo in casu cum sit unus medius tantum inter dominum distringentem & tenentem; Et in casu quando medius ille est plene etatis & in casu quando tenens, sine prejudicio alterius quam medii, attornare se potest capitali domino, quod dictum est pro mulieribus tenentibus in dotem, tenentibus per legenmAnglie, vel aliter ad terminum vite vel per feodum talliatum, quibus pro aliquibus casibus nondum est remedium provisum, set Deo dante alias providebitur.

**10.** Cum in itinere Justiciariorum proclamatum fuerit, quod omnes qui brevia liberare voluerint, ea liberent infra certum terminum post quem nullum breve recipiatur, multi de hoc confidentes cum moram fecerint usque ad predictum terminum & nullum breve super eos fuerit liberatum de licentia Justitiariorum recedunt, post quorum recessum adversarii sui ipsorum absentiam percipientes brevia sua porrigunt in cera, que aliquando per fraudem, aliquando per vicecomitem pro dono recipiuntur, & alii qui secure credebant recessisse, tenementa sua amittunt. Ut hujusmodi fraudi subveniatur imposterum, statuit Dominus Rex, quod Justitiarii in itineribus suis statuant terminum, quindecim dierum vel mensis, minoris vel majoris termini secundum quod comitatus fuerit major vel minor, infra quem terminum publice proclametur, quod omnes qui brevia liberare voluerint ea liberent citra illum terminum, & in adventu illius termini certificet vicecomes capitalem Justitiarium itineris quot brevia habent & que & quod ultra illum terminum nullum breve recipiatur, quod si receptum fuerit processus per illud factus pro nullo habeatur, excepto quod breve cassatum durante toto itinere relevari poterit; brevia etiam de Dote, de viris qui obierint infra summonitionem itineris, assise Ultime presentationis, Quare impedit de ecclesiis vacantibus infra summonitionem predictam, quocumque tempore ante recessum justitiariorum, recipiantur; brevia etiam Nove disseisine quocumque tempore facta fuerit disseisina recipiantur.

In itineribus Justitiariorum concedit Dominus Rex de gratia speciali quod illi qui tenementa habent in diversis comitatibus in quibus Justiciarii itinerant, vel de quibusdam tenementis in comitatu in quo Justitiarii itinerant timent implacitari, & de aliis tenementis in comitatu in quo Justitiarii non itinerant implacitantur coram Justitiariis apud Westministerium vel in Banco Domini Regis vel coram Justitiariis ad assisas capiendas assignatis, vel in aliquo comitatu coram vicecomite vel in aliqua curia Baronum, facere possint attornatum generalem ad sequendum pro eis in omnibus placitis in itinere Justitiariorum pro ipsis vel contra ipsos motis vel movendis durante itinere, qui quidem attornatus vel attornati habeant potestatem in placitis motis in itinere, quousque placitum terminetur vel dominus suus ipsum amoverit; nec per hoc excusentur si fuerint in juratis, vel assisis coram eisdem Justitiariis.

**11.** De servientibus, ballivis, camerariis & quibuscunque receptoribus, qui ad compotum reddendum tenentur concorditer est statutum & ordinatum, quod cum dominus hujusmodi servientium dederit eis auditores compoti, & contingat ipsos esse in arreragiis super compotum suum, arrestentur corpora ipsorum per testimonium auditorum ejusdem compoti, et mittantur aut liberentur proxime gaole domini Regis in partibus illis, & a vicecomite seu custode ejusdem gaole recipiantur & mancipentur carceri in ferris sub bona custodia, & in illa prisona remaneant de sue proprio viventes, quousque dominis suis de arreragiis plenarie satisfecerint. Attamen si quis sic gaole liberatus, conqueratur quod auditores compoti ipsum injuste gravaverunt, onerando de receptis que non recepit, vel non alilocando expensas aut liberationes rationabiles, & inveniat amicos qui eum manucapere voluerint ad ducendum coram baronibus de scaccario, liberetur eis; & scire faciat vicecomes in cujus prisona fuerit domino quod sit coram Baronibus de Scaccario ad aliquem certum diem, cum rotulis & talliis per quos compotum reddiderit, & in presentia Baronum vel auditorum, quos assignare voluerint recitetur compotus & fiat partibus justitia, ita quod si fuerit in arreragiis committatur gaole de Flete ut supradictum est. Et si diffugerit & gratis compotum reddere noluerit sicut alibi in aliis statutis continetur, distringantur ad veniendum coram Justiciariis ad compotum suum reddendum, si habeant per quod distringi possint. Et si ad curiam venerint dentur auditores compoti, coram quibus si fuerint in arreragiis, si statim arreragia solvere non possint committantur gaole custodiendi in forma predicta. Et si diffugerint & testatum fuerit per vicecomitem quod non sunt inventi exigantur de comitatu in comitatum quousque utlagentur

& sint hujusmodi incarcerati irreplegiabiles. Et caveat sibi vicecomes vel custos ejusdem gaole, sive sit in libertate sive non, quod per commune breve quod dicitur Replegiarum vel alio modo sine assensu domini, ipsum a prisona exire non permittat, quod si federit, & super hoc convincatur, respondeat domino de dampno per hujusmodi servientem sibi illato, secundum quod per patriam verificare poterit & habeat suum recuperare per breve de Debito. Et si custos gaole non habeat per quod justicietur vel unde solvat, respondeat superior suus, qui custodiam hujusmodi gaole sibi commisit per idem breve.

**12.** Quia multi per malitiam volentes alios gravare procurant falsa appella fieri, de homicidio & aliis feloniis, per appellatores nichil habentes unde domino Regi pro falso appello nec appellatis de dampnis respondere possunt; statutum est quod cum aliquis sic appellatus de felonia sibi imposita se acquitaverit in curia Regis modo debito, vel ad sectam appellatoris vel domini Regis, Justitiarii, coram quibus auditum erit hujusmodi appellum & terminatum, puniant appellatorem per prisonam unius anni & nichilominus restituant hujusmodi appellatores appellatis dampna secundum discretionem Justitiariorum, habito respectu ad prisonam vel arrestationem, quam occasione hujusmodi appellorum sustinuerunt appellati, & ad infamiam, quam per imprisonamentum vel alio modo incurrerunt, & nichilominus versus dominum Regem gravius redimantur. Et si forte hujusmodi appellatores non habeant unde predicta dampna restituere posssint, inquiratur per quorum abettum formatum fuerit hujusmodi appellum per malitiam, si appellatus hoc petat, & si inveniatur per illam inquisitionem quod aliquis fit abettator per malitiam, per breve de Judicio ad sectam appellati, distringatur ad veniendum coram Justiciariis, & si legitimo modo convictus fuerit de hujusmodi abetto per malitiam, puniatur per prisonam & ad restitutionem dampnorum sicut superius dictum est de appellatore. Nec jaceat de cetero appellatori in appello de morte hominis essonium, in quacumque curia appellum fuerit terminandum.

**13.** Quia vicecomites fingentes multotiens coram eis aliquos in turnis suis indicatatos de furtis & aliis malefactis, capiunt homines non culpabiles nec legitimo modo indictatos & eos imprisonant, & ab eis pecuniam extorquent, cum legitimo modo per duodecim juratos non fuerint indictati; statutum est quod vicecomites in turnis suis & alibi, cum inquirere habeant de malefactoribus per preceptum Regis vel ex officio suo, per legales homines ad minus duodecim, faciant inquisitiones suas de hujusmodi malefactoribus, qui inquisitionibus suis sigilla sua apponant, & illos quos per hujusmodi inquisitiones invenerint culpabilies, capiant & imprisonent secundum quod alias fieri consuevit. Et si alios imprisonaverint, quam per hujusmodi inquisitiones invenerint indicatatos, habeant hujusmodi imprisonati actionem suam per breve de Imprisonamento versus vicecomites sicut haberent versus quamcumque aliam personam que eos imprisonaret sine waranto. Et sicut dictum est de vicecomitibus observetur de quolibet ballivo libertatis.

**14.** Cum de vasto facto in hereditate alicujus per custodes, tenentes in dotem, per legem Anglie, vel aliter ad terminum vite consueverit fieri breve de Prohibitione vasti, per quod breve multi fuerunt in errore, credentes quod illi qui vastum fecerunt non habuerunt necesse respondere nisi tantum de vasto facto post prohibitionem eis directam, dominus Rex ut hujusmodi error de cetero tollatur statuit quod de vasto quocumque modo ad nocumentum alicujus facto non fiat de cetero breve de Prohibitione, set breve de Summonitione, ita quod illle de quo queritur respondeat de vasto facto quocumque tempore. Et si post summonitionem non venerit, attachietur, & post attachiamentum distringatur. Et post districtionem si non venerit, mandetur vicecomiti, quod in propria persona assumptis secum duodecim, &c. accedat ad locum vastatum, & inquirat de vasto facto, & returnet inquisitionem, & postquam retornata fuerit inquisitio procedatur ad judicium, secundum quod continetur in statuto prius edito apud Westministerium.

**15.** In omni casu quo minores infra etatem implacitari possunt, concessum est, quod si hujusmodi minores elongati sint, quo minus personaliter sequi possint, propinquiores amici admittantur ad sequendum pro eis.

**16.** In casu quo alicui minori descendatur hereditas ex parte patris qui tenuit de uno domino, & ex parte matris, que tenuit de alio domino, dubitatio hucusque exiterit de maritagio hujusmodi minoris, ad quem de duobus dominis pertineat; concordatum est de cetero quod ille dominus habeat maritagium, de quo antecessor suus prius fuit feoffatus, non habito respectu ad sexum nec ad quantitatem tenementi, set solummodo ad antiquius feoffamentum per servicium militare.

**17.** In itinere Justitiariorum non admittatur de cetero essonium de malo lecti de tenemento in eodem comitatu, nisi ille qui se facit essoniari veraciter sit infirmus; quia si excipiatur a petente quod tenens non est infirmus nec in illo statu quo venire potuit coram justiciariis, admittatur ejus calumpnia. Et si hoc per inquisitionem convinci poterit vertatur illud essonium in defaltam. Nec jaceat de cetero illud essonium in brevi de Recto inter duos clamantes per unum descensum.

**18.** Cum debitum fuerit recuperatum vel in curia Regis recognitum, vel dampna adjudicata, sit de cetero in electione illius qui sequitur pro hujusmodi debito aut dampnis, sequi breve, quod vicecomes fieri faciat de terris & catallis, vel quod vicecomes liberet ei omnia catalla debitoris, exceptis bobus & affris caruce & medietate terre sue, quousque debitum fuerit levatum per rationabile pretium vel extentam. Et si ejiciatur de illo tenemento, habeat recuperare per breve Nove disseisine & postea per breve Redisseisine si necesse fuerit.

**19.** Cum post mortem alicujus decedentis intestati & obligati aliquibus in debito, bona deveniant ad ordinarios disponenda, obligetur de cetero ordinarius ad respondendum de debitis, quatenus bona defuncti sufficiunt, eodem modo quo executores hujusmodi respondere tenerentur si testamentum fecisset.

**20.** Cum Justitiarii in placito Mortis antecessoris admittere consueverint responsionem tenentis, quod petens non est propinquior heres antecessoris de cujus morte tenementum petitur & hoc paratus est per assisam inquirere, concordatum est quod in brevibus de Consanguinitate,

Avo, & Proavo, & que sunt ejusdem nature, admittatur illa responsio & inquiratur & secundum illam inquisitionem ad judicium procedatur.

**21.** Cum in statuto edito apud Gloucestriam contineatur quod si quis dimiserit terram alicui, ad reddendum valorem quarte partis tenementi vel majoris, habeat ille qui dimisit vel ejus heres, postquam fuerit a solutione cessatum per biennium, actionem petendi tenementum sic dimissum in dominico. Eodem modo concordatum est quod si quis detineat domino suo servicium debitum vel consuetudinem per biennium, habeat dominus actionem petendi tenementum in dominico per tale breve: Precipe A. quod juste &c. reddat B. tale tenementum quod C. de eo tenuit per tale servicium, et quod ad predictum B. reverti debet, eo quod predictus A. in faciendo servicium predictum per biennium cessavit ut dicit. Et non solum in isto casu, set in casu de quo fit mentio in predicto statuto Gloucestriam, fiant brevia de Ingressu heredi petenti super heredem tenentis & super eos quibus alienatum fuerit hujusmodi tenementum.

**22.** Cum duo vel plures teneant boscum, turbariam, piscariam vel alia hujusmodi in communi absque hoc quod aliquis sciat suum seperale, & aliquis eorum faciat vastum contra voluntatem alterius, moveatur actio per breve de Vasto; & habeat defendens cum ad judicium venerit electionem capiendi partem suam in certo loco per vicecomitem, & visum & sacramentum & assignationem vicinorum ad hoc electorum & juratorum, vel quod concedat quod nichil capiet de cetero in hujusmodi bosco, turbaria, & aliis nisi secundum quod participes sui capere voluerint. Et si eligat capere partem suam in certo loco assignetur ei in sua parte locus vastatus secundum quod fuit antequam vastum fecit. Breve in hoc casu: Cum A. & B. teneant boscum pro indiviso, B. fecit vastu, &c.

**23.** Habeant de cetero executores breve de Compoto reddendo & eandem actionem & processum per illud breve, qualem habuit mortuus, & haberet si vixisset.

**24.** In casibus quibus conceditum breve in Cancellaria de facto alicujus de cetero non recedant quereates a curia Regis sine remedio, pro eo quod tenementum transfertur de uno in alium et in registro de Cancellaria non est inventum aliquod breve in illo casu speciale, sicuti de domo, muro, mercato, conceditur breve super eum qui levavit. Et si transferatur domus, murus, & hiis consimilia, in aliam personam breve denegatur; set de cetero cum in uno casu conceditur breve & in consimili casu simili remedio indigente sicut prius fit breve: Questus est nobis A. quod B. injuste, &c. levavit domum, murum, mercatum, & alia que sunt ad nocumentum. Si hujusmodi levata transferantur in aliam personam de cetero fiat breve sic: Questus est nobis A. quod B. & C. levaverunt, &c. Eodem modo, sicut persona alicujus ecclesie recuperare potest communiam pasture per breve Nove disseisine, eodem modo de cetero recuperet successor super disseisitorem vel ejus heredem, per breve Quod permittat, licet hujusmodi breve prius a Cancellaria non fuit concessum. Eodem modo sicut conceditur breve utrum aliquod tenementum sit libera elemosina alicujus ecclesie, vel laicum feodum talis, de cetero fiat breve utrum sit libera elemosina talis ecclesie, vel alterius ecclesie, in casu quo libera elemosina unius ecclesie transfertur in possessionem alterius ecclesie.

Et quotienscumque, de cetero evenerit in Cancellaria quod in uno casu reperitur breve, & in consimili casu cadente sub eodem jure & simili indigente remedio, concordent clerici de Cancellaria in brevi faciendo, vel atterminent querentes in proximo parleamento, & scribant casus in quibus concordare non possunt, & referant eos ad proximum parliamentum, & de consensu jurisperitorum fiat breve; ne contingat de cetero quod curia diu deficiat querentibus in justitia perquirenda.

**25.** Quia non est aliquod breve in cancellaria per quod querentes habent tam festinum remedium sicut per breve Nove disseisine; dominus Rex voluntatem habens ut celeris fiat justitia & dilationes in placitis motis amputentur vel abbrevientur, concedit quod breve Nove disseisine locum habeat in pluribus casibus quam prius habuit, & concedit, quod de estoveriis bosci, proficuo capiendo in bosco, de nucibus & glande & aliis fructibus colligendis, de corrodio, liberatione bladi, aut aliorum victualium aut necessariorum in certo loco annuatim recipiendorum, tolneto, tronagio, passagio, pontagio, & hiis similibus in certis locis capiendis, custodiis parcorum, boscorum, forestarum, chacearum, warenarum, portarum, & aliis ballivis & officiis in feodo, jaceat de cetero assisa Nove disseisine. Et in omnibus supradictis, modo consueto fiat breve de Libero tenemento; & sicut prius jacuit & locum habuit in comuna pasture ita de cetero locum habeat in comuna turbarie, piscarie, & aliis communiis hiis similibus, quas quis habet pertinentes ad liberum tenementum vel etiam sine tenemento per speciale factum ad minus ad terminum vite. In casu etiam quando quis tenens tenementum ad terminum annorum, vel in custodia, illud alienat in feodum & per illam alienationem transfert liberum tenementum in feoffatum, fiat remedium per breve Nove disseisine & habentur pro disseisitoribus tam ille qui feoffat quam feoffatus, ita quod vivente altero eorum, locum habeat predictum breve. Et si per mortem Personarum cesset remedium per predictum breve fiat remedium per breve de Ingressu. Et quamvis superius fiat mentio de aliquibus casibus, de quibus locum non habuit prius breve Nove disseisine, non propter hoc credat aliquis illud breve non competere ubi prius competebat. Et licet dubitaverint quidam utrum in casu quo quis pascit alterius separale, fieri poterit remedium per predictum breve, teneatur pro certo quod in casu illo per predictum breve bonum & certum est remedium. Et caveant de cetero qui nominati sint disseisitores, quod non proponant falsas exceptiones per quas captio assise differatur, dicendo quod assisa alias transivit inter easdem partes de eodem tenemento, vel dicendo & mentiendo quod breve de altiori natura pendet inter easdem partes de eodem tenemento, & super hiis & consimilibus vocent rotulos vel recordum ad warantum ut per illam vocationem asportare possint vesturam, levare reditus, & alia proficua ad magnum detrimentum querentis. Et quia licet prius aliam penam non habuit qui hujusmodi falsas exceptiones mendaciter proposuit, nisi tantum quod post mendacium suum convictum processum fuit ad captionem assise, Dominus Rex, cui odiose sunt hujusmodi false exceptiones, statuit quod si quis disseisitor nominatus personaliter proponat illam exceptionem, ad diem sibi datum, si defecerit de warranto quod vocavit, habeatur pro disseisitore absque recognitione assise, & restituat dampna ipsia, prius inquisita, vel post inquirenda in duplo, & nichilominus pro falsitate sua puniatur per prisonam unius anni. Et si illa exceptio proponatur per ballivum non propter hoc differatur captio assise & judicium super restitutionem tenementi & dampnorum; ita tamen quod si dominus illius ballivi, qui absens fuerit postmodum veniat coram Justiciariis qui assisam ceperint, & offerat verificare per recordum vel per rotulos quod assisa alias transivit, de eodem tenemento inter easdem partes, vel quod querens alias se retraxerit de consimili brevi, vel placitum pendet per breve de altiori natura, fiat ei breve de Faciendo venire super hoc recordum; & cum illud habuerit et videat Justitiarius quod recordum ita ei missum valeret ante judicium, quod per illud excluderetur querens ab actione sua, statim faciat Justitiarius scire parti que prius recuperavit quod sit ad certum diem, ad quem rehabeat defendens seisinam suam & dampna si que prius solvit post primum judicium redditum, que ei restituantur in duplo ut supradictum est, & nichilominus puniatur ille qui primo recuperavit per prisonam, secundum discretionem Justiciarii. Eodem modo si defendens, contra quem transivit assisa in sua absentia ostendat cartas vel quietas clamantias super quarum confectione non fuerunt juratores examinati nec examinari poterunt, pro eo quod de eis non fiebat mentio in placitando, et probabiliter ignorare poterunt confectiones hujusmodi scriptorum, Justitiarii visis scriptis illis, faciat scire parti que recuperavit, quod sit ad certum diem, et venire faciant juratores illius assise, et si per veredictum juratorum vel forte per irrotulamentum scripta illa verificaverit puniatur ille qui assisam impetravit contra factum suum per penam supradictam. Et non capiat de cetero vicecomes bovem ad disseisito, set a disseisitore tantum, set si plures sint disseisitores in uno brevi nominati nichilominus de uno bove sit contentus; nec exigat bovem nisi de precio quinque solidorum et quatuor denariorum, vel precium.

**26.** In brevibus de Redisseisina adjudicentur de cetero dampna in duplo, & sint redisseisitores de cetero irreplegiabiles per commune breve. Et sicut in statuto de Merton provisum fuit illud breve de hiis qui disseisiti fuerunt postquam recuperaverunt per assisas Nove disseisine, Mortis antecessoris, aut per alias Juratas, ulterius habeat de cetero illud breve locum illis qui recuperaverunt per defaltam, redditionem, vel alio modo sine recognitione assisarum vel juratarum.

**27.** Postquam aliquis posuerit se in inquisitionem ad proximum diem allocetur ei essonium, set ad alios dies sequentes per essonium non differatur captio inquisitionis, sive prius habuit essonium sive non; nec admittatur essonium post diem datum prece partium in casu quo partes venire consentiunt sine essonio.

**28.** Cum per statutum Gloucestriam statuatur quod postquam tenens semel comparuerit in curia, non allocetur ei essonium in brevibus assisarum, eodem modo de cetero observetur de petentibus.

**29.** Breve de Transgressione ad audiendum & terminandum de cetero non concedatur coram aliquibus Justitiariis, exceptis Justitiariis de utroque banco, & exceptis Justitiariis itinerantibus nisi pro enormi transgressione ubi necesse est festinum apponere remedium, & Dominus Rex de speciali gratia hoc duxerit concedendum. Nec etiam concedatur de cetero breve ad audiendum & terminandum appella coram Justitiariis assignatis nisi in casu speciali & certa causa cum Dominus Rex hoc preceperit. Set ne hujusmodi appellati vel indictati diu detineantur in prisona, habeant breve de Odio & Atya, sicut in Magna Carta & alius statutis dictum est.

**30.** Assignentur de cetero duo Justiciarii jurati coram quibus & non aliis capiantur assisie Nove disseisine, Mortis antecessoris & Attincte, & associent sibi unum vel duos de discretioribus militibus comitatus in quem venerint & capiant assisas predictas & attinctas ad plus ter per annum, videlicet semel inter quindenam sancti Johannis Baptiste & gulam Augusti & iterum inter festum Exaltationis sancte Crucis & octabas sancti Michaelis, & terti inter festum Epiphanie & festum Purificationis beate Maria. Et in quolibet comitatu ad quamlibet captionem assisarum antequam recedant, statuant diem de reditu suo, ita quod omnes de comitatu scire possint eorum adventum, & de termino in terminum adjornent assisas, si per vocationem waranti, per essonium, per defectum recognitorum si ad unum diem captio earum differatur. Et si aliqua de causa viderint quod utile sit quod assise Mortis antecessoris per essonium vel vocationem waranti respectuate adjornentur in Banco, liceat eis hoc facere, & tunc mittantur Justitiariis de Banco recordum cum brevi originali. Et cum loquela perveniatur ad captionem assise remittatur loquela cum brevi originali per Justitiarios de Banco ad priores Justitiarios coram quibus capiatur assisa. Set de cetero dent Justiciarii de Banco in hujusmodi assisis ad minus quatuor dies per annum coram prefatis Justiciariis assignatis, ut parcatur laboribus & expensis atterminentur inquisitiones capiende de transgressionibus placitatis coram Justiciariis de utroque Banco, nisi ita enormis sit transgressio, quod magna indigeat examinatione. Atterminentur etiam coram eis inquisitiones de aliis placitis placitatis in utroque Banco in quibus facilis est examinatio, ut quando dedicitur ingressus vel seisina alicujus, vel in casu cum de uno articulo fit inquirendum. Set inquisitiones de grossis & pluribus articulis que magna indigent examinatione, capiantur coram Justitiariis de Bancis, nisi ambe partes petant quod inquisitio capiatur coram aliquibus de societate cum in partes illas venerint, quod de cetero non fiat nisi per duos Justiciarios vel unum cum aliquo milite de comitatu, in quem partes consentiunt. Nec atterminentur hujusmodi inquisitiones coram aliquibus Justiciariis de Banco nisi statuantur certus dies & locus in comitatu in presentia partium & dies & locus inserantur in brevi de Judicio per hec verba: Precipimus tibi quod venire facias coram Justitiariis nostris apud Westministerium in octabis sancti Michaelis, nisi talis & talis, tali die & loco, ad partes illas venerint, xii. &c. Et cum hujusmodi inquisitiones capte fuerint retornentur in Bancis, & ibi fiat judicium & irrrotulentur. Et si omissa forma predicta alique inquisitiones capiantur, pro nullis habeantur, excepto quod assisa Ultime presentationis & inquisitiones super Quare impedit atterminentur in proprio comitatu coram uno Justitiario de Banco & uno milite, ad certos tamen diem & locum in Banco statutos, sive defendens consentiat sive non, & ibi statim reddatur judicium. Habeant de cetero omnes Justitiarii de Bancis & itineribus clericos irrotulantes omnia placita coram eis placitata, sicut antiquitus habere consueverunt. Item ordinatum est quod Justitiarii ad assisas capiendas assignati, non compellant juratores dicere precise si sit disseisina vel non, dummodo voluerint dicere veritatem facti, & petere auxilium Justitiariorum. Set si sponte velint dicere quod disseisina est vel non, admittatur eorum veredictum sub suo periculo. Et de cetero non ponant Justitiarii in assisis aut juratis aliquos juratores nisi eos qui ad hoc primo fuerunt summoniti.

**31.** Cum aliquis implacitatus coram aliquibus Justitiariis proponat exceptionem & petat quod Justitiarii eam allocent, quam si allocare noluerint si ille qui exceptionem proponet, scribat illam exceptionem & petat quod Justitiarii apponant sigilla in testimonium Justitiarii sigilla sua apponant, & si unus apponere noluerit, apponat alius de societate. Et si forte ad querimoniam de facto Justitiariorum venire faciat Dominus Rex recordum coram eo, & si illa exceptio non inveniatur in rotulo, & querens ostendat exceptionem scriptam cum sigillo Justitiarii appenso, mandetur Justitiario quod sit ad certum diem ad cognoscendum sigillum suum vel dedicendum. Et si Justitiarius sigillum suum dedicere non possit, procedatur ad judicium secundum illam exceptionem prout admittenda esset vel cassanda

**32.** Cum viri religiosi & alie persone ecclesiastice implacitent aliquem & implacitatus fecerit defaltam ob quam tenementum amittere debeat, quia Justitiarii hucusque timuerunt quod si implacitatus fecerit defaltam per collusionem, ut cum petens occasione statuti per titulum doni aut alterius alienationis seisinam de tenemento consequi non posset, per illam defaltam consequeretur & fieret fraus statuto; ordinatum est per Dominum Regem & concessum, quod in hoc casu postquam defalta facta fuerit, inquiratur per patriam utrum petens habeat jus in sua petitione aut non. Et si compertum fuerit quod petens jus habet in sua petitione procedatur ad judicium pro petente & recuperet seisinam suam; et si jus non habuerit, incurratur tenementum proximo domino feodi, si illud petat infra annum a tempore inquisitionis capte; Et si infra annum non petat, superiori domino incurratur si petat infra dimidium annum post illum annum; Et sic habeat quilibet dominus post proximum dominum spacium dimidii anni ad petendum successive, quousque perveniatur ad Regem, cui ad ultimum pro defectu aliorum dominorum tenementum incurratur. Et ad calumpniandum juratores inquisitionis admittantur quicumque capitales domini feodorum, & similiter pro Rege qui calumpniare voluerit; & remaneat terra, postquam judicium clarum fuerit, in manum Domini Regis, quousque tenementum per petentem vel aliquem capitalem dominum disrationetur, & oneretur vicecomes ad respondendum inde ad Scaccarium.

**33.** Quia multi tenentes erigunt cruces in tenementis suis aut erigi permittunt, in prejudicium dominorum suorum, ut tenentes per privilegium Templariorum & Hospitalariorum tueri se possint, contra capitales dominos feodorum; statutum est quod hujusmodi tenementa capitalibus dominis aut Regi incurrantur, eodem modo quo statuitur alibi de tenementis alienatis ad mortuam manum.

[Purveu est que si homme ravist femme, espouse, damoiselle ou autre femme desoremes, par la ou ele ne se est assentue ne avaunt ne apres, eit jugement de vie & de membre. E ensement par la ou home ravist femme, dame espouse damoiselle, ou autre femme a force, tut seit ke ele assente apres, eit tel jugement come avaunt est dit si il feit ateint a la suite le Rei, e la eit le Rei sa suite.]

**34.** De mulieribus abductis cum bonis viri habeat Rex sectam de bonis sic asportatis. Et uxor si sponte reliquerit virum suum, & abierit & moretur cum adultero suo, amittat imperpetuum actionem petendi dotem suam, que ei competere posset de tenemento viri, si super hoc convinccatur; nisi vir suus sponte, & absque cohertione ecclesiastica eam reconciliet & secum cohabitare permittat, in quo casu restituatur ei actio. Qui monialem a domo sua abducat, licet monialis consentiat punietur per prisonam trium annorum, & satisfaciat domui a qua abducta fuerit competenter, & nichilominus redimetur ad voluntatem Regis.

**35.** De pueris sive masculis sive femellis, quorum maritagium ad aliquem pertineat, raptis & abductis, si ille qui rapuit non habens jus in maritagio, licet postmodum restituat puerum non maritatum, vel de maritagio satisfecerit, puniatur tamen pro transgressione per prisonam duorum annorum. Et si non restituerit, vel heredem post annos nubiles maritaverit et de maritagio satisfacere non poterit, abjuret regnum vel habeat perpetuam prisonam, & super hoc habeat querens tale breve. Si A. fecerit te securum de clamoro suo prosequitur tunc pone per vadium, &c. quod sit coram Justiciariis &c. ostensurus quare talem heredem infra etatem existentem, cujus maritagium ad ipsum pertinet, tali loco inventum rapuit & abduxit, contra voluntatem ipsius A. & contra pacem nostram, &c. Et si heres sit in eodem comitatu tunc addatur ista clausula: Et diligenter inquiras, ubi ille heres sit in balliva tua, & ipsum ubicumque fuerit inventus capias, & salvo & secure custodias, ita quod eum habeas coram prefatis Justitiariis nostris ad prefatum terminum ad reddendum cui predictorum A. vel B. reddi debeat. Et fiat secta versus partem de qua queritur quousque per districtionem venerit, si habeat per quod possit distringi, vel per contumaciam si non sit justitiabilis exigatur & utlagetur. Si forte hujusmodi heres ducatur & transferatur in alium comitatum tunc vicecomiti illius comitatus fiat breve in hac forma. Questus est nobis A. quod B. nuper talem heredem, infra etatem & in custodia sua existentem, tali loco in comitatu tali rapuit & de comitatu tali ad talem locum in comitatu tuo abduxit, contra voluntatem ipsius A. & contra pacem nostram. Et ideo tibi precipimus quod predictum heredem ubicumque in balliva tua invenire poteris capias & salvo & secure eum custodias ita quod eum habeas coram Justitiariis nostris tali loco & die, quem diem idem A. habet versus predictum B. ad reddendum, cui de jure reddi debeat. Et si heres antequam invenire poterit, vel antequam restituatur querenti obierit nichilominus procedat placitum inter eos quousque terminetur cui restitui deberet si superstes fuisset. Nec excusabitur ille aut alleviabitur ille qui injuste rapuit hujusmodi heredem de pena supradicta post mortem heredis cujus extitit male fidei possessor dum vixit. Et si querens obierit ante placitum terminatum, si jus ei competebat ratione proprii feodi sui, resumoneatur loquela ad sectam heredis querentis & procedat placitum debito ordine. Si vero per alium titulum competat ei jus, sicut titulo donationis, venditionis vel alio hujusmodi titulo, tunc resumoneatur loquela ad sectam executorum querentis & procedat placitum ut predictum est. Eodem modo si moriatur pars defendens antequam placitum terminetur vel heres restituatur, procedat placitum per resumonitionem inter querentem vel ejus heredem seu executores, & executores defendentis, vel ejus heredem si executores non sufficient, quoad satisfactionem de valore maritagii, secundum quod in aliis statutis continetur, set non quoad penam prisone, qua quis pro alieno facto non est puniendus. Eodem modo cum pendeat placitum inter partes de custodia terre, & heredis vel utriusque per commune breve quod incipit, Precipe tali quod reddat &c. fiat resumonitio inter heredes & executores querentis, & similiter heredes aut executores defendentis, si mors alteram partem preveniat ante placitum terminatum. Et cum perveniatur ad magnam districtionem detur terminus, infra quem tres comitatus teneantur ad minus, in quorum quolibet comitatu fiat publica proclamatio, quod deforciator veniat ad bancum ad diem in brevi contentum, responsurus querenti, ad quem diem si non venerit & si proclamatio sic semel secundo & tertio testificata fuerit, procedatur ad judicium pro querente, salvo jure defendentis si postmodum inde loqui voluerit. Eodem modo fiat in brevi de transgressione cum quis queritur se ejectum fuisse de hujusmodi custodiis.

**36.** Et quia domini curiarum & alii qui curias tenent & senescalli, volentes gravare subditos suos cum non habeant legalem viam eos gravandi, procurant alios movere querelas versus eos & dare vadium & offerre plegios, vel impetrare brevia & ad sectas hujusmodi querentium compellunt eos sequi comitatum hundredum & curiam quousque finem fecerint cum ipsis pro voluntate sua; statutum est quod de cetero hoc non fiat. Et si quis per hujusmodi falsas querimonias fuerit attachiatus replegiat districtionem suam sic captam, & poni faciat loquelam coram Justitiariis, coram quibus vicecomes vel alius ballivus vel dominus postquam sic districtus formaverit querimoniam suam & advocaverit justam districtionem ratione hujusmodi querimoniarum coram eis factarum, & replicetur quod hujusmodi querimonie vesus eos movebantur malitiose ad instantiam seu procurationem vicecomitis aut aliorum ballivorum aut dominorum, admittatur illa replicatio. Et si super hoc convicti fuerint versus dominum regem redimantur & nichilominus hujusmodi sic gravatis dampna in triplo restituant.

**37.** Quia etiam ballivi, ad quos ex officio pertinent districtiones facere, volentes subditos suos gravare ut ab eis pecuniam extorqueant, mittunt ignotos ad faciendes districtiones ea intentione ut subditos gravare possint, per hoc quod sic districti non habentes notitiam personarum non permittunt hujusmodi districtiones super eos fieri; statutum est quod nulla districtio fiat nisi per ballivos juratos & notos. Et distringentes si alio modo fecerint & de hoc convicti fuerint, si gravati breve de Transgressione impetraverint, restituant gravatis dampna, & versus Regem graviter puniantur.

**38.** Quia etiam vicecomites, hundredarii, & ballivi libertatum consueverunt gravare subditos suos, ponendo in assisis & juratis, homines langidos, decrepitos, perpetua vel temporali infirmitate languentes, homines etiam tempore summonitionis sue in patria non commorantes; sumonendo etiam effrenatam multitudinem juratorum ita ut a quibusdam eos in pace dimittendo pecuniam extorqueant, & sic fiunt assise & jurate multotiens per pauperiores, divitibus pro suo dando domi comorantbus; statutum est de cetero, quod non summoneantur in una assisa plures quam viginti & quatuor. Senes etiam videlicet ultra sexaginta & decem annos, perpetuo languidi, vel tempore summonitionis infirmi, vel in patriam non comorantes non ponantur in juratis vel minoribus assisis. Nec etiam ponantur in assisis aut juratis, licet in proprio comitatu capi debeant, aliqui qui minus habeant tenementum, quam ad valentiam viginti solidorum per annum. Et si hujusmodi assise & jurate extra comitatum capi debeant non ponatur in eis aliquis qui minus tenementum habeat quam ad valentiam quadraginta solidorum per annum, hiis exceptis, qui testes sunt in cartis, vel aliis scriptis quorum presentia necessaria est, dum tamen potentes sint ad laborandum. Nec debet istud statutum extendi ad magnas assisas in quibus aliquando oportet apponere milites in patria non residentes, propter paucitatem militum, dum tamen in comitatu habeant tenementum. Et si vicecomes vel subballivi sui vel ballivi libertatis contra istud statutum in aliquo articulo venerint, & super hoc convincantur, restituant dampna gravatis, & nichilominus sint in misericordia Domini Regis. Et habeant justitiarii ad assisas capiendas assignati cum in comitatum venerint, potestatem audiendi querimonias singulorum conquerentium, quoad articulos in isto statuto contentos & justitiam in forma predicta exhibendam.

**39.** Quia Justitiarii, ad quorum officium spectat unicuique coram eis placitanti justitiam exhibere, frequentius impeniuntur quo minus officium suum debito modo exequi possent, per hoc quod vicecomites brevia originalia & judicialia non returnant, per hoc etiam quod ad brevia Regis falsum returnant responsum, providit Dominus Rex & ordinavit, quod illi qui timent maliciam vicecomites liberent brevia sua originalia & judicialia in pleno comitatu, vel in retro comitatu, ubi fit collectio denariorum Domini Regis, & capiatur bilettum de vicecomite presente vel subvicecomite in quo biletto contineantur nomina petentur & tenentur que nominantur in brevi, & ad requisitionem illius qui breve liberabit apponatur sigillum vicecomitis vel subvicecomitis in testimonium & fiat mentio de die liberationis brevis. Et si vicecomes vel subvicecomes hujusmodi biletto sigilla sua apponere noluerint, capiatur testimonium militum & aliorum fide dignorum qui presentes fuerint, qui sigilla sua hujusmodi biletto apponant. Et si vicecomes brevia sibi liberata non returnaverit, & super hoc Justitiariis querimonia perveniat, mandetur per breve de Judicio Justitiariis ad assisas capiendas assignatis, quod inquirant per eos qui presentes fuerint qundo breve vicecomiti liberatum fuit si sciverint de illa liberatione, & inquisitio retornetur. Et si compertum fuerit per inquisitionem quod breve fuit ei liberatum, adjudicentur petenti vel querenti dampna, habito respectu ad quantitatem & qualitatem actionis & ad periculum quod ei evinire posset per dilationem, quam patiebatur. Et per istam viam fiat remedium, quando vicecomes respondet quod breve adeo tarde venit quod preceptum Regis exequi non potuit.

Multociens etiam capiunt placita dilationem per hoc quod vicecomites respondent quod preceperint ballivis alicujus libertatis qui nichil inde fecerunt & nominant libertates que nunquam returnum brevium habuerunt, propter quod ordinavit Dominus Rex quod Thesaurarius de Scaccario liberet in rotulo omnes libertates in quibuscumque comitatibus, que habent returnum brevium. Et si vicecomes respondeat quod returnum fecit ballivis alterius libertatis quam alicujus contente in predicto rotulo, statim puniatur vicecomes tanquam exheredator Domini Regis & Corone sue. Et si forte respondeat quod retornavit ballivis alicujus libertatis, que veraciter returnum habet, mandetur vicecomiti, quod non omittat propter predictam libertatem, quin exequatur preceptum Domini Regis, & quod scire faciat ballivis quibus fecit returnum quod sint ad diem in brevi contentum ad respondendum quare de precepto Domini Regis executionem non fecerunt. Et si ad diem venerint & se acquietent quod returnum brevis eis non fuit factum statim condempnetur vicecomes domino illius libertatis & similiter parti lèsé per dilationem in restitutionem dampnorum. Et si ballivi ad diem non venerint, vel venerint & supradicto modo se non acquietaverint, in quolibet brevi de Judicio quam diu durat placitum, precipiatur vicecomiti quod non omittat propter libertatem, &c. Multotiens etiam falsum dant responsum, quoad illum articulum, Quod de exitibus, &c. mandantes aliquando & mentientes, quod nulli sunt exitus, aliquando quod parvi sunt cum de majoribus respondere possunt, aliquando non facientes mentionem de exitibus; propter quod ordinatum est & concordatum quod si querens petat auditum responsionis vicecomitis concedatur ei; & si offerat verificare quod vicecomes, de majoribus exitibus respondere potuit, fiat ei breve de Judicio ad Justitiarios ad assisas capiendas assignatos, quod inquirant in presentia vicecomitis si interesse voluerit de quibus & quantis exitibus vicecomes respondere potuit, a die receptionis brevis, usque ad diem in brevi contentum. Et cum inquisitio retornata fuerit, si de pleno prius non respondit oneretur de superplusagio per extractas liberatas ad scaccarium

& nichilominus graviter amercietur pro concelamento. Et sciat vicecomes quod redditus, blada in grangia, & omnia mobilia preter equitaturam, indumento & utensilia domus continentur sub nomine Exituum. Precipit Dominus Rex quod vicecomites pro hujusmodi falsis responsis, semel & iterum si sit necesse, per Justic' castigentur. Et si tertio deliquerint alius non apponat manum quam Dominus Rex. Multotiens etiam dant responsum mandando quod non potuerunt prosequi preceptum Regis propter resistentiam potestatis alicujus magnatis, de quo caveant vicecomites de cetero, quia hujusmodi responsio multum redundat in dedecus Domini Regis. Et quam cito ballivi sui testificantur quod invenerunt hujusmodi resistentiam, statim omnibus omissis, assumpto secum posse comitatus sui eat in propria persona ad faciendam executionem. Et si inveniat subballivos mendaces puniat eos per prisonam, ita quod alii per eorum penam castigentur. Et si inveniat eos veraces, castiget resistentes per prisonam, a qua non deliberentur sine speciali precepto Domini Regis. Et si forte vicecomes cum venerit resistentiam invenerit, certificet curiam de nominibus resistentitum, auxillantium, consentientium, precipientium & fautorum, & per breve de Judicio attachientur per corpora ad veniendum ad curiam; & si de hujusmodi resistentia convincantur, secundum quod Domino Regi placuerit. Nec intromittat se aliquis minister Domini Regis de pena hujusmodi infligenda, quia Dominus Rex hoc specialiter sibi reservat pro eo quod hujusmodi resistentes censeatur pacis sue & regni perturbatores.

**40.** Cum quis alienat jus uxoris sue, concordatum est quod de cetero secta mulieris vel ejus heredis non differatur post obitum viri, per minorem etatem heredis qui warantizare debet, sed expectet emptor, qui ignorare don debuit quod jus alienum emit, usque ad etatem waranti sui de warantia sua habenda.

**41.** Statuit Dominus Rex quod si Abbates, Priores, Custodes Hospitalium, & aliarum domorum religiosarum, fundatum ab ipso vel a progenitoribus suis alienaverint de cetero tenementa domibus ipsis ab ipso vel a progenitoribus suis collata, tenementa illa in manum Domini Regis capiantur & ad voluntatem suam teneantur, & emptor amittat suum recuperare tam de tenementis quam de pecunia quam pacavit. Si autem domus illa a Comitibus Baronibus, vel aliis fundata fuerit, de tenementis sic alienatis habeat ille a quo vel a cujus antecessore tenementum sic alienatum collatum fuerit, breve ad recuperandum tenementum illud in dominico, quod tale est: Precipe tali Abbati quod juste, &c. reddat B. tale tenementum, quod eidem domui collatum fuit in liberam elemosynam per predictum B. vel antecessores suos, & quod ad predictum B. reverti debet per alienationem quam predictus Abbas fecit de predicto tenemento contra formam collationis predicte ut dicit. Eodem modo de tenemento dato pro Cantaria sustentanda vel luminari in aliqua ecclesia vel Capella vel aliis elemosinis sustentandis, si tenementum sic datum alienatur. Et si forte tenementum sic datum pro Cantaria, luminari, potura pauperum, vel aliis elemosinis sustentandis, vel faciendis non fuerit alienatum, sed subtracta fuerit hujusmodi elemosina per biennium, competat actio donatori vel ejus heredi ad petendum tenementum sic datum in dominico, sicut statutum est in statuto Gloucestrie, de tenementis dimissis ad faciendum vel ad reddendum quartam partem valoris tenementi vel majoris.

**42.** De marescallo Domini Regis de feodo, Camerario, Custodeo Hostiorum in Itinere Justitiariorum, & servientibus virgam portantibus, coram Justitiariis apud Westministerium, qui officium illud habent de feodo & qui plus exigunt ratione feodi sui quam exigere consueverunt secundum quod multi queruntur, per eos qui statum Curie a multo tempore viderunt & sciunt; Dominus Rex inquiri fecit quem statum predicti ministri de feodo habere consueverunt temporibus retroactis, & per inquisitionem statuit & precepit, quod Marescallus de feodo qui de novo exigit palefridum, de Comitibus, Baronibus & aliis, per partem Baronie tenentibus, palefridum quando homagium fecerunt, & nichilominus ad militiam eorum alium palefridum & de quibusdam de quibus palefridum habere non debent palefridum de novo exigunt ordinavit quod predictus Marescallus de quolibet Comite & Barone, integram Baroniam tenente, de unico palefrido sit contentus vel de precio, quale antiquitus percipere consueverunt; ita quod si ad homagium quod fecit palefridum vel precium ceperit in forma predicta, ad militiam suam nichil capiat. Et si forte ad homagium nichil ceperit ad militiam capiat. De Abbatibus & Prioribus, integram Baroniam tenentibus, cum homagium aut fidelitatem fecerint pro Baroniis suis capiat palefridum vel precium, ut predictum est. Hoc idem de archepiscopis & episcopis est observandum. De hiis autem qui partem Baronie tenent, sive sint religiosi sive seculares, capiant secundum portionem partis Baronie quam tenent. De religiosis tenentibus in liberam elemosynam, & non per Baroniam vel partem Baronie, nichil de cetero exigat mareschallus. Et concessit Dominus Rex quod per hoc statutum non precludatur marescallus suus de feodo in plus petendo, si imposterum ostendere poterit quod jus habeat plus petendi. Camerarii Domini Regis habeant de cetero de Archiepiscopis, Episcopis, Abbatibus, Prioribus, & aliis personia ecclesiasticis, Comitibus, Baronibus, integram Baroniam tenentibus, rationabilem finem cum homagium aut fidelitatem pro Baroniis suis fecerint. Et si per partem Baronie teneant, capiat rationabilem finem secundum portionem ipsos contingentem. Alii vero Abbates & Priores & alii religiosi & seculares, non tenentes per baroniam vel partem baronie, non distringantur ad finem faciendum secundum quod de tenentibus per baroniam vel partem baronie sicut dictum est, set sit camerarius de superiori indumento contentus vel de precio indumenti quod plus dictum est pro religiosis quam secularibus quia honestius est quod religiosi finem faciant pro superiori indumento quam exuantur.

**43.** Prohibetur de cetero Hospitelaris & Templariis ne de cetero trahant aliquem in placitum coram conservatoribus privilegiorum suorum, de aliqua re cujus cognitio ad forum Regium pertineat; quod si fecerint, primo restitutis dampnis parti gravate & versus Regem graviter puniantur. Prohibet etiam Dominus Rex conservatoribus privilegiorum eorundem ne de cetero ad instantiam Templariorum, Hospitelariorum, aut aliorum privilegiatorum concedant citationes quousque sciverint super qua re fieri debeat citatio. Et si viderint hujusmodi conservatores quod petatur citatio de aliqua re cujus cognitio ad forum spectat regium hujusmodi conservatores nec citationem faciant nec cognoscant. Et si aliter fecerint, conservatores respondeant parti lèsé de dampnis & nichilominus versus Regem graviter puniantur. Et quia hujusmodi privilegiati impetrant conservatores Subpriores, Precentores, Sacristas, viros religiosos, qui nichil habent unde lesis aut Domino Regi satisfacere possint, qui audaciores sunt ad ledendum dignitatem Domini Regis quam eorum superiores, quibus per eorum temporalia pena potest infligi. Caveant de cetero prelati hujusmodi obedientiariorum ne permittant obedientiarios suos assumsere sibi jurisdictionem in prejudicium Domini Regis & Corone sue; quod si fecerint pro facto ipsorum respondeant superiores sui, ac si de proprio facto convicti essent.

**44.** De custodibus hostiorum in Itinere & virgam portantibus coram Justitiariis de Banco, ordinatum est quod de qualibet assisa & jurata quam custodiunt, capiant quatuor denarios tantum, de cirographis nichil. De hiis qui recupant demandas suas, per defaltam, redditionem, vel alio modo per judicium, sine assisa & jurata, de hiis qui recedunt sine die per defaltam petentis vel querentis, nichil capiant. Et si quis recuperaverit demandam suam, versus plures per unum breve & per recognitionem assise aut jurate, de quatuor denariis sint contenti. Et similiter in uno brevi nominati, per recognitionem assise vel jurate, de quatuor denariis sint contenti. De hiis qui faciunt homagium in Banco de superiori panno sint contenti. De magnis assisis, attinctis, juratis, & de duello percusso, xii. denarii tantum capiantur. De hiis qui vocati sunt coram Justitiariis ad sequendum vel defendendum placitum suum, nichil dent pro ingressu vel egressu. Ad placita Corone de qualibet duodena xii. denarii tantum capiantur. De quolibet prisone deliberato, quatuor denarii tantum capiantur. De quolibet cujus pax proclamata fuerit xii. denarii tantum capiantur. De inventoribus vicinis & aliis villatis attachatis, quatuor hominibus & preposito decennaro nichil capiatur. De cirographariis pro cirographosa faciendo statutum est, quod de quatuor solidis sint contenti. De clericis scribentibus brevia originalia & judicialia statutum est quod pro brevi de denario sint contenti. Et injungit Dominus Rex omnibus Justitiariis suis in fide & sacramento quibus ei tenentur, quod si hujusmodi ministri contra predictum statutum in aliquo venerint &

querimonia ad eos perveniat, penam ei sinfligant rationabilem. Et si iterum deliquerint, majorem penam eis infligant qua castigari merito debeant. Et si tertio deliquerint & super hoc convicti fuerint, si sint ministri de feodo, amittant feodum suum, si alii sint amittant curiam Regis, nec redeant sine ipsius Regis speciali gratia seu precepto.

**45.** Quia de hiis que recordata sunt coram Cancellario Domini Regis & ejus Justitiariis, qui recordum habent & in rotulis eorum irrotulata, non debet fieri processus placiti per summonitionem, attachiamentum, essonium, visus terre, & alias solempnitates Curie, sicut fieri consuevit de contractibus & conventionibus factis extra curiam, observandum est de cetero quod ea que inveniuntur irrotulata coram hiis qui recordum habent, vel in finibus contenta, sive sint contractus sive conventiones sive obligationes sive servicia aut consuetudines recognitiones vel alia quecumque irrotulata, quibus Curia Regis sine juris & consuetudinis offensa auctoritatem potest prestare, talem de cetero habeant vigorem quod non sit necesse de hiis imposterum placitare. Set cum venerint conquerentes ad Curiam Domini Regis si recens sit cognitio vel finis videlicet infra annum in brevi levatus statim habeant breve de executione illius recognitionis facte. Et si forte a majori tempore transacto facta fuerit illa recognitio vel finis levatus precipiatur vicecomiti quod scire faciat parti de qua fit querimonia quod sit ad certum diem ostensura si quid sciat dicere quare hujusmodi irrotulata vel in fine contenta executionem habere non debeant. Et si ad diem non venerit, vel forte venerit & nichil sciat dicere quare executio fiere non debeat, precipiatur vicecomes quod rem irrotulatam vel in fine contentam exequi faciat. Eodem modo mandetur ordinario in suo casu observato nichilominus quod supradictum est de medio qui per recognitionem aut judicium obligatus est ad acquietandum.

**46.** Cum in statuto edito apud Merton concessum fuerit quod domini boscorum, vastorum, & pasturarum appruare se possent de boscis, vastis, & pasturis illis, non obstante contradictione tenentium suorum, dummodo tenentes ipsi haberent sufficientem pasturam ad tenementa sua cum libero ingressu & egressu ad eandem, & pro eo quod nulla fiebat mentio inter vicinum & vicinum, multi domini boscorum, vastorum, & pasturarum, hucusque impediti extiterunt per contradictionem vicinorum sufficientem pasturam habentium. Et quia forinseci tenentes non habent majus jus communicandi in bosco, vasto, aut pastura, alicujus domini quam proprii tenentes ipsius domini; statutum est de cetero quod statutum apud Merton provisum inter dominum & tenentes suos locum habeat de cetero inter dominos boscorum vastorum & pasturarum & vicinos. Ita quod domini hujusmodi vastorum boscorum & pasturarum, salva sufficienti pastura hominibus suis & vicinis, appruare se possint de residuo. Et hoc observetur de hiis qui clamant pasturam tanquam pertinentem ad tenementa sua. Sed si quis clamat communam per speciale feoffamentum, vel concessionem ad certum numerum averiorum vel alio modo quam de jure communi habere deberet, cum conventio legi deroget, habeat suum recuperare quale habere deberet per formam concessionis sibi facte. Occasione molendini ventritii, bercarii vaccarii augmentationis curie necessarie aut curtilagii de cetero non gravetur quis per assisam Nove disseisine de communa pasture. Et cum contingat aliquando quod aliquis jus habens appruare se, foffatum aut sepem levaverit, & aliqui noctanter vel alio tali tempore quo non credant factum suum sciri, foffatum vel sepem prostraverint, nec sciri poterit per veredictum assise aut jurate qui fossatum aut sepem prostraverint, nec velint homines de villatis vicinis indictare de hujusmodi facto culpabiles, distringantur propinque villato circumadjacentes levare fossatum aut sepem ad custum proprium & dampna restituere. Et cum aliquis jus non habens communicandi usurpet communam, tempore quo heredes extiterint infra etatem, vel uxores sub potestate virorum suorum existentes, vel pastura sit in manu tenentium in dotem, per legem Anglie, vel aliter ad terminum vite vel annorum, vel per feodum talliatum, & pastura illa diu usi fuerint, multi sunt in opinione quod hujusmodi pasture debent dici pertinere ad liberum tenementum, & quod hujusmodi possessori competere debet actio per breve Nove disseisine, si hujusmodi pastura deforcietur; sed de cetero tenendum est quod habentes hujusmodi ingressum a tempore quo currit breve mortis antecessoris si antea communam non habuerunt, non habeant recuperare per breve nove disseisine si fuerint deforciati.

**47.** Provisum est quod aque de Humbre, Ouse, Trente, Doon, Eyre, Deerewent, Werf, Nid, Yore, Swale, Tese, & omnes alie aque in quibus salmones capiuntur in Regno, ponantur in defenso, quoad salmones capiendos a die Nativitatis beate Marie usque ad diem sancti Martini, & similiter quod salmunculi non capiantur nec destruantur per retia vel per aliqua ingenia ad stagna molenda a medio Aprilis usque ad Nativitatem beati Johannis Baptiste. Et in partibus ubi hujusmodi ripario fuerint assignentur conservatores istius statuti, qui ad hoc jurati sepius videant & inquirant de transgressoribus. Et in prima transgressione puniantur per combustionem retium & ingeniorum suorum. Et si iterato deliquerint, puniantur per prisonam quarterii unius anni Et si tertio deliquerint, puniantur per prisonam unius anni, & sic multiplicata transgressione, crescet pene inflictio.

**48.** De visu terre ordinatum est & statutum, quod de cetero non concedatur visus, nisi in casu quando visus terre est necessarius; sicuti si aliquis amittat tenementum per defaltam & ille qui amisit suscitet aliud breve ad petendum idem tenementum. Et in casu quando quis per aliquam exceptionem dilatoriam cassat breve post visum terre, sicut per non tenuram, vel male nominando villam vel hujusmodi, si suscitet aliud breve in hoc casu, & superiori, de cetero non concedatur visus terre dummodo habuerit in prioribus brevibus. In brevi de dote cum petitur dos de tenemento quod vir uxorem alienavit tenenti vel ejus antecessori, cum ignorare non debeat tenens, quale tenementum vir uxoris alienavit sibi vel antecessori suo, licet vir non obierit seisitus, nichilominus tenenti de cetero non erit visus concedendus. In brevi etiam de ingressu, cassato per hoc quod petens male nominavit ingressum, si petens suscitet aliud breve de aliquo ingressu, si tenens in priori brevi habuit visum, in secundo non habebit. In omnibus etiam brevibus per que tenementa petuntur, ratione dimissionis, quam petens vel ejus antecessor fecit tenenti & non antecessori, sicuti quod ei dimisit dum fuit infra etatem non compos mentis, in prisona & similibus, non jaceat de cetero visus, sed si dimissio facta fuerit antecessori, jaceat de cetero visus sicut prius.

**49.** Le Chaunceller, Tresorer ne Justice, ne nul Counseil le Roy, ne clerc de la Chauncelerye, del Escheker, ne de Justice, ne autre Ministre, ne nul del hostel le Roy clerc ou lay, ne puisse resceivre esglise ne avoeson de esglise, ne terre ne tenement, ne fee ne par doun ne par achat ne a ferme, ne a chaumpart, ne en autre manere; taunt come la chose est en plee devaunt no ou devant nul de noz Ministrez, ne nul loer ne seyt pris. E ki ceste chose face, ou par lui, ou par autry, ou nul baret y face seyt puni a la volunte le Roi ausi bien celui qe le purchacera, com celui qi le fera.

**50.** Omnia predicta statuta incipiunt conservari ad festum sancti Michaelis proximo futurum, ita quod occasione delictorum contra aliquod predictorum statutorum citra predictum festum perpetratorum pena delinquentibus, de quibus mentio fit in statutis non infligatur. Super vero statutis in defectum legis & ad remedia editis, ne diutius querentes cum ad curiam venerint recedant de remedio desperati, habeant brevia sua in suo casu provisa, set non placitentur usque ad predictum festum sancti Michaelis.

## Translation

Whereas not long ago the lord king, a fortnight after the feast of St. John the Baptist in the sixth year of his reign, summoned to Gloucester the prelates, earls and barons, and his council, because many of his kingdom were suffering disinheritance, for in many cases where a remedy ought to have been applied none had been provided by his predecessors or himself, and issued certain statutes, very necessary and useful for his people, through which his people, English and Irish, subject to his rule, have obtained, in their tribulations, swifter justice than before; and yet certain cases, in which the law was inadequate, remained undetermined, and also some things remained to be enacted in order to restrain the oppression of the people; the lord king, in his parliament held at Westminster after Easter in the thirteenth year of his reign, to supplement the aforesaid statutes issued at Gloucester, caused many oppressions of the people and defects of the law to be recited, and issued statutes, as shall appear in the following.

First, concerning tenements which are often given upon condition, that is, when someone gives his land to some man and his wife and the heirs begotten of the same man and woman with the added condition expressed that, if the man and woman should die without heir begotten of them, the land so given should revert to the donor or his heir; also in the case when someone gives a tenement in frank marriage, which gift has a condition attached, though it is not expressed in the deed of gift, which is, that if the man and woman should die without heir begotten of them, the tenement so given should revert to the donor or his heir; also in the case when someone gives a tenement to somebody and to the heirs issuing of his body: it seemed, and still seems, hard to such donors and heirs of donors that their wish expressed in their gifts has not heretofore been observed and still is not observed. For in all these cases, after offspring begotten and issuing from those to whom the tenement was thus conditionally given, these feoffees have hitherto had power to alienate the tenement so given and to disinherit their own issue contrary to the wish of the donors and the form expressed in the gift. And further, when on the failure of the issue of such feofees the tenement so given ought to have reverted to the donor or his heirs by the form expressed in the deed of such a gift, notwithstanding the issue, if any there were, had died, they [the donors] have heretofore been barred from the reversion of the tenements by the deed and feoffment of those to whom the tenements were thus given upon condition, which was manifestly against the form of their gift. Wherefore the lord king, perceiving that it is necessary and useful to provide a remedy in the aforesaid cases, has enacted that the wish of the donor, according to the form manifestly expressed in his deed of gift, is henceforth to be observed, in such wise that those to whom the tenement was thus given upon condition shall not have the power of alienating the tenement so given and thereby preventing it from remaining after their death to their issue, or to the donor or his heir if issue fail either because there was no issue at all or because if there was issue it has failed by death, the heir of such issue failing. Neither shall, henceforth, the second husband of such woman have anything by the curtesy after the death of his wife in a tenement so given upon condition, or the issue of the woman and second husband have hereditary succession, but instead immediately after the death of the man and woman to whom the tenement was so given, it shall revert after their death either to their issue or to the donor or his heir as is aforesaid. And because in a new case a new remedy must be provided, the following writ is to be made as required: Command A. to render to B. justly etc. such and such a manor with appurtenances which C. gave to such and such a man and such and such a woman and the heirs of the bodies of that man and woman or which C. gave to such and such a man in frank marriage with such and such a woman and which after the death of the aforesaid man and woman ought, by the form of the aforesaid gift, as he says, to descend to the aforesaid B., the son of the aforesaid man and woman or which C. gave to so and so and the heirs of his body and which after the death of the same so and so ought by the form etc. to descend to the aforesaid B., the son of the aforesaid so and so. The writ whereby the donor has his recovery when issue fails is in common use in the chancery. And it is to be understood that this statute applies to the alienation of a tenement contrary to the form of a gift made after this, and does not extend to gifts made before it. And if a fine is levied hereafter on such a tenement, it is not to be legally binding, and the heirs or they to whom the reversion belongs will not be bound to lay their claim even if they are of full age, within England, and not in prison.

**2.** Because lords of fees who distrain their tenants for services due to them are frequently aggrieved in that their tenants replevy their distress with or without a writ, and then when the lords come by attachment on the complaint of their tenants to the county court, or to some other court having power to hold pleas of vee de naam,[1] and avow the distraint as reasonable and lawful, the tenants disavow holding or claiming to hold anything of him who took the distress and avowed it, so that he who

1 Also called *withernam* (see glossary).

distrained is in mercy and his tenants go quit and no punishment can be inflicted on them for such disavowal by record of the county or of other courts which do not have record, it is provided and enacted that henceforth as lords cannot obtain justice in county court or in such courts against tenants of theirs of this kind, as soon as they are attached at the suit of their tenants a writ shall be granted to them to bring the action before the justices, before whom and nowhere else can justice be done to such lords. And in the writ is to be inserted the clause, "Because so and so distrained in his fee for services and customs due to him." Nor by this statute is the ordinary usage of the law, which has not allowed any plea to be brought before the justices at the petition of the defendant, infringed; for though at first sight the tenant seems to be the one who is bringing the action and the lord the defendant, yet having regard to the fact that the lord is distraining and suing for services and customs due to him which are in arrears, he will appear to be rather the bringer of the action or plaintiff than the defendant. And that the justices may be certain on how recent a seisin lords can avow reasonable distraint upon their tenants, it is agreed that henceforth reasonable distraint can be avowed on a seisin of their ancestors or predecessors from the time from which the writ of *novel disseisin* runs. And because it sometimes happens that the tenant, after he has replevied his beasts, sells or eloigns them so that their return to the distraining lord, if that is adjudged, cannot be effected, it is provided that sheriffs or bailiffs are not henceforth to receive from the plaintiffs merely pledges to prosecute the suit but also to return the beasts, if judgment is given for their return, before handing the beasts over. And if anyone accepts pledges in any other form, he is to answer for the value of the beasts and the distraining lord is to have his recovery by a writ, "that he render to him such and such a number of beasts or chattels to that amount," and if the bailiff has not the means to make restitution, his superior is to make it. And because it sometimes happens that the party so distrained, after the return of the beasts to the distrainor has been adjudged and the beasts accordingly returned, replevies them again and when he sees the distrainor appearing in court ready to answer him, makes default; on which account return of the beasts to the distrainor will again be adjudged and thus the beasts will be replevied a second time, a third time, and so on indefinitely and in this case the judgments of the king's court will have no effect, and because no remedy has yet been provided for this, the following procedure is ordained in this case: that as soon as return of the beasts to the distrainor has been adjudged, the sheriff is to be ordered by a judicial writ to have the beasts returned to the distrainor; in which writ it is to be stated that the sheriff shall not hand them over without a further judicial writ in which mention is made of the judgment given by the justices, and this cannot be done except by writ issuing from the rolls of the justices before whom the action was brought. When therefore the distrained party comes to the justices and asks for his beasts to be again replevied, let this judicial writ be made for him: that the sheriff, exacting surety to prosecute and also to return the beasts or chattels or their value if judgment for return is given, is to hand over to him the beasts or chattels previously returned and let him who distrained be attached to appear on a certain day before the justices before whom the plea is to be brought in the presence of the parties. And if he who has made the replevin makes default again, or if for any other reason return of the distress, by now twice replevied, is adjudged, that distress is to remain forever irrepleviable. But if a fresh distraint is made for a fresh reason, the above-mentioned procedure is to be observed with regard to the new distress.

**3.** In cases where the husband lost by default a tenement which was the right of his wife, it was hard that the wife after the death of her husband had no recovery other than by a writ of Right: wherefore the lord king has ordained that a woman after the death of her husband may have recovery by a writ of Entry *cui ipsa in vita sua contradicere non potuit*,[1] which shall be pleaded in the following way, namely, if the tenant excepts to the woman's claim on the ground that he had entry by

1 "Whom she in his lifetime could not gainsay." Words from a writ of entry to be used by a woman against the person to whom her husband had aliened her lands and tenements during his lifetime.

judgment, and it be found that it was upon default (which the tenant must needs disclose if it be demanded of him), he must then further show his right according to the form of the writ which he first sued out against the husband and wife. And if he can prove that he has right in the tenement claimed, the woman shall take nothing by her writ; and if he cannot prove it, the woman shall recover the tenement claimed; this being observed that if a husband absent himself and refuse to defend his wife's right or wish to surrender it against his wife's will, if the wife come before judgment ready to answer the demandant and to defend her right, she is to be admitted. Likewise if a tenant in dower, by the law of England, or otherwise for term of life, or by gift wherein reversion is reserved, make default or wish to surrender, the heirs and those to whom the reversion belongs are, if they come before judgment, to be admitted to answer. And if judgment has been given upon default or surrender, then the heirs and those to whom the reversion belongs after the death of such tenants shall have recovery by a writ of Entry in which the same process shall be observed as is said above in the case of the husband losing by default his wife's tenement. Thus in the cases aforesaid two actions concur, one between the demandant and tenant, and the other between the tenant showing his right and the demandant.

**4.** When a husband impleaded of a tenement renders the tenement demanded to his adversary, clearly, after the husband's death, the judges award her dower to the widow if it is sought by writ; but when the man loses the tenement demanded by default, if the widow after his death seeks dower it is found that dower is adjudged to her by some judges notwithstanding the default of her husband, although other judges are of the contrary opinion and adjudge the opposite: in order henceforth to remove this uncertainty,[1] it is ordained for certain that a woman claiming her dower shall in both cases be heard. And if it is excepted against her that her husband lost by judgment the tenement whereof the dower is demanded, for which reason she ought not to have dower, and it is asked by what judgment and it be found that it was by default (which the tenant

1 The translation to this point in chapter 4 is by Plucknett 1922/2010 18.

must needs disclose), it then behoves the tenant to answer further and show that he had and has right in the aforesaid tenement according to the form of the writ which he first sued out against the husband. And if he can show that the woman's husband had not right in the tenement, nor anyone other than he the holder, then let him go quit and the wife recover nothing of her dower; and if he cannot show this, the wife shall recover her dower.

And so in these cases and in certain others following, that is to say, when the wife being endowed loses her dower by default, and tenants in marriage, by the law of England, or for term of life or in fee-tail, a number of actions concur: for such tenants, when they have to claim their tenements lost by default and the point is reached that the tenant is compelled to show his right, they cannot make answer without those to whom the reversion of right belongs and are therefore allowed to vouch to warranty as if they were tenants, if they have a warranty. And when the warrantor has warranted, the plea shall proceed between him who is seised and the warrantor according to the tenor of the writ that the tenant first sued out and by which he recovered by default; and so from a number of actions in the end one judgment is arrived at, which is, that such demandants shall recover what they are claiming or that the tenants shall go quit. And if the action of such a tenant, who is compelled to show his right, is brought by a writ of Right, although the Grand Assize or battle cannot be joined by the usual words they can however be joined by words suitable, for since the tenants, in that they are showing their right which belongs to them by the writ they first sued out, are thus in the position of plaintiff, the warrantor may well defend the right of the tenant, who as said is held to be in the position of demandant, and offer to defend the seisin of his ancestor by the body of his freeman or put himself on the Grand Assize and ask for a recognition to be made to determine whether he has the greater right in the disputed tenement, or the aforesaid so-and-so; or the Grand Assize may be joined in another way, thus "So-and-so, the warrantor, defends the right, etc. and acknowledges the seisin of his ancestor and puts himself on the Grand

Assize and asks for a recognition to be made whether he has the greater right in the tenement aforesaid as in that whereof he enfeoffed such a man or that which such a man released and quitclaimed etc., or the aforesaid so-and-so has."

As it sometimes happens that a woman not having right to demand dower obtains, while the heir is under age, a writ of dower against the guardian and the guardian assigns the woman dower by favor or makes default or by collusion defends the plea so faintly that the dower is adjudged to the woman to the heir's prejudice, it is provided that when he comes of age the heir shall have against such woman the action of demanding the seisin of his ancestor which he would have against any other deforciant; yet so that there be saved to the woman her exception against the demandant of showing that she has right to her dower, if she can show it she may go quit and retain her dower and the heir be in mercy and be amerced heavily at the direction of the justices, and if not the heir may recover his demand.

In like manner let the woman be protected if the heir or any other implead her for her dower if she lose her dower by default, in which case her default shall not be so prejudicial to her that she cannot recover her dower if she has right, and she may have this writ: "Command A. to render justly etc. to so-and-so, who was the wife of so-and-so, so much land with appurtenances in such-and-such vill, which she claims as her reasonable dower, or as part of her reasonable dower, and which the aforesaid so-and-so is withholding from her by force." And to this writ let the tenant have his exception showing that she has no right in the dower, and if he can prove it let him go quit; otherwise the woman shall recover the tenement which before she had in dower.

And whereas in times gone by anyone who had lost his land by default had no other recovery than by a writ of Right, which was not appropriate for those who could not claim absolute right (such as tenants for term of life, in frank marriage, or in fee-tail, in which cases a reversion is reserved) it is provided that henceforth their default shall not be so prejudicial to them that they cannot have recovery of their estate, if they have right, by another writ than by writ of Right. For land in frank marriage lost by default, let such a writ be made: "Command A. to render to B. justly etc. such-and-such manor with appurtenances, which he claims is his right and his marriage and which the aforesaid A. is unjustly withholding from him." Likewise, for a tenement held for term of life lost by default let there be made the writ "Command so-and-so to render to so-and-so justly etc. the manor etc. which he claims to hold for the term of his life and which so-and-so is unjustly etc." Similarly [for the tenant in fee-tail with the variant] "which he claims to hold to himself and the heirs of his body and which so-and-so is unjustly etc."

**5.** Whereas concerning advowsons of churches there are only three original writs, that is to say the writ of Right and two of possession, namely, *darrein presentment* and *quare impedit*, and hitherto it has been used in the realm that when anyone having no right to present presented to any church and the one so presented was admitted, he who is the true patron could recover his advowson by no other writ than by a writ of Right, which had to be determined by judicial combat or by the Grand Assize, and in this way heirs under age, by the fraud and negligence of their guardians, and heirs also, whether of full age or under age, by the negligence or fraud of tenants by the law of England, or women tenants in dower or otherwise for term of life or for years or in fee-tail, were often disinherited of their advowsons, or at least, which was better for them, were compelled to resort to a writ of Right (and in that case hitherto were utterly disinherited), it is provided that such presentations shall not be so prejudicial to such rightful heirs, or to those to whom such advowsons ought to revert after the death of any persons, that they cannot—as often soever as anyone having no right presents during such wardships or during tenancies in dower or by the law of England or otherwise for term of life or of years or in fee-tail, at the next vacancy after the heir has come of age, or when after the death of tenants of the sort aforesaid the advowson reverts to the heir of full age—have like action and exception by a possessory writ of advowson to that which the last ancestor of such heir would, being of full age, have had at the last vacancy in his time arising before his death or before demise was made for term [of life or years] or in fee-tail as aforesaid. The same shall be observed of presentations made to churches belonging to the inheritance of wives while they were under the power of their husbands: they shall be helped by this statute by the aforesaid remedy. Men of religion, bishops, archdeacons, rectors of churches and other ecclesiastical persons shall be helped, too, by that same statute if anyone having no right to present presents to churches belonging to their houses, prelacy, dignity or parsonage during a vacancy in such prelacies, dignities or parsonages.

This statute shall not, however, be so largely understood that persons for whose remedy it was ordained may have their aforesaid recovery by asserting that guardians, tenants in dower— by the law of England or otherwise for term of life or years—or husbands, have defended faintly the plea begun by them or against them, because judgments given in the king's court are not annulled by this statute; instead a judgment shall stand valid until it is annulled by the king's court as erroneous if error is found. Nor shall an assize of *darrein presentment* or an inquest by writ of *quare impedit,* if completed, be annulled by attaint or certification, which may be freely granted. And henceforth one form of pleading shall be observed among justices in writs of *darrein presentment* and *quare impedit* in this respect: if the defending party excepts the plenarty[1] of the church by reason of his own presentation, the action shall not be stayed because of that plenarty provided the writ is obtained within six months although the presentation cannot be recovered within the six months. And whereas sometimes an agreement is made between several claimants to the advowson of a church and recorded before justices in the roll or in a fine, in the form that one party shall present the first time and at the next vacancy another, at the third a third, and so on for as many as there are, but when one has presented and obtained the presentation due to him by the terms of the agreement, at the next vacancy he to whom the following presentation belongs is hindered by any party to the agreement or

1 The status when an ecclesiastical office or benefice is occupied.

someone for him, it is provided that henceforth the one so hindered shall have no need to acquire a writ of *quare impedit*, but have recourse to the roll or to the fine, and if the aforesaid agreement or concord is found on the roll or in a fine, word shall be sent to the sheriff to notify the hinderer to be ready at an early date within the next fortnight or three weeks, as the place is near or far, to show if he can say why so-and-so should not have his presentation. And if he does not come, or perhaps comes but cannot say why the one who is thus hindered should not—because of something done after the enrolling of or the making of a chirograph of the agreement—have his presentation, the latter shall recover his presentation with his damages. And where it happens that after the death of the ancestor who presented to a church the advowson of it has been assigned in the dower of any woman or is held by the law of England and those holding in dower or by the law of England have presented and, after the death of such tenants by the law of England or in dower, the true heir is hindered in presenting when the church falls vacant, it is provided that henceforth it shall be for him who is hindered to choose whether he wishes to sue by the writ of *quare impedit* or of *darrein presentment*. This is to apply also in the case of advowsons demised for term of life, or years, or in fee-tail. And henceforth damages shall be awarded in writs of *darrein presentment* and *quare impedit*, namely, if six months go by because of hindrance by anybody with the result that the bishop collates to the church and the true patron loses his presentation on that occasion, damages shall be awarded equivalent to two years value of the church; and if six months have not elapsed but the right to present is established within that time, then damages equivalent to half a year's value of the church shall be awarded. And if the hinderer has not the means to pay the damages in the case where the bishop collates by lapse of time, he shall be punished by imprisonment for two years; and if the right to the advowson is established within the six months, the hinderer shall be punished by imprisonment for half a year. And henceforth writs are to be granted for chapels, prebends, vicarages, hospitals, abbeys, priories and other houses whose advowson is someone else's which before used not to be granted. And when by a writ of *Indicavit* the rector of any church is hindered in demanding tithes in a neighboring parish, the patron of the rector so hindered shall have the writ for claiming the advowson of the tithes demanded, and when he has proved his right the plea shall proceed afterwards in the ecclesiastical court in accordance with what has been decided in the court of the king. When an advowson descends to parceners, although one presents twice and encroaches upon the coheir, he that was negligent shall not on this account be wholly excluded, but at another time, when it happens, he shall have his turn to present.

**6.** When anyone demands a tenement from another and the one sued vouches to warranty and the warrantor denies the warranty and the plea is held up a long time between the tenant and the warrantor, when it is at last proved incontestably that he who was vouched to warranty is bound to warrant, there was by the law and custom hitherto used no other punishment inflicted on the vouchee who refused to warrant save that he should warrant and be amerced because he did not warrant before, a thing which was hard on the demandant, who by collusion between the tenant and the warrantor often suffered great delays: on which account the lord the king has ordained that, just as the tenant should lose the tenement demanded if he vouched to warranty and the warrantor is able to rid himself of the warranty, the warrantor shall lose in the same way if he denies the warranty and it is proved incontestably that he is bound to warrant. And if an inquest is pending between the tenant and the warrantor and the demandant asks for a writ to summon the jury, it shall be granted to him.

**7.** The writ for measuring dower shall henceforth be granted to a guardian; but the heir shall not be barred by the guardian's suit from measuring the dower as it ought to be measured by the law of the land when he comes of age if the guardian takes proceedings against the woman tenant in dower fictively and collusively. And as well in this writ as in the writ for measuring pasture there shall in future be a speedier procedure than before, so that, when it comes to the great distress, days shall be given within which two counties may be held at which public proclamation shall be made that the defendant shall come on the day contained in the writ to answer the plaintiff: on which day, if he comes, the plea between them shall proceed, and if he dos not come and proclamation in the manner aforesaid is witnessed to by the sheriff, let them because of the default proceed to the measuring.

**8.** Since, by a plea instituted upon a writ of admeasurement of pasture, pasture is measured sometimes before the justices, sometimes in the county before the sheriff, and it often happens that after such measuring he who overloaded the pasture before again puts more cattle on it than is appropriate for him to have and up to now no remedy has been provided, it is ordained that for the second overloading remedy shall be provided for the plaintiff in this manner: if the pasture was measured before the justices, the plaintiff shall have a judicial writ that the sheriff shall, in the presence of the parties if they have been forewarned and wish to be present, inquire into the second overloading and if the finding is that it in fact occurred, this shall be returned to the justices under the sheriff's seal and the seals of the jurors; and the justices shall award the plaintiff damages and put in the estreats[1] the value of the animals which after the measurement was made the overloader put in the pasture beyond what he ought to have done, and deliver the estreats to the barons of the exchequer for them to be answerable to the lord king for the animals. If the pasture was measured in the county, then, at the request of the plaintiff, a writ shall issue out of chancery for the sheriff to inquire into such overloading, and, for the cattle put in the pasture beyond the due number, or for their value, he shall be answerable to the lord king at the exchequer. And lest sheriffs defraud the lord king in this respect, it is agreed that all such writs of overloading a second time that issue out of chancery shall be enrolled and at the end of the year a transcript sent to the exchequer under the seal of the chancery for the treasurer and barons of the exchequer to see how the sheriffs answer for the issues of such writs. In the same way writs of redisseisin shall be enrolled and sent to the exchequer at the end of the year.

1 Copies of the court records.

**9.** When chief lords distrain on their fee for services and customs due to them, and there is a mesne who ought to acquit the tenant (since it lies not in the mouth of the tenant after he has replevied the first distress to deny the demand of the chief lord who maintains in the court of the lord king that the distraint is lawfully levied upon his tenant, that is, upon the mesne tenant) many have hitherto been oppressed by such distraints, inasmuch as the mesne tenant, although he had the means by which to be distrained, made great delays before coming to court to answer his tenants on a writ of mesne, inasmuch also as it was hard when the mesne tenant had nothing, when also, if the tenant was ready to render to the chief lord the services and customs demanded, the chief lord refused to accept the services and customs due to him at the hands of any other than his nearest tenant and so such tenants in demesne lost the profit of their lands sometimes for a time, sometimes for the rest of their days, and up to now no remedy has been provided for this. There is for the future a remedy for this ordained and provided in this form. As soon as such a tenant in demesne with a mesne tenant between him and the chief lord is distrained he shall at once get himself a writ of mesne. And if the mesne tenant has land in the county but absents himself until the great distress, such day shall be given to the plaintiff in his writ of great distress that two counties can be held before it and the sheriff shall be ordered to distrain the mesne by the great distress as contained in the writ. And nevertheless the sheriff shall have it solemnly proclaimed in two full counties that such mesne shall come on the day contained in the writ to answer his tenant. If he comes on that day, the plea shall proceed between them in the usual way; if he does not come, the mesne shall lose his tenant's service, the tenant from then on not being responsible to him for anything, but, leaving out the mesne tenant, being responsible to the chief lord for the same services that previously the said mesne had to perform. Nor shall the chief lord have power to distrain, so long as the said tenant offers him the services due and accustomed. And if the chief lord exacts more than the mesne ought to render to him, the tenant shall in that case have the exception the mesne would have. If however the mesne tenant has nothing within the king's jurisdiction, the tenant may obtain his writ of mesne to the sheriff of the county in which he is distrained all the same; and, if the sheriff sends word that the mesne tenant has nothing he can be summoned by, let him, notwithstanding, sue out a writ of attachment. And if the sheriff returns that he has nothing he can be attached by, let him, nevertheless, sue out a writ of great distress and let proclamation be made in the way aforesaid. If however the mesne tenant has no land in the county in which the distress is taken but has land in another county, then an original writ shall issue to the sheriff of the county in which the distress is taken to summon him, and when it has been testified by that sheriff that the mesne has nothing in his county, a judicial writ to summon him shall issue to the sheriff of the county in which it is testified that he has a tenement and let suit be made in that county and proceed as far as the great distress and proclamation as prescribed above in the case of a mesne who has land in the county in which the distress is levied, and let suit be made nevertheless in the county in which he has nothing, as prescribed above about a mesne with nothing, and proceed as far as the great distress and proclamation; and so after proclamation in both counties the mesne shall be adjudged deprived of his fee and service. As it sometimes happens that the tenant in demesne is enfeoffed to hold by less service than the mesne tenant had to do to the chief lord, when after such proclamation the tenant has been turned over to the chief lord, to the exclusion of the mesne tenant, the tenant shall be bound to answer to the chief lord for the services and customs which previously the mesne had to render to him. And after the mesne tenant has come into court and admitted, or it is adjudged, that he ought to acquit him, if after such admission or judgment there is complaint that the mesne is not acquitting the tenant, then a judicial writ shall issue that the sheriff distrain the mesne to acquit the tenant and to appear before the justices on a certain day to show why he did not acquit him sooner. And when because of the distress he does appear, the plaintiff shall be heard, and if the plaintiff can prove that he has not acquitted him he shall compensate for damages and the tenant shall by judgment of the court be quit of the mesne and be turned over to the chief lord. And if on this first distress he does not appear, let a writ issue for another distress and let proclamation be made. And after it has been testified, the court shall proceed to judgment as said above. And it is to be understood that by this statute tenants, if they are impleaded concerning their tenements, are not precluded from producing in court the warranty of their mesnes and the heirs of these as they did before. Nor are tenants precluded either from being able to institute proceedings against their mesnes as used to be the custom, if they see that their action is more likely to be successful by the old custom than by this statute. And it is to be understood that by this statute no remedy is provided for any mesne tenant whatsoever but solely for the case where there is one mesne only between the lord who is distraining and the tenant, where that mesne is of full age, and where the tenant can turn himself over to the chief lord without prejudice to anyone other than the mesne, which is said for the benefit of women holding in dower, tenants by the law of England or otherwise for term of life or in fee-tail, for whom for certain reasons remedy is not yet provided, but, God permitting, shall be at another time.

**10.** When in the eyre it is proclaimed that all who wish to deliver writs should deliver them within a certain time, after which no writ will be received, many relying on this, when they have waited until that time and no writ has been served upon them, withdraw by license of the justices and after their departure their adversaries perceiving their absence deliver their writs late and these are accepted by the sheriff sometimes as a favor to them, sometimes in return for a gift, and they who thought they had left safely lose their tenements. To remedy such fraud hereafter, the lord king has ordained that justices in their eyres shall fix a period of a fortnight or a month, the shorter or the longer period according to the size of the county, within which, it shall be publicly proclaimed, all who wish to deliver writs shall deliver them and at the end of it the sheriff shall inform the senior justices of the eyre of how many writs he has, and which; and that after that no writ shall be accepted and if it is accepted the proceedings begun by it shall be deemed invalid, except that a writ abated can be revalidated at any time during the whole circuit; also writs of dower concerning men who die after the summons of the eyre, assizes of *darrein presentment* and *quare impedit* concerning churches falling vacant after the aforesaid summons may be accepted any time before the departure of the justices. Writs too of *novel disseisin*, at whatever time the disseisin was done, may be accepted.

In eyres, the lord king as an act of special grace grants that those who have tenements in different counties in which the justices go on eyre, or who are afraid of being impleaded concerning certain tenements in counties in which the justices go on eyre, and who are impleaded concerning other tenements in counties in which the justices are not going on eyre, before the justices at Westminster or in the king's bench or before justices assigned to take assizes or in any county before the sheriff or in any court baron can appoint a general attorney to sue for them in the eyre in all pleas moved or to be moved for them or against them during the eyre, which attorney or attorneys shall have authority in pleas moved in the eyre until a plea is finished or his principal removes him. Not that by this they are to be excused from being on juries or assizes before the same justices.

**11.** On serjeants, bailiffs, chamberlains and all manner of receivers who are obliged to render account, it is with one consent ordained and established that when the master of such servants appoints auditors of their accounts and it happens that they are in arrears on their account, they shall be arrested and on the testimony of the auditors of the account sent and delivered to the nearest gaol of the lord king in those parts and be received by the sheriff or the keeper of the gaol and committed to prison in irons and in good custody and remain in that prison living at their own expense until they have rendered full satisfaction to their masters for the arrears. If however anyone thus delivered to gaol complains that the auditors of the account have burdened him unjustly by debiting him with receipts which he did not receive or by not allowing expenses or reasonable disbursements, and finds friends willing to undertake to bring him, let him be handed over to them. And the sheriff in whose power he has been shall instruct the master to be before the barons of the exchequer on some appointed day with the rolls and tallies by which he rendered account, and in the presence of the barons, or auditors whom it is their will to appoint, the account is to be gone through again and justice done between the parties so that, if he is in arrears, he be committed to the Fleet gaol as said above; and if he should flee and not be willing to render account voluntarily, he is to be distrained as is contained elsewhere in other statutes to come before the justices to render account if he has anything he can be distrained by. And if he comes to court, auditors of account shall be appointed before whom, if he is in arrears and if he cannot pay the arrears immediately, he shall be committed to gaol for custody in the manner aforesaid; and if he should flee and it is testified by the sheriff that he is not to be found, he is to be summoned from county to county until he is outlawed and such a prisoner shall not be repleviable. And the sheriff or keeper of the gaol, whether it is in a liberty or not, shall take care not to let him out of prison on the common writ called Replevin or by other means without the assent of his master; and if he does and is found guilty of this, he shall be answerable to the master for the damage done to him by such servant as established by a jury and may have his recovery by a writ of debt. And if the keeper of the gaol has not the means by which he can be distrained or with which to pay, his superior who entrusted the keeping of the gaol to him shall be answerable by the same writ.

**12.** As many, wishing out of malice to injure others, cause false accusations of homicide and other felonies to be made by accusers who have nothing with which to satisfy the king for the false accusation or pay damages to those accused, it is ordained that when anyone so accused has in due manner acquitted himself in the king's court of the felony attributed to him, the justices before whom such accusation has been heard and determined shall, at the suit of either the person accused or the king, punish the accuser with imprisonment for a year and such accusers shall nonetheless make good to the accused their damages as decided by the justices, having regard to the imprisonment or arrest the accused sustained by reason of such accusations and to the ill-fame they incurred by imprisonment or otherwise, and shall nonetheless as regards the lord king be obliged to make grievous fine. And if perchance such accusers have not the wherewithal to make good the said damages, enquiry, if the accused desires it, shall be made on the oath of good and law-worthy men into by whose instigation such malicious accusation was framed. And if it is found by that inquest that someone was the instigator out of malice, he shall, by a judicial writ at the suit of the one accused, be distrained to appear before the justices; and if he is lawfully convicted of such malicious abetment, he shall be punished by imprisonment and be bound to make restitution of damages as said above concerning the accuser. And in future no essoin shall lie for the accuser in an accusation of homicide, in whatever court the accusation is to be determined.

**13.** As sheriffs, pretending that certain persons have been indicted before them in their tourns of thefts and other evil deeds, often arrest men who are not guilty and not lawfully indicted, and imprison them and extort money from them when they were not lawfully indicted by twelve jurors, it is ordained that sheriffs, in their tourns and elsewhere when they have to make enquiries about wrongdoers by the lord king's precept or in virtue of their office, shall make their enquiries about such wrongdoers by at the least twelve law-worthy men, who shall put their seals to those inquests, and shall arrest and imprison those whom through such inquests they find are guilty, as used aforetimes to be done. And if they imprison any other than those indicted by such inquests, such imprisoned shall have their action by writ of imprisonment against the sheriffs as they would have against any other person whatsoever who imprisoned them without warrant; and what has been said of sheriffs shall apply to any bailiff of a liberty.

**14.** Since a writ of prohibition of waste used to be granted for waste committed in anybody's inheritance by guardians [or] tenants in dower, by the law of England or otherwise for term of life, [and] many were misled by which writ, thinking that those who committed the waste needed only to answer for waste committed after the prohibition was directed to them, the lord king, to remove for the future this error, has ordained that, for waste committed in any way whatever to the harm of anyone, there shall in future be granted not a writ of prohibition of waste but a writ of summons so that he who is complained of shall answer for waste committed at any time, and if after the summons he does not appear, let him be attached, and after attachment be distrained, and if after distraint he does not appear, the sheriff shall be commanded to go personally to the place where the waste has occurred, taking with him twelve etc., and enquire into the waste and return the inquest, and after the inquest has been returned, the court shall proceed to judgment in accordance with what is contained in the statute published earlier at Westminster.[1]

**15.** In every case in which minors under age can plead, it is granted that if such minors are eloigned[2] so that they cannot sue personally, their next friends shall be admitted to sue for them.

**16.** In the case where an inheritance descends to a minor from the side of his father, who held of one lord, and from the side of his mother, who held of another lord, there has been doubt hitherto to which of the two lords the marriage of the minor should belong. It is agreed that henceforth that lord shall have the marriage by whom the ancestor was first enfeoffed, with no regard to the sex or the size of the tenement, but only to the more ancient feoffment by knight service.

**17.** In the eyre of the justices an essoin of bed-sickness shall not henceforth be allowed for a tenement in the same county unless he who is causing himself to be essoined is genuinely sick; for if the demandant excepts that the tenant is not ill or in such a state that he could not appear before the justices, his challenge shall be permitted, and if this on investigation is proved beyond doubt, the essoin shall be converted into a default. And henceforth this essoin shall not lie in a writ of right between two people claiming by one descent.

---

1 The reference is actually to chapter 5 of the Statute of Gloucester (1278).
2 Prevented from appearing.

**18.** When a debt has been recovered or acknowledged in the king's court, or damages awarded, it shall henceforth be for him who is suing for such debt or damages to choose whether to sue out a writ that the sheriff cause to be made out of the lands and chattels or have the sheriff deliver to him all the chattels (except cattle and beasts of the plough) of the debtor and half his land until, on a reasonable valuation and extent, the debt has been levied. And if he is ejected from the tenement, he shall have recovery by writ of *novel disseisin*, and afterwards, if need be, by a writ of redisseisin.

**19.** When after the death of anyone who dies intestate and is bound to any persons for debt his goods come to the ordinary to be disposed of, the ordinary shall henceforth be bound to answer for the debts (to the extent that the deceased's goods suffice) in the same way that the executors would be bound to answer if he had made a will.

**20.** As justices in a plea of *mort d'ancestor* have been accustomed to permit the tenant to answer that the plaintiff is not the next heir of the ancestor on account of whose death he claims the tenement and to inquire into this by assize, it is agreed that in writs of cosinage, aiel, and besaiel, which are of the same nature, that same answer shall be permitted and inquired into and in accordance with the inquest let the court proceed to judgment.

**21.** As in a statute made at Gloucester it is contained that if any demise to another a tenement at a rent of a quarter or more of the value of the tenement, he who demised it, or his heir, shall after cessation of payment for two years have an action for claiming in demesne the tenement so demised, in like manner it is agreed that if anyone withholds from his lord the due or customary service over a period of two years the lord shall have an action for claiming the tenement in demesne by the following writ: "Order A. that lawfully etc. he render to B. such and such tenement, which C. has held of him by such and such service and which ought to revert to the aforesaid B. because the aforesaid A. has for two years stopped doing that service, as he says." And not only in this case but also in the case mentioned in the aforesaid statute of Gloucester let writs of entry be made out for an heir claiming against the heir of the tenant, and against those to whom such a tenement may have been alienated.

**22.** When two or more hold wood, turbary, fishery or other such things in common without any of them knowing his severalty and any of them commits waste against the wish of another, an action may be brought by writ of Waste and the defendant when he comes to judgment shall have the choice either of taking his share in a particular place on the authority of the sheriff and by the view, oath and allotment of men of the neighborhood chosen and sworn for the purpose, or of agreeing not to take anything in future in such wood, turbary or other things except in accordance with what his coparceners are willing to take. And if he chooses to take his share in a particular place, let there be allotted to him in his share the place wasted at its value before he wasted it. The writ in this case: "As A. and B. hold the wood jointly, B. committed waste etc."

**23.** Executors shall henceforth have the writ of account and the same action and process by that writ as the deceased had and would have if he were alive.

**24.** In cases in which a writ is granted in chancery for an act done by somebody, plaintiffs shall not henceforth depart from the court of the king without remedy because the tenement has changed hands and for that case no special writ is provided in the chancery's register (as for instance about a house, a wall, a market, a writ is granted against him who set it up, yet if house, wall, and such like be conveyed to another person, the writ is refused). Instead from now on when a writ is granted in one case, in a like case requiring like remedy it shall be made as before: "A. has complained to us that B. unjustly etc. has set up a house, wall, market and other things which are to the nuisance etc." If such things set up to the nuisance are transferred to another person, it shall henceforth be made thus: "A. has complained to us that B. and C. have set up etc." In the same way, just as the parson of a church can recover common of pasture by a writ of *novel disseisin*, so from now on shall his successor recover against the disseisor or his heir by the writ Quod permittat although this kind of writ has not been granted from chancery before. Likewise, just as a writ is granted as to whether a tenement is the frankalmoin of some church or the lay fee of so-and-so, from now on shall a writ be made whether it is the frankalmoin of one or of another church in the case where the frankalmoin of one church is transferred into the possession of another church. And whensoever in future it happens in the chancery that a writ is found in one case, but in a similar case involving the same law and requiring similar remedy it is not,[1] the clerks of the chancery shall agree in framing a writ, or shall adjourn the plaintiffs to the next parliament and shall write down the matter on which they cannot agree and refer them to the next parliament, and a writ shall be framed by the joint opinion of the learned in the law so that it may not happen hereafter that the court long fails those who seek justice.

**25.** Because there is not any writ in the chancery whereby plaintiffs have so speedy a remedy as by a writ of *novel disseisin*, the lord king, desiring speedy justice to be done, and delays in pleas to be done away with or reduced, grants that the writ of *novel disseisin* shall have a place in more cases than it has had before and grants that an assize of *novel disseisin* shall lie for estovers of wood, the profit to be taken from gathering nuts, acorns and other fruits in a wood, a corrody[2], the delivery of grain or other victuals or necessaries due to be received annually at a certain place, the takings of toll, tronage, passage, pontage and such like in certain places, the keeping of parks, woods, forests, chaces, warrens, gates, and other bailiwicks and offices in fee; and in all the aforesaid cases the writ shall be made out in the customary way with the words "of his freehold." And as it formerly lay and had a place in common of pasture, so shall it in future have a place in common of turbary, fishery

1 The missing negative is customarily provided as necessary to the sense of the text.

2 A lifetime allowance of food, clothing, and shelter at a monastery. It could be granted by the king.

and similar common rights which anyone has appendant to a freehold or by special deed for at least term of life without a freehold. In the case too when anyone holding a tenement for term of years or in wardship alienates it in fee and by that alienation transfers the freehold to the feofee, remedy shall be by a writ of *novel disseisin* and both the feoffor and the feofee shall be considered disseisors, so that while either of them is alive the writ shall be in place. And if by the death of the parties remedy by that writ shall cease, remedy shall be given by a writ of entry. And although mention is made above of some cases in which the writ of *novel disseisin* had no place before, let no one for this reason think that that writ is not now competent where it was competent before. And though some have doubted whether there can be remedy by the aforesaid writ in the case where one pastures on the several[1] of another, let it be taken as certain that in that case there is a good and sure remedy by the aforesaid writ. And let those named as the disseisors take care henceforth not to put forward false exceptions to delay the taking of the assize, saying that an assize about the same tenement has passed between the same parties elsewhere, or saying untruthfully that a writ of a higher nature is pending between the same parties about the same tenement, and on these and like matters vouching rolls or record to warranty so that by that vouching they may be able to take away the crops and get the rents and other profits, to the great detriment of the plaintiff: because, although he who falsely advanced such untrue exceptions did not before bear any other penalty save only that on proof of his falsehood the court proceeded to take the assize, the lord king, to whom such false exceptions are hateful, has ordained that if anyone named as a disseisor puts forward personally the exception at the day given to him and fails in the warranty he has vouched, he is, without the recognition of the assize, to be adjudged a disseisor and shall make good the damages, those already ascertained and those to be ascertained later, twofold, and shall nonetheless be punished by being imprisoned for one year for his falsehood. And if the exception is put forward by an agent, the taking of

1 A several right of pasture was distinct from common of pasture.

the assize and the judgment on the restitution of the tenement and damages shall not be delayed on this account, so however that if the absent master of the bailiff appears later before the justices who took the assize and offers to prove by record or rolls that an assize about the same tenement between the same parties passed elsewhere, or that the plaintiff withdrew from his suit in a like writ elsewhere, or that a plea by a writ of a higher nature is pending, a writ calling for the record of this to be brought is to be made out for him, and when he has it and the justices see that the record so sent for him would have availed before the judgment for the plaintiff to be barred by it from his action, the justices shall straightway cause the party who before recovered to be warned to appear on a certain day for the defendant to recover his seisin and the damages, if any, he paid by the first judgment together with the damages he became liable for after the giving of the first judgment, which shall be restored to him, as is said above, twofold. And he who recovered before shall nonetheless be punished by imprisonment at the discretion of the justices. In the same way, if the defendant against whom the assize passed in his absence shows charters or quitclaims on the making of which the jurors were not examined, nor could be examined, because no mention was made of them in pleading, and probably could be ignorant of their making, the justice on seeing those writings shall cause the party who recovered to be warned to appear on a certain day and cause the jurors of the same assize to come. And if he verifies those writings by the verdict of the jurors, or it may be by an enrollment, he who requested the assize in contravention of his own deed shall be punished by the penalty aforesaid. And the sheriff shall not henceforth take an ox from the disseisee but from the disseisor only. And if there are several disseisors named in one writ he shall nevertheless be content with one ox, and shall exact an ox priced at only five shillings and fourpence, or its value.

**26.** In writs of redisseisin double damages shall henceforth be awarded and the redisseisors shall not hereafter be repleviable by the common writ. And just as in the statute of Merton[1] that writ was provided for

1 Chapter 3.

those who were disseised after they had recovered by assize of *novel disseisin*, *mort d'ancestor* or other juries,[1] that writ shall henceforth be further available for those who have recovered by default, restoration or otherwise, without a recognition of assizes or juries.

**27.** After anyone has put himself on an inquest, an essoin shall be allowed him at the next day, but at other days following, the taking of the inquest shall not be delayed by essoin, whether or not he had an essoin before. And an essoin shall not be allowed after a day given at the prayer of the parties in a case in which the parties agree to appear without essoin.

**28.** Whereas by the statute of Gloucester[2] it is provided that after tenants have once appeared an essoin shall not be allowed them in writs of assizes, in like manner it shall henceforth be observed in the case of demandants.

**29.** A writ of trespass to hear and determine shall not henceforth be granted before any justices except justices of either bench and justices in eyre, unless it be for a heinous trespass where it is necessary to apply a speedy remedy and the lord king considers it should be granted as an act of special grace. Nor, again, shall a writ to hear and determine appeals before justices assigned be granted henceforth, unless in a special case and for a definite reason the lord king orders it. But to prevent such appealed or indicted persons being kept in prison a long time, they shall have a writ *de odis et atia* as stated in Magna Carta[3] and other statutes.

**30.** Henceforth two sworn justices shall be assigned, before whom and not others assizes of *novel disseisin*, *mort d'ancestor*, and attaint shall be taken, and they shall associate with them one or two of the more discreet knights of the county into which they shall come and shall take the aforesaid assizes and attaints at most three times a year, namely once between the quindene of St John the Baptist and the Gules of August [8

1 Here meaning simply legal actions.
2 Actually the Statute of Westminster I, chapter 42.
3 Magna Carta (1215), chapter 36.

July to 1 August] and again between the feast of the Exaltation of the Holy Cross and the octave of Michaelmas [14 September to 6 October] and the third time between Epiphany and the Purification of the blessed Mary [6 January to 2 February], and in every county at every taking of assizes they shall before their departure fix the day of their return, so that every one of the county may know of their coming, and they shall adjourn assizes from date to date if on one day the taking of them is delayed by vouching to warranty, by essoin, or by default of jurors. And if they see that it would be advantageous for any reason for an assize of *mort d'ancestor* which is postponed owing to an essoin or vouching to warranty to be adjourned into the bench, it shall be lawful for them to do this. And then they shall send the record with the original writ to the justices of the bench. And when the action reaches the taking of the assize, it, together with the original writ, shall be remitted by the justices of the bench to the previous justices for the assize to be taken before them. But henceforth the justices of the bench shall appoint at least four days a year for such assizes.

To save labor and expense, inquisitions in connection with trespasses pleaded before justices of either bench shall be scheduled to be taken before the said justices assigned, unless the trespass is so heinous that it requires considerable examination. It shall also be arranged to take before them inquisitions of other pleas pleaded in either bench in which the examination is easy, as when entry or somebody's seisin is contradicted, or in the case of one article having to be inquired into: but inquisitions arising out of massive pleas and involving many articles, which require considerable examination, shall be taken before the justices of the benches unless both parties ask for the inquisition to be taken before some of them when they come to those parts, which henceforth shall not be done save by two justices or by one along with some knight of the county upon whom the parties agree, and inquisitions of this sort shall not be arranged to be taken before any unless a definite day and place in the county is settled on with the parties present and day and place inserted in a judicial writ in these words: "We command you to cause twelve etc. to appear before the justices at Westminster on the octave of Michaelmas unless so-and-so and so-and-so come to those parts on such-and-such day and place." And when such inquisitions have been taken they shall be returned in the benches and there shall judgment be given and they shall be enrolled. And if any inquisitions are taken otherwise than in the aforesaid manner, they shall be deemed invalid, except that it shall be arranged to take an assize of *darrein presentment* and inquisitions of *quare impedit* in their own county before one justice of the bench and one knight at a definite day and place decreed in the bench with or without the defendant's consent, and there judgment shall be given immediately. All justices of the bench and in eyres shall have clerks henceforth enrol all pleas pleaded before them as they have been used from of old to have them.

It is also ordained that justices assigned to take assizes shall not compel the jurors to say specifically whether it is disseisin or not, provided they are willing to speak the truth as to the facts and to seek the help of the justices, but if they volunteer that it is or is not disseisin, their statement shall be admitted at their own risk. And justices shall not henceforth put in assizes or juries any jurors other than those who were summoned for the purpose in the first instance.

**31.** When anyone who is impleaded before any of the justices puts forward an exception, praying the justices to allow it, and they will not allow it, if he who alleges the exception writes it down and requires a justice to affix his seal in witness, the justice shall affix his seal. And if one justice will not, another of them shall. And should the lord king, on complaint of the justices' action, have the record brought before him and should the exception not be found on the roll and the complainer shows the exception written out with the seal of a justice affixed, the justice shall be commanded to appear on a certain day to acknowledge his seal or deny it. And if the justice cannot deny his seal, the court shall proceed to judgment having regard to the exception and the question whether it should be admitted or be quashed.

**32.** Forasmuch as when men of religion and other ecclesiastical persons implead anyone and the party impleaded defaults (on which account he should lose the tenement), justices have hitherto feared that if the impleaded party defaults collusively, in order that the demandant (when because of the statute[1] he cannot get seisin of the tenement by right of gift or alienation of another kind) may get it because of the default, the statute would in this way be circumvented, it is ordained by the lord king and granted that in this case after the default inquiry shall be made by the community whether the demandant has a right to what he claims or not. And if it is found that the said demandant has a right, the court shall proceed to judgment for the demandant and he shall recover his seisin; but if he has not a right, the tenement shall accrue to the immediate lord of the fee if he claims it within a year from the time of the taking of the inquest. And if he does not claim it within the year, it shall accrue to the lord immediately above if he claims it within a year from the time of the taking of the inquest. And if he does not claim it within the year, it shall accrue to the lord immediately above if he claims within half a year after that year; and so each lord in turn after the immediate lord shall have half a year within which to claim, until in the end it is the king to whom in default of other lords the tenement accrues. And each of the chief lords of the fees shall be allowed to challenge jurors of the inquest, and likewise he who wishes to challenge on behalf of the king. And after the judgment is clear, the land shall remain in the king's hands until it is deraigned upon some chief lord and the sheriff shall be charged to answer for it at the exchequer.

**33.** Because many tenants erect crosses in their tenements, or permit them to be erected to the prejudice of their lords in order that the tenants can protect themselves by the privileges of the Templars and the Hospitallers against the chief lords of the fees, it is ordained that such tenements shall be forfeited to the chief lords or to the king in the same way as is provided elsewhere for tenements alienated in mortmain.

---

1 The Statute of Mortmain (1279).

**34.** It is provided that henceforth if a man rapes a married woman, a maiden, or other woman, without her consent before or afterwards, he shall have judgment of life and limb; and likewise where a man rapes a woman—married woman, maiden, or other woman—by force even though she consents afterwards, he shall have the judgment before stated if he is convicted at the king's suit, and there the king shall have his suit.

As to women taken away with the husband's goods, the king shall have the suit for the goods thus carried off. And if a wife willingly leaves her husband and goes away and stays with her adulterer, and if she is convicted thereof, she shall be barred forever of action to claim her dower which she ought to have of her husband's tenements unless her husband willingly and without the coercion of the church takes her back and allows her to live with him, in which case action shall be restored to her.

He who takes a nun away from her house, although she consents, shall be punished by three years imprisonment, make adequate satisfaction to the house from which she was abducted, and nonetheless make fine at the king's pleasure.

**35.** On children, male or female, seized and taken away, whose marriage belongs to someone: if he who seized them has no right to the marriage, he shall be punished for the offense by imprisonment for two years even if he subsequently restores the child unmarried or recompenses for the marriage. And if he does not restore, or marries the heir after marriageable age is reached and cannot recompense for the marriage, he shall abjure the realm or have imprisonment for life. And for this the complainant shall have the following writ: "If A. gives you security etc. put B. under gage etc. to be before our justices on such-and-such a day to show why he has ravished and taken away a certain heir found in such-and-such place, who is under age and whose marriage belongs to him, against the will of the said A. and against the peace etc." And if the heir is in the same county, then this clause shall be added: "And you shall diligently enquire where that heir is in your bailiwick and wherever he is found take and safely and securely keep him so as to have him before our aforesaid justices at the aforesaid term to be given back to whichever of the aforesaid A. or B. he ought to be given." And there shall be legal action against the party complained of until under distress he appears, if he has anything he can be distrained by, or, if he cannot be brought to justice he shall be exacted and outlawed for contumacy. If perchance such an heir be conducted and transferred into another county, then a writ to the sheriff of that county shall be made in this form: "A. has complained to us that B. has lately seized a certain heir under age and in his wardship in such-and-such place in the county of so-and-so and abducted him from that county to such-and-such place in your county against the will of A. and against our peace. And therefore we command you wherever you can find him in your bailiwick to take the aforesaid heir and keep him safely and securely so as to have him before our justices at such-and-such day and place, which day the said A. has against the aforesaid B. to be given back to him to whom he ought rightly to be given." And if the heir dies before he can be found or before he is restored to the plaintiff, the plea shall proceed between them nevertheless until it is determined to whom he ought to have been restored if he had survived, and he who unlawfully seized such an heir shall not be excused from or get any lightening of the punishment aforesaid after the death of the heir whose possessor in bad faith he was while he lived. And if the plaintiff dies before the plea is determined, if his right derived from his own fee, the action shall be re-summoned at the suit of the plaintiff's heir and the plea shall proceed in due order; if however the right was his by another title, such as by title of gift, sale, or other sort of title, then the action shall be re-summoned at the suit of the executors of the plaintiff and the plea proceed as aforesaid. In the same way if the defendant dies before the plea is determined or the heir restored, the plea shall proceed by re-summons between the plaintiff, or his heir or executors, and the executors of the defendant, or his heir if the executors have not means enough to compensate for the value of the marriage in accordance with what is contained in other statutes, but not as regards the penalty of imprisonment—with which penalty no one should be punished for the offense of another. In the same way when a plea is pending between parties for the custody of land or of an heir or of both by the common writ which begins, "Command so-and-so that he render etc.," re-summons shall be made between the heirs and the executors of the plaintiff, and likewise the heirs or executors of the defendant, if death overtakes either party before the plea is determined. And when the stage is reached of the grand distress a term shall be given within which at least three counties may be held, in each of which public proclamation shall be made that the deforciant shall appear in the bench to answer the plaintiff at the day contained in the writ. And if he does not appear on that day and it is certified once, a second time, and a third time, that proclamation has been made, the court shall pass judgment for the plaintiff, saving the right of the defendant if afterwards he wishes to plead in the matter. The same shall be done in a writ of trespass, when anyone complains that he has been ejected from wardships of this sort.

**36.** Because lords of courts and others who hold courts, and stewards, when they wish to harass those subject to them and have no lawful means of doing so, procure others to bring complaints against them and to give gage and offer pledges, or to sue out writs and force them, at the suit of such plaintiffs, to attend county, hundred, and [seignorial] court until they have made fine with them at their will, it is ordained that this shall not be done henceforth. And if anyone is attached upon such false complaints, let him replevy the distress there taken from him and have the action brought before the justices, before whom that replication shall be admitted if, after the one so distrained has formulated his complaint, the sheriff or other bailiff or lord avows that the distress was lawful because of the sort of complaints made before them and it is replied that such complaints were made against them maliciously at the instance or by procurement of the sheriff or other bailiffs or lords; and if they are convicted of this they shall make fine where the king is concerned and nevertheless pay triple damages to those so injured.

**37.** Because, too, bailiffs, whose office it is to take distresses, wishing to oppress those under their authority so as to extort money from them, send strangers to levy the distresses with the intention of being able to harass those under them on the ground that those distrained in this way (not knowing the persons) will not let such distresses be levied upon them, it is ordained that no distress shall be levied save by bailiffs who are sworn and known. And those who distrain, if they do otherwise and are convicted of it, shall, if injured parties sue out a writ of trespass, pay damages to the injured parties and where the king is concerned be heavily punished.

**38.** Because, also, sheriffs, hundred-bailiffs, and bailiffs of liberties have been accustomed to oppress those subject to them by putting on assizes and juries men who are ailing, decrepit, permanently or temporarily incapacitated, and even men not living in the district at the time of the summons, as well as by summoning an inordinate number of jurors in order to extort money from some of them for letting them go in peace, so that assizes and juries are often made up of poor men, the rich because of their bribes staying at home, it is ordained that henceforth there shall be summoned not more than twenty-four in one assize, and old men (that is, over seventy years old), the chronically sick, those ill at the time of the summons, and those who do not live in the district, shall not be put in juries or in petty assizes. Nor shall any be put in assizes or juries, even if these are to be taken in their own county, who hold tenements worth less than twenty shillings a year. And if such assizes and juries are to be taken outside the county, no one shall be put in them who has a tenement worth less than forty shillings a year, except those who are witnesses in charters or other writings, whose presence is taken for granted provided they are able to travel. Nor ought this statute to be extended to Grand Assizes, in which it is sometimes necessary because of the shortage of knights to put knights not resident in the district, provided they have tenements in the county. And if sheriffs or their under-sheriffs, or bailiffs of liberties, contravene in any article of this statute and are convicted of it, they shall pay damages to the injured parties and shall nonetheless be in the king's mercy. And justices assigned to take assizes shall, when they come into the county, have power to hear the plaints of all who have complaints in connection with the articles contained in this statute and to administer justice in the form aforesaid.

**39.** Because justices, whose duty it is to do justice to everyone who pleads before them, are very often hindered from being able to discharge their office in proper fashion because sheriffs do not return original and judicial writs, and also because they return a false answer to the king's writs, the lord king has provided and ordained that those who fear wrongdoing on the part of a sheriff are to deliver their writs, original and judicial, in full county or in the rere-county[1] at which the king's money is collected and a bill is to be received from the sheriff, if he is present, or the under-sheriff, giving the names of the parties and of the tenements contained in the writ. And at the request of him who delivered the writ, the seal of the sheriff or the under-sheriff is to be affixed in testimony and mention made of the day of the delivery of the writ. And if sheriffs or under-sheriffs will not affix their seals to a bill of this kind, the testimony of the knights and other trustworthy people present who affix their seals to the bill is to be accepted. And if a sheriff does not return writs delivered to him and complaint thereof reaches the justices, let order be given, by a judicial writ to the justices assigned to take assizes, to enquire of those who were present when the writ was delivered to the sheriff if they were aware of its delivery, and the inquest is to be returned. And if it is found by the inquest that the writ was delivered to him, damages shall be awarded to the demandant or plaintiff, having regard to the gravity and the nature of the action and to the danger that could have befallen him because of the delay he suffered. And in this way let remedy be given when a sheriff replies that a writ reached him so late that he could not carry out the king's command.

Pleas are very often delayed, too, because a sheriff replies that he has sent instructions to the bailiffs of some liberty or other who have done

1 A court held by a sheriff on the day after a county court.

nothing thereon, and he names liberties which have never had the return of writs; on which account the lord king has ordained that the treasurer of the exchequer shall provide a roll of all liberties having return of writs in any counties whatsoever. And if the sheriff replies that he has made return to the bailiffs of some other liberty than is contained in the aforesaid roll he is to be punished forthwith as a dis-inheritor of the lord king and of his crown. And if perchance he replies that he has made return to the bailiffs of some liberty which indeed has return, the sheriff shall be ordered not to omit to execute the lord king's command by reason of the aforesaid liberty and to make it known to the bailiffs to whom he made the return that they are on the day mentioned in the writ to answer why they did not execute the lord king's command. And if they come on the day and clear themselves on the ground that a return was not made to them, the sheriff shall forthwith be condemned to restore damages to the lord of that liberty and likewise to the party injured by the delay. And if the bailiffs do not come on the day or come but do not clear themselves in the way aforesaid, the sheriff is to be ordered in every judicial writ as long as the plea lasts not to omit by reason of the liberty etc. Sheriffs also very often give a false answer to the article about issues etc., sometimes reporting untruthfully that there are no issues, sometimes that they are small when they could return a bigger sum, sometimes not mentioning issues; wherefore it is ordained and agreed that if the plaintiff asks to hear the sheriff's reply, his request is to be granted. And if he offers to prove that the sheriff could have answered for greater issues, a judicial writ to the justices assigned to take assizes is to be made for him ordering them to enquire, in the presence of the sheriff if he wishes to be there, what were the issues and how much they were for which the sheriff could have answered from the day when the writ was received until the day contained in the writ. And when the inquest has been returned, if he did not previously answer for the full amount, he is to be charged with the deficit by estreats[1] delivered into the exchequer, and be nonetheless

1 Copies of the court records that order the fines (the "issues" of the preceding sentence).

heavily amerced for the concealment. And let the sheriff know that rents, corn in the grange, and all movables except harness, clothes, and household necessaries are included under the heading of issues. And the lord king has commanded that for such false answers sheriffs shall be punished the first time, and a second time if need be, by the justices. But if they offend a third time, no one other than the king is to handle the matter. Very often, too, they give a false answer in reporting that they could not carry out the king's command because of the resistance of the armed force of some magnate, of which answer let sheriffs beware in future, for an answer of this kind redounds greatly to the lord king's dishonor; and as soon as his bailiffs aver that they have encountered such resistance, a sheriff shall immediately put everything aside and, taking with him the posse of his county, go in person to carry out the command. And if he finds that his bailiffs have lied he shall so punish them by imprisonment that by their punishment others will be deterred. And if he finds they are telling the truth, let him punish those resisting them by imprisonment, from which they are not to be released without the lord king's special order. And if perchance the sheriff encounters resistance when he comes, let him inform the court of the names of the resisters and of those aiding, assenting, instructing or supporting them, and they are to be attached by a judicial writ to appear in person in court, and if they are convicted of such resistance, they are to be punished at the king's pleasure. Nor is any officer of the lord king to concern himself with inflicting such punishment, as the lord king specially reserves this matter to himself because resisters of this kind are deemed to be disturbers of his peace and of his realm.

**40.** When anyone alienates his wife's right, it is agreed that the suit of the woman or her heir shall not henceforth be delayed after the husband's death by the minority of the heir who ought to warrant; instead, the buyer, who ought not to have been ignorant that he was buying another's right, shall wait to have his warranty until his warrantor comes of age.

**41.** The lord king has ordained that if abbots, priors, wardens of hospitals and of other religious houses founded by him or by his progenitors alienate henceforth tenements given to those houses by him or by his progenitors, those tenements shall be taken into the hands of the lord king and held at his will and the buyer lose his recovery both of the tenements and of the money he paid. If, on the other hand, the houses were founded by earls, barons or others, he by whom or by whose ancestors a tenement so alienated was given shall, for tenements so alienated, have a writ to recover the tenement in demesne in this form: "Command the abbot of so-and-so to render to B. justly etc. such-and-such tenement which was given by the aforesaid B. or his ancestors in frankalmoin to that house and which ought to revert to the said B. because of the alienation the said abbot has made of the said tenement contrary to the form of the said gift as he says." Likewise for a tenement given for maintaining a chantry, or lights in some church or chapel or to provide other alms, if, given on such condition, it is alienated. But if a tenement so given for a chantry, for lights, for feeding the poor or other good deed is perhaps not alienated but such alms withheld over a period of two years, an action shall lie for the donor or his heir to claim in demesne the tenement so given, as is ordained in the statute of Gloucester[1] to tenements demised at a service or rent of a quarter or more of the value of the tenement.

**42.** Concerning the lord king's marshals at fee, chamberlains, doorkeepers in the eyres of the justices and sergeant-vergers before the justices at Westminster who have the office in fee who exact more by reason of their fee than they used to exact, as many complain on the authority of those who have seen and known the ways of the court for a long time, the lord king has had enquiry made what standing the aforesaid officers at fee used to have in times past. And as a result of the enquiries he has ordained and commanded that a marshal at fee who as an innovation exacts a palfrey from earls and barons and orders holding by a part of a barony when they have done homage and another palfrey, notwithstanding, when they are knighted, and as an innovation exacts a palfrey from some from whom he ought not to have one, shall be content

1 Statute of Gloucester, chapter 4. See also chapter 21 of the present statute.

with one palfrey from every earl and baron holding a whole barony or the value of it in money which of old he used to receive by custom, so that if he takes the palfrey or its value in money in the way said when he does homage, he shall take nothing when he is knighted, and if it should be that he takes nothing at the homage, he shall take it at the knighting. As to abbots and priors holding a whole barony, when they have done homage or fealty for their baronies, he shall take a palfrey or its value in money, as aforesaid. The same to be done in the case of archbishops and bishops. From those, on the other hand, who hold a part of a barony, whether they are religious or seculars, he shall take proportionately to the part they hold of the barony. From religious who hold in frankalmoin and not by barony or part of a barony, a marshal shall henceforth exact nothing. And the lord king has granted that a marshal of his at fee shall not be precluded by this statute from demanding more if hereafter he can show that he has a right to demand more. The lord king's chamberlains shall in future receive from archbishops, bishops, abbots, priors and other ecclesiastics, earls and barons, who hold a whole barony, a reasonable fine when they do homage or fealty for the barony. And they shall accept a reasonable fine proportionate to what they hold, if they hold part of a barony. Other abbots, priors, religious and seculars, however, who do not hold by barony or part of a barony, shall not be bound to make fine as is said of those who hold by barony or part of a barony, but instead a chamberlain shall be content with the outer garment—or with its value in money, which is said more for the benefit of the religious than for seculars because it is more seemly for religious to make fine for their outer garment than to be uncovered.

**43.** It shall be prohibited henceforth for Hospitallers and Templars to implead anyone in future before the conservators of their privileges on any matter cognizance of which belongs to the king's court, and if they do they shall after restoring damages to the injured party be severely punished as regards the lord king. The lord king prohibits too the conservators of those same privileges from in future granting citations at the instance of Hospitallers or Templars or other privileged persons before it is expressly stated on what matter the citation ought to be made. And if such conservators see that the citation is requested over some matter cognizance of which belongs to the king's court, they shall neither make the citation nor treat it as valid. And if they do otherwise they shall be answerable to the injured party for damages and be nonetheless severely punished as regards the lord king. And because such privileged persons procure sub-priors, precentors, sacrists and men of religion as conservators because they have nothing from which they can satisfy the injured parties or the lord king and are readier to offend the lord king's dignity than are their superiors, on whom a penalty can be inflicted through their temporalities, let the superiors of such obedientiaries take care in future not to allow them to assume to themselves jurisdiction to the prejudice of the lord king and his crown. And if they do, the superiors shall be answerable for what they do, as if it were their own doing.

**44.** With regard to doorkeepers in the eyres and vergers before the justices of the bench, it is ordained that for every assize and jury which they keep they shall take fourpence only, for chirographs nothing. From those who recover their claims by default, surrender, or in any other way by judgment without an assize and jury, from those who leave without a day through the default of the plaintiff or demandant, they shall take nothing. And if anyone recovers his claim against more than one person by the one writ and by verdict of an assize or jury, they shall be content with fourpence only. They shall similarly be content with fourpence only if several named in the one writ recover by verdict of an assize or jury. From those who do homage in the bench they shall be content with the outer garment. For Grand Assizes, attaints, juries and trial by battle they shall take twelve pence only. From those called before justices to prosecute or defend their plea they shall take nothing for going in or out. At the pleas of the crown only twelve-pence shall be taken from each jury of twelve; from each prisoner released only fourpence taken; from each person whose peace is proclaimed only twelve-pence taken. From finders, from neighbors and from others who are attached, from townships, from the four men and the reeve, from tithingmen, nothing shall be taken. As regards chirographers and the making of chirographs, it is ordained that they are to be content with four shillings. As for clerks writing original and judicial writs, it is ordained that for a writ they are to be content with a penny. And the lord king enjoins every one of his justices on the fealty and oath by which they are bound to him that if such officials contravene in any way this statute and complaint reaches them, they are to inflict on them moderate punishment, and if they offend a second time, they shall inflict on them a greater punishment, with which they shall be punished as they deserve. And if they offend a third time, and are convicted of this, they shall, if they are officers at fee, lose their fee; if [they are] other than this, they shall be dismissed from the king's court and not return without the special order or grace of the king himself.

**45.** Because on matters which are recorded before the chancellor of the lord king and justices of his who have record, and which are enrolled on their rolls, proceedings on a plea ought not to be by way of summons, attachment, essoin, view of land, and other necessary formalities of a court, as has been the customary practice with contracts and covenants made out of court, the practice in future shall be that those things which are found enrolled before those who have record, or are contained in fines, whether they are contracts, covenants, bonds, acknowledgements of services or customs, or whatever else is enrolled which the lord king's court can give authority to without breach of law and custom, shall henceforth have such force that it shall not hereafter be necessary to plead concerning them. Instead, when the plaintiff comes to the lord king's court he shall, if the recognition or fine is recent, that is to say drawn up in writing within the year, have forthwith a writ of execution of the recognition made. And if perchance the recognition was made or the fine levied longer ago than that, the sheriff shall be commanded to inform the party complained of that he is to appear on a certain day to show if he knows any reason why such things as are enrolled or are contained in the fine ought not to be put into execution. And if he does not come on that day, or comes perhaps but cannot give any reason why execution should not take place, the sheriff shall be commanded to have what is enrolled or is contained in the fine carried out. The same instructions shall be given to the ordinary if the case concerns him, subject however to what has been said above [in chapter 9] about a mesne tenant who is bound by recognizance or a judgment to acquit being observed.

**46.** Whereas in a statute published at Merton [chapter 4] it was granted that lords of wastes, woods and pastures could approve those wastes, woods and pastures, notwithstanding the opposition of their tenants, provided that those tenants have pasture adequate to their tenements and free access and egress to it, yet because no mention was made of relations between neighbor and neighbor many lords of wastes, woods and pastures have been hindered up to now by the opposition of neighbors with pasture enough, and because outsider tenants have no greater right of commoning in the waste or pasture of any lord than the lord's own tenants, it is henceforth ordained that the statute provided at Merton between lord and tenants shall in the future have effect between lords of wastes, woods and pastures and neighbors, so that such lords of wastes, woods or pastures can, saving sufficient pasture for their men and neighbors, approve the residue. And this shall be observed in the case of those who claim pasture as appurtenant to their tenements. But if anyone claims common by special feoffment or grant for a certain number of beasts or in any way other than he ought to have of common right, since covenant qualifies the law he shall have the recovery he is entitled to by the form of the grant made to him. No one shall be harassed henceforth by assize of *novel disseisin* for common of pasture because of a windmill, a sheepfold, a cattle pasture, the necessary enlargement of a court or curtilage. And as it sometimes happens that someone with a right to approve raises a bank of hedge and others, at night or some other time when they believe their action will not be noticed, level the bank or the hedge to the ground, and it cannot be ascertained by verdict of assize or jury who leveled it, nor will men of the neighboring vills indict those guilty of such deed, let the vills immediately adjoining be distrained to restore the bank or hedge at their own expense and to pay damages. And when anyone without right of commoning usurps commons while heirs are under age, or a married woman is under the power of living husbands, or while the pasture is in the hands of tenants in dower, by the law of England, or otherwise for term of life or years or in fee-tail, and has used the pasture for a long time, many are of the opinion that pastures of this sort ought to be said to be appurtenant to the free tenement and that the possessor of such ought to have action by a writ of *novel disseisin* if he is deforced of such pasture; but from now on it must be held that those acquiring entry of it in the period within which the writ of *mort d'ancestor* runs shall not have recovery of it by writ of *novel disseisin* if they are deforced, if they had not common before.

**47.** It is provided also that the waters of the Humber, Ouse, Trent, Don, Aire, Derwent, Wharfe, Nidd, Ure, Swale, Tees and all other waters in which salmon are caught shall be put in defense as regards the taking of salmon from the Nativity of the Blessed Mary [8 September] to St Martin's day [11 November]; and likewise that young salmon shall not be caught or destroyed by nets or by other engines at millponds from the middle of April to the Nativity of St John the Baptist [24 June]. And in the parts where such rivers are, let there be appointed conservators of this statute who, sworn to this, shall view frequently and enquire as to offenders. For the first offense they are to be punished by the burning of nets and engines. If they offend again, they shall be punished by imprisonment for a quarter of a year. If again they offend, they shall be punished by imprisonment for a whole year. And as the offense increases, so shall the penalty inflicted increase.

**48.** As to view of land, it is ordained and established that, in future, view shall not be granted except in cases where a view is necessary. Thus if someone loses a tenement by default, then moves another writ to demand the same tenement, or when someone by a dilatory exception abates a writ after the view of the land (on account, for instance, of non-tenure or misnomer of the vill or such like), if he moves another writ, in this case and in the previous one view shall not henceforth be granted, provided he had it in the earlier writs. In writs of dower when dower is demanded of a tenement which the woman's husband alienated to a tenant or the tenant's ancestor, view nevertheless shall not henceforth be granted to the tenant, since the tenant ought not to be ignorant of what it was the woman's husband alienated to him or his ancestor although the husband did not die seised. Likewise in a writ of entry abated because the demandant misnamed the entry, if the demandant moves another writ of entry, the tenant if he had view in the first writ shall not have it in the second. In all writs, too, by which tenements are demanded by reason of a demise which the demandant or his ancestor made to the tenant (but not to his ancestor), as something he demised to him while he was under age, not in his right mind, in prison, and the like, view henceforth shall not lie; but if the demise was made to the ancestor of the tenant, view shall lie henceforth as it did before.

**49.** The chancellor, the treasurer, a justice, or anyone of the king's council; a clerk of the chancery, of the exchequer, of a justice or other minister; or anyone of the king's household, clerk or lay, cannot accept a church or the advowson of a church, land, tenement or fee, by gift or by purchase, or at farm, or by champerty, or in any other way, so long as the thing is in plea before us or before any of our ministers; nor may any monetary reward be taken in connection with it. And he who does this, whether by himself or through another, or commits any fraud with regard to it, shall be punished at the king's pleasure, as well he who gains by it as he who does it.

**50.** All the aforesaid statutes shall come into effect next Michaelmas: consequently for any offenses against any of them committed before that feast the punishment prescribed in them for offenders shall not be inflicted. Where statutes provided to afford remedies where the law is deficient are concerned, however, suitors shall have the writs provided in their case, in order that they may no longer come to court and depart without a hope of remedy, but these shall not be pleaded until after the aforesaid Michaelmas.

## The Statute of Westminster III

This statute addresses the loss of control over their lands being experienced by demesne lords whose tenants were subinfeudating their holdings to tenants of their own, creating that chain of dependent land tenures commonly referred to as bastard feudalism. The effects of *Quia Emptores* were considerable over time and far-reaching effects are ascribed to its provisions. The most obvious consequence was the increase in escheats of tenements to lords when free-holding families died out, with the monarchy benefitting most of all over time. Maitland contended that "the one person who had all to gain and nothing to lose by the new law was the king,"[1] but Plucknett showed that, since the problem of subinfeudation was exactly the same for a major as for a minor lord, *Quia Emptores*' "policy is to protect all lords and to preserve the fruits of all lordships."[2] Perhaps more importantly, the statute recognizes a fundamental change that has been taking place in land tenure: real property is being sold for money. As Milsom points out, in *Quia Emptores* "land has been reduced to a form of property, and the parties to the tenurial transaction have been reversed. The tenant is now owner of his tenement."[3] What is really at issue is the transference of the original rights and services due to the demesne lord from the original tenant to the new purchaser as a condition of the acquisition, thus preserving the feudal incidents in exchange for which the land had originally been granted. For Plucknett, "it seems fairly clear that *Quia Emptores* slowly dissolved the *nexus* of tenures which constituted a manor, and prevented the replenishment of its freeholders as well as the creation for the future of those onerous duties of suit of court, enforced by distress, which must once have added enormously to the lord's power over his tenants."[4]

---

1 Pollock and Maitland 1898 1, 337n.
2 Plucknett 1949/1962 104.
3 Milsom 1976 112.
4 Plucknett 1949/1962 107.

# The Statute of Westminster III

We take our text from Luders, *Statutes of the Realm*, I, 106. The translation is our own.

Quia emptores terrarum & tenementorum de feodis magnatum & aliorum, in prejudicium eorumdem temporibus retroactis multociens in feodis sunt ingressi, quibus libere tenentes eorumdem magnatum & aliorum terras & tenementa sua vendiderunt, tenenda in feodo sibi & heredibus suis de feoffatoribus suis & non de Capitalibus dominis feodorum, per quod idem Capitales domini eschaetas, maritagia & custodias terrarum & tenementorum de feodis suis existentium sepius amiserunt, quod quidem eisdem magnatibus & aliis dominis quam plurimum durum & difficile videbatur, & similiter in hoc casu exheredacio manifesta: Dominus Rex in parliamento suo apud Westministerium post Pascha anno regni sui decimo octavo, videlicet in quindena sancti Johannis Baptiste, ad instantiam magnatum regni sui, concessit, providit, & statuit, quod de cetero liceat unicuique libero homini terram suam seu tenementum sive partem inde pro voluntate sua vendere; Ita tamen quod feoffatus teneat terram illam seu tenementum de eodem Capitali domino & per eadem servicia & consuetudines, per que feoffator suus illa prius tenuit. Et si partem aliquam earumdem terrarum seu tenementorum suorum alicui vendiderit, feoffatus illam teneat immediate de Capitali domino & oneretur statim de servicio quantum pertinet sive pertinere debet eidem domino pro particula illa, secundum quantitatem terre seu tenementi venditi; Et sic in hoc casu, decidat Capitali domino ipsa pars servicii capienda per manum feoffatoris ex quo feoffatus debet eidem Capitali domino juxta quantitatem terre seu tenementi venditi de particula illa servicii sic debiti esse intendens & respondens. Et sciendum est quod per predictas vendiciones seu empciones terrarum seu tenementorum, seu partis alicuius eorumdem, nullo modo possunt terre seu tenementa illa, in parte vel in toto, ad manum mortuam devenire, arte vel ingenio contra formam statuti super hoc dudum editi. Et sciendum est quod istud statutum locum tenet de terris venditis tenendis in feodo simpliciter tantum. Et quod se extendit

ad tempus futurum; Et incipiet locum tenere ad Festum sancti Andree proximo futuro.

### Translation

Because buyers of lands and tenements from the fees of magnates and others, to their prejudice, have in times past often entered into fees which free men holding lands and their own tenements of those same magnates and others have sold for the purpose of keeping them in fee to themselves and their heirs for feoffors and not for the fees' chief lords, by which the same chief lords have often lost escheats, marriage fees, and wardships of the lands and tenements pertaining to their fees, which to those same magnates and other lords very often seemed hard and difficult and like in this case to manifest disinheritance, the lord king in his parliament at Westminster following Easter, in the year of his reign the eighteenth and on the quindene of Saint John the Baptist, at the instance of his realm's magnates, granted, provided, and established that henceforth it shall be permitted to each free man to sell his own land or tenement or a part thereof per his will, so that, however, the feoffee shall hold that land or tenement from the chief lord by the same services and customs by which his feoffor first held them. And if he sells some part of their lands and tenements to someone, the one who has been feoffed shall hold it directly from the chief lord and be burdened immediately of as much service which pertains or ought to pertain to that same chief lord for that portion according to the quantity of the land or tenement sold, and so in this case let that part of the service that should be exacted fall to the chief lord through the hand of the feoffor, through whom the feoffee is obligated to be submissive and answerable to the same chief lord for that portion of the services thus owed according to the quantity of the land or tenement sold. And let it be understood that by the aforesaid sales or purchases of lands or tenements, or some part of them, in no manner can those lands or tenements, in part or in whole, come to the dead hand, by craft or scheme, against the form of the statute about this lately given out.[1] And

1 That is, the Statute of Mortmain.

let it be understood that this statute is applicable only for lands sold for holding in fee simple. And that it extends to time coming; and let it begin to be applicable at the feast of St. Andrew in the near future.

## The Statute of Quo Warranto

The question of certifying titles to various kinds of franchises had long occupied the rulers of England and their fiscal administrators, according to Plucknett since at least the Inquest of Sheriffs in 1170.[1] But it was the inquest of 1274-5 that required those making a claim to a franchise to return a writ of *quo warranto* clarifying "by what title" they professed to enjoy their holdings. This writ, relatively unused before but available, quickly created a large number of cases that lingered unsettled due to judicial uncertainty about their resolution. The statute is accordingly an attempt to clear a backlog in the courts by clarifying what constitutes a valid claim. In effect, it says that a clear claim will be founded upon a royal charter, which will be granted by the king upon a royal review of the plaintiff's suit. Plucknett's discussion[2] is essential reading. We include only the A text, ignoring the two summarizing restatements, B(1) and B(2), in Latin and French respectively. We have as well accepted without comment interlinear additions to the parliament roll.

We take our text from Luders, *Statutes of the Realm*, I, 107. The translation is our own.

Quia brevia de quo Waranto & etiam judicia super placitis eorumdem brevium reddenda diutinam ceperunt dilationem, eo quod Justicii in judiciis illis reddende de voluntate domini Regis non fuerunt hucusque certiorati; Idem dominus Rex ad parliamentum suum post Pascha apud Westministerium anno regni sui decimo octavo de gratia sua speciali, & etiam propter affectionem, quam habet erga prelatos, Comites, Barones & ceteros de regno suo, concessit quod omnes de regno suo quicunque fuerint, tam viri religiosi quam alii, qui per bonam inquisitionem patrie

1 Plucknett 1949/1962 35.
2 Ibid. 35-50.

aut alio modo sufficienti verificare poterint, quod ipsi & eorum antecessores, vel predecessores usi fuerunt libertatibus quibuscunque, de quibus per brevia predicata fuerunt implacitati, ante tempus Regis Ricardi consanguinei sui aut toto tempore suo, & hucusque sine interrruptione continuarunt, et ita quod libertatibus illis non sint abusi, quod partes adjornentur ulterius coram eisdem Justiciis usque certum diem & rationabilem, infra quem dominum Regem adire possint cum recordo Justiciorum sub sigillo suo signato, & redire; & dominus Rex statum eorum affirmabit per literas suas. Et illi qui non poterint seisinam antecessorum seu predecessorum suorum verificare, eodem modo, quo predictum est, deducantur & judicentur secundum legem communem; Et illi, qui habent cartas regales, secundum cartas illas & earumdem plenitudinem judicentur. Preterea dominus Rex de gratia sua speciali concessit quod omnia judicia, que reddita sunt in placitis de quo quaranto, per Justicios suos apud Westministerium post Pascha predictum, & pro ipso domino Rege, si partes, que amiserunt, ad ipsum dominum Regem revenire voluerint, tale habebunt remedium de gratia domini Regis sicut superius est concessum. Concessit etiam idem dominus Rex, ad parcandem misis & expensis populi de regno suo, quod placita de quo Waranto de cetero placitentur & terminentur in Itineribus Justiciis, & quod placita adhuc coram ipsos pendentia de quo Waranto readjornentur in singulis Comitatibus suis usque adventum Justiciorum in partibus illis, &c. Et quod interim post adjornacionem sic factam remaneant sine die.

### Translation

Because writs of *quo warranto* and also judgments rendered upon pleas of the same writs have suffered long delay, because justices in returning those judgments have not hitherto been certain of the lord king's will, the same lord king at his parliament after Easter at Westminster in the year of his reign the eighteenth, by his special grace and also because of the affection that he has toward his prelates, earls, barons and others of his realm, has granted that all of his realm whoever they are, as well men of religion as others, who can verify, by a good inquest of the community or by some other sufficient manner, that they and their ancestors or predecessors have enjoyed whatsoever liberties of which they have been impleaded by the aforesaid writs, before the time of king Richard his kinsman or in all his time, and have continued[1] hitherto without interruption, and so that they have not abused these liberties, that the parties shall be adjourned further until a certain and reasonable day before their same justices, within which time they can go to the lord king with the record of the justices beneath their signed seal, and return, and the lord king will affirm their estate by his letters. And those who cannot verify the seisin of their ancestors or predecessors in the same way as is aforesaid shall be brought to trial and judged according to the common law, and those who have royal charters, let them be judged according to those charters and their fullness. In addition, the lord king of his special grace has granted that all judgments that are returned in pleas of *quo warranto* by his justices at Westminster after the Easter aforesaid and for our lord king himself, if the parties who have lost should wish to come again to the same lord king, they will have such remedy by the lord king's grace as is granted above. The same lord king has also granted, in order to save the people of his realm losses and expenditures, that pleas of *quo waranto* from henceforth shall be pleaded and determined by the justices in eyre, and that pleas of *quo warranto* still pending before them shall be readjourned in every county until the arrival of the justices in those parts, etc. And that in the meantime after adjournment thus made let them remain *sine die*.[2]

1 Rothwell 1975 3, 464 emends *continuarunt* to *continuent*, but that seems to us unnecessary.

2 Without a day having been established for re-adjournment.

# TREATISES

## Leges Henrici Primi

The *Leges Henrici Primi*, traditionally taken to be an account of the state of the law in the time of Henry I rather than an account of his legislation, is one of the oldest surviving attempts to present a comprehensive view of the state of the law in England and, while it is generally judged harshly for its insufficiencies of organization and content, our knowledge of legal developments would be severely impaired without it. It is likely the second volume of the so-called *Quadripartitus*, which, as its title suggests, was intended as a four-part work that was, however, not completed or has not survived intact. More recently, the *Leges* has been considered an example of "visionary literature," a conscious forgery that represents "what the king should have promulgated" but didn't.[1]

The author describes the three systems of law operative in the land, the laws of Wessex, Mercia, and the Danelaw, as well as the procedural differences in the shire, hundredal, borough, siegnorial, and royal courts. He is not sanguine about the ability of litigants to get a fair hearing in any of them and his conclusion that legal proceedings are as uncertain as a game of dice speaks volumes about the state of affairs in his world. He does, however, acknowledge the superiority of the royal court as a bastion of uniformity and in so doing anticipates the general course that legal development will take under subsequent monarchs. Baker sees this recognition as "more significant in retrospect than a contemporary would have understood," for the price of royal justice in Henry I's England was beyond the reach of most. Yet, "the regularity of procedure which characterized the common law was already discernible" even if "royal justice was not yet the common property of all subjects."[2] Thc *Leges Henrici Primi* is often compared, to its

1 See Hanna 2005 70.
2 Baker 2002 13.

disadvantage, with *Glanvill*, which is seen as a model of focus and organization.

Text in Downer, *Leges Henrici Primi*, which contains the most extensive treatment of the text to date. The translation is our own except as otherwise indicated. We omit chapter two, which reproduces the London Charter, and offer selections deemed to be of particular interest for subsequent developments in the law. We have included all ninety-four chapter headings so that the reader can see the scope of the whole as well as its organizational inadequacies.

**Coke's *Institutes of the Lawes***

## De Libertate Ecclesie et Totius Anglie Observanda Leges Henrici.

***Proemium 1***: Hec sunt denique beata pacis ac libertatis exoptate gaudia quibus toti regno suo gloriosus cesar Henricus in diuinis legibus et secularibus institutis, scriptis et bonorum operum exhibitionibus irradiat moderatus prudens iustus fortis.

***Proemium 2***: Quem Deus felicibus auspiciis et salutari quesumus corporis et anime prosperitate cum coniuge sua inclita Matilde secunda et eorum liberis longis seculorum seculis et eterna pace gentis nostre faciat imperare.

**C. 1: Epistola eiusdem omnibus fidelibus suis.**

1, 1: Henricus Dei gratia Rex Anglorum omnibus Baronibus et fidelibus suis Francis et Anglicis salutem. Sciatis me Dei misericordia et communi consilio et assensu Baronum regni Anglie . . . optimatibus totius regni Anglie. Apud Westmonasterium quando coronatus fui.

**C. 2: The London Charter.**[1]

**C. 3: De causarum pertractatione et diffinitione (uel descriptione).**

3, 1: Omnes cause uera consilii ratione discutiende sunt a iudicibus et sine personarum acceptatione cum equalitate discernende uel si facultas admiserit potius pace honestande.

3, 1a: Et licet sanum ubique consilium in sue maiestatis luce uiguerit, pro modo tamen concausantium informari lepida moralitate non nocuit.

3, 2: Et consilium forsitan dici poterit quicquid honestum et utile propositum quoquo modo promouerit.

**C. 4: De generibus causarum.**

1 Henry's charter for the city is interpolated into the text during the reign of John. See Hanna 2005 56.

## The Laws of Henry the First for Regarding the Liberty of the Church and All of England.

**Proemium 1**: Here accordingly are the desired blessed jewels of peace and liberty with which the most glorious Emperor Henry, moderate, prudent, just, brave, illuminates all his realm in divine laws and secular ordinances, writings, and displays of good works.

**Proemium 2**: We ask that God might let him rule beneath happy auspices and healthy of body, and in prosperous life with his renowned spouse Matilda the Second and their children, forever and ever in the eternal peace of our people.

**C. 1: A letter of the same to all his faithful subjects.**

1,1: Henry, by the grace of God King of the English, to all his barons and faithful French and English subjects, greetings. Know me [to be king] by God's mercy and by the counsel of the commons and the assent of the barons of the realm of England . . . [witnesses] . . ., by the very best people of all the realm of England. At Westminster when I was crowned.

**C. 2: The Charter of London.**

**C. 3: The handling of causes and the specification (or the indictment).**

3, 1: All causes should be determined by the judges with a true reckoning of counsel and decided with fairness without respect of persons or, if practice permits, preferably graced with concord.

3, 1a: And although sound counsel everywhere has flourished in his majesty's light, nevertheless it has done no harm for the manner of the litigants to be instructed by gracious virtue.

3, 2: And perhaps worthy counsel can be pronounced and a useful proposition advanced in every way.

**C. 4: The kinds of causes.**

4, 1: Genera causarum tria sunt: deliberatiuum de faciendo et non faciendo, demonstratiuum de laude uel uituperio, iudicale de pena uel merito.

4, 1a: Status causarum duo sunt: rationalis et legalis.

4, 2: Partes quatuor: exordium provocans, narratio explicans, argumentum asserens, conclusio compl[ect]ens.

4, 3: Species quinque: honestum, commendatorium uel persuasorium; admirabile, alienatum; humile, neglectum; anceps, dubium uel promiscuum; obscurum, difficile uel tardum.

4, 3a: [Institutio equitatis duplex est]: in lege scripta, in moribus uel communi usu pro lege suscepto.

4, 4: Omne autem ius aut naturale cognatorum est aut morale extraneorum aut legale ciuium.

4, 5: Set siue lex agenda precipiat, leuia permittat, hort[e]tur maxima, uitanda prohibeat, debet esse manifesta, iusta, honesta, possibilis, in omni conditione, professione et ordine, in omni genere et statu causarum, in omni controuersia simplici uel composita, in omni iure naturali uel consuetudinis, in omni [loco] contingenti uel remoto, loco tempori persone conueniens, nullo priuato commodo precipue deseruiens, ueritatis et iustitie, non miserum peccunie querens augmentum.

4, 6: Purum uero sit et perspicua breuitate decorum perorantis elogium, inuentione, dispositione, elocutione, memoria, pronuntiatione, persuasione, naturali ingenio, doctrina sciente et assiduo usu peritum in omni d[ic]endi genere.

4, 7: Qui magna salutari grauitate pero[r]et, parua subtili lenitate deducat, media temperata moderatione delectet.

4, 7a: Nec longioribus yperbatis sensa confundat nec uerbis inanibus ambages interserat.

4, 1: There are three kinds of causes: deliberative, for what ought to be done and not done; demonstrative, for praise or disparagement; judicial, for punishment or reward.

4, 1a: There are two states of causes: rational and legal.

4, 2: There are four parts of causes: a provocative *exordium*, an explanatory narrative, an assertive argument, a summarizing conclusion.

4, 3: There are five kinds of causes: straightforward (commendatory or persuasive), astonishing (to make strange), lowly (to render insignificant), ambiguous (dubious or indiscriminate), obscure (difficult or limping).

4, 3a: Equity's establishment is twofold: in written law, [and] in customs or common usage taken as law.

4, 4: Moreover, all *ius* is either natural for kindred, moral for outsiders, or statutory for citizens.

4, 5: But whether the law orders what should be done, permits trivialities, exhorts what is most important, or bans those things that should be avoided, it ought to be manifest, just, open, [and] possible, in every condition of life, profession and order, in every kind and state of causes, in every controversy simple or complex, in all *ius* natural or customary, in every place near and far, agreeable as to time, place, [and] person, above all doing service to no private benefit, seeking not wretched wealth but the increase of truth and justice.

4, 6: Let the plea of advocacy be pure and decorous in perspicacious brevity, expert in all manner of speaking by invention, arrangement, elocution, memory, articulation, persuasion, native ingenuity, doctrinal knowledge, and assiduous usage.

4, 7: Who would entreat great matters with salutary gravity, let him bring forth little matters with subtle gentleness and with temperate moderation make pleasing the matters in between.

4, 7a: Let him not confound sense with lengthy hyperboles nor introduce ambiguities by means of inane words.

4, 7b: Qui directa locutione fatigatum congrua scematum iunctura reficiat.

4, 8: Et si quid in dicendis aptum est et ualidum finis sentiat et principium; reliquum si dissimulari uel preteriri nequeat, breuiter sit et transcursim medietatibus interiectum.

**C. 5: De causarum proprietatibus.**

5, 1: In causis omnibus ecclesiasticis et secularibus legaliter et ordine pertractandis, alii sunt accusatores alii defensores alii testes alii iudices in omni discussione probitatis ydonei nullaque simul exactione permixti.

5, 1a: Deinde causarum qualitas sincera perscrutatione pensanda et accusantium intentio, testium modus et iudicum electio.

5, 2: Ne peregrina sint iudicia uel a non suo iudice uel loco uel tempore celebrata.

5, 2a: Nec in re dubia uel absente accusato dicta sit sententia.

5, 3: Notandumque per omnia si accusatus indutias competentes et respondendi uel defendendi licentiam legittimam habuerit, ne disseisiatus uel implegiatus uel illegiatus uel surreptione aliqua circumuentus aut fraude iudicetur.

5, 5: Iudices sane non debent esse nisi quos impetitus elegerit.

5, 28b: Reum non facit nisi mens rea.

**C. 6: De tripartitione regni Anglie in diuersitate legum comitatuum uel prouinciarum.**

6, 1: Regnum Anglie triphariam diuiditur, in Westsexiam et Mircenos et Danorum prouinciam.

6, 1a: Habet archiepiscopatus duos, episcopatus multos (xv), comitatus xxxii.

4, 7b: Let him refresh a tired contrivance with straight talk in a congruent arrangement.

4, 8: And if something in the matters being presented is apt and valid, let the end and the beginning remark [it]; if the rest cannot be skipped over or let pass, let it be briefly and cursorily inserted in intermediate places.

**C. 5: The properties of causes.**

5, 1: In all ecclesiastical and secular causes that should be tried legally and orderly, some men are plaintiffs, some defendants, some witnesses, and others in every investigation judges of suitable probity not embroiled at the same time in any accusation.

5, 1a: Then the real nature of the causes, the intention of the plaintiffs, the handling of witnesses, and the selection of the judges should be considered with thoughtful scrutiny.

5, 2: Let judgments not be by a stranger or [rendered] by a judge or in a place or at a time not one's own.

5, 2a: Nor should an opinion be given in a dubious matter or in the absence of the accused.

5, 3: And above all it should be noted if the defendant has had adequate stays in the proceedings and proper license to answer and defend, lest having been disseised or forced to give sureties, or outlawed or tricked by some deceit or fraud, he is judged.

5, 5: Judges, to be sure, should be only those whom the accused has chosen.

5, 28b: One does not do a guilty thing without a guilty mind.

**C. 6: The tripartite division of the realm of England in the diversity of the laws of the counties and provinces.**

6, 1: The tripartite realm of England is divided into Wessex and Mercia and the province of the Danelaw.

6, 1a: It has two archbishoprics, many bishoprics (15), thirty-two counties.

6, 1b: Ipsi uero comitatus in centurias et sipessocna distinguntur, centurie uel hundreta in decanias uel decimas et dominorum plegios.

6, 2: Legis etiam Anglice trina est partitio ad superiorem modum, alia enim Westsexie, alia Mircena, alia Denelaga est.

6, 2a: Preter hoc tremendum regie maiestatis titulamus imperium quod preesse iugiter legibus ac salubriter frequentamus aduertendum.

6, 3: In multis autem different, set in multis conueniunt.

6, 3a: Ipsorum etiam iura comitatuum per prouincias plerumque dissentiunt sicut uidelicet cupiditas et maligna professorum detestanda studia grauiora nocendi genera legalibus statibus adiecerunt.

6, 4: Tanta quippe rerum peruersitas et malorum affluentia est ut definita legis ueritas uel stabilis medicine prouidentia raro possit inveniri, sed ad maiorem omnium confusionem nouus inplacitationis modus exquiritur, noua nocendi fraus inuenitur, tanquam parum noceat quicquid ante fuerit, et pluris esse iudicetur qui pluribus plus nocuerit.

6, 6: Tot denique sunt et tantis occupata sollicitudinibus, tot circumductionibus inuoluta sunt infortunia seculorum ut uitande potius uideantur exactiones et incerta penitus alea placitorum.

**C. 7: De generalibus placitis comitatuum, quomodo uel quando fieri debeant.**

6, 1b: The counties themselves are separated into centuries and sipessocna,[1] centuries, or hundreds, [are divided] into decanates, or tithings, and the frankpledges[2] of lords.

6, 2: The division of English law is also tripartite in the above manner, one for Wessex, another for Mercia, and the other is the Danelaw.

6, 2a: Beyond this we designate the formidable imperium of the royal majesty, which we emphasize has been perceived to be perpetually and beneficially at the head of the laws.

6, 3: They [the laws] differ in many things, but in many they agree.

6, 3a: Also, the law of the counties themselves disagrees for the most part throughout the provinces, just as the greed and the wicked detestable practices of its practitioners have suggested to the legal ranks graver ways of doing harm.

6, 4: So great is the perversity of matters and the abundance of evil men that the law's measured truth or the forethought of a firm remedy can rarely be found, but to the greater confusion of all a new way of pleading is sought out, a new fraud for inflicting harm is discovered, as if whatever went before didn't do enough damage, and he is judged the greater who does the most harm to more people.

6, 6: And accordingly the unwished misfortunes of worldly affairs are beset by so many cares, so many deceits, that the painfully uncertain dice of pleadings[3] seem rather exactions and penalties that have to be avoided.

**C, 7: The general pleadings of the counties, how and when they are obliged to be held.**

1 Hundreds obligated to furnish a ship.

2 Considered as a manorial tithing.

3 Baker 2002 13 translates "the utterly uncertain dice of pleas."

7, 1: Sicut antiqua fuerat institutione formatum, salutari regis imperio uera nuper est recordatione firmatum, generalia comitatuum placita certis locis et uicibus et diffinito tempore per singulas prouincias Anglie conuenire debere, nec ullis ultra fatigationibus agitari nisi propria regis necessitas uel commune regni commodum sepius adiciat.

7, 2: Intersint autem episcopi, comites, uicedomini, uicarii, centenarii, aldermanni, prefecti, prepositi, barones, uauasores, tungreuii et ceteri terrarum domini, diligenter intendentes ne malorum inpunitas aut grauionum prauitas uel iudicum subuersio solita miseros laceratione conficiant.

7, 3: Agantur itaque primo debita uere christianitatis iura, secondo regis placita, postremo cause singulorum dignis satisfactionibus expleantur.

7, 3a: Et quoscumque scyregemot discordantes inueniet uel amore congreget uel sequestret iudicio.

7, 4: Debet autem scyregemot et burgemot bis, hundreta uel wapentagia duodecies in anno congregari, et septem diebus antea submoneri, nisi publicum commodum uel efficientie regis dominica necessitas terminum preueniat.

7, 5: Et si aliquid in hundretis agendorum penuria iudicum uel casu aliquo transferendum sit in duos uel tres uel amplius hundredos, respectetur iusto fine claudendum.

7, 6: Et si quisquam uiolenta recti destitutione uel detentione in hundretis uel congruis agendorum locis causam suam ita turbauerit ut ad comitatus audientiam pertrahatur, perdat eam et de cetero componat sicut rectum sit.

7, 7: Si quis baronum regis uel aliorum comitatui secundum legem interfuerit, totam terram quam illic in dominio suo habet acquietare poterit.

7, 1: Just as it was fashioned in ancient law, recently by the king's salutary imperium it has been affirmed for the record that the general pleadings of the counties are obliged to meet in fixed places and terms and at definite times throughout the individual counties of England, nor to be disturbed beyond that by further meetings unless royal necessity or the convenience of the realm indicates more often.

7, 2: And the bishops, earls, sheriffs, deputies, hundred-men, aldermen, stewards, reeves, barons, vavasours, town reeves, and other lords of lands, shall be present, diligently making sure lest the impunity or grave depravity of evil men or the subversion of judges confound the wretched in their accustomed torment.

7, 3: And so the obligatory rights of Christianity shall be acted upon first, secondly the pleas of the crown, and finally the causes of individuals shall be discharged with satisfactory amends.

7, 3a: And whomsoever the shire session should find discordant, it shall bring together in love or let a judgment constrain by sequestration.

7, 4: Moreover, the shire session and town session are obliged to be brought together twice, the hundred or wapentake[1] twelve times per year, and to be summoned seven days before unless the public convenience or a domain requirement of the king's duty precludes the date.

7, 5: And if any of the proceedings in the hundreds, by a lack of judges or some other reason, must be transferred into two or three or more hundreds, they shall be adjourned for settlement by a just determination.

7, 6: And if someone by a violent deprivation or withholding of right in the hundreds or in suitable places of legal processes has so roiled his cause that it must be taken to the county, he shall lose it and finally settle just as it is right.

7, 7: If any of the king's barons or other lords is present in the county court according to law, he may acquit all land which he holds there [i.e. in that county] in his demesne.

---

1 The name for the hundred in the northern and some midlands counties.

7, 7a: Eodem modo est si dapifer eius legitttime fuerit.

7, 7b: Si uterque necessario desit, prepositus et sacerdos et quattuor de melioribus uille assint pro omnibus qui nominatim non erunt ad placitum submoniti.

7, 8: Idem in hundreto decreuimus obseruandum de locis et uicibus et iudicum obseruantiis, de causis singulorum iustis examinationibus audiendis, de domini et dapiferi uel sacerdotis et prepositi et meliorum hominum presentia.

**C. 8: De hundretis tenendis**

8, 1: Speciali tamen plenitudine si opus est, bis in anno conueniant in hundretum suum quicumque liberi tam hur[đ]efest quam folgarii ad dinoscendum scilicet inter cetera si decanie plene sint, uel qui, quomodo, qua ratione recesserint uel superaccreuerint.

8, 1a: Presit autem singulis hominum nouenis decimus et toti simul hundreto unus de melioribus, et uocetur aldremannus, qui Dei leges et hominum iura uigilanti studeat obseruantia promouere.

8, 1b: Quia nil a nullo exigi uel capi debet nisi de iure et ratione per legem terre et iustitiam et per iudicium curie sine dolo, prout statum est maxima consideratione procerum et bonorum predecessorum totius regni et multa aggregatione seruorum Dei et bonorum patrum et sapientum totius monarchie approbatum.

7, 7a: The same holds true if his steward is lawfully present.

7, 7b: If either is absent by necessity, the reeve and priest and four from among the better men of the vill shall be present for all who were summoned by name to the court.

7, 8: We have established that the same [principles] should be observed in the hundred court about places and times and the observances of judges, about hearings for the causes of each individual with just examinations, about the presence of the lord and the steward or the priest and the reeve and the better men.

**C. 8: Holding the hundreds.**

8, 1: If there is need, however, for a special plenary session, twice a year all freemen, hearth holders as well as followers, shall gather in their hundreds, namely for the purpose of determining, among other things, if the tithings are full, or how and for what reason they have shrunk or become too large.

8, 1a: Moreover, let a tithing man preside over the other nine and likewise one of the better men over the whole hundred, and he shall be called alderman who shall take care to promote with vigilant observation the laws of God and the rights of men.

8, 1b: For nothing should be demanded or seized from no one except by right and reason according to the law of the land and justice and the guileless judgment of a court, just as it has been decreed with the greatest consideration by the nobles and their worthy predecessors in the whole realm and approved in many assemblies of God's servants and of the worthy fathers and wise men of the entire monarchy.

8, 2: Communis quippe causa commodi prouida dispensatione statutum est ut a duodecimo etatis sue anno in hundreto sit et decima uel plegio liberali quisquis were uel wite uel iure liberi dignus curat estimari.

**C. 9: De qualitate causarum.**

9, 1: Qualitas causarum multa est, emendabilium et non emendabilium, et que solum pertinent ad ius regium.

9, 1a: Omnes uero cause simplices sunt aut coniuncte et in manifestatione consistunt uel in accusatione.

9, 1b: In compellatione positorum alie per uisum fiunt et auditum, alie per relationem, alie per estimationem, que magis ad uiolentam usurpationem inprobis prelatorum coniecturis inuersantur; que a legittimis causis omnibus et maxime ecclesiasticis submouentur.

9, 4: Et omnis causa terminetur uel hundreto uel comitatu uel halimoto socam habentium uel dominorum curiis uel diuisis parium uel certis agendorum locis adiacens, ne cuilibet irrogatam iniuriam fomenta dilata uel amota multiplicent, ne causarum habitudine uel aliqua recti destitutione iura pertranseant.

9, 4a: Transeunt autem multis modis, alia intrinsecis, alia extrinsecis accidentiis, secundum industriam uel inscitiam concausantium, secundum socam prelatorum quam quidam habent in suo de suis, quidam de suis et extraneis siue in omnibus siue in quibusdam causis.

8, 2: It has indeed been established for the public benefit by a foreseeing ordinance that whoever cares to be thought worthy either of his monetary valuation, or amercement for wite,[1] or the rights of freemen shall from the twelfth year of his age be in a hundred and a tithing or frankpledge.

**C. 9: The nature of causes.**

9, 1: There are many kinds of causes: those which can be settled by compensation and those which cannot be so settled, and those which fall under the king's jurisdiction.

9, 1a: All causes are simple or conjoined and consist in manifestation[2] or in accusation.

9, 1b: In the compilation of charges, some are made through seeing and hearing, others through reporting, [and] others through presumption distorted to flagrant injustice by the improbable conjectures of officials, which should be proscribed in all law-worthy causes, especially the ecclesiastical.

9, 4: And a cause concerning neighbors[3] should be determined either in the hundred or in the county [court], or in the hallmoot [manorial court] of those having soke or of lords, or in the boundary courts of peers, or in the places fixed and appointed for proceedings, lest delayed remedies of justice or removals [to higher courts] should multiply the injury supposedly inflicted upon someone, lest by the conduct of causes or by any deprivation of justice rights might pass away.

---

1 The monetary value of a freeman is established as 100 shillings in the London Charter included as chapter two of the *Leges*. See Pollock and Maitland 1898 2, 514-15, esp. n.4. "Amercement for *wite*" is a redundant restatement of "monetary value," since *wite* is the OE equivalent of amercement.

2 Downer 1972 105, translates "seizure of the accused in the act."

3 So we translate the problematical *adiacens*, which can only modify *causa*. We take the resultant bracketing phrase to refer to property line disputes, generally adjudged in the most immediate courts where the most precise local knowledge of any issue would be presumed most available.

9, 9: Nemo enim stultus aut inprobus debet esse iudex, set optimates quique secundum modum suum qui non personam set opera diiudicent [dividicent?] per legem prouincie.

**C. 10: De iure regis.**

10, 1: Hec sunt iura que rex Anglie solus et super omnes homines habet in terra sua commoda pacis ac securitatis institutione retenta: infractio pacis regie per manum uel breue date; Denagildum; placitum breuium uel preceptorum eius contemptorum; de famulis suis ubicumque occisis uel iniuriatis; infidelitas et proditio; quicumque despectus uel maliloquium de eo; castellatio trium scannorum; utlagaria; furtum mort[e] inpunitum; murdrum; falsaria monete sue; incendium; hamsocna; forestal; fyrđinga; flemenfyrme; premeditates assultus; robaria; stretbreche; presumptio terre uel peccunie regis; thesaurus inuentus; naufragium; maris [la]ga[n]um; uiolentus concubitus; raptus; foreste; releuationes baronum suorum; qui in domo uel familia regis pugnabit; qui in hostico pacem fregerit; qui burgbotam uel brigbotam uel firdfare supersederit; qui excommunicatum uel utlagam habet et tenet; borchbrege; qui in bello campali uel nauali fugerit; iniustum iudicium; defectus iustitie; preuaricatio legis regie.

10, 2: Omnes herestrete omnino regis sunt, et omnia qualstowa, id est occidendorum loca, totaliter regis sunt in soca sua.

10, 3: Et omnibus ordinatis et alienigenis et pauperibus et abiectis debet esse rex pro cong[a]tione et aduocato, si penitus alium non habent.

10, 4: Hec sunt dominica placita regis, nec pertinent uicecomitibus uel apparitoribus uel ministris eius, sine diffinitis prelocutionibus, in firma sua.

**C. 11: De placitis ecclesie pertinentibus ad regem.**

**C. 12: Que placita emendari debeant, que non.**

**C. 13: Que placita mittunt hominem in misericordia regis.**

9, 4a: They perish moreover in many ways, some by intrinsic, others by extrinsic accidents, according to the industry or ignorance of the parties, according to the soke of officials which some have in their own land over their own people, some over their own and outsiders, whether in all causes or in certain ones.

9, 9: No one foolish or evil ought to be a judge, but [only] the best men and those who in accordance with their manner would judge not the person but his deeds according to the law of the locality.

**C. 10. The king's *ius*.**[1]

10, 1: These are the *iura* which the king of England alone and over all men holds in his land, kept for the convenience of peace and the institution of security; breach of the royal peace given by his hand or writ; Danegeld; the plea of contempt of his writs or commands; the death or injury of his household everywhere; disloyalty and treason; any disrespect or slander of him; a fortification of three embankments; outlawry; theft punishable by death; murder [the deed and the fine]; forgery of the purity of his coinage; arson; house breech; stealing from his forests; military activity; the harboring of outlaws; premeditated assault; robbery; street breeches; appropriation of the king's land or money; discovered treasure; shipwreck; jetsam of the sea; rape; abduction; forests; the reliefs of his barons; he who will fight in the king's dwelling or household; he who has broken the peace in the militia; he who avoids borough service or bridge repair or military service; he who holds and keeps an ex-communicant or outlaw; tithing; he who flees in war on land or sea; lack of justice; transgression of the king's law.

10, 2: All highways designated for military use are altogether the king's, and all killing places, that is, the sites of execution, are completely the king's in his soke.

**C. 11: Pleas of the church belonging to the king.**

**C. 12: Which pleas should be amended, which not.**

1 Downer 1972 109, here translates this difficult term as "royal jurisdiction" and its plural (*iura*) as "jurisdictional rights."

13, 1: Hec mittunt hominem in misericordia regis: infractio pacis quam per manum suam dabit alicui: contemptus breuium suorum et quicquid ad propriam eius personam uel mandatorum suorum contumeliatur iniuriam; de famulis suis in ciuitate uel castello uel ubicumque occisis; infidelitas et proditio; despectus de eo; castellatio sine licentia; utlagaria (et qui eam faciet in iure regio sit, et si bocland habeat in manum regis ueniat); furtum probatum et morte dignum.

**C. 14: De releuationibus.**

**C. 15: De Denegildo.**

**C. 16: De pace curie regis.**

16, 1: [T]am longe debet esse pax regis a porta sua ubi residens erit a quatuor partibus loci illius; hoc est iii miliaria et iii quarentene et i[ii] acre latitudine et ix pedes ix palme et ix grana ordei.

16,2: Multus sane respectus esse debet ac multa diligentia ne quis pacem regis infringat, maxime in eius uicinia.

**C. 17: De placito forestarum.**

**C. 18: De lada.**

18, 1: Francigena si compellatur iuret se sexto, Anglicus liber triplici lada plane uel simplici frangenti, uel iudicio neget.

**C. 19: De iustitia regis.**

19, 1: Hec sunt que ad iustitiam uel indulgentiam regis et fiscum proprie censentur cum apendentiis suis (nec sine diffinitis prelocutionibus pertinent uicecomitibus uel prepositis eius in firma sua) ubicumque, a quocumque, in quemcumque fiant, siue terra dominica regis et socna sit, siue sit alterius.

C. 13: Which pleas put a man in the king's mercy.

13, 1: These things put a man in the king's mercy: breach of the peace that he gives anyone by his own hand; contempt of his writs and whatever slanders injuriously his own person or his commands; manslaughter upon his household in town or castle or anywhere; disloyalty and treason; contempt for him; castellation without permission; outlawry (and let who does it be in the king's *ius*, and if he has bookland[1] let it come into the king's hand); manifest theft worthy of death.

**C. 14: Reliefs.**

**C. 15: Danegeld.**

**C. 16: The peace of the king's court.**

16, 1: The king's peace should extend in distance from his gate where he is residing from the four sides of that place; this is three miles and three furlongs and the width of three acres, and nine feet and nine hand palms and nine grains of barley.

16, 2: There ought to be much consideration and much diligence lest anyone infringe the king's peace, especially in his vicinity.

**C. 17: Plea of forests.**

**C. 18: The oath of purgation.**

If a Frenchman is appealed, let him swear as one of six, and let an English freeman deny with a simple triple oath or a single strict oath or by the ordeal.

**C. 19: The king's justice.**

19, 1: These are the things which are consigned to the king's justice or mercy and fisc, with their appurtenances (they do not belong to the sheriffs or their officials in their farms without definite pre-agreements)

1 Land held by written title.

wherever and by and against whomever they are made, whether it be on the king's demesne land and soke[1] or someone else's.

19, 2: Omnium terrarum quas rex in dominio suo habet socnam pariter habet; quarumdam uero terrarum suarum maneria dedit et socnam simul singularem uel communem; quarumdam terrarum maneria dedit, set socnam sibi retinuit.

19, 3: Nec sequitur socna regis data maneria, set magis est ex personis.

**C. 20: De socna**

20, 1: Participantium quoque causarum partim in socna, id est in questione sua, rex habet, partim concedit aliis.

20, 1a: Omnis autem socna simplex est habentibus aut coniuncta, in custodia uero trina principaliter distincta: sub prepositis maneriorum in causis adiacentibus halimotis; sub prelatis hundretorum et burgorum; sub uicecomitibus.

20, 2: Archiepiscopi, episcopi, comites et alie potestates in terris proprii potentatus sui sacam et socnam habent, tol et theam et infongenþeaf (in ceteris uero per emptionem uel cambitionem uel quoquo modo perquisitis, socam et sacam habent in causis communibus et halimotis pertinentibus) super suos et in suo et aliquando super alterius homines presertim si in forisfaciendo retenti uel grauati fuerint, et illic competentem emendationem habeant.

1 Suit of court, i.e. the right to convene court and render legal judgments, or the area within which the right is exercised, in which case the word is typically rendered as "jurisdiction."

19, 2: At the same time the king has soke of all the lands which he has in his demesne; of course he has granted manors and likewise soke either singular or common[1] of some of his lands; of others of his lands he has granted manors but kept the soke to himself.

19, 3: The king's soke does not follow the manorial grant but is rather by arrangement of the parties.

**C. 20: Soke**

20, 1: The king also holds a portion of the shared causes in his soke, that is in his own jurisdiction, [and] a portion he grants to others.

20, 1a: Each soke, moreover, is simplex for those possessing it or shared, in its keeping three distinct authorities: [it is] under the reeves of manors in causes pertaining to hallmoots; under the presiding officials of hundreds and boroughs; [and] under sheriffs.

20, 2: Archbishops, bishops, earls and other high-ranking men having rule in lands of their own have soke and sake, toll and team and infongenþeaf [2] (in others acquired by purchase or exchange or any other means, they have soke and sake in common causes and those pertaining to hallmoots) over their own men and on their own land and sometimes over the men of others, especially if taken in the act and charged, and there they shall have suitable compensation.

1 That is, either exclusive or shared with the king.

2 An ancient formula: soke and sake are synonyms designating the right to hold court, toll the right to charge access and passage across land, team the right to hold a court that judged ownership of cattle and/or take the fines, *infongenþeaf* and *utfongenþeaf* the right to hold court on thieves from a manor caught on the manor and thieves from a manor caught outside its jurisdiction.

20, 3: Singulorum denique baronum [et] senatorum (clericorum, laicorum) ubicumque habeant terram, siue socna regis sit uel non, in capitalibus questionibus socna [regis] est, sicut a Edmundi, Cnuti uel Edwardi legibus per successiones posteras hereditaria dignitas successit, nisi uel propinquitate uel aliqua dignitate meritorum regis indulgentia quemcumque respexerit, cuius amanda bonitas promouet potius, et non euertit liberatatem.

**C. 21: De generibus causarum.**

**C. 22: De grithbreche et hamsocna.**

**C. 23: De foresfactis.**

**C. 24: De iudicis fiscalis iure.**

24, 1: Super barones socnam suam habentes habet iudex fiscalis iustitie legis obseruantiam, et quicquid peccabitur in eorum personam; nemo enim forisfacturam sui ipsius habuit, set fortasse dominus eius.

24, 2: Et qui furem ei promisit uel robariam uel pacis fractionem uel deinceps similia, accusatum conuincat uel inde componat.

24, 3: Et si forisfaciant, emendent sicut alii; nullus enim socnam habet inpune peccandi.

24, 4: Si prepositus regius in terra socnam habentium forisfactum prior sciat, non tamen habeat nisi socnam illam excedat.

**C. 25: De priuilegiis procerum Anglie.**

**C. 26: De furti placito.**

20, 3: Finally, in capital matters soke of each of the barons and senators[1] (of clerics [and] laymen) wherever they hold land is the king's, whether it be in the king's jurisdiction or not, just as by the laws of Edmund, Cnut and Edward this hereditary privilege has passed through subsequent successions, unless either by kinship or some other worthiness of merits the king's indulgence has honored someone whose loving goodness rather promotes and not subverts liberty.

**C. 21: The kinds of causes.**

**C. 22: *Grithbreche* and *hamsocn.*[2]**

**C. 23: Forefeitures.**

**C. 24: The *ius* of a judge of the fisc.**

24, 1: A judge of the fisc has jurisdiction[3] of the law's justice over barons who have their own soke, and whatever wrong will be done against their person; for no one has had his own *forisfactum*[4] of himself but possibly his lord.

24, 2: And he who has charged theft or robbery or breach of the peace or similar things to him [the judge], he shall successfully attaint the accused or make payment thence.

24, 3: And if they [barons] make *forisfactum*, let them make amends just like others; for no one has soke for transgressing with impunity.

24, 4: If a royal reeve learns first of *forisfactum* on the land of those having soke, he shall nevertheless not have [jurisdiction over it] unless it [the issue] is beyond that soke.

**C. 25: The privileges of England's nobles.**

**C. 26: The plea of theft.**

1 Members of the Witan, the council of advisors to Anglo-Saxon kings.
2 Breach of the peace and house-breach.
3 Note that *ius* and soke in the sense of jurisdiction are essentially synonyms in this passage. *Iudex fiscalis* designates a royal judge in the early twelfth century.
4 The right of specifying forfeitures for offenses.

**C. 27: De libertate uauasorum.**

**C. 28: De equo iudicio faciendo.**

28, 1: In omnibus agendis inoffensus esse debet iudicum affectus, non suspectus.

28, 2: Grauius enim lacerantur pauperes a prauis iudicibus quam a cruentis hostibus.

28, 3: Et diligentia testium et personarum omnium digna Dei auribus perscrutatione pensanda est ut ydonea sit et cui ab aduersario iure contradici non possit.

28, 4: Et ipsi coagentes frequenter interrogandi sunt an amplius aliquid dicere uelint an inde iudicari, quia multa per subreptionem eueniunt.

28, 6: Et licet infinita delinquentium multidudo modum miserationis incommodet, uno uerbo concludimur: quod tibi non uis fieri, alii ne feceris.

**C. 29: Qui debeant esse iudices regis.**

29, 1: Regis iudices sint barones comitatus [et] qui liberas in eis terras habent, per quos debent cause singulorum alterna prosecutione tractari.

29, 1a: Villani uero uel cotseti uel ferdingi uel qui sunt huiusmodi uiles et inopes persone non sunt inter legum iudices numerandi.

**C. 30: De libertate procerum in placitis comitatus.**

**C. 31: De capitalibus placitis.**

31, 1: In summis et capitalibus placitis unus hundretus uel comitatus iudicetur a duobus, non unus duos iudicet.

**C. 27: The franchise of vavasours.**

**C. 28: Making impartial judgments.**

28, 1: In all proceedings, the manner of the judges should be irreproachable, not suspect.

28, 2: For poor people are more gravely savaged by crooked judges than by fierce enemies.

28, 3: And the diligence of witnesses and all persons in an examination should be thought worthy for God's ears, so that it be suitable and cannot be lawfully challenged by one's adversary.

28, 4: And the parties themselves should be frequently asked whether they might wish to say more or to be judged then, because many things come to pass through concealment of the truth.

28, 6: And although the infinite multitude of offenders may not suit the mode of mercy, let us conclude with one thought: what you do not wish done to you, you should not do to another.

**C. 29: Who should be the king's judges.**

29, 1: The king's judges should be the barons of the county and those who have freeholds in his lands, by whom ought to be handled the causes of individuals in alternating presentation [accusation and defense].

29, 1a: Villeins or cottagers or ferling men[1] or those who are base-born and impoverished shall not be numbered among the judges of the laws.

**C. 30: The privilege of nobles in pleas of the county.**

**C. 31: Capital pleadings.**

31, 1: And in the highest capital pleas, one hundred or county shall be adjudicated by two, [and] one shall not judge two.

1 Small landholders.

31, 2: Si inter iudices studia diuersa sint, ut alii sic, alii aliter fuisse contendant, uincat sententia meliorum et cui iustitia magis acquieuerit.

31, 3: Interesse comitatui debent episcopi, comites et cetere potestates qui Dei leges et seculi negotia iusta consideratione diffiniant.

31, 4: Recordationem curie regis nulli negare licet; alias licebit per intelligibiles homines placiti.

31, 5: Et nemo de capitalibus placitis testimonio conuincatur.

31, 6: Si quis iudices suspectos habeat, aduocet aut contradicat.

31, 7: Vnusquisque per pares suos iudicandus est et eiusdem prouincie.

31, 7a: Peregrina uero iudicia modis omnibus submouemus.

31, 7b: Et quicquid aduersus absentes (in omni loco uel negotio) uel a non suis iudicibus agitur, penitus euacuetur.

31, 8: In quibusdam locis utrimque eligitur iudicium, medietas ab eis quorum est negotium, et ibi testes nominati et electi sunt habendi, nisi odium uel aliquid competens in nominatione proponatur cur haberi non possint.

31, 8a: In Westsexa duo modi testium sunt: nominati et electi, electi et non nominati; iudices: constituti, aduocati.

**C. 32: Ne aliquis iudicet dominum suum.**

32, 1: Nemo solus presumat uel ab aliquo cogatur iudicium celebrare.

32 1a: Nec summorum quispiam minorum iudicatione dispereat.

31, 2: If there are diverse opinions among the judges, so that some argue it was one way and others another, let prevail the sentence of the better men and the one with which justice has more agreed.

31, 3: There ought to be present at the county [court] the bishops, earls, and other powerful men who shall determine the laws of God and the affairs of the world with just deliberation.

31, 4: It is permitted to no one to deny the record of the king's court; it will be permitted elsewhere [i.e. in other courts] by men knowledgeable of the plea.

31, 5: And concerning capital pleas, let no man be convicted for his character.

31, 6: If anyone has suspect judges, he should appeal or postpone.

31, 7: Everyone should be judged by his peers from the same district.

31, 7a: Of course, we oppose in all ways unsettled judgments.[1]

31, 7b: And whatsoever is done against absentees (in every place or matter) and by judges not of their choosing, let the punishment be set aside.

31, 8: In which places the body of dooms-men is chosen by both sides, half of them is negotiated by each of them [the parties], and there named and selected witnesses should be produced, unless hostility or something sufficient is proposed in the nomination why they cannot be produced.

31, 8a: In Wessex there are two kinds of witnesses: named and [then some] selected, [and] selected and not having been named; judges [are either already] established or summoned.

**C. 32: Let no one judge his own lord.**

32, 1: Let no one presume alone, or be compelled by another, to deliver judgment.

32 1a: Let not anyone of high degree despair by the judicial judgment of lesser men.

---

1 Downer 1972 135, translates "judgments pronounced by strangers."

32, 2: Nemo dominum suum iudicet uel iudicium proferat super eum cuius ligius sit, si etiam principis causa sit.

32, 3: Si dominus placitet contra suum hominem, potest in consilio suo iudices habitos infortiare, si opus sit.

**C. 33: De placito tractando.**

33, 1: Si quis in curia sua uel in quibuslibet agendorum locis placitum tractandum habeat, conuocet pares et uicinos suos ut, infortiato iudicio, gratuitam et cui contradici non possit iustitiam exhibeat.

33, 1a: Defectus quippe iustitie et uiolenta recti eorum destitutio est, que causas protrahunt in ius regium uel in dicionem dominorum.

33, 2: Iniusto quoque iudicio contradici poterit wemminge maiori et sapientiori presertim si in reditione fuerit aduocatum.

33, 2a: Si uero sine calumpnia recipiatur, et deinceps causam illam reformare quis cupiat, non procedet in celebrationibus, ut opus sit iudicibus narrationes repetere iudicii, maxime si dominus querimonie interfuerit uel dapifer uel minister eius, uel congruum inde terminum habuerit.

33, 3: Si dominus placitet contra hominem suum, respectare potest et differre, dum uelit, quia non frangit, nisi maior iustitia intersit.

33, 3a: Erga parem uel uicinum suum uel alterius hominem agens uiderit ne pro recti penuria sine iudicio dimittat eum tertio, quia curiam suam inde perderet et placitum et emendaret.

32, 2: Let no one judge his lord or proffer judgment upon him whose liege he is, even if the cause is the prince's.

32, 3: If a lord pleads against his own man, he may reinforce the accustomed judges from his own council if it is necessary.

**C. 33: Drawing the plea.**

33, 1: If anyone has a plea that must be drawn[1] in his court or in whatsoever places of proceedings, let him call together his peers and neighbors, so that with his body of dooms-men buttressed, he may provide an acceptable justice that cannot be challenged.

33, 1a: Indeed, it is the failure of justice and the violent deprivation of their [presumably litigants] rights which draw causes into the royal *ius* or the jurisdiction of [other] lords.

33, 2: It shall also be possible to challenge an unjust judgment by a wemming[2] to a greater and wiser judge, especially if it has been noted in the response.

33, 2a: If it has been received without challenge and then someone desires to amend that cause, let him not go forward with judicial proceedings, so that there is a need to repeat to the judges the counts of the judgment, especially if his lord, or his steward or official, was present at the hearing, and he has had there an appropriate date.

33, 3: If a lord pleads against his own man, he may adjourn and delay as he wishes, because it [his cause] does not fail unless a superior justice is present.

33, 3a: Proceeding in respect of his peer or neighbor or another's man, he shall beware lest through a default of justice he sends him away thrice without judgment, because he would lose his court then and the plea and have to make amends.

1 To "draw the count" is to present a case before a court.

2 Apparently an appeal based upon a blemish (OE *wemming*) in the proceedings.

33, 4: De libro Theodosiane legis: Iniuste uictus infra iii menses reparet causam; quod si neglexerit, sententia collata perseueret.

33, 5: Iudices sane non debent esse nisi quod impetitus elegerit.

33, 6: Augustinus: Iuris forensis est qui in impetitionibus mentitus est, non ei prosit quod impetrauit.

33, 7: Ieronimus: Equum iudicium est ubi non persona set opera considerantur.

**C. 34: De iniusto iudicio.**

34, 1: Si quis ira uel odio uel timore uel amore uel cupiditate uel quoquo respectu iniustum iudicet uel unlagam constituat, cxx solidorum culpa sit et đegenscypes et omni iudiciaria dignitate priuetur nisi se erga regem redimat, sicut in eius misericordia erit;

34, 1a: (in Denelaga; lahslite, nisi super sancta iurare poterit quod melius et rectius nesciuit)—siue in comitatu uel quouis placito regis fiat, de sua uel alterius causa, uel inter compares in curiis uel diuisis uel locis suis uel inter dominum et hominem suum; ubique sit interdictum.

34, 1b: Pensandum est etiam si de peccunialibus uel capite plectendis actionibus, et an scienter uel inscienter hoc acciderit.

34, 1c: Sepe enim culpa malum aggrauat et were uel wite uel lahslite discrimen infatuat.

33, 4: From the book of Theodosian law: let one unjustly defeated renew the cause within three months; because if he neglects [to do so], the judgment gathered should stand.

33, 5: Sensibly, there ought to be no judges except those the accused has selected.

33, 6: Augustine: He is *iuris forensis*[1] who has lied in his accusations; let what he has obtained not profit him.

33, 7: Jerome: A judgment is equitable when not the person but the deeds are considered.

**C. 34: Unjust judgment.**

34, 1: If someone should give an unjust judgment or create an injustice in anger or hatred or fear or love or greed or in whatsoever regard, let his fine be 120 shillings and let him be deprived of his thaneship and every judicial office unless he redeems himself to the king, so that he will be in his mercy;

34, 1a: (in the Danelaw; let it be *lahslit*,[2] unless one can swear upon the sacred things that he did not know better and more rightly)—whether it happen in the county [court] or in whatever king's court, concerning one's own cause or another's, whether between equals in courts either on their boundaries or in their own places, or between a lord and his own man; everywhere let it be forbidden.

34, 1b: It must also be considered if this matter occurred in actionable pleas concerning monetary penalties or capital punishment, and whether knowingly or unknowingly.

34, 1c: For often blame aggravates a wrong and wergeld or wite [amercement] or *lahslit* nullifies a disaster.

1 Downer, 1972 137, translates "It is a rule of law in the courts that anyone who has lied in his accusations shall not have the benefit of what he has obtained." *Forensis,* however, also has the sense of "foreigner" or "outsider" (See Latham, s.v. *forensis,* 196) and "outside of the law" is the sense we suggest for *iuris forensis.*

2 The fine for breach of law.

34, 2: Si quis iniustum iudicet et affligat wera componat.

**C. 35: De ouerseunesse regis.**

35, 1: Ouerseunesse regis est in causis communibus xx mance que faciunt l solidos in Westsexa.

35, 1a: Regine xx mance, episcopi x mance, comitis x mance, thaini uel baronis u mance.

35, 2: In causis regiis grithbreche c solidi stretbreche c solidi, forestel c solidi, hamsocne c solidi, borhbreche c solidi, et deinceps sicut prediximus emendabitur wita, wera, iuxta culpam potius quam personam.

**C. 36: Qui perdunt ouerseunessam.**

**C. 37: De cesione nemoris.**

**C. 38: De schildwite.**

**C. 39: De forisfactura sanguinis.**

39, 1: In quibusdam locis qui blodwitam, id est forisfacturam sanguinis, fecit solummodo reus est, in quibusdam etiam qui patitur, ut nec agens impunitate superbiat nec contumeliatus fedis emendationibus assuescat.

**C. 40: De fractura pat[r]ici.**

**C. 41: Quod unusquisque ouerseunessam debeat habere.**

**C. 42: De summonitionibus.**

42, 1: Qui summonitionem regis uel communis domini domino uel cuilibet perferendam susceperit, et dimiserit uel ex industria uel ex inscitia, emendet per iudicium, sicut erit, dampnum uel ouerseunessam, si ad id deducatur, et quietus inde sit qui submonebatur, et ite[ru]m ad rectum submoneatur.

34, 2: If anyone gives an unjust judgment and inflicts harm, let wergeld lay.

**C. 35: Despite of the king.**

35, 1: Despite of the king in common causes is twenty mancuses, which make 50 shillings in Wessex.

35, 1a: Of the queen twenty mancuses, of a bishop ten mancuses, of an earl ten mancuses, of a thane or baron five mancuses.

35, 2: In royal causes, *grithbreche* [peace-breach] 100 shillings, *stretbreche* [high road-breach] 100 shillings, *forestel* [waylaying] 100 shillings, *hamsocn* [house-attack] 100 shillings, *borhbreche* [borough-breach] 100 shillings, and then, just as we have said, let amercement be paid, wergeld accordant to the crime rather than the person.

**C. 36: Those who lose [the right to] *ouerseunesse.***

**C. 37: Woodcutting.**

**C. 38: Scyldwita.**[1]

**C. 39: The offense of bloodshed.**

39, 1: In certain places the one who has committed blood*wite*, that is, the offense of bloodshed, is alone liable, in others also the one who suffers, lest anyone acting with impunity should become arrogant or anyone having been mistreated should become accustomed to sordid compensations.

**C. 40: Breach of a pound.**[2]

**C. 41: That each [lord] should have his penalty for *ouerseunesse.***

**C. 42: Summonses**

42, 1: Who has undertaken to bear the summons of the king or of a lord of the commons to a lord or to anyone, and left off either on purpose or through ignorance, let him amend by a judgment, just as it will be, the

1 A fine for a crime of violence.
2 Illegally entering a holding pen to recover distrained animals.

42, 2: Si quis uero dapiferum uel quemlibet ministrum ita rebus suis prefecerit (et hoc ubi et sicut iustum est notificauerit) et [h]omin[i] suo committet, ut quodammodo locum eius habeat, et quod fecerit factum sit, et a rege uel iustitia eius uel a communi utrorumque domino de proprio ipsorum placito per eum submoneatur, et idem coram testibus suscepit ut negari non possit submonitus iudicetur, siue dictum sit ab homine suo siue non; et si non uenerit ad placitum, rectum inde iudicetur; unde si dampnum ei euenerit, loquatur inde cum homine suo.

42, 3: Si etiam uenire non possit et mittat nuntium ad dominum suum, mittat qui diligenter et fideliter renuntiet preceptum illius.

**C. 43: Ne quis inplacitatus a rege alicui respondeat.**

43, 1: Nemo a rege inplacitatus cogitur per legem alicui respondere donec ei qui dominus omnium est satisfecerit; sic potest ei warantus esse qui in seruitio suo est.

43, 1a: Si prepositus aut debitor domini sui est, quod debet reddat aut inde componat; neque enim iustum est ut hominis sui forisfactum dominus luat, nec expectari conuenit ut quis eum in suis preueniat.

43, 1b: Pensandum tamen est ut ratione et consideratione hoc fiat ne fraudationis potius quam iuste repetitionis actio iudicetur.

damage or despite, if it should be brought to that, and he who was summoned shall be quit there and summoned again to justice.

42, 2: If someone should put his steward or some such minister in charge of his affairs (and has made this known where and just as it is proper) and he commissions this man so that in some way he may hold his place and do what should be done, and that he may be summoned through him by the king or his Justice or by a lord in common of both sides concerning his own plea, and he [the steward] has accepted [a summons] in the presence of witnesses so that it cannot be denied, let the one summoned be judged, whether it [the summons] be said [i.e. made known to him] by his man or not; and if he [the lord whose steward has neglected to inform him of the summons] has not come to the plea, let the right [of the matter] be then judged; whence if damage results to him [the lord], then let him speak with his man.

42, 3: And if he [the steward] is unable to come and sends a messenger to his lord, let him send someone who diligently and faithfully may report his instruction.

**C. 43: Let someone impleaded by the king not answer to another.**

43, 1: No one impleaded by the king is compelled by law to answer to another until he has made satisfaction to him who is lord of all; thus he [the king] is able to be warrantor to him who is in his service.

43, 1a: If one is his own lord's reeve or debtor, let him repay what he owes or pay his fine; for it is not just that a lord pay for his man's fine, nor is it fit to expect that anyone should have priority over him in respect of his own men.

43, 1b: However, it should be carefully considered so that this is done by due thought and consideration, lest the suit should be judged more of a fraud than a just restitution.

43, 2: Si quis a domino suo sine licentia discedat, utleipa emendetur et redire cogatur ut rectum per omnia faciat.

43, 3: Qui sibi facit aduocatum contra dominum suum per superbiam perdat quod deo eo tenet.

43, 4: Si quis hominem habeat qui ei nolit esse ad rectum, si quid de eo tenet post legittimam submonitionem saisiri faciat.

43, 5: Si quis diuersos diuersorum feodos teneat, de eo quod ad eorum feudum pertinet cum singulis componat, et de rebus alterius alteri non intendat.

43, 6: Qu[ot]cumque dominos aliquis habeat uel quantumcumque de aliis teneat, ei magis obnoxious est et eius residens esse debet cuius ligius est.

43, 6a: Si multis homagium fecerit, et ab aliquo eorum captus et implacitatus sit, ille cuius residens et ligius est erga quoslibet alios iure potest eum plegiare, nec debet ei denegari qui manbotam inde haberet et cui ipse magis acquieuerit.

43, 7: Qui furtum fecerit, qui proditor domini sui fuerit, quicumque ab eo in obuiatione hostili uel bello campali fugerit, uel uictus erit uel feloniam fecerit, terram suam forisfecerit.

43, 8: Si dominus terram suam uel feodum suum auferat homini suo, unde est homo suus, uel si eum in mortali necessitate deserat superuacue forisfacere potest dominium suum erga eum.

43, 9: Sustinere tamen debet homo dominum suum, si faciat ei contumeliam uel iniuriam eiusmodi, in werra xxx dies, in pace unum annum et unum diem; et interim priuate per compares, per uicinos, per domesticos et extraneos per legem requirere eum de recto.

43, 2: If someone should leave his lord without permission, let him be fined *utleipa*[1] and forced to return so that he may do what is just in every respect.

43, 3: Anyone who through pride appoints an advocate against his own lord shall lose what he holds from him.

43, 4: If anyone has a man who does not wish to be just with him, [and] if he [the man] holds anything from him, he may cause it to be seised after a lawful summons.

43, 5: If anyone holds different fees of different men, let him settle with each of them from that which pertains to their fee, and not satisfy the one from the things of the other.

43, 6: However many lords someone may have, or however much he may hold of others, he owes more obedience to him, and ought to be his vassal, whose liege he is.

43, 6a: If one has done homage to many and is taken and impleaded by any of them, that one whose vassal and liege man he is may stand pledge for him in respect of any others, nor should this be denied to him who has *manbot*[2] thereupon and to whom he himself has to a greater extent submitted.

43, 7: Anyone who has committed theft, who has committed treason against his lord, and whoever has fled from him in an encounter with the enemy or on the battlefield, who has been defeated or committed a felony[3] shall forfeit his land.

43, 8: If a lord should take away his man's land or fee by virtue of which he is his man, or if he deserts him without cause in his mortal need, he may forfeit his lordship with respect to him.

43, 9: A man is obligated, nevertheless, to sustain his lord for thirty days in war and a year and a day in peace if he [the lord] does him contumely

1 A serf's payment for flight.
2 Synonym for *wergeld.*
3 Defeated, that is, in a judicial combat or feloniously breached the feudal bond.

**C. 44: De plegiis dominorum suorum.**

44, 1: Si quis a domino suo missus sit in plegium ut ostendere possit quod ei ex sponsione uel fideiussione illa dampnum uenit, non cogitur ex lege de quauis peccuniali inplacitatione respondere ei donec totum restituat quod amiserit pro eo.

44, 2: De contumelia uero domini semper est homini suo respondendum, prima uice etiam sine alio compellante; deinde qui sacramentum vel legem abnegandi uult habere, querat accusantem.

**C. 45: De inculpationibus.**

45 1: Multe sunt et multorum inculpationes in quibus non necesse est secumdum legem responderi, ut in quauis compellatione simplici promptum est inueniri.

45 1a: Simplex enim et uacua compellatio est ubi ex neutra parte, compellantis scilicet aut compellati, testis est, nec causa huiusmodi que bello uel iudicio uel lege sacramentali uel timore uel amore mereatur promoueri.

45, 2: Et si quis monacho uel monache, seruo uel ancilla sine prelatorum suorum licentia aliquid committat, ut negauerit nil recipiat.

45, 3: Item si quis sponse uel puero uel puelle sine permissu domini sui quamcumque commendationem uel aliquam commutationem uel traditionem fecerit, non opus est eos uel eorum dominos respondere super hiis si complaceat abnegare quamdiu sub uirga sunt.

or injury of such kind; and in the meantime to pursue him for his rights according to the law through peers, neighbors, family members, and outsiders.

**C. 44: Pledges of their own lords.**

44, 1: If anyone has been put in pledge by his lord so that he can show that damage has come to him by his guarantee or surety, he cannot be compelled by law to answer to him [the lord] for any monetary action until he [the lord] restores to him [the liege man] all that he has lost for him.

44, 2: It is necessary for a man always to answer to his lord for contumely, and on the first occasion without another appellor; afterward let he who wishes to have an oath or law by denial obtain [another] accuser.

**C. 45: Accusations.**

45, 1: Many accusations there are and of many people in which it is not necessary according to law for an answer to be made, as is readily to be found in any simple appeal.

45, 1a: For an accusation is simple and null and void when there is no witness from either party, that is, accuser or accused, nor [is there] a cause of this kind which deserves to be promoted by judicial combat or ordeal or lawful oath or fear or love.

45, 2: And if someone entrusts anything to a monk or nun, a serf or a maid servant, without license of their superiors, let him receive nothing if he or she has denied [it].

45, 3: Likewise, if someone has entrusted or handed anything over to or exchanged it with a wife or a boy or a girl without the consent of their lord, there is no need for them or their lords to answer for these things if it pleases them to deny by oath as long as they are under the rod.

45, 4: Et de nemore inoperatio per tihlam nemo respondeat nisi sit ibi captus uel sit homo eius cuius est nemus.

45, 5: Et si quis delegiatus legalem hominem accuset, funestam dicimus uocem eius.

**C. 46: De inplacitatis a dominis.**

46, 1: Si quis a domino suo uel iustitia per suam uel alterius suggestionem inplacitetur, submoneatur ad vii dies in eodem comitatu, de nominatis uel innominatis placitis.

46, 1a: Et si lex domino uadietur differat cetera placita donec lex deducatur per burgi legem, nisi de furto uel capitalibus sit, in quibus statim oportet responderi.

46, 2: De quibuscumque inplacitetur aliquis, furst et fandung habeat, et nominentur ei placita, et inde ad vii dies respondeat quod uelit.

46, 2a: Si autem hoc uel alio modo uentum erit ad placitum siue contra dominum siue contra alium, tacite se inplacitari patiatur in omnibus placitis super eum.

46, 3: Et si quis de felonia compellitur, remaneat de cetero donec inde finiatur.

46, 4: In aliis querat accusatus consilium et habeat ab amicis et parentibus suis (quod nulli iure debet defendi), maxime eorum quos secum adduxerit uel ad placitum suum rogauerit; et in consilio suo fiducialiter rerum ueritatem fateatur, ut de placito uel de pace salubrius uideatur.

45, 4: And no one shall answer to an accusation for unworked wood[1] unless he has been seized there or is his man whose wood it is.

45, 5: And if someone not law-worthy accuses a lawful man, we declare his voice worthless.

**C. 46: Those impleaded by their lords.**

46, 1: If anyone is impleaded by his lord or a justice by his own or another's instigation, let him be summoned to appear in seven days in the same county, for specified or unspecified pleas.

46, 1a: And if the law is wagered by the lord, let him defer other pleas until the law is carried out according to borough law, unless it concerns theft or capital matters, in which cases it should be answered immediately.[2]

46, 2: And for whatever anyone is impleaded, let him have *furst* and *fandung*,[3] and let the pleas be specified to him, and then after seven days let him respond as he wishes.

46, 3: And if anyone is charged with felony, let him stay about other matters until it is thence finished.

46, 4: In other matters, let the accused seek counsel and have [it] from his friends and kin (which by law should be denied to no one) especially of those whom he has brought with him or called to his pleading; and in his counsel let him faithfully disclose the truth of matters, so that it may seem beneficial for his plea or his peace.

---

1 Downer 1972 155, translates *nemore inoperato* as "wood which has been cut but not carried away."

2 To suggest the additional layer of translation often necessary in working with the *Leges* we offer Downer's 1972 157 translation of this passage: "If the accused person commits himself to making an oath of compurgation to his lord, the person holding the court shall defer all other pleas until the oath is performed in accordance with the law appropriate to the particular court, unless it is a matter of theft or of one of the more serious charges, in respect of which an answer in defense must be given immediately."

3 OE "time" and "proof." Liebermann 1906 2,76 translates "*Frist zum Beweis,*" that is, "time to prove."

46, 5: Bonum autem est ut cum alicuius consilium in placito redditur, cum emendatione dicendum predicatur, ut si forte perorator uel superadiecerit aliquid uel omiserit, emendari liceat ei.

46, 6: Sepe enim fit ut in sua causa quis minus uideat quam in alterius, et in ore alterius plerumque poterit emendari quod in suo non liceret.

**C. 47: De causis criminalibus uel capitalibus.**

47, 1: De furto et murdro et proditione domini et robaria et utlagaria et husbreche et bernet et falsaria et causis criminalibus uel capitalibus nemo querat consilium quin inplacitatus statim perneget sine omni petitione consilii, cuiuscumque nationis uel condicionis sit; uel eius affirmationem uel negationem defensor aut dominus prosequatur competenti termino comprobandam.

**C. 48: Quomodo possunt uti consilio.**

48, 1: In aliis omnibus potest et debet quilibet uti consilio; in consulendo etiam consulte agere consilium est.

48, 1a: Si quis enim a iustitia regis inplacitatus ad consilium exierit et ad inculpationem non responderit, xx manca[rum] uel ouerseunesse regis culpa sit.

48, 1b: Quando itaque aliquid habetur in inplacitationibus pretendendum, in inculpationibus ostendatur et ad consilium de inplacitatione non exeat qui placitare non deliberat.

48, 1c: Iudicium enim est: qui sine contradictione uel preoccupatione super implacitationem exit ad consilium, intrat in placitum, et de quibus non responderit, concesserit.

48, 2: Si totus comitatus uel sep[ara]t[i]m hundreta super aliquibus inplacitentur et ad aliquem specialiter uel singulariter inculpatio dirigatur, petat ut ei comitatum suum, qui eiusdem esse dicitur, habere liceat, et cum eo respondeat ut, sicut omnium una est inculpatio, una emundatio uel emendatio sit.

46, 5: It is best when anyone's advice is given in a plea that it be said in advance that it is spoken subject to a right of correction, so that he is allowed to correct it if the speaker has said too much or left anything out.[1]

46, 6: For it is often the case that somebody is less perceptive in his own case than in the case of another; and commonly what he could not amend if he had spoken himself can be amended if spoken by another.

**C. 47: Criminal or capital causes.**

47, 1: Let no one seek counsel concerning theft, murder, treason against his lord, robbery, outlawry, *husbreche*, arson, forgery/counterfeiting, and criminal or capital causes unless he, immediately having been impleaded, denies [the charge] without any counsel having been sought, of whatsoever people or condition he is; let his warrantor or lord follow up on his affirmation or denial when a suitable date has been set.

**C. 48: How they [the accused] are able to employ counsel.**

48, 1: In all other matters, anyone [accused] may and should enjoy counsel, and in taking counsel, the advice is to act advisedly.

48, 1a: For if someone impleaded before the king's justice withdraws to take counsel, and has not answered to the charge, let his liability [i.e. fine] be twenty mancuses or [a charge of] despite of the king.

48, 1b: When, therefore, anything is contained in the impleadings that should be alleged, let it be revealed in the charges, and let one who has not decided how to plea not go out for counsel concerning the charge.

48, 1c: For it is the judgment that he who goes out for counsel without a denial or objection upon the charge enters into the plea and has conceded those things to which he has not answered.

48, 2: If an entire county, or the hundreds separately, have been impleaded upon matters and a charge is directed to someone specially or individually, let him seek that he be permitted to have with him the

1 This passage and the following are so translated by Brand 1992 10.

48, 2a: Si eis alternatim uerum de se testantibus, quia Francorum et Anglorum plenum est testimonium, ita sit; si secus est eligantur de melioribus iuraturi secundum rerum meritum et cause modum.

48, 3: Nec aliquis baro solus de hundreto uel de eo placitet quod at plures pertinet.

48, 4: Nec liceat domino uel iustitie testibus aliquem sine contradictione uincere.

48, 5: Si quid in comitatu uel in quouis placito per iustitiam dictum factumue negetur, per homines qui interfuerint et per alterius dominii testes agatur.

48, 6: Et de omni causa ubi plures fuisse dicuntur, unum ad minus intelligibilem de placito erit rectum haberi.

48, 7: Et qui contra dominum partem confitetur ceterum probabit.

48, 8: Qui nichil inculpationis recognoscit totum si uult abnegabit.

48, 9: Nec testes audientes uel uidentes habendi sunt de eo quod non fuerit, set quod accusatus fuisse contendit.

48, 10: Et de cremento feudi debet haberi testis eiusdem dominii, uel ex sua uel ex parte domini etiam inuocatus.

48, 11: De primo feudo habeantur quicumque liberi, si non possint, alii.

county, which is said to be his, and respond with it, so that, just as there is one charge, let there be one exculpation or compensation.

48, 2a: If they [Frenchmen and Englishmen] by turns give truthful witness about something, since the testimony of Frenchmen and Englishmen is valid, let it be settled; if it is otherwise, let those who are sworn be chosen from the more respectable men according to the merit of the matter and the manner of the cause.

48, 3: Nor should any baron plead alone for a hundred or about anything that pertains to several.

48, 4: Nor should it be permitted a lord or a Justice to convict anyone by witnesses without rebuttal.

48, 5: If anything said or done by a justice in a county or other court is denied, let it be argued by men who were present and by the witnesses of another lord.

48, 6: And for every cause where several were said to have been, it will be just that at least one person knowledgeable about the plea be produced.

48, 7: And he who confesses a part [of a charge] against his lord shall prove the rest [by judicial combat or ordeal].

48, 8: He who acknowledges nothing of the charge may clear himself by oath of the whole if he wishes.

48, 9: Nor do witnesses who heard or saw something have to be produced for that which did not happen, but that which the accused claims did.

48, 10: And for an incremented fee[1] a witness from the same demesne should be produced, and he should be summoned either on his own [the man's] or his lord's behalf.

48, 11: Freemen should be had [as witnesses] concerning a prime fee,[2] others if they cannot.

---

1 A fee to which property has been added after the original grant.
2 An ancestral fee.

48, 12: Et in diratiocinatione feudi precedere debet feudatus testem suum ad bellum uel aliam legem.

**C. 49: Quibus causis statim responderi debeat, quibus non.**

**C. 50: De supersessionibus placiti.**

**C. 51: De summonitione hundreti.**

**C. 52: De proprio placito regis.**

**C. 53: De supersessione comitatus.**

**C. 54: De discessione sociorum unius peccunie.**

**C. 55: De priuilegio domini super hominem suum.**

**C. 56: De firma tenenda.**

**C. 57: De querela uicinorum.**

**C. 58: De homine uagante.**

**C. 59: De contramandatione placiti.**

**C. 60: De contramandatione placiti per iustitiam positi.**

**C. 61: De placito alicuius domini cum preposito suo et sibi subditis.**

**C. 62: De obseruatione temporis leges faciendi.**

**C. 63: De inplacitatione iudicis fiscalis.**

**C. 64: De tractatione locutionum secundum quod sunt.**

**C. 65: De dimissione furis.**

**C. 66: De occisione ministri altaris.**

**C. 67: De homine infamato.**

48, 12: And a feudatory in deraigning[1] a fee should precede his witness[2] to arms or to another law.[3]

**C. 49: In which causes it ought to be answered at once, in which not.**

**C. 50: Defaults of a plea.**

**C. 51: The summoning of the hundred.**

**C. 52: The king's plea proper.**

**C. 53: Default of the county court.**

**C. 54: Dissolution by partners of common wealth.**

**C. 55: A lord's privilege over his man.**

**C. 56: Holding in farm.**

**C. 57: Complaints of neighbors.**

**C. 58: A vagrant man.**

**C. 59: Deferment of a plea.**

**C. 60: Deferment of a plea scheduled by a justice.**

**C. 61: The plea of any lord with his reeve and his subjects.**

**C. 62: Observance of the time for applying the laws.**

**C. 63: Impleading by a judge of the fisc.**

**C. 64: Drawing[4] of impleadings according to what they are.**

**C. 65: Release of a thief.**

**C. 66: The killing of a minister of the altar.**

**C. 67: The infamous man.**

---

1 In establishing a claim to.
2 In this meaning, his champion, but his compurgator in the second instance.
3 That is, another method of proof.
4 To draw the count is to give a narrative description of a case at its outset.

**C. 68: De solutione liberi aut serui occisi.**

**C. 69: De occisione Anglici.**

**C. 70: Consuetudo Westsexe.**

**C. 71: De homicidio malefic[or]um.**

**C. 72: Diffinitio homicidii.**

**C. 73: De ordinatis homicidis.**

**C. 74: De purgatione occisorum.**

**C. 75: De occisoribus dominorum suorum.**

**C. 76: De pretio cuiuslibet.**

**C. 77: De solutione liberi uel servi occisi.**

**C. 78: De liberatione serui.**

**C. 79: De emendatione filioli uel patrini.**

**C. 80: De homicidio in curia regis, exercitu, burgo uel castello.**

**C. 81: De pace regis danda in potatione.**

**C. 82: De aliquibus inimicis ad inuicem.**

**C. 83: Quod unicuique liceat se defendere in quodlibet negotio preter contra dominum suum.**

**C. 84: De uerberatione.**

**C. 85: Quod quiuis liberet eum quem in malum duxerit.**

**C. 86: Ne quis se uindicet de suo homine sine lege.**

**C. 87: De delicto ex armis accommodatis.**

**C. 88: De commissione armorum quibus aliquis occidatur.**

**C. 89: Qui aliquem de propinquis occiderit.**

**C. 90: Si quis uolens aliquos inter se dimicantes diuidere occidatur.**

**C. 91: De solutione murdri.**

**C. 92: De solutione murdri.**

**C. 93: De emendatione uulneris.**

**C. 94: De uerberatione absque sanguinis effusione.**

**C. 68: Payment for a freeman or a slain slave.**

**C. 69: The killing of an Englishman.**

**C. 70: The custom of Wessex.**

**C. 71: Homicide by necromancers.**

**C. 72: The definition of homocide.**

**C. 73: Homicides by ordained persons.**

**C. 74: Expiation of the slain.**

**C. 75: Slayers of their lords.**

**C. 76: The price of anyone.**

**C. 77: Payment for a slain freeman or serf.**

**C. 78: Emancipation of a serf.**

**C. 79: Compensation for a godson or godfather.**

**C. 80: Homicide in the king's court, army, fortress, or castle.**

**C. 81: The king's peace given during convivial drinking.**

**C. 82: Concerning mutual enemies.**

**C. 83: That anyone is permitted to defend himself in any activity except agains his lord.**

**C. 84: Battery.**

**C. 85: That anyone shall relieve him whom he has led into evil.**

**C. 86: No one may avenge himself for his man outside the law.**

**C. 87: Transgression with borrowed arms.**

**C. 88: The employment of arms by which someone is killed.**

**C. 89: He who kills any of his relatives.**

**C. 90: If anyone is killed desiring to separate others fighting amongst themselves.**

**C. 91: Payment for murder (1).**

**C. 92: Payment for murder (2).**

**C. 93: Compensation for a wound.**

**C. 94: Battery without loss of blood.**

**Exchequer**

## Dialogus de Scaccario

*(Begun in 1177, completion date unknown, perhaps late 1180s)*

The author of this important treatise was Richard fitzNigel, king's treasurer from 1160 until his death in 1198 and Bishop of London from 1189-1198. An early version of the text is in Stubbs (1870), from Madox' *History of the Exchequer* (1711), which collates the Black and the Red Book of the Exchequer, where fitzNigel is named as author. A public servant and ecclesiastic from a distinguished family, the author composed this indispensable account of the functioning and functionaries of the exchequer as it had come to be by the late twelfth century. Cast in the familiar form of a discussion between a master and a student, albeit a rather unusual one, it breaks out in great detail the organization and workings of the exchequer's upper and lower halves. The first part discusses the lower half, which handled the receipt and expenditure of funds, and the second part discusses the upper, in which sheriffs were held to account for the payment due on their county farms. The presiders, known as barons for their rank, sat as a fiscal court, whose roots the author locates in a Norman institution superimposed upon Anglo-Saxon tradition. FitzNigel's dialogue shows clearly how fiscal affairs and the administration of the law are tightly interwoven in Plantagenet England.

There has been some discussion about interpolations in the text, but this has been inconclusive and we have accordingly omitted the brackets once customary for the disputed passages. The *Dialogus* has been well represented and studied over the centuries, from Thomas Madox to Stubbs to Felix Liebermann and more recent editors and translators.[1] Although we have consulted the recent editions and translations, we have followed our practice throughout in translating fairly literally in

1 Madox 1711; Liebermann 1875; Stubbs 1913/2012; Poole 1912 esp. 3-12.

order that readers can move more easily back and forth between Latin and English.

The game of chess is more of an introductory device than an applied operative metaphor for the functioning of the treasury. The speaker is the treasurer of England, the chess-master of royal finances, the individual responsible to the king for the receipt, record, and expenditure of royal revenues. His companion is someone of age and substance who has played often at the board, and apparently often lost, and he is angry when he addresses the master, the both of them sitting in an "outlook" on the Thames, probably to be considered as a public house, especially in the light of the master's mention of his "tipsy memory" at the dialogue's end. The master invites his pupil-to-be to arise from his "adversarial" seat opposite and come and sit with him. This irate adversary should perhaps be taken as a sheriff, perhaps the sheriff of London, Middlesex County—of which London is the county seat—or Winchester or several other sites where the exchequer also sat. Contemporaries may well have recognized him. At the time of composition, the exchequer is much occupied with the bi-annual audits of England's sheriffs, who had to appear at the Easter session to make a preliminary payment on the annual rent for their county farms and at Michaelmas to settle what they yet owed, receive a refund in the unlikely event they had overpaid, or go quit. The discussion that follows is, accordingly, a bit wry in making a sheriff a pupil of the treasurer for the purposes of the exposition that follows, an explanation of the game of finances conceived very generally, in two separate senses, as a chess game. In the first sense the various officials and functionaries of the exchequer are the pieces whose moves (responsibilities) must be understood if success at the chessboard is to be achieved. In the second sense a play at the board occurs when the sheriff's clerk places tally sticks in the appropriate squares of the tablecloth, to be matched by the Exchequer's counter tallies. Any difference between the two tally counts must be paid in or out, depending upon whose "play" has been superior. The extraordinary popularity of chess at the time of composition has been well documented, and chess was a popular metaphor for detailed analyses in many frames of reference.[1]

FitzNigel's account is, as would be expected of a prominent member of the clergy, grounded everywhere in biblical references and the reader will hear the echo of familiar passages throughout. We have attempted with our selections to represent the most important parts of the text, but we have also included the chapter headings of omitted passages so that the reader can derive some sense of the whole.

We have used the edition of Hughes, Crump and Johnson 1902, but we have consulted and incorporated suggestions from Johnson 1983 and Amt 2007.

1 See Adams 2006 1-14.

## Praefatio

Ordinatis a deo potestatibus in omni timore subici simul et obsequi necesse est. Omnis enim potestas a domino deo est. Non ergo videtur absurdum vel a viris ecclesiasticis alienum regibus quasi praecellentibus et ceteris potestatibus seruiendo sua jura servare; praesertim in hiis quae veritati vel honestati non obuiant. Oportet autem hiis seruire non in conseruandis tantum dignitatibus per quas gloria regie potestatis elucet, verum in mundanarum facultatum copiis que eos sui status ratione contingunt. Ille enim illustrant, hec subueniunt. Porro mobilium copia vel defectus principum potestates humiliat vel exaltat. Quibus enim hec desunt hostibus preda fiunt, quibus autem hec suppetunt hiis hostes in predam cedunt. Sane licet hec regibus plerumque, iure non prorsus examinato set patriis quandoque legibus quandoque cordium suorum consiliis occultis vel solius interdum suae voluntatis arbitrio, prouenire contingat; eorum tamen facta ab inferioribus discutienda vel condempnanda non sunt. Quorum enim corda et motus cordium in manu dei sunt et quibus ab ipso deo singulariter est credita cura subditorum, eorum causa divino tantum non humano judicio stat aut cadit. Nemo tamen quantumlibet diues si secus egerit de impunitate sibi blandiatur, cum de huiusmodi scriptum sit, "Potentes potenter tormenta patientur." Igitur qualiscumque sit vel videatur adquirendi causa vel modus, hiis qui ad eorum custodiam ex officio deputantur cura remissior esse non debet, set in eisdem congregandis, conseruandis vel distribuendis sollicitam decet esse diligentiam quasi rationem reddituris de regni statu qui per hec incolumis perseuerat. Nouimus quidem prudentia, fortitudine, temperantia siue iustitia, ceterisque virtutibus principaliter regna regi iuraque subsistere, vnde et hiis

# Dialogus de Scaccario

## Preface

To the powers ordained by God it is necessary to be subject in all dread and likewise to obey. For all power is from the Lord God. Therefore it does not seem an absurd or strange thing for ecclesiastical men to serve His law in serving kings, as it were eminences and other powers, above all in those matters that do not go against truth or honesty. It is suitable, moreover, to serve them not so much in preserving their dignities, through which the glory of regal power shines forth, but rather in the riches of worldly means that belong to them by reason of their state, for the former adorn them, the latter assist. But an abundance of moveable goods, or a lack, exalts or humbles the power of princes. For to whom these are lacking, they are plunder to enemies; however, to whom these suffice, enemies yield to them in plunder. Truly, although it happens that these things mostly come to kings not altogether by strict right but sometimes by ancestral laws, sometimes by the secret counsels of their hearts, or sometimes by the exercise of their individual will, nevertheless their actions must not be struck down or condemned by their subjects. For their hearts and the impulse of their hearts are in God's hand and the case of those to whom the sole care of subjects is entrusted by God Himself stands or falls by divine judgment only [and] not human. Nevertheless, no man howsoever wealthy should delude himself if with impunity he should act contrarily, since of such a kind it is written [that] "The mighty shall endure torments mightily." Therefore, howsoever the case or manner of the acquisition is or seems, to those who are assigned by their office to the keeping of them [riches] there should be no less relaxation in care, but in the care of their gathering, conserving, or distributing there should be rendered solicitous diligence, so to speak reason, for the state of the realm which through them endures unharmed. Indeed we know that kingdoms are ruled and laws endure chiefly by prudence, fortitude, temperance or justice, and the other virtues, whence

mundi rectoribus totis est viribus insistendum. Set fit interdum vt quod sano consilio vel excellenti mente concipitur intercedente pecunia citius conualescat et quod difficile videbatur per hanc quasi per quandam negotiorum metodum facilem consequatur effectum.

Non solum autem hostilitatis set etiam pacis tempore necessaria videtur. Illo enim in municipiis firmandis, in stipendiis ministrandis et in aliis plerisque locis pro qualitate personarum ad conseruandum regni statum effunditur; hoc vero licet arma quiescant, a deuotis principibus construuntur basilice, Christus alitur et vestitur in paupere et ceteris operibus misericordie insistendo mamona distribuitur. In vtriusque vero temporis strenuis actibus gloria principum est; set excellit in hiis vbi pro temporablibus impensis, felici mercimonio mansura succedunt.

Ea propter, rex illustris, mundanorum principum maxime, quia sepe te vidimus vtroque tempore gloriosum, non parcentem quidem pecunie thesauris, set pro loco, pro tempore, pro personis, legitimis sumptibus insistentem, modicum opus excellentie tue deuouimus, non de rebus quidem magnis vel luculento sermone compositum, set agresti stylo de scaccarii tui necessariis obseruanciis. Porro super hiis te vidimus quandoque sollicitum, adeo vt missis a latere tuo viris discretis de eodem dominum tunc Eliensem conueneris. Nec fuit absurdum tam excellentis ingenii virum, tam singularis potentie principem, inter cetera maiora hec etiam curasse. Sane scaccarium suis legibus non temere set magnorum consideratione subsistit cuius ratio si seruetur in omnibus poterunt singulis sua iura seruari also these must be pursued by the world's rulers with all their might. But it happens sometimes that something conceived by sound counsel or an excellent mind prospers more quickly when money intervenes and what seemed difficult in this way may achieve an easy result just as by some method of negotiations.

Not only, moreover, in times of hostility but also of peace it [i.e. *pecunia*] seems necessary. For there [times of hostility] it is poured out on fortified towns, in paying wages and in many other places for the quality of people needed to preserve the state of the realm, but here [times of peace] although arms are quiet, basilicas are constructed by devout princes, Christ is fed and clothed in the poor and wealth is distributed in pursuing other works of mercy. But in whichever times, the glory of princes is in vigorous actions, but it excels in those things where through temporal expenditures they attain—in a happy exchange—things destined to endure.

On account of these things, illustrious king, greatest of worldly princes, because we have seen you glorious in both times, not sparing indeed of the treasury's money, but for the place, for the time, for the persons, steadfast in proper expenditure, we devote this modest work to your excellence, not indeed about grand matters or composed in splendid language, but in a rude style about the necessary observances of your exchequer. Formerly we have seen you sometimes concerned about these matters to such a pass that you have convened discreet men released from your side by the same lord then at Ely.[1] Nor was it out of place that such a man of excellent nature, such a prince of singular power, undertook these matters also among greater issues. Truly the exchequer exists by its own laws, not blindly but by the deliberation of great men, whose reason, if preserved in all respects, the rights for each can be

1 That is, fitzNigel's father, the Bishop of Ely.

et tibi plene prouenient que fisco debentur, que possit oportune nobilissime mentis tue ministra manus effundere.

## Diologus Liber Primus

Anno xxiii. regni regis Henrici secundi cum sederem ad fenestram specule que est iuxta fluuium Tamensem factum est verbum hominis in impetu loquentis ad me dicens "Magister, nonne legisti, quod in scientia vel thesauro abscondito nulla sit vtilitas?" Cui cum respondissem "Legi;" statim intulit. "Cur ergo scientiam de scaccario que penes te plurima esse dicitur alios non doces et ne tibi commoriatur scripto commendas." Tum ego, "Ecce frater ad scaccarium iam per multa tempora resedisti et nihil te latet cum scrupulosus sis. Sic et de ceteris qui assident probabile est." At ille, "Sicut qui in tenebris ambulant et manibus palpant frequenter offendunt, sic illic multi resident qui videntes non vident et audientes non intelligunt." Tum ego, "Irreuerenter loqueris, nec enim scientia tanta est vel de tantis; sed forte sunt illis, qui magna aucupantur, corda ut pedes aquile qui parua non retinent et quos magna non effugiunt." Et ille, "Esto, set licet aquile celsius volent, tamen in humilibus quiescunt et reficiuntur, et ob hoc humilia nobis exponi petimus ipsis aquilis profutura." Tum ego, "Veritus sum de hiis rebus opus contexere que corporeis sensibus subiecta sunt et cotidianis vsibus vilescunt, nec est vel esse potest in eis subtilium rerum descriptio vel iocunda nouitatis inventio."

served and fully provide to you those things owed to the fisc,[1] which your attendant hand, suiting your most noble mind, can stream forth.

## Diologus First Book

In the twenty-third year of the reign of king Henry the second, while I sat at the window of an outlook hard by the river Thames, the word of a man speaking in haste came to me, saying, "Master, have you not read that there is no utility in knowledge or treasure hidden away?" To which when I had answered, "So I have read," he put in at once, "Why then don't you teach others the knowledge of the exchequer that is said to be mostly in your hands and entrust it to writing lest it perish with you?" Then I said, "Behold, brother, you have sat at the exchequer many times now and nothing escapes your notice since you are very precise. And that's also likely for the others who sit there."

But he said, "Just as they who walk in darkness and feel with their hands frequently stumble, so there are many resident there who seeing do not see and hearing do not understand. Then I said, "You have spoken disrespectfully, for there is neither so much to know nor is it about such great matters; but perhaps they are those who are fowling for big game, their minds like the feet of an eagle which do not grasp small things but which big ones cannot escape. And he said, "That is so, but although eagles fly higher, nevertheless they rest and are restored in lowly places, and on account of this we ask that the lowly matters be explained to us for the benefit of the eagles themselves."

Then I said, "I have feared to compose a work about these matters that have been governed by the corporeal senses and are held cheap in everyday usages; there cannot be in them either a description of refined matters or a pleasing discovery of something new."

1 The royal treasury.

Et ille, "Qui nouitatibus gaudent, qui subtilium rerum fugam appetunt, habent Aristotelem et libros Platonicos, audiant illos. Tu scribe non subtilia set utilia." Tum ego, "De hiis rebus quas petis impossibile est nisi rusticano sermone et communibus loqui verbis." At ille velut succensus in iram, desideranti enim animo nihil satis festinatur, ait, "Artium scriptores ne multa parum scisse viderentur et ut ars difficilior cognitu fieret, multa conquisierunt et verbis incognitis palliarunt. Tu scribendam artem non suscipis set quasdam consuetudines et iura scaccarii, que quia communia debent esse, communibus necessario vtendum est verbis ut sint cognati sermones rebus de quibus loquimur. Preterea quamvis plerumque noua liceat nomina fingere, rogo tamen si placet vt vsitatis rerum ipsarum vocabulis, que ad placitum sunt, vti non pudeat, nec noua difficultas ex insolitis verbis oborta amplius perturbet." Tum ego, "Sensi te iratum, set animequior esto; faciam quod hortaris. Surgens ergo sede ex aduerso et de hiis qui te offendunt interroga. Quod siquid inauditum proposueris non erubesco dicere "Nescio," set conueniamus ambo discretiores." Et ille "Ad vota respondes. Licet autem turpis et ridicula res sit elementarius senex, ab ipsis tamen elementis incipiam."

And he, "They who rejoice in novelties, seek the escape of refined matters, have Aristotle and the Platonic books; let them hear those. You must write not refined but useful things."

Then I, "It is impossible to speak about these matters which you seek except in uneducated speech and commonplace words."

But he, as if on fire in anger, for nothing hurries sufficiently for a desiring mind, said, "Authors of the arts did not seem to have known many matters at all and so that art might be made more difficult in perceiving, they gathered up many matters and cloaked them in unknown words. You are not undertaking art to be written but those certain customs and rights of the exchequer that, because they should be common matters, it is necessary must be deployed in common words so that our discussions are kindred to the matters about which we speak. Moreover, although it may be permitted generally to devise new names, I ask nevertheless, if it please you, that it not be shameful to use the customary terms, which are at your pleasure, of the matters themselves, lest a new difficulty flowing from unfamiliar words should cause further confusion."

Then I, "I sense that you are angry, but be calm; I will do what you urge. Arising accordingly from your adversarial seat, ask then about these things that bother you. If you put forward something unheard of, I won't blush to say, 'I don't know, but we can together approach wiser men.'"

And he, "You answer my prayers. Moreover, although an elementary old man may be a disgraceful and ridiculous thing, nevertheless let me begin from first principles themselves."[1]

---

1 The author is being playful. Latin students learned their LMNs (thus the word "element") the way English beginners do their ABCs. The gentleman that fitzNigel encounters is presented as someone, presumably with some legal training or knowledge, who has had considerable experience of the Exchequer and been frustrated by it. He is not a beginning student who needs to begin with his ABCs or with first principles in the other sense of elements. His anger, plainly expressed to such a powerful figure as the treasurer, and the deference with which fitzNigel treats him, suggest he is a figure of some authority, likely a disgruntled sheriff.

**I. Quid sit Scaccarium et que ratio huius nominis.**

**Discipulus.** Quid est scaccarium?

**Magister.** Scaccarium tabula est quadrangula quae longitudinis quasi x. pedum latitudinis v. ad modum mense circumsedentibus apposita, vndique habet limbum altitudinis quasi iiii. digitorum ne quid appositum excidat. Superponitur autem scaccario [superiori] pannus in termino Pasche emptus, non quilibet, sed niger virgis distinctus, distantibus a se virgis vel pedis vel palme extente spatio. In spatiis autem calculi fiunt iuxta ordines suos de quibus alias dicetur. Licet autem tablula talis scaccarium dicatur, transumitur tamen hoc nomen vt ipsa quoque curia, que consedente scaccario est, scaccarium dicatur, adeo ut si quis per sententiam aliquid obtinuerit, vel aliquid de communi consilio fuerit constitutum, dicatur factum ad scaccarium illius vel illius anni. Quod autem hodie dicitur ad scaccarium, olim dicebatur ad taleas.

**Discipulus.** Que est ratio hujus nominis?

**Magister.** Nulla mihi verior ad presens occurrit quam quia scaccarii lusilis similem habet formam.

**Discipulus.** Numquid antiquorum prudentia pro sola forma sic nominavit? Cum et simili ratione posset tabularium appellari?

**I. What the Exchequer is and what the reason for this name.**

**Pupil.** What is the exchequer?

**Master.** The exchequer is a rectangular writing board whose length is perhaps ten feet and its width five, set up in the manner of a table for those sitting around it, and it has everywhere a raised edge, perhaps four fingers, lest something placed thereupon should fall off. Moreover, a cloth, purchased in Easter time, is placed on top of the surface, not just any sort but black divided by lines, the lines distant from each other either by a foot or the space of an extended palm. In the spaces are counters according to their own order, about which more will be said. Moreover, although such a board is called an exchequer, this name nevertheless has been transferred so that the court itself that sits around the chessboard[1] is called the exchequer, to the extent that if someone obtains something through a sentence or something is decided by common counsel, it is said to have been done at the exchequer of this or that year. Moreover, what is today called "at the exchequer" was once called "at the tallies."

**Pupil.** What is the reason for this name?

**Master.** Nothing truer occurs to me at the moment than that it has the same shape of a chess game.

**Pupil.** Surely the prudence of our ancestors can't have called it that for the shape alone? For the same reason couldn't it also have been called the checkerboard?[2]

---

1 The literal meaning of exchequer.

2 The chess- and checkerboard has sixty-four squares, with eight along each side. The exchequer tablecloth had but seven squares down the long side and four on the short.

**Magister.** Merito te scrupulosum dixi. Est et alia set occultior: sicut enim in scaccario lusili quidam ordines sunt pugnatorum et certis legibus vel limitibus procedunt vel subsistunt, presidentibus aliis et aliis procedentibus, sic in hoc quidam president quidam assident ex officio, et non est cuiquam liberum leges constitutas excedere quod erit ex consequentibus manifestum. Item, sicut in lusili pugna committitur inter reges, sic in hoc inter duos principaliter conflictus est et pugna committitur, thesaurarium scilicet et vicecomitem qui assidet ad compotum, residentibus aliis tanquam iudicibus vt videant et iudicent.

**Discipulus.** Numquid a thesaurario compotus suscipitur cum illic multi sint qui ratione potestatis maiores videantur?

**Magister.** Quod thesaurarius a vicecomite compotum suscipiat hinc est manifestum quia idem ab eo cum regi placuerit requiritur. Nec enim ab ipso requireretur quod non sucepisset. Sunt tamen qui dicunt thesaurarium et camerarios obnoxios tantum hiis que scribuntur in rotulis "In Thesauro" vt de hiis compotus ab eis exigatur. Sed verius creditur vt de tota scriptura rotuli respondeant, quod ex consequentibus constare poterit.

**II. Quod aliud est inferius, aliud superius; vna tamen origo vtriusque.**

**Discipulus.** Numquid solum illud scacarium est in quo talis conflictus est?

**Master.** Deservedly I have called you precise. There is another [reason] but more obscure: for just as in the chess game there is a certain order of the combatants and they move or stay by certain rules or limits, some in precedence and others in movements, so in this one some preside, some sit there ex officio, and none of them is free to exceed the established rules, which will be clear from what follows. Likewise, just as battle is joined between kings in the game, so in this there is dispute between two principles and a battle is joined, namely the treasurer and the sheriff who sits to a reckoning before the other residents, as it were as judges, as they watch and decide.[1]

**Pupil.** Why is the account received by the treasurer when there are many there who by reason of their power seem greater?

**Master.** It is clear that the treasurer receives that account from the sheriff because it is required from him when it pleases the king. For that cannot be required of him what he has not received. However, there are those who say that the treasurer and the chamberlains are liable only for those things written in the rolls "In the Treasury," so that an account of these may be exacted from them. But it is more correctly considered that they should answer for all the writings of rolls, which will be apparent from what follows.

**II. That one is the lower and the other the higher and both from one origin.**

**Pupil.** Is that exchequer in which such a contest occurs the only one?

---

1 The "pieces" in the exchequer, that is, the barons (or their stand-ins), move only when they adjourn to an adjoining chamber to discuss difficult matters out of the hearing of those attending and in order not to disrupt the proceedings. The real game of chess was played in "Receipts," especially at the Michaelmas session where the annual accounts were settled, when the sheriff's clerk placed his tally sticks in the appropriate squares of the tablecloth, which seems to have functioned as an abacus, and a teller matched them with the exchequer's counter-tallies.

**Magister.** Non. Est enim inferius scaccarium quod et "Recepta" dicitur vbi pecunia recepta numeratur et scriptis et taleis committitur vt de eisdem postmodum in superiori compotus fiat. Vna tamen vtriusque origo est, quia quicquid solvendum esse in maiore deprehenditur hic soluitur et quod hic solutum fuerit ibi computatur.

**III. Que sit ratio vel institutio inferioris per singula officia.**

**Discipulus.** Que est ratio vel institutio inferioris scaccarii?

**Magister.** Vt video nullius horum ignorantiam sustines. Noueris autem quod inferius illud scaccarium suas habet personas ratione quidem officiorum a se distinctas, set in regis vtilitatem, salua tamen equitate, pari intentione deuotas; omnes quidem dominorum suorum nominibus non propriis militantes, exceptis duobus dumtaxat, milite scilicet qui preest examinibus, et fusore. Horum enim officia de regis tantum pendent arbitrio, vnde magis ad superius quam ad inferius pertinere videntur, sicut infra dicetur.

Illic est clericus thesaurarii cum sigillo eius. Sunt et duo milites camerariorum. Est et miles quidam qui argentarius dici potest quia ex officio argento examinando preest. Est et fusor qui argentum examinat. Sunt et quatuor computatores ad numerandam pecuniam. Est et hostiarius thesauri et vigil.

Horum autem hec sunt officia. Clericus thesaurarii cum fuerit numerata pecunia et in forulos missa per centenas libras apponit sigillum et deputat scripto quantum vel a quo vel ob quam causam receperit. Taleas quoque de eadem recepta a camerariis factas inbreuiat. Non solum autem pecunie saccis sed et archis et singulis forulis in quibus rotuli vel talee collocantur si libet apponit sigillum et ad omnia

**Master.** No. For there is a lower exchequer that is called "Receipts," where money received is counted and committed to writings and tallies so that later in the upper exchequer an account can be made from them. However, the source of both is the same, because whatever is held to be due in the upper is resolved here and what has been resolved here is accounted for there.

**III. What the underlying principle or foundation of the lower is according to its individual offices.**

**Pupil.** What is the underlying principle or foundation of the lower exchequer?

**Master.** I see that you endure ignorance of none of these matters. You should know moreover that the lower exchequer has it own staff, distinguished to be sure from each other by reason of their offices, but devoted with equal purpose to the kings' rights and the preservation of equity; all indeed serve in their lords' names, not their own, with only two exceptions, namely the knight who presides over the assays and the smelter. For the offices of these depend on the king's choice, whence they seem to pertain more to the upper than the lower, as will be discussed below.

There is the treasurer's clerk with his seal. There are also the two chamberlains' knights. And there is a certain knight who can be called the silverer because he presides over assaying the silver. There is also a smelter who assays the silver. There are also four tellers for reckoning the money. There is also the doorkeeper of the treasury and the watchman.

These are their duties. The treasurer's clerk, when he has counted the money and put it in bags of one hundred pounds, affixes the seal and reckons in writing how much or from whom or for what reason he has received it. He also abridges the tallies made of each receipt from the

subiecta officia diligenter prospicit et nil eum latet.

Militum, qui et camerarii dicuntur quia pro camerariis ministrant, hoc est officium. Hii clauis archarum baiulant, archae enim cuilibet due sere sunt diuersi generis; hoc est cuius neutri clauis alterius possit aptari— et hii claues earum deferunt. Circumcingitur autem quelibet archa corrigia quadam immobili in qua desuper, firmatis seris, thesaurarii sigillum apponitur vt nulli eorum nisi de communi assensu accessus pateat. Item officium horum est numeratam pecuniam et in vasis ligneis per centenos solidos compositam ponderare, ne sit error in numero, et tunc demum in forulos mittere per centenas, vt dictum est, libras. Quod si vas aliquod inuentum est minus habens, non quidem per estimationem quod deesse putatur apponitur sed statim in aceruum numerandorum id de quo dubitatur proicitur.

Et nota quosdam comitatus a tempore regis Henrici primi et in tempore regis Henrici secundi licite potuisse cuiuscunque monete denarios solutioni offerre dummodo argentei essent et ponderi legitimo non obstarent; quia scilicet monetarios ex antiqua institutione non habentes vndecunque sibi denarios perquirebant, quales sunt Norhumberland et Cumberland. Sic autem suscepti denarii, licet de firma essent, seorsum tamen ab aliis cum quibusdam signis appositis mittebantur. Reliqui vero comitatus solos vsuales et instantis monete legitimos denarios tam de firmis quam de placitis afferebant. At, postquam rex illustris cuius laus est in rebus magnis excellentior sub monarchia sua per vniuersum regnum vnum pondus et vnam monetam instituit, omnis comitatus vna legis necessitate teneri et generalis commercii solutioni cepit obligari. Omnes itaque idem monete genus quomodocunque

chamberlains. Moreover, if it pleases him he affixes the seal not only to the bags of money but also to the chests and each of the cases in which rolls or tallies are gathered. He watches all the subject offices diligently and nothing escapes him.

This is the office of the knights, who are also called chamberlains because they minister for the chamberlains. They bear the keys of the chests, for to each chest there are two locks of a different kind; so it is to neither of which the key of the other can be fit—and they carry the keys of them. Moreover, each chest is cinched about with a sturdy strap upon which, after the locks are shut, the seal of the treasurer is affixed so that none of them can be accessed except by common assent. Likewise, when the money has been counted and arranged in wooden vessels of one hundred shillings, it is their duty to weigh them, lest there be an error in the count, and then finally to lay them in bags of one hundred pounds, as was said. If some vessel is found having less, that which is thought to be missing by valuation is not added in to be sure but immediately the one about which there is doubt is put back into the stack of those yet to be counted.

And note that certain counties from the time of king Henry the first and in the time of king Henry the second have been allowed to offer payments of whatsoever coins as long as they are silver and do not differ from the lawful weight; namely because not having moneyers by ancient arrangement they searched out pennies for themselves from everywhere; such are Northumberland and Cumberland. Moreover, pennies thus received, although they were from a farm, were nevertheless put aside from the rest with a certain sign affixed. The rest of the counties brought only the usual lawful pennies of the current coinage whether from the farms or pleas. But after our illustrious king, whose distinguished praise is in his great deeds, established under his monarchy one weight and one coinage throughout his universal realm, every county began to be held by the law's sole requirement and to be obliged to payment of the common

teneantur soluunt. Sed tamen exactionis que de combustione prouenit iacturam omnes non sustinent.

Item hii taleas faciunt de receptis, et commune est eis cum clerico thesaurarii vt per breuia regis vel precepto baronum, thesaurum susceptum expendant, non tamen inconsultis dominis suis. Hii tres simul omnes vel vicissim cum thesauro mittuntur cum oportuerit. Hiis tribus precipua cura est in omnibus hiis que in inferiori scaccario fiunt.

**Discipulus.** Ergo vt video licet hiis per breue regis vel precepto eorum qui president thesaurum susceptum consultis tamen dominis suis expendere.

**Magister.** Licet, inquam hoc modo. De liberationibus seruientium inferioris scaccarii et de minutis necessariis scaccarii emendis, qualia sunt vasa illa lignea et alia de quibus infra dicetur, eorum fidei committitur. Alias autem non. Qui vero breue regis vel cartam detulerit pro pecunia, precipientibus dominis suis, hac ei lege soluatur id quod expresse nominatur in breui vt, antequam exeat, susceptam pecuniam numeret. Quod si quid defuerit redeat ad scaccarium is qui suscepit et fidei religionem prestet sub hac forma quod quantam suscepit reportauit, non apposito secundum conscientiam suam vt fit in aliis, et hoc facto solvatur ei quod restat, numerata prius eadem coram omnibus a constitutis computatoribus. Si vero, lege sibi proposita, hostium thesauri egressus fuerit quecunque fuerit persona vel quantacunque iactura non ei respondeatur.

sort. And so they all pay the same kind of coinage howsoever they are obligated. But nevertheless they do not all sustain the loss which occurs from the smelting of the payment.

Likewise they make tallies from the receipts, and, together with the treasurer's clerk, they commonly disperse received funds by the king's writ or the command of the barons, not however without consulting their masters. These three together or individually are sent with the treasure when required. They have special responsibility in everything done in the lower exchequer.

**Pupil.** So, as I see, they are permitted by the king's writ or by order of those who govern the received treasure to expend it, however in consultation with their masters.

**Master.** It is, I say, in this way. For the liveries[1] of the servants of the lower exchequer and for the purchases of small necessities of the exchequer—such are those wooden vessels and other things which will be spoken of below—is entrusted to their honesty. Not, however, otherwise. Who has brought the king's writ or charter for money, ordered by their masters, is paid precisely that which is named in the writ on condition that, before he leave, he count the received money. If something is lacking, he who received it should return to the exchequer and stand before the community of faith [i.e. swear an oath] in this formula, that as much as he received he has returned, not affixing "according to his conscience" as it is in other oaths, and having done this there is paid to him what was omitted, the same having been counted first in the presence of all the appointed tellers. But if, the law having been propounded to him, he has passed out the door of the treasury, whatsoever person he is or howsoever much the loss, it should not be returned to him.

---

1 Livery is an allowance, which may include clothing and identifying devices and badges.

Militis argentarii et fusoris officia sibi videntur annexa et ad superius scaccarium magis pertinentia et ob hoc ibidem cum ceteris officiis explananda.

Quatuor computatorum officium hoc est. Cum in scaccarium numeranda pecunia mittitur, vnus eorum diligenter totam commiscet vt non seorsum meliores et seorsum deteriores sint set mixti vt ponderi respondeant. Quo facto camerarius ad libram scaccarii ponderat quantum oportet in trutina; quod si numerus xx. solidorum plusquam sex nummis excreuerit respectu libre, indigna recipi dicitur. Si vero vel ad vi. vel infra se cohibet, suscipitur et a computatoribus dilgenter per centenos solidos vt predictum est numeratur. Si vero de firma sunt denarii et sint examinandi, facta commixtione xliiii. solidorum de aceruo in loculum seorsum mittuntur, et huic vicecomes signum suum apponit vt ex hiis postmodum examen, quod vulgo essaium dicitur, fiat sicut ex sequentibus liquebit. Erit autem cure eorum qui presunt recepte gratia dominorum suorum, hoc est, clerici thesaurarii et camerariorum vt recepta pecunia seorsum mittant examinati argenti pondera et denarios de firma, appositis quibusdam signis saccis eorum, vt si rex vasa argentea ad cultum domus dei vel ad domus proprie obsequium vel forte monetas transmarinas fieri voluerit ex hiis fiant.

**Discipulus.** Est aliquid in praedictis quod me pulsat.

**Magister.** Dic ergo.

**Discipulus.** Dixisti si bene memini quod ad scaccarium quandoque soluenda differtur pecunia que iudicatur indigna recipi. Si scilicet pensata cum libra ponderis de scaccario inuenta est minus habens

The offices of the knight silverer and smelter seem connected to each other and pertain more to the upper exchequer and because of this will be explained there with its other offices.

The office of the four tellers is this. When money that has to be counted is sent to the exchequer, one of them diligently mingles it so that the better and the poorer [coins] are not separate but mingled so that they may answer to their weight. That done, a chamberlain weighs on a weighing beam as much as is necessary for the exchequer's pound, which [i.e. the amount weighed], if the sum of twenty shillings accrues more than six pence with respect to the pound, it is declared unworthy of acceptance. But if it contains either up to six [pence] or less, it is accepted and by the tellers diligently counted by hundreds of shillings as aforesaid. But if the pennies are from a farm and have to be assayed, after the mixing is done forty-four shillings from the heap are put separately in a money box and the sheriff affixes his seal on it so that from these afterwards the test that is commonly called the assay can be made, just as will be clear from the following. Moreover, it will be in the care of those who preside over the receipt by the grace of their masters, that is, the clerk of the treasury and the chamberlains, that they set aside from the money received, for assay, weights of silver and the pennies from farm, in sacks affixed with their certain seal, so that if the king wishes silver vessels to adorn the house of God or for services in his own home or perhaps coins to be sent abroad, they can be made up from these.

**Pupil.** There is something in the aforesaid that strikes me.

**Master.** Speak then.

**Pupil.** You said, if I have remembered well, that sometimes money paid at the exchequer which was judged unworthy to be received was declined. That is, if it was found to have more than six pence less by weight when you have weighed it by the exchequer pound. Therefore,

vltra vi. Cum ergo quilibet moneta regni huius impressam habere debeat regis imaginem et ad idem pondus omnes monetarii teneantur operari qualiter fieri potest vt non omne eorum opus eiusdem ponderis sit?

**Magister.** Magnum est quod queris et alterius egens inquisitionis. Attamen fieri potest per falsarios et nummorum decurtatores vel detonsores. Noueris autem monetam Anglie in tribus falsam deprehendi, in falso scilicet pondere, in falsa lege, in falsa imagine. Hiis tamen falsitatibus par poena non debetur. Sed de hiis alias.

**Discipulus.** Si placet, persequere de officiis vt cepisti.

**Magister.** Ad hostiarii curam: spectat vt excludat vel admittat quod oportet et diligens sit in custodia omnium que hostio concluduntur. Vnde et ratione hostii de singulis breuibus exitus duos habet denarios. Hic ministrat forulos ad pecuniam reponendam et rotulos et taleas et cetera necessaria per annum et pro singulis forulis duos habet denarios. Hic in omnem receptam ligna oportuna ministrat ad taleas recepte et compotorum, et semel, hoc est, in termino sancti Michaelis, v. solidos pro lignis talearum percipit. Hic vascula lignea cnipulos, loculos et corrigias et cetera minuta necessaria de fisco inuenit. In termino eodem pro incausto totius anni ad vtrumque scaccarium ii. solidi debentur quos sibi de antiquo iure vendicat sacrista maioris ecclesiae Westmonasteri.

Vigilis officium idem est ibi quod alibi, diligentissima scilicet de nocte custodia thesauri principaliter et omnium eorum que in domo thesauri reponuntur.

Sic habes omnium officia distincta qui inferius ministrant. Sunt et hiis liberationes constitute dum scaccarium est; hoc est a die qua

since whatsoever coinage of the realm is obliged to have the impressed image of its king and all moneyers are held to operate by the same pound, how can it be that each work of them is not of the same weight?

**Master.** What you have asked is a great matter and in want of further investigation. Nevertheless, it can happen through counterfeiters and clippers and trimmers of coins. You should know, moreover, that the coinage of England is found false in three manners, that is, in false weight, in false alloy, [and] in false image. For these three falsenesses, however, the punishment is not bound to be the same. But about these matters elsewhere.

**Pupil.** If it pleases, persevere about the offices as you began.

**Master.** To the doorkeeper's care: he watches so that he might exclude or admit what is proper and diligently be in charge of all the things enclosed by the door. Whence and by reason of the door for each writ of issue he has two pennies. He supplies the forels[1] for storing money and the rolls and tallies and the other necessary materials and for each forel he has per year two pennies. In each receipt [i.e. session of the exchequer] he provides suitable wood for the tallies of receipt and accounts, and one time, which is in the term of St Michael, he gets five shillings for the wood of the tallies. He provides from the fisc the wooden vessels, knives, money bags, and straps and other small necessities. In the same term, for the entire year's ink for both exchequers, two shillings are owed, which by ancient law the sacristan of the greater church of Westminster claims for himself.

The office of watchman there is the same that [is] elsewhere, namely most diligently during the night the custody of the treasure chiefly and of all the things that are kept in the treasure house.

1 Bins for loose money.

conuocantur usque ad diem qua generalis est secessio. Clericus thesaurarii qui infra est, v. denarios habet in die. Scriptor eiusdem thesaurarii in superiori scaccario similiter v. Scriptor cancellarii v. Duo milites baiuli clauium quisque in die viii. ratione militiae; asserunt enim quod equis necessariis et armis instructi fore teneantur vt cum thesauro missi quod sui officii fuerit opportunius sic exequantur. Miles argentarius xii. in die. Fusor v. Hostiarius maioris scaccarii v. Quatuor computatores quisque iii. si Londoniis sunt, si Wintonie, quia inde solent assumi, ii. quisque habet. Vigil, vnum denarium. Ad lumen cuiusque noctis circa thesaurum, obulus.

**Discipulus.** Hostiarius thesauri qua ratione liberationem solus non percipit?

**Magister**. Non satis noui, sed tamen quia videtur aliquid percipere ratione hostii et pro forulorum et talearum ministerio liberationem forte non recipit vel forte quia non regi sed magis thesaurario et camerariis seruire videtur in custodia hostii domus eorum. Hac lege minoris scaccarii vel recepte ratio subsistit.

**Discipulus.** Sic mihi satisfactum est in hac parte vt nil decesse videatur. Nunc ergo si placet prosequere de maiore.

**IIII. Que sit auctoritas superioris et unde sumpsit originem.**

**Magister.** Licet eorum qui ad maius scaccarium resident, officia quibusdam videantur proprietatibus esse distincta vnum tamen officium omnium est et intentio vt regis vtilitati prospiciant, salua tamen equitate, secundum constitutas leges scaccarii. Eius autem ratio vel institutio cum ipsa temporis antiquitate tum magnorum qui assident auctoritate

Thus you have the separate offices of all who serve the lower exchequer. And there are liveries [allowances] for these while the exchequer is constituted; that is from the day when they are convened until the day on which adjournment is general. The treasurer's clerk, who is in the lower exchequer, receives five pennies per day. The same treasurer's scribe in the upper exchequer likewise five. The chancellor's scribe five. The two knights bailiff of the keys each per day eight pennies by reason of knighthood, for they claim that they are held to be equipped with the necessary horses and arms so that when sent with treasure it will be that their offices thus might be carried out more suitably. The knight silverer twelve per day. The smelter five. The doorkeeper of the greater exchequer five. The four tellers each three if they are in London, if in Winchester each has two because they are wont to be supposed there. The watchman, one penny. For the lighting around the treasury, an obolus [halfpenny] each night.

**Pupil.** For what reason does the treasury's doorkeeper alone not receive livery?

**Master.** I haven't quite understood, but nevertheless perhaps he does not receive livery because he seems to receive something by reason of the door and for the bailiwick of the forels and tallies, or perhaps because he is seen to serve not the king but more the treasurer and the chamberlains in the custody of their house's door. The plan of the lesser exchequer or receipt subsists in this manner.

**Pupil.** I am satisfied accordingly in this part as nothing seems to have been left out. Therefore now, if it please, continue about the greater [exchequer].

**IIII. What the authority of the upper is and whence it took its beginning.**

**Master.** Although the offices of those who sit at the greater exchequer seem to be distinct in their certain characteristics, nevertheless the one

roborata subsistit. Ab ipsa namque regni conquisitione per regem Willelmum facta cepisse dicitur sumpta tamen ipsius ratione a scaccario transmarino. Verum in plurimis et pene maioribus dissident. Sunt etiam qui credant vsum eius sub regibus Anglicis extitisse hinc sumentes huius rei argumentum quod coloni et iam decrepiti senes fundorum illorum qui corone annominantur quorum in hiis cana memoria est optime nouerint a patribus suis edocti quantum de albo firme pro singulis libris soluere teneantur. Sed hec ratio cogens est de firme solutione non de scaccarii sessione. Videtur autem eis obuiare qui dicunt album firme a temporibus Anglorum cepisse quod in libro iudicario in quo totius regni descriptio diligens continetur et tam de tempore regis Edwardi quam de termpore regis Willelmi, sub quo factus est, singulorum fundorum valencia exprimitur nulla prorsus de albo firme fit mentio. Vnde probabile videtur quod facta illa descriptione tempore iam dicti regis de albo firmarum fuerit a studiosis eius constitutum propter causas que inferius annotantur. Quocumque vero tempore ceperit vsus eius, certum est quod magnorum auctoritate roboratur adeo vt nulli liceat statuta scaccarii infringere vel eis quauis temeritate resistere. Habet enim hoc commune cum ipsa domini regia curia in qua ipse in propria persona iura discernit quod nec recordationi nec sententie in eo late licet alicui contradicere. Huic autem curie tam insignis auctoritas est cum propter regie ymaginis excellentiam que in sigillo eius in thesauro indiuidua lege seruatur tum propter eos qui assident vt dictum est quorum sollertia totus regni status indempnis

office and purpose of all is that they watch out for the king's profit, preserving equity, however, according to the established laws of the exchequer. Its manner or arrangement, moreover, maintains itself by its own temporal antiquity together with the valid authority of the magnates who sit there. For it is said from the very conquest of the realm by king William to have taken its appropriated arrangements from the overseas exchequer,[1] although in its own way. Indeed they [i.e. the Norman and English exchequers] are at variance in many and mostly major matters. There are also those who believe that its use existed under the Anglo-Saxon kings, here assuming the argument of this matter because the villeins and now infirm old men of those farms that are named for the crown,[2] whose memory in these matters is wise, learned very well, taught by their fathers, how much they are obliged to pay for the blanching of a farm for every pound [in rent].[3] But this reason is cogent for the payment of the farm, not for the sitting of the exchequer. Moreover, it seems to go against those who say the blanching of a farm took its origins from the times of the Anglo-Saxons that in the judgment book [Domesday], in which is contained a careful description of the entire realm both from the time of king Edward and the time of king William, under whom it was made, and there is expressed the valuation of each single farm, absolutely no mention is made about the blanching of a farm. Whence it seems probable that the blanching of farms was constituted with the already-mentioned king's census by his zealous men, for reasons discussed below. In whatever time its use took its origins, it is certain that it was strengthened by the authority of the magnates to such a degree that it was permitted to no one to infringe upon the statutes of the exchequer or to resist them with whatsoever temerity. For it has this in common with the court of the lord king itself, in which he in his own person decides the law, that it is permitted to no one to contradict either a

1 That is, the Norman exchequer.
2 The crown lands.
3 A blanch farm paid rent in coins whose silver had to be assayed.

seruatur. Illic enim residet capitalis domini regis iustitia, primus post regem in regno ratione fori, et maiores quique de regno qui familiarius regiis secretis assistunt vt quod fuerit sub tantorum presentia constitutum vel terminatum inuiolabili iure subsistat.

Verum quidam ex officio, quidam ex sola iussione principis resident. Ex officio principaliter residet, immo et presidet, primus in regno, capitalis scilicet iustitia. Huic autem assident ex sola iussione principis momentanea scilicet et mobili auctoritate quidam qui maiores et discretiores videntur in regno siue de clero sint siue de curia. Assident inquam ad discernenda iura et dubia determinanda que frequenter ex incidentibus questionibus oriuntur. Non enim in ratiociniis sed in multiplicibus iudiciis excellens scaccarii scientia consistit. Facile enim est, proposita summa que exigitur et suppositis ad collationem eius hiis que soluta sunt, per subtractionem discernere, si satisfactum est vel si quid restat. At cum ceperit multiplex inquisitio fieri de hiis rebus, que varie fisco proueniunt, et diuersis modis requiruntur et a vicecomitibus non eodem modo perquiruntur, discernere si secus egerint quibusdam graue est et ob hoc circa hoc scientia scaccarii maior esse dicitur. Dubiorum vero vel dubitalium iudicia que frequenter emergunt sub vna tractatus serie comprehendi non valent quia nec dum omnia dubiorum

recording or a sentence received in it. Moreover, the authority of this court is manifest both on account of the excellence of the royal image that is preserved on its seal in the treasury by special law and because of those who preside, as has been said, whose skill has kept safe the entire state of the realm. For there sits the chief justice of the lord king,[1] first after the king in the realm by reason of his *forum*, and great men of the realm[2] who intimately assist with the king's secrets, so that what has been constituted or concluded in the presence of so many may stand by imperishable law.

Indeed, some of them sit *ex officio*, some solely by the command of the prince. *Ex officio* chiefly sits, indeed presides, the first man in the realm, namely the chief justice [i.e. the justiciar]. With him, moreover, sit solely by order of the prince, of course with curtailed and dismiss-able authority, certain men in the realm who are considered greater and more distinguished, whether they are from the clergy or the court. They sit, I say, to discern the law and to determine the doubtful matters that frequently arise from incidental questions. For not in accountings but in complex judgments consists the surpassing knowledge of the exchequer. For it is easy, from the proposed sum which has been exacted and from the submissions to its payment which have been made, to discern by subtraction if it has been satisfied or if something remains. But when a complex inquest is held to levy money about these matters, which come to the fisc variously, are required in diverse manners, and are not pursued by the sheriffs in the same way, it is a serious matter to discern if they have acted improperly about them, and accordingly the treasury's expertness in respect of this is said to be more important. Truly the

1 The justice referred to is the Justiciar, at the time fitzNigel writes the king's viceroy when the monarch is in country and regent in his stead when he is abroad. *Forum* is used in the ecclesiastical sense, in which it designates an area of administrative responsibility or jurisdiction.

2 These *maiores* who sit with the Justiciar are specifically, to his right the Bishop of Winchester, and to his left, in order, the Chancellor, the Constable, both Chamberlains, and the Marshal.

genera in lucem prodierunt. Quedam tamen ex hiis que proposita vel determinata cognouimus suis locis inferius annotabimus.

**V. Quod sit officium presidentis in illo et que sint singulorum sibi assidentium officia.**

**VI. Quis sit tenor breuium regis factorum ad scaccarium siue de exitu thesauri sive de computandis, siue de perdonandis.**

**VII. A quibus et ad quid instituta fuit argenti examinacio, set hoc incidenter.**

**VIII. Que sint iura et dignitates residentium ad scaccarium vel ex officio vel ex solo regis mandato, et quedam incidentia necessaria.**

**IX. Quid scutagium et quare sic dicatur.**

**X. Quid murdrum et quare sic dictum.**

**XI. Quid danegeldum et quare sic nominatum vel institutum.**

**XII. Quid foresta regis et que ratio appellationis.**

**XIII. Quid essartum vel quid vastum et que rationes horum nominum.**

**XIIII. Quod thesaurus dicitur interdum ipsa pecunia, interdum locus in quo seruatur.**

**XV. Quis sit vsus sigilli regii quod est in thesauro.**

**XVI. Quid liber iudiciarius et ad quid compositus.**

**XVII. Quid hyda, quid centuriata, quid comitatus secundum vulgarem de hiis opinionem.**

judgment of doubtful or questionable matters which frequently arise cannot be seriously comprehended within one *tractatus*, because all the varieties of doubtful matters have not yet come to light. However, some of them proposed or asserted that we we have examined we will note in their places below.

**V. What the office of the presider is in it and what the offices are of each of those who have a seat.**

**VI. What the wording is of the king's writs made at the exchequer either for the issue of treasure or for reckonings or pardons.**

**VII. By whom and to what purpose the assay of silver was established, but this incidentally.**

**VIII. What the rights and dignities are of those sitting at the exchequer, either ex officio or by the king's command alone, and certain incidental necessities.**

**IX. What scutage [is] and why it is so called.**

**X. What murdrum[1] [is] and why so called.**

**XI. What danegeld [is] and why thus named and established.**

**XII. What the king's forest [is] and what the reason of its appellation.**

**XIII. What assart[2] [is] or what waste and what the reasons of their names.**

**XIIII. That money itself is sometimes called *thesaurus*, sometimes the place in which it is kept.**

**XV. What the use is of the king's seal that is in the treasury.**

**XVI. What the book of judgment[3] [is] and to what end composed. XVII. What hides, what hundreds, what counties [are] according to the common opinion of them.**

---

1 *Murdrum* is both the act of murder and the fine associated with it.
2 Land cleared of trees.
3 Domesday Book.

## XVIII. Quid rotulus exactorius.

### Diologus Liber Secundus

Audi me frater et auribus audiendi percipe que loquar tibi. Non penitebit te modicum tempus ereptum otiis impendere velle negotiis. Sunt enim non nulli qui non erubescunt dicere in cordibus suis, "qui apponit scientiam apponit et dolorem." Hiis onerosa est doctrina et iocundum [est] desipere: propter hoc ab hiis longe facta est veritas, quia metuentes iocundum discipline laborem incidunt in errorem. Fiunt igitur ceci corde, viarumque pericula non videntes pronis gressibus in precipitium ruunt. Verum te, frater, nullus dies otiosum inueniat ne te forte vacantem pessimis quibusque subiciat, pronior in malum infirmitatis humane conditio. Quod si forte tibi nulla sunt, honesta tamen finge negotia, vt semper exercitatus animus expeditior sit ad doctrinam. Hiis igitur negotiis in que nos impegisti paulisper attende, non vt ex eis magni laboris metas fructus, set tantum ne otiosus [sis].

**Discipulus.** Vereor ne instantis noctis crepusculum precipitem inponat finem negotiis, et omissis pluribus necessariis acceleres, vt careas inportunitate querentis.

**Magister.** Immo ego magis veritus sum, ne te post longa silentia, propter agrestem stilum, diu suppressus cachinnus succuteret, vel forte tacitus tecum pertractasses qualiter sine nostra molestia ab

**XVIII. What the roll of exactions [is].**[1]

### Diologus Second Book

Hear me brother and perceive, with the ears of one hearing, what I would tell you. You will not be sorry to wish to devote to business matters a little time snatched from leisure affairs. For there are some who have not blushed to say in their hearts, "who serves up knowledge serves up also sorrow." To these learning is onerous and [it is] agreeable to act foolish: on account of this truth has become tedious to them, because those fearing the agreeable labor of knowledge fall into error. Therefore they have become blind in heart, and, not seeing the dangers of their ways, rush with inclined[2] steps into the precipice. Truly, brother, let no day find you otiose nor idle lest perchance the human condition should make you submissive to the worst things, more inclined unto the evil of weakness. But if perchance they [i.e. the worst things] are nothing to you, nevertheless fashion honest affairs, as always a disciplined mind is more prepared for knowledge. Therefore attend to these affairs into which you have thrust us for a little while, not that from them you will earn the fruits of a great labor, but only lest you be idle.

**Pupil. I** fear lest the darkness of approaching night should impose a precipitate end upon our affairs, and, leaving out many necessary matters, you might hurry, that you absent yourself from the insolence of my complaining.

1 The Roll of Farms.

2 FitzNigel puns on the meaning of *pronus*, which means both literally inclined, like a blind sinner following a downward path into the abyss, but also prone to do something, that is, blindly lead an idle and accordingly dangerous life.

hiis auelli posses ad que nos coegisti. Ob hoc fateor me finem intempestuum pene posuisse dicendis. Set tamen cum docilis sis, et in te nondum tepuerit attentionis industria cepto ferar itinere. Vt igitur disposite rationis ordini satisfiat, de summonitionibus primo loco dicendum est, ex quibus scilicet, et qualiter, et ad quid fiant; atque vt de hiis tibi plenius constet, sit trium premonstrandorum primo prius ultimum, hoc est ad quid fiant.

**I. Ex quibus et qualiter et ad quid fiunt summonitiones.**

**II. Que sit differentia summonitionum vtriusque termini.**

**III. De agendis vicecomitis multipliciter.**

**Magister.** Omnes igitur vicecomites et ballivi, ad quos summonitiones diriguntur, eadem necessitate legis constringuntur, hoc est auctoritate regii mandati, vt scilicet die nominato designatoque loco conueniant et de debitis satisfaciant; quod vt manifestius fiat ipsius summonitionis tenorem diligentius intuere. Ait enim, "Vide, sicut te ipsum et omnia tua diligis, vt sis ad scaccarium ibi tunc et habeas tecum quicquid debes de veteri firma et noua et hec debita subscripta." Attende igitur, quia duo dicuntur que duobus sequentibus coaptantur, hoc enim "vide sicut te ipsum diligis" refertur ad "sis ibi tunc," illud vero "et sicut omnia tua diligis" referri videtur ad hoc "et habeas ibi tecum hec debita subscripta," ac si aperte dicatur "Absentia tua, tu, quicunque suscipis summonitionem, nisi necessariis et lege diffinitis causis possit excusari, in capitis tui periculum redundabit; videris enim sic regium spreuisse mandatum et in contemptum regie maiestatis irreuerenter egisse, si citatus super regiis, quibus addictus es, negotiis, nec veneris nec excusatorem miseris. Verum si per te steterit quominus

**Master.** No, to the contrary I was more afraid that after your long silence laughter suppressed for a long time was shaking you by reason of my wretched style, or, silent, you were perhaps thinking to yourself how you could be torn without our annoyance from these matters to which you have compelled us. On account of that, I confess almost to have put an untimely end to our discourses. But nevertheless, since you are attentive and the effort of application has not yet grown tepid in you, I submit to being borne along by our journey. Therefore, so that it might be sufficient to the order of the proposed plan, in the first place we must speak about summonses, namely from what, and how, and to what end they are made; but so that it might be more fully clear to you concerning these matters, in the beginning let the last of the three matters that must be shown be first, that is, to what end they are made.

**I. From what and how and to what end summonses are made.**

**II. What the difference is of the summonses of both terms.**

**III. About the sheriff's many obligations.**

**Master.** Therefore all sheriffs and bailiffs, to whom summonses are directed, are constrained by the same necessity of the law, that is, by the royal authority of the command, to wit, that on the day named and in the designated place they shall convene and make amends for their debts; thereby, that it become more manifest, consider more diligently the wording of the summons itself. For it says, "See, just as you value yourself and all yours, that you shall be there at the exchequer then and have with you whatever you owe from the old farm and the new and the below written debts." Pay close attention, therefore, because two things are said that are fit together with two following, for this "see just as you value yourself" refers to "you shall be there then," and that "and just as you value all yours" is seen to be referred to this "and you shall have there with you these below written debts," as if it should openly say, "You, who have received the summons, your absence, unless for

debita subscripta soluantur, tunc de firma, quam soluturus es, aliena debita de quibus summonitus es, capientur; firma vero de catallis tuis et fundorum tuorum redditibus perficietur, te interim, si barones dicreuerint, in loco tuto sub libera custodia collocato."

Cum ergo premissa fuerit et a vicecomite suscepta summonitio, ipsa die nominata veniat et ostendat se presidenti, si adesse eum contigerit, vel thesaurario, si presidens ille presens non fuerit. Deinde, salutatis maioribus, ipsa die sibi vacet, in crastino et deinceps die qualibet ad scaccarium rediturus. Quod si forte nec venerit nec iustam premiserit excusationem, prima die regi condempnabitur in c. solidis argenti de quolibet comitatu, sequenti vero in x. libris argenti, similiter in centum. Tertia, sicut ab hiis accepimus qui nos precesserunt, in beneplacito regis erunt quecunque mobilia possidet. Quarto vero, quia iam ex hoc contemptus regie maiestatis conuincitur, non solum in rebus suis sed in propria persona soli regie misericordie subiacebit. Sunt tamen qui credant ad omnem summam solam penam pecuniariam sufficere, vt scilicet in prima die in c. solidis, secunda similiter in c. solidis, et ita deinceps per singulos dies in singulis centenis puniantur absentes. Hiis ego non dissentio, si tamen is, cui delinquitur, in hoc ipsum consenserit. Hunc autem pene modum velle regem admittere satis probabile

necessary and lawfully defined causes it can be excused, will cascade danger upon your head; for you will thus seem to have spurned a royal command and acted irreverently in contempt of his royal majesty, if having been summoned upon royal affairs, to which you are bound, you have neither come nor sent someone with your excuse. But if it has been established that through you the below written debts are not paid, then the unconnected debts for which you have been summoned will be taken from the farm for which you are going to pay; but the farm will then be completed from your chattels and from the returns of your tenements, you meanwhile, if the barons[1] should have judged, having been put in a secure place under loose guard.

When therefore the summons has been sent and received by the sheriff, let him come on the same day named and show himself to the presider [i. e. the justiciar], if it happens that he is present, or the treasurer, if the presider is not present. Then, after greeting the more important members,[2] he may absent himself for that day, returning to the exchequer on the morrow and every day following. But if perchance he has neither come nor sent ahead a valid excuse, he shall be held in contempt of the king in [the sum of] one hundred silver shillings on the first day for each county [of his], but on the following in ten pounds of silver, [then] likewise in one hundred. On the third [day], just as we have learned from those who preceded us, any moveables he may possess will be at the king's pleasure. But on the fourth, because now he has been convicted by this contempt of royal majesty, he shall be subject to royal amercement[3] alone, not only in his things but in his own person. However, there are those who believe that a penalty of money alone suffices for the entire sum, namely that the absent persons should be

1 The judges of the exchequer.

2 *Maior* can mean "magnate," but here designates the barons certainly and other principal men probably.

3 As royal treasurer, fitzNigel is more likely to have the technical fiscal meaning in mind.

est cum eius gratia singularis "ad penam pigra sit et hec ad premia velox."

**Discipulus.** Imprudentis pariter et impudentis est auditoris currentem calamum ante prouisum dicendorum finem preoccupare: ideoque sustinui voluens in animo quod ex parte me turbat. Dixisti enim, si per vicecomitem steterit quominus debita subscripta soluantur, tunc de firma quam soluturus est, capientur. Si ergo vicecomes per breuia regis vel in operationes vel alias vniuersa distribuerit que hic fuerat soluturus, quid fiet?

**Magister.** Cum ex regis mandato vel in camera curie vel in operationibus, vel quibuslibet aliis firmam comitatus expenderit, si in debitis soluendis minus egisse deprehenditur, per fidem suam, vbi mairores decreuerint, detinebitur donec de hiis satisfiat, sicut de firma satisfacturus fuerat.

**Discipulus.** Cum citatum vicecomitem et non venientem vel excusantem tum rerum mobilium tum immobilium tum etiam proprii corporis grauis iactura sequatur nisi suam non voluntariam sed necessariam absentiam excusauerit, rogo te, si placet, vt quas citatus pretendere possit absentie sue sufficientes causas, aperire non differas.

**IV. Quibus de causis absentia uicecomitis valeat excusari.**

**V. Quid sit quosdam fundos dari blancos, quosdam numero.**

**VI. Que sint vicecomiti computanda, elemosine scilicet, decime, liberationes utriusque generis, et terre date.**

**VII. Que sint per solam consuetudinem scaccarii vicecomiti computanda, hoc est sine breui.**

punished on the first day in [the sum of] one hundred shillings, on the second likewise in one hundred shillings, and thus thereafter for each day in single hundreds. I do not disagree with these men, if, however, he to whom he is delinquent has himself consented in this. Moreover, it is likely enough that the king mostly wishes to admit this manner, since his singular grace "is slow to a punishment and swift to rewards."

**Pupil.** It is alike imprudent and impudent of a listener to anticipate the flowing pen [!] before the intended conclusion of those speaking; therefore, I have held back, turning over in my mind something that disturbs me somewhat. For you have said, if it is through the sheriff that the below written debts [i. e. in the summons] are not paid, then they are taken from the farm which he is going to pay. Therefore, if the sheriff has distributed by the king's writ or on his operations or other general affairs what he had been going to pay, what will happen?

**Master.** Since, by the king's command, he has spent the county's farm either in the court's chamber [the exchequer] or on operations, or on whatsoever other things, if he is discovered to have done too little in paying off his debts, per his oath, where the great ones [the barons] have decreed, he shall be detained until he has made satisfaction for these matters, just as if he had been going to make satisfaction for the farm.

**Pupil.** Since a serious cost attends a sheriff summoned and not come or excused, both of his moveable and his immoveable goods, even of his own body, unless he has alleged not a willful but his necessary absence, I ask you, if it please, that you not delay to disclose what kind of sufficient causes of his absence the one summoned is able to allege.

**IV. For which causes the sheriff's absence is able to be excused.**

**V. Why it is that some tenements are paid blanched [coins smelted for purity], others by number [face value].**

**VI. What the sheriff's accounts are, namely alms, tithings, liveries of both kinds, and granted lands.**

**VII. What the sheriff's accounts are by the exchequer's custom only, that is, without a writ.**

**VIII. Quo ordine computanda sunt vicecomiti que in operibus missa sunt per breue regis numerum non determinans.**

**IX. Quod non absoluitur quis a debito per breue regis numerum non habens etsi causam determinet.**

**X. De excidentibus et occupatis quod vsitatius dicimus de purpresturis et excaetis.**

**XI. De censu nemorum qualiter de hiis compoti fieri debeant.**

**XII. De placitis et conuentionibus quo ordine de hiis compoti fiant cum exacta soluuntur.**

**XIII. De distinctione personarum que soluendo non sunt, de quibus a vicecomite fides offertur et sub quo tenore verborum detur.**

**XIV. Que catalia debitorum vendenda sint cum ipsi non soluunt et quis in vendendis ordo sit obseruandus.**

**XV. Quod vicecomes a debitoribus debitoris illius, qui regi non soluit, debitam regi summam prius suscipiat.**

**XVI. Quod vicecomes, a fundis eius qui non soluit, quod requiritur percipiat etiam si eosdem ex quo regi teneri ceperit quomodolibet alienauerit.**

**XVII. Quod non licet vicecomiti debitam sibi pecuniam a non soluentibus suscipere et quid sit agendum si forte susceperit.**

**XVIII. Qualiter vir pro vxore vel vxor pro viro conuenienda est cum ille vel illa soluendo non est**

**XIX. Quod non sit idem modus coercionis baronum regis et aliorum in penis pecuniariis.**

**VIII. How sheriffs have accounts who have been sent on works by a king's writ not designating an amount.**

**IX. That someone is not absolved from debt by a king's writ not designating a specific amount, even if it designates the cause [of the debt].**

**X. About windfalls and encroachments, that we more customarily call purprestures and escheats.**

**XI. About the cess[1] of woods, how these ought to be accounted.**

**XII. About pleas and covenants, in what manner these should be accounted when the exactions are paid.**

**XIII. About the distinction of persons who are insolvent, for which an oath is pledged by the sheriff and in which manner of words it should be given.**

**XIV. What chattels of debtors may be sold when they are insolvent and the order that should be observed in any sale.**

**XV. That the sheriff should first undertake the sum of that debt owed the king by debtors.**

**XVI. That the sheriff should secure, from his tenements who has not paid, what is required even if he has alienated them in some way because he has taken them to be held by the king.**

**XVII. That it is not permitted a sheriff to accept money owed him by insolvents and what should be done if he perhaps has.**

**XVIII. How a husband should be summoned for his wife and a wife for her husband when he or she is not solvent.**

**XIX. That in monetary penalties the manner of exaction of the king's barons and of others should not be the same.**

1 A rent paid by the sheriff for the royal forests in his farm.

**XX. Quid faciendum cum economus qui fidem dedit de satisfaciendo non comparet.**

**XXI. Quid cum veniens non satisfacit, si miles est. Quid, si non miles.**

**XXII. Qualiter ipse dominus puniendus est qui sponte militem exposuit vt possit interim liberari.**

**XXIII. Quid de sponte offerentibus faciendum cum et ipsi non soluunt.**

**XXIV. Quid de releuiis sponte non solutis.**

**XXV. Quid de auibus oblatis faciendum et quo tempore summonende.**

**XXVI. De auro regine.**

**XXVII. Quod aliter de firmis atque aliter de custodiis respondendum et sub alio tenore fides danda.**

**XXVIII. Quod fides vicecomitis semel data de legittimo compoto sufficiat per vniuersum.**

**Magister.** Consummato vero, sicut dictum est, de corpore comitatus compoto, a marescallo fides vicecomitis sub forma predicta semel suscipitur et sic absolutus dimittitur. Fuerunt tamen, qui crederent de singulis per fidem firmandis singillatim fidem a vicecomite dandam vt, quotiens diceret sic esse aliquid, quod sola posset fide confirmari, totiens fidem daret.

**XX. What should be done when a steward who has given his oath does not appear for making amends.**

**XXI. What [should be done] when the one coming does not make satisfaction, if he is a knight. What, if not a knight.**

**XXII. How a lord should be punished who willingly exposes a knight so that in the meantime he himself is able to be freed.**

**XXIII. What should be done about those willingly offering when then they do not pay.**

**XXIV. What [should be done] about reliefs[1] not paid willingly.**

**XXV. What should be done about obleys[2] for hunting birds and when summoned.**

**XXVI. About the queen's gold.**

**XXVII. That it should be accounted differently for farms and differently for custodies and pledges given in another manner.**

**XXVIII. That the sheriff's oath once given about a lawful account suffices for all.**

**Master.** Now, just as it has been said, when the account for the corpus of the county has been concluded, the sheriff's oath is taken on one occasion only by the Marshal in the aforesaid form, and thus he is sent away absolved. Nevertheless, there were those who believed that for several farms paid for by pledge, an oath for each should be given by the sheriff, so that as often as he said something to be so, which could be confirmed by an individual oath, he would swear an oath. But by prudent men and those experienced of divine law such a subtlety was considered very pernicious, since he gave his oath once that he had acted lawfully, with a clear conscience, by all of his accounts.

---

1 Payment made by an heir to an overlord upon succession to an estate.

2 Payment rendered by a vassal to a lord, often in kind as the subsequent discussion makes clear.

Set a prudentibus et legis diuine peritis perniciosa satis visa est subtilitas, cum semel fidem dederit se legitimum per omnia compotum, salua conscientia, fecisse. Ea propter hec sententia post modicum meruit cum suo auctore contempni et vna fide, hoc est semel data, contenti sunt, quia in vnius fidei confessione vnum sunt.

**Discipulus.** Sentio iam languente stilo quod dicendorum finis adesse festinat. Verum, licet instantis noctis crepusculum et productioris operis laborprolixior ad alia nos euocent et paullulum respirare compellant, vellem tamen, si fieri posset, vt suspensam, et hactenus fluctuantem in verbo tuo, discipuli tui mentem confirmares, ostendens quid sit, quod ab initio dixisse te recolo, totam scilicet scaccarii discriptionem quedem esse sacramentorum latibula que reuelanda sunt cum omnium libri aperti erunt et ianua clausa.

**Magister.** Magnum est quod queris et alterius egens inquisitionis, nec his exponendis ex promisso debitor tibi factus sum. His igitur ad presens supersedeo in alterius diei disputationem eadem reseruans. Vereor quidem ne, si pluribus onerato nouam sarcinam imponerem, sub pondere deficeres. Item si iam dictis et memorie commendandis nouarum rerum studia consuerem, vtraque te fastidire compellerem. Contentus ergo iam dictis esto ad que me coegisti. Habes enim in his, quantum madide se potuit offerre memorie, quecumque circa scaccarii scientiam potiora tibi visa sunt, initialiter vtcunque distincta. Ceterum ad singula, que tractu temporis videri poterunt necessaria, vngue tenus explananda nec virtus hominis, nec vita forte, sufficeret. Ex variis enim et insolitis casibus vel nulla fiet vel adhuc incognita disciplina; vnde fit vt detractoriis linguis hinc potius exponar dum, succedente tempore, pleraque dubia

On that account, this opinion after a short time deserved, together with its author, to be scorned, and they were content with one oath, that is given just once, because they are one in the confession of one faith.

**Pupil.** I sense already by your listless stylus [!] that it hastens to be at the end of our discourses. But although the darkness of approaching night and the extended exertion of a rather prolonged work summon us to other things and compel us to find a little relief, nevertheless, if it is possible, I wish that you strengthen your pupil's mind, anxious and up to now awash in your talk, showing what it is that I recall you to have said in the beginning, namely that the entire arrangement of the exchequer is a den of mysteries which are going to be revealed when all the books have been opened and the door shut.

**Master.** That is a large matter that you complain about and needful of another inquest, nor have I been made your debtor in these explanations by a promise. Therefore at the present time I refrain from these matters, reserving the discussion until some other day. I fear indeed lest, if I will load a new burden on the many I have imposed, you will sink beneath the weight. Also, if to the things already said I stitched together a study of new things that had to be committed to memory, I might drive you to scorn both. Therefore, be content with the matters already said to which you have driven me. For in them you have, to the extent my tipsy memory is able to offer, whatever important matters have been shown to you about the science of the exchequer, basically clarified to some extent. Moreover, neither a man's strength nor perhaps his lifetime would suffice for explaining smoothly to their end all the matters which in the course of

necdum audita proponi continget. De quibus aut consimilibus cum hic nil inuenerint, incipiant illudere, dicentes, “hic homo cepit edificare et non potuit, vel non nouit, consummare.” His ego non dissentio, pessimum namque magistrum, me ipsum, secutus sum. Feci tamen, te cogente, quod potui duce carens et exemplari: de intacta namque rudique silua regiis edificiis missa securi ligna secui prudentioris architecti dolabro complananda. Cum, igitur, ex his regie domus structura surrexerit, is, qui dedit initia, primam, licet non precipuam, gratiam mereatur. Valeat rex illustris.

Explicit liber secundus.

time have seemed necessary. For either nothing or a still untried body of knowledge can be made from unresolved and unrefuted cases; whence it is that I am liable to be abandoned by detracting tongues hence when, in coming times, it will come to pass that many doubtful and yet unheard matters will be put forward. For which, or similar things when they have found nothing here, they may begin to mock, saying, "this man began to build and could not, or knew not how, to finish." I do not disagree with them, for I have followed the worst master, namely myself. Nevertheless, compelled by you, I have accomplished what I can, lacking guidance and example. For from the wild and virgin forest I have hewn, my ax laid to the wood, for the broad-axe of a more skilled architect to smooth for the king's structures. When, therefore, out of these [timbers] the realm's house has arisen constructed, let he who has provided the beginnings have earned the first, although not especial, thanks. May our illustrious king prevail.

The second book ends.

## GLANVILL[1]

The text known as *Glanvill*, "traditionally but questionably attributed to Sir Ranulf de Glanvill," as J. H. Baker puts it, continues to take its name from Henry II's justiciar (1180-89) even if its actual authorship remains a mystery.[2] The significance of *Glanvill* for legal history can hardly be exaggerated. Baker, for instance, compares the English lawbook in its effect to Gratian's famous concordance of discordant ecclesiastical canons.[3] As the canon lawyer imposed order on the mass of conflicting rules for the church's administration by creating legal theory, so too did *Glanvill* create order out of late twelfth-century English legal practice by concentrating on the procedures of the royal courts and the writs that provided access to them. In so doing, it marks a significant step in the common law's long path towards nation-wide legal coordination. It is the natural point at which Paul Brand begins a discussion of "the process of integrating the older courts into a single legal system with [the] new royal courts" begun by Henry II and his advisors.[4] While still recognizing that all beginnings grow out of endings, we cannot nevertheless go far wrong by seeing the *Leges Henrici Primi* as the end of one phase of English law and *Glanvill* as the beginning of another. R. C. Van Caenegem clearly identifies it as "our first treatise on the Common Law."[5]

The differences between the *Leges Henrici Primi* and its associative manner of organization, considered to be the rhetorical influence of

---

1 Although the work is generally referred to simply as *Glanvill,* the full title is *Tractatus de Legibus et Consuetudinibus Regni Anglie Qui Glanvilla Vocatur (The Treatise on the Laws and Customs of the Realm of England Which is Called Glanvill).*

2 Baker 2002 13. Milsom 1969 27, considers the justiciar himself "no doubt the shadowy figure who wrote the book we know by Glanvill's name."

3 Baker 2002 13-14.

4 Brand 1992 97.

5 Van Caenegem 1973 30.

Isidore of Seville, and *Glanvill* are considerable. T. F. T. Plucknett says the author of the latter work "realized that the arrangement of his treatise was dictated by essentially legal considerations of the sort of remedy sought, and the nature of the proceedings used. There is no fumbling or hesitation; we are, for the first time in the history of our law, presented with a law-book, written by a lawyer, framed upon principles derived from the law, and not from those of any other science."[1] S. F. C. Milsom calls its author "the most businesslike of English legal writers."[2] Going beyond the usual praise accorded *Glanvill* for clarity, Plucknett finds as well the presence of a keenly analytical legal mind, above all in Books VI (Dower) and VII (the Marriage Portion), in which the discussion of procedure followed by the presentation of appropriate writs gives way to a "clarity of exposition" independent of procedural authority.[3]

We follow the standard edition and translation, with some variation, by G. D. G. Hall 1985, which supersedes that by G. E. Woodbine (New Haven: Yale, 1932).We have tried to select some of the most important passages of the text and summarized the rest in an effort to represent the movement of thought throughout.

1 Plucknett 1958 36.
2 Milsom 1976 122.
3 See Plucknett 1958 37.

## Incipit

*— For a summary of Latin section headings, see Appendix I —*

Incipit tractatus de legibus et consuetudinibus regni Anglie tempore Regis Henrici Secundi compositus, iusticie gubernacula tenente illustri uiro Rannulfo de Glanuilla, iuris regni et antiquarum consuetudinum eo tempore peritissimo.

## Prologus

Regiam potestatem non solum armis contra rebelles et gentes sibi regnoque insurgentes oportet esse decoratam, sed et legibus ad subditos et populos pacificos regendos decet esse ornatam, ut utraque tempora, pacis scilicet et belli, gloriosus rex noster ita feliciter transigat, ut effrenatorum et indomitorum dextra fortitudinis elidendo superbiam et humilium et mansuetorum equitatis uirga moderando iusticiam, tam in hostibus debellandis semper uictoriosus existat quam in subditis tractandis equalis iugiter appareat.

Quam eleganter autem, quam strenue, quam callide hostium obuiando maliciis excellentissimus rex noster hostilitatis tempore armatam exercuerit miliciam nemini uenit in dubium, cum iam in omnen terram exierit laus eius et in omnes fines orbis terre magnalia eius. Quam iuste eciam, quam misericorditer et quam discrete erga subditos suos tempore pacis ipse pacis auctor et amator se habuerit non ambigitur, cum tante equitatis sit sue celsitudinis curia quod in ea nullus iudicum tam attrite frontis tam temerarie sit presumptionis quod a iusticie tramite aliquaternus declinare aut uiam ueritatis ullatenus presumat excedere. Ibi etenim pauperem non opprimit aduersarii potentia, nec a liminibus iudiciorum propellit quemquam fauor uel gratia. Legibus namque regni et consuetudinibus de ratione introductis et diu obtentis et, quod laudabilius est, talium uirorum licet subditorum non dedignatur regi consilio,

## Incipit

*— For a summary of English section headings, see Appendix II —*

Here begins the treatise on the laws and customs of the realm of England, composed in the time of King Henry the Second when justice was under the direction of the illustrious Ranulf Glanvill, the most learned of that time in the law and ancient customs of the realm.

## Prologue

Not only must royal power be furnished with arms against rebels and nations which rise up against the king and the realm, but it is also fitting that it should be adorned with laws for the governance of subject and peaceful peoples; so that in time of both peace and war our glorious king may so successfully perform his office that, crushing the pride of the unbridled and ungovernable with the right hand of strength and tempering justice for the humble and meek with the rod of equity, he may both be always victorious in wars with his enemies and also show himself continually impartial in dealing with his subjects.

No one doubts how finely, how vigorously, how skilfully our most excellent king has practiced armed warfare against the malice of his enemies in time of hostilities, for now his praise has gone out to all the earth and his mighty works to all the borders of the world. Nor is there any dispute how justly and how mercifully, how prudently he, who is the author and lover of peace, has behaved towards his subjects in time of peace, for his Highness's court is so impartial that no judge there is so shameless or audacious as to presume to turn aside at all from the path of justice or to digress in any respect from the way of truth. For there, indeed, a poor man is not oppressed by the power of his adversary, nor does favor or partiality drive any man away from the threshold of judgment. For truly he does not scorn to be guided by the laws and customs of the realm which had their origin in reason and have long prevailed; and, what is more, he is even guided by those of his subjects

quos morum grauitate in peritia iuris et regni consuetudinibus peritissimos sue sapientie et eloquencie prerogatiua alios nouit precellere, et ad causas mediante iusticia decidendas et lites dirimendas, nunc seuerius nunc micius agendo prout uiderint expedire, ipsis rerum argumentis comperit cum ratione promptissimos.

Leges autem Anglicanas licet non scriptas leges appellari non uideatur absurdum, cum hoc ipsum lex sit "quod principi placet, legis habet uigorem," eas scilicet quas super / dubiis in concilio diffiniendis, procerum quidem consilio et principis accedente auctoritate, constat esse promulgatas. Si enim ob solum scripture defectum leges minime censerentur, maioris proculdubio auctoritatis robur ipsis legibus uideretur accomodare scriptura quam uel decernentis equitas aut ratio statuentis.

Leges autem et iura regni scripto uniuersaliter concludi nostris temporibus omnino quidem impossibile est, tum propter scribentium ignoranciam tum propter eorundem multitudinem confusam. Verum sunt quedam in curia generalia et frequentius usitata, que scripto commendare non mihi uidetur presumptuosum, set plerisque perutile et ad iuuandum memoriam admodum necessarium. Horum utique particulam quandam in scripta redigere decreui, stilo uulgari et uerbis curialibus utens ex industria ad eorum noticiam comparandam eis qui in huiusmodi uulgaritate minus sunt exercitati. Ad quorum euidentiam causarum secularium genera in hunc modum duxi distinguendum:

most learned in the laws and customs of the realm whom he knows to excel all others in sobriety, wisdom and eloquence, and whom he has found to be most prompt and clear-sighted in deciding cases on the basis of justice and in settling disputes, acting now with severity and now with leniency as seems expedient to them.

Although the laws of England are not written, it does not seem absurd to call them laws—those, that is, which are known to have been promulgated about problems settled in council on the advice of the magnates and with the supporting authority of the prince—for this also is a law, that "what pleases the prince has the force of law." For if, merely for lack of writing, they were not deemed to be laws, then surely writing would seem to supply to written laws a force of greater authority than either the justice of him who decrees them or the reason of him who establishes them.

It is, however, utterly impossible for the laws and legal rules of the realm to be wholly reduced to writing in our time, both because of the ignorance of scribes and because of the confused multiplicity of those same laws and rules. But there are some general rules frequently observed in court which it does not seem to me presumptuous to commit to writing, but rather very useful for most people and highly necessary to aid the memory. I have decided to put into writing at least a small part of these general rules, adopting intentionally a commonplace style and words used in court in order to provide knowledge of them for those who are not versed in this kind of inelegant language. To make matters clear, I have distinguished the kinds of secular cases in the following manner:

## Liber I

### Distinctio causarum secularium

**1.** Placitorum aliud criminale aliud ciuile. Item placitorum criminalium aliud pertinet ad coronam domini regis, aliud ad uicecomites prouinciarum. Ad coronam domini regis pertinent ista:

### Capitula

**2.** Crimen quod in legibus dicitur crimen lèsé maiestatis, ut de nece uel seditione persone domini regis uel regni uel exercitus; occultatio inuenti thesauri fraudulosa; placitum de pace domini regis infracta; homicidium; incendium; roberia; raptus; crimen falsi, et si qua sunt similia: que scilicet ultimo puniuntur supplicio aut membrorum truncatione.

**3.** Excipitur crimen furti quod ad uicecomites pertinet et in comitatibus placitatur et terminatur. Ad uicecomites etiam pertinet per defectum dominorum cognoscere de melletis, de uerberibus, de plagis etiam nisi accusator adiciat de pace domini regis infracta.

### Distinctio causarum ciuilium

Placitum ciuile aliud in curia domini regis tantum placitatur et terminatur, aliud ad uicecomites prouinciarum pertinet. In curia domini regis habent ista tractari:

### Capitula

Placitum de baroniis; placitum de aduocationibus ecclesiarum; questio status; placitum de dotibus unde mulieres ipse nihil penitus perceperunt; querela de fine facto in curia domini regis non obseruato; de homagiis faciendis et releuiis recipiendis; de propresturis; placitum de debitis laicorum. Et ista quidem placita solummodo super proprietate rei prodita sunt. De illis autem que super possessione loquuntur et per recognitiones terminantur inferius suo loca dicetur.

## Book I

### The division of secular cases

**1.** Pleas are either criminal or civil. Some criminal pleas belong to the crown of the lord king, and some to the sheriffs of counties. The following belong to the crown of the lord king:

### The Chapters

**2.** The crime that civil lawyers call *lèse-majesté*, namely the killing of the lord king or the betrayal of the realm or the army; fraudulent concealment of treasure trove; the plea of breach of the lord king's peace; homicide; arson; robbery; rape; the crime of falsifying and other similar crimes: all these are punished by death or the cutting off of limbs.[1]

**3.** The crime of theft is not included because this belongs to the sheriffs, and is pleaded and determined in the counties. If lords fail to do justice, then sheriffs also have jurisdiction over brawling, beatings, and even wounding, unless the accuser states in his claim that there has been a breach of the peace of the lord king.

### Division of civil cases

Some civil pleas are to be pleaded and determined only in the court of the lord king; others belong to the sheriffs or counties. The following must be drawn in the court of the lord king:

### The Chapters

Pleas concerning baronies; pleas concerning advowsons of churches; the question of status; pleas of dower, when the woman has so far received none; complaints that fines made in the lord king's court have not been observed; pleas concerning the doing of homage and the receiving of relief; purprestures; debts of laymen.

---

1 Compare this and the following paragraph with the *Leges Henrici Primi* Chapter 10, "Concerning the royal jurisdiction."

### Placita ciuilia ad uicecomites pertinentia

**4.** Ad uicecomites pertinent ista: placitum de recto de liberis tenementis per breue domini regis ubi curie dominorum probantur de recto deficisse, quod qualiter fieri debeat inferius dicetur; placitum de natiuis, sed per breue domini regis.

### Placitorum initia

**5.** Cum quis clamat se domino regi aut eius iusticiis de feudo uel libero tenemento suo, si fuerit loquela talis quod debeat uel dominus rex uelit eam in curia sua deduci, tunc is qui queritur tale breue de submonitione habebit:

### Breve de prima summonitione facienda

**6.** Rex uicecomiti salutem. Precipe[1] N. quod iuste et sine dilatione reddat R. unam hidam terre in illa uilla unde idem R. queritur quod predictus N. sibi deforciat. Et nisi fecerit, summone eum per bonos summonitores quod sit ibi in crastinum post octabas clausi Pasche coram me uel iusticciis meis ostensurus quare non fecerit. Et habeas ibi summonitores et hoc breue. Test Rannulfo de Glanuill' apud Clarendunam.

### Quid iuris sit ad primam summonitionem quando summonitus neque uenit neque essonium mittit

**7.** Summonitus autem ad diem prefixum aut uenit aut non uenit. Item si non uenit, aut nuncium aut essonium mittit aut neutrum.

1 This is the writ of right *precipe quod reddat,* by which a seisin issue is initiated in *curia regis*. For initiating an action for right in a lord's feudal court, the writ of right *de recto,* which will not be mentioned until later in the text, would be employed. *Glanvill*'s primary concern is the royal law. The action of right could be taken from the seignorial court to a county court by *tolt* and then by a writ of *pone* from a county court to the royal court, at which point it becomes identical with an action begun by *precipe quod reddat.*

All these pleas concern solely claims to the property in the disputed subject matter: those pleas in which the claim is based on possession and that are determined by recognitions will be discussed later in their proper place.

### Civil pleas belonging to the sheriffs

**4.** The following belong to the sheriffs: pleas concerning the right to free-holdings, begun by a writ from the lord king, where default of right is proved against the lords' courts in the manner stated below; pleas concerning villeins begun by a writ from the lord king.

### The beginning of pleas

**5.** When anyone complains to the lord king or his justices concerning his fee or free tenement, and the case is such that it ought to be, or the lord king is willing that it should be, tried in the king's court, then the complainant shall have the following writ of summons:

### The writ for making the first summons

**6.** The king to the sheriff, greeting. Command N. to render to R., justly and without delay, one hide of land in such-and-such a vill, which the said R. complains that the aforesaid N. is withholding from him. If he does not do so, summon him by good summoners to be before me or my justices on the day after the octave of Easter, to show why he has not done so. And have there the summoners and this writ. Witness Ranulf Glanvill, at Clarendon.

### What the law is when the party summoned neither comes nor sends an essoiner in response to the first summons

**7.** On the appointed day the party summoned either comes or does not. If he does not come, then he sends a representative or an essoiner, or neither. If he neither comes nor sends anyone, the other party who is claiming against him should appear before the justices on the appointed

Si neque uenit neque mittit, aduersarius eius qui petit aduersus eum die statuta coram iusticiis appareat et se aduersus eum liti offerat, et ita in curia per tres dies expectabit. Si uero nec quarta die uenerit, apparentibus summonitoribus et asserentibus se bene eum summonuisse, et idem probare se offerentibus iuxta considerationem curie, tunc secundum considerationem curie iterum per aliud breue summonebitur per interualla quindecim dierum ad minus. Et erit breue ut ueniat responsurus tam super capitali placito quam super eo quod ad primam summonitionem non uenit.

Et ita tribus summonitionibus sub hac forma emissis, si nec ad terciam summonitionem uenerit neque miserit, capietur terra in manum domini regis et ita per quindecim dies remanebit. Et si infra illos quindecim dies non uenerit, aduersario eius adiudicabitur saisina ita quod de cetero non audietur nisi super proprietate per breue de recto. Si uero infra illos quindecim dies uenerit uolens replegiare tenementum, precipietur ei quod ad quartum diem ueniat et habebit quod de iure habere debebit, et ita poterit saisinam recuperare si uenerit.

Si uero ad terciam summonitionem uenerit et premissas summonitiones recognouerit, statim amittit saisinam nisi dies saluare possit per dominum regem guarantum, et per breue quod incontinenti ostendat:

return day and present his case against the tenant; and he shall wait three days in court. If the tenant does not come on the fourth day, but the summoners appear and allege that he has been properly summoned and offer to prove this in whatever way the court may decide, then the court shall direct that the tenant be summoned again by a further writ to come on a return day at least a fortnight later. This writ shall direct him to come and answer both as to the principal plea and as to his not coming at the first summons.

Three summonses shall be sent out in this way. If the tenant neither comes nor sends anyone at the third summons, then the land shall be taken into the lord king's hand, and shall remain thus for a fortnight; if the tenant does not come within the fortnight, seisin shall be adjudged to the other party, and the tenant shall not be allowed to reopen the issue except on the question of property by means of a writ of right. If, however, the tenant comes within the fortnight and wishes to replevy the tenement, he shall be ordered to come on the fourth day, when he shall have justice done to him; and so, if he comes then, he can get back his seisin.

If the tenant does come at the third summons and admits the previous summonses, he immediately loses his seisin unless he is able to save the previous return days by royal warrant; this is done by showing straight away the following writ:

### The writ for saving a return day by royal warrant

**8.** The king to his justices, greeting. I warrant that by my command N. was in my service at such-and-such a place on such-and-such a day, and therefore could not appear before you on that day at your assizes. Therefore I command you that you shall not put him in default for his absence on that day, nor shall he in any way lose thereby. Witness, etc.

If he deny all the summonses, he shall, for each of them, swear by the oaths of twelve. And if it happen on the appointed day that either of the

### Breue de saluando die per regem warantum

**8.** Rex iusticiis salutem. Warantizo N. quod fuit apud illum locum per preceptum meum illo die in seruicio meo, et ideo coram uobis eo die assisis uestris interesse non potuit. Et uobis mando quod pro absentia sua illius diei eum non ponatis in defaltam nec in aliquo sit perdens. Teste etc.

Si summonitiones omnes negauerit, pro qualibet iurabit duodecima manu; et si unus iuratorum die statuta defecerit aut persona alicuius eorum iuste excipi possit sine recuperatione alterius, eadem hora saisinam amittit propter defaltam. Si uero sufficienter iuratum fuerit, eodem die de placito respondebit.

Si ad primum diem non uenerit summonitus sed se essoniauerit, si essonium fuerit rationabile recipietur. Et ita tribus uicibus continue poterit se essoniare. Et quia uariis ex causis contingit aliquem se essoniare et iuste, de diuersis generibus essoniorum uideamus.

[I.9-32 omitted]

### De absentia utriusque partis

**33.** Quandoque contingit utrumque abesse, et tunc in uoluntate domini regis uel eius iusticiarum erit si uoluerit uersus utrumque prosequi contemptum curie uel falsum clamorem.

compurgators are absent, or if the person of either of them be justly excluded and the vacancy occasioned by this not be filled, at that moment the tenant shall lose his seisin because of his default. But if the tenant sufficiently disprove the summonses, on that same day he shall answer the plea.

If the tenant, when summoned, does not come on the first day, but essoin himself, the essoin shall be allowed, if it is reasonable. And he may in the same manner essoin himself three times consecutively. And since there are various reasons why a person may legitimately essoin himself, let us consider the various kinds of essoins.

[I.12-32 omitted]

### About the absence of both parties.

When it happens that the demandant and the tenant are both absent, then the king or his justices may at their pleasure, if they so wish, punish both parties, one for contempt of court, the other for his false claim.

[Books II-V omitted]

[Book II presents the procedures for moving the issue of a contested piece of land. A writ orders the sheriff to send a number of "*liberos et legales homines*" to view the contested land, four of which will then be made available to the presiding judge as witnesses. The demandant makes his claim in court after as many as three essoins and the defendant then must choose whether he will defend the land by battle or put himself upon the grand assize for judgment. After a discussion of champions and attendant matters, the text presents the appropriate writ for delivering seisin to the victorious individual who has elected to prove his claim by combat. The rest of Book II explains the nature of the grand assize and the appropriate writs that establish it, the permissible essoins, the manner of its conduct, and concludes with the writ that delivers seisin following judgment.

Book III discusses the procedures to be followed, and the writs to be employed, when the tenant holds the disputed property from a third party who gave or let it to the defendant. The case now will be presented against this warrantor, who may also be allowed essoins in the course of presenting his claim. If necessary, the lord from whom the land is held in fee may ultimately be required to testify as the chain of sub-infeudation is legally established.

Book IV discusses advowson, the assignment of benefices by patrons, and the manner of resolution in the event contrary claims to their presentation should be made. The discussion is oriented to the writ of right advowson and not the petty assize of *darrein presentment*.

Book V discusses the question of status, that is, the legal issues that arise when someone claims another as villein or when a villein claims freedom. The writ of naifty applies in the first instance. If the person claimed asserts the status of a free man but the sheriff wishes to pursue the matter, he may appeal to the king's justice, for which another writ is provided. The book concludes with accounts of manumission and the ways in which people become villeins].

**Court of King's Bench**

## Liber VI

### Placitum de dotibus

**1.** Dos duobus modis dicitur. Dicitur enim dos uilgariter it quod aliquis liber homo dat sponse sue ad hostium ecclesie tempore desponsationis sue. Tenetur autem unusquisque tam iure ecclesiastico quam iure seculari sponsam suam dotare tempore sue desponsationis. Cum quis autem sponsam suam dotat, aut nominat dotem aut non. Si non nominauerit dotem, tercia pars tocius liberi tenementi sui intelligetur dos eius, et apellatur rationabilis dos cuiusliber mulieris tercia pars tocius iberi tenementi uiri sui quod habet tempore disponsationis, ita quod inde fuerit saisitus in dominico. Si uero dotem nominat is qui mulierem desponsat et plus tercia parte, dos ipsa in tanta quantitate stare non poterit. Amensurabilitur enim usque ad terciam partem, quia minus tercia parte tenementi potest quis dare in dotem, plur uero tercia parte non.

### De amplianda dote ratione questus

**2.** Contingit autem quandoque quod si modicum tenementi habeat is qui mulierem aliquam desponsat, possit dotem ipsam ampliare, scilicet de questu suo in terciam partem uel minus. Si uero nichil de questu fuerit expressum in dotis assignatione, licet parum habeat tenementi tempore desponsationis et postea multum adquisierit, non poterit in dotem clamari plus tercia parte illius tenementi quod habuit is qui mulierem dotauit tempore desponsationis. Idem dico si quis in denariis uel in aliis catallis, terram non habens, sponsam suam dotauerit, et postea magnum questum fecerit in terris et tenementis, quia nihil de questu de cetero in dotem de iure clamari poterit. Quia hoc generaliter uerum est quod quantacumque uel qualiscumque fuerit dos assignata alicui mulieri, si inde satisfactum fuerit ipsi mulieri ad hostium ecclesie quantum ad dotem, numquam de cetero poterit amplius ad dotem petere.

## Book VI

### Pleas of dower

**1.** The word *dos* is used in two senses. In common English law usage it means that which a free man gives to his wife at the church door at the time of his marriage. Moreover, every man is bound both by ecclesiastical and by secular law to endow his wife at the time of his marriage. When a man endows his wife either he nominates certain property as dower, or he does not. If he does not nominate dower, then one third of the whole of his free tenement is deemed to be her dower, and the reasonable dower of any woman is one third of the whole of the free tenement of which her husband was seised in demesne at the time of the marriage. If, however, the husband nominates dower and it amounts to more than one third, it cannot stand at such a level, but will be measured up to one third; for a man can give less but not more than one third of his tenement in dower.

### Increase in dower as a result of later acquisitions

**2.** It sometimes happens that a husband who has a little land can increase the dower by adding one third or less of his later acquisitions. However, if nothing was said about acquisitions when the dower was originally assigned, then, even if the husband had little land at the time of the marriage and afterwards acquired much land, no more can be claimed in dower than one third of the land which he had at the time of the marriage. I state the same rule when a man who has no land endows his wife with money or other chattels and afterwards acquires many lands and tenements, for nothing can in future lawfully be claimed as dower from these acquisitions. For it is a general rule that however much dower and of whatever kind is assigned to a woman, if she consents to this assignment of dower at the church door she cannot in future lawfully claim any more in dower.

**3.** Sciendum autem quod mulier nichil potest disponere circa dotem suam in uita sui mariti. Quia cum ipsa mulier plene in potestate uiri sui de iure sit, non est mirum si tam dos ipsius mulieris quam cetere res eius omnes plene intelligantur esse in dispositione ipsius uire. Potest itaque quilibet uxorem habens dotem uxoris sue donare uendere et alio quo uoluerit modo alienare in uita sua, ita quod tenetur uxor sua in hoc sicut et in aliis rebus omnibus que contra Deum non sint ei consentire. Adeo autem uiro suo tenebitur mulier obedire quod si uir eius dotem eius uendere uoluerit et ipsa ei contradixerit, si postea ita uendita fuerit et empta dos ipsa, mortuo uiro suo non poterit mulier dotem ipsam uersus emptorem petere, si confessa fuerit in curia uel super hoc conuicta quod ea contradicente uiro suo uendita fuerit dos ipsa a uiro suo.

**4.** Mortuo siquidem uiro alicuius mulieris, aut uacat dos eius si fuerit nominata aut non uacat. Si uacat, ponere se poterit mulier ipsa in dotem suam et tenere se in saisina cum consensu heredis. Si uero non uacet, aut tota non uacat aut quedam pars uacat et quedam non uacat. Si quedam pars uacat quedam non, in parte que uacat ponere se poterit predicto modo et de residuo habebit breue de recto ad warantum suum, scilicet quod teneat ei plenum rectum de illa terra quam clamat pertinere ad rationabilem dotem suam. Breue autem tale erit:

#### Breue de recto de pertinentia dotis

**5.** Rex W. salutem. Precipio tibi quod sine dilatione plenum rectum teneas M. que fuit uxor Rodberti de una hida terre in illa uilla, quam clamat pertinere ad rationabilem dotem suam quam tenet de te in eadem uilla per liberum seruicium decem solidorum per annum pro omni seruicio, quam N. ei deforciat. Et nisi feceris uicecomes faciat, ne oporteat eam amplius inde conqueri pro defectu recti. Teste etc’.

**3.** It should be known that a woman cannot alienate any of her dower during the life of her husband. For since legally a woman is completely in the power of her husband, it is not surprising that her dower and all her other property are clearly deemed to be at his disposal. Therefore any married man may give or sell or alienate in whatever way he pleases his wife's dower during her life, and his wife is bound to consent to this as to all other acts of his which do not offend against God. Indeed, to such an extent is a woman bound to obey her husband that if he wishes to sell her dower and she opposes him, and afterwards the dower is in fact sold and purchased, she cannot when her husband is dead claim the dower from the purchaser if she confesses, or it is proved against her, in court that it was sold by her husband against her will.

**4.** When a woman's husband dies and dower has been nominated, either it lies vacant or it does not. If it is vacant, the woman may enter on the dower and remain in seisin with the consent of the heir. If, however, it is not vacant, then either none is vacant, or else some part is vacant and some is not; in the latter case she may enter on the vacant part in the manner stated above, and in respect of the rest she shall have a writ of right to her warrantor, directing him to do full right to her concerning certain land which she claims as belonging to her reasonable dower. The writ will be as follows:

### The writ of right for land belonging to dower

5. The king to W., greeting. I command you to do full right without delay to M. the widow of Robert, in respect of one hide of land in such-and-such a vill, which she claims as belonging to the reasonable dower which she holds of you in that vill by the free service of ten shillings a year for all service, and which N. is withholding from her. If you do not do it the sheriff will, that she need no longer complain for default of right in this matter. Witness, etc.

**6.** Tractabitur autem placitum illud per hoc breue in curia waranti donec probetur curia ipsius ei de recto defecisse, quod qualiter fieri debeat inferius dicetur. Quo probato, procedet loquela usque ad comitatum et ita, mediante comitatu, pro uoluntate domini regis uel capitalis iusticie poterit loquela ipsa ad capitalem curiam domini regis eciam iuste transferri, et per hoc breue:

### Breue de transferendo placito a comitatu in curiam

**7.** Rex uicecomiti salutem. Pone[1] coram me uel iusticiis meis tunc loquelam que est in comitatu tuo inter M. et N. de una hida terre in illa uilla quam ipsa M. clamat uersus predictum N. ad rationabilem dotem suam. Et sumone per bonos sumonitores predictum N. qui terram illam tenet quod tunc sit ibi cum loquela sua. Et habeas ibi summonitores et hoc breue. Teste etc'.

## Liber VII

### De maritagiis

**1.** In alia acceptione accipitur dos secundum leges romanas, secundum quod proprie appellatur dos id quod cum muliere datur uiro, quod uilgariter dicitur maritagium. Potest itaque quilibet liber homo terram habens dare quandam partem terre sue cum filia sua uel cum alia qualibet muliere in maritagium, siue habeat heredem siue non, uelit heres si habuerit heredem siue non uelit, imo eciam eo contradicente et reclamante. Cuilibet eciam cuicumque uoluerrit potest quis quandam partem sui liberi tenementi donare in remunerationem seruicii sui uel loco religioso in elemosinam:

---

1 Here is the imperative verb by which this writ is known. It is the standard mechanism for removing a case from a county court into *curia regis*.

**6.** This plea will be drawn by the above writ in the warrantor's court until his court is proved to have failed to do right to the widow: the method of proving this is stated below [XII, 7]. When default of right has been proved, the case shall go to the county court and so, with that court as middle stage, the case can be lawfully transferred even to the chief court of the lord king if he or his chief justice will it. This is done by the following writ:

#### The writ for transferring a plea from the county court to the Curia

**7.** The king to the sheriff, greeting. Put before me or my justices on a certain day the plea which is in your county court between M. and N. concerning one hide of land in such-and-such a vill, which the said M. claims against the aforesaid N. as part of her reasonable dower. And summon by good summoners the aforesaid N. who holds that land to be there with his plea. And have there the summoners and this writ. Witness, etc.

[Book VI continues with an extensive discussion of various situations that affect dower along with the writs and procedures that apply].

### Book VII

#### Marriage portions

**1.** In Roman law the word *dos* has a different meaning: there *dos* is properly used for that which is given with a woman to her husband, which is commonly called *maritagium*, a marriage portion. Every free man who has land can give a certain part of his land with his daughter, or with any other woman, as a marriage portion, whether he has an heir or not, and whether the heir if he has one is willing or not, and even if he is opposed to it and protests. For he can give a certain part of his free tenement to whom he pleases in recompense for his service, or to a religious place as alms. If seisin follows the gift, the land will remain forever with the donee and his heirs, it it was given to them heritably;

ita quod si donationem ipsam saisina fuerit secuta, perpetuo remanebit illi cui donata fuerit terra illa et heredibus suis, si iure hereditario fuerit eis concessa: si uero donationem talem nulla fuerit secuta saisina, ex tali donatione nihil post mortem donatoris contra uoluntatem heredis efficaciter peti potest, quia id intelligitur secundum consuetam regni interpretationem potius esse nuda promissio quam aliqua uera donatio.

**[Book VII 2-6 omitted]**

### Breve de faciendo stare rationabilem diuisam

**7.** Rex uicecomiti salutem. Precipio tibi quod iuste et sine dilatione facias stare rationabilem diuisam N., sicut rationabiliter monstrari poterit quod eam fecerit et quod ipsa stare debeat. Teste etc.

**[The rest of Book VII, and all of Books VIII-XII omitted]**

however, if no seisin follows such a gift, then after the donor's death nothing can be claimed in reliance on such a gift against the will of the heir, because, according to the interpretation customary in the realm it is deemed to be a naked promise[1] rather than a true gift.

[After a lengthy discussion of issues pertaining to heirs and inheritance of the marriage portion, *Glanvill* offers the applicable writ].

### The writ for upholding a reasonable division

**7.** The king to the sheriff, greeting. I command you to uphold, justly and without delay, the reasonable division made by N., if it can reasonably be shown that he made it and that it ought to stand. Witness, etc.[Book VII concludes, after a lengthy discussion of inheritance issues and bastardy, with an account of the various kinds of marriage portion.

Book VIII discusses written agreements, whether pertaining to land or not. The book discusses various situations and provides examples of appropriate chirographs and writs.

Book IX discusses homage and relief (the payment required when an individual renders homage and assumes a fee) and provides the relevant writs that pertain to issues that arise between lord and vassal. Of particular significance is the writ for summoning the Grand Assize between lord and vassal.Book X discusses debt, purchase and sale, and theft.

Book XI discusses the appointment of a spokesperson to represent the principal in court proceedings. This person is called responsalis, however, and not attornatus. The writ for designating a representative is provided and a discussion of the available essoins and applicable distraints in such cases.

---

1 A promise "unclothed" by legal obligation and therefore non-binding.

**Scales of Justice tilted toward the Poor.**

Book XII discusses and illustrates the writ of right. This is the sole point in Glanvill where the focus is on the county and manorial courts, the appropriate venues for initiating most issues of right, which may, however, be subsequently removed into the royal courts. Since villeins are property, there is a writ of right for naifty just as there is a writ of right for replevying cattle and restoring chattels. A freeholder and even a freeholder's tenant may, however, seek relief from a lord via a writ forbidding vexing. The book concludes with an explanation for the omission of any discussion of pleas belonging to the sheriff, since the book's plan concerns the custom and law of the king's court].

# Liber XIII

## De diuersis recognitionibus

**1.** Generalia que circa premissa placita de recto frequentius in curia contingunt hactenus in parte sunt expedita. Nunc uero ea que super saisinis solummodo usitata sunt restant prosequenda. Que quia ex beneficio constitutionis regni que assisa nominatur in maiore parte transigi solent per recognitionem, de diuersis recognitionibus restat tractandum.

**2.** Est itaque quedam recognitio que uocatur de morte antecessoris. Quedam autem est de ultimis presentationibus personarum in ecclesiis; quedam utrum aliquod tenementum sit feodum ecclesiasticum uel laicum feodum; quedam utrum aliquis fuerit saisitus de aliquo libero tenemento die qua obiit ut de feodo uel ut de uadio; quedam utrum aliquis sit infra etatem uel plenam habeat etatem; quedam utrum aliquis obierit saisitus de aliquo libero tenemento ut de feodo uel ut de warda; quedam utrum aliquis presentauerit personam ad aliquam ecclesiam ultimam occasione feodi sui quod in dominico suo habuerit uel occasione alicuius warde: et si que sunt similes que in curia frequenter emergunt presentibus partibus, tum ex consensu ipsarum parcium tum eciam de consilio curie considerate, ad aliquam controuersiam terminandam. Item recognitio que dicitur de noua dissaisina.

Cum quis itaque moritur saisitus de aliquo libero tenemento ita quod inde fuerit saisitus in dominico suo sicut de feodo suo, heres eandem saisinam antecessoris sui recte petere potest, et si maior fuerit habebit tale breue:

## Breve de morte antecessoris

**3.** Rex vicecomiti salutem. Si G. filius O. fecerit te securum de clamore suo prosequendo, tunc sumone per bonos sumonitores duodecim liberos et legales homines de uisneto de illa uilla quod sint coram me uel iusticiis meis eo die, parati sacramento recognoscere si O.

# Book XIII

## The various kinds of recognitions

**1.** So far the questions which most often arise in pleas about right have been dealt with. There remain for discussion those which are concerned with seisin only. By virtue of a constitution of the realm called an assize these questions are for the most part settled by recognition, and therefore the various kinds of recognition must now be considered.

**2.** One kind of recognition is called *mort d'ancestor*. Another concerns the last presentation of parsons to churches; another, whether a tenement is ecclesiastical or lay fee; another, whether a man was seised of a free tenement on the day he died as of fee or as of gage; another, whether a man is under age or of full age; another, whether a man died seised of a free tenement as of fee or as of wardship; another, whether a man presented the last parson to a church by virtue of his fee which he had in his demesne, or by virtue of the wardship of someone. And if similar questions arise as they frequently do when both parties are present in court, then recognitions are used to settle the dispute, whether with consent of the parties or by award of the court. There is also the recognition called *novel disseisin*.

When anyone dies seised of a free tenement, if he was seised in his demesne as of fee, then his heir can lawfully claim the seisin which his ancestor had, and if he is of full age he shall have the following writ:

## The writ of mort d'ancestor

**3.** The king to the sheriff, greeting. If G. son of O. gives you security for prosecuting his claim, then summon by good summoners twelve free and lawful men from the neighborhood of such-and-such a vill to be before me or my justices on a certain day, ready to declare on oath whether O. the father of the aforesaid G. was seised in his demesne as of his fee of one virgate of land in that vill on the day he died, whether he died after

pater predicti G. fuit saisitus in dominico suo sicut de feodo suo de una uirgata terre in illa uilla die qua obiit, si obiit post primam coronationem meam, et si ille G. propinquior heres eius sit. Et interim terram illam uideant, et nomina eorum imbreuiari facias. Et summone per bonos sumonitores R. qui terram illam tenet quod tunc sit ibi auditurus illam recognitionem. Et habeas ibi summonitores et hoc breue. Teste etc.

Si uero antecessor ipse predicto modo saisitus iter arripuerit eundi in aliquam peregrinationem, tunc erit breue tale:

### Breue de eodem

**4.** Rex uicecomiti salutem. Si G. filius O. fecerit te securum de clamore suo prosequendo, tunc sumone per bonos sumonitores duodecim liberos et legales homines de uisneto de illa uilla quod sint coram me uel iusticiis meis eo die, parati sacramento recognoscere si O. pater predicti G. fuit saisitus in dominico suo sicut de feodo suo de una uirgata terre in illa uilla die qua iter arripuit uersus Ierusalem, uel uersus sanctum Iacobum, in quo itinere obiit, et si iter ipsum arripuit post primam coronationem meam, et si prefactus G. propinquior eius heres sit. Et interim terram illam uideant etc., ut prius.

### Quo ordine perueniatur ad hanc assisam

7. Recepto itaque breui de morte antecessoris ab ipso uicecomite et in comitatu data securitate de clamore prosequendo, tunc hoc ordine peruenitur ad assisam. Ab inicio elegendi sunt duodecim liberi et legales homines de uisneto secundum formam in breui expressam, presentibus partibus scilicet tam petente quam tenente, uel absente eciam ipso tenente dummodo summonitus fuerit saltem semel quod interesset illi electioni. Quia semel inde sumonendus est ut presens sit et audiat qui eligendi sint ad ipsam recognitionem faciendam, et quosdam eciam ex rationabili causa si uoluerit recuset ut ab illa recognitione excludantur. Si uero ad primam sumonitionem in curia recte testatam non uenerit, ulterius non expectabitur; imo eciam eo absente ipsi eligentur duodecim iuratores, et deinde ex transmissione uicecomitis facient uisum terre uel alterius tenementi cuius saisina petitur.

my first coronation, and whether the said G. is his next heir. And meanwhile let them view the land; and you are to see that their names are endorsed on this writ. And summon by good summoners R., who holds that land, to be there then to hear the recognition. And have there the summoners and this writ. Witness, etc.

If, however, the ancestor who was seised in the manner stated above has set out on a pilgrimage, then the writ shall be as follows:

**4.** The king to the sheriff, greeting. If G. son of O. gives you security for prosecuting his claim, then summon by good summoners twelve free and lawful men from the neighborhood of such-and-such a vill to be before me or my justices on a certain day, ready to declare on oath whether O. the father of G. was seised in his demesne as of his fee of one virgate of land in that vill on the day he set out for Jerusalem (or for St. James), on which journey he died, and whether he set out after my first coronation, and whether G. is his next heir. And meanwhile let them view the land, etc., as above.

[Two more variant writs are given for *mort d'ancestor*].

### The procedure leading to this assize

**7.** When the sheriff has received the writ of *mort d'ancestor* and security for prosecuting the claim has been given in the county court, then the procedure leading to the assize is as follows. First, in accordance with the terms of the writ, twelve free and lawful men from the neighborhood must be selected in the presence of both demandant and tenant, or even in the absence of the tenant provided he has been summoned at least once to attend the election. He must be summoned once to come and hear who are elected to make the recognition, and he can if he wishes reject some of them for reasonable cause so that they are excluded from the recognition. If, however, he has not come when the first summons is properly attested in court, then he shall be waited for no longer, and in

Vnicam tamen et super hos habebit summonitionem ille qui tenet. Nomina eciam illorum duodecim electorum faciet ipse uicecomes imbreuiari.

Deinde autem sumonere faciet uicecomes ipse ipsum tenentem, quod die per breue domini regis uel eius iusticiarum statuta sit coram rege uel eius iusticiis auditurus illam recognitionem. Die autem prima et secunda essoniare se poterit is qui tenet si maior fuerit is qui petit: tercia uero die non poterit, imo ad tercium terminum capietur recognitio siue ueniat siue non is qui tenet, quia in nulla recognitione super saisina tantum prodita currunt nisi duo essonia. In recognitione uero de noua dissaisina nullum essonium locum habet. Tercio itaque die siue uenerit tenens siue non capietur ut dictum est assisa. Et si uratores ipsi dixerint pro petente, adiudicabitur ei inde saisina et precipietur uicecomiti quod ei saisinam illam habere faciat per hoc breue:

### Breve de facienda saisina post recognitionem

**8.** Rex vicecomiti salutem. Scias quod N. dirationauit in curia mea saisinam tante terre in illa uilla per recognitionem de morte illius antecessoris sui uersus R. Et ideo tibi precipio quod saisinam illam ei sine dilatione habere facias. Teste etc.

### De recognitione de ultimis presentationibus ecclesiarum

**18**. Sequitur de recognitione de ultimis presentationibus personarum. Contingente itaque aliquam ecclesiam uacare, si fuerit controuersia super presentatione, poterit controuersia illa per recognitionem de ultima presentatione decide, alterutro litigantium id in curia postulante, super quo tale breue impetrabit:

his absence the twelve jurors shall be elected and sent by the sheriff to view the land or other tenement of which seisin is claimed. Here again the tenant shall have one summons only. The sheriff shall see that the names of the elected twelve are endorsed on the writ.

Then the sheriff shall arrange for the tenant to be summoned to be before the king or his justices on the day stated in the writ of the king or his justices, to hear the recognition. If the demandant is of full age, the tenant can essoin himself on the first and second return days but not on the third day, for then the recognition shall be taken whether the tenant comes or not, because no more than two essoins are allowed in any recognition which concerns only seisin. Indeed, in the recognition of *novel disseisin* no essoin is allowed. On the third return day, then, as stated above, the assize shall be taken whether the tenant has come or not. And if the jurors declare in favor of the demandant, seisin shall be adjudged to him and the sheriff ordered by the following writ to have him put in seisin:

### The writ for delivering seisin after the recognition

**8.** The king to the sheriff, greeting. Know that N. has proved in my court, by a recognition concerning the death of a certain ancestor of his, his right against R. to the seisin of so much land in such-and-such a vill. And therefore I command you to have him put in seisin without delay. Witness, etc.

[A lengthy discussion of issues, variations, procedures, and writs follows].

### The recognition of darrein presentment to churches

**18.** Now there follows the recognition of *darrein presentment* of parsons. When a church is vacant and there is a dispute about the presentation, it can be decided by a recognition of *darrein presentment*, if either party asks for this in court; and he shall request the following writ:

### Breve de summonende recognitione de ultimis presentationibus ecclesiarum

**19**. Rex uicecomiti salutem. Sumone per bonos sumonitores duodecim liberos et legales homines de uisneto de illa uilla quod sint coram me uel iusticiis meis eo die, parati sacramento recognoscere quis aduocatus presentauit ultimam personam que obiit ad ecclesiam de illa uilla, que uacans est ut dicitur et unde N. clamat aduocationem. Et nomina eorum imbreuiari facias. Et sumone per bonos sumonitores R. qui presentationem illam deforciat, quod tunc sit ibi auditurus illam recognitionem. Et habeas ibi summonitores et hoc breue. Teste etc.

### De recognitione noue desaisine

**32**. Postremo de illa recognitione que appellatur de noua dissaisina restat dicendum. Cum quis itaque infra assisam domini regis, id est infra tempus a domino rege de consilio procerum ad hoc constitutum quod quandoque maius quandoque minus censetur, alium iniuste et sine iudicio desaisierit de libero tenemento suo, desaisito huius constitutionis beneficio subuenitur, et tale breue habebit:

### Breve de noua desaisina

**33**. Rex uicecomiti salutem. Questus est mihi N. quod R. iniuste et sine iudicio desaisiuit eum de libero tenemento suo in illa uilla post ultimam transfretationem meam in Normanniam; et ideo tibi precipio quod si predictus N. fecerit te securum de clamore suo prosequendo, tunc facias tenementum illus resaisiri de catallis que in ipso capta fuerunt, et ipsum tenementum cum catallis esse in pace usque ad clausum Pascha.

### The writ for summoning a recognition of darrein presentment to churches

**19.** The king to the sheriff, greeting. Summon by good summoners twelve free and lawful men from the neighborhood of such-and-such a vill to be before me or my justices on a certain day, ready to declare an oath which patron presented the last parson who is now dead to the church in that vill, which is alleged to be vacant and of which N. claims the advowson. And you are to see that their names are endorsed on this writ. And summon by good summoners R., who withholds the presentation, to be there then to hear the recognition. And have there the summoners and this writ. Witness, etc.

[A lengthy discussion of variations and writs follows].

### The recognition of novel disseisin[1]

**32.** Lastly there remains for discussion the recognition called *novel disseisin*. When anyone has unjustly and without a judgment disseised another of his free tenement within the assize of the lord king—that is, within the limit of time which is appointed for this purpose by the lord king on the advice of his great men, which varies in length—then the disseisee can claim the benefit of this constitution, and shall have the following writ:

### The writ of novel disseisin

**33.** The king to the sheriff, greeting. N. has complained to me that R. unjustly and without a judgment has disseised him of his free tenement in such-and-such a vill since my last voyage to Normandy. Therefore I command you that, if N. gives you security for prosecuting his claim, you are to see that the chattels which were taken from the tenement are restored to it, and that the tenement and the chattels remain in peace until the Sunday after Easter. And meanwhile you are to see that the tenement

1 This action is fully discussed by Sutherland 1973. For a specific case, see the Cases section in this anthology.

Et interim facias duodecim liberos et legales homines de uisneto uidere tenementum illud, et nomina eorum inbreuiari. Et sumone eos per bonos sumonitores quod tunc sint coram me uel iusticiis meis parati inde facere recognitionem. Et pone per uadium et saluos plegios predictum R., uel bailiuum suum si ipse inventus non fuerit, quod tunc sit ibi auditurus illam recognitionem. Et habeas ibi summonitores et hoc breue et nomina plegiorum. Teste etc.

### Quod nullum essonium in hac recognitione admittitur

**38**. In hac autem recognitione nullum admittitur essonium. Prima enim die siue uenerit siue non is qui desaisinam fecit, procedet recognitio; quia hic nemini parcitur, nec minori nec maiori, nec eciam warantus expectatur. Si enim quid desaisinam talem in curia recognouerit sed warantum inde uocans, eo ipso remanet recognitio, et ille qui hoc recognouerit in misericordiam domini regis incidet; et postea sumonebitur warantus et erit placitum inter eum et alium qui super hoc eum uocauit warantum.

Illud autem sciendum quod semper uictur, siue fuerit appellans siue appellatus, in misericordia domini regis remanet propter uilentam desaisinam. Preteres si apellans diem suum non fuerit prosecutus, tunc plegii quoque in misericordiam incident. Simile quoque accidit circa personam alterius si se absentauerit ad diem statutam. Pena autem huius constitutionis est misericordia domini regis tantum.

In hac autem recognitione potest cum effectu desiderare is qui nouam desaisinam probauit ut precipiatur uicecomiti quod catalla et fructus per preceptum domini regis uel eius iusticiarum interim arestatos faciat habere illi qui dissaisinam probauit.

is viewed by twelve free and lawful men of the neighborhood, and their names endorsed on this writ. And summon them by good summoners to be before me or my justices on the Sunday after Easter, ready to make the recognition. And summon R., or his bailiff if he himself cannot be found, on the security of gage and reliable sureties to be there then to hear the recognition. And have there the summoners, and this writ and the names of the sureties. Witness, etc.

[Variations of this writ are presented].

### No essoin is allowed in this recognition

**38.** No essoin is allowed in this recognition. Whether or not the disseisor comes on the first day, the assize shall proceed; for the full rigor of this assize applies to all, to minors as well as to those of full age, and there is no waiting even for a warrantor. However, if anyone confesses a disseisin in court but also vouches a warrantor, the recognition shall not proceed, and he who confessed shall be liable to amercement by the lord king; afterwards the warrantor shall be summoned, and there shall be a plea between him and the party who vouched him.

It should be known that the losing party, whether appellor or appellee, shall always be liable to amercement by the lord king on account of the violent disseisin. Moreover, if the appellor does not prosecute his claim on the appointed day, his sureties also shall be liable to amercement; and the same rule applies to the other party if he absents himself on the appointed day. The liability to amercement by the lord king is the sole penalty provided by this constitution.

In this recognition the party who has proved disseisin can require that the sheriff be ordered to see that the chattels and fruits, which have in the meantime been seized by command of the lord king or his justices, are restored to him. In no other recognition does the judgment make mention

In nulla autem alia recognitione mentio solet fieri per iudicium de catallis uel de fructibus. Et nisi uicecomes de fructibus et catallis ei satisfacere prouiderit, tunc tale breue inde impetrabit is qui queritur:

### Breve de catallis reddendis

**39.** Rex uicecomiti salutem. Precipio tibi quod iusticies N. quod iuste et sine dilatione reddat R. catalla sua etc.

Hoc breue suprascriptum reperiri potest [at XII, 18].

[Book XIV 1-5 omitted]

### Placitum de crimine raptus

**6.** Raptus crimen est quod aliqua mulier imponit uiro quo proponit se a uiro ui oppressam in pace domini regis. Tenetur autem mulier que tale quid patitur mox dum recens fuerit maleficium uicinam uillam adire, et ibi iniuriam sibi illatam probis hominibus ostendere et sanguinem si quis fuerit effusus et uestium scissiones. Dehinc autem apud prepositum hundredi idem faciat. Postea quoque in primo comitatu id publice proponat. Deinde autem facta super hoc querimonia, iudicium ut predictum est ordinabitur [XIV, 1]. Auditur itaque mulier in tali casu aliquem accusans sicut et de qualibet alia iniuria corpori suo illata solet audiri. Sciendum tamen quod in electione accusati erit in tali casu uel honus purgationis subire uel mulieris probationem contra se sustinere.

of chattels or of fruits. And if the sheriff has not seen to it that he gets the fruits and chattels, the complainant shall have the following writ:

### The writ for restoring chattels

**39.** The king to the sheriff, greeting. I command you to constrain N. to restore, justly and without delay, to R. his chattels, etc.

This writ can be found written above.

[Unlike the books up to this point, which have discussed civil pleas, Book XIV concerns criminal actions. The discussion begins with treason, provides a general account of procedures for all manner of felonies, and then considers in turn concealment of treasure trove, homicide, arson, robbery, rape, falsifying, and theft].

### The plea of the crime of rape

**6.** In the crime of rape a woman charges a man with violating her by force in the peace of the lord king. A woman who suffers in this way must go, soon after the deed is done, to the nearest vill and there show to trustworthy men the injury done to her, and any effusion of blood there may be and any tearing of her clothes. She should then do the same to the reeve of the hundred. Afterwards she should proclaim it publicly in the next county court; and when she has made her complaint, the form of proceeding to judgment shall be as stated above [XIV, 1]. In such a case a woman is allowed to make an accusation just as in every case of injury done to her body. It should be known that in such a case it is for the accused to choose whether he will submit to the burden of the ordeal, or will rely on disproving the accusation of the woman.

Moreover, it should be known that if anyone is convicted in this kind of plea the judgment against him shall be the same as in the crimes discussed earlier. Nor can the wrongdoer escape this by expressing his willingness, after judgment, to marry the woman he has defiled. For if he could it would frequently happen as a result of a single defilement that

Preterea sciendum quod si quis in huius modi placito conuictus fuerit, simili modo ac in predictis iudiciis de eo est iudicandum. Non enim sufficit post iudicium malefactorem ipsum corruptam illam uelle ducere in uxorem. Sic enim frequenter contingeret seruilis conditionis homines generosissimas mulieres unius pollutionis occasione perpetuo fedare, uel generosos homines per mulieres ignobiles fedari, et ita claram parentum eorum famam indecenter denigrari. Ante iudicium tamen ita receptum est quod de licencia principis uel eius iusticiarum cum parentum assensu possunt mulier accusans et accusatus beneficio coniugi sibi inuicem reconciliari.

men of servile status disgraced forever women of good birth, or that men of good birth were disgraced by women of low estate, and thus the fair repute of their families would be unworthily blackened. But before judgment is given the woman and the accused can be reconciled to each other by marriage, if they have license from the king or his justices and the consent of their families.

***Bracton***

## Bracton

*Bracton*, as the *De Legibus et Consuetudinibus Angliae* is conventionally called, was for centuries considered to have been exclusively from the hand of Henry Bracton (a corruption of Bratton), a distinguished English jurist from Devonshire. However, the earliest reference to him as author dates from 1277 and scholars have long since concluded that several hands at least are responsible for the work as it is now before us. Nevertheless, it is still convenient and conventional to name Bracton as the original author even if he was, at least initially, but a clerk of a distinguished jurist named William Raleigh, perhaps given the task of copying materials and continuing a process of composition Raleigh himself had performed when he clerked for another well-known legal figure named Martin Pateshull. Paul Brand proposes that "the initial impulse for the writing of *Bracton* may have come from the work done in preparing a statement of English law for promulgation in Ireland by King John in his charter of 1210."[1] Samuel Thorne, *Bracton*'s modern translator, locates parts of the book in the 1220s and 1230s, too early to be Bracton's, concludes that much of it was written by 1236 and the appearance of the Statute of Merton, and that the last additions were made in 1258.[2] We are unlikely ever to get a better picture than the one Thorne has sketched. Beginning apparently as a series of tracts on a variety of topics more or less practically arranged by items and paragraphs along the lines of the civil law *Digest*, *Bracton* came to its present shape in the late 1250s and had an active life for perhaps a century before it fell into disuse and obscurity, to be recovered again in early modern times. It was several times recast and updated, most notably in *Britton* and, to a lesser extent, *Fleta* and *Thornton*.

*Bracton* is remarkable for its use of Roman law in an attempt to create a theoretical system out of the mass of English laws and customs. As

1 Brand 1981 112.
2 Thorne 1968-1977 3, xiv-xv.

Thorne puts it, "Bracton's resort to Roman law was neither a display of virtuosity nor an ostentatious introduction to the main body of his work; nor was he simply a practical English lawyer adding Roman flourishes to a book on English law complete without them. He was a trained jurist with the principles and distinctions of Roman jurisprudence firmly in mind, using them throughout his work, wherever they could be used, to rationalize and reduce to order the results reached in the English courts. Roman law supplied him not only with a number of concepts under which his English matter could be subsumed, and thus fashioned, for the first time, into an articulated system of principles, but with a precise technical vocabulary, infinitely more subtle than the language of the plea rolls, with which to describe and analyze it."[1] As for the errors and misapplications of that law that earlier legal historians thought they saw, Thorne concluded that "Bracton's principal task was not to copy or make an abstract of the texts before him. To reproduce the teachings of Justinian and Azo was not his aim, but to use the ideas and language he found in their books for English purposes. Departures from them were thus not distortions or perversions of the texts he was using, for a treatise on English law required some modifications of Roman material, some remodeling of Roman doctrines, some adaptations of Roman terms to English institutions."[2]

*Bracton* is also distinctly different from anything that preceded it in its employment of approximately five hundred actual law cases, most of them presided over by the above-referenced Martin Pateshull and William Raleigh, introduced in the course of legal discussions.[3] While

---

1 Thorne 1968-1977 3, xxxiii.

2 Ibid.

3 Bracton's *Notebooks* contain over 2,000 cases. Raleigh was a clerk for Pateshull and Bracton in turn clerked for Raleigh. See Turner 1985 216-17. Thorne thinks that Raleigh is a likely candidate for author and Bracton his clerical assistant for the gathering of materials.

historians do not consider the use of those cases to be yet the beginnings of *stare decisis* ("to stand by decisions"), the foundational concept of English case law, nevertheless the idea that the records of cases should be consulted for guidance does begin with *Bracton*. Moreover, the rolls on which cases were recorded were not available to legal practitioners and when Bracton had them copied for use in his own writings he did something apparently new. However, it will be several generations yet before legal records begin to be seen as public information not restricted to the use of officialdom, and Bracton himself was finally ordered to return the rolls he had taken to have copied.

The precise nature and source of *Bracton*'s knowledge of Roman law led in the mid-twentieth century to a spirited discussion that involved the most distinguished legal historians of several generations, notably marked by a heavyweight bout between George E. Woodbine and Hermann Kantorowicz not without bitterness further exacerbated by undiplomatic contributions from others.[1] However, the altercation established once and for all a massive Civil, Roman, and Canon Law presence in *Bracton* and its exact location in the knowledge and employment of Romanism as practiced by the authors' European contemporaries. The many problems concerning both Roman and English law contained in the text are accounted for by the redacted manuscript that was the source of all the extant copies, as Kantorowicz suggested. Thorne's careful and painstaking translation and emendation of Woodbine's cautious and sometimes incorrect edition has given us something as close to the original text as we shall ever have. That original, presumably Bracton's own, with its variously located notes, glosses, interleaved insertions, marginalia and *addiciones* that required editorial disposition within the text, disappeared after it was transcribed

1 See Kantorowicz's *Bractonian Problems*, George E. Woodbine's review in the *Yale Law Review,* 52, 428, and, for a balanced view, Charles H. McIlwain's review in the *Harvard Law Review,* 57, 220.

by a redactor faced sometime between 1272 and 1277 with the difficult task of creating a unified text out of Bracton's original and its accretion of commentary. Subsequent contributors and their clerks not only perpetuated the corrupt text but likely added further confusions in the course of augmentation and transmission, no doubt thinking all the while they were being as true as possible to the alpha text.

The structure of *Bracton* is modeled on that of Justinian's *Digest*, comprising a series of titles further broken down into paragraphs, some of which were likely original with the opening exposition of a topic and others that were appended at a later date as additional relevant material was folded into the text. A lengthy introduction and *addicio* establishing Roman principles and definitions is followed by topics subdivided into varying numbers of paragraphs and further *addiciones* for more detailed discussion and illustration. The so-called Vulgate edition was divided into the Introduction and five additional chapters, titled Of Persons, Of Things, Of Acquiring the Dominion of Things, Of Actions, and Of Pleas of the King and Thorne has retained the headings in the body of his text even if they are not used in the table of contents. This is the material we reproduce, which constitutes volume 2 of Thorne's translation.

Thorne's edition is not an easy work for the uninitiated reader. Important information is scattered throughout the introductions to the various volumes and the translation is ordered by a calendar of MS folios given as a table of contents. Whereas Woodbine was reluctant to reorder obviously mislocated materials in the Latin text, Thorne properly does move elements about in order to recreate sense out of passages that are otherwise hopelessly jumbled. Accordingly, the reader who wishes to move from the Latin to the English is often required to be agile.

We have generally followed Thorne's translation, but at the same time adjusted it in numerous places to help the student follow the movement of the Latin into English. Passages within italic brackets indicate interlinear additions or supplementary passages later taken into the text by an editor or redactor. Materials within square brackets are Thorne's transitional and explanatory additions. Pointed brackets mark addiciones in the text. As with the *Leges Henrici Primi, and Glanvill* we have reproduced the chapter headings of omitted materials in the interest of continuity.

## Introductio

### Quae sunt regi necessaria.

*— For a summary of section headings in Latin, see Appendix I —*

In rege qui recte regit necessaria sunt duo haec, arma videlicet et leges, quibus utrumque tempus bellorum et pacis recte possit gubernari. Utrumque enim istorum alterius indiget auxilio, quo tam res militaris posssit esse in tuto, quam ipsae leges armorum podio sint servatae. Si autem arma defecerint contra hostes rebelles et indomitos, sic erit regnum indefensum: si autem leges, sic exterminabitur iustitia, nec erit qui iustus faciat iudicium. Cum autem fere in omnibus regionibus utatur legibus et iure scripto, sola Anglia usa est in suis finibus iure non scripto et consuetudine. In ea quidem ex non scripto ius venit quod usus comprobavit. Set non erit absurdum leges Anglicanas licet non scriptas leges appellare, cum legis vigorem habeat quidquid de consilio et consensu magnatum et rei publicae communi sponsione, auctoritate regis sive principis praecedente, iuste fuerit definitum et approbatum. Sunt etiam in Anglia consuetudines plures et diversae secundum diversitatem locorum. Habent enim Anglici plura ex consuetudine quae non habent ex lege, sicut in diversis comitatibus, civitatibus, burgis et villis, ubi semper inquirendum erit quae sit illius loci consuetudo et qualiter utantur consuetudine qui consuetudines allegant.

### Si insipiens et indoctus cathedram iudicandi ascenderit.

Cum autem huiusmodi leges et consuetudines per insipientes et minus doctos, qui cathedram iudicandi ascendunt antequam leges didicerint, saepius trahantur ad abusum, et qui stand in dubiis et in opinionibus et multotiens pervertuntur a maioribus, qui potius proprio arbitrio quam legum auctoritate causas decidunt, ad instructionem saltem minorum ego, Henricus de Brattone, animum erexi ad vetera

# Bracton

## Introduction

### What the needs of a king are.

*— For a summary of section headings in English, see Appendix II —*

To rule well a king requires two things, arms and laws, that by them both times of war and of peace may rightly be ordered. For each stands in need of the other, that the achievement of arms be conserved [by the laws], the laws themselves preserved by the support of arms. If arms fail against hostile and unsubdued enemies, then will the realm be without defense; if laws fail, justice will be extirpated, and no man will be able to render just judgment.

[England alone uses within her boundaries unwritten law and custom.] Though in almost all lands use is made of the *leges* and the *ius scriptum*, England alone uses unwritten law and custom. There law derives from nothing written [but] from what usage has approved. Nevertheless, it will not be absurd to call English laws *leges*, though they are unwritten, since whatever has been rightly decided and approved with the counsel and consent of the magnates and the general agreement of the *res publica*, the authority of the king or prince having first been added thereto, has the force of law. England has as well many local customs, varying from place to place, for the English have many things by custom that they do not have by law, as in the various counties, cities, boroughs and vills, where it will always be necessary to learn what the custom of the place is and how those who allege it use it.

### If an unwise and unlearned man ascends the judgment seat.

Since these laws and customs are often misapplied by the unwise and unlearned who ascend the judgment seat before they have learned the laws and stand amid doubts and the confusion of opinions, and frequently subverted by the greater [judges] who decide cases according to their own will rather than by the authority of the laws, I, Henry de Bracton, to

iudicia iustorum, perscrutando diligenter non sine vigiliis et labore, facta ipsorum, consilia et responsa, et quidquid inde nota dignum inveni in unam summam redigendo sub ordine titulorum et paragraphorum, sine praeiudicio melioris sententiae, compilavi, scripturae suffragio perpetuae memoriae commendanda, postulans a lectore ut si quid superfluum vel perperam positum in hoc opere invenerit, illud corrigat et emendet, vel conniventibus oculis pertranseat, cum omnia habere in memoria et in nullo peccare divinum sit potius quam humanum.

### Prohemium auctoris.

In hoc autem tractatu sicut in aliis tractatibus consideranda sunt haec, scilicet, quae sit materia, quae intentio, quae finis et cui parti philosophiae supponatur.

### Quae sit materia.

Et sciendum quod materia est facta et casus qui quotidie emergunt et inveniunt in regno Angliae, ut sciatur quae competat actio et quod breve, secundum quod placitum fuerit reale vel personale, et super huiusmodi conficienda acta sive irrotulationes, secundum proposita et obiecta, agendo et probando, defenendo et excipiendo et replicando et huiusmodi.

### Quae intentio.

Intentio autem auctoris est tractare de huiusmodi et instruere et docere omnes qui edoceri desiderant, qualiter et quo ordine lites et placita decidantur secundum leges et consuetudines Anglicanas, et de huiusmodi habere tractatum, ut doceantur et corrigantur errantes, puniantur contumaces. Item communis intentio est de iure scribere ut rudes efficantur subtiles, subtiles subtiliores, et homines mali

instruct the lesser judges, if no one else, have turned my mind to the ancient judgments of just men, examining diligently, not without working long into the night watches, their decisions, *consiliis* and *responsa*, and have collected whatever I found therein worthy of note into a *summa*, putting it in the form of titles and paragraphs, without prejudice to any better system, by the aid of writing to be preserved to posterity forever. I ask the reader, if he finds in this work anything superfluous or erroneous, to correct and amend it, or pass it over with eyes half closed, for to keep all in mind and err in nothing is divine rather than human.

### The author's preamble.

In this tractate, as in others, these must be considered: the matter with which it deals, its intention, its utility, the end it serves and the division of learning into which it falls.

### The matter with which it deals.

Its matter consists of the judgments and the cases that daily arise and come to pass in the realm of England.[1]

### The author's intention.

The intention of the author is to treat of such matters and to instruct and teach all who desire to be taught what action lies and what writ, *[*and*]*, according as the plea is real or personal, how and by what procedure, *[*by suing and proving, defending and excepting, replicating and the like,*]* suits and pleas are decided according to English laws and customs, and [the art] of preparing records and enrollments according to what is alleged and denied, and to treat of these so that those who err may be instructed and set right and those who obstinately do otherwise punished. The general intention is to treat of law that the unskilled may be made expert,

1 Thorne's note at this point reads:"The remainder of this paragraph, which supplements the next section, [is] transposed below." The transposition is marked in the translation by italicized brackets.

efficiantur boni et boni meliores, tum metu poenarum tum exhortatione praemiorum, iuxta illud,

Oderunt peccare boni virtutis amore,

Oderunt peccare mali formidine poenae.[1]

### Quae utilitas.

Utilitas autem est quis nobilitat addiscentes et honor es conduplicat et profectus et facit eos principari in regno et sedere in aula regis et in sede ipsius regis quasi in throno dei, tribus et nationes, actores et reos, ordine dominabili iudicantes, vice regis quasi vice Ihesu Christi, cum rex sit vicarius dei. Iudicia enim non sunt hominis sed dei, et ideo cor regis bene regentis dicitur esse in manu dei.

### Quis finis.

Item finis huius rei est ut sopiantur iurgia et vitia propulsentur, et us in regno conservetur pax et iustitia. Ethicae vero supponitur quasi morali scientiae quia tractat de moribus.

### Leges iubent et vetant.

Huismodi vero leges Anglicanae et consuetudines regum auctoritate iubent quandoque, quandoque vetant, quendoque vindicant et puniunt transgressores. Quae quidem, cum fuerint approbatae consensu utentium et sacramento regum confirmatae, mutari non poterunt nec distrui sine communi consensu eorum omnium quorum consilio et consensu fuerint promulgatae. In eorum omnium quorum consilio et consensu fuerint promulgatae. In melius tamen converti possunt etiam sine eorum consensu, quia non destruitur quod in melius commutatur. Si autem aliqua nova et inconsueta emerserint et quae prius usitata non fuerint in regno, si tamen similia evenerint per simile iudicentur, cum bona sit occasio a

1 Horace, *Epistles*, 1.16.52.

the expert more expert, the bad good and the good better, as well by the fear of punishment as by the hope of reward, according to this [verse]:

Good men hate to err from love of virtue;

The wicked from fear of pain.

### The utility.

The utility [of this work] is that it ennobles apprentices [i.e. pleaders] and doubles their honors and profits and enables them to rule in the realm and sit in the royal chamber, on the very seat of the king, on the throne of God, so to speak, judging tribes and nations, plaintiffs and defendants, in lordly order, in the place of the king, as though in the place of Jesus Christ, since the king is God's vicar. For judgments are not made by man but by God, which is why the heart of a king who rules well is said to be in the hand of God.

### The end served.

The end of this work is to quiet disputes and avert wrongdoing, that peace and justice may be preserved in the realm. It must be set under ethics, moral science, as it were, since it treats of customary principles of behavior.

### Laws command and forbid.

[And because] in truth these English laws and customs, by the authority of kings, sometimes command, sometimes forbid, sometimes castigate and punish offenders. Since they have been approved by the consent of those who use them and confirmed by the oath of kings, they cannot be changed without the common consent of all those by whose counsel and consent they were promulgated. They cannot be nullified without their consent, but may be changed for the better, for to change for the better is not to nullify. If new and unusual matters arise which have not before been seen in the realm, /If like matters arise let them be decided by like, since the occasion is a good one for proceeding *a similibus ad similia.]*

similibus procedere ad similia. Si autem talia prius numquam evenerint, et obscurum et difficile sit eorum idicium, tunc ponantur iudicia usque ad magnam curiam ut ibi per consilium curiae terminentur: licet sint nonnulli qui de propria scientia praesumentes, quasi nihil iuris ignorent, nolint alicuius consilium expetere. Et quo casu honestius et consultius foret eis consilium habere quam aliquid temere definire, cum de singuilis dubitare non sit inutile.

### Sapiens esse debet qui iudicat.

Sedem quidem iudicandi, quae est quasi thronus dei, non praesumat quis ascendere insipiens et indoctus, ne lucem ponat tenebras et tenebras jucem, et ne manu indocta modo furientis gladio feriat innocentem et liberet nocemtem, et ex alto corruet quasi a throno dei, qui volare inceperit autequam pennas assumat. Et cum quis iudicare debeat et iudex fieri caveat unusquisque sibi, ne perverse iudicando et contra leges prece vel pretio, pro temporalis lucelli commodo, eiterni luctus maetitiam sibi comparare praesumat.

### Quae sit poena male iudicantis.

Et ne in die furoris domini sentiat ipsum vindicantem, qui ait, *Mihi vindictam et ego retribuam*, et ubi flebunt et planent reges et principes terrae cum viderint filium hominis, propter timorem tormentorum eius, ubi aurum et argentum non valebit liberare eos. Quis autem non timeat illud examen, in quo erit dominus accusator, advocatus et iudex? A sententia autem sua non poterit provocari, quia pater omne iudicium dedit filio, qui claudit et nemo aperit, aperit et nemo claudit. O districtum iudicium, quo non solum de actibus, verum etiam de omni verbo otioso quodcumque locuti fuerint homines, reddituri sunt rationem. Quis ergo effugere poterit a ventura ira? Mittet enim filius hominis angelos suos, qui colligent de regno dei omnia scandala et eos qui faciunt iniquitatem, et ex eis alligabunt fasciculos ad

and their judgment is difficult and unclear, let them be adjourned to the great court to be there determined by counsel of the court, /though there are some who, presuming on their own knowledge, as though nothing connected with the law were beyond their competence, are unwilling to seek the counsel of anyone,/ [since] it is more becoming and more lawyer-like to take counsel rather than to determine anything rashly, nor is it discreditable to be in doubt as to individual cases.

### He who judges ought to be wise.

Let no one, unwise and unlearned, presume to ascend the seat of judgment, which is like unto the throne of God, lest for light he bring darkness and for darkness light, and, with unskilful hand, even as a madman, he put the innocent to the sword and set free the guilty, and lest he fall from on high, as from the throne of God, in attempting to fly before he has wings. And though one is fit to judge and to be made a judge, let each one take care for himself lest, by judging perversely and against the laws, because of prayer or price, for the advantage of a temporary and insignificant gain, he dare to bring upon himself sorrow and lamentation everlasting.

### What the punishment for evil judging is.

And lest in the day of the wrath of the Lord he feel the vengeance of Him who said, "Vengeance is mine, I will repay," on that day when kings and princes of the earth shall weep and bewail when they behold the Son of Man, because of fear of his torments, where gold and silver will be of no avail to set them free. Who shall not fear that trial, where the Lord shall be the accuser, the advocate and the judge? From his sentence there is no appeal, for the Father has committed all judgment to the Son; he shuts and there is none to open; he opens and there is none to shut. O how strict shall that judgment be, where we shall give account not only of our acts but even of every idle word that men utter. Who can escape his impending wrath? For the Son of Man shall send His angels and they

comburendum, et mittent eos in caminum ignis, ubi erit fletus et stridor dentium, gemitus et ululatus, eiulatus, luctus et cruciatus, stridor et clamor, timor et tremor, dolor et labor, ardor et foetor, obscuritas et anxietas, acerbitas et asperitas, calamitas et egestas, angustia et tristitia, oblivio et confusio, tortiones et punctiones, amaritudines et terrores, fames et sitis, frigus et cauma, sulphur et ignis ardens in saecula saeculorum. Caveat etiam quilibet iudicium illud ubi iudex terribiliter districtus, intolerabiliter severus, immoderate offensus, vehementer iratus, sentenntia eius incommutabilis, carcer irremeabilis, tormenta sine fine, sine intervallo, tortores horribiles qui numquam lassescunt, numquam miserentur, timor rerum conturbat, conscientia damnat, cogitationes increpant, et fugere non licet. Unde beatus Augustinus, *O quam magna peccata mea sunt nimis! Unde cum quis deum habuerit iustum iudicem, et conscientiam suam testem, nihil timeat nisi causam suam.*

### Quid sit lex et quid consuetudo.

Videndum est etiam quid sit lex. Et sciendum quod lex est commune praeceptum virorum consultum prudentium, delictorum quae sponte vel irnorantis contrahuntur coertio, rei publicae sponsio communis. Item auctor iustitiae est deus, secundum quod iustitia est in creatore. Et secundum hoc ius et lex idem significant. Et licet largissime dicatur lex omne quod legitur, tamen specialiter significat sanctionem iustam, iubentem honesta, prohibentem contraria. Consuetudo vero quandoque pro lege observatur in partibus ubi fuerit more utentium approbata, et vicem legis obtinet. Longaevi enim usus et consuetudinis non est vilis auctoritas.

### Quid sit iustitia.

Quia iustitia quasi a quodam fonte omnia iura emanant, et quod vult iustitia ius idem prosequitur, videamus igitur quid sit iustitia et unde dicatur. Item quid sit ius et unde dicatur, et quae sint eius praecepta. Item quid sit lex, et quid consuetudo, sine quibus non poterit quis esse iustus, ut faciat

shall gather out of His kingdom all things that offend and them that do iniquity and bind them into bundles to be burnt, and shall cast them into the fiery furnace, where there will be wailing and gnashing of teeth, groans and screams, outcries, lamentation and torment, roaring and shouting, fear and trembling, sorrow and suffering, fire and stench, doubt and anxiety, violence and cruelty, ruin and poverty, distress and dejection, oblivion and brimstone and burning fire for ever and ever. Therefore let each beware of that judgment where the judge is terribly strict, intolerably severe, offended beyond measure and vehemently angered, whose sentence none can commute, from whose prison there is no escape, whose punishments are without end, his tormentors horrible, who never grow weary, never pity, whom fear does not disturb, conscience condemn, thoughts reproach, and who may not flee. Hence the blessed Augustine, "O how far too great are my sins, wherefore when one has God as a rightful judge and his conscience as witness, let him fear nothing except his cause."

### What law is and what custom.

We must see what law is. Law is a general command, the decision of judicious men, the restraint of offenses knowingly or unwittingly committed, the general agreement of the *res publica*. Justice proceeds from God, assuming that justice lies in the Creator, [*jus* from man], and thus *jus* and *lex* are synonymous. And though law (*lex*) may in the broadest sense be said to be everything that is read (*legitur*) its special meaning is a just sanction, ordering virtue and prohibiting its opposite. Custom, in truth, in regions where it is approved by the practice of those who use it, is sometimes observed as and takes the place of *lex*. For the authority of custom and long use is not slight.

### What justice is.

Since from justice, as from a fountain-head, all rights arise and what justice commands *jus* provides, let us see what justice is and whence it is

iustitiam et iustum iudicium inter virum et virum. Est autem iustitia constans et perpetua voluntas ius suum cuique tribuens. Cuius definitio poterit intellegi dubus modis, uno prout est in creatore, altero prout est in creatura. Et si intellegatur prout est in creatore, id est in deo, plana sunt omnia, cum iustittia sit dei dispositio, quae in omnibus rebus recte constituit et iuste disponit. Ipse enim deus tribuit unicuique secundum opera sua. Ipse non est variabilis neque temporalis in dispositionibus et voluntatibus suis, immo eius voluntas est constans et perpectua. Ipse enim non habuit principium, nec habet nec habebit finem. Altero modo intellegitur prout est in creatura, id est in homine iusto. Homo enim iustus habet voluntatem tribuendi unicuique ius suum, et ita illa voluntas dicitur iustitia. Et dicitur voluntas tribuere ius suum, non quantum ad actum sed quantum ad afffectionem. Sicut dicitur imperator Augustus, non quod semper augeat imperium, sed quia eius propositi est ut augeat. Sicut dicitur de matrimonio, quod dicitur individua coniunctio quia eius sunt animi ut numquam dividantur, postmodo tamen dividuntur ex causa. Item dicitur iustitia *constans* secundum definitionem, prout iustitia est in creatura, ut per hoc quod dicit *voluntas* intellegatur mens, et per hoc quod dicit *constans* intellegatur bonum. Constantia enim semper accipitur in bonum, unde et sancti dicuntur fuisse constantes, ubi dicitur, *O constantia martyrum*! Item *Constantes estote*. Constantia enim non admittit variationem. Per hoc autem quod dicit *perpetua* intellegatur habitus, quia iustitia est habitus mentis bonus, vel mentis bene constitutae. Vel iustitia est voluntarium bonum. Nec enim potest dici bonum proprie nisi intercedente voluntate. Tolle enim voluntatem et erit omnis actus indifferens. Affectio quidem tua nomen imponit operi tuo. Item crimen non contrahitur nisi voluntas nocendi intercedat. Item voluntas et propositum distinguunt maleficia. De hoc autem quod dicit *ius suum*, id est hominis meritum, nam propter delictum vel pactum non servatum, vel

so called. Also what *jus* is and whence it is so called and what its precepts are, and what law is and what custom, without which one cannot be just, so as to do justice and give just judgment between man and man. Justice is the constant and unfailing will to give to each his right. This definition may be understood in two ways, according as justice is taken to be in the Creator or in the created. If in the Creator, that is, in God, the matter is clear, since justice is the disposition of God which in all things rightfully orders and justly disposes. God himself gives to each man in accordance with his deserts. He is neither variable nor inconstant in his dispositions and wills, but is constant and unfailing. For he had no beginning, nor has nor will have any end. The definition may be understood in another way, that justice is in the created, that is, in the just man. The just man has the will to give to each his right, and thus that will is called justice. His will to give each his right refers to what is intended not to what is done, as the emperor is called Augustus not because he always augments his empire but because it is his intention to do so [and] as matrimony is said to be an inseparable conjoining because the parties intend never to be separated though they may afterwards be separated for just cause. Thus justice is said to be constant, in accord with the definition. [Justice may also be understood in another way, according to the definition] which defines justice as in the created: by the word "will," "mind" may be understood, and by "constant," "good," for constancy is always taken to be good; hence the saints are said to have been constant, and we say "O the constancy of the martyrs"! By the word "unfailing," "habit" may be understood [also by the word "constant"], "Be ye constant," for constancy does not admit of variation, as though the definition read "justice is a good habit of mind" or "the habit of a mind well constituted" or "justice is a willed good," for it cannot properly be called good unless will plays a part. Remove will and every act will be indifferent. It is your intent that differentiates your acts, nor is a crime committed unless an intention to injure exists; it is will and purpose which distinguish *maleficia*. As for the words "his right," they mean his

similia, privatur quis iure suo. De hoc autem quod dicit *cuique*, id est hominis meritum, nam propter delictum vel pactum non servatum, vel similia, privatur quis iure suo. De hoc autem quod dicit *cuique*, id est sibi ipsi, ut honeste vivat. Item deo, ut deum diligat. Item proximo, ut eum non laedat.

### Quid sit ius.

De hoc autem quod dicit *ius suum*, id est iustitiae, et sic dicitur ius iustitia quia in ea stant omnis iura. Ius ergo derivatur a iustitia, et habet varias significationes. Ponitur enim quandoque pro ipsa arte, vel pro eo quod scriptum habemus de iure, quod ius dicitur ars boni et aequi, cuius merito quis nos sacerdotes appellat. Iustitiam namque colimus et sacra iura ministramus. Item ius quandoque supponitur pro iure naturali, quod semper bonum et aequum est. Quandoque pro iure civili tantum. Quandoque pro iure praetorio tantum. Quandoque pro eo tantum quod competit ex sententia. Praeter enim ius dicitur reddere, et cum inique decernit, relatione facta non ad it quod praetor fecit, sed ad illud quod praetor facere debuit. Item supponit quandoque ius pro loco in quo redditur ius. Supponit etiam quandoque pro necessitudine, sicut pro iure cognationis vel affinitatis. Supponit etiam ius quandoque pro actione. Quandoque pro obligatione qualibet. Quandoque pro hereditate, sicut pro proprietate rei. Quandoque pro bonorum possessione. Quandoque pro potestate, ut cum dicitur *iste est sui iuris*. Quandoque pro rigore iuris, ut cum dicitur *inter ius et aequitatem*. Item ponitur pro ipsa arte, non pro quolibet iure quod invenitur in ipsa arte: nec enim omne ius praecipit, immo quoddam permittit. Vel ponitur pro omni iure quod praecipit honeste vivere, alterum nonn laedere, ius suum cuique tribuere.

**Addicio. Quid iuris prudentia. Quid aequitas. Quae iuris praecepta. Quid sit ius privatum. Quid sit ius naturale. Quid sit ius civile. Quid sit jus gentium. Quid sit manumissio.**

merited right, for because of delict or a pact broken or the like one is [*de jure*] deprived of his right. Or say "to each" means to him, that he live virtuously, and to God, that he love God, and to his neighbor, that he not harm him. Or say "*suum jus*" means "her right," that is, [to each what justice entitles him to]; she is called justice because in her all rights reside.

### What jus is.

*Jus* is derived from justice and is used in a number of different senses. For it is sometimes used for the *ars boni et aequi* itself, or for the written body of *jus*. It is called the art of what is fair and just, of which we are deservedly called the priests, for we worship justice and administer sacred rights. *Jus* is sometimes used for natural law which is always fair and right; sometimes for the civil law only; sometimes for praetorian law only; sometimes for that which results from a judgment, for the praetor is said to do *jus* even when he does it unjustly, the word referring not to what he in fact did but what he ought to do. *Jus* is sometimes used for an action, sometimes for an obligation, sometimes for an inheritance, as for the *proprietas* of a thing, sometimes for the possession of goods. Sometimes it signifies *potestas*, as when it is said "He is *sui juris*." Sometimes it stands for law in all its rigor, as when we distinguish between law and equity. *Jus* is [here] put for the art as such, not for everything contained within it, for not all *jus* enjoins since some permits. Or it is here used for all the *jus* that enjoins, [for all the *jus* that enjoins] us to live virtuously, to harm no one and to give each his right.

**Addicio. What jurisprudence is. What equity is. What the praecepta iuris are. What private law is. What natural law is. What the civil law is. What the jus gentium is. What manumission is.**

## De Personis.

### Quod omne ius pertinet vel ad personas, vel ad res, vel ad actiones.

Dictum est supra de iure naturali, gentium et civili, sed quia omne ius de quo tractare proponimus pertinet vel ad personas, vel ad res, vel ad actiones secundum leges et consuetudines Anglicanas, et cum digniores sint personae, quarum causa statuta sunt omnia iura, ideo de personis primo videamus et earum statu, qui varius est et diversus, et postmodum de iure personarum quod vertitur circa eas.

### De prima divisione personarum.

Est autem prima divisio personarum haec et brevissima, quod omnes homines aut liberi sunt aut servi, id est, omnis homo aut est liber, aut est servus, et ita resolvatur pluralis oratio in singularem. Sed sic opponi poterit de ascripticio, ut videtur, quia vere liber est, licet quodam servitio sit astrictus. Et de eo brevis poterit esse solutio, quia ei qui liber est villenagium vel servitium nihil detrahit libertati[s], habita tamen distinctione, utrum tales sint villani et tenuerint in villano socagio de dominico domini regis, de quibus inferius tractabitur plenius. Item nec obstat quod dicitur de statuliberis, quia quamvis servus fuerit in possessione libertatis, re vera servus est, quamvis se et sua aliquando defendere possit contra dominum suum, petentem ipsum ut nativum suum, per exceptionem privilegii. Cum autem omnis homo sit liber vel servus, expedit videre quid sit libertas et quid servitus et qualiter contingat servitus.

### Quid sit libertas.

Est autem libertas naturalis facultas eius, quod cuique facere libet, nisi quod iure aut vi prohibetur. Sed secundum hoc videtur quod servi sint liberi, nam et ipsi liberam habent facultatem nisi vi aut iure prohibeantur. Set definitur libertas eo iure quo prodita est, ex qua liberi vocantur. Licet enim servi efficiantur liberi, tamen quoad ius gentium servi sunt, quoad

## Of Persons

### That all law relates either to persons, things or actions.

We have spoken above of natural law, the *jus gentium*, and the civil law, but since the whole of the law with which we propose to deal relates either to persons or to things or to actions, according to English laws and customs, and since persons, because of whom all rights are established, are of the greater dignity, therefore let us first look to them and their conditions, which are various and diverse, and then to the law of persons which is directed to them.

### The first classification of persons.

The first and shortest classifications of persons is this, that all men are either free or bond, that is, every man is either free or bond, that the plural number may so be reduced to the singular. Against this can be cited the *ascripticius*, so it seems, for he is truly free though bound to a certain service. But to this a brief answer may be given, for from him who is free a villeinage or villein service detracts in no way, [this] distinction [only] being taken, whether such persons are villeins or [free men who] hold in villein socage of the demesne of the lord king, of whom more will be said below. Nor is what is said of *status liberi* an objection, for though a bondsman is in possession of his freedom he is in truth bond, though against his lord claiming him as his villein he sometimes can defend himself and his goods by an exception based upon his privilege. Since, then, every man is either free or bond, we must see what freedom and bondage are, and how bondage comes about.

### What freedom is.

"Freedom is the natural power of every man to do what he pleases, unless forbidden by law or force." But if so, it then appears that bondsmen are free, for they have free power [to act] unless forbidden by force or law.

ius vero naturale liberi, et ita liberi et servi diversis tamen respectibus, et sic omnino liber et omnino servus et non pro parte, et secundum quod praedictum est. Et in hac parte ius civile vel gentium detrahit iuri naturali.

**Quid sit servitus. Servi aut nascuntur aut fiunt: qualiter nascuntur. Qualiter servi fiunt. Quis dici possit liber et quis ingenuus. Qui dicuntur libertini. Qui dici poterunt liberi et computari debeant inter pueros et qui non. Alia divisio hominum. De hermaphrodito. De manumissione.**

### QUOD NULLA ACCEPTIO PERSONARUM APUD DEUM EST, TAMEN APUD HOMINES, QUIA QUIDAM PRINCIPANTUR IN TERRIS IN REBUS SPIRITUALIBUS, ET QUIDAM IN TEMPORALIBUS.

Liberorum autem hominum quorumcumque nulla est acceptio apud deum nec etiam servorum, quia non est personarum acceptor deus, quia quantum ad deum qui maior est fiat tamquam minor, et qui praecessor fiat tamquam ministrator. Apud homines vero est differentia personarum, quia hominum quidam sunt praecellentes et prelati et aliis principantur: dominus papa in rebus spiritualibus quae pertinent ad sacerdotium, et sub eo archiepiscopi, episcopi, et alii prelati inferiores. Item in temporalibus imperatores, reges, et principes in his quae pertinent ad regnum, et sub eis duces, comites et barones, magnates sive vavasores, et milites, et etiam liberi et villani, et diversae potestates sub rege constitutae. Comites videlicet qui a comitatu sive a societate nomen sumpserunt, qui etiam dici possunt consules a consulendo. Reges enim tales sibi associant ad regendum populum dei, ordinantes eos magno honor e et potestate et nomine quando concingunt eos gladiis, id est ringis gladiorum.

**Quid sint ringae. Quid significat gladius.**

But freedom is defined by that law by which it is created, by virtue of which they are called free. For though bondsmen may be made free,since with respect to the *jus gentium* they are bond, they are free with respect to the *jus naturale,* thus free and bond, but from different points of view, and so wholly free [or] wholly bond, not in part one and part the other, as was said above. And in this connection the civil law or the *jus gentium* detracts from natural law.

**What bondage is. Bondsmen are either born unfree or are made such; how they are born unfree. How men are made bond. Who may be called free and who freeborn. Who are called freedmen. Who may and may not be called children and reckoned as such. Another classification of men. Of the hermaphrodite. Of manumission.**

### That God is no respecter of persons though men are, since some rule over lands in spiritual matters, some in temporal.

God is no respecter of any men whomsoever, free or bond, "for there is no respect of persons with God," for as to Him, "he that is greatest, let him be as the smallest; and he that is chief as he that doth serve." But with men, in truth, there is a difference between persons, for there are some of great eminence /who/ are placed above others and rule over them: in spiritual matters which belong to the priesthood, the lord pope, and under him archbishops, bishops and other less exalted prelates; in temporal matters which pertain to the kingdom, emperors, kings and princes, and under them dukes, earls and barons, magnates or vavasours and knights, also freemen and bondsmen. Various powerful persons are established under the king, namely, earls, who take the name "comites" from "comitatus," or from "societas," a partnership, /who may also be called consuls from counseling/, for kings associate such persons with themselves in governing the people of God, investing them with great honor, power and name when they gird them with swords, /that is with sword belts/.

**What belts are. What the sword signifies.**

### Rex non habet parem.

Parem autem non habet rex in regno suo, quia sic amitteret praeceptum, cum in parem non habeat imperium. Item nec multo fortius superiorem, neque potentiorem habere debet, quia sic esset inferior sibi subiectis, et inferiores pares esse non possunt potentioribus. Ipse autem rex non debet esse sub homine sed sub deo et sub lege, quia lex facit regem. Attribuat igitur rex legi, quod lex attribuit ei, videlicet dominationem et potestatem. Non est enim rex ubi dominatur voluntas et non lex. Et quod sub lege esse debeat, cum sit dei vicarius, evidenter apparet ad similitudinem Ihesu Christi, cuius vices gerit in terris. Quia verax dei misericordia, cum ad recuperandum humanum genus ineffabiliter ei multa suppeterent, hanc potissiman elegit viam, qua ad destruendum opus diabioli non virtute uteretur potentiae sed iustitiae ratione. Et sic esse voluit sub lege, ut eos qui sub lege erant redimeret. Noluit enim uti viribus, set iudicio. Sic etiam beata dei genetrix, virgo Maria, mater domini, quae singulari priveligio supra legem fuit pro ostendendo tamen humilitatis exemplo legalibus subdi non refutit institutis. Sic ergo rex, ne potestas sua maneat infrenata. Igitur non debet esse maior eo in regni suo in exhibitione iuris, minimus autem esse debet, vel quasi, in iudicio suscipiendo si petat. Si autem ab eo petatur, cum breve non currat contra ipsum, locus erit supplicationi, quod factum suum corriat et emendet, quod quidem si non fecerit, satis sufficit ei ad poenam, quod deum expectet ultorem. Nemo quidem de factis suis praesumat disputare, nec multo fortius contra factum suum venire.

**Alia divisio personarum, quod aut sunt sui iuris aut alieni aut dubii. De his qui sunt sui iuris. De his qui sunt in potestate patrum. Qualiter dissolvitur patria potestas et dominca. Quidam sunt sub tutela vel cura vel custodia. Sub potestate dominorum sunt servi. De dominico domini regis et de condicione personarum tenentium de dominico: non dico de manerio. Sunt etiam liberi in manerio domini regis. Sub potestate dominorum sunt liberi homines.**

### The king has no equal.

The king has no equal within his realm, *[*Subjects cannot be the equals of the ruler, because he would thereby lose his rule, since equal can have no authority over equal.*]* nor *a fortiori* a superior, because he would then be subject to those subjected to him. The king must not be under man but under God and under the law, because law makes the king, *[*Let him therefore bestow upon the law what the law bestows upon him, namely, rule and power.*]* for there is no *rex* where will rules rather than *lex*. Since he is the vicar of God, *[*And that he ought to be under the law appears clearly in the analogy of Jesus Christ, whose vice-regent on earth he is, for though many ways were open to Him for his ineffable redemption of the human race, the true mercy of God chose this most powerful way to destroy the devil's work, he would use not the power of force but the reason of justice. Thus he willed himself to be under the law that he might redeem those that live under it. For He did not wish to use force but judgment. And in that same way the Blessed Mother of God, the Virgin Mary, Mother of our Lord, who by an extraordinary privilege was above law, nevertheless, in order to show an example of humility, did not refuse to be subjected to established laws. Let the king, therefore, do the same, lest his power remain unbridled.*]* there ought to be no one in his kingdom who surpasses him in the doing of justice, but he ought to be the last, or almost so, to receive it, when he is plaintiff. If it is asked of him, since no writ runs against him there will *[*only*]* be opportunity for a petition, that he correct and amend his act; if he does not, it is punishment enough for him that he awaits God's vengeance. No one may presume to question his acts, much less contravene them.

**A second classification of persons, that they are in their own potestas, or another's, or their status is doubtful. Those who are [not] sui juris. Those who are in the potestas of fathers. How paternal potestas and seignorial potestas are extinguished. Some are under tutelage or curatorship or wardship. Bondsmen are under the potestas of their lords. Of the demesne of the lord king and the condition of persons who**

## De Rebus

### De rebus et rerum divisione: prima divisio.

Superius dictum est de personis et statu hominum et iure personarum, consequenter dicendum erit de rebus per divisionem, quia res per divisionem melius aperiuntur. Rerum autem prima divisio haec est, quod rerum quaedam sunt in patrimonio nostro, et quaedam extra. Quae sunt in patrimonio satis patebit inferius. Extra patrimonium autem dicuntur res sacrae et communes. Quaedam vero nec sunt in patrimonio nec extra, sicut iura et servitutes, ususfructus, iter et actus, via et aquae ductus et huiusmodi. Et ideo non dicuntur servitutes esse in bonis, quia per se sine fundo alienari non possunt. Item praediales servitutes per se non censentur, et ideo videntur non esse, vel extinctae esse, si censeantur per se. Nam et manica videtur extincta, cum non accedit vestimento, et tignum videtur non possideri cum accedit aedificio. Sed tamen non dicuntur istae servitutes esse extra bona, cum possidentes exceptionem, et non possidentes habeant actionem.

### Divisio secunda.

Fit et alia et secunda divisio rerum, quia aliae sunt corporales aliae incorporales. Corporales vero quae tangi possunt, sicut terra, fundus, res immobiles vel res mobiles, quae se movere possunt, sicut animalia et huiusmodi, vel moveri. Incorporales vero sunt sicut sunt iura, quae videri non possunt neque tangi, ut ius eundi, agendi, aquamve ducendi, et huiusmodi quae non possidentur sed quasi.

**are tenants of the demesne; I say nothing of the manor. Free men in the manor of the lord king. Free men under the potestas of lords.**

## Of Things

### Things and the classification of things: the first division.

We have spoken above of persons, the status of men and the law of persons; we must now speak of things, dividing [them] into classes, for in that way a subject is more clearly set forth. The first division into which things fall is this: some are within our patrimony, some outside it. What things are within our patrimony will appear adequately below. Outside our patrimony are sacred things and things owned in common. Some are neither within nor without our patrimony, as rights and servitudes, a usufruct, a right of passage [or] of driving beasts, a right of way over or a right to conduct water over another man's land and other similar arrangements. Servitudes are said not to be owned because they cannot be aliened by themselves apart from the land. Praedial servitudes cannot be thought of as having an existence of their own, and thus are taken not to exist, or to be extinguished, when regarded separately, for a sleeve is taken no longer to exist as such when [not] attached to a garment and a beam is taken not to be possessed when [not] attached to a house. Nevertheless, these servitudes are not thought of as things unowned, since [for them] possessors have an exception and those who do not possess an action.

### A second division.

There is another, a second, classification of things, for some are corporeal, others incorporeal. Corporeal are those that can be touched, [that is], immovables, as land, an estate, or movables, whether animate, as animals and such, or inanimate. Incorporeal things, such as rights, are those which can neither be seen nor touched, as a right of way over

### Divisio tertia.

Est etiam tertia divisio rerum, quod aliae sunt communes, aliae publicae, aliae universitatis, aliae nullius, et aliae singulorum, quae variis ex causis cuique adquiruntur.

### Quaedam res sunt communes.

Naturali vero iure communia sunt omnium haec: aqua profluens, aer et mare et litora maris, quasi mari accessoria. Nemo igitur ad litus maris accedere prohibetur, dum tamen villis et aedificiis abstineat, quia litora non sunt iure gentium communia sicut et mare. Immo aedificia, si in mari sive in litore posita fuerint, aedificantium sunt de iure gentium, et ita in hoc casu solum cedit aedificio, licet alibi contrarium, quod aedificium cedit solo.

### Quaedam publicae.

Publica vero sunt omni flumina et portus. Ideoque ius piscandi omnibus commune est in portu et in fluminibus. Riparum etiam usus publicus et iuris gentium sicut ipsius fluminis. Itaque naves ad eas applicare, funes arboribus ibi natis religare, onus aliquod in his reponere, cuilibet liberum est sicuti per ipsum flumen navigare. Sed proprietas earum est illorum quorum praediis adhaerent, et eadem de causa arbores in eisdem natae eorundem sunt. Et haec intellegenda sunt de fluminibus perennibus, quia temporalia possunt esse privata. Publica autem ita accipiuntur, quae sunt omnium populorum, id est quod spectant ad usum hominum tantum. Communia vero dici poterunt aliquando, quae sunt omnium animantium.

### Quaedam universitatis.

Universitas vero sunt, non singulorum, quae sunt in civitatibus ut theatra, stadia et huiusmodi, et si qua

another's land, a right to drive beasts or conduct water over it and other such, which cannot be possessed only *quasi*-possessed.

### A third division.

There is as well a third classification of things: some are common, others are public, others are the property of the *universitas*; some belong to no one, others, acquired for each by a *causa* of some king, belong to individual persons.

### Some things are common.

By natural law these are common to all: running water, air, the sea, and the shores of the sea, as though accessories of the sea. No one therefore is forbidden access to the seashore, provided he keeps away from houses and buildings [built there], for by the *jus gentium* shores are not common to all in the sense that the sea is, but buildings built there, whether in the sea or on the shore, belong by the *jus gentium* to those who build them. Thus in this case the soil cedes to the building, though elsewhere the contrary is true, the building cedes to the soil.

### Some things are public.

All rivers and ports are public, so that the right to fish therein is common to all persons. The use of river banks, as of the river itself, is also public by the *jus gentium* [and] consequently everyone is free to moor ships to them, to fasten ropes to the trees growing there and to land cargoes upon them, just as he is free to navigate the river itself. But the ownership of the banks belongs to those of whose lands they are part, and theirs, for the same reason, are the trees growing upon them. This is to be understood of permanent rivers, for streams that do not flow uninterruptedly may be privately owned. Those things are taken to be public that belong to all people, that is, which are for the use of mankind alone. Those that belong to all living things may sometimes be called common.

sunt in civitatibus communia. Dicuntur vero theatra a theorando, id est inspiciendo. Stadium vero dicitur octava para miliarii, quod, ut dicitur Hercules uno anhelitu currebat et postea stabat. Et dicuntur ista universitatis dominio et usu. Alia autem dicuntur universitatis esse non usu, sed dominio et fructu, ut fundi autem dicuntur universitatis esse non usu, sed dominio et fructu, ut fundi et servi civitatum, qui ita sunt omnium civium, ita quod nullius per se.

### Quaedam singulorum.

Item sunt res singulorum, ut mea, tua, dominio et usus, sicut fundi, civitates et servi.

### Quaedam sacrae et religiosae quae sunt deo consecratae.

Res vero sacrae, religiosae, et sanctae in nullius bonis sunt. Quod enim divini iuris est, id in nullius hominis bonis est, immo in bonis dei hominum censura. Et sunt sacra quae rite et per pontifices deo consecrata sunt, veluti aedes sacrae et religiosae et dona quae rite ad ministerium dei dedicata sunt, ut calices, cruces, et turibula, quae alienari prohibentur, excepta causa redemptionis captivorum. Item loca sacra sunt coemiteria et ecclesiae et capellae, et licet aedificia diruantur, adhuc locus sacer manet. Et differt sacrum a sacrario quia sacrarium dicitur locus ubi sacra reponuntur. Sacrae etiam res sunt, veluti muri et portae civitatum, et ideo dicuntur sancti quia poena capitalis constituta est in eos qui aliquid in muros sanctos delinquunt, violando aliquid in his vel immittendo, vel transcendendo, scalis adhibitis, vel alia qualibet ratione. Quia hostile est et abominabile alias ingredi quam per portas. Dicitur etiam sanctum quod defensum est et munitum ab iniuria hominum, et lex illa specialiter dicitur sanctio quae poenam imponit iniurioso. Muros vero municipales reficere non licet alicui ad privatum commodum, sed ad publicam utilitatem.

### Some things belong to the universitas.

Things in cities belong not to individuals but to the *universitas*, as theaters, stadia and the like; if there are any [such] they are the common property of the citizenry. Theatres are so called from "*theorando*," that is "watching as a spectator." A stadium is so called from the eighth part of a mile, which, so it is said, Hercules ran at a single breath and then stopped. Such are said to be the property of the *universitas* in dominion and use. Other things are said to belong to the *universitas* not in use, but in dominion and profit, as the lands and the slaves of a city, which belong to all the citizens in such a way that they belong to none individually.

### Some things belong to individuals.[1]

There are things that belong to individuals, as mine and thine, in dominion and use, as the lands and the slaves of the citizens.

### Some things are sacred and holy, those consecrated to God.

Sacred, holy and inviolable things belong to no one, for what is subject to divine law is no one's property but the property of God by the common opinion of mankind. Sacred things are those properly consecrated to God by priests, such as sacred and religious buildings and gifts solemnly dedicated to the service of God, as chalices, crosses and censers, which it is forbidden to alienate except to ransom captives. Cemeteries are also sacred places, as are churches and chapels, and though the buildings are destroyed their sites still remain sacred. A sacred thing differs from a *sacrarium*, for that is the place where sacred things are kept. There are also things subject to a sanction, as the walls and gates of cities, which are called such because capital punishment is decreed for those who commit any outrage upon them, violating them either by admitting persons through them or scaling them by ladders or in any other way, for it is a hostile and disgraceful act to enter in any way except by the gates.

---

1 This section and the one following are reversed in the Latin text. The English and Latin contents have been realigned by the editor.

### Quaedam nullius.

Res quidem nullius esse dicuntur pluribus modis: natura, sive iure naturali, ut ferae bestiae, volucres et pisces. Item censura, ut dictum est, sicut res sacrae, religiosae et sanctae. Item casu, sicut est hereditas iacens ante aditionem. Sed fallit in hoc, quia sustinet vicem personae defuncti, vel quis sperantur futurae heredis qui adibit. Dicuntur etiam res in nullius bonis esse quae habitae sunt pro derelicto. Item tempore dicuntur res nullius esse ut thesaurus. Item ubi non apparet dominus rei, sicut de wrecco maris. Item de his quae pro wayvio habentur, sicut de averiis, ubi non apparet dominus, et quae olim fuerunt inventoris de iure naturali, iam efficiuntur principis de iure gentium. Item sunt res natura nullius, ubi natura non patitur, quod possint esse alicuius, sicut sunt liberi homines. Liberi enim homines exempti sunt a dominio et commercio, et illud idem dici poterit in servo aegrotante, quem dominus abiecit. Lex enim facit ei ut sit liber.

## Rerum Dominio

### Qualiter dominia rerum adquiruntur de iure naturali vel gentium.

Dictum est supra de rerum divisione. Nunc autem dicendum est qualiter dominia rerum adquiruntur de iure naturali sive gentium, ut a vetustiore iure incipiatur, quod cum ipso genere humano rerum natura prodidit, et post dicendum erit de iure civili, quod postea esse coepit, cum et civitates condi et magistratus creari et leges scribi coeperunt.

**De feris bestiis. De piscatione, venatione, apprehensione. Apes cum includuntur. De mansuetis bestiis et avibus. Adquiritur iure gentium per accessionem. De accessione quae fit humana natura operante per adiunctionem specierum. De accessione quae fit divina natura et humana cooperante. Item adquiruntur res per specificationem. Item per**

That is said to be subject to a sanction which is protected and fortified against the wrongs of men, and that law especially called a sanction which imposes a penalty on a wrongdoer. No person is permitted to rebuild the city walls for his private advantage, only for the public welfare.

### Some things belong to no one.

Things are said to be *res nullius* in several different ways: by nature or the *jus naturale*, as wild beasts, birds and fish; by the common opinion of mankind, as was said [above], as things sacred, religious or subject to a sanction; by accident, as an inheritance lying vacant before it is taken up. But the rule fails in this case because the inheritance represents the *persona* of the deceased or because [the advent] of a future heir who will take it up is expected. Things taken as derelict are likewise said to be *res nullius*. They are also said to become such through lapse of time, as treasure trove. Also where there is no apparent owner of the thing, as in wreck, and the same is true of things regarded as waif, as cattle, where there is no apparent owner, all of which formerly belonged to the finder by natural law but are now made the property of the prince by the *jus gentium*. There are things that are *res nullius* by nature, which nature does not permit to be anyone's property, as free men. Free men are not subjects of ownership and commerce and the same may be said of a sick slave his lord has cast off. The law declares him to be free.

## Of Acquiring The Dominion Of Things

### How the dominion of things is acquired by the jus naturale or the jus gentium.

We have treated above of the classification of things. Now we must explain how the dominion of things is acquired according to natural law or the *jus gentium* (to start first with the older law, which, with the human race itself, proceeded from the nature of things) and then how it is acquired according to the civil law, which came into existence later, after

**confusionem. Item per inventionem. Item ex causa donationis. Ista pertinent ad materiam supra de rerum divisione. De servitutibus.**

### De rerum dominio ex causa donationis inter vivos.

Quoniam inter alias causas adquisitionis magis celebris est et famosa causa donationis, ideo sibi vindicat secundum locum, quia per eam magis adquiritur et saepius quam per aliam. Et unde imprimis videndum est quid sit donatio, et qualiter dividatur, quis donare possit, et quis non. Item quae res donari possit et quae non, et cui dari possit et cui non. Item quae exigatur ad hoc quod valeat donatio. Item qualiter adquiratur possessio, et ab uno ad alium transferatur, et cum fuerit adquisita qualiter amittatur, et cum amissa fuerit qualiter restituatur.

### Quid sit donatio.

Est autem donatio quaedam institutio quae ex mera liberalitate nullo iure cogente procedit, ut rem transferat ad alium. Et est dare rem accipientis facere cum effectu, alioquin inutilis erit donatio quae irritari poterit et revocari. Ut si fiat de re aliena, quia non videtur quis possessionem adeptus qui eam ita nactus est ut illam retinere non possit. Et tamen si res aliena donetur, erit donatio valida quoad dantem et quoad incipientem ab initio, licet invalida sit quantum ad verum dominum et illum qui ius habet, erga quem nullo tempore erit valida, nisi per confirmationem eius qui illam infirmare poterit, scilicet veri domini vel eius heredis, vel per eorum ratihabitionem, vel per cursum temporis, quod omnem excludit actionem.

**Qualiter donatio dividatur. Quis donare possit. Quis donare non possit. Cui donari possit. Quae res dari possit. [Quae res dari non possit.][1] Quae exigantur ad hoc quod valeat donatio. Breve vicecomiti directum ad**

1 Bracketed subtitles in Thorne's text indicate his translations of interleaved or marginal notations in the text. Since Woodbine's Latin text does not provide these, we have for the student's sake attempted reasonable representations.

states came to be founded, magistrates created and laws reduced to writing.

**Of wild beasts. Of fishing, hunting, [and] capture. When bees are in hives. Of tame beasts and birds. [Dominion] is acquired by accession according to the jus gentium. Of accession made by human action, by joining together materials. Of accession made by natural and human forces jointly. Things are acquired by specification. By confusion. By finding. By gift. This belongs above with the matter on the classification of things. Of servitudes.**

## Of acquiring the dominion of things by gift inter vivos.

Since the most celebrated and famous of the *causae acquisitionis* is that of gift it may lay claim to pride of place, for in that way more is acquired, and acquired more often, than in any other. Hence we must first see what a gift is and into what divisions it falls; who may give and who may not; [then] what may be given and what not, and to whom a gift may be made and to whom not. Then the requirements of a valid gift. Then how possession may be acquired and how transferred from one to another; [and finally], when it has been acquired, how it may be lost, and when lost how recovered.

## What a gift is.

A gift is a disposition arising from pure liberality and without legal compulsion, that is, neither of civil or natural law, payment, duress or force playing no part. It proceeds from the full and free disposition of a donor [wishing] to transfer his property to another. "To give" is to make a thing the property of the taker effectively, otherwise it will be useless, as a gift made of another's property which may be invalidated and revoked, for he who obtains possession in such a way that he cannot retain it is not considered to have gained it at all. Nevertheless, if another's property is given the gift will be valid from the first as between donor and donee, though invalid as against the true lord, him who has the right, against whom it will never be valid except by the confirmation of

**inquirendum in quo statu fuit donator quando fecit donationem. Aliud breve de eodem si sit compos mentis. Breve de summonendo tenentem. Quod certa res sit quae dari debet. Quod donatio sit gratuita et non coacta. Alia divisio donationum, quod alia simplex et pura, alia condicionalis vel sub modo. [Donationes sub modo.] Item fieri possunt donationes sub modo et adiecta condicione. Si fiat donatio sub condicione. Si ex facto praecedente vel ex causa. Quod condicio impedit descensum ad proprios heredes. Si terra data fuerit bastardo per se vel in maritagium. De dote uxoris bastardi. Si terra data fuerit in maritagium, videndum qualiter fiat donatio in maritagium. [Et est maritagium aliquando liberum.] [Quod maritagium aliud liberum aliud non.] Quod maritagium revertitur pro defectu heredum. Si servis fiat donatio. Si fiat donatio servo sub potestate domini sui constituto. Si fiat donatio ei qui fuerit extra potestatem domini. Si servus donationem facere possit. Si fiat donatio alicui ad terminum vitae donatoris vel donatarii. Fit donatio in liberam elemosinam. Item pluribus fieri poterit donatio simul et in eodem tempore sicut diversis temporibus et successive. Si pluribus bastardis simul de concubina. Si vir uxori donationem facere possit constante matrimonio. Si felo post feloniam donationem facere possit. Si fiat donatio de re aliena. Mutatur quandoque per donationem una causa possidendi in aliam causam possidendi. Si fiat donatio alicuius rei excepta aliqua parte. Donator poterit ponere legem et condicionem donatione. Si fiat donatio pro homagio et servitio vel sine homagio.**

## De distinctione cartarum.

Et sciendum quod cartarum alia regia, alia privata. Et regiarum alia privata, alia communis, alia universitatis. Item privatarum alia de puro feoffamento et simplici, alia de feoffamento condicionali, sive conventionali. Et secundum omnia genera feoffamentorum fieri poterit. Item privatarum alia de recognitione pura vel condicionali. Item alia de quieta clamantia. Item alia de confirmatione. Et de hac

him who may invalidate it, that is, the true lord himself or his heir, as by their ratification, or by the lapse of time which bars all actions.

**How gifts are classified. Who may give. Who may not give. To whom a gift may be made. What things may be given. [What things may not be given.] What the requirements of a valid gift are. Writ directed to the sheriff to inquire into a donor's condition at the time of his gift. Writ of the same kind: whether he is compos mentis. Writ to summon the tenant. That the thing given be certain. That a gift be free and not extorted. A second classification of gifts: some are simple and absolute, others conditional or subject to a modus. [Gifts subject to a modus]. Gifts may be made subject to a modus with a condition attached. If a gift is made subject to a condition. If a gift is made because of a precedent act or causa. That a condition prevents descent to right heirs. If land is given to a bastard alone or in maritagium. The dower of a bastard's wife. If land is given in maritagium; how a gift in maritagium is made. [Some maritagia are free.] [Some maritagia are not free.] That a maritagium reverts for failure of heirs. Whether a gift may be made to bondsmen. If a gift is made to a bondsman within the potestas of his lord. If a gift is made to one beyond the potestas of his lord. Whether a bondsman may make a gift. If a gift is made to another for the life of the donor or donee. A gift made in free alms. A gift may be made to several together, and at the same time, just as at different times and successively. [A gift made] to the several bastards of a concubine. Whether a husband may make a gift to his wife during marriage. Whether a felon may make a gift after the felony. If a gift is made of another's property. By a gift one causa possidendi is sometimes changed to another. If a gift is made of a thing excepting some portion of it. A donor may impose a law and a condition on a gift. If a gift is made for homage and service or for service alone.**

## OF THE KINDS OF CHARTERS.

It is clear that some charters are royal, others private. Of the royal, some are private, some common, some universal. Of the private, some are of

materia inveniri poterit infra de finali concordia. Carta vero de puro feoffamento est de simplici feoffamento sine aliqua adiectione. Condicionalis, ut si condicio donationi sit adiecta, ut supra videri poterit. Item de recognitione, ut si tenens rem quam detinet et ab eo petitur, recognoverit esse ius petentis. Vel e converso, si petens rem quam tenens tenet recognoverit esse ius tenentis, tenendam de se vel de alio, vel si illam remiserit et quietam clamaverit. Item de pura quieta clamantia, ut si petens pure remiserit et quietam clamaverit tenenti terram, quam petiit ut ius suum. Item carta de confirmatione, quae alterius factum consolidat et confirmat tantum, et nihil novi attribuit, sed aliquando confirmat et addit. Item earum quae sunt privatae et simplices de pura donatione remanent donatario et eius heredibus. Si autem communes sint duplicari debent, quod quilibet habeat partem suam, vel deponi in aequa manu cuilibet partium, cum necessarie fuerit exhibenda. Et si penes donatarium remanserit, donator eo quod sua interest petat exhibitionem, cum donatarius forte aliquid petat a donatore, quod donator negaverit vel de quo dubitetur, vel si donator petat et donatarius neget, tunc donatarius vel exhibeat instrumentum, vel ei denegetur actio si petens fuerit, vel si ab eo petatur remaneat indefensus. Communis enim esse poterit, ut si terra detur ad terminum annorum vel ad firmam. Item communis esse poterit alia ratione et perpetua, ut si quis donationem fecerit alicui de aliqua re, retenta sibi aliqua parte illius rei, ut si quis manerium dederit retenta sibi quarta parte vel de eius pertinentiis. Ut si quis manerium dederit retenta sibi advocatione ecclesiae vel huiusmodi, et si tenens dicat se totum tenere, cum donator petat ostendere debet tenens cartam ad probandam exceptionem suam, quod si non fecerit, exceptio sua nulla et amittat sicut indefensus. Si autem cartam forte exhibere non possit, quia illam ad manum non habuerit, de necessitate erit ad patriam recurrendum. Et eodem modo si casum allegaverit et casum probaverit. Et sciendum quod privatorum instrumentorum tres sunt species, unde facit aliquando quis

absolute and unconditional feoffment, others of conditional feoffment or feoffment subject to an agreement. /A charter/ may be drawn in accordance with each of the various kinds of feoffments. Some are charters of acknowledgement, absolute or subject to a condition; others of quitclaim, others of confirmation: /On this matter may be found below [in the portion] on final concords./ of absolute feoffment, [that is], of simple feoffment, without any addition; of conditional feoffment, as where a condition is attached to the gift, as may be seen above; of absolute acknowledgement, as where a tenant acknowledges that the thing he detains which is being claimed from him, is the demandant's right; or conversely, where the demandant acknowledges that the thing the tenant holds is the tenant's right, to hold of him or of another. Of absolute quitclaim, as where the demandant remits and quitclaims absolutely to the tenant the land he claimed as his right. There is also a charter of confirmation, which only strengthens and confirms the deed of another, adding nothing new, though sometimes it confirms and adds. Charters that are private and unconditional, of an absolute gift, remain to the donee and his heirs. Those that are common ought to be duplicated, that each may have his portion, or if not, deposited in a third hand to be produced to each of the parties when required. If it remains in the donee's possession, when he claims something from the donor which he denies, or as to which there is doubt, let the donor, because of his interest, demand its production, and let the donee either produce the instrument or be denied his action. If it is the donor who claims and the donee who denies, let him either produce the instrument or be without defense. A charter may /also/ be common if land is given for a term of years or to farm. It may be common for another reason, and in perpetuity, as where one gives a thing to another reserving some part of it to himself, as where one gives a manor saving to himself the fourth part, or /part/ of its appurtenances, as where he gives the manor reserving the advowson of the church or the like; if when the donor claims the tenant says that he holds the whole, he must produce the charter to prove his exception; if he

scripturam sibi ipsi, et tali scripturae non erit fides adhibenda, aliquando facit contra se, et tali scripturae fides adhibetur, aliquando tamen facit quis scripturam sibi et alii, et contra se et pro se, quae communis est et de qua superius dicitur, et de quibus agitur de conventionibus factis inter privatas personas. Et talis scriptura dicitur carta cirograffata, quae scinditur per medium, et unde una pars remanet parti uni et altera alteri. Et unde quamvis non liceat alicui partium a conventionibus recedere, tamen non solet aliquando necessitas imponi curiae domini regis, de huiusmodi conventionibus privatis discutere. Set tamen si quis a conventione recedat, succuritur alteri parti per actionem de conventione, secundum quod inferius dicetur. Et notandum quod omnium scripturarum privatarum quibus quis uti voluerit in iudicio pro se, copiam faciat adversario suo contra se. Sed petens petere non debet quod tenentis instrumento exhibeantur ad suam intentionem fundandam, cum non teneatur armare adversarium suum contra se, nisi forte instrumenta sua sint communia. Nec etiam poterit tenens petere quod exhibeantur ei instrumenta petentis ad exceptionem suam probandam, secundum quod praedictum est, maxime nisi sint communia.

### Quod de cartis regiis non debent iustitiarii disputare nec eas iudicare.

De cartis vero regiis et factis regum, non debent nec possunt iustitiarii nec privatae personae disputare, nec etiam si in illis dubitatio oriatur possunt eam interpretari. Etiam in dubiis et obscuris, vel si aliqua dictio duos contineat intellectus, domini regis erit expectanda interpretatio et voluntas, cum eius sit interpretari cuius est condere. Et etiam si omnino sit falsa propter rasuram, vel quia forte signum appositum est adulterinum, melius et tutius est quod coram ipso rege procedat iudicium. Item factum regis nec cartam potest quis iudicare ita quod factum regis irritetur. Sed dicere poterit quis quod rex iustitiam fecerit, et bene, et si hoc eadem ratione quod male, et ita imponere ei quod iniuriam emendet, ne incidat rex et iustitiarii in iudicium viventis dei propter iniuriam. Rex habet superiorem, deum scilicet. Item legem per quam factus est rex.

does not his exception will be void and he will lose as though without defense. If he cannot produce the charter because he does not have it ready, recourse must of necessity be had to the country. And so if he alleges an accidental loss and proves the accident. /It is clear that there are three kinds of private instruments, for sometimes one makes a writing in his own interest, to which no credit will be given; sometimes against his own interest, to which credit will be given; and sometimes in another's favor as well as his own, against his own interest as well as for it. /Such a document/ is common and of it [something] is said above; it is with such that [the portion] on agreements made between private persons is concerned. A writing of that kind is called a chirographic charter which is cut through the middle, one portion remaining with one party, the other with the other./ Hence, though it is not usual, the necessity of considering such private agreements is sometimes imposed upon the king's court, for it is not lawful for either of the parties to withdraw from agreements, since if one withdraws the other is aided by an action based on the agreement, as will be explained below. And note that a party shall make available to his adversary all private writings he wishes to use on his own behalf in a judicial proceeding, /to be used/ against himself. But the demandant cannot ask that the tenant's deeds be produced in order to found his case upon them, for one is not bound to arm his adversary against himself, unless his deeds are common. Nor may the tenant claim that the demandant's deeds be produced to prove his exception, as was said above, unless they are common.

### That the justices must not question royal charters nor pass upon them.

Private persons cannot question the acts of kings, nor ought the justices to discuss the meaning of royal charters: not even if a doubt arises in them may they resolve it; even as to ambiguities and uncertainties, as where a phrase is open to two meanings, the interpretation and pleasure of the lord king must be awaited, since it is for him who establishes to explain his deed. And even if the document is completely false, because

Item curiam suam, videlicet comites et barones, quia comites dicuntur quasi socii regis, et qui socium habet, habet magistrum. Et ideo si rex fuerit sine fraeno, id est sine lege, debent ei fraenum apponere nisi ipsimet fuerint cum rege sine fraeno. Et tunc clamabunt subditi et dicent, *Domine Iheus in chamo et fraeno maxillas eorum constringe.* Ad quos dominus, *Vocabo super eos gentem robustam et longinquam et ignotam, cuius linguam ignorabunt, quae destruet eos et evellet radices eorum de terra, et a talibus iudicabuntur, quia subditos noluerunt iuste iudicare*. Et in fine ligatis pedibus eorum et manibus, mittet eos in caminum ignis et tenebras exteriores, ubi erit fletus et stridor dentium.

**Cum res certa dari debeat, oportet quod certa sint servitia quae venire debent in compensationem pro re data. [Verba scripturum.] De servitiis et consuetudinibus praestandis. [Servitia forinseca.] De servitiis forinsecis quae aliquando in cartis exprimuntur certa et determinata quandoque non specificantur. [Clausula warrantazio.] [Fides adhibenda huiusmodis scripturiis si in curia impugnetur.] Quod non valet donatio nisi subsequatur traditio, et ideo videndum de divisione possessionum et qualiter adquiratur possessio rerum.**

### Quid sit possessio.

Quid sit possessio videndum. Et sciendum quod possessio est corporalis rei detentio, id est corporis et animi cum iuris adminiculo concurrente. De re autem corporali ideo dicitur, quia incorporalia non possunt possideri nec usucapi, nec sine corpore tradi, quia per se traditionem non patiuntur. Ideo dicuntur quasi possideri. Tradi enim possunt vel quasi per patientiam et per usum. Et possessio ideo dicitur rei detentio, quia naturaliter tenetur ab eo qui ei insistit, id est corporaliter. De hoc autem quod dicit *corporis et animi cum iuris adminiculo concurrente*, dicetur

of an erasure or because the seal affixed is a forgery, it is better and safer that the case proceed before the king himself. <No one may pass upon the king's act *[or his charter]* so as to nullify it, but one may say that the king has committed an *injuria*, and thus charge him with amending it, lest he *[and the justices]* fall into the judgment of the living God because of it. The king has a superior, namely, God. Also the law by which he is made king. Also his *curia*, namely, the earls and barons, because if he is without bridle, that is without law, they ought to put the bridle on him. *[That is why the earls are called the partners, so to speak, of the king; he who has a partner has a master.]* When even they, like the king, are without bridle, then will the subjects cry out and say "Lord Jesus, bind fast their jaws in rein and bridle." To whom the Lord *[will answer]*, "I shall call down upon them a fierce nation and unknown, strangers from afar, whose tongue they shall not understand, who shall destroy them and pluck out their roots from the earth." By such they shall be judged because they will not judge their subjects justly, and in the end, bound hand and foot, He shall send them into the fiery furnace and into outer darkness, where there will be wailing and gnashing of teeth.>

**Since a thing certain must be given, the services which must come in exchange for it should be certain. [The words of charters.] Of services and customs to be performed. [Forinsic services.] Of forinsec services that sometimes are set forth in certain and specified in charters and sometimes not. [The warranty clause.] [The credit to be given charters and other instruments if impugned in court.] That a gift is invalid unless livery follows. Of the kinds of possession and how the possession of things is acquired.**

### WHAT POSSESSION IS.

What possession is must be looked at. It must be understood that possession is the control [*detentio*] by body and mind of a corporeal thing, with the concurrent support of right. Therefore it is said about a corporeal thing, because incorporeal things cannot be possessed or be the

infra plenius. Et cum quis in possessione fuerit et ei controversiam moveamus, aut pertinet ad hoc ut nostrum quod non possidemus, et forte iniuste fuerimus eiecti de possessione propria, vel si alienam sicut antecessorum nostrorum petierimus quod nobis restituatur, vel ad hoc quod per interdictum nobis retinere liceat libere et quiete, bene et pacifice possidemus. Restituendae enim possessionis ordo per actionem expeditur. Retinendae vero duplex est, aut exceptio vel interdictum. Exceptio vero datur multis de causis.

**De divisione:qualiter dividatur possessio. De traditionibus.**

### Quid est traditio.

Videndum est imprimis quid sit traditio. Et est traditio de re corporali, propria vel aliena, de persona in personam, de manu propria vel aliena, sicut procuratoria, dum tamen de voluntate domini, in alterius manum gratuita translatio. Et nihil aliud est traditio in uno sensu nisi in possessionem inductio. *De re corporali* ideo dicit quia res incorporalis non patitur traditionem, sicut ipsum ius quod rei sive corpori inhaeret, et quia non possunt possideri, sed quasi. Ideo traditionem non patiuntur, sed quasi, nec adquiruntur nec retinentur nisi per patientiam et usum. *De re propria vel aliena* dicit quia refert quis traditionem facere possit.

**Quis traditionem facere possit. [Qualiter traditio fieri debeat.] [Item si traditio non interveniat.] [Item quid transferat qui tradit.] Facta traditione, videndum quando donatarius incipit possidere et quando donator desinit. Item per quas personas adquiratur possessio. Si de una re pluribus facta fuerit donatio simul vel successive.**

### Quibus modis amittatur possessio.

Cum autem semel fuerit possessio adquisita, amitti poterit multis modis: videndum igitur quibus modis amittatur. Et sciendum quod eisdem quibus adquiritur. Adquiritur enim non tantum corpore vel animo tantum, sed utroque. Animo tamen retineri poterit sine corpore, amitti tamen non

subjects of usucaption /possession over time/ or be transferred apart from some corporeal thing, since they do not admit of livery by themselves. They therefore are said to be *quasi*-possessed /and/ can be transferred or *quasi*-transferred by acquiescence and use. Possession is also said to be the control of a thing because it is held naturally by him who has it, that is, physically. With respect to what is said /to be/ "by body and mind with the concurrent support of right," more will be said below. When one is in possession and we dispute it against him, the dispute involves either that there be restored to us what is ours but we do not possess /as where we have been wrongfully ejected from our own possession, or another's, as that of our ancestors,/ or that (by interdict) we be allowed to retain (freely and quietly, properly and peacefully, what we do not possess. For the restoration of possession, process is by action; for its retention it is twofold, exception or interdict. An exception is given for many reasons.

**How possession is divided. Of liveries.**

### What livery is.

First it must be seen what livery is. It is the transfer of a corporeal thing, one's own or another's, from person to person, by one's own hand or another's, such as a procurator's, while nevertheless by the lord's consent, into the hand of the other, a gratuitous transference. In one sense, livery is nothing other than an induction into possession. It is said [to be] *of a corporeal thing* because an incorporeal thing does not admit of livery, as the right itself which inheres in a thing or a body, because they [rights] cannot be possessed, only *quasi*-possessed. They therefore do not admit of livery, only of *quasi*-livery, nor are they acquired or retained except by acquiescence and use. *Of one's own property or another's* is said because it matters who is able to make livery.

**Who may take livery. How livery must be made, [If livery is not made]. [What he who gives livery transfers]. When the donor begins and the donor ceases to posses. By what persons possession may be acquired. [forus]. Where the gift of a single thing is made to several, together**

poterit sine utroque, scilicet animo et corpore, quia retinetur animo sine corpore et corpore sine animo, et cum utrumque defecerit, amittitur ex toto. Qualiter vero amissa contra voluntatem possidentis restituatur, satis dicetur infra de assisa novae disseisinae.

**Si ille cui datum est rem datam ulterius dare possit. [Item donatio subiecta condicioni vel servituti.] Qualiter quis uti debeat seisina. Qualiter amittatur possessio adquisita. Qualiter adquiratur possessio per usucapionem. De adquirendo rerum dominio incorporalium sicut de iuribus, libertatibus et servitutibus.**

## Qualiter quis uti debeat servitute in communa pastura.

Item videndum qualiter quis uti debeat iure sibi concesso ad retinendam possessionem et iuris sui declarationem. Et primo de servitutibus, ut si cui concedatur in alieno ius pascendi, statim cum possit immittat pecora sua, unum vel plura, et per hoc retinebit seisinam suam. Unum dico, quia si ad plura usque ad mille, vel sine numbero, sufficit ad seisinam retinendam si unicum immittat. Item si ius pascendi per totum fundum concedatur, sufficit ad seisinam retinendam per totum fundum si unicum immittat eo animo ut per totum pascat: quod quidem si ei permissum non fuerit, quod uti non possit omnino vel commode, competit ei assisa novae disseisinae, licet antea usus non fuerit in veritate, propter quasi seisinam et quasi usum ex prima voluntate concedentis. Et cum sic in veritate usus fuerit, illud ius cum usu transmittit ad heredes suos et assignatos, quod prius facere potuit sine usu, et extunc ad extraneos illud ius transmittere poterit cum usu et seisina, quod prius non potuit sine usu. Et quod dictum est de iure pascendi, fiat de iure eundi, agendi, aquamve ducendi, et de omnibus aliis servitutibus, quae sunt infinitae et non refert.

**Qualiter in iure praesentandi et qualiter transfertur seisina. De libertatibus et quis concedere possit libertates et quae sint regis. Si quis aliquem vexaverit contra libertates concessas per regem. Breve quare quis alium vexaverit contra libertatem. De intentione querentis proponenda. De responsione illorum contra intentionem querentium. De confirmationibus.**

**or successively.**

### In what ways possession may be lost.

When possession has once been acquired, however, it can be lost in many ways: therefore it should be seen in what ways it may be lost. And it should be understood that [is] by the same as it is acquired. For it is acquired not so much physically or so much mentally but by both. Nevertheless, it can be held in mind without body and in body without mind, and when both cease it is completely lost. How it can be restored without the possessor's consent when lost will be sufficiently discussed below concerning the assize of *novel disseisin.*

**Whether he to whom a thing is given may give the thing given to another. [Gifts subject to a condition or a servitude.] How one ought to use his seisin. How possession once acquired may be lost. How possession of a right not subject to livery is acquired by long use. How possession [and dominium] may be acquired by usucaption. On acquiring the dominion of incorporeal things, as rights, liberties, and servitudes.**

### How one ought to use his servitude in common of pasture.

And it must be seen how one must use a right granted him so as to retain possession and as evidence of his right. And first of servitudes, as where one is granted the right of pasturing cattle on another's land. Let him, as soon as possible, drive in his beasts, one or several; by that he will retain his seisin. *[*"One," I say, because if *[*his grant is*]* for more, as for a thousand, or an indefinite number, it suffices for retaining seisin if he puts in one, and so if a right of pasturing over an entire estate is granted, it suffices for retaining seisin of the whole if he puts *[*it in one place*]* with the intention that it graze over the whole*]*. If that is not allowed him, so that he cannot use it at all or can do so only with difficulty, he is entitled, though there has been no real use, to the assize of *novel disseisin*, because of his *quasi*-seisin and *quasi*-use [arising] out of the original agreement of the grantor. And when he has so used it in fact, he

**[Quid sit confirmatio.] [Quando quis possit confirmare.] De donationibus inter mortuos et mortis causa. [Testamenta.] De adquirendo rerum dominio ex causa emptionis. De locato et conducto. De usu vestimentorum.**

## De adquirendo rerum dominio ex causa successionis et qualiter heredes succedunt parentibus.

Est etiam alia causa adquirendi rerum dominia quae dicitur causa successionis, et quae competit singulis heredibus de omnibus de quibus antecessores eorum obierint seisiti ut de feodo, vel etiam seisiti aliquo tempore ut de feodo et iure hereditario, quod quidem descendere debet heredibus propinquioribus, masculis et feminis, recta linea vel transversali venientibus. Descendit itaque ius quasi ponderosum quid cadens deorsum recta linea vel transversali, et numquam reascendit eadem via qua descendit propter mortem antecessorum. A latere tamen ascendit aliquando propter defectum heredum inferius provenientium. Et si seisina sive possessio aliquando exorbitet ita quod ius merum non sequatur, in fine tamen ad proprietatem revertetur si sit heres qui petat. Item descendit ius vero heredi ubicumque fuerit natus, vel in utero matris, citra mare vel ultra. Nec potest aliquis sibi facere heredem, quia solus deus heredem facit. Et quia heres dicitur ab hereditate, et non hereditas ab herede, ideo primo videndum est quid sit hereditas, postea quis sit heres legitimus, et quis ex pluribus praeferatur.

## [Quid sit hereditas.]

Et sciendum quod hereditas est successio in universum ius quod defunctus habuit ex quacumque causa adquisitionis vel successionis, cum seisina vel sine, ut si cum seisina quocumque tempore seisitus fuerit in vita vel in morte, scilicet die quo obiit. Et si ius ad plures heredes descendat successive sine seisina,

transmits that right and use to his heirs and assigns which, without use, he could do before, and thenceforward he can transfer that right to strangers, with use and seisin, which he could not do before, without use. And let what was said concerning the right of pasturing apply as well concerning rights of way, of driving cattle, or of conducting water, and concerning all other servitudes, which are infinite and it makes no difference.

**How [one ought to use] a right to present and how seisin is transferred. Of liberties and who may grant liberties and which belong to the king. If one has troubled another contrary to liberties granted by the king. Writ: why one has troubled another contrary to his liberty. On putting forward the plaintiff's case. Of their reply to the plaintiff's claim. Of confirmations. [What a confirmation is.] [When one may make a confirmation.] Of gifts inter mortuos and mortis causa. [Wills.] On acquiring dominion by purchase. Of letting and hiring. Of the use of clothing.**

### Of acquiring the dominion of things by succession and how heirs succeed ancestors.

There is another *causa* for acquiring dominion called succession, which entitles every heir to everything of which his ancestors die seised as of fee, or of which they once were seised as of fee and hereditary right, which ought to descend to nearer heirs, male and female, in the right or transverse line, for the right descends, like a weight falling downwards, in the right or transverse line and never re-ascends by the same path by which it descends on the death of ancestors. It sometimes, however, ascends collaterally because of the failure of heirs below. And if seisin or possession sometimes turns aside so that it does not follow the mere right, in the end it will revert to the *proprietas*, if there is an heir who claims. Right descends to the true heir no matter where he is born, [and though he is not yet born,] on this side of the sea or beyond it. Nor can anyone make himself heir, for only God can make an heir. Since an heir is called such from inheritance and not conversely, we must first consider

tamen eadem seisina competit heredi quam antecessor habuit in vita vel in morte. Et cum ius proprietatis concursum habuerit cum seisina, statim et sine mora adquiritur heredi liberum tenementum.

### Quis dici debeat heres legitimus.

Item videndum quis dici debeat heres legitimus, quia secundum quod inferius dicitur liberorum quidam sunt filii et heredes sicut sunt illi qui ex iustis nuptiis procreati sunt et progeniti, et ibi plenius. Legitimus vero heres et filius est quem nuptiae demonstrant esse legitimum, sicuti ille qui natus est ex legitimo matrimonio, vel ille qui in facie ecclesiae legitimus reputatur, quamvis in veritate matrimonium non fuerit, cum ambo tam vir quam uxor coniuncti sunt bona fide credentes se legitime copulatos esse, cum sint re vera consanguinitate vel affinitate coniuncti, vel alio modo quod matrimonium stare non posset, vel dum modo alter eorum tantum hoc credat. Quia cum mulier alicui coniugato nubat bona fide credens eum est solutum, cum sit alteri mulieri copulatus, et ex eo filios suscipiat, tales legitimi iudicantur et heredes, sive post matrimonium contractum progeniti sint et nati, sive ante matrimonium geniti et in matrimonio nati, sive in matrimonio geniti et post matrimonium nati, sive solutum sit matrimonium per mortem parentum vel in vita parentum ex quacumque causa per divortium: et hoc sive inter parentes publice contrahantur sponsalia vel matrimonium, dum tamen si divortium in vita parentum celebretur et inter tales clandestina fuerint coniugia ab initio, vel contracta contra interdictum ecclesiae in gradu prohibito, etiam ignoranter, soboles de tali coniunctione suscepta prorsus illegitima est censenda, de parentum ignorantia nullum habitura subsidium, cum illi taliter contrahendo clandestina coniugia non expertes scientiae vel saltem affectatores ignorantiae videantur. Pari modo proles illegitima est censenda, si ambo parentes impedimentum scientes legitimum etiam praeter omne interdictum in facie ecclesiae contrahere praesumpserunt, quod quidem non esset si in facie ecclesiae hoc facerent ignoranter, uterque scilicet vel eorum alter. Set in omni casu ubi

what inheritance is, then who may be a lawful heir, and who among several such shall be preferred.

### [What inheritance is.]

It is clear that inheritance is succession to the entire right the deceased had, no matter by what *causa*, acquisition or succession, with seisin or without it: with seisin, as where he was seised at some time, during his lifetime or at his death, that is, on the day he died; [without seisin] as where the right descends to several heirs successively without seisin; the heir is entitled to the same seisin the ancestor had in his lifetime or at his death, and when the proprietary right is joined with seisin the heir immediately has a free tenement.

### Who ought to be called a lawful heir.

We must see who ought to be called a legitimate heir, because /as said below, and there more fully/ of children, some are sons and heirs, as those conceived and begotten of lawful marriages, [and some are sons but not heirs]. A legitimate heir is a son whom the marriage proves to be legitimate, as he who was born in lawful wedlock, or one recognized as legitimate in face of the church though in truth there has been no marriage, /as/ when both the husband and wife were joined in good faith, believing themselves joined in a lawful union, though in truth they are related by blood or affinity, or in some other way, so that no marriage could exist, or if only one of them so believes, for if a woman weds a married man, believing him in good faith to be single though he is married to another, and has children by him, they are adjudged legitimate and heirs, whether conceived and born after marriage, or conceived before marriage and born in wedlock, or conceived during marriage and born after it has ended, whether it was dissolved by death or, for some reason, by divorce during their lives, /This is true if the espousals or marriage are publicly contracted between the parents./ provided that if a divorce is pronounced during their lives and their union was clandestine from the outset or contracted, even unwittingly, within a forbidden

clandestina sunt coniugia non excusabit ignorantia, nec etiam si publice contracta, si hoc fuerit praesumptive contra interdicta ecclesiae. Et ad hoc facit decretale cuius verba sunt haec, *Cum inter I. virum et B. mulierem divortii sententia canonice sit prolata, filii eorum non debent exinde sustinere iacturam, cum parentes eorum publice et sine contradictione ecclesiae inter se contraxisse noscantur. Ideoque sancimus ut filii eorum quos ante divortium habuerunt, et qui concepti fuerunt ante latam sententiam, non minus habeantur legitimi, et quod in bona paterna hereditario iure succedant, et de parentum facultatibus nutriantur.*

**Qualiter illegitimi legitimantur. De praesumptionibus quod partus debeat esse legitimus eo quod nascitur ex uxore. De differentia puerorum. De qualitate heredum, qui propinqui, qui propinquiores, et de eorum seisina. Quid faciat heredem propinquiorem. Item propinquiores heredes esse possunt plures sicut unus. De gradibus successsionis et parentelae. De personis eorum qui aliis succedere debent et de ordine successionum. De heredibus qui succedunt non ex successione sed substitutione per modum donationis. De partu supposito, et cum uxor se fecerit praegnantem cum non sit, ad exheredationem veri heredis. Breve de videnda muliere ut sciatur utrum praegnans sit vel non. Breve constabulario quod recipiat eam in castro suo. Item de eodem ad querelam heredis quod videatur. Item de eodem quod vicecomes faciat eam venire coram iustitiariis apud Westmonasterium. De eo qui nutriverit aliquem in domo sua ut filium et heredem qui nec est filius nec heres. Breve de habendo corpus talis et uxoris suae coram iustitiariis. Item si cum verus heres infra aetatem moriatur, supponat custos alium extraneum vel habeatur suspicio quod mortuus sit, breve quod producatur et videatur. Item cum verus heres mortuus sit et supponatur alius a custode vel marito fraudulenter. Breve si hereditas heredis mortui debeat esse eschaeta domini regis. Cum talis mulier in iudicio convicta fuerit vel confessa quod praegnans non sit, breve de faciendo seisinam vero heredi.**

degree contrary to church law, the issue of such a union must be taken as altogether illegitimate, to be aided in no way by the parents' ignorance,for in so contracting a clandestine marriage they are taken to be not lacking in knowledge but rather affecting ignorance. Similarly, the issue must be regarded as illegitimate if both parents, knowing a lawful impediment to exist, presume, despite every prohibition, to wed in face of the church, though this would not be so if they marry in face of the church in ignorance of the impediment, both, that is, or only one. But in all cases of clandestine union ignorance will be no excuse; nor is it such, even if the marriage is publicly contracted, if it is presumptively contrary to ecclesiastical prohibition. This is established by a decretal in these words: "If between J. and B., man and woman, sentence of divorce has been canonically pronounced, their children should not suffer injury on that account if their parents are known to have been married publicly and without any ecclesiastical objection. Therefore we ordain that their children, born before the divorce or conceived before the final judgment of divorce was pronounced, shall nonetheless be held legitimate and shall succeed to the paternal property by hereditary right and be supported by parental resources."

**How bastards are legitimized. Of the presumption that the issue ought to be legitimate because born of the wife. Of the differentiation of children. The nature of heirs, who are near and who nearer, and their seisin. What may make one a nearer heir. Nearer heirs may be many as well as one. Degrees of kinship and succession. Of those who ought to succeed others and the order of succession. Of heirs who succeed not be succession but by substitution, by the modus of the gift. Of supposititious birth and when a woman claims to be pregnant though she is not, to the disherison of the true heir. Writ for viewing a woman to discover whether or not she is pregnant. Writ ordering the constable to receive her into his castle. Writ at the complaint of the heir that she be examined. Writ that the sheriff cause her to come before the justices at Westminster. Of one who raises another in his house as son and heir who is neither. Writ for having the bodies of such a one and his wife before the justices. Where**

### De heredibus instituendis.

Mortuo tenente alicuius, imprimis debet dominus capitalis seisire in manum suam feodum suum et tenementum quod de eo immediate tenetur, et tenere in manu sua donec ei constiterit si defunctus heredem habuerit vel non: et hoc dico si vacuam invenerit possessionem. Si autem heres apparens sit, tunc aut unus aut plures, plures qui sunt quasi unus heres vel contendunt se esse heredes cum non sint, et nescitur quis eorum propinquior, quo casu licitum erit domino capitali tenere feodum suum in manu sua quousque discussum fuerit inter coheredes quis eorum rectus et propinquior. Si autem in seisina invenerit aliquem qui se facit heredem, talem eicere non poterit quin faciat disseisinam. Tenere tamen se poterit in seisina cum tali donec talis, si heres fuerit, ipsum recognoscat ad dominum, secundum quod inferius dicitur in assisa mortis antecessoris in principio. Cum autem sit heres apparens, unus vel plures unum ius habentes ut praedictum est, et sint plenae aetatis, sive inveniantur in astro sive non, imprimis capiat eorum homagium et rationabile relevium, et postea habeant seisinam hereditatis. Et qualiter hoc fieri debeat inferius dicetur plenius. Si autem heres vel heredes plures fuerint infra aetatem, qui recogniti fuerint ad heredes, non prius habeat capitalis dominus custodiam heredum et maritagium antequam ceperit eorum homagium, et capto homagio, tunc remaneant in custodia dominorum sicut de feodo militari, usque ad legitimam aetatem suam. Et de custodia et maritagio inferius dicetur plenius post tractatum de homagio capiendo et relevio.

**Si fieri debeat partitio inter coheredes. De iustitiariis constituendis ad partitionem faciendam. De iustitiariis constituendis ut intersint partitioni. Breve cum partes elegerint aliquos de communi consensu ad partitionem faciendam. Breve alterius modi sed de eodem, ubi partitio minus rite facta est per alios. Breve de eodem. Breve de seisina facienda coheridibus cum convenerit inter eos de partitione. Item aliud de eodem si particeps tenens recognoverit participi partem suam, et quod fiat extensio. Breve quod quis set ad**

**the true heir dies within age and the guardian substitutes another, a stranger; or if it is suspected that he is dead, a writ that he be produced and viewed. When the true heir is dead and another is fraudulently substituted by the guardian or husband. Writ where the inheritance of the deceased heir ought to be the escheat of the lord king. When in a judicial proceeding a woman has been proved not to be pregnant or has confessed that she is not, a writ for giving seisin to the true heir.**

**THE INSTITUTION OF HEIRS.**

When his tenant dies the chief lord ought first to seize into his hand his fee and the tenement which is held immediately of him, and keep it there until it is clear whether the deceased has an heir or not. *[*I say this if he finds the possession vacant. If he finds someone in seisin who claims to be the heir he cannot eject him without committing a disseisin, but may hold himself in seisin concurrently with him until he, if he is indeed the heir, acknowledges him as lord, as is explained below in the [portion on] assize of *mort d'ancestor*, at the beginning.*]* If there is an heir apparent, either one or several who are so to speak a single heir, *[*if there are several who claim to be heirs though they are not and there is doubt as to which of them is the nearer, it will be lawful for the chief lord to hold the fee in his hand until it has been decided among them which of them is the right and nearer heir,*]* and they are of full age, let him, whether they are found on the hearth or not, first take their homage and rightful relief and then let them have seisin of the inheritance. How this ought to be done will be explained more fully below, *[[*in*]* the tractate on the taking of homage and relief.*]* If the heir, or the several heirs acknowledged as heirs, are within age, the chief lord may not have the wardship and marriage of the heirs until he has taken their homage, and that being taken, let them then remain in the wardship of the lords until they are of lawful age. Wardship and marriage will be dealt with more fully below.

**Where partition ought to be made among co-heirs. [Writ for] appointing justices to make a partition. [Writ] appointing justices to be present at a partition. Writ when the parties by common consent choose others to make the partition. Writ in another form but of the same kind, where**

**capiendum sacramentum de extensoribus, si facienda sit extensio extra comitatum.**

**Breve ubi extensores nihil fecerint ad primum mandatum. Breve si milites venerint et vicecomes negligens fuerit. Breve si extensio minus sufficienter facta fuerit. Breve interlaqueatum, ubi milites de duobus comitatibus convenire debent ad faciendam extensionem. Item breve de eodem. Breve de querela filiae primogenitae et participis quae non habet rationabilem partem suam nec aesnesciam, et de partitione rationabiliter facienda per milites. Breve de habendis corporibus extensorum ad certificandum. De officio extensorum. Breve vicecomiti de seisina facienda coheredibus post partitionem. De homagiis faciendis et capiendis. [Homagium.]**

### Quid sit homagium et qualiter contrahatur.

Quid sit homagium? Sciendum quod homagium est iuris vinculum quo quis tenetur et astringitur ad warantizandum, defendendum, et adquietandum tenentem suum in seisina sua versus omnes per certum servitium in donatione nominatum et expressum, et etiam vice versa quo tenens reobligatur et astringitur ad fidem domino suo servanduam et servitium debitum faciendum. Item contrahitur homagium de utriusque voluntate tam domini quam tenentis per contrariam utriusque voluntatem dissolvendam si uterque voluerit. Non enim sufficit si unus tantum hoc voluerit, quia nihil tam conveniens est naturali aequitati etcetera. Est itaque tanta et talis connexio per homagium inter dominum et tenentem suum, quod tantum debet dominus tenenti quantum tenens domino praeter solam reverentiam.

**Quis teneatur homagium capere. Quis teneatur homagium facere. Item quando. Item quotiens. De quibus rebus. Per quas personas. Item qualiter et per quae verba.**

### De sacramento fidelitatis.

Hoc audis domine N. quod fidem portabo de vita et membris, corpore et catallis et terreno honor e, sic me deus adiuvet et haec sancta. Et quidam

**partition was improperly made by others. A writ on the same matter. Writ to deliver seisin to co-heirs when they have agreed among themselves as to the partition. Another writ of the same kind: where a tenant parcener has acknowledged his share to his parcener; that an extent be made. Writ that one be present to take the oath of the extenders if the extent is to be made outside the county. Writ where the extenders have done nothing in response to the first order. Writ where the knights appear but the sheriff is negligent. Writ where an extent has been improperly made. An interlaced writ, where knights of two counties must come together to make an extent. Another writ on the same matter. Writ on the complaint of an eldest daughter and parcener who does not have her rightful share nor her seniority; and of making a reasonable partition by knights. Writ to produce the bodies of extenders so they may certify. The duty of extenders. Writ to the sheriff for giving seisin to co-heirs after partition. Of performing and taking homages. [Homage.]**

### What homage is.

What is homage? Homage is a legal bond by which one is bound and constrained to warrant, defend, and acquit his tenant in his seisin against all persons for a service certain, described and expressed in the gift, and also, conversely, whereby the tenant is bound and constrained in return to keep faith to his lord and perform the service due. *[*Homage is contracted by the will of both, the lord and the tenant, *[*and*]* is to be dissolved by the contrary will of both, if both so wish, for it does not suffice if one alone wishes, because nothing is more in conformity with natural equity etc.*]* The *nexus* between a lord and his tenant through homage is thus so great and of such quality that the lord owes as much to the tenant as the tenant to the lord, reverence alone excepted.

**Who is bound to take homage. Who is bound to do homage. When. How often. From what things. By what persons. How and by what words.**

hic adiciunt in sacramento et bene, quod fideliter et sine diminutione, contradictione, vel impedimento et dilatione iniusta, terminis statutis faciet servitium suum domino suo et heredibus suis. Et fieri debet homagium non privatim, sed loco publico et communi, coram pluribus in comitatu, hundredo, vel curia, ut si forte tenens per malitiam homagium vellet dedicere, posset dominus facilius probationem habere de homagio facto et servitio recognito: quia homagium faciendum praecedere debet diligens examinatio, si ille qui heredem se facit sit filius naturalis eius cuius heredem se facit, et heres rectus et propinquus quantum ad ius possessionis, et non solum rectus et propinquus, sed si sit heres propinquior quantum ad ius proprietatis. Quilibet autem heres propinquior utrumque ius habere debet, possessionis videlicet et proprietatis, quamvis eo alius maius ius habuerit.

**Quid sunt inquirenda et tenenda in sacramento fidelitati.**

### Quis effectus homagii.

Effectus vero homagii est, quod si quis homagium alteri fecerit domino vel non domino, a tali domino vel homagio suo recedere non poterit sine iudicio quamdiu tenuerit tenementum, per quod obligatur ad homagium, in dominico vel servitio. Item nihil poterit tenens facere propter obligationem homagii, quod vertatur domino ad exheredationem vel atrocem iniuriam, nec dominus tenenti e converso. Quod si fecerint, dissolvitur et extinguitur homagium omnino et homagii connexio et obligatio, et erit iustum iudicium cum venerint contra homagium et fidelitatis sacramentum. <Quod in eo in quo delinquunt puniantur, scilicet in persona domini quod amittat dominium, et in persona tenentis quod amittat tenementum, secundum quod inferius dicetur plenius. Et sic dissolvi poterit homagium.>

**Qualiter homagium dissolvitur et extinguitur. Si dominus attornare possit homagium et servitium tenentis sui contra voluntatem tenentis. Si dominus captionem homagii tenentis sui differat vel recuset per malitiam. Si tenens propria auctoritate divertat se ad alium relicto**

### The oath of fealty.

"Hear this, lord N., that I will bear you fealty in life and limb, in body, goods, and earthly honor, so help me God and these sacred [relics]." And some add the following to the oath, and properly, that at the agreed terms he shall do his service to his lord and his heirs faithfully and without diminution, contradiction, impediment, or wrongful delay. Homage ought not to be done in private, but in a public place and openly, in the presence of many, in the county or hundred court or the court of the lord, so that if, through malice, the tenant should wish to deny his homage the lord could more readily produce proof of the homage done and the service acknowledge.

**What should be ascertained before homage is done.**

### What the effect of homage is.

The effect of homage is this, that if onc has done homage to another, his true lord or a non-lord, he cannot withdraw from such lord or his homage without judgment, as long as he holds the tenement, either in demesne or in service, by which he is bound to homage. Because of the bond of homage the tenant may do nothing to the disherison of his lord or his severe injury, nor conversely, may the lord so act toward the tenant. If either so acts homage is completely dissolved and extinguished, /and the *nexus* and obligation of homage,/ since they act contrary to homage and the oath of fealty, and it will be a just judgment <that they be punished with respect to that in which they offend, that is, /if/ it is the lord, that he lose his lordship; /if/ the tenant, his tenement, as will be explained more fully below. In this way homage may be dissolved.>

**How homage is dissolved and extinguished. Whether a lord may attorn the homage and service of his tenant against the tenant's will. If a lord wrongfully defers or refuses to take his tenant's homage. If a tenant on his own authority abandons his lord and turns to another and does him homage. If a mesne lord when he has received service from his tenant**

**domino suo et faciat ei homagium. Si dominus medius cum servitium receperit a tenente suo non adquietaverit eum versus superiorem dominum. De illis qui tenentur ad sacramentum fidelitatis.**

### De releviis dandis.

Cum homagia capta fuerint et fidelitates ab illis qui plenae aetatis extiterint, oportet statim quod tenementum quod fuit in manibus antecessorum, et hereditas quae iacens fuerit per eorum decessum relevetur in manus heredum, et propter talem relevationem facienda erit ad heredibus quaedam praestatio quae dicitur relevium, de feodis militaribus et seriantiis et aliis de quibus fit homagium et regale servitium, vel de socagiis de quibus de iure nullum fieri debet homagium. Fit quaedam praestatio quae non dicitur relevium sed quasi, sicut herietum quasi loco relevii, et quod dari debet aliquando ante sacramentum fidelitatis, aliquando post. Et unde videndum imprimis quale sit rationabile relevium, et quis debeat dare relevium, et quibus sit dandum, et quotiens et quando. Et imprimis de feodo militari.

**Quid sit rationabile relavium. Qui teneatur ad relevium. Quibus teneatur. Item quotiens. Item quando. Si de socagio dari debeat relevium et quid. Si de feodi firma et quid. De custodia heredum. [Sunt autem diversae aetates secundum diversitatem heredum et tenementorum.] De herede sokemanni, sub cuius custodia esse debeat. De maritagiis heredum et ad quem pertinere debeat maritagium. Si plures et diversae hereditates sint alicui descendentes tam ex parte patris quam ex parte matris. Quando feodum alicuius deliberetur quod ad dominum pertineat maritagium heredis. Cum plures sint domini capitales tam ex parte patris quam ex parte matris. Cum autem maritagium petatur, refert quis fuerit in seisina de herede, unus ex dominis vel extraneus. Ad quem pertineat maritagium de socagio. Provisio si quis heredem subtraxerit.**

**does not acquit him against the superior lord. Of those who are bound to an oath of fealty.**

## Of the giving of reliefs.

When homages and oaths of fealty have been taken from those of full age, the tenement which was in the hands of their ancestors, and the inheritance which lies vacant by their decease, is raised again in the hands of the heirs, and because of such *relevatio* a certain payment must be made by heirs which is called a relief, /from military fees and serjeanties and other [tenements] from which homage is done and royal service; from socages, from which *de jure* no homage ought to be done a payment is made which is not called a relief but is a kind of relief, like a heriot, [given], so to speak, in place of a relief, which ought sometimes to be given before the oath of fealty, sometimes after it./ Thus we must first see how much a reasonable relief is, who ought to give a relief, to whom it is to be given, how often and when. And first of the military fee.

**What a reasonable relief is. Who is bound to relief. To whom he is bound. How often. When. Whether relief ought to be given from socage and how much. Whether relief is payable from a fee farm and how much. Of the wardship of heirs. There are different ages according to the different kinds of heirs and tenements. Of the heir of a sokeman, in whose wardship he ought to be. Of the marriages of heirs and to whom the marriage ought to belong. If several different inheritances descend to an heir from the father's side and the mother's. When one's fee is [so] delivered that the marriage of the heir belongs to the lord. When there are several chief lords, both on the father's side and the mother's. When a marriage is claimed it is important to determine who is in seisin of the heir, one of the lords or a stranger. To whom a marriage belongs in the case of socage. A provision applicable where one has ravished an heir.**

### De donationibus propter nuptias ob causam dotis et de constitutione dotis.

Quoniam utile est mulieres esse dotatas multis de causis, adquiruntur enim eis eum fuerint maritandae rerum dominia ex causa donationis, ut cum femina fuerit maritanda, fit ei donatio a viro suo multis modis propter nuptias de re propria viri, vel de re patris vel matris, fratris vel sororis, vel alterius amici, de eorum consensu et voluntate: quae quidem donatio dicitur dos, et quae quidem perfecta esse non potest ante mortem viri, nec quamvis in vita viri possit constitui, tamen ante mortem suam non poterit assignari. Imprimis igitur videndum quid sit dos, et quae sit dos rationabilis, et quis possit dotem constituere, et cui. Item quando, et ubi, et de qua re, et quantum. Item quis possit dotem assignare, et quando, et infra quod tempus, et ubi assignetur, quae competat actio mulieri ad dotem suam consequendam.

### Quid sit dos.

Et sciendum quod dos est id quod liber homo dat sponsae suae ad ostium ecclesiae propter onus matrimonii et nuptias futuras, ad sustentationem uxoris et educationem liberorum cum fuerint procreati, si vir praemoriatur.

### Quid sit rationabilis dos.

Rationablis autem dos est cuiuslibet mulieris de quocumque tenemento tertia pars omnium terrarum et tenementorum quae vir suus tenuit in dominico suo, et ita in feodo quod eam inde dotare poterit die quo eam desponsavit.

### Quis possit dotem constituere.

Item quis possit dotem constituere? Et sciendum quod tam minor quam maior masculus. Cui? Uxori tam maiori quam minori. Poterit enim ille qui infra aetatem est uxorem suam dotare quamvis existentem infra aetatem, dum tamen possit dotem promereri, et virum sustinere, et quamvis vir infra aetatem moriatur, uxor sua sive infra aetatem fuerit

### Of gifts propter nuptias by way of dower and the constitution of dower.

*Dominium* is acquired by the *causa* of gift in many ways, as when a woman is to be married. Since it is proper, for a number of reasons, that women be endowed, a gift *propter nuptias* is made by her husband /from his own property, or that of his father or mother, brother or sister, or another, with their leave and consent,/ which is called dower, /which cannot be complete before the husband's death, /because/ though it may be constituted in the husband's lifetime, it cannot be assigned before his death./ Thus we must see what dower is, what is rightful dower, who may constitute dower, and to whom. Also, when and where, out of what, and how much. Also, who may assign dower and when, and within what time, and /if it is not/ assigned what action is available to the woman for obtaining her dower.

### What dower is.

Dower is that which a free man gives his spouse at the church door [on the marriage day], because of the burden of matrimony and the future marriage, for the maintenance of the wife and the nurture of the children when they are born, should the husband predecease her.

### What rightful dower is.

The rightful dower of every woman is the third part /of each tenement,/ of all the lands and tenements her husband held in his demesne and so in fee that he could endow her on the day he married her.

### Who can constitute dower.

Who can constitute dower? Any male, whether he is a minor or of full age. To whom? To any wife, of full age or a minor. For he who is under age may endow his wife though she is under age, provided that she may merit dower and is mature enough to take a husband; and though the

sive non dotem obtinebit. De hac materia inveniri poterit de termino Paschae anno regis Henrici nono, comitatu Devoniae, de Sarra quae fuit uxor Willelmi Burnel.

### Item quando et ubi.

Quando? Et sciendum quod ante desponsationem in initio contractus. Ubi? Et sciendum quod in facie ecclesiae et ad ostium ecclesiae. Non enim valet constitutio facta in lecto mortali vel in camera, vel alibi ubi clandestina fuerint coniugia, quia si non valeant clandestina coniubia heredibus quoad successionem, numquam valebunt uxoribus quoad dotis exactionem. Oportet igitur quod constitutio dotis sit facta publice, et cum solemnitate ad ostium ecclesiae: et ubi nullum omnino matrimonium, ibi nulla dos. Igitur videtur a contrario sensu ubi matrimonium, ibi dos, quod quidem verum est si matrimonium in facie ecclesiae contrahatur. Et ad ostium ecclesiae fiat dotis constitutio inter quascumque personas consanguinitate vel affinitate coniunctas, vel etiam extraneas, dum tamen matrimonium in vita contrahentium accusatum non fuerit nec dissolutum. Si autem accusatum et dissolutum quacumque ratione, desinit esse dos cum deficiat matrimonium, et desinit esse dotis exactio. Nec debet aliquis ratione unius viri in dotis petitione duabus uxoribus respondere.

**De duabus speciebus dotia. De qua re. Quod uxor vidua remanere debet in capitali mesuagio per quadraginta dies post mortem viri donec dos sua fuerit ei assignata. Qualiter dos fuerit ei assignanda. Quod dos libera esse debeat.**

husband dies within age, his wife will have her dower whether she is within age or not. On this matter may be found [in the roll] of Easter term in the ninth year of king Henry in the county of Devon, [the case] of Sarah wife of William Burnel.

### When and where.

When? Before the marriage, at the beginning of the marriage. Where? In the face of the church and at the church door. A constitution of dower made on the death bed or in a private chamber is invalid, /or elsewhere when the marriage is clandestine, for if secret nuptials are sufficient for heirs with respect to succession, they will never suffice to provide dower for wives,] and it therefore must be made publicly and with a ceremony at the church door. Where there is no marriage at all there is no dower, and thus it appears conversely that wherever there is a marriage there is dower, which is true if the marriage is contracted in the face of the church. A [valid] constitution of dower may be made at the church door between any persons whatever, those related by blood or affinity as well as strangers, provided the marriage is not challenged or dissolved in the lifetime of the parties; if it is challenged and dissolved, for whatever reason, dower ceases to exist, since the marriage comes to an end, and any claim for dower fails: one need [never] answer in an action of dower to two wives claiming through one husband.

**Of the two kinds of dos. Of what thing. That a wife who is a widow ought to remain in the chief messuage for forty days after the death of her husband until her dower has been assigned her. How dower is to be assigned her. That dower ought to be free.**

## De Actionibus

### De actionibus et quid sit actio.

Dictum es supra de personis et rebus. Nunc autem dicendum est de actionibus. Et videndum quid sit actio, et unde oriatur, et qualiter dividatur, et qualiter proponatur et intentetur, et qualiter proposita fundetur, et qualiter proponatur et intentetur, et qualiter proposita fundetur, et qualiter fundata probetur. Quid sit actio? Et sciendum quod actio nihil aliud est quam ius persequendi in iudicio quod alicui debetur. *Ius* autem ponitur ad differentiam eorum quae non sunt iuris vel eorum qui quamvis ius habeant et actionem, elidi tamen poterit per legitiman exceptionem contrapositam. Vel dicitur ius ad differentiam officii iudicis, quod latissimum est et non actio. Multa enim expediuntur per officium iudicis quae non expediuntur iure actionis. Et ius non est ipsum officium, set appellari poterit factum. Sed si sit qui quaerat cur dicatur quis persequi per actionem cum proponat actionem iniuriarum, cum ibi ex officio iudicis summa constituatur, respondeo, Bene potest dici actio cum agitur ex iniuria, et est ratio, quia habet querens ius querendi et petendi et aliquid ei debetur. Si quaeras quid, respondeo, Id videlicet quod querens aestimaverit. Nam antequam querens in iudicio conqueratur, aestimare poterit iniuriam sibi factam, sciliciet quale damnum sustinuerit ex qualitate facti et iniuriae enormitate. Quae quidem aestimatio si iniusta fuerit vel superflua, bene permittitur iudici ex officio suo summam quam querens aestimavit moderare et minuere, non autem augere, nisi forte ita sit quod ille de quo queritur se gratis posuerit in voluntatem et gratiam conquerentis. Et quo casu aestimatio et taxatio erit in voluntate conquerentis, et aufertur iudici officium et potestas taxandi. Item dicitur *persequendi.* Hoc autem ponitur ad differentiam exceptionis, qua non persequimur alium, sed magis ab alio persecuti nosmet ipsos defendimus, licet in exceptione partes actoris sustineamus.

## Of Actions

### Of actions and what an action is.

We have spoken above of persons and things. Now we must turn to actions and see what an action is and whence it arises, into what divisions actions fall, how an action is brought and formulated, and how, after being brought, it is supported, and having been supported, proved.

What is an action? It is nothing other than the right of pursuing in a judicial proceeding what is due to one. The word "right" is used to distinguish it from cases where there is no right, or those where, though one has right and an action it may be avoided by the interposition of a valid exception. Or "right" is used to differentiate an action from matters dealt with by the judge *ex officio* (his powers in this respect being very wide) rather than by action, for many matters are dealt with by a judge acting *ex officio* which do not proceed by right of action. A judge's *ex officio* act is not a matter of *jus* but rather a matter of fact. If it should be asked why one is said to pursue by action when he brings an *actio injuriarum*, since there the sum due in damages is fixed by the judge *ex officio*, I answer, "When suit is brought on an *injuria* the proceeding may well be termed an action, the reason being because the plaintiff has a right to complain and claim and something is due to him." If you ask "what?" I reply, "The amount at which he assesses the wrong." For before the plaintiff may claim in a judicial proceeding he may estimate the wrong done him, that is, what damage he has sustained, taking into account the character of the act and the extent of the wrong, which estimate, if it is inaccurate or exorbitant, the judge, acting *ex officio*, is permitted to moderate and reduce, but not to increase, unless the defendant freely throws himself on the plaintiff's mercy. The estimate and the taxation of damages will then be at the plaintiff's discretion and the judge's duty and power to tax them is taken away.

Item de eo quod dicit *in iudicio*, hoc etiam ponitur ad differentiam eorum quae non in iudicio sed extra persequimur, sicut furem nocturnum vel diurnum, sicut praedonem vel alium, et ubi licebit unicuique se sine iudicio vindicare, hoc excepto, quod si tales vivi capiantur, vita et mors et membra pertinent ad regem. Item *quod sibi debetur* ponitur ad differentiam criminalium actionum, quibus non solum mihi debitum persequor, sed cuilibet de populo propter pacem regis et communem utilitatem.

### Unde actio oriatur.

Videndum est etiam unde actio oriatur. Et sciendum quod ex obligationibus praecedentibus tamquam a matre filia. Obligatio autem quae est mater actionis originem ducit et initium ex aliqua causa praecedente, sive ex contractu vel quasi, sive ex maleficio vel quasi. Ex contractu vero oriri poterit multis, sicut ex conventione, per interrogationes et responsiones, ex verborum conceptione quae voluntates duorum in unum trahit consensum, sicut sunt pacta conventa, quae nuda sunt aliquando, aliquando vestita. Quae si nuda fuerint exinde non sequitur actio, quia ex nudo pacto non nascitur actio. Oportet igitur quod habeat vestimenta de quibus inferius dicendum. Et huiusmodi causa ex contractu vel quasi semper erit civilis. Item nascitur obligatio ex maleficio vel quasi, et maleficium provenit ex delicto et iniuria, quae quidem sub se plures continet species, ut si quis crimen laesae maiestatis commiserit, homicidium vel furtum et huiusmodi. Vel quasi ex maleficio, ut si iudex scienter male iudicaverit, obligatus esse videtur quasi ex delicto. Sed quia neque praecise ex maleficio, neque ex contractu obligatus est, et aliquid peccasse intellegitur, licet per imperitiam, ideo videtur quasi ex maleficio teneri.

**Quid sit obligatio et qualiter contrahatur. Si fiat stipulatio sub condicione. Facta in stipulationem deducuntur. Iudicialis stipulatio. Si res plures in stipulationem deducantur. Quis non possit stipulari.**

The word "pursuing" is used to distinguish an action from an exception, by which we do not pursue another but rather, when pursued by another, defend ourselves, though in putting forward an exception we assume the role of plaintiff. The words "in a judicial proceeding" are used to distinguish an action from matters we pursue not in a court but outside it, as when we pursue a thief who steals by night or by day, a robber or another, where it will be permissible for each to do right for himself without legal proceedings, with this exception, that if such are taken alive, life, death and member belong to the king. Finally the words "what is due to one" are inserted to distinguish it from criminal proceedings; by the latter I seek not only what is due to me but to every person, because of the king's peace and the common welfare.

### Whence an action arises.

We must see whence an action arises. It is clear that actions are born of precedent obligations, as a daughter is born of a mother. The obligation, the mother of the action, takes its own origin and beginning from some precedent cause, either *ex contractu* or *quasi ex contractu* or *ex maleficio* or *quasi ex maleficio*. An obligation may arise *ex contractu* in many ways, as from an agreement, but questions and answers, from a form of words which brings the wills of the two parties into accord, as agreements by way of pact, which sometimes are nude, sometimes vested. If they are nude no action follows, for an action does not arise from a nude pact. A pact must therefore have vestments, of which something is said below. From a cause of this kind, *ex contractu* or *quasi*, [the action] will always be civil. An obligation also arises *ex maleficio* or *quasi, [*also *ex delicto* [or] *quasi ex delicto,* [for] *injuriae* are of several kinds,*]* *ex maleficio*, as where one commits the crime of lèse-majesté, homicide or theft and the like; *quasi ex maleficio,* as where a judge wittingly renders a false judgment.

### Quis non possit stipulari.

In fine autem videndum quis non possit stipulari neque promittere, ut sciri possit quis possit stipulari. Et sciendum quod mutus neque stipulari potest neque promittere, eum loqui non possit, nec verba stipulationi congruentia proferre. Quod quidem in surdo receptum est, quia is qui stipulatur verba promittentis et is qui promittit verba stipulantis audire oportet, nisi sit qui dicat quod hoc facere possint per nutus vel scripturam. Nec dicitur hoc de eo qui tardius audit, sed de eo qui omnino non exaudit. Et quod per scripturam fieri possit stipulatio et obligatio videtur, quia si scriptum fuerit in instrumento aliquem promisisse, perinde habetur ac si interrogatione praecedente responsum sit. Furiosus autem stipulari non potest nec aliquod negotium gerere, quia non intellegit quid agit. Eodem modo nec infans vel qui infanti proximus est, et qui multum a furioso non distat, nisi hoc fiat ad commodum suum et cum tutoris auctoritate.

**De obligationibus quae quasi ex contractu nascuntur. De traditione et iunctura. Per quas personas adquiritur obligatio. Quibus modis tollitur obligatio. Item oriuntur obligationes ex delicto vel quasi.**

That he is bound is clear, but because he is bound neither properly *ex maleficio* nor *ex contractu* and yet is understood to have done something wrong, though only through lack of skill, he therefore is taken to be bound *quasi ex maleficio.*

**What an obligation is and how it is contracted. If a stipulation is made subject to a condition. Acts as the objects of stipulations. The judicial stipulation. If several things are made the object of a stipulation. Who cannot stipulate. The judicial stipulation. If several things are made the object of a stipulation.**

### Who cannot stipulate.

Finally we must consider those who can neither stipulate nor promise, that we may know those who may enter into a stipulation. It is clear that one who is dumb can neither stipulate nor promise, since he cannot speak or utter the words appropriate to a stipulation. The same is true of a deaf mute, for it is essential that the stipulator hear the words of the promisor and the promisor those of the stipulator, unless one says that they may enter into a stipulation by a nod or a writing. What we have said applies not to one who is hard of hearing but to him who is stone-deaf. That a stipulation and obligation may be created by a writing is obvious, because if it is written in an instrument that a person has promised, it is treated exactly as if an answer had been made to some preceding question. A lunatic cannot stipulate or conduct any transaction because he does not understand what he is doing. Nor can an infant or one just out of infancy (who does not greatly differ from a lunatic) unless what is done is to his advantage and done with the authority of his tutor.

**Why stipiulations and obligations were devised. Of obligations which arise quasi ex contractu. Of traditio and conjunction. By what persons an obligation is acquired [for us]. In what ways an obligation is extinguished. Obligations arise ex delicto or quasi.**

### De prima divisione actionum.

Dictum est supra quid sit actio et qualiter de obligationibus oriatur. Nunc autem videndum qualiter dividatur. Et sciendum quod omnium actionum sive placitorum, ut inde utatur aequivoce, haec est prima divisio, quod quaedam sunt in rem, quaedam in personam et quaedam mixtae. Item earum quae sunt in personam alia criminalia alia civilia, secundum quod descendunt ex maleficiis vel contractibus. Item criminalium alia maior, alia minor, alia maxima, secundum criminum quantitatem. Sunt enim crimina maiora, et dicuntur capitalia, eo quod ultimum inducunt supplicium vel truncationem membrorum vel exilium perpetuum vel ad tempus. Minora vero quae fustigationem inducunt, vel poenam pilloralem vel twymboralem vel carceris inclusionem, quandoque cum infamia quandoque sine, secundum quod causa fuerit talis vel talis. Ictus enim fustium infamiam non irrogat, sed causa, propter quam id pati meruit. Item earum quae sunt in personam et quae ex delicto oriuntur vel quasi, sicut actio iniuriarum de qua civiliter agitur quaedam maior est quaedam minor. Est enim atrox iniuria et est levis, et secundum hoc sequetur poena maior vel minor, iuxta illud. Quod tamen admissum quae sit vindicta docebo. Nec debet poena ad alios extendi quam ad suos auctores, nec ulterius progredi quam se extendit delictum. Item poterit iniuria sub se continere transgressionem, ut si quid praesumatur contra statuta regis et regni excedendo modum et mensuram vel faciendo citra debitum, videlicet minus quam deberet, per malitiam et fraudem, negligentiam et omissionem. Item sunt actiones in personam civiles quae oriuntur ex contractu vel quasi, ut supra dictum est, videlicet ubi quis alteri tenetur ad aliquid dandum vel faciendum ex aliqua causa praecedente. Et notandum quod nulla actio in personam civilis criminaliter potest nec debet intentari. Unde oportet quod iudex in qualibet actione tali factum et initium diligenter examinet, et secundum hoc procedat actio civiliter, etiam si utraque pars vellet criminaliter agere in civili.

### The first division of actions.

We have explained above what an action is and how actions arise out of obligations. Now we must see the divisions into which actions fall. The first classification of actions or pleas (to use these terms synonymously) is this, that some are *in rem*, some *in personam* and some mixed. Of those *in personam*, [some] descend *ex maleficio*, [others] *ex contractu*. [Of those *ex maleficio*], some are criminal, others civil. Of the criminal, some are major, others minor, and others of the heaviest kind, according to the magnitude of the crimes committed. There are the major crimes, called capital because they involve the supreme penalty or the loss of members or exile, perpetual or temporary. The minor, which entail flogging, or the pillory or ducking-stool or imprisonment, sometimes with, sometimes without infamy, depending upon what the reason is. "It is not the beating that imposes the stigma of infamy, but the reason for which it merited imposition" [*Digest* 3.2.22]. And so of those that are *in personam* and arise *ex delicto* or *quasi*, as the *actio iniuriarum*, which is sued civilly, for an *injuria* may be grievous or slight, and accordingly a heavier or a lighter punishment will follow, according to the verse, "I will show you what the punishment is when the wrong is admitted" [Ovid, *Metam.* 1.210]. Punishment ought not to be extended to those who do not offend nor go beyond the nature of the offense. *[*An *injuria* may amount to a trespass, as where something is done contrary to the statutes of the king and the kingdom by exceeding mean and measure or by doing less than what is due, that is, less than he ought, through malice and fraud [or] negligence and neglect.*]* *[*There are also civil actions *in personam* which arise *ex contractu* or *quasi*, as was said above, where one is bound to another for the giving or doing of something, by force of some preceding *causa.]* [Thus] no civil action *in personam* can or ought to be sued criminally.

Ut si quis actionem institueret contra alium criminaliter cum sit civilis, et diceret quod per feloniam excussisset pulverem de capa sua, vel quid tale, et hoc paratus esset disrationare: iudex factum examinando et causam pronuntiare deberet appellum esse nullum, et causam civilem et non criminalem. Et etiam si per imperitiam esset inter eos duellum vadiatum, deberet devadiari per iudicium. Set restat quaerendum utrum talis ulterius ad civilem actionem habere possit regressum vel non. Cum autem actio fuerit mere criminalis, institui poterit ab initio criminaliter vel civiliter. Sed cum criminalis semel fuerit instituta civiliter, quaeritur an accusans mutare possit et agere criminaliter, et e contrario. Dicunt quidam quod a criminali descendere non poterit ad civilem minuendo, sed a civili ad criminalem augendo. Quibus tamen ego non assentio, cum in hoc casu admitti non deberet variatio. Personales vero actiones sunt quae competunt contra aliquem ex contractu vel quasi, ex maleficio vel quasi, cum quis teneatur ad aliquid dandum vel faciendum, et licum habent adversus eum qui contraxit et heredem suum, nisi sint poenales. Et dicuntur actiones nativae, eo quod nascuntur ex contractibus. Et omnes fere personales actiones sunt ex contractu, sicut mutui, commodati, depositi, mandati, ex empto vendito, locato et conducto. Personales vero actiones quae nascuntur ex maleficio, aliae persequuntur poenam tantum ut actio furti aliae vero persequuntur ipsam rem et poenam sicut actio vi bonorum raptorum, et ita sint duplices eo quod sunt rei persecutoriae et poenae, et ita tam in rem quam in personam. Et cum sint uno modo rei persecutoriae, competunt contra omnes qui possunt restituere, sive ille possideat qui spoliavit sive alius. Secundum vero quod fuerint poenales, non persequuntur nisi tantum auctores delicti.

Hence in every [criminal] action let the judge carefully examine the deed and origin, and let the action proceed accordingly, civilly even though both parties should wish to proceed criminally in a civil matter, as where one has instituted an action against another criminally (though it is civil) and said that he had feloniously shaken the dust from his cloak (or something of the sort) and that this he would be ready to deraign; the judge by examining the deed and the reason for the action ought to pronounce the appeal void and the suit civil and not criminal. And so even though the appellee should be prepared to defend himself by his body. And so even though the judicial combat has inadvertently been waged between them, it ought to be de-waged by judgment. The question remains whether he may or may not have recourse over to a civil action. When an action is purely criminal it may be brought criminally or civilly, [that is], at the outset, but once a criminal action has been brought civilly *quaere* whether the complainant can change and proceed criminally, or conversely. Some say that he cannot descend from a criminal to a civil action by diminishing it but may [ascend] from a civil to a criminal action by augmenting it. But I do not agree with this, for no variance ought here to be countenanced. Actions *in personam* are those which lie against one *ex contractu* or *quasi*, *ex maleficio* or *quasi*. [If *ex contractu*], when one is bound to give or do something, they lie against him who contracted and his heir, unless they are penal. They are called "born" actions because they are born of contracts. [All actions *in rem* are for the recovery of a thing]. And so are almost all personal actions [which] arise *ex contractu*, as those arising from a loan for consumption, a loan for use, from deposit, mandate, sale and purchase or letting and hiring. Some personal actions arising *ex maleficio* pursue the penalty only, as the *actio furti*, some the thing and the penalty, as the action *vi bonorum raptorum*, and thus are double, since they are recuperatory and penal, and thus [mixed] both *in rem* and *in personam*.

Et quandoque competunt versus unum qui deliquit cum possit restituere, cum sint coniunctae in una persona: et quandoque versus duos vel plures, cum sint disiunctae et bifurcatae, cum ille qui deliquit non possideat nec restituere possit, et ille qui possidet non deliquerit sed restituere possit. Item illarum quae sunt in personam ex maleficio vel quasi, quaedam sunt criminales et quaedam civiles. Criminalium quaedam maiores, quaedam minores. Et civilium eodem modo, secundum quod superius in parte tangitur.

**Quae sunt actiones in rem de re mobili. Quae sit actio mixta. Quaedam conceptae sunt in simplum et sic. De actionibus in rem [alia confessoria alia negatoria]. De actionibus civilibus in personam, qualiter nascuntur.**

### De possessoria hereditatis petitione, quae dici poterit assisa novae disseisinae.

Possessoria vero hereditatis petitio est de possessione propria, et quae dicitur actio unde vi per quam restituitur spoliato sua possessio, et dici poterit assisa novae disseisinae. Item dicitur possessoria petitio de possessione aliena, sicut alicuius antecessoris, de aliquo de quo antecessor obiit seisitus ut de feodo, quae dicitur actio quorum bonorum sive assisa mortis antecessoris.

**Cui competant actiones quae oriuntur ex maleficio, et contra quem. Item cui actio iniuriarum competat, et contra que. Item cui actio quod metus causa, et contra quem. Item cui et contra quem competat interdictum quod vi aut clam. Item cui et contra quem competat interdictum de itinere actuque privato. De interdicto quorum bonorum. Alia divisio actionum.[1] Si plures competant super una re et una fuerit electa. Si quis se retraxerit ab una [in rem] cum fuerit electa. Item actionum tertia divisio. Ubi terminari debeant actiones criminales.**

1 The translation of this section is missing from Thorne's edition. See 2, 296.

Since they are in part recuperatory, they lie against any who can restore, whether the possessor is he who despoiled or another; in so far as they are penal they lie only against those who committed the wrong. They sometimes lie against one person, the wrongdoer, since he can restore, when both aspects are conjoined in one individual, and sometimes against two or several, when they are separated and divided, since the wrongdoer does not possess and cannot restore and the possessor did not commit the wrongful act but can restore. Of personal actions arising *ex maleficio* or *quasi* some are criminal, others civil. Of the criminal, some are major, others minor; of the civil the same is true, as was touched upon briefly above.

**Actions in rem for an immovable. Actions in rem for movables. What a mixed action is. Some actions are in simplum. Of civil actions in rem, [some are on the possession, others on the property]. Of civil actions in personam; how they arise.**

### Of the possessory action for an inheritance, which may be called the assize of novel disseisin.

The hereditatis petitio possessoria [lies] on the possession of some ancestor, for a thing of which the ancestor died seised as of fee, [and] is called the action quorum bonorum or the assize of mort d'ancestor. There is also a petitio possessoria on one's own possession, which is called the action unde vi [or] the assize of novel disseisin, by which his own possession is restored to the person despoiled.

**For whom actions arising ex maleficio lie and against whom. For whom the actio iniuriarum lies and against whom. For whom the actio quod metus causa lies and against whom. For whom the interdict quod vi aut clam lies and against whom. For whom the interdict de itinere actuque privato lies and against whom. Of the interdict quorum bonorum. Another division of actions. If several actions are available for the same thing and one has been chosen. If one has withdrawn from an action [in rem] after having chosen it. A third division of actions. Where criminal proceedings ought to be determined.**

### **De generibus poenarum quibus homines afficiuntur propter eorum iniquitates.**

Genera poenarum quibus afficiuntur malefactores sunt haec. Sunt autem quaedam quae adimunt vitam vel membra. Sunt autem quae auferunt civitatem, burgum, vel provinciam. Sunt autem quae continent exilium perpetuum vel ad tempus, vel corporis coertionem, scilicet imprisonamentum vel ad tempus vel imperpetuum. Sunt quaedam quae fustigationem, verberationem, poenam pilloralem et twymboralem et damnum cum infamia inducunt. Sunt etiam quaedam quae dignitatis et ordinis inducunt depositionem vel alicuius actus privationem vel prohibitionem. Et non alio modo puniatur quis quam secundum quod se habeat condemnatio, ut si gladio animadverti debeat in aliquem, tunc non securi neque telo neque fustibus vel laqueo alio quove modo. Item qui vivi exuri debent non eis verberibus noceatur, nec virgis, nec tormentis: quia plerique deficiunt dum torquentur, et hoc nisi aliter exigat enormitas delicti. Solent praesides in carcere continendos damnare ut in vinculis contineantur, sed huiusmodi interdicctae sunt a lege, quia carcer ad continendos homines et non puniendos haberi debet. Respiciendum est iudicanti ne quid aut durius aut remissius constituatur quam causa deposcit, nec enim aut severitatis aut clementiae gloria affectanda est, sed perpenso iudicio prout quaeque res expostulat statuendum. In levioribus causis proniores esse debent ad lenitatem. In gravioribus vero poenis severitatem legum cum aliquo temperamento benignitatis subsequi. Et poenae potius molliendae sunt quam exasperandae. effractorem, et furem diurnum a nocturno. Quantitas discernit furem ab abigeo, secundum quod furtum fuerit maius vel minus, ut si quis suem surripuerit, fur, et si quis gregem, abigeus erit. Eventus, ut si ex voluntate et conscientia certa fecerit quis aliquid, sicut homicidium, an ex eventu, ut supra. Et secundum hoc aut erit felonia aut infortunium. Item est poena pecuniaria sicut corporalis, et qualibet poena corporalis quamvis minima maior est qualibet poena pecuniaria. Delinquunt latrones

**Of the kinds of punishments set upon men because of their iniquities.**

The kinds of punishments visited upon malefactors are these. Some take away life or member; some entail the abjuration of a city, borough or county, others abjuration [of the realm], permanent or temporary, or bodily restraint, that is, imprisonment, for a time or for life. Others entail cudgeling, flogging, the pillory and the ducking-stool and a judgment with infamy. Others bring about deposition from a dignity or an order or the prohibition or denial of some activity. One is not punished in any way other than that provided in his condemnation, as where he ought to be executed by the sword he shall not be put to death in any other way, neither by the axe nor the spear, by cudgels nor by the rope. Similarly, those condemned to be burned alive ought not to be injured by floggings, whippings, or tortures, since many perish while under torture; this [is so] unless the enormity of the offense demands otherwise. It is the custom of the authorities to injure those detained in prisons by keeping them in chains, but such things are forbidden by law, for a prison ought to be used to detain men not to punish them. It is the duty of the judge to impose a sentence no more and no less severe than the case demands; he must seek a reputation neither for severity nor clemency but, having weighed the circumstances, should determine as each case requires. In less serious cases they ought to be more inclined to leniency; in the imposition of the heavier penalties to temper the severity of the law with a degree of benignity. Punishments are rather to be mitigated than increased. [Offenses are committed intentionally, by impulse or by accident]. Robbers commit offenses intentionally, by deliberation; those who are drunk, by impulse, moved by their drunkenness, when a matter comes to blows or the sword; by accident, when they occur through misadventure, as where in hunting one kills a man by a spear thrown at a beast, or does some similar act.

proposito per factionem. Ebrii, impetu per ebrietatem cum ad manus vel ferrum pervenitur. Casu, cum per infortunium, ut si aliquis venando per telum in feram missum hominem interfecerit, et similia perpetraverit. Crimen vel poena paterna nullam maculam filio infligere potest. Igni concremantur qui saluti dominorum suorum insidiaverint. Facta puniuntur, ut furta, homicidia. Scripta, ut falsa et libelli famosi. Consilia, ut coniurationes. Sed haec quatuor genera consideranda sunt septem modis, causa, perona, loco, tempore, qualitate, quantitate et eventu. Causa, ut in verberibus quae impunita sunt a magistro vel parente nisi modum excedant, quia emendationis et non iniuriae gratia videntur adhiberi, et puniuntur eum quis per iram ab extraneo pulsatus est. Persona dupliciter spectatur, eius scilicet qui fecit et eius qui passus est. Aliter enim puniuntur ex eisdem factionibus servi quam liberi, et aliter qui quid in dominum parentemve commiserit quam in extraneum, in magistratum quam privatum. Et similiter aetatis ratio habenda est. Locus facit ut idem sit furtum vel sacrilegium, et secundum hoc minor poena vel maior. Tempus discernit praedonem a fure vel

### Ubi terminandae sunt actiones civiles.

Dictum est superius in cuius curia actiones criminales debeant terminari, sive in comitatu vel extra, sive in curia domini regis vel alibi. Nunc autem dicendum ubi terminandae sunt actiones civiles quae sunt in rem vel in personam. Et sciendum quod earum quae sunt in rem, sicut rei vindicationes per breve de recto, terminari debent in curia baronum vel aliorum de quibus ipse petens clamaverit tenere, si plenum rectum ei tenere voluerit, vel possit vel sciverit. Si autem noluerit vel non possit vel nesciverit, tunc probato a tenente quod curia domini sui ei de recto defecerit, tunc transferri debet placitum ad comitatum ut vicecomes rectum teneat, et sic a comitatu transferri poterit ad magnam curiam ex certa causa, si dominus rex voluerit, et ibi terminari. Sed fieri non debet

*[The crime or punishment of the father can impose no stigma on the son.] [Those who plot against the safety of their lord are burned by fire.]* Deeds are punished, as thefts and homicides; [words, as insults and unfaithful advocacy]; writings, as forgeries and libels; advices, as conspiracies. But these four kinds of offenses must be considered from seven points of view: motive, person, place, time, quality, quantity and fortuity. Motive, as in whippings, which are not punishable if imposed by a master or parent (unless they are immoderate) since they are taken to be inflicted to correct, not injure, but are punished when one is struck in anger by a stranger. Person has two aspects, he who committed the act and he who suffered it. Because of the same misdeeds bondsmen are punished differently from free men; he who commits an offense against his lord or his father from him who injures a stranger, one who injures a magistrate from one who injures a private citizen. Age must also be taken into account. Place, for that determines whether the same act is theft or sacrilege, and accordingly brings about a lesser or a greater punishment. Time distinguishes one who exceeds his furlough from a deserter, or a burglar or thief by day from one by night. [Quality, whether the theft is large or small, distinguishes a thief from a cattle-lifter; if one steals a pig, he is a thief, if a herd of swine, a cattle-lifter. Fortuity, as where one does some act intentionally and with full understanding, as homicide, or does it accidentally, as above. Depending upon this his deed will be either felony or misadventure. There is pecuniary as well as corporal punishment, but every corporal punishment, though of the slightest, is greater than any pecuniary one.

### Where civil actions are to be determined.

We have indicated above in whose court it is that criminal actions must be determined, whether in the county or outside it, in the king's court or elsewhere. Now we must consider where civil actions *in rem* or *in personam* are to be determined.

contra voluntatem dominorum, sicut olim fieri solet per *praecipe* nisi ex praedictis causis, vel si dominus curiae sponte curiam suam remiserit ipsi regi. Et de hac materia habetis plenius infra, de actionibus civilibus in rem super ipsa proprietate per breve de recto. In comitatu vero terminari poterit placitum per breve de recto et coram vicecomite, si ad magnam curiam translatum non fuerit ut praedictum est. Item quaestio status sicut placitum de nativis, nisi ille qui petitur excipiendo se dicat esse liberum, et coram iustitiariis domini regis in adventu ipsorum se esse probaturam. Et quo casu pacem habebit usque adventum ipsorum, vel transferri poterit probatio et iudicium ad magnam curiam si domino regi placuerit. Item in comitatu et coram vicecomite placitari possunt plura placita in quibus vicecomes est iustitiarius constitutus per breve quod iustitiet, sicut de servitiis et consuetudinibus, de debitus, et aliis placitis infinitis. Item placitum de vetito namii in quo vicecomes iustitiarius est et vicecomes. Et qualiter huiusmodi terminentur inferius dicetur. Et quare non potest vicecomes et comitatus iudicare de alicuius libertate, sicut de ipsius nativitate, cum probatio libertatis sit quasi incidens placito de nativis, sicut posset in curia domini regis? Nescio aliam causam assignare nisi hoc sit propter favorem libertatis, quae est res inaestimabilis, et quae insipientibus et minus discretis committi non debet ad discrimen. Placita vero civilia in rem et in personam in curia domini regis terminanda coram diversis iustitiariis terminantur. Habet enim plures curias, curiam propriam, sicut aulam regiam, et iustitiarios capitales qui proprias

Those *in rem,* as *rei vindicationes* by writ of right, must be determined in the court of the lords or others of whom the demandant claims to hold, if the lord is willing to do him full right, and is able and has the requisite knowledge to do so. If he is unwilling or unable or without the requisite knowledge, then, after the tenant has proved that his lord's court has failed to do him right, the plea must be transferred to the county court, that the sheriff may do him right, and in the same way it may be transferred from the county court to the great court, for specific cause [or] if the king so desires, and there be determined. But this ought not be done against the will of lords, as once used to be done by *praecipe,* except for the causes mentioned above, or if the lord voluntarily remits his court to the king. On this matter there is more below, [in the portion] on civil actions *in rem* on the property by writ of right. A plea by writ of right, if it has not been removed to the great court as was said above, may be determined in the county court and before the sheriff. So may the question of status, as the action *de nativo habendo,* unless the person claimed as a villein by excepting alleges that he is free and that he will prove his freedom before the justices of the lord king on their arrival. He will then have his peace until they come, or, if it pleases the lord king, the proof and trial may be transferred to the great court. In the county court and before the sheriff many pleas may be pleaded in which the sheriff is constituted judge by the writ *justicies,* as in writs of services and customs, of debts, and innumerable other pleas. Also the plea *de vetito namii* in which the sheriff is both judge and sheriff. How such pleas are determined will be explained below.

causas regis terminant, et aliorum omnium per querelam vel per privilegium sive libertatem. Ut si sit aliquis qui implacitari non debeat nisi coram ipso domino rege. Habet etiam curiam et iustitiarios in banco residentes qui cognoscunt de omnibus placitis de quibus auctoritatem habent cognoscendi, et sine waranto iurisdictionem non habent necqe coertionem. Habet etiam iustitiarios itinerantes de comitatu in comitatum, quandoque ad omnia placita, quandoque ad quaedam specialia, sicut assisas novae disseisinae et mortis antecessoris capiendas, et ad gaolas deliberandas, quandoque ad unicam vel duas et non plures. In his casibus omnibus erit curia domini regis. Et sunt duae recognitiones, scilicet de nova disseisina et de morte antecessoris, quae capi non debent nisi in suis comitatibus per communem libertatem, et hoc nisi inceptae fuerint in comitatibus, quia si inceptae fuerint in comitatu, extra comitatum transferri poterunt de loco in locum et extra comitatum terminari cum omnibus sequelis suis, sicut convictionibus et certificationibus cum evenerint. Et sive huiusmodi recognitiones in comitatu terminatae fuerint sive non, non est prohibitum quin convictiones et certificationes extra comitatum trahi possint. Et sicut praedictum est in parte, trahuntur placita causis supradictis a curiis baronum usque ad comitatum, et ibi terminantur quandoque et quandoque inde transferuntur, et ponuntur coram iustitiariis itinerantibus in comitatu, et inde coram iustitiariis de banco vel coram rege multis de causis. Sunt etiam inter alia placita quaedam quae non per translationem, sed immediate terminari debent coram iustitiariis vel coram rege, scilicet placita de baroniis, ubi ipse petens tenere clamat immediate de domino rege in capite per breve de recto quod vocatur *praecipe in capite*, et hoc ideo quia hoc tangit ipsum regem in toto vel in parte. Item immediate in curia domini regis terminari debent placita de advocationibus ecclesiarum et capellarum, et assisa ultimae praesentationis. Et est ratio, quia si alius a rege mandaret episcopis de admittendo clericum et ipse non obtemperaret, alius a rege coertionem non haberet, et quia episcopus ad alterius mandatum quam regis clericum admittere non tenetur.

Why cannot the sheriff and the county court determine, as the king's court may, the question of a man's freedom, as it may that of his villeinage, since proof of liberty is incidental, so to speak, to the plea of villeinage? I know of no other reason except that this is a concession made in favor of liberty, a priceless thing, not to be entrusted to the discretion of the unlearned and inexperienced. Civil pleas *in rem* and *in personam* to be determined in the court of the lord king are determined before various kinds of justices. For the king has many courts, his own court, /as the *aula regia,]* and the chief justices who determine the king's own suits and those of all others by plaint or by reason of a privilege or liberty, as where a person ought not to be impleaded save before the lord king himself. He also has a court and justices resident in the bench, who take cognizance of all pleas they are authorized to entertain, who, in the absence of a warrant, have neither jurisdiction nor the power to coerce. He also has justices itinerant who travel from county to county, somctimcs appointed to hear all pleas, sometimes only pleas of a certain kind, as assizes of *novel disseisin* and *mort d'ancestor* and gaol deliveries, sometimes to hear a single assize or two and no more. In all these cases the court will be the court of the lord king. There are two recognitions, namely, *novel disseisin* and *mort d'ancestor*, which by Magna Carta [1215, ca. 18; 1225, ca. 12] must not be taken save in their counties, and that /they must not be taken outside unless they have been begun in their counties, for once they have been begun there they may be transferred outside, from place to place, and determined outside*]* with all their consequential proceedings, as convictions and certifications, when such occur. If such recognitions have been begun within the county, convictions and certifications may be carried outside it. As was said briefly above, pleas are transferred, for the reasons stated, from seignorial courts to the county court; sometimes they are decided there, sometimes transferred thence and put beforc thc justiccs itinerant in the county, and thence (for many reasons) before the justices of the bench or *coram rege*.

Item immediate in curia domini regis placitantur placita de dotibus ubi mulier nihil habet. Et est ratio, quia si contra mulierem dotem petentem exciperetur quod dotem habere non posset, eo quod viro cuius nomine dotem petit numquam fuit legitimo matrimonio copulata, nullus alius praeter regem posset episcopo demandare inquisiitonem faciendam. Item immediate pertinet ad regem querela finis factae in curia domini regis et non observatae. Et est ratio, quia nemo potest finem interpretari nisi ipse rex in cuius curia fines fiunt. Est enim eius interpretari cuius est condere. Item in curia domini regis immediate placitantur plura placita propter impotentiam aliorum ex necessitate, cum non possit aliquis baro, vicecomes, vel alius de liberis tenementis cognoscere, nec tenens tenetur respondere, sine waranto vel praecepto domini regis, nec etiam possunt aliquem de huiusmodi ad sacramentum sine waranto compellere. Et huiusmodi placita sunt infinita. Qualiter autem placita de curia in curiam transferuntur propter necessitatem multipliciter, vel propter indulgentiam privilegiatorum sicut Templariorum et huiusmodi, infra dicetur plenius per translationem per pone.

There are some pleas which do not reach them by transfer but must in the first instance be determined before the justices or *coram rege*, namely, pleas of baronies, where the demandant claims to hold immediately of the lord king in chief, [brought] by the writ of right called *praecipe in capite*; the reason is because the matter touches the king himself, in whole or in part. Similarly, pleas concerning the advowsons of churches and chapels and the assize of *darrein presentment*, because if someone other than the king should order bishops to admit a clerk and the bishop should not obey, no person other than the king would have the power to coerce him, for a bishop is not bound to admit a clerk except at the direction of the king. Pleas of dower *unde nihil habet* are also pleaded in the court of the lord king in the first instance. The reason is because if against the woman claiming dower the exception is raised that she ought not to have it because she was never joined in lawful wedlock to the man in whose name she claims dower, no one but the king could order the bishop to makc an invcstigation. The plaint concerning a fine made in the court of the lord king and not observed also belongs to the king in the first instance. The reason is because no one may interpret a fine except the king himself, in whose court fines are made, for he who establishes, interprets. Pleas of this sort are infinite. Many pleas are pleaded directly in the king's court of necessity, because others are powerless to hear them, since no baron, sheriff or other person may take cognizance of free tenements without the warrant or precept of the lord king, nor can they compel anyone to take an oath with respect to his free tenement without such warrant. Nor is a tenant bound to answer. How pleas are transferred from court to court of necessity, [or] through translation by *pone*, or because of the favor of the privileged, as the Templars and others, will be explained more fully below.

### Ubi et coram quibus personis proponendae sunt actiones et probandae.

### Quid sit iudicium, et in quibus consistit officium iudicis, scilicet in tribus.

Videndum est igitur quid sit iudicium. Et sciendum quod iudicium est in qualibet actione trinus actus trium personarum: iudicis, videlicet, actoris et rei, secundum quod large accipi possunt huiusmodi personae, scilicet quod duae sint personae ad minus inter quas vertatur contentio, et tertia persona ad minus quae iudicet. Alioquin non erit iudicium, cum istae personae sint partes principales in iudicio sine quibus iudicium consistere non potest. Iudex vero sive iustitiarius uti debet veritate, et veritas iudicii in tribus consistit, scilicet in indifferenti et aequali partium susceptione, ut legitur in Deuteronomio primo, *Audite illos et quod iustum fuerit, iudicate, sive civis sit iste sive peregrinus.*

*Nulla erit distantia personarum, ita parvum audietis ut magnum, nec accipietis cuiusquam personam, quia dei iudicum est.* Item in eodem libro capitulo sexto decimo, *Non accipies personarum nec munera, quia munera excaecant* etcetera, ut infra de iustitiariis. Item consistit in diligenti examinatione quia oportet iudicem cuncta rimari. Hoc intellegens Iob ait, vicesimo nono, *Causam quam ignorabam diligentissime investigabam.* Non enim dicit diligenter sive diligentius, immo diligentissime. Debet enim iudex per examinationem de dubiis facere certum, et de credulitate veritatem, de ignorantia notitiam, et notorium sive notitiam de ignoto. Item consistit veritas iudicii in iusta sententiae prolatione et iusta et diligenti executione, ut in Deuteronomio sexto decimo, *Iuste quod iustum est persequeris, ut vivas et possideas terram quam dominus deus daturus est tibi.* Et in secundo libro Paralipomenon nono decimo ubi dicitur, *Videte quid faciatis, non enim hominis exercetis iudicium sed dei, et illud idem quod iudicaveritis in vos redundabit. Sit timor domini vobiscum, et cum diligentia cuncta facite. Non enim est apud dominum deum nostrum iniquitas neque personarum acceptio, nec cupido menerum,* quae excaecant oculos sapientum et

### *Where and before what persons [civil] actions are to be instituted and proved.*

### What a judicial proceeding is [and how civil actions are to be instituted.]

We must see, therefore, what a judicial proceeding is. It is clear that, no matter what the action, it is the threefold act of three persons, the judge, the actor and the *reus*. It is clear that though the word "persons" may be taken in a larger sense, [unless] there are at least two parties between whom the dispute arises and at least a third who acts as a judge, there will be no judicial proceeding, for they are the principal parties to such a proceeding and without them it cannot exist. The judge must employ the truth of judgment, and truth in judgment consists in three things, in the indifferent and impartial acceptance of the parties, as it is written in the first book of Deuteronomy, "Hear them and judge righteously between them, whether he be one of your country or a stranger. Ye shall not respect persons in judgment, but shall hear the small as well as the great; neither shall ye respect any man's person, for the judgment is God's. And in the same book, chapter sixteen, "Thou shalt not respect persons nor take gifts, for gifts blind [the eyes of the wise]," as below [in the portion] on justices. [Secondly], it consists in diligent investigation, for it behoves a judge to seek out everything. Perceiving this Job says, in twenty-nine, "The cause which I knew not, I searched out most diligently." He does not say "diligently" or "more diligently," but "most diligently." For a judge by investigation must draw certainty from doubt, truth from credulity, knowledge from ignorance and information or what is known from what is unknown. [Thirdly], truth in judgment consists in the just pronouncement of judgment and its just and diligent execution, as in Deuteronomy sixteen, "That which is just shalt thou follow justly, that thou mayest live and possess the land, which the Lord thy God giveth to thee." And in the second book of Chronicles nineteen, "Take heed what

pervertunt verba iustorum: ut legitur in Ecclesiastico vicesimo capitulo, *Xenia et dona excaecant oculos iudicum*. Et qui dona sive munera dixit, omne genus muneris intellexit. Munus, scilicet a manu, quale scilicet est res corporalis quae praestatur. Munus a lingua, quale est blandiens et adulatoria supplicatio, laudum celebre praeconium, vanae gloriae symphonia. Item munus ab obsequio, quale est servitium impensum et acceptum, pro quo extorquetur iudicii rectitudo. Item nec minus munus a sanguine vocari meretur, cum pro sanguinis linea recti iudicii linea recurvatur. In hoc enim tangit sanguis sanguinem. Haec profecto genera munerum sordidorum nomine nuncupantur, et lex humana graven poenam infligit iudici corrupto per sordes, id est per munera sordida, ut si iudex sive iustitiarius paciscatur cum litigatore ad certam partem litis, ut C. *ad legem Iul. Repet. 1. omnes, ubi dicitur, Omnes cognitores et iudices a pecuniis manus abstineant, neque alienum iurgium putent suam praedam. Etenim privatarum quoque litium cognitor idemque mercator statutam legibus cogetur subire iacturam*. Iactura enim sive poena erit quod id quod recepit restituat in quadruplum, ut C. eodem 1. ult. In fine, quia ibi tenentur in quadruplum, sive tempore administrationis aliquid receperint sive post, quocumque titulo vel quocumque velamento, ut si finxerint intervenisse titulum donationis vel venditionis. Re vera sordidus est ille quem iudicii veritas non adornat, ut si favor vel odium, timor, invidia vel praemium inducant contrarium, ut iudicii veritas corruat in plateis, de quo dici poterit, Vae illi sordido per quem veritas sordescit in paludibus platearum. Nec erit inter beatos connumerandus de quibus dicitur, Beatus qui excutit manus suas ab omni munere. Ab omni tamen munere non est abstinendum, quia licet ab omnibus et passim avarissimum sit accipere et vilissimum a nemine tamen accipere erit inhumanum, ut si amicus recipiat ab amico solo intuitu amicitiae et amoris. Actor vero, sive sit petens sive querens, ut debet intentione. Docere enim debet et rationem praetendere quod ad ipsum pertineat actio et quod pars esse possit in iudicio.

ye do, for ye judge not for man but for the Lord, and whatsoever you judge, it shall redound to you. Let the fear of the Lord be upon you and do all things with diligence for there is no iniquity with the Lord our God, nor respect of persons, nor taking of gifts, which blind the eyes of the wise and pervert the words of the just, as is written in Ecclesiasticus, the twentieth chapter, "Presents and gifts blind the eyes of judges." And he who said "gifts" or "presents" understood every kind of present. That is, a gift made by the hand, such as the offer of a corporeal thing; a gift made by the tongue, as a flattering and fawning entreaty, a public eulogy, a symphony of vain glory; a gift made by obedience, as a service bestowed and accepted, for which the probity of judgment is strained. Nor does a gift by reason of kinship deserve to be called anything else, when the line of right judgment is bent for the sake of the tie of blood. For in this blood touches blood. Gifts of this kind are truly called sordid and the *lex humana* imposes a grave penalty upon the judge corrupted by filth, that is, by sordid gifts, as where the judge or justice bargains with the litigant for a share in the suit, as C. 9.27.3, where it is said, "Let all attorneys [*cognitores*] and judges refrain from taking money, and let them not regard the controversies of others as a source of plunder. The attorney [*cognitor*] who is nothing more than a trader in private litigation shall be compelled to suffer the penalties prescribed by the laws." The forfeiture or penalty shall be that he restore fourfold what he has received, as C. 9.27.6 *in fine,* for there they are held to a fourfold penalty whether they receive the gift at the time of their administration or afterwards, whatever the pretext or guise, as where they feign it to be a gift or a sale. In truth he is defiled whom the truth of judgment does not adorn, as where bias or hatred, fear, envy or reward leads him to do the contrary, so that the truth of judgment falls in the streets, of which it may be said, "Woe to him defiled, through whom the truth is muddied in the puddles of the streets"; nor shall he be numbered among the blessed of whom it is said "Blessed is he that freeth his hands from all bribes." But one need not reject every gift, for although to accept presents from all

Proponere enim debet in iudicio coram eo qui ius dicturus est intentionem suam, et illam fundare et probare. Reus vero uti debet exceptione et defensione, secundum quod inferius dicetur plenius.

**De potestate iudicis. De divisione iurisdictionum sacerdotii et regni. De regimine iurisdictionum regni, quia de sacerdotis nihil ad praesens.**

### De sacramento quod rex facere debet in coronatione sua.

Imprimus se esse praecepturum et pro viribus opem impensurum ut ecclesiae dei et omni populo christiano vera pax omni suo tempore observetur. Secundo, ut rapacitates et omnes iniquitates omnibus gradibus interdicat. Tertio, ut in omnibus iudiciis aequitatem praecipiat et misericordiam, ut indulgeat ei suam misericordiam clemens et misericors deus, et ut per iustitiam suam firma pace gaudeant universi.

### Ad quid creatus sit rex, et ordinaria iurisdictione.

Ad hoc autem creatus est rex et electus, ut iustitiam faciat universis, et ut in eo dominus sedeat, et per ipsum sua iudicia discernat, et quod iuste iudicaverit sustineat et defendat, quia si non esset qui iustitiam faceret pax de facili posset exterminari, et supervacuum esset leges condere et iustitiam facere nisi esset qui leges tueretur. Separare autem debet rex cum sit dei vicarius in terra ius ab iniuria, aequam ab iniquo, ut omnes sibi subiecti honeste vivant et quod nullus alium laedat, et quod unicuique quod suum fuerit recta contributione reddatur. Potentia vero omnes sibi subditos debet praecellere. Parem autem habere non debet nec multo fortius superiorem maxime in iustitia exhibenda, ut dicatur vere de eo, magnus dominus noster, et magna virtus eius etcetera.

indiscriminately is most contemptible and avaricious, to accept them from no one is almost inhuman, as where friend accepts from friend, moved solely by friendship and affection. The *actor*, whether he is demandant or plaintiff, must employ an *intentio*, [which] he must put forward in court before him who is to decide upon it, support it, /show and give the reasons why the action is his and that he is entitled to be party to the proceedings,/ and prove it. The *reus* must employ exception and defense, as will be explained more fully below.

**Of the judge's power. Of the division of jurisdictions; of the church and the realm. Of the regulation of jurisdictions in the realm (as to the ecclesiastical estate nothing for the present).**

### Of the oath the king must swear at his coronation.

In the first place, that to the utmost of his power he will employ his might to secure and will enjoin that true peace shall be maintained for the church of God and all Christian people throughout his reign. Secondly, that he will forbid rapacity to his subjects of all degrees. Thirdly, that he will cause all judgments to be given with equity and mercy, so that he may himself be shown the mercy of a clement and merciful God, in order that by his justice all men may enjoy unbroken peace.

### For what purpose a king is created; of ordinary jurisdiction.

To this end is a king made and chosen, that he do justice to all men /that the Lord may dwell in him, and he by His judgments may separate/ and sustain and uphold what he has rightly adjudged, for if there were no one to do justice peace might easily be driven away and it would be to no purpose to establish laws (and do justice) were there no one to enforce them. The king, since he is the vicar of God on earth, must distinguish *jus* from *injuria*, equity from iniquity, that all his subjects may live uprightly, none injure another, and by a just award each be restored to that which is his own. He must surpass in power all those subjected to

Licet in iustitia recipienda minimo de regno suo comparetur, et licet omnes potentia praecellat, tamen cum cor regis in manu dei esse debeat, ne sit effrenata frenum apponat temperantiae et lora moderantiae, ne cum effrenata sit trahatur ad iniuriam. Nihil enim aliud potest rex in terris, cum sit dei minister et vicarius, nisi id solum quod de iure potest, nec obstat quod dicitur quod principi placet legis habet vigorem, quia sequitur in fine legis cum lege regia quae de imperio eius lata est, id est non quidquid de voluntate regis temere praesumptum est, sed quod magnatum suorum consilio, rege auctoritatem praestante et habita super hoc deliberatione et tractatu, recte fuerit definitum. Potestas itaque sua iuris est et non iniuriae, et cum ipse sit auctor iuris non debet inde iniuriarum nasci occasio unde iura nascuntur, et etiam qui ex officio suo alios prohibere necesse habet, id ipsum in propria persona committere non debet. Exercere igitur debet rex potestatem iuris sicut dei vicarius et minister in terra, quia illa potestas solius dei est, potestas autem iniuriae diaboli dum declinet ad iniuriam. Dicitur enim rex a bene regendo et non a regnando, quia rex est dum bene regit, tyrannus dum populum sibi creditum violenta opprimit dominatione. Temperet igitur potentiam suam per legem quae frenum est potentiae, quod secundum leges vivat, quod hoc sanxit lex humana quod leges suum ligent latorem, et alibi in eadem, digna vox maiestate regnantis est legibus, scilicet alligatum se principem profiteri. Item nihil tam proprium est imperii quam legibus vivere, et maius imperio est legibus submittere principatum, et merito debet retribuere legi quod lex tribuit ei, facit enim lex quod ipse sit rex.

him, /He ought to have no peer, much less a superior, especially in the doing of justice, that it may truly be said of him, "Great is our lord and great is his virtue," etc. [Psalm 146:5], though in suing for justice he ought not to rank above the lowliest in his kingdom./ nevertheless, since the heart of a king ought to be in the hand of God, let him, that he be not unbridled, put on the bridle of temperance and the reins of moderation, lest being unbridled, he be drawn toward injustice. For the king, since he is the minister and vicar of God on earth, can do nothing save what he can do *de jure*, /despite the statement that the will of the prince has the force of law [*Inst.* 1.2.6; *Dig.* 1.4.1], because there follows at the end of the *lex* the words "since by the *lex regia*, which was made with respect to his sovereignty" [*Inst.* 1.2.6]; nor is that anything rashly put forward of his own will, but what has been rightly decided with the counsel of his magnates, deliberation and consultation having been had thereon, the king giving it *auctoritas/*. His power is that of *jus,* not *injuria* /and since it is he from whom *jus* proceeds, from the source whence *jus* takes its origin no instance of *injuria* ought to arise, and also, what one is bound by virtue of his office to forbid to others, he ought not to do himself./ as vicar and minister of God on earth, for that power only is from God, /the power of *injuria*, however, is from the devil, not from God, and the king will be the minister of him whose work he performs,/ whose work he performs. Therefore as long as he does justice he is the vicar of the Eternal King, but the devil's minister when he deviates into injustice. For he is called *rex* not from reigning but from ruling well, since he is a king as long as he rules well but a tyrant when he oppresses by violent domination the people entrusted to his care. Let him, therefore, temper his power by law, which is the bridle of power, that he may live according to the laws, for the law of mankind has decreed that his own laws bind the lawgiver, and elsewhere in the same source [*Dig.* 2.2; 2.2.1], it is a saying worthy of the majesty of a ruler that the prince acknowledge himself bound by the laws [*Cod.* 1.14.4]. Nothing is more fitting for a sovereign than to live by the laws, nor is there any greater

Item cum non semper oporteat regem esse armatum armis sed legibus, addiscat rex sapientiam, et conservet iustitiam, et deus praebebit illam sibi, et cum illam invenerit beatus erit si tenuerit illam, cum sit honor et gloria in sermone sensati, et lingua imprudentis subversio ipsius, et principatus sensati stabilis, et rex sapiens iudicabit populum suum. Si autem fuerit insipiens perdet illum, quia a capite corrupto descendit corruptio membrorum, et si sensus et vires non vigeant in capite, sequitur quod cetera membra suum non poterunt officium exercere. Non solum autem sapiens esse debet sed misericors, et cum sapientia misericorditer iustus, et licet tutius sit reddere rationem pro misericordia quam pro iudicio. Tutissimum tamen est ut ita palpebrae eius praecedant gressus suos quod iudicium non vacillet per imprudentiam, nec misericordia desipiat per incircumspectionem. Misericordia siquidem iniusta est cum incorrigibili, et non est in eos liberalitatis augustae referenda humanitas qui impunitatem veteris admissi consuetudini potius quam emendationi deputarunt. Et cum indulgeat iudex indigno, nonne ad prolapsionis contagium provocat uniiversos? Sic ergo misereatur indigno ut semper homini condoleat. Item pauperis non misereatur quis in iudicio, misericordia scilicet remissionis, cui tamen misericordia compassionis est sicut et omnibus miserendum. Et quibus et qualiter sit miserendum, eum doceant merita vel demerita personarum.

**Item ad quid iustitiarii, et iurisdictione delegata.**

Dictum est in proximo de ordinaria iurisdictione quae pertinet ad regem, consequenter dicendum est de iurisdictione delegata ubi quis ex se ipso nullam habet auctoritatem, sed ab alio sibi commissam, cum ille qui delegat non sufficiat per se omnes causas sive iurisdictiones terminare.

sovereignty than to govern according to law, and he ought properly to yield to the law what the law has bestowed upon him, for the law makes him king. And since it is not only necessary that the king be armed with weapons and laws but [with wisdom], let the king learn wisdom that he may maintain justice, and God will grant wisdom to him, and when he has found it he will be blessed if he holds to it, for there is honor and glory in the speech of the wise and the tongue of the imprudent is its own overthrow; the government of the wise man is stable, and the wise king will judge his people, but if he lacks wisdom he will destroy them, for from a corrupt head corruption descends to the members, and if understanding and virtue do not flourish in the head it follows that the other members cannot perform their functions. A king ought not only to be wise but merciful, his justice tempered with wisdom and mercy. Yet though there is greater safety in having to render a final account for mercy rather than judgment, it is safest that [a judge's] eyes precede his steps, that judgment not become uncertain through unconsidered discretion nor mercy debased by indiscriminate application, for mercy is indeed unjust when it is extended to the incorrigible. Nor does the grace of our august liberality extend to those who, having been pardoned an earlier offense, take it to be approved by custom rather than deserving of punishment. And when a judge is indulgent to the unworthy, does he not expose all to the infection of regression? Let him therefore be merciful to the unworthy in this way, as always to feel compassion for the man. And let him not in judgment show mercy to the poor man, that is, the mercy of remission, though to him there ought to be shown, as to all men, the mercy of compassion. And to whom and in what fashion a judge should be merciful, the merits or demerits of persons shall instruct him.

### Why there are justices and of delegated jurisdiction.

We have spoken in the next [preceding] of ordinary jurisdiction which belongs to the king. Now we must discuss delegated jurisdiction, where one having no authority of his own has authority committed to him by

Ut si ipse dominus rex ad singulas causas terminandas non sufficiat, ut levior sit ei laborin plures personas partitio onere, eligere debet de regno suo viros sapientes et timentes deum in quibus sit veritas eloquiorum et qui oderint avaritiam, quae inducit cupiditatem, et ex illis constituere iustitiarios, vicecomites, et alios ministros et ballivos suos, quibus referantur tam quaestiones super dubiis quam querimoniae super iniuriis, et qui ad dextram neque ad sinistram viae propter prosperitatem terrenam vel adversitatis metum a tramite iustitiae non declinent, set iudicent populum dei in aequitate, ut dici possit de eis cum psalmista quod de vultu eorum iudicium prodiit aequitatis. Et considerent efficaciter quid oportuerit secundum necessitatem, quid expedierit secundum utilitatem, quid liceat secundum permissionem, quid deceat secundum honestatem. Et tale iudicium diligit honor regis, cuius personam in iudicando repraesentant. Nulli autem iuris beneficium denegent, a nullo praemium petant ut praedictum est vel recipiant, ut quis ius suum libere prosequatur, ut causa viduae ad eos libere ingrediatur, ut sint orphano et pupillo adiutores, ut nulli calumniam fieri patiantur, ut constitutiones eorum et edicta iuri et consuetudinibus approbatis et communi utilitati sint convenientia. Coram eis nullum deprimat advesariorum potentia, sed agat quilibet quod causa sua desiderat et se temperet ab iniuria, nec a liminibus iudiciorum iustorum avertat eos odium, favor, vel gratia, ut dici possit de eis, Iustus es, domine, et rectum iudicium tuum, etcetera. Item sapientes oportet esse eos qui iudicant ut honestatem iudicandi ab aliis non mendicent. Si quis autem minus sapiens et indoctus sedem iudicandi conscendere et honestatem iudicandi sibi praesumpserit, ex alto corruet quia volare satagit antequam pennas assumat, et qui tali potestatem iudicandi dederit perinde erit ac si gladium poneret in manum furientis. Item non solum oportet iudicantem esse sapientem immo potentem, iuxta illud Salomonis, *Noli quaerere fieri iudex nisi virtute valeas irrumpere iniquitates, ne forte extimescas faciem potentis et ponas scandalum in agilitate tua.*

another. [But] since he cannot unaided determine all causes [and] jurisdictions, that his labor may be lessened, the burden being divided among many, he must select from his realm wise and God-fearing men in whom there is the truth of eloquence, who shun avarice which breeds covetousness, and make of them justices, sheriffs, and other ministers and officials, to whom there may be referred doubtful questions and complaints of wrongdoing; "prosperity or fear of adversity, but who will judge the people of God equitably, so that one may say of them, with the psalmist, that from their countenance came forth the judgment of equity [*Ps.* 16:2]. And let them consider effectually what is required by necessity, what desirable by expediency, what allowable by license and what becoming to honesty. Such a judgment delights the honor of the king, whose person they represent as they sit in justice. Let them deny to none the benefit of the law, */nor seek or accept reward from anyone, as was said above,]* that each may freely pursue his right, that the cause of the widow proceed freely before them, they be counsellors to the orphan and the ward, they permit false actions to be brought against no one, and that their ordinances and edicts be in accordance with the law and the approved customs and with the common welfare. Before them let no one be oppressed by the power of his adversaries but each proceed as his cause requires, and let them refrain from unlawfulness, nor let hatred, partiality or favor turn them from the threshold of just judgments, that it may be said of them, "Thou are just, O Lord, and thy judgment is right etc." [*Ps.* 118:137 Those who judge must also be wise, that they need not beg soundness in judgment from others. If any man witless and unlearned [presumes] to ascend the judgment seat, taking his ability to do justice for granted, he shall fall from on high, as venturing to fly before he has wings; to give such a one the power of judgment is in no way different from putting a sword in the hand of a madman. And a judge ought not only to be wise but strong, according to the saying of Solomon [*Eccl.* 7:6], "Seek not to be made a judge unless thou art strong in virtue, with the strength to break down iniquities, lest thou quail before the face of the mighty and lay a stumbling block in the way of the activity."

### De differentia iustitiariorum.

Item iustitiariorum quidam sunt capitales, generales, perpetui et maiores a latere regis residentes, qui omnium aliorum corrigere tenentur iniurias et errores. Sunt etiam alii perpetui certo loco residentes, sicut in banco, loquelas omnes de quibus habent warantum terminantes, qui omnes iurisdictionem habere incipiunt praestito sacramento. Item sunt alii itinerantes deo loco in locum, sicut de comitatu in comitatum, quandoque ad omnia placita, quandoque ad quaedam specialia, sicut ad assisas tantum et gaolas, et qui auctoritatem habere incipiunt sine sacramento cum breve domini regis receperint de waranto. Sunt etiam iustitiarii constituti ad quasdam assisas, duas vel tres vel plures, qui quidem perpetui non sunt quia expleto officio iurisdictionem amittunt.

**De potestate iustitiariorum. Qualiter et quando finiatur eorum potestas et iurisdictio. Qualiter constituendi sunt iustitiarii ad itinerandum de comitatu in comitatum generaliter ad omnia placita vel ad specialia.**

### De sacramento quod iustitiarii facient cum iustitiariam receperint.

Et sacramentum tale erit. Iurabit quilibet post alium quod rectam iustitiam facient pro posse suo in comitatibus in quibus fuerint itineraturi, tam pauperibus quam divitibus, et quod assisam servabunt secundum capitula subscripta et inferius exprimanda, et quod facient omnes rectitudines et iustitias spectantes ad coronam domini regis. Et post suum sacramentum dicatur eis expresse quod pro posse suo intendant ad faciendum commodum domini regis.

**Breve uni eorum clausum. Breve omnibus iustitiariis simul quod erit eorum warantum et publice legetur in comitatu patens. Breve de eodem omnibus iustitiariis simul patens. Breve clausum vicecomiti quod venire faciat coram iustitiariis omnia placita. Breve de generali summonitione clausum. Breve cum ipsi iustitiarii fecerint summonitionem nomine proprio et per breve suum. Item omnibus quatuor iustitiariis simul ubi constituuntur ad specialia et non ad omnia placita. Breve clausum vicecomiti quod venire faciat assisam. Si autem quatuor constituantur**

[and see what kinds of justices delegate they are, what their power is, and how their power or jurisdiction may be determined].

### Of the kinds of justices.

Some justices are major, general, permanent and of greater importance, who remain at the side of the king and whose duty it is to correct the wrongs and errors of all others. There are also other permanent judges, sitting in a place certain, that is, in the bench, who determine all pleas for which they have a warrant, all of whom begin to have jurisdiction after having taken an oath. There are other justices, traveling from place to place, as from county to county, sometimes for all pleas, sometimes for certain special pleas, as for assizes only and [the delivery of] gaols, who begin to have authority without an oath, when they have received the lord king's writ of warrant. There are also justices appointed for certain [named] assizes, two or three or several, who are not permanent, and who lose their jurisdiction once they have discharged their office.

**Of the power of justices. In what way and when their power and jurisdiction may be determined. How justices to travel from county to county generally ad omnia placita or to hear pleas of a particular kind are to be appointed.**

### Of the oath the justices shall swear when they have received the office of judge.

The oath shall be this. Each will swear, one after the other, that in the counties into which they are to travel they will do right justice to the best of their ability to rich and poor alike, and that they will observe the assize according to the articles set out, to be expounded below, and that they will execute all that is right and just in matters pertaining to the crown of the lord king. And after his oath let each of them be instructed to promote, to the best of his ability, the advantage of the lord king.

**Writ close for one of the justices. Amn't patent for all the justices together, which shall be their warrant and be read publicly in the county.**

**milites iustitiarii ad unicam assisam capiendam. Breve de eodem vicecomiti clausum quod venire faciat assisam. Si iustitiarius de banco solus constituatur et quod assumat. Breve vicecomiti clausum de eodem. Breve si de banco transferatur assisa usque ad comitatum ad certos iustitiarios. Breve clausum de eodem vicecomiti dirigendum. Si assisa transferatur a quatuor iustitiariis usque ad iter iustitiariorum extra comitatum cum in comitatu incepta fuerit. Breve de constituendo iustitiarios ad inquisitionis faciendas super contentionibus ad querelam. Breve vicecomiti clausum super eodem.**

### In adventu iustitiariorum de ordine proponendi actiones et eorum officio.

In adventu iustitiariorum ad omni placita ex iuridictione sibi delegata, pertinet ad eos audire querelas singulorum et petitiones, ut unicuique fiat iustitia et quod suum fuerit tribuatur. Et si sit qui putet se petitionem habere, actionibus debet experiri, quia nemo sine actione experitur, et hoc non sine brevi et libello conventionali, quia nemo de libero tenemento suo sine brevi vel eius pertinentiis nisi gratis voluerit respondebit. Quod si ad hoc iniuste artatus fuerit, subvenitur ei per tale breve domini regis vicecomiti directum in hac forma.

**Breve ne quis implacitetur sine brevi et praecepto domini regis. De ordine actionum. Quod prius agendum est super possessione quam super proprietate. Fallit in quatuor casibus. De actione vi bonorum raptorum triplici.**

## De Placitis Coronae

### Qualiter iustitiarii procedere debent in itinere suo et quo ordine.

Facta coram iustitiariis itinerantibus generali summonitione ad certos diem et locum, quae ad minus continere debet spatium quindecim dierum, videndum erit in primis qualiter procedere debeant et quo ordine. Et sciendum quod in primis incipere debent de placitis coronae, in quibus terminantur actiones criminales tam maiores quam minores, nisi ipse dominus rex forte in aliqua parte aliter duxerit faciendum. Et in primis

**Writ patent on the same subject to all the justices together. Writ close to the sheriff to cause all pleas to come before the justices. Writ close of general summons. Writ when the justices themselves issue a summons in their own name and by their own writ. [Writ] to all four justices together, where they are appointed for special and not for all pleas. Writ close to the sheriff to cause the assise to come. Writ if four knights are appointed justices for the taking of a single assise. [Writ] if a justice of the bench is appointed sole judge with power to assume others. Writ close to the sheriff on the same matter. Writ where an assise is transferred from the bench to the county [and] to specified justices. Writ close on the same matter to be directed to the sheriff. [Writ] if an assise is transferred from the four justices to the eyre of the justices outside the county after it is begun in the county. Writ for the appointment of justices for inquiries into contentions on complaint. Writ close to the sheriff on the same matter.**

## On the arrival of the justices [ad omnia placita]; their duty. Of the order of bringing actions.

On the arrival of the justices *ad omnia placita* it is their duty, by virtue of the jurisdiction delegated to them, to hear the plaints and claims of all, that justice may be done to each and each receive his due. If one believes that he has a claim he must proceed by actions, for no one can prosecute a claim without an action. [that is], without a writ or *libellus conventionalis*, for no one, unless he willingly does so of his own accord, will answer for his free tenement or its appurtenances without a writ. Which, if he be wrongfully constrained to do, he is aided by a writ of the lord king directed to the sheriff in this form.

**Writ that no one be impleaded without the writ and order of the lord king. The order of actions. That suit must first be brought on the possession rather than on the property. Failure in four cases. Of the threefold action for things taken by force.**

## Pleas of the Crown

legantur brevia quae dant eis auctoritatem et potestatem itinerandi, ut sciri possit de eorum auctoritate. Quibus auditis, si iustitiariis placuerit, quidam maior eorum et discretior publice coram omnibus proponat quae sit causa adventus eorum, et quae sit utilitas itinerationis, et quae commoditas si pax observetur. Et proponi solent verba ista per Martinum de Pateshilla. In primis de pace domini regis et iustitia eius violata per murdritores et robbatores et burgatores, qui malitiam suam exercent die ac nocte, non solum in homines de loco in locum itinerantes, sed in homines in lectis suis dormientes, et quod dominus rex mandat omnibus fidelibus suis quod in fide qua ei tenentur, et sicut salvare sua voluerint, efficax et diligens praestent consilium et auxilium ad pacem et iustitiam suam conservandam, et malitiam praedictorum tollendam et reprimendam, et huiusmodi plura. Quibus propositis, debent iustitiarii se transferre in aliquem locum secretum, et vocatis ad se quatuor vel sex vel pluribus de maioribus de comitatu, qui dicuntur buzones comitatus et ad quorum nutum dependent vota aliorum, et sic inter se tractatum habeant iustitiarii ad invicem, et ostendant qualiter a domino rege et consilio suo sit provisum, quod omnes tam milites quam alii qui sunt quindecim annorum et amplius, iurare debent quod utlagatos, robbatores et burgatores non receptabunt, nec eis consentient nec eorum receptatoribus. Et si quos tales noverint, illos attachiari facient et hoc vicecomiti et ballivis suis monstrabunt. Et si huthesium vel clamorem de talibus audiverint, statim audito clamore sequentur cum familia et hominibus de terra sua. <Ad quod notari poterit quod si quis feloniam fecerit et statim captus fuerit, levato huthesio, cessabit secta. Et unde si homo per infortunium oppressus fuerit, submersus, vel aliquo alio modo mortuus, vel interfectus, statim levetur hutheisium, sed sequi non oportet de terra in terram, villa in villam, cum malefactor captus sit, scilicet la bane.> Et traciam conducent per terram suam, et in fine terrae suae illam monstrabunt dominis terrarum vicinarum. Et quod sic fiat secta de terra in terram cum omni diligentia donec malefactores comprehendantur. Et quod non remaneat tracia facienda nisi impedimentum interveniat per noctem supervenientem, vel alia rationabili causa, et quod illos quos

### How the justices ought to proceed in their eyre and in what order.

We must first see how /a general summons having been issued [to attend] before the justices in eyre at an appointed day and place, a summons which ought to allow at least a fortnight's interval/, they ought to proceed and in what order. /They ought first to begin with the pleas of the crown, in which both major and minor criminal actions are determined, unless the lord king has ordered them to proceed in another way in some particular place./ First let the writs be read which authorize and empower them to proceed on eyre, that their authority may be known. When these have been heard, and if the justices so wish, let one of the senior and more distinguished among them publicly declare in the presence of all the reason for their coming, the purpose of the eyre and the advantage to be derived from keeping the peace. These words used to be said by Martin of Pateshull. First of all, of the king's peace and justice and the breaches thereof by murderers, robbers and burglars, who commit their crimes by day and night, not only against those who journey from place to place but even against those asleep in their beds. And [let him declare] that the king orders all his lieges, in the faith whereby they are bound to him and as they wish to save their possessions, to lend effective and diligent counsel and aid for the preservation of his peace and justice and the suppression and extirpation of wrongdoing. And more [may be said] to the like effect. These remarks having been made, the justices ought to betake themselves to some private place and call before them four or six or more of the greater men of the county, who are called the "buzones" of the county and on whose nod the views of the others depend, and let them consult with those men in turn and explain how the king and his council have ordained that all those who are fifteen years of age and more, knights as well as others, must swear that they will not harbor outlaws, robbers or burglars, nor join with them /nor with those who harbor them, and if they

suspectos habebunt pro posse suo arrestabunt, non expectato mandato iustitiarii vel vicecomitis, et quid inde fecerint scire faciant iustitiariis vel vicecomiti. Iurabunt etiam quod si aliquis venerit in villam vel burgum vel alibi, et emerit panem, cervisiam, vel alia victualia, et suspectus habeatur quod hoc sit ad opus malefactorum, ipsum arrestabunt et arrestum vicecomiti vel ballivis suis liberabunt. Iurabunt etiam quod nullum de nocte recipient in domun suam ad hospitandum nisi bene notus sit, et si forte ignotum aliquem hospitaverint, quod non permittent eum in crastino recedere ante clarum diem, et hoc sub testimonio trium vel quatuor proximorum vicinorum. Convocentur postmodum servientes et ballivi hundredorum, et per ordinem irrotulentur hundreda sive wapentakia et nomina servientum, quorum quilibet affidabit quod de quolibet hundredo eliget quatuor milites, qui statim veniant coram iustitiariis ad faciendum praeceptum domini regis, et qui statim iurabunt quod eigent duodecim milites vel liberos et legales homines si milites non inveniantur, qui neminem appellent nec sint appellati, nec male crediti de pace infracta, de morte hominis, vel alio maleficio, et per quod negotia domini regis possint melius et utilius expediri. Et nomona ipsorum duodecim statim imbreviari faciant in quadam cedula et illam liberent iustitiariis, qui etiam cum venerint iurabunt in hac forma, primus sic.

### De sacramento duodecim militum electorum ad dicendum veredictum in placito coroner.

Hoc auditis iustitiarii quod veritatem dicam de hoc quod a me interrogabitis ex parte domini regis, et fideliter facia id quod mihi praecipietis ex parte domini regis, et pro aliquo non omittam, quin ita faciam pro posse meo, sic me deus adiuvet et haec sancta. Et post eum iurabit quilibet aliorum separatim et per se, ita: Tale sacramentum quale A. primus iurator scilicet hic iuravit, ego tenebo ex parte mea, sic me deus adiuvet et haec sancta. Et cum ita iuraverint omnes, legantur eis capitula per ordinem, de quibus coram iustitiariis respondebunt.

know of any such they will cause them to be attached and show what they have done to the sheriff and his bailiffs]. And that if they have heard the hue and cry raised against such men that immediately on hearing it they and their household, the men of their land being assembled, will follow the trail through their own land and at its boundary show it to the lords of the neighboring lands, that pursuit may thus be made from estate to estate with all diligence until the wrongdoers are apprehended, such pursuit not to end unless some obstacle intervenes, darkness or other reasonable cause. <By which it may be noted that if one has committed a felony and, after the hue has been raised, is arrested at once, pursuit shall end. And hence if a man has been crushed, drowned, or has died or been killed in some other way by misadventure, let the hue be raised at once but pursuit need not be made from estate to estate [or] from vill to vill since the malefactor has been arrested, to wit, the "bane."> and will arrest as best they can those they suspect, without waiting for an order from justice or sheriff, and inform the justices or the sheriff of what they have done. They shall also swear that if anyone comes to a township or borough or any other place and buys bread, ale or other victuals and is suspected of doing this for the benefit of wrongdoers, that they will arrest him and deliver him under arrest to the sheriff or his bailiffs. Also that they will take no guest into their house by night unless he is well known, and that if they give lodging to a stranger they will not permit him to depart on the morrow before daylight, and then only with three or four of the nearer neighbors as witnesses. Let the serjeants and bailiffs of the hundreds then be called together, and the names of the hundreds or wapentakes and their serjeants enrolled in order, each of whom shall undertake on oath to choose four knights from each of the hundreds, who shall at once come before the justices to do the king's bidding. These shall immediately take an oath that they will choose twelve knights, or free and law-abiding men if knights may not be found, who are not appealing anyone nor being appealed themselves and are not under suspicion of breach of the peace, homicide or other crime, through whom the king's business may best and most profitably be expedited.

Quibus auditis, statim dicatur eis quod de quolibet capitulo, separatim et per se sufficienter, distincte et aperte respondeant in veredicto suo, et illud habeant ad certum diem. Et secreto dicatur eis quod si sit aliquis in hundredo vel wapentakio suo qui male creditus sit de maleficio aliquo, illum statim capiant si possint. Si autem non, tunc secreto habere faciant iustitiariis nomen talis, et omnium illorum qui male crediti sunt in quaedam cedula,et praecipietur vicecomes quod illos statim capiat et captos venire faciat coram iustitiariis ut iustitiarii de his faciant iustitiam. Capitula vero quae illis duodecim proponenda sunt, quandoque variantur secundum varietatem temporum et locorum, et quandoque augentur, quandoque minuuntur. Sed tamen aliquid dicatur de capitulis exempli causa qualiter per ordinem proponuntur.

### Capitula de quibus duodecim respondebunt.

Imprimis de veteribus placitis coronae quae alias fuerunt coram iustitiariis, et non fuerunt terminata. De novis placitis coronae quae postea emerserunt, per quod natari poterit per capitula ista quod non erit quaerendum de placitis illis quae emerserunt ante aliud iter iustitiariorum, et quae coram eis proposita non fuerunt. Et si aliquis de huiusmodi fuerit accusatus, inde habebit exceptionem, et etiam possent iuratores duodecim de alio itenere argui de periurio, ut de termino Sancti Michaelis anno regis Henrici nono incipiente decimo, de quodam Henrico Rumbaud comitatu Hertfordiae. De illis qui sunt in misericordia domini regis et non sunt amerciati, ad quod videndum qualiter quis sit amerciandus. Et sciendum quod miles et liber homo non amerciabitur nisi secundum modum delicti, secundum quod delictum fuerit magnum vel parvum, et salvo contenemento suo. Mercator vero non nisi salva mercandisa sua. Et villanus autem non nisi salvo waynagio suo. Et hoc per iudicium proborum hominum de visneto qui affidabunt simul cum serviente. Comites vero et barones non sunt amerciandi nisi per pares suos et secundum modum delicti, et hoc per barones de scaccario vel coram ipso rege. Clericus vero non amerciabitur secundum beneficium

And let the knights cause the names of these juries of twelve to be noted down at once on a schedule and deliver it to the justices. When the jurors arrive they also shall take an oath, in this form, the first of them as follows:

### The oath of the twelve knights chosen to speak the truth in a plea of the crown.

"Hear this, ye justices, that I will speak the truth as to that on which you shall question mc on the lord king's behalf, and I will faithfully do that which you shall command me on the lord king's behalf, and for nothing will I fail so to do to the utmost of my power, so help me God and these holy relics." And after him each of the others, separately and individually, shall swear an oath in this form: "The oath that A. (that is, the first juror) has here sworn I will for my part keep, so help me God and these holy relics." When all have thus taken the oath let the chapters [of the eyre], as to which they shall answer before the justices, be read to them in order. Having heard them, let them be told to answer in their *veredictum* fully, clearly and openly to each chapter, separately and by itself, and to have that *veredictum* ready at an appointed day. And let them be told in private that if anyone in their hundred or wapentake is suspected of some crime they are to arrest him at once if they can. If they cannot, let them give his name, and the names of all those who are under suspicion, privately to the justices in a schedule and the sheriff will be ordered to arrest them at once and bring them under arrest before the justices, that the latter may do justice upon them. The chapters to be put before the jurors sometimes vary, depending on the time and place; they sometimes are enlarged, sometimes curtailed. Nevertheless something may be said of the chapters by way of illustrating how they are put forward in order.

suum ecclesiasticum, sed secundum quantitatem laici feodi sui, et secundum modum delicti. Et ad hoc fideliter faciendum affidabunt amerciatores, et quod neminem gravabunt per odium nec alicui deferent per amorem, et quod celabunt ea quae audiverint. De valletis et puellis qui sunt et esse debent in custodia domini regis, qui sunt et qui illos habent et per quem, et quantum terrae illorum valent. De dominabus quae sunt et esse debent de donatione domini regis sive sint maritatae sive non, et si sint maritatae, quibus et per quem et quantum terrae illarum valent. De ecclesiis quae sunt de donatione domini regis, quae ecclesiae illae sunt et qui illas habent et per quem. De eschaetis domini regis, quae sunt et qui illas tenent et per quod servitium, tam de terris Normannorum quam de aliis, et si teneantur sine waranto. De seriantiis domini regis, quae sunt et qui illas tenent et per quem, et iuiusmodi seriantiae illae sunt et quantum valent. De purpresturis factis super dominum regem, sive in terra, sive in mari, sive in aqua dulci, sive infra libertatem, sive extra, sive alibi ubicumque. De mensuris factis et iuratis per regnum, si servatae sint sicut provisum fuit, et si custodes mensurarum mercedem ceperint ab aliquo quod possint per alias emere et per alias vendere, quod quidem intellegatur de omnibus mensuris, tam ulnis quam ponderibus, et si assisa de latitudine pannorum servata sit sicut fuit provisum, et si quis denarios ceperit pro pannis contra assisam venditis. De vinis venditis contra assisam et quis ea veniderit. De illis qui ceperunt denarios ab illis qui extraneos hospitati sunt contra assisam inde factam anno praeterito. De vicecomitibus et aliis ballivis domini regis qui tenuerunt placita coronae et quae placita, et qui convenire faciunt hundreda sive wapentakia pro inquisitionibus faciendis de morte hominis vel aliis placitis coronae, et si ceperint misericordias pro defaltis vel pro huthesio non levato vel non secuto. De usurariis christianis mortuis, qui fuerunt et quae catalla habuerunt et quis ea habuerit.

**The chapters to which the juries shall answer.**

First of all, pleas of the crown heard in the last eyre but not then determined. New crown pleas which have arisen since the last eyre. /By these chapters it may be seen that there is to be no investigation of pleas that had arisen prior to that eyre and were not put before the justices. If anyone is accused of a matter of that kind he will have an exception, and the jurors of the other eyre may be charged with perjury, as [in the roll] of Michaelmas term in the ninth and the beginning of the tenth years of king Henry, [the case] of one Henry Rumbaud of the county of Hertford./ Of those who are in the king's mercy and have not been amerced. /Here we must see how one is to be amerced. It is clear that a knight and a free man shall only be amerced according to the gravity of the offense, according as it is great or small, and excepting his contenement;[1] a merchant excepting his merchandise; a villein excepting his wainage. And it is to be done by the assessment of trustworthy men of the neighborhood, who shall be put on oath together with the serjeant. Earls and barons are not to be amerced save by their peers and according to the gravity of the offense; the assessment to be made by the barons of the exchequer or before the king himself. A clerk shall be amerced not in terms of his ecclesiastical benefice but of his lay fee and according to the gravity of the offense. And the amercers shall swear an oath that they will do this faithfully and will harass no one through hatred nor benefit him through affection and that they will keep secret the things they hear./ Of young men and maidens who are and ought to be in the king's wardship: who they are, who have them and through whom, and how much their lands are worth. Of ladies who are and ought to be in the king's gift: whether they are married or not, and if they are married, to whom and by whom, and how much their lands are worth. Of churches in the king's gift: which churches they are, who hold them and by whom they were presented.

1 Property necessary for the maintenance of his position.

De catallis Iudeorum occisorum, et vadiis et debitis et cartis eorum et quis ea habeat. De falsonariis et retonsoribus denariorum. De moneta et cambio domini regis, scilicet quis fecit monetam et cambium sine domino rege vel iustitiariis suis. De burgatoribus et malefactoribus et eorum receptatoribus tempore pacis. De fugitivis, et si quis redierit post fugam sine waranto domini regis. De utlagatis et eorum catallis, quis ea habet, et si qui utlagati redierint sine waranto. De his per quorum terras utlagati vel burgatores transierunt, qui non fecerunt sectam post eos sicut facere debuerunt. De mercatis remotis ab uno die in alium sine licentia domini regis, nisi de die dominica, et si quod mercatum de novo levatum fuerit sine praecepto domini regis. De novis consuetudinibus levatis, sive in terra sive in aqua, quis eas levavit et ubi. De mercede capta pro blado et aliis catallis dimittendis ne caperentur ad castella, et similiter de prisis factis per vicecomitem, constabularium, vel alios ballivos contra voluntatem eorum quorum catalla illa fuerunt. De defaltis, scilicet de his qui summoniti fuerunt ad esse hic coram iustitiariis et non sunt, et qui non venerunt primo die. De gaolis deliberatis sine waranto domini regis, et similiter de illis qui tenuerunt placita de probatoribus sine waranto. De evasione latronum. De wrecco maris. De malefactoribus in parcis et vivariis, qui illi sint, et eodem modo de columbariis et qui columbas capiunt revertentes ad columbaria. De rapinis et prisis factis extraneis, per quos hoc factum fuerit, et quando et ubi et in cuius potestate. De illis qui non permittunt ballivos domini regis intrare in terras suas ad summonitiones et attachiamenta vel districtiones faciendas, pro debitis domini regis vel pro placitis et aliis rebus sine speciali libertate. De ballivis qui ceperunt dona vel denarios pro recognitoribus removendis de iuratis et assisis, et similiter de vicecomitibus et ballivis qui ceperunt redemptionem de valletis integrum feodum militis tenentibus, vel viginti libratas terrae habentibus, ne milites fierent ad mandatum domini regis, cum vicecomites et alii ballivi praeceptum domini regis inde haberent speciale de talibus plenae aetatis existentibus milites faciendi.

Of the king's escheats: which they are and who hold them, [by whose grant] and by what service, having regard to the lands of the Normans as well as other lands, and whether they are held without warrant. Of the king's serjeanties: which they are and who hold them, by whose grant and what kind of serjeanties they are, and how much they are worth. Of purprestures made against the king, whether on land or in the sea or in fresh water, whether within a liberty or without or elsewhere, no matter where. Of measures established and sworn throughout the realm: whether they have been adhered to as ordained, and whether the keepers of measures have taken a bribe from anyone that he may buy by one set of measures and sell by another, which is to be understood of all measures, by ell as by weight, and whether the assise concerning the measurement of cloth has been kept as ordained, and whether anyone has taken money to allow cloth to be sold contrary to the assise. Of wines sold contrary to the assise and who has sold them. Of those who take money from those who have given lodging to strangers contrary to the assise made thereon in the past year [i.e. 1236]. Of sheriffs and other bailiffs of the lord king who held pleas of the crown: what pleas they held, and [of those] who convene the hundred or wapentake courts in order to inquire as to homicide or other pleas of the crown, [and then] take amercements for not answering the summons or for not raising the hue or for not pursuing it. Of deceased Christian usurers: who they were, and what chattels they had, and who has them. Of the chattels of slain Jews and their pledges, debts and charters, and who has them. Of forgers and clippers of coins. Of the king's money and exchange: that is, who has counterfeited money and exchanged money without [leave of] the king or his justices. Of burglars and malefactors and their harborers in time of peace. Of fugitives: if any have returned after flight without the permission of the lord king. Of outlaws and their chattels: who has them, and whether outlaws have returned without warrant. Of those who have not pursued as they ought outlaws and burglars who crossed their lands. Of markets altered from one day to another without the king's license, except from a

De vicecomitibus et aliis ballivis qui placita coronae et namii vetiti placitant et terminant in comitatibus et hundredis, vel per sacramentum vel alio modo, cum nullam inde habeant potestatem sine speciali mandato domini regis et per breve suum, nisi tantum vicecomes qui est in hoc iustitiarius domini regis super iniusta captione et detentione. De excessibus vicecomitum et aliorum ballivorum, si aliquam litem suscitaverint occasione habendi terras vel custodias vel perquirendi denarios vel alios profectus, vel per quod iustitia et veritas occultetur vel dilationem capiat. De vicecomitibus et aliis ballivis ambidextris qui capint ex utraque parte. De thuthingis, hundredis, sive wapentakiis, et aliis ballivis domini regis positis ad firmam tempore praedictorum vicecomitum. De prisis domini regis in terra, sive in aqua dulci vel salsa, et libertatibus spectantibus ad castella sua, sive ad comitatum sive ad burgos suos sive ad alia quaecumque loca, quae sunt et quantum valeant per annum, et quis ea occupaverit vel celaverit et detinuerit. De vicecomitibus et aliis ballivis qui ceperunt denarios ab illis qui rettati fuerunt de morte hominis, ut dimitteret eos per plevinam cum non essent replegiandi sine speciali praecepto domini regis. De vicecomitibus et aliis ballivis qui imprisonaverunt illos qui rettati fuerunt de latrocinio per indictamenta vel appellum probatoris, et illos in prisona detinuerunt quousque haberent de illis redemptionem, cum possent et deberent per legem terrae replegiari sine aliqua redemptione, vel si a talibus redemptionem ceperunt ne imprisonarentur. De vicecomitibus et aliis ballivis qui bis vel pluries denarios ceperunt ab aliquo, ac si pluries esset amerciatus cum amerciatus non esset nisi semel. De vicecomitibus et aliis ballivis qui distrinxerunt plures unum nomen habentes pro pluribus amerciamentis, ubi non fuit amerciatus nisi unum tantum.

Sunday; and whether any market has recently been established without the permission of the lord king. Of new customs assumed, whether on land or water: who has assumed them and where. Of bribes taken for ensuring that corn and other goods shall not be seized for munitioning castles; and also of prises taken by the sheriff, constable or other bailiffs without the consent of those who owned the said chattels. Of defaults, that is, of those who have been summoned to be here before the justices and are not present, and of those who did not come on the first day. Of gaols delivered without the warrant of the lord king; also of those who have held the pleas of approvers without warrant. Of the escape of thieves. Of wreck of the sea. Of poachers in parks and fishponds; who they are; also of pigeon-houses: those who catch pigeons returning to pigeon-houses. Of rapine and prises inflicted upon strangers: by whom done, when, where, and who now holds. Of those who, having no special liberty, do not allow the king's bailiffs to enter their lands to make summonses, attachments or distraints for the king's debts or for pleas or other things. Of bailiffs who have taken gifts or bribes for removing recognitors from juries and assises; also of sheriffs and bailiffs who have taken ransoms from squires holding a whole knight's fee or having twenty pounds worth of land, that they not be made knights at the king's command, though the sheriffs and other bailiffs have had special instructions thereon from the king about making such as are of full age knights. Of sheriffs and other bailiffs who hold and determine pleas of the crown and of replevin, either by oath or in some other way, in county or hundred courts, though they have no jurisdiction therein without the special mandate of the lord king and by his writ, with the sole exception of the sheriff, who in matters of unlawful taking and detainer is the king's justice in this regard. Of the excesses of sheriffs and other bailiffs: whether they have fomented litigation for the purpose of acquiring lands or wardships or of obtaining money or other profits by which justice and truth are stifled or suffer delay. Of sheriffs and other ambidextrous bailiffs who take bribes from both sides.

De vicecomitibus et aliis ballivis qui distrinxerunt aliquem ad pacandum plus quam id at quod fuit amerciatus per summonitionem scaccarii. De ballivis qui faciunt cervisias suas quas quandoque vocant Scotale, quandoque Filastale, ut pecuniam extorqueant ab eis qui sequuntur hundreda sua et ballivas suas, et de illis similiter qui licet cervisam non faciunt, blada tamen colligunt in autumno, agnos et alia, praetextu ballivae suae, per quod pauperes gravant et molestant. De catallis extraneorum de potestate regis Franciae existentium dum rex fuit in Wasconia, quo devenerunt etcetera. De denariis captis pro defaltis per ballivos de his qui non venerunt ad summonitionem vicecomitis, quis eos ceperit et quantum. De his levaverunt warenam sine sufficienti waranto. De his qui manuceperunt habendi aliquem coram iustitiariis in adventu ipsorum, et non habuerunt eum prime die. De his qui traxerunt brevia et alteri parti vendiderunt, per quod dominus rex amisit id quod ad ipsum inde pertinebat. De thesauris inventis.

**Breve de generali summonitione ad itinerandum apud Shipweye in comitatu Cantiae infra libertatem quinque portuum. Breve vicecomiti Norfolciae et Suffolciae quod scire faciat hominibus de Gernemue et Donewyz.**

### De crimine laesae maiestatis.

Cum sint quaedam crimina capitalia quae corporalem poenam inducunt, quandoque ultimum supplicum, quandoque membrorum truncationem, secundum quod fuerint maiora vel minora, et quorum quaedam sunt publica et quaedam privata, et publicorum quaedam maiorem poenam inferunt propter personam contra quam praesumitur, sicut est crimen laesae maiestatis, ut si contra personam ipsius regis sit praesumptum, quod quidem crimen omnia alia crimina excedit quoad poenam, ideo primo dicendum est de hoc crimine laesae maiestatis.

Of the ridings, hundreds or wapentakes or other bailiwicks of the lord king let to farm in the time of former sheriffs. Of the king's prises on land or in fresh or salt water, and the liberties pertaining to his castles or his counties or his boroughs or any other places whatsoever: what they are, and how much they are worth a year, and who has taken them or concealed them or withheld them. Of sheriffs and other bailiffs who have taken bribes from those accused of homicide for releasing them on bail though they should not be replevied without the special order of the lord king. Of sheriffs and other bailiffs who have imprisoned those accused of theft by indictments or an approver's appeal and have kept them in prison until they could obtain ransom from them, though they may and ought to be allowed bail by the law of the land without any ransom, or if they took ransom from such men that they not be imprisoned. Of sheriffs and other bailiffs who have twice or several times taken money from someone, as though he had been amerced several times when he had been amerced only once. Of sheriffs and other bailiffs who have distrained several men bearing the same name for several amercements when one only had been amerced. Of sheriffs and other bailiffs who have distrained anyone to pay more than the sum at which he was amerced by summons of the exchequer. Of bailiffs who hold their ale-drinkings, which they sometimes call scot-ales, sometimes filast-ales,[1] in order to extort money from those who owe suit to their hundreds and their bailiwicks; and also of those who, though they do not hold ale-drinkings, extort gifts in harvest time, corn, lambs and other things, by virtue of their office, by which they aggrieve and harass the poor. Of the chattels of foreigners owing allegiance to the king of France seized while the king was in Gascony, to whom they have come, etc. Of money for defaults taken by bailiffs from those who did not come at the sheriff's summons: who took it and how much. Of those who have established a warren without proper warrant. Of mainpernors who understood to have someone before the justices at their coming and did not produce him on the first day. Of those

---

1 A *scotale* (ML *cervisia*) or ale-feast held by a bailiff or other official, for which an enforced contribution was levied.

Habet enim crimen laesae maiestatis sub se multas species, quarum una est ut si quis ausu temerario machinatus sit in mortem regis, vel aliquid egerit vel agi procuraverit ad seditionem domini regis vel exercitus sui, vel procurantibus auxilium et consilium praebuerit vel consensum, licet id quod in voluntate habuerit non perduxerit ad effectum. Ad accusationem vero huius criminis admittitur quilibet de populo, liber homo et servus et minor infra aetatem constitutus, dum tamen accusatus attachietur usque ad aetatem accusantis. Et hoc dico dum tamen sit ille qui accusat integrae famae et non criminosus, quia criminosi ab omni accusatione repelluntur, ut si accusans fuerit latro cognoscens vel utlagatus, vel aliquo genere feloniae convictus vel convicendus. Nec etiam admittuntur ad accusationem in crimine laesae maiestatis aliquo casu conspiratores vel crimini consentientes, et in hoc casu pertinet actio tota ad accusantem et ad ipsum regem. Continet etiam sub se crimen laesae maiestatis crimen falsi, quod quidem multiplex est, ut si quis falsaverit sigillum domini regis vel monetam reprobam fabricaverit, et huiusmodi, secundum quod inferius dicetur. Si sit aliquis qui alium noverit esse inde culpabilem vel in aliquo criminosum, statim et sine aliquo intervallo accedere debet ad ipsum regem si possit, vel mittere si venire non possit, vel ad aliquem regis familiarem, et omnia ei manifestare per ordinem. Non enim debet morari in uno loco per duas noctes vel dies antequam personam regis videat, nec debet ad aliqua negotia quamvis urgentissima se convertere, quia vix permittitur ei quod retro aspiciat. Quod autem si ad tempus dissimulaverit et subticuerit, quasi consentiens et assentiens, erit seductor domini regis manifestus, sive accusatus proprius fuit homo vel alienus. Et si post intervallum accusare velit, non erit de iure audiendus nisi docere possit se fuisse iustis rationibus impeditum. Si quis autem de hoc crimine fuerit diffamatus, tunc videndum erit utrum appareat accusator vel non.

who have carried off writs and sold them to the other party whereby the king lost what he was entitled to. Of treasure trove.

**The writ of general summons for an eyre at Sheppey in the county of Kent within the liberty of the Cinque Ports. Writ to the sheriff of Norfolk and Suffolk to inform the men of Yarmouth and Dunwich.**

## Of the crime of lèse-majesté.

[Since of those crimes that are called] capital, which lead to corporal punishment, sometimes death, sometimes dismemberment, according as they are major or minor, some are public and some private, and of the public crimes some carry a heavier punishment because of the person against whom they are directed, as the crime of lèse-majesté, as where something is done against the person of the king himself, a crime which surpasses all others with respect to the punishment inflicted, we therefore must first turn to this crime of lèse-majesté. The crime of lèse-majesté takes many forms, one of which is where one rashly compasses the king's death, or does something or arranges for something to be done to the betrayal of the lord king or of his army, or gives aid and counsel or assent to those making such arrangements, even though what he has in mind is not carried into effect. Anyone, a free man or a bondsman, is admitted to make accusation of this crime, or a minor under age, provided the accused is attached until the accuser comes of age. I say this provided that the accuser is a man of good reputation and is not himself a criminal, for criminals are debarred from making any accusation, as where the accuser is a self-confessed thief or an outlaw, or one convicted or about to be convicted of a felony of some kind. Nor are conspirators or those consenting to the crime ever admitted to make an accusation in the crime of lèse-majesty. In this crime accusation belongs to the accuser, the action to the king himself. *[The crime of lèse-majesté also embraces the crime of forgery, which takes many forms, as where one forges the seal of the lord king or counterfeits money and the like, as will be explained below.]*

Si autem nullus appareat nisi sola fama, quae tamen apud bonos et graves oriatur, hic salvo attachiabitur per salvos et securos plegios, vel si plegios non habuerit, per carceris inclusionem, donec de crimine sibi imposito veritas inquiratur. Et si condemnandus fuerit, ultimum sustinebit supplicium cum poenae aggravatione corporalis et omnium bonorum amissione, et heredum suorum perpetua exheredatione, ita quod nec ad hereditatem paternam nec maternam admittuntur. Est enim tam grave crimen istud quod vix permittitur heredibus quod vivant. Et si aliquando forte ad successionem admittantur tales, hoc magis erit de gratia quam de iure. Si autem appareat accusator, tunc primo capiatur ab eo securitas de prosequendo, et si plegios non habuerit, sufficit pro securitate sola fidei datio, et hoc ideo quia si ad plegios inveniendos districte teneretur, alii se abstinerent a consimili accusatione. Facta igitur securitate de prosequendo ut praedictum est, statim capiatur accusatus et carcerali custodiae mancipetur, nec erit per plegios dimittendus, neque per ballivum sine speciali praecepto domini regis, non magis quam de homicidio perpetrato, et si libere et sine districtione venire voluerit et libere respondere, libere debet recedere nisi iudicium eum incumberet. Utroque autem apparente, tam accusante quam accusato, proponat accusans appellum suum in hunc modum, scilicet dicere debet se interfuisse et vidisse certo loco, certo die, certa hora, et scivisse ipsum accusatum prolocutum fuisse mortem regis vel seditionem suam vel exercitus sui, vel consensisse, vel consilium vel auxilium impendisse, vel ad hoc auctoritatem praestitisse, et hoc eo iuxta considerationem curiae disrationare parato. Accusato etiam e contra per ordinem negante solet appellum illud per duellum terminari, nec erit locus concordiae nisi hoc sit de voluntate ipsius regis. Poterit tamen accusatus ad appellum respondere et illud declinare antequam duellum vadietur. Dicere enim poterit appellatus cum feloniam defenderit et seditionem domini regis et totum quidquid ei imponitur, et petere sibi allocari quod appellans est latro cognoscens et latro captus et imprisonatus pro latrocinio, et quod fregit prisonam et a prisona evasit, vel quod utlagatus fuit, ita quod

[Thus] if one knows that another is guilty thereof or incriminated in some way he ought to come immediately and without delay, in his own person if he can, or through another if he cannot, to the king himself, or to some member of his household, and reveal everything to him exactly as it happened. For he ought not to remain in one place for two nights or days before he sees the king in person, nor ought he to turn aside to any business, however urgent, for he is scarcely allowed a backward glance. If he dissembles for a time and keeps silent, as though consenting and assenting, he will be a manifest betrayer of the lord king, whether the accused is his own man or another's. If after such lapse of time he wishes to make an accusation he is not to be heard *de jure* unless he can show that he was hindered by just cause. If one has been accused of this crime we must then see whether the accuser appears or does not. If no accuser appears, only public suspicion, but that originates among good and reputable men, he will be carefully attached by safe and secure pledges, or if he has no pledges, by imprisonment, until the truth as to the crime imputed to him is investigated. If he is convicted he shall suffer the extreme penalty with torture, the loss of all his goods, and the perpetual disherison of his heirs, who are admitted neither to their paternal nor their maternal inheritance. For this crime is so serious that his heirs are hardly permitted their lives. If they are sometimes admitted to the succession it will be more as a matter of grace than of right. If the accuser appears, let pledges for prosecuting first be taken from him: if he has no pledges his simple affidation provides sufficient security, for this reason, because were he strictly bound to find pledges others would be deterred from making any similar accusation. Security for prosecuting having been furnished, as aforesaid, let the accused be arrested at once and consigned to gaol, nor is he to be released by pledges or by bail without special instructions from the lord king, any more than if he had committed homicide. *[If he is willing to appear voluntarily without distraint and to answer freely he ought to depart freely, until judgment has fallen upon him.]*

nihil restat deo eo iudicandum nisi tantum executio iudicii. Item petere poterit sibi allocari quod cum dicat appellans quod alii plures fuerunt cum eo ubi prolocutio facta fuit, quod ipsi numquam simul fuerunt aliquo tempore de die neque de nocte. Item petere poterit sibi allocari quod cum idem appellans post diem quo prolocutio illa fiere debuit et seditio, ductus esset alias coram iustitiariis pro alia transgressione, nihil locutus fuit de tali seditione domini regis. Item petere poterit sibi allocari quod ex quo appellans talem scivit seditionem esse prolocutam, statim et sine mora non accessit ad regem ut hoc ei ostenderet, sed hoc per tantum tempus subticuit, quod interim posset domino regi si ita esset periculum imminere. Et unde in appello suo audiri non deberet, sicut inimicus et traditor domini regis et consentiens feloniae. Item petere poterit sibi allocari quod cum hoc fieri deberet tali tempore, et appellans esset saepius in curia domini regis et cum rege saepius loqueretur, vel loqui posset si vellet, de hoc nihil ei ostendit. Item petere poterit sibi allocari quod cum ipse appellatus veniret coram ipso appellante et staret inter plures, ipsum non cognovit nec scivit ipsum ab aliis discernere. Poterit etiam plura alia petere sibi allocari, de die et hora et variatione, et aliis pluribus, secundum quod inferius dicetur de appellis. Ad exceptiones istas oportet quod appellans respondeat ad singulos articulos per ordinem, ut sic remaneat appellum ad iudicium. Et tunc videndum quis possit et debeat iudicare. Et sciendum quod non ipse rex, quia sic esset in querela propria actor et iudex in iudicio vitae et membrorum et exheredationis, quod quidem non esset si querela esset aliorum. Item iustitiarius non, cum in iudiciis personam domini regis cuius vices gerit repraesentet. Quis ergo iudicabit. Videtur sine praeiudicio melioris sententiae quod curia et pares iudicabunt, ne maleficia remaneant impunita, et maxime ubi periculum fuerit vitae et membrorum vel exheredationis, cum ipse rex pars actrix esse debeat in iudicio.

When both appear, the accuser as well as the accused, let the accuser put forward his appeal in this way: he ought to say that he was present and a witness at a certain place on a certain day and hour and knew that the accused had plotted the death of the king, or his betrayal, or that of his army, or had assented or given counsel or aid or lent authority thereto. If he is ready to prove this as the court may award and the accused denies the charge completely, the appeal is usually decided by judicial combat, nor will it be possible for them to compromise the matter except with the king's consent. The accused may answer and avoid the appeal before the duel is waged. He may allege (after he has denied the felony and the betrayal of the lord king and everything else imputed to him) and pray that it be allowed on his behalf that the appellor is a self-confessed thief and a thief arrested and imprisoned for theft and that he broke prison and escaped from prison, or that he was outlawed, so that nothing further remains save the execution of judgment. He may also pray that it be allowed on his behalf that though the appellor alleges that there were several others with him when the plot was made, such persons never met together at any time, by day or night; [or] that though the appellor was brought before the justices for another offense on another occasion, after the day on which the said plot and treason were supposed to be committed, he said nothing of any such betrayal of the lord king; [or] that since the appellor knew that the said treason had been plotted and did not go at once and without delay to the king to disclose it to him, but kept silent about it for so long a time that peril, if such there were, might in the meanwhile have befallen the king, that he therefore ought not to be heard in his appeal, as the king's enemy and betrayer and as one consenting to the felony; [or] that though this was said to have been done at such a time, and the appellor has since frequently been in the lord king's court and has often spoken with the king, or could have spoken with him had he so wished, he made no mention of it; [or] that though he, the appellee, came into the presence of the appellor and stood among several others, he neither recognized him nor was able to distinguish him from them.

Sed in hac parte ut videtur erit distinguendum quale sit factum de quo proponitur appellum, utrum scilicet sit ibi felonia vel transgressio, quia quaelibet transgressio dici non debet felonia, quamvis e converso. Si autem ibi fuerit felonia, tunc iudicanda sunt verba appelli, ordo et processus, ut sciri possit si inter appellantem et appellatum iungi possit duellum, quia si ad appellum accusantis paratus esset appellatus sine responsione vadiare duellum, praecedere deberet examinatio ut praedictum est. Et si sine examinatione contra iustitiam esset vadiatum, per examinationem posset devadiari. Si autem tale sit factum quod debeat ibi magis transgressio qum felonia denotari remanebit duellum, sed tunc videndum utrum transgressio illa quae tangit regem gravis fuerit vel levis, sive sibi, sive uxori et pueris. In suis vero poterit rex iniuriari. Si autem levis fuerit transgressio quae poenam infligat pecuniariam tantum et levem, bene possunt iustitiarii sine paribus iudicare. Si autem gravis fuerit et proxima exheredationi, quod redemptionem inducat, ibi debent pares iustitiariis associari, ne ipse rex per seipsum vel iustitiarios suos sine paribus actor sit et iudex.

**De crimine falsi et suis speciebus. De occultatione thesauri. Quid sit wreccum, et de grosso pisce, scilicet sturgio et balena. De assisis regni iuratis si non observentur.**

### De crimine homicidii et qualiter dividitur.

Est etiam inter alia crimina crimen capitale quod in parte tangit ipsum regem, cuius pax infringitur, et in parte privatam personam, quae nequiter et contra pacem domini regis occiditur. Et unde imprimis videndum de homicidio, quid sit homicidium, et unde dicatur, quae eius species, et qua poena homicidiae puniantur. Et est homicidium hominis occisio ab homine facta. Si enim a bove, cane, vel alea re, non dicetur proprie homicidium. Est enim dictum homicidium ab homine et caedo, caedis, quasi hominis caedium. Species homicidii sunt plures, nam aliud spirituale, aliud corporale. De spirituali vero ad praesens non est hic

He may also pray that many other things be allowed him, a variance as to the day and the hour and many others, as will be explained below [in the portion] on appeals. The appellor must answer each of these exceptions in order, [and if] so, let the appeal remain. If [it proceeds] to judgment, we must then see who may and ought to judge. It is clear that it cannot be the king himself in his own suit, for he would thus be both *actor* and judge in a cause involving life and members and disherison, though this would not be so if the suit were another's. Nor can it be a justice, since in judicial matters he represents the person of the king whose deputy he is. Who then shall judge when the king himself must be the *actor* at the trial? Without prejudice to any better opinion, it is submitted that the court and the peers shall render judgment, lest wrongful deeds remain unpunished, particularly where life and members or disherison are at stake; [But in this connection we must distinguish the kind of deed for which the appeal is brought, that is, whether there is a felony or a trespass, for every trespass ought not to be termed felony though the converse is true. If it is adjudged felony the words of the appeal, the order and process, are then to be examined in order to ascertain whether the judicial combat may be joined between appellor and appellee; even if the appellee be prepared towage the duel against the accuser's appeal without making answer an examination ought to come first, as was said above, and if the duel has been unlawfully waged without examination it may be de-waged by examination If the deed is such that it ought to be designated trespass rather than felony the duel will remain.] [if it is a trespass], whether [done] to him or his wife or children, for the king may be wronged in the persons of his family, we must see whether it is grievous or slight. If it is a slight trespass which calls for a pecuniary penalty only, that is, a light pecuniary penalty, the justices may well sit without the peers. But if it is serious enough to involve ransom, the next thing to disherison, the peers ought there to be associated with the justices, lest the king, in person or through his justices without the peers, be plaintiff and judge.

dicendum. Sed corporale est quo homo occiditur corporaliter, et hoc dupliciter committitur, lingua vel facto. Lingua tribus modis, scilicet praecepto, consilio, defensione sive tentione. Facto quatuor modis, scilicet iustitia, necessitate, casu et voluntate. Iustitia, ut cum iudex vel minister reum iuste damnatum occidit. Istud autem homicidium si sit ex livore vel delectatione effundendi humanum sanguinem, licet ille iuste occidatur, iste tamen peccat mortaliter propter intentionem corruptam. Si vero hoc fiat ex amore iustitiae, nec peccat iudex ipsum condemnando ad mortem, et praecipiendo ministro ut occidat eum, nec minister si missus a iudice occidit condemnatum. Et peccat uterque si hoc fecerint iuris ordine non servato. Necessitate, quo casu distingendum erit utrum necessitas illa fuit evitabilis vel non. Si autem evitabilis et evadere posset absque occisione, tunc erit reus homicidii. Si autem inevitabilis, quia occidit hominem sine odii meditatione in motu dolore animi, se et sua liberando cum aliter evadere non posset, non tenetur ad poenam homicidii. Casu, sicut per infortunium, cum aliquis proicit lapidem ad avem vel animal et alius transiens ex insperato percutitur et moritur, vel si quis arborem inciderit, et per casum arboris aliquis opprimatur, et huiusmodi. Sed hic erit distinguendum utrum quis dederit operam rei licitae vel illicitae. Si illicitae, ut si lapidem proiciebat quis versus locum per quem consueverunt homines transitum facere, vel dum insequitur quis equum vel bovem, et aliquis a bove vel equo percussus fuerit, et huiusmodi, hic imputatur ei. Si vero licitae rei operam dabat, ut si magister causa disciplinae discipulum verberat, vel si cum quis deponebat foenum de curru, vel arborem incidebat, et huiusmodi, hic si adhibuit diligentiam quam potuit, scilicet respiciendo et proclamando, sed non nimis tarde vel dimisse, sed tempore congruo et alte, et ita quod si aliquis ibi erat vel illuc veniebat posset aufugere et sibi praecavere, vel magister non excedendo modum in verberando discipulum, non imputatur ei. Sed si dabat operam rei licitae et non adhibuit

**Of the crime of forgery and its species. Of the concealment of treasure. What wreck is; and concerning great fish, that is, sturgeon and whale. If the sworn assizes of the realm are not observed.**

### The crime of homicide and the divisions into which it falls.

Among other crimes there is a capital crime [called homicide], which partly concerns the king, whose peace is broken, and partly the private individual who is slain wickedly and in breach of the king's peace. Hence we must see what it is and why it is so called, its various kinds, and the punishment imposed. Homicide is the slaying of man by man. If it is done by an ox, a dog or some thing it will not properly be termed homicide. For it is called "homicide" from "homo" and "caedo, caedis," "man-killing" so to speak. There are several kinds of homicide, for one is spiritual, the other corporal, but of spiritual homicide we have nothing to say here at the moment. Corporal homicide is where a man is slain bodily, and this is committed in two ways: by word or by deed. By word in three ways, that is, by precept, by counsel, and by denial or restraint. By deed in four ways, that is, in the administration of justice, of necessity, by chance and by intention. In the administration of justice, as when a judge or officer kills one lawfully found guilty. But it is homicide if done out of malice or from pleasure in the shedding of human blood [and] though the accused is lawfully slain, he who does the act commits a mortal sin because of his evil purpose. But if it is done from a love of justice, the judge does not sin in condemning him to death, nor in ordering an officer to slay him, nor does the officer sin if when sent by the judge he kills the condemned man. But both sin if they act in this way when proper legal procedures have not been observed. Of necessity, and here we must distinguish whether the necessity was avoidable or not; if avoidable and he could escape without slaying, he will then be guilty of homicide; if unavoidable, since he kills without premeditated hatred but with sorrow of heart, in order to save himself and his family, since he could not otherwise escape [danger], he is not liable to the penalty for homicide. By chance, as by misadventure, when one throws a stone at a

diligentiam debitam, imputabitur ei. Voluntate, ut si quis ex certa scientia et in assultu praemeditato, ira vel odio vel causa lucri, nequiter et in felonia et contra pacem domini regis aliquem interfecerit. Et fit aliquando huiusmodi homicidium pluribus astantibus et videntibus, aliquando vero clanculo et nemine vidente, ita quod sciri non possit quis sit occisor, et huiusmodi homicidium dici poterit murdrum, secundum quod inferius dicetur. Poena vero homicidii duplex, spiritualis videlicet et corporalis. Spiritualis tollitur per paenitentiam. Et occidit quis alium dupliciter, quandoque lingua, quandoque facto. Lingua, ut si quis dissuadet et sic dissuadendo retrahit aliquem a bono proposito volentem aium liberare a morte, et sic quodam modo indirecte facit quis homicidium. Poena vero homicidii commissi facto variatur. Pro homicidio vero iustitiae iusta et recta intentione facto, non est aliqua poena infligenda. Si sit aliquis qui mulierem praegnantem percusserit vel ei venenum dederit, per quod fecerit abortivum, si puerperium iam formatum vel animatum fuerit, et maxime si animatum, facit homicidium. Possunt etian esse plures culpabiles de homicidio sicut unus, ut si plures rixati fuerint inter se in aliquo conflictu, et aliquis sit interfectus inter tales, nec appareat a quo nec ex cuius vulnere, omnes dici poterunt homicidae, et illi qui percusserunt et qui tenuerunt malo animo dum percussus fuit. Item et illi qui nec occiderunt nec voluntatem occidendi habuerunt, sed venerunt ut praestarent consilium et auxilium occisoribus, quamvis aliquando eorum violentia repellatur. Item non solum tenetur ille qui percutit et occidit, verum etiam ille qui praecipit percutere et occidere, quia cum non sint immunes a culpa, immunes esse non debent a poena. Nec etiam ille qui cum posset hominem a morte liberare non liberavit. Item fit homicidium in bello, et tunc videndum utrum bellum sit iustum vel iniustum. Si autem iniustum tenebitur occisor. Si autem iustum, sicut pro defensione patriae, non tenebitur nisi hoc fecerit corrupta intentione.

bird or elsewhere and another passing by unexpectedly is struck and dies, or fells a tree and another is accidentally crushed beneath its fall and the like. But here we must distinguish whether he has been engaged in a proper or an improper act. Improper, as where one has thrown a stone toward a place where men are accustomed to pass, or while one is chasing a horse or ox someone is trampled by the horse or ox and the like, here liability is imputed to him. But if he was engaged in a lawful act, as where a master has flogged a pupil as a disciplinary measure, or if [another is killed] when one was unloading hay from a cart or cutting down a tree and the like, and if he employed all the care he could, that is, by looking about him and shouting out, not too tardily or in too low a voice but in good time and loudly, so that if there was anyone there, or approaching the place, he might flee and save himself, or in the case of the master by not exceeding mean and measure in the flogging of his pupil, liability is not imputed to him. But if he was engaged in a lawful act and did not employ due care, liability will be attributed to him. By intention, as where one in anger or hatred or for the sake of gain, deliberately and in premeditated assault, has killed another wickedly and feloniously and in breach of the king's peace. Homicide of this kind is sometimes done in the sight of many bystanders, sometimes in secret, out of the sight of all, so that who the slayer is cannot be ascertained; homicide of that kind may be termed murder, as will be explained below. The punishment for homicide is of two kinds [since homicides are of two kinds], namely, spiritual and corporal. The spiritual is discharged by penance. One slays another in two ways, sometimes by word, sometimes by deed: by word, as where one dissuades another and by such dissuasion restrains him from doing the good he intended when he wished to rescue someone from death; thus in an indirect way he commits homicide. The punishment for homicide committed by deed varies; for homicide committed in doing justice, with a proper and lawful intention, no punishment is to be inflicted. If one strikes a pregnant woman or gives

### De officio coronatorum.

Cum autem contingat homicidium fieri quandoque in domibus, quandoque in villa vel vicis, quandoque in campis extra villam et in nemoribus, et ad coronatores pertineat de huiusmodi occisis, cum de interfectore quis ille fuerit nesciatur, diligentem facere inquisitionem, ideo bonum est videre quale sit eorum officium in hac parte. Est igitur eorum officium, quod quam cito habuerint mandatum a ballivo domini regis vel a probis hominibus patriae illius accedere debent ad occisos sive ad vulneratos, sive ad submersos vel subito mortuos, et ad domorum fractiones et ad locum ubi dicitur thesauri fuisse inventum. Et hoc facere debent statim et sine mora aliqua, et in adventu ipsorum versus partes illas mandare debent quatuor vel quinque vel sex villis vicinis quod statim veniant coram eis, et per eorum sacramentum faciant inquisitionem de homine occiso, cum a coronatoribus fuerint requisiti.

### De inquisitionibus ubi occisus fuerit.

Imprimis scilicet ubi mortuus occisus fuerit, in domo vel in campo. Item si ad luctam vel ad tabernam vel aliam congregationem, et ubicumque inventus fuerit mortuus, tunc diligenter erit inquirendum qui tunc interfuerunt, sive masculus sive femina, maior vel minor, et qui illorum de facto fuerunt culpabiles, et qui de forcia, consilio vel praecepto, et qui fuerunt in causa aliqua illius facti. Et facta inquisitione diligenti, quotquot per inquisitionem inventi fuerint culpabiles aliquo praedictorum modorum, si praesentes fuerint vel alicubi inveniri possint, statim et sine mora capiantur et vicecomiti liberentur et in gaolam detrudantur. Quotquot, etiam inventi fuerint per inquisitionem in domibus vel ubi mortuus fuerit interfectus, licet culpabiles non fuerint, attachiandi tamen sunt usque ad adventum iustitiariorum, et nomina plegiorum irrotulentur in rotulis coronatorum.

**De attachiendo culpabiles. Si in campis vel boscis. Si notus vel ignotus. Si occisor fugerit. De submersis. De thesauris.**

her poison in order to procure an abortion, if the foetus is already formed or quickened, especially if it is quickened, he commits homicide. Several may be guilty of homicide just as one may be, as where several have quarreled among themselves in some dispute and one of them is slain; [if] it does not appear by whom nor by whose blow it was done all may be called homicides, those who struck, those who with evil intent held the victim while he was struck, and those who came with the intention of slaying though they struck no blow. Also those who neither slew nor had any intention of slaying but came to lend counsel and aid to the slayers, sometimes even though their [the slayers'] violence is repulsed. Not only is he who strikes and slays liable, but he who orders him to strike and slay, for since they are not free of guilt, they ought not to be free of punishment; nor ought he to be free who, though he could rescue a man from death, failed to do so. Homicide also occurs in war, and we must then ascertain whether the war is just or unjust. If it is unjust he who kills will be liable; if just, as a war in defense of the *patria,* he will not, unless he acts with evil intent.

### Of the office of coroners.

[Wherever men are found dead, which may] sometimes be in the houses of a town, or the streets, sometimes outside the town in fields or woods, */*or when a homicide occurs*/*, it is the business of the coroners to make diligent inquiry with respect to such */*and if they have been slain, as to the slayer, when he is unknown,*/* and therefore, as soon as they have their order from the bailiff of the lord king or from the responsible men of the district, they ought to go */*to those who have been slain or wounded or drowned or have met untimely deaths, [or] to where there has been housebreaking [or] where it is reported that treasure has been found,*/* at once and without delay to the place where the dead man has been found, and on their arrival there to order four, five or six [men] of the neighboring vills to come before them at once and by their oath hold an inquest. When they are required [to hold an inquest] on a slain man, [they must enquire].

### Si raptus virginum.

Est etiam eorum officium in raptu virginum quod si quis ad aliqua de raptu fuerit appellatus, et factum recens fuerit, secundum quod multotiens videri poterit per iudicia certa, ut si huthesium levatum fuerit et recenter secutum et ruptum vestimentum, et si non ruptum, sanguine tamen intinctum, tunc attachietur appellatus per quatuor vel sex vel plures si tot inveniri possint, sin autem, ad minus per duos quod sit etcetera, ut supra. Si autem factum recens non fuerit nec huthesium recenter levatum nec signa appareant qua praesumptionem inducant, sufficit si appellatus attachiatur per duos.

**De pace et plagis. De officio vicecomitis in appello de pace et plagis et de plagis mensurandis. Si plaga periculosa sit ponantur appellati in prisonam, nec sunt per plegios dimittendi, sed videndum in cuius prisona sint custodiendi, scilicet in prisona illius qui potestatem habet iudicandi tales. De probatore. Prisones non debent de terris suis disseisiri sed inde debent sustentari. Breve de inquisitione facienda, utrum appellati sint odio vel atya. Si per inquisitionem culpabilis inveniatur. De pace et plagis cum adiectione feloniae. Si non sit culpabilis quod dimittatur per plegios. Aliud breve de eodem. Si captus infra libertatem et dilata fuerit deliberatio, et captor attachiatur quod sit ad respondendum quare talem cepit et imprisonavit. Si clericus captus fuerit pro morte hominis et petatur curia christianitatis de eo, qualiter committendus erit episcopo, et qualiter episcopus debeat eum custodire. Cum in curia christianitatis defecerit in purgatione. Si ordinarius noluerit ei purgationem indicere cum sit ei liberatus, tunc fiat ei tale breve. De custodia reorum qui sunt in prisonam mittendi et qui per plegios dimittendi, et de fractione carceris. De criminosis qui statim fugiunt post feloniam, et tunc qualiter secta fieri debeat post tales, et quorum quidam sunt in franco plegio et quidam de manupastu alicuius.**

### Of inquests: where he was slain.

First of all, where he was slain, in a house or in the fields. [If in a house or] at a wake, or in a tavern or at a gathering of some sort, they must then enquire who were then present, and which of them, man or woman, adult or minor, were in any way the cause of that deed, and which of those were guilty as principals and which as accessories, counsellors or instigators. A careful inquiry having been made, let as many as the inquest has found guilty in any of the aforesaid ways be arrested at once, if they are present or can be found elsewhere, and handed over to the sheriff and clapped into gaol. Also let those the inquest has found [to have been] in the house or [at the gatherings] where the dead man was slain, though they are not guilty of any wrongdoing, be attached until the coming of the justices and the names of their pledges entered on the coroners' rolls.

**Of attaching the guilty. If [the slain man is found] in fields or woods. If the slain man is known or unknown. If the slayer has taken to flight. Of those who are drowned. Of treasure.**

### Where there is rape of virgins.

This is their [the coroners'] official duty in connection with the rape of virgins: if a man has been appealed of rape by a woman and the deed is of recent occurrence, as may often be ascertained by certain signs, as where the hue has been raised and recently pursued, or her garments are torn, or if not torn, stained with blood, let the appellee be attached by four or six pledges, or more if that many may be found, or if not, by at least two, that he be etc., as above. But if the deed is not recent, nor was the hue recently raised, nor do signs sufficient to raise a presumption appear, it suffices if the appellee is attached by two pledges.

**Of breach of the peace and wounding. Of the duty of the [coroner and] sheriff in an appeal of breach of the peace and wounding; and of the measuring of wounds. If the wound is dangerous let the appellees be put in prison, nor are they to be released on finding pledges; but we must see**

### Ad visum de franco plegio.

Omnis qui est aetatis duodecim annorum facere debet sacramentum in visu franci plegii quod nec latro vult esse nec latroni consentire, et in franco plegio esse debent omnes qui terram tenent et domum, qui dicuntur husfastene, et etiam alii qui illis deserviunt, qui dicuntur folgheres, quia nec debet quis a se repellere servientem suum antequam purgatus sit de omni calumnia unde prius fuerit calumniatus. Item de manupastu alicuius est ille et familia qui est ad victum et vestitum, vel ad victum tantum cum mercede, sicut sunt famuli domus mercenarii. Item secundum antiquam consuetudinem dici poterit de familia alicuius qui hospitatus fuerit cum alio per tres noctes, quia prima nocte dici poterit uncuth, secunda vero gust, tertia nocte hoghenehine Et in fine notandum quod potest quis alium recipere in franco plegio, sicut borghyaldre, quando voluerit pro voluntate sua, sed non poterit illum a franco plegio dimittere cum voluerit, nec vice versa ut videtur cum quis se posuerit in francum plegium alicuius vel decennam, vel ex antiquo secutus fuerit cum decenna, non poterit se retrahere cum voluerit.

**Qualiter reus criminosus sit requirendus, et si non venerit qualiter utlagandus. Cum malefactor fugam ceperit, qualiter interrogandus erit in comitatu et de comitatu in comitatum, et qui sequi debeant et possint.**

### Item quis utlagari possit et debeat.

Item videndum quis utlagari possit et debeat ad alicuius sectam et quis non. Et sciendum quod quilibet masculus, dum tamen sit duodecim annorum et amplius, quia omnes talis aetatis aut sunt aut esse debent in decenna vel in eo quod tantundem valet, sicut in manupastu et huiusmodi ut supra.

**in whose prison they are to be kept, that is, in the prison of him who has the power of judging such men. Of an approver. Prisoners ought not to be disseised of their lands but maintained therefrom. The writ for holding an inquest as to whether they were appealed because of hate and spite. Where a man is found guilty by the inquest. Of breach of the peace and wounding with the addition of felony. Where one is not guilty, [a writ] that he be released on finding pledges. Another writ concerning the same. Where a man is arrested within a liberty and his release has been delayed; let him who arrested him be attached to answer why he arrested the said man and imprisoned him. Where a clerk has been arrested for homicide and court christian claims him; how he is to be committed to the bishop and how the bishop ought to keep him in custody. When a man fails in his purgation in court christian. Where the ordinary refuses to impose purgation on a man when he is delivered to him; a writ then should issue to him as follows. Of the custody of the accused; who are to be committed to prison and who released on finding pledges; and of breach of prison. Of criminals who flee immediately after a felony; and then how pursuit should be made after such men, some of whom are in frankpledge and some in another's mainpast.**

### At the view of frankpledge.

*[*Every (male) who has reached the age of twelve years must take an oath at the view of frankpledge that he does not intend to be a thief nor a party to thieving. All who hold land and house, who are called "householders," ought to be in frankpledge, and also those who serve them, who are called "followers." No one ought to dismiss his servant before he is cleared of every accusation, those with which he has previously been charged.*]* A man belongs to the mainpast and household of him from whom he has food and clothing, or food only with wages, as in the case of hired household servants. He may also be called a member of another's household, according to ancient custom, who has lodged with another for three nights, because on the first night he can be described as "stranger," on the second as "guest," and on the third as "one of the household." And in conclusion note that one, as a "borgholder," may

### Minor non.

Minor vero et qui infra duodecim annos fuerit, utlagari non potest nec extra legem poni, quia ante talem aetatem non est sub lege aliqua nec in decenna, non magis quam femina, quae utlagari non potest quia ipsa non est sub lege, id est inlaghe anglice, scilicet in franco plegio sive decenne, sicut masculus duodecim annorum et ulterius. Et ideo non poterit utlagari. Wayviari tamen bene potest et pro derelicta haberi, cum pro aliqua felonia fugam ceperit. Est enim wayvium quod nullus advocat, nec princeps eam advocabit nec tuebitur cum fuerit rite wayviata, sicut fit de masculo qui secundum legem terrae rite fuerit utlagatus: extunc enim gerunt caput lupinum ita quod sine iudiciali inquisitione pereunt, et secum suum portant iudicium, et merito sine lege pereant qui secundum legem vivere recusaverunt. Et hoc ita si cum capiendi fuerint fugiant vel se defendant. Si autem vivi capti fuerint vel se reddiderint, vita illorum et mors erit in manu domini regis.

**Qualiter quis sequi debeat et ad quot comitatus. Cum fuerit interrogatus ante utlagationem poterit se ponere in prisonam et respondere appellantibus et excipere contra appellum. Si sectam resumere noluerit, sine secta non procedatur ad utlagationem. Item quae causa utlagationis subesse debeat vera vel praesumptiva. Causa praesumptiva. Item si nulla subfuit causa. Item si plaga non fuit periculosa. Si quis fuerit utlagatus ob nullam causam vel minus rationabilem, fiat ei gratia maior quantum ad inlagationem. Item poterit utlagatio pronuntiari nulla et fiat breve regis super hoc, et nulla dici poterit multis rationibus. Quae dici poterit nulla et quibus rationibus, quia minus rite facta. Item nulla dici poterit in casibus subscriptis. Si tam ille de forcia quam ille de facto fugerint, et utlagatur quis tam propter factum quam propter forciam, et e contrario.**

receive another in frankpledge when he wishes and at his pleasure, but cannot extrude him from frankpledge when he pleases; nor, it is submitted, is the converse true, for one who has put himself in the frankpledge of another, or in a tithing, or in times past has followed [the hue] with the tithing, cannot withdraw himself at his pleasure.

**How a defendant accused of crime is to be summoned and how outlawed if he does not appear. When a wrongdoer has taken to flight: how he is to be exacted in the county court and from one county court to another and who may and ought to prosecute.**

### WHO MAY AND OUGHT TO BE OUTLAWED.

We must also see who may and ought to be outlawed at the suit of another and who ought not. It is clear that any male may be outlawed /provided he is twelve years of age or more, for all of that age are or ought to be in a tithing or the equivalent, as in mainpast and the like, as above./

### A MINOR CANNOT BE OUTLAWED.

A minor, however, one who is under twelve years of age, cannot be outlawed or put outside the law because until he reaches that age he is not under any law, [nor in a tithing], any more than a woman, who cannot be outlawed because she is not under the law (in English, "in law"), that is, in frankpledge or tithing, as is a male of twelve years and upwards; thus she cannot be outlawed, but when she has taken to flight for a felony she may well be waived and regarded as one abandoned, for waif is that which no one claims, nor will the prince claim her or protect her when she has been properly waived, any more than he will a male who has been properly outlawed according to the law of the land. Henceforth they bear the wolf's head and in consequence perish without judicial inquiry; they carry their judgment with them and they deservedly perish without law who have refused to live according to law.This is so if they take to flight or resist when they are to be arrested; if they are arrested alive or give themselves up, their life and death will be in the hands of the lord king.

**Qualiter et quando pronuntiari debeat utlagaria de facto et quando de forcia, an statim et eodem die diversa opinio. Si ille de forcia praesens sit et ille de facto fugerit, vel si uterque. Si quis in quarto comitatu velit manucapere non audietur. Ille de forcia non est interrogandus donec factum convincatur. Cum autem uterque praesens fuerit et ille de facto convictus, qualiter sit procedendum contra illum de forcia.**

### Quid utlagatus forisfaciat per utlagationem.

Cum quis ita fuerit utlagatus rite et secundum legem terra, videndum quae forisfaciat per utlagariam cum sic quarto vocatus non comparuerit. Et sciendum quod imprimis forisfaciat patriam et regnum, et exsul efficitur, et talem vocant Anglici utlaghe, et alio nomine solet nominari antiquitus, scilicet frendlesman, et sic videtur quod forisfacit amicos. Et unde si quis talem post utlagariam et expulsionem scienter paverit, receptaverit, vel cum eo communicaverit aliquo modo, vel occultaverit vel receptaverit, eadem poena puniri debet qua puniretur utlagatus, ita quod careat omnibus bonis suis et vita nisi rex ei parcat de sua gratia. Scienter dico quia aut potest esse notus et cognitus vel ignotus et incognitus, et unde qui notum et cognitum receptaverit, pari poena puniendus est, qui dicitur cuthutlaghe.

**Cuthutlaghe qui scienter talem receptaverit. Si non fugerit nec se defenderit. Sola fuga inducit. Item ea quae legis sunt. Item ea quae iuris sunt. Item nulli tenetur nec aliquis ei. Item forisfacit actionem. Item dissolvit donationes, venditiones, et omnes contractus et obligationes. Item catalla sua sunt regis. Si terram liberam habuerit, statim capiatur in manum regis. Breve de inquisitione facienda si extiterit in manu regis per tantum tempus. Breve de restituenda terra domino capitali post annum et diem. Aliud breve de eadem materia de restituenda terra. Si terra data in maritagium cum filia alicuius de hereditate materna extiterit in manu regis per annum et diem, per feloniam quam vir ipsius filiae fecerit, breve de restitutione.**

**How one ought to prosecute; at how many county courts. When one has been exacted he may surrender himself to prison before outlawry and answer appellors and except against the appeal. If he refuses to resume his suit; no proceedings to outlawry may take place without suit. Which cause of outlawry ought to be regarded as true and [which as] presumptive. Presumptive cause. Where there was no cause. Where the wound was not dangerous. Where one has been outlawed without cause or for an inadequate cause let more grace be shown in inlawing him. An outlawry may be pronounced void and a royal writ issued thereon; an outlawry may be declared void for many reasons. Why an [outlawry] may be called void and for what reasons; because incorrectly made. It may be called void in the following cases. Where both principal and accessory have fled; one is outlawed for being an accessory as well as for being a principal, and conversely. How and when outlawry should be promulgated in the case of principals and when in the case of accessories; opinions differ whether it should be immediately and on the same day. Where the accessory is present and the principal has fled, or both [have fled]. If one wishes to mainprise at the fourth county court he shall not be heard. The accessory is not to be exacted until the principal is convicted. When both are present and the principal has been convicted, how proceedings are to be taken against the accessory.**

### What an outlaw forfeits by outlawry.

When one has thus been outlawed, properly and according to the law of the land, we must see what he forfeits by the outlawry, when having been summoned for the fourth time he has failed to appear. It is clear that he first forfeits the country and the realm and is made an exile, such as the English call an "outlaw"; in ancient times he used to be called by another name, that is, "friendless man," from which it is apparent that he forfeits his friends. Hence if anyone wittingly feeds him after his outlawry and expulsion, or harbors him or communicates with him in some way or hides or keeps him, he ought to receive the same punishment as the outlaw, and thus he may be deprived of all his goods and of his life, unless the king spares him of his grace. /I say "wittingly," because [an outlaw]

**Breve, si rex alienaverit infra terminum suum vel ballivi sui. Item aliud breve de eadem materia. Si donationem fecerit ante convictionem vel post. Nihil forisfacit antequam fuerit convictus. Quod terra felonis revertatur ad capitales dominos pro defecta heredum quia inde processit. Sed quid dicetur de hereditate uxoris cum vir fuerit utlagatus, an sit statim restituenda?**

### QUALITER UTLAGATI POST UTLAGATIONEM EX CAUSA ADMITTUNTUR AD PACEM.

Cum quis ita fuerit utlagatus qualitercumque et ex quacumque causa, non erit ei tutum quod compareat antequam fuerit de gratia principis inlagatus. Rex enim poterit utlagatum de gratia sua inlagare, et recipere eum ad pacem suam extra quam prius positus fuit et reponere eum in legem, ita quod si utlagatio rite facta fuerit et secundum legem terrae et sive ex causa vera sive praesumptiva, perdonare poterit ei fugam et utlagationem. Si autem contra legem terrae, debet eam pronuntiare esse nullam. Et quidam sic utlagati secundum legem terrae facilius recipiuntur ad pacem, secundum quod ibi subfuerit causa vera vel nulla vel minus sufficiens, ut si ille qui interfici debuit producatur vivus et sanus. Si autem factum tale quod non sit criminosum eodem modo, vel si factum contingat per infortunium, vix autem aut numquam admittuntur. Si factum fuerit criminale et feloniam contineat, tales quidem ad pacem recipi non deberent, ne ex facilitate veniae aliis tribuatur materia sive audacia delinquendi. Et qualitercumque inlagetur, ita debet inlagari quod omnibus respondeat qui versus eum loqui voluerint, et fiant ei litterae domini regis patentes et testificantes quod pacem suam ei dederit in hac forma.

**Breve quod dominus rex perdonat fugam et utlagariam omnibus ballivis dirigendum de tempore suo. Aliud breve, quod rex perdonat quantum ad ipsum pertinet utlagariam factam tempore patris sui. Item quod rex perdonat utlagariam quia tempore quo appellum factum fuit, ipse appellatus in alio comitatu appellatus de eodem roberia rex remittit.**

may be known and recognized or unknown and unrecognized; thus he who harbors a known and recognized outlaw, who is called the "outlaw's friend," is to be punished with a like punishment/.

**The "outlaw's friend" who knowingly harbors an outlaw. If he does not flee or defend himself. Flight alone involves. He [forfeits] the things pertaining to law. He [forfeits] the things pertaining to right. He is bound to no one nor anyone to him. He forfeits actions. [Outlawry] dissolves gifts, sales and all contracts and obligations. His chattels belong to the king. If he has free land let it be seized into the king's hand at once. A writ for taking an inquest as to whether [land] has been in the king's hand for such a length of time. A writ for restoring land to a chief lord after the year and day. Another writ on the same matter for the restoration of land. Where land given in maritagium with a daughter from her mother's inheritance has been in the king's hand for a year and a day by reason of a felony committed by that daughter's husband [for which] he has been outlawed in the county court; the writ for restoration. A writ where the king has alienated within his term or his bailiffs [have done so]. Another writ on the same subject. Where one has made a gift, before conviction or afterwards. He forfeits nothing before he has been convicted. That the land of a felon may revert to the chief lords for lack of heirs because it came from them. But what shall be said of a wife's inheritance when her husband has been outlawed; is it to be restored at once?**

### [INLAWRY]: HOW OUTLAWS AFTER OUTLAWRY ARE ADMITTED FOR GOOD REASON TO THE PEACE.

When one has thus been outlawed, no matter in what way and regardless of the cause, it will not be safe for him to appear until he has been in-lawed by grace of the prince. For the king may of his grace in-law and outlaw, admit him to his peace outside of which he had earlier been placed. [He may] put him back within the law provided that /If the outlawry has been properly done according to the law of the land, whether the cause is true or presumptive, he may pardon him his flight and outlawry; if contrary to the law of the land,

**Si quis falso coram iustitiariis fuerit indictatus, et postea se reddiderit prisonae regis, remittit rex utlagariam. Item si ille qui interfici debuit sanus et vivus redierit. Breve de eo qui interfici debuit, si sanus et vivus revertatur. De inlagatione et ad quae restituatur inlagatus. Iudicanda erit causa primo ante inlagationem pro qua fuit utlagatus, ut facilius admittatur ad pacem secundum causam utlagationis. Item nulla omnino causa. Non restituitur quis nisi tantum ad pacem. Item iuste utlagatus et rite non restituitur nisi tantum ad pacem quod ire possit et redire et pacem habere, et ad actiones restitui non potes nec ad alia, quia est quasi infans modo genitus et homo quasi modo genitus. Quid felo forisfaciat. Item restituuntur legi maxime in criminalibus, quod ipsi aliis respondeant, et alii ipsis non. In civilibus vero ipsi aliis. Rex remittit eis suam sectam sine praeiudicio aliorum. Si sit qui versus eum loqui voluerit cum fuerit inlagatus, oportebit quod versus ipsum loquatur per verba appelli. Item si antenatus filius ex pluribus feloniam fecerit in vita patris, et fuerit utlagatus in vita patris. Cum utlagatus captus fuerit, non alicui licitum est eum interficere nisi in ipsa captione se defendat. Aliquando poterit rex de sua gratia vitam concedere restitutis.**

### De homicidio quod palam et pluribus astantibus perpetratum est, et postea de homicidio quod nullo praesente perpetratum est, et quod dicitur murdrum.

Dictum est supra de homicidio quod palam et pluribus astantibus quandoque perpetratur. Nunc autem dicendum de homicidio quod nullo praesente, nullo sciente, nullo audiente, nullo vidente clam perpetratur, quod dicitur murdrum. Unde imprimis videndum quid sit murdrum, quae causa inventionis, et qualiter quis a murdro excusetur. Murdrum vero est occulta extraneorum et notorum hominum occisio a manu hominum nequiter perpetrata, et quae nullo sciente vel vidente facta est praeter solum interfectorem et suos coadiutores et fautores, et ita quod non statim assequatur clamor popularis. Occulta dicitur quia occisor ignoratur, nec scitur quis ille fuerit qui occidit. Item extraneorum et notorum hominum, ut comprehendatis tam masculum quam feminam, et sic excludatis animalia bruta quae ratione carent.

he ought to pronounce it void.*]* *[*Some so outlawed according to the law of the land are more readily admitted to the peace [than others], *[*according as there was a true cause, or none, or an insufficient cause*]*, as where he alleged to be slain is produced alive and well, [or] if the deed was not criminal, or occurs by misadventure. If the deed is criminal and amounts to a felony, they ought not to be taken back into the peace lest easy forgiveness furnish others with excuse for or temerity in offending*]*. he answer all who wish to proceed against him. Let the lord king's letters patent testifying that he has granted him his peace be drawn in this form:

**A writ addressed to all bailiffs to the effect that the lord king pardons a fight and outlawry occurring in his reign. Another writ: that the king pardons, as far as it lies in his power, an outlawry made in the time of his father. [A writ to the effect] that the king pardons an outlawry because the appeal was made when the appellee had been appealed in another county of the same robbery. The king remits the outlawry. Where one has been falsely indicted before the justices and has afterwards surrendered himself to the king's prison; the king remits the outlawry. Where he who was said to be slain returns alive and well. A writ where one said to be slain returns alive and well. Of inlawry and to what an inlaw may be restored. Before inlawry the cause for which he was outlawed must first be considered, that he may be admitted more readily to the peace according to the cause of the outlawry. Where there is no cause at all. A man is restored to nothing but the peace. A man lawfully and properly outlawed is restored to nothing but the peace so that he may come and go and have peace; he cannot be restored to his actions nor to other things because he is as it were a child newly born and a man newly created. What a felon may forfeit. They are restored to the law, especially in criminal matters, that they may answer others, but others need not answer them.**

**In civil matters they [are to answer] others. The king pardons them his suit without prejudice to others. If one wishes to sue against him when he has been inlawed, he must proceed against him by words of appeal. Where the eldest of several sons commits felony in his father's lifetime and is outlawed in his father's lifetime.**

Extraneorum dico quia sive interfector cognitus fuerit vel incognitus, dicitur Francigena nisi Englescheria, id est quod Anglicus sit, probetur per parentes et coram iustitiariis praesentetur.

**Quae causa inventionis murdrorum.**

Causa vero inventionis murdrorum talis fuit: quod in diebus Knuti regis Danaorum qui post Angliam adquisitam et pacificatam rogatu baronum Anglorum remisit ad Daciam exercitum suum, et ipsi barones Angliae erga ipsum regem Knutum fideiussores extiterunt, quod quotquot rex in Anglia secum retineret firmam pacem per omnia haberent, ita quod si quis Anglorum aliquem hominum quos rex secum adduxit interficeret, si se super hoc defendere non posset iudicio dei, scilicet aqua vel ferro, fieret de eo iustitia. Si autem aufugeret et capi non posset, solverentur pro eo sex et sexaginta marcae, et colligebantur in villa ubi quis esset interfectus, et ideo quia interfectorem non habuerunt: et si in tali villa pro paupertate colligi non possent, colligerentur in hundredo in thesauro regis deponendae.

**Quid dicitur murdrum.**

Et dicitur murdrum extraneorum occisio et notorum, quia sive notus sit vel extraneus, ille qui interfectus est semper reputabitur Francigena nisi Englescheria rite fuerit coram iustitiariis praesentata, per quod fieri possit quod Anglicus extiterit. Et qualiter Englescheria praesentari debeat infra dicetur plenius suo loco. Item a manu hominum dicitur ad differentiam eorum qui a bestiis et animalibus quae ratione carent occiduntur vel devorantur, et qui non possunt dici murdriti in felonia, quia animalia quae ratione carent non possunt dici murdriti in felonia, quia animalia quae ratione carent non possunt dici fecisse iniuriam neque feloniam. Vel hoc dici poterit ad differentiam eorum qui mortui sunt per infortunium, sicut de submersis et oppressis et huiusmodi per infortunium ubi nulla subest felonia, secundum quod inferius dicetur.

**When an outlaw has been arrested it is unlawful for anyone to slay him unless he resists arrest. The king of his grace may sometimes grant their lives to those restored to the peace.**

### Of homicide committed openly and in the presence of many bystanders; and of homicide committed in the absence of witnesses, which is called murder.

We have spoken above of homicide committed openly and in the presence of many bystanders. Now we must turn to homicide committed in secret, in no one's presence, to no one's knowledge, and in no one's sight or hearing, which is called murder. First we must see what murder is, why it was devised, and how one may be discharged [payment] of a murder-fine. Murder is the secret slaying of man by the hand of man, *[whether those slain are known or strangers]*, *[committed wickedly]*, done out of the sight of and unknown to all except the slayer alone and his accomplices and abettors so that no public hue and cry immediately pursues them, and [where] who the slayer is cannot be ascertained. The word "secret" is used because the slayer is unknown; "of man," so as to include male and female and exclude brute animals lacking reason. I say "of strangers and men who are known" because whether the slain man is known or unknown he is called a Frenchman, unless englishry, that is, that he is an Englishman, is presented before the justices [and] proved by his kinsmen.

### The reason for devising murder-fines

The reason for the devising of murder-fines was this: in the days of Cnut, king of the Danes, when at the prayer of the English barons he sent his army back to Denmark after he had conquered and pacified England, the barons of England offered themselves as sureties to the said King Cnut that, whatever the force the king kept with him in England they would

**Qualiter patria excusatur a murdro. Si interfector captus fuerit nullum erit murdrum. Si mortui fuerint per infortunium. Item si in mari vel eius ripa. Si mortuus ignoretur licet Anglicus, murdrum erit.**

### Qualiter debeat murdrum praesentari secundum consuetudinem diversorum comitatuum. In quibus vero comitatibus praesentatur sic.

Et sciendum quod statim in ipsa inquisitione et coram coronatoribus, sed diversimode secundum diversas consuetudines comitatuum. In quibusdam vero comitatibus praesentatur Englescheria, sive mortuus fuerit masculus vel femina, per duos masculos ex parte patris et per duas feminas <In quibusdam vero comitatibus praesentatur per unum masculum ex parte patris et per unam feminam ex parte matris. Item in quibusdam comitatibus secundum quosdam, si masculus inveniatur interfectus, praesentatur Englescheria per unum masculum ex parte patris et per unum masculum ex parte matris. <Vel ex parte patris tantum vel ex parte matris tantum.> Et si femina modo praedicto per duas feminas. Quorum quidem nomina irrotulari debent in rotulis coronatorum coram iustitiariis in itinere suo praesentanda, et ubi mutari non possunt personae nec nomina nec variari, quod si contra factum fuerit nulla erit Englescheria cum sit minus rite facta. Et ideo dabitur murdrum. Et ideo sic praesentatur ut sciri possit utrum interfectus Anglicus fuerit vel Francigena.

**Pro Anglico vero et de quo constare possit quod Anglicus sit, non praesentatur Englescheria. Si autem dubium fuerit utrum Anglicus et utrum parentes producti eius sint vel non.**

### Si malefactores fugiant ad ecclesiam, qualiter debeant regnum abiurare si cognoscant latrocinium et feloniam.

Sunt etiam quidam qui cum capi deberent fugiunt ad ecclesiam vel ad alium locum religiosum vel privilegiatum, et se tenent in ecclesia: et quo casu nihil medium, nisi quod veniant ad pacem domini regis ad standum recto si quis versus eos loqui voluerit, vel quod cognoscant maleficium propter quod se tenent in ecclesia, et sic habebit electionem.

make his defense against the charge by the judgment of God, that is, by water or iron, justice would be done upon him. If he fled away and could not be arrested they would pay on his behalf sixty-six marks, to be collected in the vill where he was slain, because the inhabitants did not produce the slayer. And if the marks could not be collected in that vill because of its poverty, they would be collected in the hundred for deposit in the king's treasury.

### What is called murder.

He will always be reputed a Frenchman unless it can be shown that he is English, englishry having been properly presented before the justices. *[*How it ought to be presented will be more fully explained below in its proper place*]*. The words "by the hand of man" are used to distinguish it from the case of those slain or devoured by beasts and animals which lack reason; such persons cannot be said to be murdered feloniously since animals which lack reason cannot be said to commit *injuria* or felony. Or the words may be used to distinguish it from the case of those who have died by misadventure, as those drowned, crushed and the like; by misadventure where there is no concealed felony, as will be explained below.

**How the countryside is discharged of a murder-fine. If the slayer has been arrested there will be no murder-fine. If they have died by misadventure. If the dead man is found in the sea or on the shore. If the slain man is not identified there will be a murder-fine, though he is an Englishman.**

### How englishry ought to be presented according to the custom of divers counties; in some counties it is presented thus:

*[*It is clear that [it ought to be presented] at once, at the taking of the inquest and before the coroners, but in divers ways according to the varied customs of the counties. In some counties, whether the dead is man or woman, it is presented by two males on the father's side and two

Et quo casu si recognito maleficio elegerit regnum abiurare, eligere debet portum aliquem per quem transire possit ad terram aliam extra regnum Angliae, quia non tenetur abiurare terram et potestatem regis praecise sed tantum regnum Angliae. Et computari debent ei rationabiles dictae usque ad portum illum, et debet ei interdici ne exeat regiam viam, nec moram faciat alicubi per duas noctes, nec alicubi divertat, nec multum declinet a via nisi hoc fuerit ex magna necessitate vel hospitandi causa. Sed semper tendat recta via ad portum ita quod ibi sit ad diem sibi datum, et quod transfretabit quam cito navem habuerit et ventum, nisi tempestate fuerit impeditus.. Si autem contra fecerit erit in periculo. Forma autem sacramenti haec est.

### De sacramento qualiter debent regnum abiurare.

Hoc auditis iustitiarii vel O vos coronatores quod exibo a regno Angliae, et illuc iterum non revertar nisi de licentia domini regis vel heredum suorum, sic me deus adiuvet etcetera. Et in sacramento faciendo nulla fiat mentio de aliquo impedimento. Sed quid dicetur si nullum eligere voluerit portum? Quia sine portu et mari exire poterit usque in aliud regnum, tunc non incompetenter dici poterit ubi dictum est quod elegit portum, quod elegit transitum per talem villam via quae ducit versus Scotiam, vel Hiberniam, vel alibi. Sed quod cognoscere debeat maleficium non est semper necesse, quia subicere poterit. Si ad ecclesiam confugerit postquam fuerit per patriam condemnatus, sive ante iudicium sive post, vel si fugerit ad ecclesiam cum captus fuerit seisitus, et in nullo istorum casuum cum ad ecclesiam confugerit morari poterit in ecclesia per quadraginta dies, sicut quidam dicunt, sed statim in adventu iustitiariorum vel coronatorum exire debet et facere legem terrae. Spatium vero quadraginta dierum olim dari solet damnatis per assisam de Clarendona, qui cum exire deberent regnum possent per quadraginta dies moram facere et quaerere subsidia amicorum.

females on the mother's side from among the nearer kinsmen of the slain man, who were described of old as "two long and two broad." In others it is presented by one male on the father's side and one female on the mother's side. In still others, according to some, if a man is found slain englishry is presented by one male on his father's side and one male on his mother's side, <or by one on the father's side or one on the mother's side only>, and if it is a woman who is found, by two females similarly chosen. If it is done in some other way the englishry will be void because improperly presented and a murder-fine will be given. The names of those who presented ought to be entered in the coroners' rolls to be presented before the justices in their eyre, where the persons who presented cannot be changed, nor their names, nor any variance introduced*]*.

**For an Englishman who can be proved to be an Englishman no murder-fine will be given. Where it is doubtful whether he is an Englishman and whether the kinsmen produced are his or not.**

### Where evildoers fly to a church: how they ought to abjure the realm if they confess theft and felony.

There are some who when they ought to be arrested flee to a church or other sacred or privileged place and maintain themselves there. They then have no alternative but to come to the king's peace and stand trial if anyone wishes to proceed against them or to confess the crime because of which they remain there. He will thus have his choice, *[*If after confessing the crime he chooses to abjure the realm, he must select some port from which he can cross to another land, beyond the realm of England, for he is not bound to abjure the land and jurisdiction of the king in those precise terms but only the realm of England. A reasonable number of days' journeys to the said port ought to be reckoned for him and he ought to be forbidden to leave the king's highway, or to make stay in any one place for two nights together, or to turn aside anywhere, or stray far from the highway except because of great necessity or to seek shelter. Let him always keep on the direct road to the port so as to be

### Quod non debet morari in ecclesia per quadraginta dies, et si velit quid tunc agendum sit.

Constitutio quidem talis fuit quod quamvis aliquis se purgaret iudicio aequae vel ignis, hic nihilominus regnum abiuraret, et habuit spatium illud occasione praedicta, quod quidem non est aliis concedendum. Sed quid si ille qui ad ecclesiam confugerit exire noluerit ab ecclesia, numquid poterit per vim extrahi per manum laicalem? Non, ut videtur, quia hoc esset horribile et nefandum. Videtur ergo quod ordinarius loci sicut archidiaconus vel officialis suus, decanus vel persona, hoc facere possent et deberent, scilicet compellere eum exire, quia gladius debet iuvare gladium et iuris executio non habet iniuriam. Et cum talis exire noluerit nisi compulsus, praesumitur vehementer contra ipsum quod malus sit, <cum sit latro publicus maxime>, et defendere eum in ecclesia nihil aliud erit quam facere contra pacem et contra ipsum regem qui pacem tueri debet ad securitatem omnium. Et si talis exire compelli non possit, saltem cum in ecclesia fuerit per unam noctem ad plus, sic poterit se tenere in ecclesia per quadraginta dies et per annum et biennium, si hoc fuerit in voluntate malefactoris. Quid igitur fiet cum ordinarii timeant irregularitatem et laici excommunicationem? Nihil aliud ergo video nisi quod tali denegentur cibaria, ut gratis exeat et petat quod contemptibiliter recusavit, et qui tali super hoc cibaria ministraverit tamquam inimicus regis et praesumptor contra pacem censeatur. Et sic fiat de illis qui debent regnum abiurare et in exilium mitti.

### De divisione exiliorum.

Est enim exilium triplex ad minus, aut certorum locorum interdictio, sicut provinciae alicuius, civitatis, burgi vel villae, imperpetuum vel ad tempus, secundum quod exposcit qualitas delicti secundum quod fuerit maius vel minus. Item est exilium propter crimen et latam culpam, et omnium locorum interdictio imperpetuum, et nisi etcetera. Vel in insulam deportatio imperpetuum vel ad tempus, quod quidem exilium dici poterit abiuratio regni sive utlagatio. Et si quis ita exulatus exilio non

there on the day assigned him, and, provided he is not hindered by a storm, cross as soon as he gets a ship and a wind. If he does anything to the contrary he will be in peril. The form of the oath is this:

### Of the oath: how he ought to abjure the realm.

"Hear this, ye justices (or "O ye coroners"), that I will go forth from the realm of England and hither I will not return save by leave of the lord king or his heirs, so help me God, etc." And in taking the oath let no mention be made of any impediment. But what if he refuses to select a port, for without port and sea he may still depart to another kingdom. It may then, not unfittingly, be said, where it is said that he chooses a port, that he chooses a passage through such a vill, a road which leads toward Scotland or Ireland or elsewhere*]*, but to confess the crime is not always necessary, as where he flies to a church after conviction by the country, or when he has been taken seised of stolen property, before conviction or after. In neither of these cases may he remain in the church for forty days, as some say, but ought to come forth immediately upon the arrival of the justices or the coroners and submit to the law of the land. *[*An interval of forty days used formerly to be given accused persons by the assise of Clarendon, who, when they had to depart from the realm could make stay for forty days and seek assistance from their friends.

### That [a wrongdoer] ought not to stay in a church for forty days, and if he attempts to do so what is then to be done.

The constitution was this, that though one had cleared himself by the judgment of water or fire he should nevertheless abjure the realm, and for so doing he had that period, which is not to be granted to others*]*. But what if he refuses to leave it; may he not be dragged out forcibly by the lay power? No, as is evident, for to do so would be abominable and impious. It seems therefore that the ordinary of the place, the archdeacon or his official, dean or parson, may and ought to do so, that is, compel

obtemperaverit, poena capitali puniatur, hoc est, si post exilium tale sine licentia revertatur.

**De homicidio per infortunium et casuali. De illis qui capti sunt, quod non debent spoliari bonis suis sed debent inde sustentari. Quod de bonis suis sustententur.**

### Qualiter captus produci debeat coram iustitiariis.

Cum autem taliter captus coram iustitiariis producendus fuerit, produci non debet ligatis manibus quamvis aliquando compeditus propter periculum evasionis, et hoc ideo ne videatur coactus ad aliquam purgationem suscipiendam. Cum autem productus fuerit et de crimine ei imposito accusatus, si crimen statim confiteatur satis planum erit iudicium.

### Si sit aliquis eum appellet.

Si autem negaverit et crimen defenderit praecise, et sit aliquis qui eum appellet per verba legitima appellum facientia, tunc autem defendit praecise omnia quae ei imponuntur, et sicut ei imponuntur, et nihil excipit contra appellantem.

### Habet potestatem eligendi quod ponat se super patriam, vel se defendat per corpus suum.

Habebit electionem utrum se velit ponere super patriam, utrum culpabilis sit de crimine ei imposito vel non, vel defendendi se per corpus suum. Si autem patriam elegerit ad defensionem per corpus suum ex paenitentia reverti non poterit, sed per patriam negotium terminabitur, nec e contrario. Si autem per corpus suum intret in defensionem nihil excipiendo, statim vadietur inter eos duellum, si omni rite concurrant et principalia maxime appellum facientia et quae iungunt duellum. Et si forte appellatus hoc omiserit iustitiarius ex officio suo debet omnia examinare.

him to come out, for sword ought to aid sword, nor does the execution of the law constitute a wrong. Since he has refused to come out unless compelled there is a strong presumption as to his guilt <especially if he is a known thief> and to protect him in the church (at least after he has been there for one night or more) will be to act contrary to the peace and the king himself, who ought to safeguard the peace for the security of all. And if he cannot be compelled to come out he may then keep himself there for forty days or for a year or two, [and] if this is what the wrongdoer intends what shall then be done, since ordinaries fear the charge of irregularity and laymen excommunication? I see no remedy except that food be denied him, that he may come forth voluntarily and seek what he has scornfully refused, and that he who supplies food to him be deemed the king's enemy and one contemptuous of the peace. And let the same be done with respect to those who ought to abjure the realm and be sent into exile.

### Of the kinds of exile.

Exile is of at least three kinds: either exclusion from certain places, as from a certain region, a city, borough, or vill, forever or for a time, as the character of the offense demands, according as it is serious or slight, [or] exile for crime and *lata fuga* [*Digest* 48.22.5, imposed banishment], as exclusion from all places except [a certain place] forever, or deportation to an island, forever or for a time, which may be termed abjuration of the realm or outlawry. If one so exiled has not complied with the exile he is punished by capital punishment, that is, if he returns without license after being so exiled.

**Of homicide through misadventure and accident. Of those who are arrested; that they ought not to be despoiled of their goods but receive sustenance therefrom. That they may be sustained out of their goods.**

### Quod in duello iungendo iustitiarius debet omnia diligenter examinare.

Imprimis factum et causam appelli, et si factum et causa sufficient, tunc imprimis examinare debet sectam si bene facta fuerit, et quod nulla sit variatio, ut si appellans unum dixerit in comitatu et coram coronatoribus et aliud modo dicat coram iustitiariis. Non enim admittitur hic variatio, secundum quod inferius dicetur plenius. Si autem omnia bene concurrant quae iungant duellum, tunc det appellatus vadium defendendi et appellator vadium disrationandi.

### Vadiatio duelli, et si appellatus victus fuerit vel appellans.

Et si appellatus victus fuerit, capitalem subibit sententiam cum exheredatione et omnium bonorum suorum amissione, et sicut esse debet in quolibet genere feloniae. Si autem appellans victus fuerit, gaolae committatur tamquam calumniator puniendus, sed nec vitam amittit neque membra, licet secundum leges ad talionem teneretur si in probatione deficeret, et appellatus quietus recederet de appello illo, nisi forte iustitiarii pro aliqua alia suspicione vel recto duxerint ulterius retinendum. Quod aliquando faciunt ex cause sicut contigit aliquando de Roberto Brodegha in comitatu Berkeriae coram M. de Pateshilla. Et haec vera sunt quod appellatus per corpus suum se defendere poterit cum appellatus fuerit, nisi aliqua violenta praesumptio faciat contra ipsum.

### In casu non est necesse probare per corpus neque per patriam, ubi praesumptio violenta facit contra appellatum.

Quae probationem non admittat in contrarium per quam dedicere vel defendere possit mortem et feloniam, sicut esse potest cum quis captus fuerit super mortuum cum cultello cruentato, mortem dedicere non poterit. Et haec est constitutio antiqua, in quo casu non est opus alia probatione. Item si quis iacuerit in domo aliqua de nocte solus cum alio qui fuerit interfectus, vel si duo ibi fuerint vel plures et huthesium non levaverint,

### How an arrested man ought to be brought before the justices.

When the person thus arrested is to be brought before the justices he ought not to be brought with his hands tied (though sometimes in leg-irons because of the danger of escape) lest he may seem constrained to submit to any form of trial. When he is brought and accused of the crime alleged against him, if he confesses it at once, the judgment will be evident enough.

### When there is one [who] appeals him.

If he enters a denial and denies the crime, and there is someone who appeals him by words lawfully constituting an appeal, he either denies everything charged against him absolutely, just as it is charged against him, raising no exception against the appellor, [or he does not. If he denies everything absolutely].

### He has the power of choosing whether to place himself on a jury or defend himself by his body.

He will have the choice of putting himself on the country,[1] as to whether or not he is guilty of the crime alleged against him, or of defending himself by his body. If he elects the country he cannot then repent and revert to defending himself by his body but the matter will be determined by the country. Nor may he act conversely. If he enters upon his defense by his body, raising no exception, let the judicial combat be waged between them at once if everything is in proper order, especially the principal matters on which the appeal is founded and which lead to joinder of the duel. If the appellee has omitted to make sure of these the justice ought to investigate them *ex officio.*

1 The word used, *patria*, does not refer to the nation state, but to the district or region. Note how Thorne translates *per patriam* as "on a jury" in the heading.

nec plagam a latronibus vel aliis qui interfecerint in defensione facienda non receperint, vel nec quis hominem interfecerit ostenderint de se vel de aliis, mortem dedicere non poterunt, ut de termino Sancti Michaelis anno regis Henrici nono incipiente decimo comitatu Cantiae, de Ada de Burgham. Eodem modo fere dici poterit ut videtur, ut si quis in domum suam notum vel ignotum receperit hospitandi causa vel alia, et qui sanus et vivus visus fuit intrare, et numquam postea nisi mortuus, dominus domus, si tunc domi fuerit, vel alii de familia qui tunc praesentes fuerint, poenam capitalem non evadent, nisi forte per patriam fuerint liberati si iustitiarii perspexerint veritatem per pattriam debere inquiri.

**Ne quis extraneum hospitetur nisi de clara die. De quibus loqui debeat appellans in appello suo. A. appelat B. per talia verba de morte fratris sui, et si ipse defecerit, tunc per talem, et ita quod sint plures de uno et eodem facto. Item possunt plures appellari sicut unus de morte alterius. Verba appelli de morte fratris vel alterius. Item et de forcia. Qualiter debent appellati defendere. Si duellum declinare voluerit per hoc quod transiit aetatem. Si omnia concurrant quae iungunt appellum statim vadietur duellum. Si plures appellaverint unum, sed de diversis factis sicut de diversis plagis.[1] Si ante duellum percussum omnes appellantes mori contingat. Si appellatus victus fuerit de facto, tunc demum procedatur versus alios de forcia et praecepto. Si plures unum appellaverint de morte alicuius de pluribus plagis. Si unus plures appellaverit de diversis plagis mortalibus. Appellatus det vadium defendendi et appellans det vadium disrationandi. Sunt quaedam exceptiones quae generales sunt ad omnia appella et quaedam speciales et diversae, secundum diversitatem placitorum et appellorum.**

1 The translation of this heading is absent in Thorne's translation and the sense of the passage is partially blended into the preceding section.

### That in waging the duel the justice must investigate everything with care.

First of all, the deed and the cause of the appeal. If deed and cause are sufficient he ought then to examine the suit, whether it has been properly made and that there is no variance, as where the appellor has said one thing in the county court and before the coroners and now says another before the justices, for here no variance is allowed, as will be explained more fully below. If everything that leads to the duel is in proper order, let the appellee then give a gage for defending and the appellor for deraigning.

### The wager of the duel: if the appellee or the appellor is vanquished.

If the appellee is vanquished he will suffer capital punishment with disherison and the loss of all his goods, as for a felony of any kind. If the appellor is vanquished let him be committed to gaol to be punished as a false accuser (but he will lose neither life nor members, though according to the laws he would be liable to the talionic[1] penalty if he had failed in his proof) and let the appellee withdraw quit of the appeal, unless the justices cause him to be held because of some other suspicion or charge, which they sometimes do if there is reason for it, as happened [in the case] of Robert Brodegha in the county of Berkshire before Martin of Pateshull. That the appellee may defend himself by his body [or by the country] when he is appealed is true unless some strong presumption of guilt lies against him.

1 Lawfully authorized retaliation in which the punishment corresponds to the injury in kind and degree.

### Prima exceptio et generalis in omni appello de secta, si bene et secundum legem terrae facta sit.

Est quidem ista generalis exceptio et prima in omni appello, scilicet si secta non fuerit bene facta, quia qui appellare voluerit et bene sequi, debet ille cui iniuriatum erit statim quam cito poterit huthesium levare, et cum huthesio ire ad villas vicinas et propinquiores, et ibi manifestare scelera et iniurias perpetratas. Et continuo accedere debet ad servientes domini regis si inveniri possint, et deinde ad coronatores, et sic inde sine intervallo ad proximum comitatum, vel si in crastino feloniae perpetratae vel secundo die teneatur comitatus, sufficit pro secta, dum tamen praecesserit huthesium, si ad comitatum venerit, servientibus et coronatoribus non quaesitis, quia die comitatus tenentur omnes adesse. Item sufficit pro secta si continuo ostendantur regi vel iustitiariis si praesentes fuerint, scelera perpetrata, et ibi dicetur ei quod eat ad vicecomitem et coronatores. Ad proximum vero et primum comitatum in praesentia vicecomitis et coronatorum fiat appellum per verba appellum facientia, et inferius dicenda. Et ipsi vicecomes et coronatores omnia verba appelli, secundum quod proposita fuerint coram eis, [irrotulari faciant] per ordinem et modum appelli, illud scilicet tantummodo nec plus nec minus. Et imprimis ad quem comitatum venit appellans post feloniam perpetratam, utrum scilicet ad primum, secundum vel tertium, et qualiter et quae verba proposuit in appello de morte hominis. Item si de pace et plagis, quales plagae fuerunt, recentes vel non recentes, in quo loco, cuius longitudinis et latitudinis. Item si de roberia, de quibus rebus, propriis vel alienis. Et si de pecunia numerata, exprimere debet numerum et genus pecuniae. Si autem massa rudis, exprimere debet valorem. Si autem formata, qualitatem et pretium. Item si vestis, colorem et pretium. Si pannis, colorem, pretium, et numerum ulnarum. Item si animal, tunc genus, pilum et pretium. Item si de pace et imprisonamento, tunc inquirendum quale fuerit imprisonamentum, utrum carcer vel simplex detentio.

### Occasionally neither proof by judicial combat nor the country is necessary: where an overwhelming presumption lies against the appellee.

In some cases neither by his body nor the country, where a strong presumption lies against the appellee which does not admit of proof to the contrary, proof by which he may repudiate or deny the death and the felony, as when he is arrested over the body of the dead man with his knife dripping blood; he cannot deny the death nor is further proof necessary. This is an ancient constitution. Other proof is not necessary. [If one lies a night in a house with another who is slain, or if two or more do so and have not raised the hue nor received a wound in defending themselves from the thieves or others who did the slaying, and are unable to show who slew the man, whether one of themselves or others, they cannot deny responsibility for the death, as [in the roll] of Michaelmas term in the ninth and the beginning of the tenth years of king Henry in the county of Kent, [the case] of Adam de la Burgh.] if one has received a known man or a stranger into his house, as a guest or for some other reason, who was seen to go in alive and well and never seen afterwards except as a corpse; the owner of the house, if he was there at the time, or others of his household who were then present, will not escape capital punishment, unless they are acquitted by the country, if the justices come to the conclusion that the truth ought to be investigated by the country. But since the country cannot learn the truth of so secret an act, how will he who has put himself on the country be acquitted? In truth it gives an adequate acquittal since it does not expressly condemn, as may be said of a charter which acquits since it does not burden specifically.

**No one is to take a stranger into his house except in broad daylight. The things of which an appellor ought to speak in his appeal. A. appeals B. by such words for the death of his brother, and, should he fail, by such a one, and so on, so that there are several appealing him of one and the same deed. Several may be appealed of another's death just as one may**

Item utrum in vinculis vel sine. Item utrum in ferro, vel lingno vel in utroque. Item si de combustione, qua hora facta fuit et de omnibus cicumstantiis. Item si de raptu, tunc de scissione vestimentorum et de sanguinis effusione per corruptionem. Item oportet mentionem facere in irrotulatione appelli de anno quo felonia debuit perpetrari, quia ex hoc dabitur appellato exceptio si in rotulis coronatorum aliter contineatur de anno et aliter coram iustitiariis in narratione. Ut si in rotulis coronatorum fiat mentio de decem annis et in narratione coram iustitiariis fiat mentio de quinque, per hoc cadit appellum propter variationem. Item fit mentio de die ad quod eadem ratio poterit assignari et etiam alia, quia si appellatus docere poterit per certa indicia per proborum hominum testificationem se ea die fuisse alibi, ita quod nullo modo praesumi posset contra ipsum quod interesse posset tali facto ea die propter locum ita remotum, quod hoc esset impossibile, tunc cadit intentio appellantis. Item fit mentio aliquando de hora, sed hoc non est multum de substantia negotii, licet variatum sit de hora, quia appellans in arto positus bene potuit horam ignorare, cum metus in se iustam contineat ignorantiam, et si variatum sit de hora ad hoc quod detur exceptio vel non, discretioni iustitiariorum relinquatur. Item fit mentio de loco praedicta ratione propter variationem. Item de comitatu fit mentio, sed non propter variationem, quia licet inter vicecomitem et coronatores de comitatu habeatur contentio, ex hoc non praeiudicatur appellanti nec appellato. Sed si appellans ad primum comitatum non venerit per se, cum commode venire possit, vel per aliam coniunctam personam cum per se venire non possit, tunc sibi praeiudicat quantum ad appellum et ad exceptionem appellato, sicut in casibus supradictis. Et si ita variatum fuerit in appello et in narratione, quod appellans unum dicat et rotuli coronatorum protestentur contrarium vel diversum, ut si appellans unum nominaverit in appello suo coram iustitiariis et rotuli coronatorum dicant quod alium, vel si ibi unum de facto et coram iustitiariis eundem de forcia, vel e contrario.

**be. The words of the appeal for the death of a brother or another. The appeal against an accessory. How those appealed ought to make their defense. Where he wishes to avoid the duel on the ground that he is over age. Where all the elements of the appeal are in order let the duel be waged at once. If all the appellors die before the duel is fought. If the person appealed as principal is vanquished let proceedings then first be taken against accessories and instigators. Where several appeal one for a death resulting from several wounds. Where one has appealed several of different mortal wounds. Let the appellee give gage for defending and the appellor for deraigning. Some exceptions are common to all appeals; some are special and vary according to the different kinds of pleas and appeals.**

### THE FIRST EXCEPTION AND A GENERAL ONE IN EVERY APPEAL OF A SUIT, WHETHER IT WAS WELL MADE AND ACCORDING TO THE LAW OF THE LAND.

There is this general exception, the first in every appeal, that suit has not been properly made, for he who wishes to appeal ought to sue properly. He to whom an *injuria* has been done ought to raise the hue at once, as soon as he can, and go with it to the neighboring and nearer vills and there make known the wicked and wrongful acts that have been done. He ought next to go to the king's serjeants, if they can be found, and then to the coroners, and thence without delay to the next county court, [if it is held on the first or second day after the felony committed his suit is sufficient (provided he has raised the hue) if he comes to the county court without seeking out the serjeants and coroners, because they are all bound to be there on the day of the county court. It suffices for suit if the evil deeds committed are immediately shown to the king or to the justices if they are present, and there he will be told to go to the sheriff and coroners]. The first, [where], in the presence of the sheriff and coroners let him make his appeal by words constituting an appeal, as will be explained below. And let the sheriff and coroners cause all the words of the appeal, just as they are pronounced before them, to be enrolled in

Item si in genere armorum variatum sit, quod ibi de baculo et hic de gladio, et generaliter qualitercumque variatum fuerit cadit appellum per exceptionem.

**Si de recordo inter iustitiarios contentio habeatur, tunc quid agendum sit. Non potest quis in appello suo variare nec appellum mutare. Poterit adicere et accrescere appellum et non minuere. Contra appellum poterit excipere appellatus. Exceptiones contra appellum. Exceptiones quod appellum non iacet. Si appellans se retraxerit: aliud est si defaltam fecerit. Cun nulla sit exceptio, tunc statim vadiatur duellum.**

### Forma sacramenti talis est.

Hoc audis homo quem per manum teneo qui te facis appellari A. per nomen baptisterii, quod ego patrem tuum vel fratrem vel alium talem non occidi, nec plagam ei feci tali genere armorum per quod remotior esse deberet a vita et morti propinquior, nec tu hoc vidisti, sic me deus adiuvet et haec sancta.

order, and the form of the appeal, that is, only this, neither more nor less: first, to which county court the appellor came after the felony committed, that is, to the first, the second or third, and, in an appeal of homicide, how and in what words he propounded it. If it is an appeal of breach of the peace and wounding, what kind of wounds they were, fresh or old, and in what part of the body and of what length and depth. If the appeal is one of robbery, of what goods, and whether his own or another's. If of coined money, he must state the number and kind of coins; if of bullion, its value, and if of wrought metal, its nature and value; if of clothes, their colour and value; if of cloth, the color, value and number of ells; if of an animal, then the kind, the garment, and the value. If it is an appeal of breach of the peace and imprisonment, inquiry must then be made into what kind of imprisonment, whether prison or mere detention, and whether in fetters or without, in irons or in stocks or both. It it is an appeal of arson, when it occurred and all the circumstances. If an appeal of rape, then whether robes were torn and whether blood was shed by the ravishment. In enrolling the appeal mention must be made of the year in which the felony was supposed to be committed, because the appellee will thereby be furnished an exception should the coroners' rolls refer to one year and the count before the justices to another, as where ten years are mentioned in the coroners' rolls and five in the count before the justices; the appeal falls because of the variance. Mention is made of the day for the same reason, and also for another, for if the appellee can show by sure proofs, by the testimony of responsible men, that he was elsewhere on that day, so that the presumption that he could have been present at the commission of the act on that day cannot rise against him, because the remoteness of the place makes that impossible, the appellor's *intentio* then falls. Mention sometimes is made of the hour, but though there is a variance as to the hour that does not touch the substance of the action, because an appellor, finding himself in a tight corner, might well not know the hour, since fear provides an excuse for his lack of knowledge; if there is a variance as to the hour, whether an exception

### Sacramentum faciendum in campo.

Hoc auditis iustitiarii quod ego non comedi neque bibi nec aliquis pro me nec per me, propter quod lex dei depirimi debeat et lex diaboli exaltari, sic me deus etcetera.

### Fiat bannus regis.

Et facto tali modo sacramento statim fiat bannus regis sub voce praeconia, et facto silentio per haec verba: Praeceptum regis et iustitiariorum est quod nullus sit ita ausus vel audax quod quidquid audiat vel videat se moveat vel verbis proferat, et si quis contra hoc fecerit, captus erit et positus in prisonam, et ibi iacebit per annum et diem usque dominus rex de eo praeceperit voluntatem suam. His igitur taliter peractis congrediantur campiones et pugnent. Et si appellans victus fuerit, vel si appellatus se defenderit contra ipsum tota die usque ad horam qua stellae incipiunt apparere, tunc recedet appellatus quietus de appello ex quo se obligavit appellans ad convincendum eum una hora diei, quod quidem non fecit.

may be raised or not is left to the discretion of the justices. Mention is also made of the place, for the reason aforesaid, because of the variance. The county court is also mentioned, not because of the variance, for though there is disagreement between the sheriff and the coroners as to the county court that prejudices neither appellor nor appellee, but [because] if the appellor has not come to the first county court, in person when he could do so without difficulty, or if unable to come himself, by another, a kinsman, he then prejudices himself with respect to his appeal and gives an exception to the appellee, as in the cases aforesaid. [And so] if there is a variance between the appeal and the count, so that the appellor says one thing and the coroners' rolls bear witness to the contrary or to something different, as where the appellor names one person in his appeal before the justices and the coroners' rolls indicate that he named another, or if he there named a man as principal and before the justices names him as accessory, or conversely, [or] if there is a variance as to the kind of weapons so that there he spoke of a club and here of a sword. Speaking generally, no matter what the variance the appeal falls by an exception.

**If there is disagreement as to the record [before] the justices, what is then to be done. One cannot vary his appeal or change it. He may add to it and increase it but not reduce it. The appellee may except against the appeal. Exceptions against the appeal. Exceptions: that an appeal does not lie [i.e. pertain or apply]. Where the appellor has retracted his appeal; if he has made default it is otherwise. Where there is no exception let the judicial combat be waged at once.**

### The form of the oath is as follows:

"Hear this, O man, whom I hold by the hand, who call yourself A. by the name of your baptism, that I did not slay your father (or your brother or some other, such a one) nor did I deal him the wound with a weapon of such a kind by which he is alleged to be farther from life and nearer to

Et non solum quietus dimittetur appellatus de facto, immo omnes alii qui appellati sunt de forcia et praecepto, nec ipse appellatus de facto solummodo quietus recedet versus ipsum primum appellantem, verum etiam versus omnes appellantes qui ipsum appellaverint de eodem facto, secus si de diversis.

### Si appellatus victus fuerit.

Si autem appellatus victus fuerit, ultimo punietur supplicio cum poena gravi vel graviori secundum criminis qualitatem, cum exheredatione heredum suorum et omnium bonorum amissione, secundum quod supra dictum est de utlagatis. Si autem plures unum appellaverint, vel plures de diversis plagis et factis, si appellatus se defenderit versus unum, procedant alii appellantes versus eundem modo supradicto quousque omnes de facto convicti fuerint, et tunc deinde procedatur contra ipsos de forcia et praecepto de eodem facto, quia factum et praeceptum ita connexa sunt quod separari non possunt.

**Si appellans in campo se retraxerit. Cum omnes de facto victi fuerint, tunc procedatur contra eos de forcia. Sacramentum faciendum ab appellante.**

### Si primo appellans de facto mortuus fuerit vel defaltam fecerit.

Si autem ille qui primo appellaverit de facto mortuus fuerit, vel defaltam fecerit, vel praesens se retraxerit, vel cum sequi velit appellatus per exceptionem appellum declinaverit, nihilominus tamen subesse poterit felonia, quae si non convincatur ita remanebunt maleficia impunita, quod esse non debet. Et quoniam non solum iniuriatur ei qui occiditur, immo domino regi cuius pax infringitur, et quia adhuc subesse poterit felonia, quamvis appellatus appellum declinaverit nec adhuc defensus erit de felonia, sed semper stabit praesumptio propter appellum donec probetur contrarium, nec remanere debent maleficia impunita.

death, nor did you see it, so help me God and these holy relics." And in his oath let him make mention of the year, the day and the place in accordance with the terms of the appeal. And afterwards let the appellor swear to the contrary in these words: "Hear this, O man, whom I hold by the hand, who call yourself B. by the name of your baptism, that you are a perjurer, and for this reason, because in such a year and on such a day and hour and in such a place you slew C., my father (or brother or some other of his kinsmen, or his lord) wickedly and feloniously (or in another way: wickedly and feloniously and in premeditated assault you dealt such a one a wound, at such a place, with a weapon of such a kind, of which he died within three days.) And this I saw, so help me God, etc." Thus let the oath always be taken in accordance with the terms of the appeal, a rule to be observed in every kind of oath whenever an oath is to be taken on both sides.

**The oath having been taken by both parties, let the defender be at once committed to two knights.**

### The oath to be taken on the field.

"Hear this, ye justices, that I have neither eaten nor drunk, nor [caused anything to be done] for me or by me by which God's law may be abased and the devil's exalted, so help me God, etc."

### Let the king's ban be proclaimed.

When the oath has been taken in this way and silence obtained, let the king's ban be proclaimed at once by the herald's voice in these words: "It is the command of the king and of his justices that none be so hardy or rash as to move or utter a word no matter what he may see or hear; if anyone acts to the contrary he shall be arrested and put in prison, to lie there for a year and a day until the lord king has expressed his will concerning him." These things having been accomplished, let the champions engage and fight. If the appellor is vanquished or if the appellee defends himself against him the whole day long, until the hour

### Rex potest procedere ex officio suo.

Procedat igitur rex ex officio et pro pace sua ad inquisitionem propter praesumptionem appelli, ac si appellatus sine appello esset legitime indictatus, et quod ad regem pertineat accusatio et secta pro pace sua. Videtur et quod appellatus non solum tenetur appellanti, immo domino regi, sicut videre poterit per verba appelli, ut si dicatur, talis appellat talem quod nequiter et in felonia et contra pacem domini regis etcetera, per quod videri poterit manifeste quod appellatus non solum tenetur appellanti, immo domino regi. Et quo casu cum se defendere obtulerit per corpus, non audietur, quia rex non pugnat, nec alium habet campionem quam patriam, nec si esset qui diceret quod pugnare deberet duello caderet, ex quo sectam non fecit, nec loqui potest de visu et auditu. Recurrendum est igitur de necessitate ad patriam ut videtur, quam quidem si inculpatus recusaverit videtur quod sit indefensus, et per hoc quasi convictus, et quod cogendus sit videtur propter defectum alterius probationis. Ut si femina appellum fecerit de morte viri sui, non tenetur duellum facere propter sexum. Cogendus est igitur appellatus quod se defendat per patriam, quia cadit duellum propter sexum femineum, et ita fit in appello de raptu virginum.

**Item defenditur quis ab appello propter mahemium. Si mulier per vim oppressa. De indictatis per famam patriae ex suspicione. Diligenter inquirendum a quibus didicerint id quod dicunt quia quidam mentiuntur per odium, quidam propter cupiditatem. Debet a iustitiariis dici ei qui suspectus habetur, quod omnes a iurata amoveat quos aliqua sufficienti ratione suspectos habuerit.**

that the stars begin to appear, the appellee will then depart quit of the appeal, since the appellor undertook to conquer him that day and has not done so. And not only will he appealed as principal be discharged, but all those appealed as accessories and instigators; and not only will he appealed as principal depart quit against this first appellor, but against all appellors who have appealed him of the same deed. It is otherwise if they have appealed him of different deeds.

### If the appellee is vanquished.

[If the appellee has been vanquished he shall suffer capital punishment, with severe or more severe torture according to the seriousness of the crime, with the disherison of his heirs and the loss of all his goods, as was said above [in the portion] on outlaws.] [for there] if the appellee successfully makes his defense against one, let the other appellors proceed against him in the manner described above until he is convicted of one deed; then let him proceed against the accessories and instigators of that same deed, because deed and instigation are so linked together that they cannot be separated.

**If the appellor retracts on the field. When all the principals have been vanquished, let proceedings then be taken against accessories. The oath to be taken by the appellor.**

### If the first appellor against the principal dies or defaults.

If he who has first appealed the principal dies or defaults, or being present retracts his appeal, or though he wishes to prosecute the appellee avoids the appeal by an exception, the felony may nonetheless exist, and if it is not convicted wicked deeds will thus remain unpunished, which ought not to be, [It may still exist because, though the appellee has avoided the appeal, he has not as yet disproved it, and the presumption raised by the appeal will always stand until the contrary is proved.] and since a wrong is done not only to him who is slain but to the lord king whose peace is broken, therefore, lest evil deeds remain unpunished.

### Debet a iustitiariis dici ei qui suspectus habetur, quod omnes a iurata amoveat quos aliqua sufficienti ratione suspectos habuerit.

Cum igitur procedendum sit de huiusmodi ad inquisitionem, ut ad iudicium securius procedatur et ut periculum et suspicio tollatur, iustitiarius dicat indictato quod si aliquem ex duodecim iuratoribus suspectum habeat, illum iusta ratione amoveat. Et illud idem dicatur de villatis, ut si capitales inimicitiae fuerint inter aliquos ipsorum et indictatum, vel si ob cupiditatem terrae suae habendae, ut praedictum est, qui omnes ex iusta suspicione amovendi sunt, ut inquisitio absque omni suspicione procedat.

**Quod villatae iurabunt per se vel omnes simul erectis manibus. Forma sacramento haec est. Verba quae a iustitiariis proponenda sunt post sacramentum factum. Generalis forma observanda in sacramentis coram iustitiariis faciendis. De pace et plagis factis contra pacem. Verba appelli. B. venit et defendit. Duellum: et B. det vadium defendendi et A. disrationandi. Vicecomes cum coronatoribus testatur. Declinatur quandoque huiusmodi appellum per exceptiones: ideo de exceptionibus.**

### Sed quid dicetur de eo qui virilia abscidit alicuius?

Sed quid dicetur si quis alterius virilia absciderit, et illum cum libidinis causa vel commercii castraverit? Tenetur, sive hoc fecerit volens vel invitus, et sequitur poena, aliquando capitalis, aliquando perpetuum exilium cum omnium bonorum ademptione. Item si quis mulieris visceribus vim intulerit quo partum abegerit, tenetur. Item si quis furem nocturnum occiderit, ita demum impune feret si parcere ei sine periculo suo non potuit. Si autem potuit, aliter erit. In manu enim regis sunt vita et mors hominum.

**The king may proceed ex officio.**

Let the king proceed to an inquest *ex officio* for the preservation of his peace because of the presumption raised by the appeal, as though the appellee had not been appealed but lawfully indicted. That an accusation and suit for breach of his peace belongs to the king is evident, and that the appellee is bound to answer not only the appellor but the lord king may be seen by the words of the appeal, where it is said "such a one appeals such a one for that wickedly and feloniously and against the king's peace, etc.," from which it may clearly be seen that the appellee is bound to answer not only the appellor but the lord king. When the appellee offers to defend himself by his body he will not be heard, because the king does not fight, nor has he any champion other than the country [i.e. the jury], and if one were to say that he ought to fight, the duel would fall, since he has made no suit, nor may he speak of his own sight and hearing. Recourse must thus of necessity be had to the country, [if the accused refuses it he is without defense and thus, so to speak, convicted], to which he is forced because of the lack of other proof, as where a woman sues an appeal on the death of her husband; she is not bound to fight the duel because of her sex and therefore the appellee is compelled to defend himself by the country. The same is true, that the appeal falls because of the feminine sex, in an appeal of rape.

**One is protected from an appeal on account of mayhem. Where a woman is ravished by force. Of those indicated by popular rumor [and] suspicion. Careful inquiry must be made from whom they have learned what they say, for some lie from hatred, some from greed. The justices must inform the man under suspicion that he may remove from the jury all those whom he holds suspect for some sufficient reason.**

<Sicut coram rege apud Wyndesore de quodam homine de Cocham coram Willelmo de Ralegha tunc iustitiario, cui dominus rex in tali casu perdonavit mortem.> Item erit idem si quis hamsoken, quae dicitur invasio domus contra pacem in domo sua se defenderit, et invasor occisus fuerit, impersolutus remanebit si ille quem invasit aliter se defendere non potuit. Dicitur enim quod non est dignus habere pacem qui non vult obsevare eam. Item Iudaeis filios suos circumcidere licet, sed non alterius religionis hominem, quod si fecerit, castrati poena irrogatur.

**Appellum de plagis et mahemio. B. defendit. Iudicandae sunt plagae ut si sit ibi mahemium.**

### Quid dici debeat mahemium.

Mahemium vero dici poterit ubi aliquis in aliqua parte sui corporis effectus sit inutilis ad pugnandum, et maxime per illum quem appellat, ut si ossa extrahantur a capite et scherda magna levetur ut praedictum est. Item si os frangatur, vel pes, vel manus, vel digitus, vel articulus pedis vel manus, vel aliud membrum abscidatur, vel per plagam factam contacti sint nervi et membrum aliquod, vel quod digiti curvi reddantur, vel si oculus effosus fuerit, vel aliud fiat in corpore hominis per quod minus habilis vel utilis reddatur ad se defendendum. Sed quid dicetur de eo qui dentes habet fractos, si fractio dentium iudicari debeat ad mahemium? Ad quod sciendum quod est quoddam mahemium quo quis inutilis efficitur ad pugnandum, de quo supra dictum est.

### Item si deformitas et non mahemium.

Est de aliud quod deformitatem corporis inducit. Et unde refert utrum fracti sint dentes praecisores, molares, sive maxillares, quia si molares sive maxillares, cum latens sit mahemium non multum inducit corporis

### The justices must inform the man under suspicion that he may remove from the jury all those whom he holds suspect for some sufficient reason.

Therefore, when proceedings of this kind have reached the point of an inquest, in order that judgment may be reached with greater certainty and risks and doubts removed, let the justice inform the indicted man that if he suspects any of the twelve jurors he may remove him for just cause, and let the same be said of the [jurors of] the vills, as where there are deadly enmities between some of them and the indicted man, or there is a greedy desire to get his land, as was said above; if there is ground for suspicion, all are to be removed, that the inquiry may proceed free of all doubts.

**That the [jurors of the] townships shall take an oath individually or all together, with hands raised. The form of the oath. The words to be pronounced by the justices after the oath taken. The general form to be observed in taking oaths before the justices. Of the peace and woundings committed in breach of the peace. The words of the appeal. B. Comes and makes denial. The duel: let B. give gage for defending and A. for deraigning. The sheriff testifies with the coroners. An appeal of this kind is sometimes avoided by exceptions: therefore about exceptions.**

### But what is to be said of one who castrates another?

But what is to be said where a man cuts off another's testicles and castrates him on account of debauchery or in order to sell him? He is liable whether he does it with his consent or against his will. Sometimes capital punishment follows, sometimes permanent exile with the forfeiture of all property. If anyone forcibly interferes with a woman's internal organs in order to produce abortion, he is liable. If anyone slays a night thief, he will do so with impunity only if he could not spare him without danger to himself; if he could it will be otherwise. For the life and death of men are in the hands of the king, <as in the case of a certain

deformitatem nec inhabilitatem ad pugnandum. Si autem praecisores, videtur quod ex hoc inducitur utrumque, huiusmodi vero dentes multum coadiuvant ad devincendum. Castratio vero quamvis latens sit, adiudicatur ad mahemium. Sunt et alia genera mahemii pro quibus non remanebit duellum ut videtur, ut si auricula abscidatur vel nasus, hoc enim magis erit ad deformitatem corporis quam ad virium defectum.

**Appellum de pace et imprisonamento. Verba appelli. B. venit et defendit. De exceptionibus contra huiusmodi appellum. In appello isto agi poterit civiliter vel criminaliter, cum adiectione feloniae vel non. De actione criminali sicut de pace et roberia, et de appellis. B. defendit. Ubi quis alium appellat de alterius rebus. De appellis de felonia et pace regis, et de verbis appelli. B. venit et defendit. Appellum de iniqua combustione et roberia. A. appellat B.**

### Appellum de raptu virginum.

Est inter alia appella quoddam appellum quod dicitur de raptu virginum. Et est raptus virginum quoddam crimen quod femina imponit alicui, de quo se dicit esse violenter oppressam contra pacem domini regis, quod quidem crimen si convincatur, sequitur poena, scilicet amissio membrorum, ut sit membrum pro membro, quia virgo cum corrumpitur membrorum amittat, propter aspectum decoris quo virginem concupivit. Amittat etiam testiculos qui calorem stupri induxerunt. Non autem sequitur huiusmodi poena de qualibet femina, licet vi opprimatur. Sequitur tamen alia gravis et gravior, secundum quod fuerit nupta vel vidua honeste vivens, sanctimonialis, vel matrona. Item concubina legitima, vel alia quaestu faciens sine delectu personarum, quas quidem omnes debet rex tueri pro pace sua, sed non erit de qualibet par poena. Olim quidem corruptores virginitatis et castitatis [suspendebantur] et eorum fautores, cum nec tales ab homicidii crimine vacui essent, maxime eum virginitas et castitas restitui non possint. Modernis tamen temporibus aliter observatur, quod pro corruptione virginis amittuntur membra ut praedictum est, et de aliis sequitur gravis poena corporalis, sed tamen sine amissione vitae vel membrorum.

man of Cookham *coram regi*[1] at Windsor before William of Ralegh, then justice, to whom the king granted a pardon for a death in such circumstances.> And so where one defends himself against hamsocn, which [the English call] the entering of a house in breach of the peace, and the intruder is slain, he will be free of liability if he who killed could defend himself in no other way. For it is said that he is unworthy of the peace who is unwilling to preserve it. The Jews are allowed to circumcise their sons but those of other religions are not; if they do so the punishment for castration is imposed.

**An appeal of wounding and mayhem. B. makes denial. Wounding is to be tried if there is [no] mayhem.**

### What ought to be termed mayhem.

It may be said to be mayhem when one is rendered incapable of fighting, especially by him whom he is appealing, as where bones protrude from his head or a large splinter of bone projects, as was said [or] a bone is broken in some part of his body, or a foot or hand, or part of a foot or hand, or a finger or other member is cut off, or where sinews and limbs are crippled by the wound dealt, or fingers have become crooked, or an eye has been gouged out, or some other thing done to a man's body whereby he is rendered less able and effective in defending himself. But what shall be said of him who has his teeth broken? Ought the breaking of teeth to be deemed mayhem? The answer is that there is one kind of mayhem by which a man is rendered incapable of fighting, of which we have spoken above.

### Where there is disfigurement and not mayhem.

And another that results in disfigurement of the body. Hence we must see whether the teeth broken are incisors, molars or grinders, for if molars or grinders the mayhem, since it is hidden, causes no great disfigurement of

1 Literally "in the king's presence," but later used also as a synonym for the royal court known as King's Bench.

Et cum virgines et viduae necnon sanctimoniales deo sint dedicatae, corruptio earum non solum ad iniuriam hominum, verum etiam ad ipsius dei omnipotentis irreverentiam committitur, et sine vindicta talis non quiescat infamia. Cum igitur virgo sic corrupta fuerit et oppressa contra pacem domini regis, statim et dum factum recens fuerit, cum clamore et huthesio accedere debet ad villas vicinas et ibi iniuriam sibi illatam probis hominibus ostendere, sanguinem et vestes suas sanguine tinctas, et vestium scissiones. Et sic ire debet ad praepositum hundredi, et ad servientem domini regis et ad coronatores et ad vicecomitem. Et ad primum comitatum faciet appellum suum, nisi ita sit quod immediate statim faciat querelam suam domino regi vel iustitiariis suis, ubi dicetur ei quod sequatur ad comitatum. Et in rotulis coronatorum irrotuletur appellum suum et omni verba appelli, secundum quod illud proposuerit per ordinem, et annus et dies quibus fecerit appellum suum. Et dabitur dies in adventu iustitiariorum, ad quem iterum proponat eoram eis appellum suum per eadem verba quibus proposuit in comitatu, et a quibus recedere non licet, ne cadat appellum propter variationem, sicut in aliis appellis. Et cautela est in appello isto et in aliis appellis, quod primo audiatur appellum ab appellante et postea irrotulatio coronatorum, qualiter appellum illud factum fuit in comitatum, et hoc ideo ne si rotuli coronatorum prius legerentur, posset appellans per illos suum formare appellum. Verba autem appelli sunt haec.

the body nor any inability to fight. But if the incisors are broken it seems that both are consequent thereon, for such teeth are of great assistance in winning a fight. Castration, though it is hidden, is deemed mayhem. There are also other kinds of mayhem for which, as is evident, the judicial combat will not remain[1], as where an ear or nose is cut off, for this will be disfigurement of the body rather than diminishment of strength.

**The appeal of breach of the peace and imprisonment. The words of the appeal. B. comes and makes denial. Of the exceptions against an appeal of this kind. This appeal may be sued civilly or criminally, with or without the assignment of felony, [and] depending on the words of the appeal a [corporal] punishment, or [a pecuniary penalty] according to the seriousness of the offense follows. Of the criminal action of breach of the peace and robbery, and of appeals. B. makes his denial. Where one appeals another of a third person's goods. Of appeals of felony and breach of the king's peace [and robbery]: the words of the appeal. B. comes and makes denial. An appeal for malicious arson and robbery. A. appeals B.**

### An appeal concerning the rape of virgins.

Among other appeals there is an appeal called the rape of virgins. The rape of virgins is a crime imputed by a woman to the man by whom she says she has been forcibly ravished against the king's peace. [If he is convicted of this crime [this] punishment follows: the loss of members, that there be member for member, for when a virgin is defiled she loses her member and therefore let her defiler be punished in the parts in which he offended. Let him thus lose his eyes which gave him sight of the maiden's beauty for which he coveted her. And let him lose as well the testicles which excited his hot lust. Punishment of this kind does not follow in the case of every woman, though she is forcibly ravished, but

1 Probably meaning "default." See Latham, *Revised Medieval Latin Word-List, s.v. remaneo.*

### De verbis appelli mulieris querentis de raptu.

Femina. talis scilicet appellat B. quod sicut esset tali loco, tali die, tali anno etcetera ut supra, vel cum iret a tali loco usque ad talem locum, vel cum esset tali loco facienda tale opus, venit idem B. cum vi sua, et nequiter et contra pacem domini regis concubuit cum ea et abstulit ei pucelagium suum sive virginitatem, et eam secum detinuit per tot noctes: et sic totum exponat factum et veritatem. Et quod hoc fecit nequiter et in felonia, offert probare versus eum sicut curia domini regis consideraverit.

**De defensione appellati. De exceptionibus contra appellum.**

### Si appellatus per patriam fuerit convictus, quae poena sequatur.

Cum autem nihil sit per quod declinari possit appellum, si appellatus per patriam fuerit condemnatus sine aliqua redemptione, oculos amittat et testiculos supradicta ratione, nisi ita sit quod femina sic corrupta eum petat in virum ante iudicium redditum, quia hoc est tantum in voluntate mulieris et non viri, quia si hoc esset in voluntate viri sic sequeretur istud inconveniens, servum videlicet vel ignobilem mulierem nobilem et generosam unius pollutionis actione perpetuo foedare, et in opprobrium generis sui ducere in uxorem. Sed esto quod vir raptor sit nobilis et femina quam rapuit ignobilis, numquid erit in electione feminae corruptae eligendi et nubendi viro nobili vel non? Quia illud idem ut videtur sequeretur inconveniens ex parte viri nobilis. Respondeo, quod sive vir nobilis sive ignobilis, femina nobilis sive ignobilis sit, voluntas semper erit in femina et electio, quia quod in femina est voluntarium, in viro erit necessarium, ut membra sua redimat ex necessitate. Cum igitur mulier habeat electionem et spreto iudicio petat ipsum in virum, conceditur ei de gratia regis ob favorem matrimonii. Si autem iudicium elegerit, facta executione iudicii de corruptore, procedat appellum versus eos qui appellati sunt de forcia.

some other severe punishment does follow, according as she is married or a widow living a respectable life, a nun or a matron, a recognized concubine or a prostitute plying her trade without discrimination of person, all of whom the king must protect for the preservation of his peace, though a like punishment will not be imposed for each. In times past the defilers of virginity and chastity [suffered capital punishment], as did their abettors, since such men were not free of the crime of killing, especially since virginity and chastity cannot be restored, and since virgins and widows as well as nuns are dedicated to God [and] their defilement is committed not only to the hurt of mankind, but indeed, in scorn of Almighty God Himself, and [since] without punishment of this kind such infamy may not be put down. But in modern times the practice is otherwise and for the defilement of a virgin they lose their members, as aforesaid, and their abettors suffer severe corporal punishment but without loss of life or members. She must go at once and while the deed is newly done, with the hue and cry, to the neighboring townships and there show the injury done her to men of good repute, the blood and her clothing stained with blood, and her torn garments. And in the same way she ought to go to the reeve of the hundred, the king's serjeant, the coroners and the sheriff. And let her make her appeal at the first county court, unless she can at once make her complaint directly to the lord king or his justices, where she will be told to sue at the county court. Let her appeal be enrolled in the coroners' rolls, every word of the appeal, exactly as she makes it, and the year and day on which she makes it. A day will be given [her] at the coming of the justices, on which let her again put forward her appeal before them, in the same words as she made it in the county court, from which she is not permitted to depart lest the appeal fall because of the variance, as is true in other appeals. The rule in this and in other appeals is this: let the appeal of the appellor be heard first and then the coroners' enrollment of that appeal as made in the county court; the reason for this is that if the coroners' rolls were read

Possunt enim plures esse in forcia, sed tamen unus tantum tenebitur de corruptione, licet plures teneri possint de concubitu. Et cum ibi diversa sint facta, videtur quod in utroque facto sequi non deberet consimilis poena, quia corrumpere virginem, et concumbere cum corrupta, non sequitur utrumque factum eadem poena: quod quidem verum est, sed non nisi propter forciam quae ita coniuncta est primo facto de corruptione.

**Addicio.**

<Raptus mulieris ne fiat defendit tam lex humana quam divina. Et sic fuit antiquitus observatum, quod si quis obiaverit mulieri vel alicubi invenerit, si sola vel socios habuerit cum pace dimittat eam, quam si per inhonestatem tetigerit, frangit edictum regis, et emendabit secundum iudicium comitatus. Si autem contra voluntatem eius iactet eam ad terram, forisfaciat gratiam suam: quod si impudice discooperuerit eam et se super eam posuerit, omnium possessionum suarum incurrit damnum: quod si concubuerit cum ea, de vita et membris suis incurrit damnum. Adelstane. Lege Romanorum, Francorum, et Anglorum, equus eius etiam ad dedecus suum dedecorabitur desuper ballenro, et cauda quam proprius natibus abscidi poterit. Canis si secum habet, leporarius vel alius, eodem modo dedecorabitur. Si habet ancipitrem, perdat beccum et ungues et caudam. Terra vero et pecunia quam ipse raptor perdidit pro sua misericordia dabitur mulieri, warantizante sibi omni rege. Et si meretrix fuerit ante, tunc not fuit meretrix, cum nequitiae eius reclamando consentire noluit. Quod autem modo fiunt quaedam dispensationes, scilicet quod ipsi raptores accipiunt violatas in matrimonium, non est de lege sed de permissione sanctae ecclesiae et regis. Et illa permissio solius regis est in regno. Et primo surrexit in Francia pro quodam comite qui hospitatus est quendam ioculatorem cum uxore sua pulchra. Quo mortuo, quali morte non curamus evolvere, ipse quidem comes habuit eam nolentem. Ipsa enim quadam nocte exivit a castello, et fugiens venit Parisiis ubi invenit regem Robertun, quae cadens ad pedes eius narravit eventum rei.

first the appellor could phrase her appeal accordingly. The words of the appeal are these:

### The words of the appeal of a woman complaining of rape.

"Such a woman, A., appeals B. for that whereas she was at such a place on such a day in such a year, etc." (as above) (or "when she was going from such a place to such," or "at such a place, doing such a thing") "the said B. came with his force and wickedly and against the king's peace lay with her and took from her her maidenhood (or 'virginity') and kept her with him for so many nights (and let her thus set out all the facts and the truth). And that he did this wickedly and feloniously she offers to prove against him as the king's court may judge."

**The appellee's denial. Of exceptions against the appeal.**

### If the appellee is convicted by the country, what penalty follows.

When there are no grounds for avoiding the appeal and if the appellee has been convicted by the country, let him, without any [question of] ransom, lose his eyes and his testicles for the reason aforesaid, unless, before judgment rendered, the woman thus defiled claims him for her husband, for this lies wholly in her discretion, not in that of the man, for if it lay in his discretion this unseemliness would result, namely, that a villein or a common person might bring perpetual disgrace upon a woman of nobility and good family by a single act of defilement and take her to wife to the disgrace of her family. But suppose that the ravisher is a noble man and the woman raped [is] a common person; will it be for the defiled woman to exercise a choice and decide whether she will marry the noble man or not? For apparently the same unseemliness would result on the side of the noble man. I answer that whether the man is noble or common, the woman noble or common, the choice and the decision will always rest with the woman, for what is a voluntary act on her part will be a necessary act on his, that he may redeem his members.

Quam ut rex audivit, misit propter episcopos et barones qui tunc erant cum eo ad curiam, et praecepit mulieri ut narraret eis monia sicut sibi fecerat, quod et ipsa fecit. Rex autem consilio episcoporum et baronum misit propter comitem, ut statuto die veniret ad curiam ad disrationandum se si posset. Comes autem ut audivit verba regis, timens iram regis pro suo maleficio, respondit quod ad hunc terminum non posset ire ad curiam, sed consilio amicorum suorum mandavit regi propter pacificandam iram suam quod daret ei ducentas libras Beluacensis monetae, et decem equos de pretio. Ioculatrici autem centum libras, et eam daret in coniugem diviti burgensi aut militi qui eam honeste custodiret omnibus diebus vitae suae. Rex quidem omnia haec subsanando renuit, dicens quod non esset iustus vicarius dei si tantam nequitiam inultam venderet pro argento, et cum magna ira fecit summonere exercitum, disponens ire super eum. Sed barones precati sunt regem ut eis indutias octo dierum daret, et quod possent eum adducere ad misericordiam suam. Quod vix concessit, et sic ipse comes consilio baronum venit ad curiam. Et cum rex comparuit quod vellet cadere ad pedes eius, divertit se dicens aut pateretur iustitiam aut discederet a curia. Quid plura? Omnes barones clamaverunt et confirmaverunt contra regem quod ipse rex concesserat ei misericordiam quando miserunt pro eo. Tandem rex vix concessit. Episcopi, comites et barones locuti cum comite disposuerunt quod ipse comes subarravit eam quae nimis erat pulchra et sapiens, et quae largita est multas elemosinas ecclesiis et pauperibus. Quae tamen de Iudeis nata, a patre et matre et cunctis parentibus. Haec dispositio a talibus et tantis facta in tantum excrevit et sublimata est, quod iam multis locis quasi consuetudinaria habetur.>

**In quibus casibus mulier habet appellum. De appello de morte viri sui. De appellatis attachiandis. Breve de attachiando. Aliud breve ad idem de eodem. Breve de faciendo venire appellum coram iustitiariis. Aliud breve ad idem de eodem, et nisi inveniatur quod utlagetur et interrogetur de comitatu in comitatum. Breve quod tradatur per vallium dudeci. Breve de summonendo appellum coram rege. Breve si appellum factum fuerit**

Thus since she has that choice, and, spurning a judgment, she claims him for her husband, let him by grace of the king be granted to her, in furtherance of marriage. If she chooses the judgment, execution of the judgment having been had against the defiler, let the appeal proceed against those appealed as accessories. Several may be accessories, but only one shall be held for the defilement, though the several may be liable for lying with her, for to defile a virgin and to lie with one defiled [are different deeds]. And since the deeds are different, it is evident that the same punishment ought not to follow in both cases. That the same punishment does not follow upon both is true, that is, unless the accessory's act is so closely linked to the first act of ravishment [that they cannot be separated].

**Of those appealed as accessories.**

### ADDITION.

<Man-made as well as divine law forbid the rape of women. [In ancient times the practice was as follows: if a man meets a woman or comes across her somewhere, whether she is alone or has companions, he is to let her go in peace; if he touches her indecorously, he breaks the king's ordinance and shall give compensation in accordance with the judgment of the county court; if he throws her upon the ground against her will, he forfeits the king's grace; if he shamelessly disrobes her and places himself upon her, he incurs the loss of all his possessions; and if he lies with her, he incurs the loss of his life and members. Athelstan.] By the law of the Romans, the Franks and the English, even his horse shall to his ignominy be put to shame upon its scrotum and its tail, which shall be cut off as close as possible to the buttocks. If he has a dog with him, a greyhound or some other, it shall be put to shame in the same way; if a hawk, let it lose its beak, its claws and its tail. The land and money which the ravisher lost through his amercement shall be given to the woman, the king warranting the whole to her. And if she was a whore before, she was not a whore then, since by crying out against his wicked deed she

**immediate coram rege. Breve vicecomiti de faciendo recordum in comitatu coram custodibus. Aliud breve deo eodem vicecomiti.**

### Si quis fecerit feloniam de se ipso.

Eodem modo quo quis feloniam facere poterit interficiendo alium, ita feloniam facere poterit interficiendo se ipsum, quae quidem felonia dicitur fieri de se ipso. Feloniam quidem facit de se ipso, ut si quis reus fuerit alicuius criminis ita quod captus fuerit pro morte hominis vel cum furto manifesto, vel cum utlagatus fuerit, vel in aliquo scelere et maleficio deprehensus, et metu criminis imminentis mortem sibi consciverit, heredem non habebit. Quia sic convincitur felonia prius facta, sicut furtum vel mors hominis vel huiusmodi. Sed qui criminis rei postulati non sunt vel in crimine deprehensi manus sibi intulerint, bona eorum fisco non vindicentur, non enim facti sceleritatem esse obnoxiam, sed conscientiae metus in reo veluti pro confesso habetur. Et ideo si rei postulati fuerint vel in scelere deprehensi, si se ipsos interfecerint, bona eorum confiscentur, scilicet bona eorum qui reatum mortis sibi consciverint, ut si eius criminis fuerint quod damnarentur morte vel deportatione. <Si se submerserint vel praecipitaverint ex alto, vel alio modo, tales heredes habebunt, quia non convincitur felonia, nec praecedat aliquod crimen propter quod periculum mortis vel membrorum sustinere deberet.> Si quis autem taedio vitae vel impatientia doloris alicuius se ipsum interfecerit, successorem habere poterit: talis non amittit hereditatem sed tantum bona mobilia, sed bona eius mobilia confiscentur. Sed si quis sine causa manus sibi intulerit per iram et malam voluntatem, ut cum alteri nocere vellet adimpleere non posset quod voluit se ipsum interfecerit, puniendus est et successorem non habebit, quia convincitur et punitur felonia quam in personam alterius facere proposuit, quia qui sibi ipsi non parcit, multo minus aliis parceret si facultatem haberet. Sed de furioso quid dicetur qui rationem non habet? Et de mente capto, et de frenetico, vel de infantulo? Vel si ille qui laborat in acuta se ipsum submerserit vel interfecerit, quaeritur an talis feloniam faciat de se ipso.

refused her consent. If some dispensations are nowadays provided, for instance, that the ravishers may receive those they have ravished in marriage, that is not by law but by permission of Holy Church and the king. That permission belongs to the king alone within the realm. It first arose in France in the case of a certain count who gave hospitality to a jester and his beautiful wife. When the jester died (and how he died we do not care to recount) the count had her against her will. One night, however, she escaped from the castle and fled to Paris, where she found King Robert,[1] and falling at his feet told him what had happened. As [soon as] the king had heard her he sent for the bishops and barons who were then at court and ordered the woman to tell them what she had told him, which she did. The king, on the advice of the bishops and barons, ordered the count to come to court on an appointed day to clear himself if he could. When the count had heard the king's words, fearing the king's anger for his wicked deed, he answered that he could not attend at that time, but, on the advice of his friends, in order to appease the king's anger, advised him that he would give him two hundred pounds in Beauvais money and ten costly horses, and the jester's wife a hundred pounds, and would give her in marriage to a wealthy burgess or knight who would keep her respectably all the days of her life. The king refused all this with derision, saying that he would not be a righteous vicar of God if he sold for money immunity from punishment for such great wickedness, and in great wrath ordered his army summoned and arrangements made for marching against him. But the barons prayed the king to give them a week's respite that they might bring the count to seek his mercy. This the king reluctantly granted, and thus by advice of the barons the count came to court. When the king appeared and he attempted to fall at his feet the king turned away, saying that he should either submit to justice or leave the court. What more is to be said? All the barons cried out and affirmed as against the king that he had granted the count mercy when they sent for him. Finally the king reluctantly

1 King Robert the Pious (996-1031).

Videtur quod non, nec hereditatem forisfaciunt nec catalla, eo quod sensu carent et ratione, non magis quam brutum animal iniuriam facere possunt nec feloniam, cum non multum distent a brutis, secundum quod videri poterit in minore, qui si alium interficeret in minori aetate, iudicium non sustineret. Et haec vera sunt quod furiosus non tenetur, nisi hoc federit simulato furore cum dilucidis gaudeat intervallis. <De submersis et oppressis et per infortunium mortuis. Sed si quis se ipsum suspenderit, non propter hoc exheredantur heredes secundum quosdam, nec uxor dotem amittit, nisi in casu ut supra, quia felonia de se ipso facta convinci non poterit.>

## De actione furti.

## Quid sit furtum.

Igitur imprimis videndum quid sit furtum, quot eius species. Et sciendum quod furtum est secundum leges contrectatio rei alienae fraudulenta cum animo furandi, invito illo cuius res illa fuerit. Fraudulenta dico, quia sine animo furandi non committitur. Est etiam quasi furtum, rapina, quae idem est quantum ad nos quod roberia, et aliud genus contrectationis contra voluntatem domini, et similis poena sequitur utrumque delictum, et unde praedo dicitur fur improbus. Quis enim magis contrectat rem aliquam invito domino quam ille qui vi rapit?

agreed. The bishops, earls and barons spoke with the count and arranged that he should espouse her, for she was fair and wise, and gave much alms to churches and the poor, though born of Jews, both father and mother and all her kin. This arrangement, made by such persons of consequence, grew and became of such authority that it is now in many places regarded as a customary.>

**The cases in which a woman has an appeal. The appeal for the death of her husband. The attachment of appellees. The writ of attachment. Another writ on the same matter for the same purpose. The writ for causing an appeal to come before the justices. Another writ on the same matter for the same purpose, that unless he is found he be exacted from county court to county court and outlawed. A writ to the effect that he be committed to the security of twelve men. Writ for summoning an appeal before the king. The writ where an appeal has been made directly before the king. The writ to the sheriff for making a record in the county court before the keepers [of the pleas of the crown]. Another writ to the sheriff on the same matter.**

### Where a man commits felony upon his own person.

Just as a man may commit felony by slaying another, so may he do so by slaying himself, which felony is said to be done to himself, as where one has been accused of some crime and been arrested [or outlawed] [as] for homicide or with the proceeds of theft, or apprehended in the course of some evil deed and crime, and kills himself in fear of the crime that hangs over him; he will have no heir, because the felony previously committed, the theft or homicide or the like, is thus convicted. But the goods of those who destroy themselves when they are not accused of a crime or taken in the course of a criminal act are not appropriated by the fisc, for it is not the wickedness of the deed that is reprehensible but that the fear of guilt in the accused takes the place of a confession. Therefore if they are accused of or apprehended in the course of a crime and kill

### Quot species furti.

Species autem furti sunt duae, quia aliud publicum aliud privatum, videlicet manifestum et non manifestum. Non manifestum est ubi aliquis suspectus est de latrocinio per famam patriae, per indictamentum et rectum, et ubi graves praesumptiones faciunt contra ipsum. Sed si seisitus non inveniatur de aliquo latrocinio, non habet quis potestatem inquirendi nec procedendi contra ipsum ad inquisitiones, nisi ipse dominus rex in curia sua. Sed de hac specie nihil amplius ad praesens, quia superius per praecedentia perpendi poterit quid in hac parte sit agendum. Et si coram ballivis vel coronatoribus furtum cognoverit, tamen non tenetur ex tali confessione sine seisina, licet cum seisina recordum haberent. Furtum vero manifestum est ubi latro deprehensus est seisitus de aliquo latrocinio, scilicet hondhabbende et bacberende, et insecutus fuerit per aliquem cuius res illa fuerit qui dicitur sakabor. Et si sine secta cognoverit se inde esse latronem coram vicecomite vel coronatoribus vel serviente regis cum testimonio proborum hominum, extunc furtum dedicere non poterit, quia tales in hoc habent recordum. Et secundum quosdam illud idem erit etiam sine seisina.

themselves, let their goods be confiscated, that is, the goods of those who know they deserve death, as where if they were found guilty of their crime they would be condemned to death or exile. But if a man slays himself in weariness of life or because he is unwilling to endure further bodily pain <as where he drowns himself or throws himself from a height, or kills himself in some other way,> he may have a successor, but his movable goods are confiscated. He does not lose his inheritance, only his movable goods, <because no felony is proved, nor is there any precedent crime for which he ought to be in peril of life or members.> <[This is true] of those who drown or are crushed, who die by misadventure, but if a man hangs himself are his heirs not thereby disinherited? [No], according to some, nor does his wife lose her dower, except in the case above, because [of] a felony done to himself he cannot be convicted.> But if one lays violent hands upon himself without justification, through anger and ill-will, as where wishing to injure another but unable to accomplish his intention he kills himself, he is to be punished and shall have no successor, because the felony he intended to commit against the other is proved and punished, for one who does not spare himself would hardly have spared others, had he had the power. But what shall we say of a madman bereft of reason? And of the deranged, the delirious and the mentally retarded? Or if one laboring under a high fever drowns himself or kills himself? Query: whether such a one commits felony against himself. It is submitted that he does not, nor do such persons forfeit their inheritance or their chattels, since they are without sense and reason and can no more commit an *injuria* or a felony than a brute animal, since they are not far removed from brutes, as is evident in the case of a minor, for if he should kill another while under age he would not suffer judgment. [That a madman is not liable is true, unless he acts under pretense of madness while enjoying lucid intervals.]

**Of the action of theft.**

**King Henry II on throne disputing with Thomas à Beckett**

### What theft is.

[Therefore let us first see what theft is and how many kinds there are. Theft, according to the laws, is the fraudulent mishandling of another's property without the owner's consent, with the intention of stealing, for without the *animus furandi* [the intention of thieving] it is not committed. I say "fraudulent" [because] there is also another kind of mishandling without the owner's consent, rapine, which is the same with us as robbery. That is why a robber is a thief *a fortiori* [from the more powerful {reasoning}], for who appropriates another's property more against the owner's will than he who seizes by force?

### How many kinds of theft there are.

The kinds of theft are two, [a like punishment follows each offense,] for one is open and the other secret, that is to say, manifest and not manifest. It is not manifest where one is suspected of theft through ill-repute in the community, through indictment and accusation, where serious presumptions lie against him but he is not found seised of any stolen property. But of this kind of theft we say nothing more at present because what is to be done as to that may be drawn from what has been said above. Manifest theft is where a thief is apprehended seised of the stolen property, that is, hand-having and back-bearing, and is sued by him whose property it is [or one] called the sacrabar.[1] If, without any suit against him he confesses that he is the thief thereof before the bailiffs or the coroners or the king's serjeant, with reputable men as witnesses, he may not subsequently deny the theft, [according to some the same will be true even if he is not found seised,] because such persons have record in this matter. [If he is not found seised of any stolen property], no one has the power of inquiring or of proceeding to inquests against him except the lord king in his court. And if he confesses the theft before the bailiffs or coroners he is not bound by such confession, [that is], if he is not found seised, though they would have record if he were seised.

1 The public prosecutor in a local court.

**Poterit quis ab initio agere civiliter vel criminaliter. De appello de latrocinio. Si defendat, vadietur duellum. Si appellatus patriam elegerit. Breve de faciendo venire warantum per auxilium. Quod quandoque intrat aliquis in warantiam malitiose et per fraudem. Habenda est ratio utrum res magna sit an minima. Si furtum in manu alicuius inveniatur. Si uxor teneatur ex furto viri. Item si cum viro convicta fuerit.**

### De furto manifesto et probatore cognoscente.

Cum furto manifesto deprehensus sine aliqua probatione cognoscit latrocinum et se esse latronem, vel cognoscit homicidium vel roberiam, vel quod aliam feloniam fecerit, vel quod utlagatus fuerit, vel gaolam fregerit, vel regnum abiuraverit, vel quid tale fecerit per quod secum suum portat iudicium, poterit dominus rex, si voluerit, ei concedere vitam et membra per sic quod patriam deliberet a malefactoribus, per corpus vel per patriam vel per fugam, secundum quod convenerit de numbero et de modo. Appellare poterit quos voluerit de societate et latrocinio vel alia quacumque felonia, dum tamen si sit aliquis fidelis et in franco plegio, et dominum habuerit qui ipsum advocaverit, et velit se ponere super patriam. Si fidelis appellatus per patriam fuerit deliberatus, probator infidelis quasi mendax et convictus condemnabitur. <Et qui sic convicti sunt et secum suum portant iudicium, sicut sententialiter condemnati, nullum habent appellum versus aliquem fidelem nec infidelem, quia omnino frangitur eorum baculus. Sed non erit ita de probatore, quia licet crimen confessus fuerit, tamen propter hoc non est iudicatus.> Si autem in decenna non fuerit, nec dominum habuerit qui advocet eum, et patriam recusaverit, forte tunc cum omnia bona ei deficiant et per hoc par sit appellanti, procedat inter eos duellum. Et eodem modo si ad appellum probatoris posuerit se quis super patriam de roberia et latrocinio, vel alia felonia ei imposita a probatore, et per patriam fuerit inde male creditus, tunc cum sit par probatori procedat inter eos duellum.

**One may at the outset sue civilly or criminally. Of the appeal of larceny. Where he makes denial, let battle be waged. If the appellee chooses the country. The writ for causing a warrantor to appear by aid. A warranty is sometimes entered into maliciously and fraudulently. Account must be taken of whether what is stolen is large or very small. If stolen property is found in another's possession. If a wife is held liable for her husband's theft. Where [the wife] has joined with her husband.**

### Manifest theft and the confessing approver.[1]

When one caught with the proceeds of theft [sometimes without any (such) proof] confesses the theft and that he is a thief, or confesses the homicide or robbery, or that he has committed some other felony, or been outlawed, or has broken gaol, or abjured the realm, or has done something because of which he bears his judgment with him, the lord king may if he wishes grant him his life and members on condition that he rid the country of [so many] criminals, by his body or by the country or by flight, according as the number and method is agreed upon between them. He may appeal any he wishes of confederacy and theft, or of any other felony, unless he is law-abiding and in frankpledge, [or] has a lord who avows him, [or] is willing to put himself on the country. <[Those who] bear their judgment with them, that is, those condemned by sentence of the court, have no appeal against anyone, law-abiding or not, because their rod is completely broken. But this will not be true of an approver, for though he has confessed the crime he has not received judgment.> [If the law-abiding appellee is delivered by the country, the lawless approver will be condemned as a liar and taken as convicted.] [If he is not in a tithing and has no lord who avows him and refuses to put himself on the country, then, since there is nothing to be said in his favor and he is thus on a par with the appellor, let a duel proceed between them. And so if on the appeal of an approver he puts himself on the

---

1 A *probator* was an informer, initially someone who provided information against accomplices. The usual translation is "approver."

Non enim habet felo vel latro cognoscens versus aliquem fidelem vocem qui velit et possit se ponere super patriam de fidelitate. Cum autem quis latrocinium vel aliam feloniam cognoverit, aut perseverat in eadem voluntate coram iustitiariis aut non perseverat. Si autem non perseveraverit, sed se retraxerit quandocumque, et recordatum sit a vicecomite et coronatoribus vel aliis qui recordum habent, quod coram eis latrocinium cognovit, extunc habebitur probator pro convicto et pro condemnato propter cognitionem. Si autem in eodem proposito coram iustitiariis perseveraverit, ubi numquam se retraxerit, tunc coram eis suam de novo faciat cognitionem, et obliget se ad convincendum tot, quot appellaverit, ut habeat vitam et membra ut praedictum est. Quod quidem nemo ei concedere poterit nisi ipse rex, vel iustitiarius suus.

**Breve quod rex concedit iustitiariis potestatem concedendi probatori vitam et membra. Quod vicecomes attachiet eos quos probator appellaverit. De capiendo appellatos per probatorem qui se cognoscit esse latronem. Cum autem praesens fuerit appellatus, qualiter probator proponere debet intentionem suam et appellum suum. Item plures appellat, et unde sic. De modo defendendi. De forma sacramenti tam appellantium quam appellatorum: et primo appellatus iuret per verba negativa. Postea iuret appellans per verba affirmativa. Si appellatus victus fuerit. Si autem probator victus fuerit. Si autem defensionem non susceperit in propria persona, sed excipit et iudicium petat, si contra talem cognoscentem se esse latronum debeat respondere. De defensione appellati. Si probator fecerit quod promisit, teneatur ei conventio. Si comitatus vel curia alicuius potentis appellum tenuerit de probatore, veniat recordum ad curiam regis per tale breve. Item breve vicecomiti quod probatorem habeat coram rege et omnes qos ipse appellaverit de societate, quia plures propter appellum probatoris se subtrahunt.**

country with respect to the robbery and theft, or the other felony alleged against him by the approver, and is found suspect by the country, let the duel proceed between them.] For a felon or a self-confessed thief has no right to speak against a law-abiding man who is able and willing to put himself on the country regarding his obedience to the law. When a man has confessed theft or other felony and become an approver before any who have record with respect to such confession, he either persists in that intention before the justices or he does not. If he does not, but retracts [his appeal], no matter at what time, and the sheriff and coroners, or others who have record, record that he confessed to the theft before them, the approver will henceforth be regarded as convicted and condemned because of the confession. If he persists in that intention before the justices, though he has not retracted, let him then make his confession afresh before them and bind himself to convict so many, as many as he appeals, in order to have his life and members, as was said above. This concession no one may grant him save the king himself or the king's justice.

**A writ in which the king grants authority to his justices to grant an approver life and members. That the sheriff attach those whom the approver appeals. Of arresting those appealed by an approver who confesses that he is a thief. When the appellee has appeared; how the approver should set forth his purpose and appeal. The approver may appeal several as follows. Of the method of making denial. Of the form of oath sworn by appellors and appellees; the appellee shall first swear in words of denial. The appellor shall then swear affirmatively. If the appellee is vanquished. If the approver is vanquished. If he does not undertake the defense in his own person but excepts and prays judgment whether he ought to answer a confessed thief. Of the appellee's defense. If the approver has done what he promised let the agreement with him be kept. If a county or a seignorial court entertains the appeal of an approver; let the record come to the king's court by this writ. A writ to**

**Si autem appellati venerint et finem fecerint, quod redire possint et esse sub plegiis. Ubi quis appellatus per patriam fuerit deliberatus, et quod habeat catalla sua. Breve de replegiando aliquem quem talis cepit et captum detinet.**

***Quod nemo potest curiam suam habere de probatore vel latrone cognoscente. Et quae placita pertinent ad curiam et quae ad comitatum, et de libertatibus singulorum.***

**Dictum est supra quod nemo potest habere curiam suam de probatore et latrone cognoscente. Videamus igitur quae placita pertineant ad curiam et quae ad comitatum. Sunt quidam barones et alii qui libertates habent, scilicet sok, sak, tol et theam, infangenethef, utfangenethef. Isti possunt iudicare in curia sua si quis inventus fuerit infra libertatem suam seisitus de aliquo latrocinio manifesto, sicut hondhabbende et bacberende, et insecutus fuerit per saccabor: quia nisi fuerit in seisina, licet aliquis sequatur versus eum sicut versus latronem, non pertinebit ad curiam, hundreda, vel wapentakia cognoscere de huiusmodi furtis, nec inde facere inquisitionem per patriam utrum talis qui non fuerit seisitus culpabilis sit vel non. Nec quod vadietur inter aliquos duellum sine seisina. De hoc quod dicit infangenethef, videndum quid sit. Et dicitur infangenethef latro captus in terra licuius de hominibus suis propriis seisitus de latrocinio. Utfangenethef vero dicitur latro extraneus veniens aliunde de terra aliena, et qui captus fuerit in terra ipsius qui tales habet libertates. Sed non sequitur quod ille possit hominem suum proprium captum extra libertatem suam reducere usque infra libertatem suam, et ibi eum iudicare ex tali libertate. Debet enim quis iuri subiacere ubi delinquit. Proprios enim latrones et alienos infra libertatem suam captos iudicare possunt. Item cognoscere possunt de medletis et hominibus verberatis, vulneratis, ubi felonia et pax regis vel vicecomitis non apponitur. Poterit tamen apponi pax domini regis et ballivorum. Item de equis, bobus, et aliis animalibus vulneratis et mahemiatis. Talis quidem transgressio emendari poterit per vicinos. Item cognoscere potest de debitis quae exiguntur sine brevi domini regis, et etiam de aliis querelis sine brevi.**

**the sheriff that he have the approver and all whom he appeals of confederacy before the king. If those appealed come and make fine for permission to return and be under pledges. Where an appellee has been discharged by the country; that he have his chattels. The writ for replevying a man arrested and detained.**

### That no one may hold his court on an approver or confessing thief; the pleas that belong to a seignorial court and to the county court; and concerning the liberties of individuals.

It was discussed above that no one is permitted to hold court on an approver and a confessing thief. Let us see therefore what pleas belong to the [seignorial] court and which to the county [court]. There are some, barons and others, who have liberties, that is, soke, sake, toll and team, infangthief, [and] outfangthief.[1] These may judge in their court [if [the thief] is found within their liberty seised of his manifest theft, that is, hand-having and back-bearing, because unless he is in seisin, despite the fact that someone sues against him as a thief, or he is prosecuted by the sacrabar, jurisdiction over such thefts will not belong to the seignorial court, [nor to those of the hundred or wapentake,] nor will it be permitted to inquire by the country [i.e. the grand assize] whether one not found so seised is guilty or not, nor to decide that judicial combat be waged between him and his accuser.] [Infangthief means a thief taken on someone's land seised of his theft, the thief being one of his own men. Outfangthief means an outsider thief, coming from another's land, who is arrested on the land of the possessor of that liberty]. their own thieves and those that are the men of others if they are taken within their liberties. [It does not follow, however, that he may bring back into his liberty and judge there one of his own men arrested outside his liberty.

1 This is a common formula. Soke and sake gave the lord petty jurisdiction over the inhabitants on his estate; toll and team gave him a share in trade conducted on his estate; infangthief gave him jurisdiction over his own men caught thieving on his estate; outfangthief gave him jurisdiction over another lord's men caught thieving on his estate.

### Ad vicecomites pertinet huiusmodi placita.

Ad vicecomites vero pertinent huiusmodi placita in comitatu. Cognoscere quidem potest de medletis, plagis, verberibus, et consimilibus pro defectu dominorum, nisi querens adiciat de pace domini regis infracta vel feloniam apponat, extunc enim vicecomes non debet intromittere, cum hoc tangat personam domini regis et coronam suam. Et ideo coronatores querelam illam sive appellam irrotulare debent, annum et diem et locum, et omnia verba appelli per ordinem, et omnes circumstantias ut supra de appellis, usque ad adventum iustitiariorum. Sed si tantum agatur de pace vicecomitis, non erit ibi amissio vitae vel membrorum, sed sequitur poena pecuniaria de convictis. Potest quidem vicecomes facere placita non ex officio vicecomitis, sed vice ipsius regis ex causa necessaria, non sicut vicecomes sed sicut iustitiarius regis, si hoc specialiter ei demandetur quod iuratam capiat et faciat inquisitiones, extensiones et partitiones, licet in quibusdam iudicium reddere non possit. Item habet ex speciali mandato regis, non ex officio vicecomitis, ubi mandatum habet quod iustitiet aliquem, et quo casu videtur quod omnia habere debet ut iustitiarius, sine quibus placitum illud terminari non possit. Habet etiam ut iustitiarius, et non ex officio vicecomitis, quod cognoscere potest de averiis captis et detentis contra vadium et plegios, quod quidem placitum pertinet ad coronam, et quod ei ex necessitate conceditur ad terminandum ratione inferius dicenda. Item pertinet ad ipsum cognoscere de assisis in regno constitutis et iratis per regnum, si fuerint servatae vel non, sicut panis et cervisiae et falsis mensuris quae pertinent ad coronam, et de quibus attachiamenta facere poterit simul cum coronatoribus usque ad adventum iustitiariorum. Item pertinet ad vicecomitem visus franci plegii in turnis suis duobus singulis annis per hundreda et wapentakia faciendis. Et ideo qualiter fieri debent turni videndum erit.

For every man ought to be subject to the law where he commits the offense]. They may also have jurisdiction over affrays and men beaten and wounded where felony and breach of the king's peace or the sheriff's are not assigned, only that of the lord and bailiffs. Also over the wounding and maiming of horses, oxen and other animals. Trespasses of that kind may be given redress by neighbors. They may also have jurisdiction over debts exigible[1] without the king's writ and also of other plaints without writ.

### These pleas belong to the sheriffs.

These pleas belong to sheriffs in the county. He is able to have jurisdiction over melees, woundings, beatings and the like, over the default of lords, unless the complainant adds "in breach of the king's peace" or assigns felony; after that the sheriff must not intermeddle since this concerns the person of the king and his crown, and therefore the coroners ought to enroll the said plaint or appeal, the year and the day and place and all the words of the appeal in order, and all the circumstances, (as above [in the portion] on appeals) pending the coming of the justices. If only the sheriff's peace is invoked, there will be no loss of life or members by those convicted but a pecuniary penalty follows. The sheriff may [also] hold pleas not by virtue of his office as sheriff but in the king's place, because of necessity, not as sheriff but as the king's justice, where it is specially required of him that he take a jury and make inquests, extents and partitions, though in some instances he cannot render judgment. When he receives instructions to justice someone, his authority issues from the special command of the king, not from his office as sheriff, and there it is evident that he ought to have the full authority of a justice, without which the said plea cannot be determined. It is also as a justice and not by virtue of his office as sheriff that he has jurisdiction over beasts taken and detained against gage and pledges, a plea that belongs to the crown and is of necessity granted to him to

1 Debts that may be summoned before a court.

**De minoribus et levioribus criminibus quae civiliter intentantur.** Dictum est supra de maioribus criminibus et appellis quae criminaliter intentantur, et aliquando ultimum inducunt supplicium, aliquando membrorum truncationem, aliquando exilium perpetuum vel ad tempus. Nunc autem dicendum est de minoribus et levioribus criminibus quae civiliter intentantur, sicut de actionibus iniuriarum personalibus, et quae pertinent ad coronam, eo quod aliquando fiunt contra pacem domini regis. Videndum igitur quid sit iniuria. Et sciendum quod iniuria est quidquid non iure fit. Et unde supra in parte dicitur quod si quis interfectus fuerit, videndum erit an iniuria sit interfectus vel sit talis qui nullo iure occiditur. Igitur qui latronem occiderit non tenetur, nocturnum vel diurnum, si aliter periculum evadere non possit, tenetur tamen si possit. Item non tenetur si per infortunium et non animo et voluntate occidendi, nec dolus nec culpa eius inveniatur, de quo supra dictum est, et de gratia principis cum eo mitius agitur hoc probato. Non iure occiditur quis, ut si in assultu praemeditato et felonia et animo occidendi fuerit quis interfectus ob iram et cupiditatem. Item si quis unum percusserit et occiderit cum alium percutere vellet in felonia, tenetur. Item si cum levius credidit percussisse, gravius percusserit et occiderit, tenetur. Debet enim quilibet modum et mensuram adhibere in suo facto. Et est iniuria talis quae inducit ultimum supplicium cum criminaliter agatur. Est et alia quae non nisi poenam pecuniariam tantum, et quandoque eandem poenam cum carceris inclusione, secundum facti qualitatem. Fit autem iniuria non solum cum quis pugno percussus fuerit, verberatus, vel fustibus caesus, verum etiam cum ei convitium dictum fuerit, vel de eo factum carmen famosum et huiusmodi.

determine for a reason to be explained below. He also has jurisdiction over the assizes established and sworn throughout the realm, as the assizes of bread and beer and false measures, which are the concern of the crown, in order to ascertain whether they have been kept or not, as to which he and the coroners may make attachments until the coming of the justices. The view of frankpledge also belongs to the sheriff, to be made in his two turns each year through the hundreds and wapentakes. We therefore must see how the turns ought to be made.[1]

### Of minor and lesser crimes brought by civil action.

Above we discussed major crimes and appeals that are brought by criminal action and sometimes lead to the supreme penalty, sometimes to the loss of members, sometimes to exile, permanent or temporary. Now we must speak of the minor and lesser crimes that are brought by civil action, such as the personal actions for *iniuria*, which belong to the crown since they are [sometimes] committed against the peace of the lord king. Therefore we must see what *iniuria* is. And it must be seen that *iniuria* is whatever does not happen by right. Whence above[2] it is said in part that we must see whether *iniuria* is someone wrongfully slain or such a one who has been slain without right. That is why he who kills a thief, either a day thief or a night thief, is not liable, [that is], if he could not otherwise escape danger; if he could he is liable. Nor is he liable who kills by misadventure, without intention and wish to kill, of which we have spoken above, and is guilty neither of guile or fault.[3] He, that having been proved, is dealt with more leniently by grace of the prince. He is slain without right if he is slain in premeditated assault and felony and with intent to kill, through anger and greed. And so if he has struck and killed one person when he intended to strike another feloniously, he is liable. And so if, thinking to strike a light blow, he has struck a heavy

1 The subject is, however, never addressed.
2 In the section titled "The first division of actions."
3 In "The Crime of homicide and how it is divided."

### Qualiter quis patitur iniuriam per suos.

Patitur autem iniuriam quis non solum per se ipsum, sed etiam per illos quos habet in potestate, sicut per liberos suos et uxorem suam. Vir autem agere poterit de iniuria facta uxori suae, sed non e contrario. Defendi enim uxores a viris, non viros ab uxoribus, dignum est. Item iniuriam patitur quis per illos quos habuerit in familia sua, sicut servientes suos et servos si pulsati fuerint et verberati in contumeliam suam, vel quaternus sua interfuit operibus eorum non caruisse. De plagis vero et verberibus sibi factis habent ipsi actionem et non dominus.

### In quibus casibus servi habent personam standi in iudicio contra dominos suos.

Habent enim servi personam standi in iudicio contra omnes de iniuriis sibi factis contra pacem domini regis, et multo fortius servientes. Habent etiam servi personam standi in iudicio contra dominos suos de seditione domini regis, et aliis quae fiunt contra personam eius, quia ibi admittitur quilibet de populo, et contra dominum suum de atroci iniuria, ubi agitur de vita vel membris, vel roberia. Poena igitur iniuriam quandoque erit corporalis, quandoque pecuniaria. Et si fuerit pecuniaria et certa et in iudicium deducta, tamen erit a iudice taxanda, cum sit omne interesse incertum, et quandoque minuitur cum sit in iudicium deducta, secundum qualitatem delicti et personae cui iniuriatur. Numquam tamen crescere debet de iure.

one and killed, he is liable. For everyone ought to observe mean and measure in what he does. An *iniuria* of this kind entails the ultimate penalty when a criminal action is brought. There is also another kind of *iniuria* that is punished by nothing more than a monetary penalty, sometimes that and imprisonment, depending on the nature of the deed. [An *iniuria* is committed not only when a man is struck with a fist or flogged or beaten with clubs but when he has been insulted or victimized by defamatory verses and the like].

### How one may suffer an iniuria through his dependents.

One may suffer an *iniuria* not only in his own person but in the persons of those he has in his *potestas*, as his children and his wife. A husband may sue for an *iniuria* done to his wife, but the converse is not true, for wives ought to be protected by husbands, not husbands by wives. One may also suffer an *iniuria* through those of his household, as his servants and bondsmen, if they have been beaten and flogged to his dishonor and shame, or to the extent of his interest in not being deprived of their labor. For the actual wounds and beatings suffered by them they and not their lord have the action.

### In which cases servants have personam standi[1] in court against their lords.

For bondsmen have a standing in court against all men for *iniuriae* done them in breach of the king's peace, and by much stronger reasoning [do] servants. Bondsmen even have a standing in court against their lords for heinous wrongs, where life and member are involved, or for robbery, and for treason against the lord king and other acts committed against his person, for in that case everyone is allowed to speak. If it is monetary, [though] a sum certain is made the subject of the action it must nevertheless be taxed by the judge, [it is sometimes reduced, [but] since it is the sum claimed, he ought never rightfully to increase it,] since the

1 Status [standing], the right to be heard in court. See Latham, s.v. *persona*.

### Quod atrox iniuria aestimatur multis modis.

Est quidem iniuria levis et est atrox. Atrocitas vero aestimatur ex ipso facto, ut si quis fuerit male vulneratus, verberatus et male tractatus contra pacem. Item ex loco, si in curia regis vel dominorum, si coram iustitiariis vel in comitatu coram vicecomite. Item si in theatro, in nundinis, vel in foro, vel alibi coram omni populo. Item locus vulneris, ut si in fronte vel in oculo magis quam in loco secreto. Item ex persona aestimatur iniuria, ut si magistratibus, ballivis fiat, parentibus vel patronis. Item non solum tenetur actione iniuriarum qui fecit iniuriam, hoc est qui percussit, sed ille qui dolo fecit vel curavit, ut cui mala pugno percuteretur.

### Quod iniuria per dissimulationem aboletur.

Haec autem actio per dissimulationem aboletur. Et ideo si quis iniuriam passus hoc statim ad animum non revocaverit, postea ex paenitentia remissam iniuriam per dissimulationem ad animum recolligere non poterit.

**De vetito namii. Si captio fuerit iniusta. Si querens queratur de captione scilicet et detentione. Si dominus post legem vadiatam defaltam fecerit. Quod non potest quis aliquid dedicere de recordo adversarii.**

### De officio vicecomitis.

Officum vero vicecomitis est si quis conqueratur de iniusta captione vel iniusta detentione contra vadium et plegios, quod cum breve domini regis susceperit, quod tale est: Rex vicecomiti salutem. Praecipimus tibi quod sine dilatione replegiari facias tali averia sua quae talis cepit et iniuste detinet ut dicit. Et postea eum inde iuste deduci facias, ne amplius inde clamorem audiamus pro defectu iustitiae.

extent of the plaintiff's interest is wholly uncertain [because], depending on the nature of the delict and the status of the injured party.

### A grievous iniuria is assessed in many ways.

An *iniuria* may be slight or grievous. In assessing damages, it is adjudged grievous from the deed itself, as where one has been badly wounded, beaten and mistreated in breach of the peace. Or from the place where it was committed, in the king's court or a seignorial court, before the justices or in the county court before the sheriff, in a theatre at a fair, or in a market place, or elsewhere in the presence of many people. Or from the position of the wound, as where it is on the forehead or in the eye rather than in a hidden part. Or from the status of the person concerned, as where an *iniuria* is done to magistrates or bailiffs, to parents or patrons. Not only is he who committed the wrong, that is, who struck the blow, liable in an *actio iniuriarum* but he who maliciously aided or abetted or caused another to be struck.

### An iniuria may be annulled by dissimulation.

This action is lost by dissimulation. Thus if a man suffers an *iniuria* and lets it slip from his mind at once he cannot subsequently regret his decision and recall it to mind in order to have it punished.

**Of replevin. If the seizure is unlawful. If the plaintiff complains of both seizure and detainer. If the lord defaults after the wager of law. One cannot deny anything in his opponent's record.**

### The sheriff's duty.

The sheriff's duty, when someone complains of an unlawful taking [and] detainer against gage and pledge, is [when he has received the king's writ, which is this: The king to the sheriff, greeting. We order you to cause to be replevied to such a one without delay the beasts which such a one took and unlawfully detains, as he says, and afterwards cause him to receive lawful judgment therein, lest we hear further complaint for

Teste etcetera. Vel etiam ad querelam alicuius sine brevi, accepta prius ab eo securitate de prosequendo. In propria persona sua si ad hoc intendere possit, accedat ad locum ubi averia detenta sunt, ut dicitur, vel si ipse non possit, mittat servientem suum, et statim cum venerit petat visum de averiis illis ubicumque inclusa fuerint. Et si sit aliquis contradictor quod inde visum habere non possit, vel propter hoc in eum manus violentas iniecerit, statim levet huthesium et clamorem, et cum huthesio et clamore capiat delinquentes, sicut illos qui sunt manifeste contra pacem domini regis, et in gaolam proiciat quousque dominus rex praeceperit inde voluntatem suam, et averia capta deliberet si inveniantur. Si autem inveniri non possint, eo quod alibi fugata sunt forte vel extra comitatum in fraudem, et captor terram habuerit in comitatu et catalla, capiat serviens regis de averiis illius in duplum, et illa detineat donec averia sic abducta reducantur. Sed quid si captor nullam terram habuerit in comitatu nec catalla? Quid erit? Cum potestas vicecomitis non extendatur usque ad alium comitatum, et hoc fiat in fraudem ad impedienduam potestatem vicecomitis, tunc recurrendum est ad potestatem regis, et fiat tale breve.

**Breve de attachiendo, quare cepit averia et fugavit extra comitatum. Cum vicecomes vel serviens regis visum habuerit de averiis sine impedimento. De responsione captoris, quod iuste quia in damno suo. Si lex vadiatur et utraque parte. Si serviens alicuius ceperit averia alicuius in absentia domini sui. Cum averia alicuius semel fuerint per iudicium deliberata et iterum capta. Breve quod deliberentur. Sunt etiam catalla quae petuntur sub nomine averiorum cum quis in solo alieno fecerit opus manifestum, si instrumento sua sicut utensilia capiantur quasi in namium propter delicta.**

default of justice. Witness, etc. or [if] it is on someone's *querela* without writ, having first taken from him sureties for prosecuting] to go in his own person, if he can attend to the matter himself, or if he cannot, to send his serjeant, to the place where the beasts are said to be detained, and immediately on his arrival to demand the view of the said beasts, [no matter where they are impounded, and if someone denies him the view, or lays violent hands upon him on that account, let him raise the hue and cry at once, and with the hue and cry arrest the wrongdoers, as men manifestly opposed to the king's peace, and cast them into gaol until the king declares his will in the matter,] and [cause] the said beasts, [if they can be found; if they cannot be found, because they have been driven elsewhere [in the county] or perhaps outside it with intent to defraud, and [if] the distrainor has lands and chattels within the county, let the king's serjeant take twice the number of the taker's beasts and retain them until the beasts so driven away have been brought back. But what if the taker has neither land nor chattels within the county? What then? Since the authority of the sheriff does not extend to the other county and [if] it is done fraudulently in order to escape his authority, let recourse then be had to the king's authority; let this writ issue:

**The writ of attachment why a man seized beasts and drove them outside the county. When the sheriff or the king's serjeant has viewed the beasts without hindrance. Of the seizor's answer, that the taking was lawful because the beasts caused him damage. If law is waged on both sides. If a servant takes another's beasts in his lord's absence. When one's beasts have one been released by judgment and seized a second time. The writ that beasts are to be released. Chattels are also claimed under the name of beasts, as when one has constructed something on another's land and his implements or tools are seized as a kind of pledge because of the delict.**

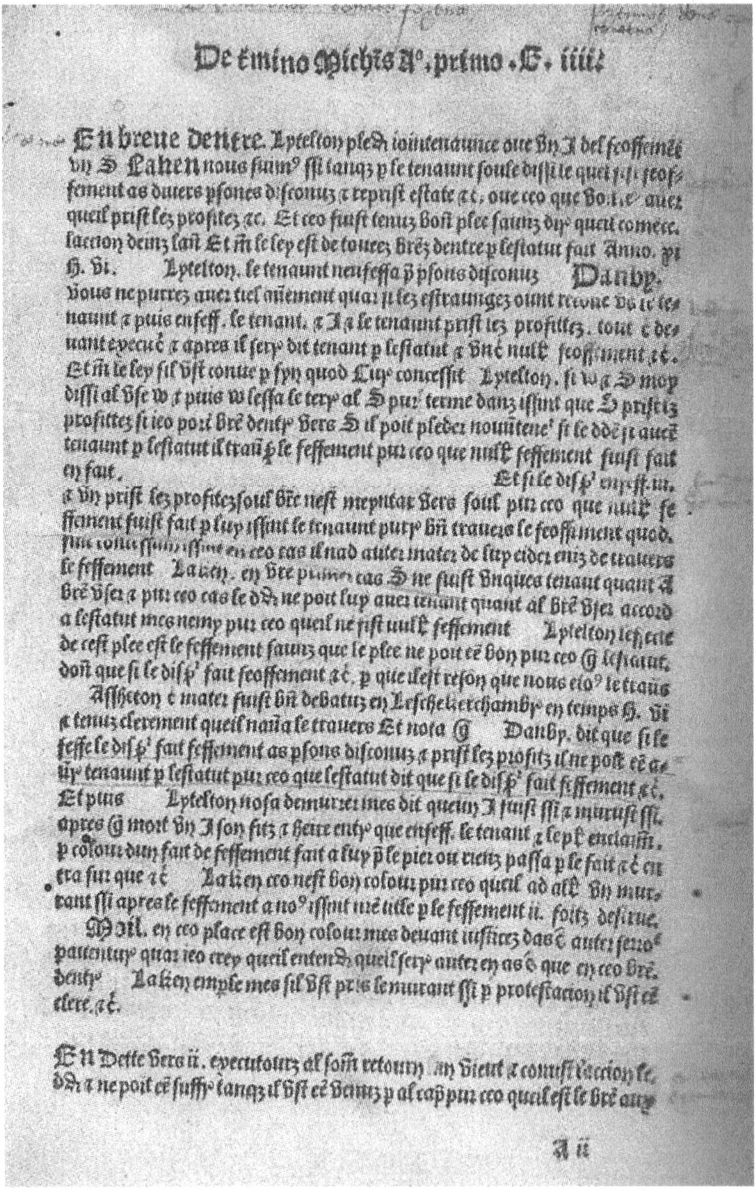
De termino Michis A°. primo. E. iiii.

En breue dentre. Lytelton pled ioinctenaunce oue vn I del feoffment vn S. Laken nous suim⁹ ssi tanqz p le tenaunt soule dissi le quel I fist feoffement as diuers psones disconuz & reprist estate ⱥc, oue ceo que vo. l. e. auer quel prist lez profitez ⱥc. Et ceo fuist tenuz bon plee sauns dire quel comence lacciō deinz lan Et m le ley est de toutez brēz dentre p lestatut fait Anno. pi. H. vi. Lytelton. le tenaunt neufessa p psons disconuz Danby. vous ne purrez auer tiel auerment quar si lez estraungez oint recouē vs le tenaunt & puis enfeff. le tenant. & I & le tenaunt prist lez profittez. tout cō deuant execuē & apres il serr dit tenant p lestatut & vnc nulle feoffment ⱥc. Et m le ley sil vst conue p fyn quod Litt. concessit Lytelton. si W & S moy dissi al vse W & puis W lessa le terr al S pur terme danz issint que S prist lez profittez si ieo port brē dentr vers S il poit pleder nountenē si le ddē ii auer tenaunt p lestatut il trauⱥ le feffement pur ceo que nulle feffement fuist fait en fait. Et si le disp enfeff. W. & vn prist lez profitez soul brē nest meyntar vers soul pur ceo que nulle feffement fuist fait p luy issint le tenaunt purr bn trauers le feoffment quod fuit concessum issint en ceo cas il nad auter mater de luy eider eniz de trauers le feffement Laken. en vre primer cas S ne fuist vnques tenant quant A brē vser & pur ceo cas le ddē ne poit luy auer tenant quant al brē vser accord a lestatut mes nemy pur ceo quel ne fist nulle feffement Lytelton le effecte de cest plee est le feffement sauns que le plee ne poit estre bon pur ceo (sic) lestatut, don que si le disp fait feoffement ⱥc. p que il est reson que nous eiō le trauers Assheton cē mater fuist bn debatuz en Leschekerchamber en temps H. vi & tenuz clerement quel nauā le trauers Et nota (sic) Danby. dit que si le fesse le disp fait feffement as psons disconuz & prist lez profitz il ne poit estre auer tenaunt p lestatut pur ceo que lestatut dit que si le disp fait feffement ⱥc. Et puis Lytelton nosa demurrer mes dit que vn I fuist ssi & murust ssi. apres (sic) mort vn I son fitz & heire entr que enfeff. le tenant & leps enclaim. p colour dun fait de feffement fait a luy p le pier ou tientz passa p le fait ⱥc en tra sur que ⱥc Laken ceo nest bon colour pur ceo quel ad alle vn murrant ssi apres le feffement a no⁹ issint nē ulle p le feffement ii. foitz destrue. Moil. en ceo place est bon colour mes deuant iustices das cō auter seront pauentur quar ieo crey quel entend quel serr auter en as cō que en ceo brē dentr Laken emple mes sil vst pris le murrant ssi p protestacion il vst estre clere. ⱥc.

En Dette vers ii. executourz al somō retourn. vn vient & confist laccion le dd & ne poit estre suffr tanqz il vst estre veinz p al cap pur ceo quel est le brē aūy

A ii

**Year Book**

## Modus Componendi Brevia

The *Modus Componendi Brevia*, which makes mention of the Statute of Westminster II (1285) as something recently enacted, was apparently composed by an unknown author shortly after that legislation. It is a workmanlike account of some of the most common writs that a practitioner is likely to need to know and covers its subject efficiently and effectively. It is in all likelihood the first part of a two-part project that was completed by the *Exceptiones ad Cassandum Brevia*, an Anglo-Norman account of exceptions that fulfills the thrice-repeated promise of a discussion of exceptions made in the last paragraph of the *Modus*, in which likewise is noted the English custom of employing French in pleadings and records. Paul Brand remarks that "it reads as though it was composed with the needs of the law student as well as the junior chancery clerk in mind. The manuscripts in which it is found normally also include a number of other contemporary legal treatises, suggesting that it went into general circulation as a fairly basic treatise containing information that was useful to law students at an early stage in their careers and perhaps to non-experts, too. It is conceivable that it was derived from what was originally a lecture but more probable that it was only ever a written treatise."[1]

The text is printed in Woodbine, *Four Thirteenth Century Law Tracts,* 143-62, followed by the *Exceptiones ad Cassandum Brevia*, which the editor proposes was separated over time from its companion piece. The text Woodbine presents is problematical, perhaps nowhere more noticeably than in its opening, and we have silently corrected and emended obvious errors and translated accordingly. Our translation represents the first time this text has been made available in English.

---

1 Brand 1992 118.

**1.** Cum sit necessarium conquerentibus in curia domini Regis ut sibi in suis casibus exhibeatur remedium congruum et festinum, ad instantiam quorundam sociorum subscriptam, ut sciatur quod breve et in quo casu, tam in actione reali quam personali, ubi minores maioribus indigeant documentum, [ut] dare debeam non modo quo debui sed quod scivi componere dignum duxi. Videndum est primo si actio conquerentis sit realis vel personalis, aut si utramque tangat naturam tam actionem personalem quam realem. Et secundum hoc intellegendum est breve de placito terrae, vel transgressionis, vel quod utramque tangat naturam. Omne igitur placitum quod deducitur in curiam domini Regis generaliter dicitur placitum terrae vel transgressionis. Istud vero placitum in quo exit breve de iudicio quod vocatur magnum Cape vel parvum propter defaltam tenentis, ad capiendum tenementum in manum domini Regis, dicitur placitum terrae. Istud vero placitum in quo exit breve de iudico de magna districtione, ut defendens distringatur per terras et catalla, ut veniat ad respondendum, dicitur placitum transgressionis. Verumtamen quaedam eorum brevium quae placitantur per districtiones, ut de consuetudinibus et servitiis, de medio, et huiusmodi, tangunt utramque naturam; quia sicut tam ratione tenementorum quam personarum iniuriam inferentium. Audito casu conquerentis videatur si actio sit realis, et in ea detur competens remedium per breve de placito terrae. Et secundum quod actio fuerit realis diversa diversificanda sunt forma brevis. Et istud concordat cum suo casu; nec per aliquam exceptionem valeat cassari.

## The Manner of Composing Writs.

**1.** Since it is necessary for plaintiffs in the Lord King's court that a suitable and speedy remedy be shown them in their cases, at the request of some associates I considered what's written below to be worth compiling, so that it might be known which writ I should provide in which case, whether in real or personal actions when subordinates need proof against superiors, [that it might be known] not only how I should provide [the writ] but what I have learned [about the law]. First it should be seen if the plaintiff's suit is real or personal, or if it touches each sort, as much a personal suit as a real. And according as this has been understood, the writ is a plea of land or a plea of trespass, or [it will have been understood] that it touches each sort. Therefore every plea that is brought to trial in the court of the Lord King generally is called a plea of land or of trespass. That plea which results in a writ of judgment called *magnum Cape* [the great *cape*] or *parvum* [the petit *cape*][1] by reason of the tenant's default, for the taking of tenements into the Lord King's hand, is called a plea of land. That plea which results in a writ of judgment by grand distress, so that the defendant is distrained in his lands and chattels, so that he might come to account, is called a plea of trespass. Nevertheless, some of their writs which are pled through distraints, as *e.g.* by customs and servitudes, mesne, and suchlike, touch each nature, because [they are] as much by reason of tenements as of the injury inflicted on persons. When the plaintiff's case has been heard, it should be apparent if the suit is real, and a suitable remedy should be given in it by a writ *de placito terrae* [of plea of land]. And according as the suit was real, the forms of the writ must be varied as required. And that should accord with its case; nor should it be able to be shaken by

---

1 *Cape* (the imperative of *capio*, to take) writs, whether *magnum* or *parvum* (*petit*), order the return of a tenement whose disposition has already been determined in a previous action. A *cape magnum* writ was issued after a defendant had failed to appear in court and a *cape parvum* writ after he had appeared. *Cape magnum* writs accordingly address the failure to appear as well as the original default.

**2.** In omni casu de placito terrae ubi aliquis petit tenementum aliquod de seisina propria, vel per descensum hereditarium, potest fieri breve de recto patens, quod est omnium aliorum in sua natura supremum. Sed propter istius brevis de recto nimiam dilationem et manifesta pericula sunt evitanda. In multis casibus possunt fieri per alia brevia remedia celeriora, ad cuius remedia exhibenda videndum est quot et quibus modis petens poterit petere tenementum aliquod in dominico, et utrum narrare vouerit de seisina propria aut de seisina antecessorum suorum cuius heres ipse est per descensum hereditarium, aut de tenemento quod ad ipsum reverti debet per formam donatoris alicuius, aut tanquam eschaeta sua. Et si petens de propria seisina narrare voluerit, videndum est utrum ipse disseisitus fuit in ipso tenemento, aut quod ipse alicui gratis dimisit. Si autem disseisitus fuerit, detur ei breve de nova disseisina versus disseisitorem et versus tenentem. Si alius sit tenens quam ipse disseisitor detur ei breve de ingressu. Si autem disseisitor mortuus fuerit, et heres eius vel aliquis per ipsum disseisitorem feoffatus de eodem tenemento sit tenens, detur disseisito breve de ingressu super novam disseisinam fundatum, de gradibus faciens mentionem, vel sine mentione graduum, secundum industriam componentis, ut breve debito modo cum suo casu concordet. Si autem petens petat tenementum quod alicui gratis dimisit hoc potest esse dupliciter, aut illud videlicet quod dimisit alicui ad terminum qui praeteriit, vel illud quod alicui dedit in feodo. Si autem petit tenementum quod alicui dimisit ad terminum decem annorum, vel vitae alicuius, post terminum elapsum, detur petenti breve de ingressu ad terminum qui praeteriit cum casu habente concordantiam. Si vero alicui petit tenementum quod dedit in feodo, videatur si tempore donationis petens fuit plenae aetatis, bonae memoriae, et extra prisonam. Et sic non competit ei acto per aliquod breve, ex quo donum illud in tali statu ratificavit.

any exception.

**2**. In every case of a plea of land where someone claims any tenement of his own seisin, or through hereditary descent, the writ *de recto patens* [of right patent] can be made, which is of all others supreme in its nature. But too many delays and obvious dangers must be avoided which arise in the case of this writ of right. In many cases speedier remedies can be had by other writs, looking at whose remedies it must be seen how many and in which ways the demandant can claim some tenement in demesne, and whether he would wish to plead of his own seisin or of the seisin of his ancestors whose heir he himself is by hereditary descent, or of a tenement that should have reverted itself by the formula of some donor or as it were by his escheat. And if the demandant wished to plea of his own seisin, it must be seen whether he himself was disseised in his own tenement, or that he demised[1] to someone freely. If, however, he was disseised, the writ *de nova disseisina* [of novel disseisin] should be given him against the disseisor and against the tenant. If someone is tenant other than the disseisor, let him be given the writ *de ingressu* [of entry]. If, however, the disseisor has died, and his heir or someone feoffed of the same tenement by the disseisor himself is the tenant, let the writ of entry be given the disseised for disseisin founded upon novel disseisin, making mention of degrees,[2] or without mention of degrees, according to the diligence of the writer, so that the writ should agree with its case in the required manner. If, however, the demandant claims a tenement that he freely demised to someone, this can be in two ways, namely either because he demised it to someone for a term which has passed, or because he gave it to someone in fee. If, however, after the term elapsed he claims a tenement that he demised to someone for a term of ten years, or of someone's life, let the writ of entry *ad terminum qui praeteriit* [at a terminus which has passed] be given to the claimant when the case

1 Conveyed the tenement to someone by inheritance.

2 That is, degrees of inheritance (from father, grandfather, or great-grandfather) if the suit is pursued as an inheritance.

Et si tempore donationis fuit infra aetatem, detur sibi breve de ingressu iuxta casum suum formatum, prout patet in registro cum non fuerit plenae aetatis. De tenemento autem quod petens dedit dum non fuit compos mentis suae, detur sibi breve de ingressu iam recuperata bona memoria, secundum casum petentis ordinatum. Si vero inprisonatus fuerit tempore donationis, ipso deliberato detur incontinenti breve de nova disseisina versus ipsum feoffamentum, per cuius vim ipse detentus fuit in prisona, et cartam de feoffamento fieri fecit.

**3.** Femina quaedam narrare debet de seisina propria petendo illud tenementum in dominico per breve de ingressu iuxta casum suum signatum, ut ius et hereditatem suam, aut dotem suam, aut maritagium suum de primo viro suo, quod vel quam vir suus alienavit vel aliter dedit, cui ipsa in vita contradicere non potuit.

**4.** Item si aliquis dederit terram vel tenementum alicui pro certo servitio annuatim sibi in mediate faciendo, et ille feoffatus, vel heres eius, aut aliquis qui de ipso donatore tenuerit, de felonia convictus fuerit, ob quam causam decollatus fuerit vel regnum Angliae abiuraverit, post annum et diem detur donatori vel eius heredi breve de eschaeta. Et illud idem breve detur sibi ad petendum illud tenementum in dominicum quod alicui bastardo dedit, qui sine herede de se obiit.

comes to settlement. If he claims from someone a tenement that he gave in fee, let it be seen if at the time of the grant the claimant was of full age, of good memory, and out of prison. And if this is [not] the case he is not competent in his suit by any writ, for the reason he ratified that grant in such a state. And if at the time of the grant he was under age, let him be given the writ of entry formed according to his case, just as it stood in the register when he was not of full age. However, for the tenement which the demandant granted when he was not in his sound mind, let him be given the writ of entry now that his sound mind has been recovered, shaped according to the demandant's case. If he was imprisoned at the time of the grant, by the same reasoning let the released man be given the writ of novel disseisin against the feoffment itself, by whose power he himself was detained in prison, and let a charter of feoffment be made.

**3.** A wife should plead of her own seisin by seeking that tenement in demesne by a writ of entry marked according to her case, on the basis of right and her inheritance, or her dowry, or her marriage gift from her first husband, which either her husband alienated or gave otherwise, to which she could not object in his lifetime.[1]

**4.** Likewise if someone has given land or a tenement to someone for a certain service done for him annually as a mesne, and that feoffee, or his heir, or someone who has held from the same donor, has been convicted of a felony on account of which case he has been beheaded or has abjured the kingdom of England, let the writ of escheat[2] be given to the donor or his heir after a year and a day. And let that same writ be given to

1 A dowry was the portion of a husband's estate, to be no more than a third, that became the wife's if her husband predeceased her. A marriage gift was a portion that the husband gave his wife upon the occasion of the wedding. While the husband lived these portions were under his control, to be assigned as he saw fit, but came to the wife upon his death. If he had alienated (transferred) them to someone else, the wife had to sue for recovery.

2 A writ of escheat effects the reversion of a tenement to the immediately superior feudal lord.

**5.** Determinata iam via in generali per quam petens poterit petere tenementum aliquod in dominico de seisina sua narrando. Restat videre quot et quibus modis poterit petere tenementum de seisina antecessoris sui per descentionem hereditariam cuius heres ipse est. Unde videndum est utrum ipse antecessor obiit seisitus in dominico suo ut de feodo de tenemento petito, aut inde disseisitus fuerit, aut quo modo ipse antecessor alicui gratis dismisit. Et si modo praedicto obiit seisitus, videatur quo gradu consanguinitatis ipse antecessor attingat petentem; et si de morte patris vel matris, fratris vel sororis, avunculi vel amitae, fiat petenti breve de morte antecessoris. Et si vero plures participes eiusdem hereditatis petant aliquod tenementum communis antecessoris, et antecessor eorum fuerat pater vel mater, frater vel soror, unus vel plures, et in remotiori gradu respectu aliorum, fiat pro eisdem participibus breve de morte antecessoris iuxta formam statuti Gloucestriae. De seisina avi vel aviae, proavi vel proaviae, fiat breve de avo vel avia, proavo vel proavia, de tenemento unde talis antecessor obiit seisitus in dominico suo ut de feodo post tempus limitationis brevium. De seisina quidam consanguinei vel consanguineae qui modo praedicto obiit seisitus, detur petenti breve de consanguinitate, prout vocatur in registro in quadam regula ante breve istud contenta. Si vero antecessor illius petentis de aliquo tenemento fuerit disseisitus, detur heredi petentis breve de ingressu super novam disseisinam fundatum versus tenentem; ita quod fiat debita mentio graduum in quibuscumque casibus ubi fieri poterit. Et si antecessor petentis alicui dimiserit aliquod tenementum, videndum est utrum illa dimissio facta fuerit ad terminum vel in feodo. Et de tenemento ad terminum dimisso, elapso termino, fiat pro herede breve de ingressu quod dicitur ad terminum qui praeteriit, observata semper graduum mentione.

**6.** Si autem antecessor alicuius tenementum aliquod alicui dimiserit vel donaverit in feodo, videatur in quo statu fuerit tempore donationis, videlicet utrum fuerit infra aetatem, aut non compos mentis suae. Et est utraque donatio revocanda per breve de ingressu, secundum utrumque casum pro herede antecessoris illius formatum, cuius modi donationis

him for claiming that tenement in demesne that he gave to some bastard, who has died without an heir of his own.

**5.** The way has now been determined in general by which the demandant can claim some tenement in demesne by pleading his own seisin. It remains to see how many and in which ways he can claim the tenement by hereditary descent of seisin of his ancestor whose heir he himself is. Whence it must be seen whether the ancestor himself died seised in his demesne as of fee of the claimed tenement, or he was thence disseised, or in what way the ancestor himself freely demised to someone. And if he died seised in the aforesaid way, it should be seen in what degree of consanguinity the ancestor himself touched the demandant, and if [the ancestor died seised] by the death of father or mother, brother or sister, paternal uncle or paternal aunt, make for the demandant the writ of *mort d'ancestor.* And if several coparceners of his same inheritance should claim some tenement of a common ancestor, and their ancestor had been father or mother, brother or sister, one or several, and in a more remote degree with respect to the others, make for his coparceners the writ of *mort d'ancestor* according to the formula of the Statute of Gloucester.[1] For the seisin of grandfather or grandmother, great-grandfather or great-grandmother, make the writ *de avo* [of grandfather] or *avia* [grandmother], *proavo* [great-grandfather] or *proavia* [great-grandmother], for the tenement where such an ancestor died seised in his demesne as of fee after the time of determination of writs. For seisin of a male or female relative who died seised in the aforesaid way, let the demandant be given the writ of consanguinity, just as it is named in whatever register contained before that writ [that is, *mort d'ancestor*]. If the demandant's ancestor has been disseised of some tenement, let the demandant's heir be given a writ of entry based upon novel disseisin against the tenant, just so that the required mention of degrees be made in whatever cases where it can be. And if the demandant's ancestor demised some tenement to somebody, it must be seen whether that demission has been made to term or in fee. And of a tenement demised

1 See the Statute of Gloucester (1278), c. 6.

revocatio in aliis casibus fieri non poterit de hereditate donatoris per suum heredem.

**7.** Si autem mulier quae tenementum aliquod tenuerit in dotem alicui donaverit, ipsa vivente, detur remedium heredi; et debet fieri reversio dotis illius iuxta formam statuti Gloucestriae. Et de huiusmodi tenemento quod mulier ante confectionem illius statuti alienaverit, fiat breve de ingressu pro herede ipso in suis gradibus formatum. Si autem aliquis intruserit se in aliquibus tenementis post mortem mulieris, quae illa tenuit in dotem vel aliter ad terminum vitae, detur heredi breve de intrusione versus tenentem; ita quod semper fiat mentio graduum ubi fieri poterit. Et in casibus ubi mentio graduum fieri non poterit, fiat breve de huiusmodi ingressu post intrusionem, sicut in omnibus aliis brevibus de ingressu ubi non poterit fieri mentio de gradibus dicitur post disseisinam vel post dimissionem. Pro viris religiosis, et pro abbatibus, prioribus, magistris, hospitellariis, ubi tenementum aliquod sit ius ecclesiarum suarum, fiant brevia super novam disseisinam fundata. Et ut de termino qui praeteriit et alia brevia sibi congrua; tam in omnibus ubi narrant de seisina propria quam praedecessorum suorum; quia sicut ius hereditatis descendit ab antecessoribus in heredem, sic generaliter descendit ius cuiuscumque ecclesiae, de praedecessore in successoribus. De tenementis quidem alienatis per abbates, priores, aut eorum ballivos, sine assensu sui capituli, fiant pro eorum successoribus brevia de ingressu debito modo in suis casibus formata.

to term, the term having lapsed, make for the heir the writ of entry that is called *ad terminum qui praeteriit* [at the terminus which has passed], always observing mention of degrees.

**6.** If, however, someone's ancestor demised or gave in fee some tenement to someone, it should be seen in what state he was at the time of the gift, namely whether he was under age or not enjoying the presence of his mind. And whichever of the two, the gift must be revoked by a writ of entry, according to each case formed for the heir of that ancestor, whose revocation by the manner of the gift in some cases cannot be done by the heredity of the donor through his heir.

**7.** If, however, a woman who has held some tenement in dower has given [it] to another, herself being alive, let remedy be given to the heir, and let a reversion of that dowry be made according to the form of the Statute of Gloucester.[1] And for a tenement of this sort that the woman alienated before the making of this statute, make the writ of entry for the heir himself informed in his degrees. If, however, someone has intruded himself in some tenements after the woman's death, which she held in dower or otherwise to the term of her life, let the heir be given the writ *de intrusione* [of trespass] against the tenant; in so doing let mention always be made of degrees where it can be. And in cases where mention of degrees cannot be made, let the writ of entry of this sort be made according to trespass, just as in all other writs of entry where mention of degrees cannot be said according to disseisin or according to demission. For religious men, and for abbots, priors, masters, hospitellers, where some tenement is the right of their churches, let the writs be made based on novel disseisin.

1 See the Statute of Gloucester, c. 7.

**8.** Accidit aliquando quod plures heredes, tam fratres de aliquibus tenementiis quam sorores, fiunt participes unius hereditatis de quibus aliqui deforciant aliis rationabilem partem suam. Et in tali casu pro participibus nullam partem habentibus, fiat breve de rationabili parte quod dicitur Nuper obiit, si eorum antecessor obiit a tempore quo currit illud breve qui terminus patet in magno statuto domini Regis Edwardi filii Regis Henrici. Si antecessor eorum participum decesserit ante terminum illum, fiat breve de recto de rationabili parte pro illis petentibus; et illud idem breve pro eisdem participibus partem habentibus et partem non, de sua hereditate, licet eorum antecessor obiit post terminum praenominatum.

**9.** Item per breve de recto patens potest dominus alicuius feodi petere tenementum illud in dominico, quod tenens eius de eo tenuit pro homagio et servitio versus ipsum tenentem. Quod quidem tenementum ipse tenens in curia domini Regis coram iusticiariis qui inde portant recordum de domino suo tenere dedixit, propter eiusdem tenentis ingratitudinem qui domino suo homagium et servitium sibi debitum malitiose subtrahere proposuit.

And as for a term that has expired and other writs congruous to it, whether in all matters where they plead of their own seisin or of their predecessors, because just as the right of inheritance descends from ancestors upon the heir, so generally descends the right of whatever church from the predecessor upon the successors. For tenements alienated by abbots, priors, or their bailiffs, without assent from their chapter, make for their successors the writ of entry formed in the required manner in such cases.

**8.** It happens sometimes that several heirs, whether brothers of some tenements or sisters, became coparceners of one inheritance of which some deforced others their reasonable share. And in such a case for coparceners having no share, make the writ *de rationabili parte* [of reasonable part] that is called *nuper obiit* [he/she recently deceased] if their ancestor died from the time when that writ runs, which limit is available in the great statute of the Lord King Edward, the son of King Henry.[1] If the ancestor of the coparceners died before that limit, make the writ of right of reasonable part for those demandants, and that same writ for their coparceners having a part and not [having] a part from his inheritance, although their ancestor died after the aforenamed limit.

**9.** Likewise by the writ of right patent the lord of any fee can claim that tenement in demesne that his tenant held of him for homage and service against that same tenant. Which certain tenement the tenant himself, in the court of the Lord King, before the justices who from there bear record, has denied to hold from his lord, because of his tenant's ingratitude who has wickedly proposed to withdraw from his lord the homage and service owed him.

1 See the Statute of Winchester I (1275), c. 39, which sets the limits of writs. Writs of right cannot be issued for claims of seisin by an ancestor from before the time of King Richard, writs of *novel disseisin* and *nuper obiit* are to have the limitation "since the first crossing of king Henry, father of our lord the king who now is, to Gascony," and writs of *mort d'ancestor, cosinage, ael*, entry, and *naifty* "from the coronation of king Henry." Henry III was crowned in 1216 and made the specified crossing in 1242.

**10.** Solum autem fit remedium per breve de utrum pro persona ecclesiarum quae per suos praedecessores ab eisdem fuerint alienata.

**11.** Vidua vero post mortem viri sui, secundum communem legem Angliae, petere poterit in dotem suam tertiam partem totius tenementi quod vir suus tenuit in feodo die quo ipsam desponsavit, vel unquam postea; nisi contingat ipsam de minori tenemento dotari. Et est generaliter intellegendum quod per quatuor brevia possunt mulieres petere dotes suas; videlicet per breve de recto de dote, per breve de dote unde nihil habet, per breve de certa dote per virum de proprio tenemento assignato, et per breve de certa dote assignata ad hostium ecclesiae quod dicitur de assensu patris, videlicet quando filius et heres ad hostium ecclesiae dotat uxorem suam de certo tenemento patris sui, ipso patre vivente et praesente ad hoc voluntatem suam et assensum praebente. In quibus autem casibus sunt brevia de dote de recto unde nihil habet, in primis statutis Regis Edwardi filii Regis Henrici sufficienter declaratum est.

**12.** In maneriis quidem de antiquo dominico coronae Angliae fit in omni casu pro tenentibus huiusmodi maneriorum parvum breve de recto clausum, ad petenda tenementa illa in dominco, ubi in aliquo modo ius vendicant in eisdem tenementis quae tenentur secundum consuetudinem maneriorum. Triplex enim fit remedium ad petendam advocationem alicuius ecclesiae, integrae, vel partis eiusdem ecclesiae, in qua advocatione ipse petens ius clamat habere; videliet per breve de recto de advocatione ecclesiae patens vel clausum, ubi ipse petens narrare debet, vel poterit, de longinqua seisina, ut de feodo et iure ab antecessore suo, cuius heres ipse est, sibi descendendo. Et per breve Quare impedit, quod fieri poterit in casu ubi petens ius clamat in advocatione alicuius ecclesiae, eo quod tenementum illud ad quod pertinet ipsa advocatio de quo quidem tenemento aliquis ipsum feoffavit, vel antecessorem suum cuius heres ipse est, una cum advocatione eiusdem ecclesiae, licet ipse vel antecessor eius ad ecclesiam illam non praesentaverit.

**10.** The only remedy, however, for the parson of churches which have been alienated from him by his own predecessors is by the writ of *utrum*.

**11.** A widow after the death of her husband, according to the common law of England, can claim in dower her third part of the whole tenement that her husband held in fee on the day he espoused her, or at any time afterwards, unless it happens that she was dowered of a lesser tenement. And it is generally understood that women can claim their dowries by four writs: namely by a writ *de recto de dote* [of right of dower], by a writ of dower *unde nihil habet* [where she has nothing], by a writ *de certa dote* [of dower in certain] through a husband of his own assigned tenement, and by a writ *de certa dote*, assigned as an offering to a church, that is called *de assensu patris* [by the father's assent], namely when a son and heir as an offering to a church dowers his wife his father's tenement of certain, his father being alive and the offering being presented at his own wish and assent. In which cases, moreover, there are writs of right of dower *unde nihil habet*; it has been made sufficiently clear in the first statute of King Edward the son of King Henry.[1]

**12.** To be sure, in manors of the ancient demesne of the crown of England there is in every case for tenants of manors of this kind the little writ of right close, for claiming those tenements in demesne where in some manner they claim right of those same tenements that are held according to the custom of the manors. For there is a three fold remedy for claiming advowson of some church, of the whole or of a part of the same church, in which by advowson the demandant claims to have right; namely by the writ of right of advowson of a church patent or close, where the demandant himself ought to plead, or can, of long-standing seisin, as of fee and right from his ancestor, whose heir he himself is, by descent from him. And by the writ *Quare impedit* [why he hinders], which can be made in a case where the demandant claims right in the advowson of some church, for the reason that someone feoffed him that

1 The Statute of Winchester I, c. 49.

Et per breve ultimae praesentationis, quod fieri potest ubi aliquis clamat advocationem alicuius ecclesiae ad donationem suam pertinere; eo quod ipse vel antecessor eius cuius heres ipse est, ultimam personam, per cuius mortem illa ecclesia sit vacans, ad eandem ecclesiam praesentavit.

**13.** Cum autem falsum iudicium datum fuerit in aliqua loquela in comitatu vel in curia alicuius deducta, licitum est parti cui illa est iniuria procurare recordum illius loquelae, per breve de falso iudicio poni coram iusticiariis de Banco vel in itinere. Et ibi secundum legem terrae iudicium illum determinare per discretionem iusticiariorum, qui partibus coram eis iustitiae complementum exhibebunt.

**14.** Si aliquis districtionem fecerit per averia vel catalla alicuis, et contra vadium et plegios detinuerit, ille cuius averia vel catalla sunt potest facere ea replegiari per breve domini Regis, et in comitatu vel coram iusticiariis de Banco, vel in itinere, loquelam illam per breve quod vocatur Pone coram eis positam; utrum huiusmodi captio sive detentio fiet iusta vel iniusta determinari.

tenement to which the advowson of which certain tenement pertains, or his ancestor whose heir he himself is, together with the advowson of the same church, although he or his ancestor has not presented to that church. And by the writ of *darrein presentment* [last presentation], which can be made where someone claims that the advowson of some church pertains to his donation; for the reason that he or his ancestor, whose heir he himself is, presented the last parson to that same church, through whose death that church is vacant.

**13.** When, however, a false judgment has been given in some grievance in the county or in someone's conducted court, the wronged party is permitted to provide a record of that grievance, through a writ of false judgment, to be placed before the justices of the bench[1] or in eyre. And there according to the law of the land to decide that judgment by the discernment of the justices, who shall deliver the fulfilment of justice to the parties in their presence.

**14.** If anyone has made a distraint of someone's beasts or chattel, and has detained them against surety and pledges, he whose beasts or chattel they are can cause them to be replevied through the writ [*in curia*] *domini Regis* [in the court of the Lord King], and in the county or before the justices in bench or in eyre, [can cause] that grievance [to be] placed before them by the writ that is called *pone*,[2] to be determined whether a seizure or detention of this sort was just or unjust. For many various assignments can be assigned in this plea, in order to affirm that a distraint which someone has made upon someone is just and reasonable. However, any lord whatsoever can avow a distraint which he made upon his own

1 Before the central courts, King's Bench and Common Pleas, in Westminster.
2 A writ directing competent authority to "place" a suit before a specified court.

Multae enim et variae assignationes possunt assignari in hoc placito, ad affirmandam districtionem quam aliquis fecerit super aliquem esse iustam et rationabilem. Quilibet autem dominus potest advocare districtionem quam faciat super tenentem suum pro amerciamentis levandis per considerationem curiae suae sibi adiudicatis, et etiam pro aliis iustis executionibus iudicorum suae curiae faciendis, et etiam districtionem factam per averia alicuius in dampno suo; ut in bladis, pasturis suis, et aliis locis ut in separabilibus, et etiam facta in feodo suo pro arreragiis et servitiis suis, de quo fuit seisitus per manum tenentis, vel etiam si continuo post mortem antecessoris sui cuius heres ipse est pro servito sibi debito districtionem illam in feodo suo fecerit, licet de eodem seisitus non extiterit. Et si dominus alicuius distringat tenentem suum pro servitiis inde debitis, exigendo ab eo consuetudines et plura servitia quam ipse tenens et antecessores sui cuius heres ipse est pro tenementis suis facere solebant domino suo, vel eius antecessori cuius heres ipse est, ipse tenens duplex habet remedium in tali casu versus dominum suum, videlicet per praedictum breve districtionem illam facere replegiari, et huiusmodi petitiones iniustas ut praedictum est determinari, vel per breve quod dicitur Prohibemus tibi ne iniuste vexes, etc., quod quidem breve per duellum vel per magnam assisam saepius contingit determinari; ob quod magis periculum imineret in hoc placito quam per viam praedictam.

**15.** Item si aliquis feoffaverit aliquem de aliquo tenemento pro quodam servitio sibi annuatim sic faciendo, pro quo ipse feoffator per cartam suam acquietabit feoffatum, exigendo ab eo servita sibi debita de eodem tenemento, vel etiam de aliis tenementis eiusdem feodi, ipse feoffatus in hoc casu per breve domini Regis faciat averia sua replegiari; et loquela illa inter ipsum et capitalem dominum coram iusticiariis pendente, potest impetrare breve de medio versus feoffatorem suum de quo tenet tenementum illud; ut ipsum acquietet de servitiis quae contra tenorem cartae suae ab eo exiguntur.

tenant for levied amercements awarded him by deliberation of his own court, and also for any just executions of judgments made by his own court, and also distraint made through someone's beasts to his damage, as in grain fields, in his pastures, and in other places such as those held in severalty,[1] and also made on his fee for arrears and his services, for which he was seised *per manum tenentis* [through the tenant's hand], or also if he made that distraint on his fee continually after the death of the ancestor whose heir he himself is for service owed to him, although he was not seised of the same. And if someone's lord distrains his tenant for services thence owed, by exacting from him the customs and the several services which the tenant himself and his ancestors whose heir he himself is were accustomed to perform for their lord for their tenements, or his ancestors whose heir he himself is, the tenant himself has a twofold remedy in such a case against his lord, namely by the aforesaid writ to cause that distraint to be replevied, and the unjust claims of this manner to be determined as was aforesaid, or by the writ that is called *prohibemus tibi ne iniuste vexes,* etc. [we forbid you to trouble unjustly, etc.], which writ indeed often happens to be decided by a duel or by the grand assize, although greater danger inheres in this plea than by the aforesaid way.

**15.** Likewise if someone has feoffed someone of some tenement for which thus doing service to him annually, for which the feoffer himself will acquit the feoffee by his charter, claiming from him services owed to him of that same tenement, or also of other tenements of his same fee, let the feoffee in this case by the writ [*in curia*] *domini Regis* cause his beasts to be replevied; and this grievance between him and the lord in chief pending before the justices, he can purchase a writ *de medio* [of mesne] against his feoffor from whom he holds that tenement, so that he acquit himself of services which are exacted from him against the stipulation of his charter.

1 Land not shared with others.

**16.** Si autem capitalis dominus non potest distringere tenentem suum pro homagiis et aliis servitiis sibi debitis de feodo suo de quibus seisitus fuerit, fiat pro ipso domino breve de consuetudinibus et servitiis, ut in redditibus arreragiis et aliis, quod quidem breve dicitur de possessione, et quod ipse dominus de seisina propria narrabit et dampna sua una cum arreragiis recuperabit. Et in casibus ubi oportet ipsum dominum de seisina antecessoris sui, cuius heres ipse est, de huiusmodi servitiis per descensum hereditarium narrare, fiat pro eodem breve de recto de consuetudinibus et servitiis, in quo non debet fieri mentio de redditibus et arreragiis, quia ipsa verba seisinam petentis semper supponunt. Cum autem petat evidenter tam per regulas in registro contentas quam per formam plurimorum brevium quae placitantur per districtiones, in quibus casibus ipsa brevia dari debent; et de eorum compositione in suis casibus non est necesse ut aliquid in praesenti doctrina tangatur; quia habito pleno intellectu brevium communium et casuum eorundem brevium habetur plenarie cognitio.

**17.** In quibus autem casibus componuntur aliqua brevia quae iuxta tenorem statutorum sunt formata ista statuta in se sufficienter declarant; sed quia pastura multipliciter poterit haberi de ipsius divisione est aliquid dicendum. Pastura quidem alia communis alia separabilis. De pastura separabili in qua quis habet ius feodi et liberum tenementum, possunt omnia remedia quae in praedictus casibis de terris et tenementia assignantur assignari. Pastura quidem communis potest esse dupliciter vel quia pertinet ad liberum tenementum alicuius, vel aliquis clamat ea ratione alicuius feoffamenti ad certum numerum averiorum, non autem ratione alicuius tenementi ad quod ipsa pastura pertinet.

**16.** If, however, the lord in chief cannot distrain his tenant for homages and other services owed him of his fee of which he [the tenant] was seised, let there be made for the lord himself the writ *de consuetudinibus et servitiis* [of customs and services], as in recovered arrears and other matters, which writ to be sure is pled of possession, and which the lord himself will plead of his own seisin and will recover his damages together with arrears. And in cases where it behooves the lord himself of seisin of his ancestor, whose heir he himself is, to plead of these kinds of services by hereditary descent, let it be by the same writ of right of customs and services, in which mention should not be made of renderings and arrears, because those words always support the seisin of the demandant. Since, however, he should claim clearly, whether by the *regulae*[1] contained in a register or by the formula of several writs that are pleaded for distraints, in which cases the writs themselves should be given; and of their composition in his cases it is not necessary that anything in the doctrine of presentment [of benefice] be touched upon, because cognizance is fully had by having full understanding of the writs of commons and the writs of their cases.

**17.** In which cases, however, some writs are composed which are formed according to the wording of statutes; these statutes verify sufficiently in themselves; but because pasture can be held in many different ways, something should be said of its division. Some pasture, to be sure, [is] common, some separate. Of separate pasture in which someone has the right of fee and free tenement, all remedies can be assigned which are assigned in the aforesaid cases for lands and tenements. Common of pasture can be twofold either because it pertains to someone's free tenement or someone claims it by reason of someone's feoffment to a certain number of beasts, not, however, by reason of someone's tenement to which the pasture pertains. And pasture of this sort for a certain

1 Perhaps meaning simply ruled lines in a register that recorded land holdings. For such registers, see Clanchy, *From Memory to Written Record*, 103-4.

Et potest huiusmodi pastura ad certum numerum averiorum dari alicui ad terminum vitae suae, vel sibi et heredibus suis in feodo, et in utroque casu potest fieri pro conquerente breve quod vocatur Quod permittat.

**18.** De communia pasturae in quo non fiet ea mentio de numero averiorum. In narratione **tam** de termino debet fieri mentio. Et si in brevi ponatur **le solet**, vel in eo omittatur, secundum quod conquerens de seisina propria aut de seisina antecessoris sui cuius heres ipse est, voluerit narrare.

**19.** De pastura communi pertinens ad liberum tenementum alicuius inquirendum est si conquerens fuit inde in seisina vel non. Et si de seisina sua eiectus fuerit iniuste, fiat pro ipso disseisito breve de nova disseisina de communia pasturae super suum disseisitorem, et mortuo disseisitore fiat breve quod vocatur Quod permittat, in quo fiat mentio de disseisina sibi facta versus heredem disseisitum. Si autem conquerens de ista pastura seisitus non fuerit, inquirendum est ab eo si antecessor eius, cuius heres ipse est, obiit seisitus de pastura illa tamquam pertinente ad liberum tenementum suum, vel inde disseisitus fuerit. Si inde disseisitus fuerit, detur ipsi querenti breve quod vocatur Quod permittat versus disseisitorem sui antecessoris, vel versus eius heredem. Si ipse disseisitor mortuus fuerit, et heres eius pasturam illam sibi deforciaverit, in quo brevi fiet mentio de disseisina antecessoris ipsius querentis facta. Et si alius fuerit inde deforcians quam ipse disseisitor vel eius heres, sicut extraneus perquisitor, disseisitus vel eius heres non poterit habere breve de huiusmodi disseisina faciens mentionem versus extraneum ipsum. Sed in tali casu habebit breve de recto de communia pasturae, non faciens mentionem de disseisina. Et illud videtur durissimum in lege eo quod idem breve de recto per duellum vel per magnam assisam vult determinare, licet antecesor conquerentis de pastura illa fuerit disseisitus.

number of beasts can be given to someone for the term of his life, or to him and his heirs in fee, and in whatsoever case the writ that is called *quod permittat* [that he permit] can be made for the complaint.

**18.** Of common of pasture in which mention is not made of the number of beasts. In the plea mention should also be made of the term. And whether *le solet* (he alone) is put in the writ, or is omitted in it, according as the plaintiff has wished to plea of his own seisin or of the seisin of the ancestor whose heir he himself is.

**19.** For common of pasture pertaining to someone's free tenement, it must be asked if the plaintiff was thence in seisin or not. And if he has been unjustly dispossessed of his seisin, make for that person disseised the writ of novel disseisin of common of pasture against his disseisor, and if the disseisor is dead make the writ that is called *quod permittat*, in which let mention be made of the disseisin made against him as opposed to [disseisin made against] his disseised heir. If, however, the plaintiff has not been seised of that pasture, it must be asked of him if his ancestor, whose heir he himself is, died seised of that pasture whether pertaining to his free tenement or he has been thence disseised. If he was thence disseised, let him be given the writ of complaint that is called *quod permittat* against his ancestor's disseisor, or against his heir. If the disseisor himself has died, and his heir has deforced him that pasture, in which writ mention shall be made of the disseisin made of his own complaining ancestor. And if someone has thence been deforcing, whether the disseisor himself or his heir, as a third party acquirer, the disseisor or his heir cannot have a writ of disseisin of this manner making mention against the outsider himself. But in such a case he shall have the writ of right of common of pasture, not making mention of disseisin. And that seems a hard thing in the law because that same writ of right wishes to decide by duel or grand assize, although the plaintiff's ancestor has been disseised of that pasture.

**20.** Cum pateat evidenter per ea quae praescripta sunt, quot et quibus modis tenens peti poterit in dominico secundum legem Angliae tempore confectionis huiusmodi doctrinae usitatam, animavertendum est ulterius quot et quibus modis a Rege Edwardo filio Regis Henrici ulterius remedium conceditur ad petendum tenementum in dominicum in magnis statutis suis, anno regni sui tertiodecimo apud Westmonasterium editis, ut in casibus de forma donationis de tenementis quorum servitium detinetur per biennium, et de tenementis in liberam elemosinam datis, et contra formam huiusmodi collationis alienatis. In ipsis itaque statutis diversificantur remedia in quibusdam casibus usitata, ut in casibus ubi prius fieri solebat breve de prohibitione vasti, et super hoc attachimentum si necesse fuisset. Nunc facto vasto fit breve de summonitione. Et etiam ubi fieri solebat breve de corrodio subtracto, nunc si corrodium subtrahatur breve de nova disseisina in illo casu datur, sicut etiam illud idem breve datur in multis aliis casibus in quibus liberum tenementum prius recuperari non potuit per idem breve, sicut plenius in eisdem statutis continetur. Multa etiam brevia originalia in istis statutis sunt provisa que prius fieri non consueverunt, et in quibus casibus ipsa brevia dari debent in ipsis statutis sufficenter declaratur. Et quia [brevia] de placito per varias exceptiones dilatiorias saepius cassantur, cum quia debito modo in suis casibus non assignantur, tum quia licet debito modo assignantur, tum quia vitium reperitur in forma et hoc potest esse multipliciter secundum quod multiplex est exceptio dilatoria quae cassat breve per iudicium. Et ad evitandum periculum huiusmodi exceptionum aliquid est subsequenter dicendum, ut minores in confectione brevium praemuniantur de multimodis vitiis per quae brevia cassantur.

**20.** Since it is clearly evident, through the things which have been written above, how many and in what ways a tenant can be sued in demesne according to the law of England practiced at the time of preparation of an instruction of this sort, it should be noted furthermore of what number and in what ways remedy for claiming a tenement in demesne has been granted in addition in his great regulations by King Edward, the son of King Henry, issued at Westminster in the thirteenth year of his reign,[1] as in cases of the form of donation of tenements whose service is distrained for two years, and for tenements given in frankalmoign,[2] and otherwise than the form for alienations of a collation of this sort. And so in the regulations themselves the remedies used are different in whatsoever cases, as in cases where the writ *de prohibitione vasti* [of forbidding waste] used to be made at first, and against it an attachment if it became necessary. Now for waste committed the writ of summons is made. And also where used to be made the writ *de corrodio subtracto* [for possessions carried off], now if the possession has been carried off, the writ of novel disseisin should be given in that case, just as also that same writ is given in many other cases in which a free tenement could not be recovered before by the same writ, just as is more fully found in his same regulations. And many original writs are provided in these regulations which were not accustomed to be made before, and in which cases these writs themselves should be given is more adequately stated in the regulations themselves. And because [writs] of a plea are often quashed by various dilatory exceptions, whether because they are not assigned in their cases in the required manner, or because although they are assigned in the required manner then because a flaw is discovered in the form, and this can be in many different ways, according to which the dilatory exception that quashes a writ by judgment is complex. And something must subsequently be said about avoiding the danger of this sort of

---

1 The Statute of Westminster II in 1285. See esp. c. 1, which forbids tenants to alienate tenements held through subinfeudation.

2 A tenure by which a religious corporation holds a tenement in perpetuity.

Et si aliquis exceptiones dilatorias per quae brevia cassantur perfecte intellegeret de huiusmodi vitiis in confectione brevium praemuniri posset hac de causa, tamen contrariorum contrarii sunt effectus; de huismodi exceptionibus inferius dicetur, ut ipsis intellectis brevis adeo perfecte conficiantur, ne per illas exceptiones cassantur. Sicut enim effectus exceptionis dilatoriae est breve vitiosum cassare, sic effectus brevis debito modo in suo casu confecti est sustinere contra quamlibet exceptionem ne valeat cassari.

**21.** Exceptionum aliae sunt dilatoriae, aliae peremptoriae. Dilatoriae sunt quae cassant breve et remanet actio petenti. Peremptoriae sunt quae perimunt tam breve quam actionem, et tam harum quam illarum quaedam proponuntur ratione petentis, quaedam ratione rei petitae, quaedam ante visum terrae, quaedam post visum terrae habitum, quaedam per ipsum tenentem in dominicum, quaedam per vocatum ad warrantum. Et qualiter et quibus modis, videlicet quae primo, quae secundo, quae tertio, et sic deinceps proponi debent, inferius patebit evidenter. Sed quia consuetudo regni Angliae talis est, quod placita coram iusticiariis per narratores in romanis verbis, et non in latinis, pronunciantur; idcirco huiusmodi exceptiones lingua romana in scriptis rediguntur.

exceptions, so that in the preparation of writs novices are forewarned of the many sorts of faults by which writs are quashed. And if someone understood perfectly the dilatory exceptions by which writs are quashed for these kinds of faults in the preparation of writs, he could be forewarned for this reason, yet the effects of opposites are opposites; these kinds of exceptions are discussed below, so that themselves having been understood let writs be prepared truly perfectly, lest they be quashed by those exceptions. For just as the effect of a dilatory exception is to quash a flawed writ, thus the effect of a writ fashioned in its case in the required manner is to prevail against whatsoever exception so that it is not able to be quashed.

**21.** Some exceptions are dilatory, others peremptory. Dilatory are those that quash a writ and stay the demandant's suit. Peremptory are those that thwart, either the writ or the suit, and whether of the former or the latter some are proposed on account of the demandant, some on account of the defendant's request, some before the viewing of the land, some after the customary viewing of the land, some by the tenant himself in demesne, some by having been called to warrant. And how and in what ways, namely which first, which second, which third, and thus according as they should be proposed, will be clearly shown below. But because such is the custom of the realm of England that pleas are delivered before the justices by pleaders in French words, and not in Latin, therefore exceptions of this sort are recorded in writing in the French language.[1]

1 This sentence is generally taken as a transition to the discussion, in French, of exceptions that formed the second part of the treatise.

# CASES

## Disputes about a Castle

**1.** A dispute about the manor of Bredwardine. In March 1199 Thomas de Baskerville complains that Ralph/Raoul de Baskerville has unlawfully taken possession (disseized) his holding in Bredwardine (the modern spelling) Castle. This castle, no longer standing, was in Herfordshire in western England on a manor, given at the Norman Conquest to John de Bredwardine and later owned by the Baskerville family. The castle and manor were subjects of several legal actions, two of which are given here. The first is a case of *novel disseisin* (see the section below on this assize).

Curia Regis Roll 51 in *Curia Regis Rolls* p. 76.

Herefordshire. §Assisa venit recognitura si Radulfus de Baschervill' injuste et sine judicio disseisivit Thomam de Baschervill' de liber tenemento suo in Bredewarthin infra assisam. Juratores dicunt quod ita desseisivit eum. Judicium. Thomas habeat inde seisinam suam, et Redulfus in misericordia. Dampnum disseisine est xviii marce: illud reddat.

Herefordshire. An assize was held to determine if Ralph of Baskerville unjustly and without legal cause disseized Thomas of Baskerville of his freehold in Bredwardine[1] within the time limit of the assize. The jurors say that he did so disseize him. The judgment: Thomas shall hereafter have his possession and Ralph shall be amerced (= fined). The fine for the disseizin is 18 Marks. Let him pay it.

2. Another dispute: on 8 July 1199 Nesta of Baskerville complains that she has been deprived of her inheritance, the castle of Bredwardine, by Robert de Wastre.

---

1 Probably the manor, not the castle. What connection there is between these two suits is unknown.

From *Rotuli Curiae Regis*, vol. 1 p. 426

Hereford'. Loquendum de Nesta de Baskerville que petit castellum de Bredeworth cum pertinentibus suis, quod Robertus de Wastre ei deforciat, et quod ipsa Nesta dicit esse jus et hereditatem suam. Et dominus Rex precepit vicecomitem quod caperet castellum illud in manum suam. Et vicecomes dicit quod castellum illud est ex baillia sua et non est ausus apponere manum suam in illo castello. Quod non est in sua potestate. Et William de Brause dicit quod nec rex nec justiciarius nec vicecomes debent manum suam apponere in libertate sua.

Loquela remanet sine die donec sciatur inde voluntas domini Regis.

Herefordshire. A plea of Nesta de Baskerville who demands the Castle of Bredeworth (Bredwardine) with its appurtenances, which Robert de Wastre has deprived her of, which this Nesta says is her right and inheritance. And the Lord King directed that the sheriff should take the castle into his own hands. And the sheriff says that that castle is out of his bailiwick [i.e. because it is a liberty], and that he dares not lay a hand on that castle, that it is not in his power. And William de Brause[1] says that neither king, nor justiciar, nor sheriff have any right to lay their hands on his liberty.

The plea remains without a day [appointed], until the will of the Lord King is known.

This case exhibits some of the technical Latin vocabulary of the law:

*Baillia* (also *balliva*), 'bailiwick', originally the area of responsibility of a bailiff (*ballivus*), a sheriff's assistant. In # 1 the sheriff refers to his own area of responsibility as his bailiwick. His area would usually have been the entire county (*comitatus*).

1 William of Braose (died 1211) was sheriff of Herfordshire at the time. A great landowner, he was a favorite of King John, but later fell out with the king and fled to France. His wife and child were starved to death by the king in Windsor Castle.

*Libertas*, 'liberty', the district subject to someone's jurisdiction, not the king's (e.g. London was a liberty); an area of local administration.

*Seisina* and its derivatives, 'seisin', 'possession without ownership'; *Disseizire,* 'to disseise or disseize', 'to dispossess', usually of an estate.

*Misericordia*, 'an amercement', 'a fine imposed by a lord or a court'. The common meaning in Latin is 'mercy', but in law *in misericordia esse* 'to be in someone's mercy' means to be subject to a fine.

Here is the image of the original entry of item #2 in the roll as printed in the 19th century.[1]

***H'ford.*** ¶ Loquend̄ de *Nesta de Bask'uill* que petit castellū de *Bredewrth* c̄ ptiñ suis qđ *Rob de Wastre* ei deforciat. ⁊ qđ ip̄a *Nesta* dic̄ ēē jus ⁊ h̄editatē suam. ⁊ dñs Rex p̄cep̄ vic̄ qđ capet castellum illđ in manū suā. ⁊ vic̄ dic̄ qđ castellū illđ ÷ exª bailliā suā ⁊ ñ ÷ ausus appoñe manū suā in illo castello. qđ ñ ÷ in sua potestate. ⁊ *Will de Brause* dic̄. qđ nᵉ rex nᵉ justic̄. nᵉ vic̄ debñt mañ suā appoñe in lib̄tate sua. ¶ Loq̄la remanet sñ die. donᵉ sciatʳ iñ voluntas dñi Reḡ.

---

1 This image is an example of "Record type," a typeface which attempts to reproduce near-facsimiles of medieval manuscripts, abbreviations and all. First created in the 1770s to print a "facsimile" of the Domesday Book, it was widely used in the 19th century. With the development of photographic reproduction, and in view of the difficulty of setting this type, its use was abandoned early in the 20th century. It still remains useful for the student who is learning to read medieval handwriting.

## A False Charge of Robbery

At an uncertain date during the reign of King John (1199-1216) Hugh Peche, who must have lived near Winfrith in Dorset, was accused of robbery. He is now suing for damages on the grounds that the charge was false. Previously there had been a duel between Hugh and Robert of Availles, the champion of the present defendant Theodoricus / Thierry Harang' (this is an example of trial by combat), and Hugh had won the duel. The king decided that the original charge of robbery stemmed from hatred, not Hugh's guilt. The defendant Theodoricus' appearance was postponed (an *essoin*) and he had pledges, or men who could vouch for his truthfulness, but they apparently were not sufficient, according to this record. The last lines mean that a writ *recordari facias* should be directed at the sheriff to remove the case to the king's jurisdiction. The eventual decision, as in most cases, is unknown.[1]

From Baildon, *Select Civil Pleas* p. 73

Hugo filius Willielmi Peche optulit se iiii die versus Theodoricum Harang' de petitio quare ipse fecit ipsum Hugonem appellari de latrocinio, unde duellum vadiatum fuit inter eundem Hugonem et Robertum de Availles, et unde inquisitum fuit per preceptum domini Regis quod Hugo appellatus fuit inde per attiam[2] et odium et non quia ipse erat culpabilis. Et Therricum non venit et habuit diem per essoinem suum et postea positus fuit per plegios, Hugonem de Bosco et Robertum de Warmewell. Et ideo consideratus est quod Thierricus

---

1 Latin terminology: *Duellum vadiatum,* a formal, legally arranged duel to settle the case, trial by combat; *Essoin*, a legal postponement; *Plegius*, 'a person who becomes surety for another, a member of a frank-pledge' (from Late Latin *plegium*, security', 'pledge').

2 *attia, atyiae, atia*, various spellings – 'hatred,' 'spite'; perhaps cognate with Ang.-Sax. *hete* and Mod. Eng. hate. Appellants often claimed that a charge had been brought *de odio et atia*, 'by hatred and spite'.

ponatur per meliores plegios. Et primi plegii summonentur adesse coram domino Rege die Veneris proxima post festum Sancti Michaelis etc. Et quia idem Hugo queritur quod suum judicium factum fuit ei inde in Hundredo de Winfrod quod Robertus de Novo burgo habet in manu sua, Vicecomes faciat fieri recordum in Hundredo et Robertus habeat recordum illud coram Regem ad predictum terminum per iiii milites de Hundredo, etc.

Hugh, son of William Peche, offered himself on the fourth day against Thierry Harang of a plea wherefore he caused Hugh to be appealed of robbery, touching which a duel was waged between the said Hugh and Robert de Availles, and as to which it was found, by the King's command, that Hugh was appealed thereof by spite and hate, and not because he was guilty. Thierry did not come, and he had a day for his essoin;[1] and he was first put [i.e. produced] by these pledges, Hugh Wood and Robert de Warmwell. It is therefore considered that Thierry be put by better pledges, and let the first pledges be summoned to be before the King on the Friday next after Michaelmas, etc. And because Hugh complains that the judgment thereof was made against him in the Hundred [-court] of Winfrith, which Robert de Newburgh[2] has in his hand, let the sheriff cause the record in the Hundred [-court] to be made, and let Robert have that record before the King at the said term, by four knights of the Hundred, etc.

1 An excuse for his absence; essoins were readily given, understandable in a pre-technological society where transport was difficult.

2 Robert de Newburgh (1175-1230), lord of Winfrith manor, Dorset, now the town of Winfrith Newburgh.

An image of the 1890 volume, which uses Record type:

[3] ¶ Hug̃ fił Wiłłi Peche op . se . iiij . die ꝟsꝰ Theodoricũ [4] Harang̃ de pł̄ito qr̃ ip̃e fecit ip̃m Hug̃ appłłari de latͦcinio uñ duellũ vadiatũ fuit inͭ eunđ Hug̃ ⁊ Rob̃ de Availleſ ⁊ uñ ĩquisitũ fuit p ꝓceptũ dñi Ꝛ q̃d Hug̃ appłłatꝰ fuit inde ꝑ attiã ⁊ odiũ ⁊ ñ quia ip̃e ẽet culpabił . ⁊ Therricꝰ ñ veñ ⁊ ħuit diẽ p essoñ suũ ⁊ pͭꝰ põitꝰ fuit ꝑ pleg̃ s . Hug̃ de Bosco ⁊ Rob̃ de Warmeweł. Et iđo cõsiđatũ est q̃d Therricꝰ ponatͬ ꝑ met pleg̃ . ⁊ pͥmi pleg̃ sum̃oñ adẽe corã dño Ꝛ die veñis ꝓxima post festũ Sc̃i Mich ⁊c. Et quia idẽ Hug̃ q̃ritͬ q̃d suũ Judm fc̃m fuit ei iñ in hundr̃ de Winfrod q̃d Rob̃ de Novo burgo ħt ĩ manu sua. Vic̃ faciat fͤri recordũ ĩ Hundr̃ ⁊ Rob̃ ħat recorđ illud corã Ꝛ ad p̃dc̃m ͭminũ ꝑ iiij . milites de Hundr̃ ⁊c.

## The Assize of *Novel Disseisin*

The assize of *novel disseisin* ("recent ejectment" or "recent dispossession") was instituted by Henry II after the Assize of Clarendon in 1166. One who had been ejected from his property (*liberum tenementum*) by superior force was to be restored immediately. Only after the restoration would the rights and wrongs of the dispute be adjudicated. Before this assize, the ejected party had the difficult task of asserting his rights (by a writ of right) against a stronger party who was in possession and who could interpose interminable delays in order to retain what might be unjust seisin. The assize of *novel disseisin* (at least in theory) alleviated this difficulty. The assize is "recent," since a date was specified after which the assize took effect; thus the *intra assisam* below, "within the period of the assize."

The following is a case of *novel disseisin*. In October 1199 John son of Godric and Aifled his wife brought suit against Gilbert of Norfolk and others alleging that they had been disseised of their property in Creake (on the town of Creake see "A Case of Nonpayment" below). The hearing was set for the next Martinmas term. It was finally heard in April of 1200, when John and Aifled lost. The jury determined that Gilbert had disseised them by judgment of his own court. The spelling of proper names varies in the source.

From *Rotuli Curiae Regis*, vol. 2 pp. 28, 194.

October 1199:

Norfolk: §Assisa de nova disseisina inter Johannem filium Godrici et Aifledam uxorem eius querentes ut Gilbertus de Norfolk et Willielmus Scriba et Radulfus Brunig' disseisiverunt de libero tenemento eorum in Creca. Ponitur in responsum usque in octabis Sancti Martini . . .

Norfolk. An assize of novel disseisin brought by John son of Godric and Aifled his wife who complain that Gilbert of Norfolk and William

Scriba and Radulfus Brunig disseised them of their free tenement in Creake. This is put for response at the octabis [eighth day] of Martinmas . . .

April 1200:

Norfolk: § Assisa venit recognitura si Gwillelmus de Norfolk injuste et sine judicio disseisivit Johannem filium Godrici et Aifledam uxorem suam de liber tenemento suo in Creca infra assisam. Juratores dicunt quod Gillielmus de Norfolk non desseisivit eos. Et postea interrogati dixerunt quod Gillielmus disseisivit eos per judicium curie sue.

Norfolk. An assize was held to determine if William of Norfolk unjustly and without legal cause disseized John son of Godric and Aifled his wife of their freehold in Creake within the time limit of the assize. The jurors say that he did not disseise them, and when later questioned, they said that William disseised them by a judgment of his own court.

Additional Reading:
Baker and Milsom 2010 29.
Plucknett 1956/2010 358-60.

## The Case of Sir William Septvans, 1366.

In the 14th century, Parliament acted as a court of appeals in which the judgments of lower courts could be reversed, as in this 1366 case of what we would call fraud. In 1351 Sir William Septvans (or Septvauns), the lord of Aldington Septvauns manor in Kent, died and left his extensive property to his minor son, also called William. In feudal England all land was considered to be nominally the property of the king: an "owner" like Septvans was said to hold the property "of the king." In turn, any of Septvans' tenants would be said to hold his property "of William Septvans," and so on. The tenant-in-chief, the tenant who held the property directly from the king, was said to hold the property *in capite,* as was the case here. On the death of a tenant *in capite*, an inquiry was held to determine the nature of the tenant's tenure, the value of his lands, and the name and age of his heir. If the heir was under age, the king took control of the property as a guardian of the heir, who was the king's ward. When the heir came of full age, he sued for a writ *de aetate probanda* "to prove his age" which was then issued to the escheator, the royal official who supervised inheritances for the king (among other duties), to inquire into the age of the child, another writ being issued to the sheriff to impanel a jury on this matter. If the heir proved to be of age, he obtained "livery of seisin" of this lands, i.e. they were returned to his hands.[1]

Thirteen years later in 1364, when his mother died, the heir, in his late teens and as insightful as young men of his age and status usually are, was convinced by several men to falsely establish that he was of age, over 21. The men mentioned as instigators in the document below included William de Chirchehull, Lucas de Whetynden, John Gower (usually identified as the poet, but there is no direct evidence), and

1 *seisin*, 'possession of land by freehold'; the opposite is *disseisin*, 'dispossession'. In modern legal English a possessor is said to be 'seized/seised of his land' i.e. in possession of.

several others. There was no shortage of vultures circling. In the escheat proceedings twelve jurors testified that William the heir had been born in 1344 and that he was of age. The escheator, John de Tye, certified the testimony and declared William son of William (*Willelmus filius Willelmi* in Latin, *William fitz William* in French) to be of age. Immediately thereafter the heir alienated much of his property to the men mentioned above. John Gower got a large share of Aldington Manor plus other properties and rents.

Someone must have complained, because in 1366 King Edward III ordered that a new inquiry be held on this matter. If the alienation had been improper, then the king had been cheated of his due (rents and services from the properties). The inquiry determined that the previous proof of age had been false, that William the son had not been of age in 1344, and that the alienation of lands had therefore been illegal. The men who had received the property, i.e. "taken it out of the king's hands," were ordered to restore it all.

Following is the Parliamentary record of the Septvans hearing. Note the mixture of languages. First comes a summary of the decision (in French), next the actual writ (in Latin) issued by King Edward III ordering a new inquiry, then a summary of the results of the inquiry (in Latin) which includes a record (in French) which gives details of the testimony in this case. Undoubtedly most of the actual testimony had been in English. The document concludes with the Latin decision of Parliament.

The Septvans family continued its career in Kent until it died out in the $15^{th}$ century.[1]

---

1 Latin vocabulary: *Feoffare*, 'to feoff', 'to put in legal possession of' (Latin *feodum,* 'a fee', 'a fief' meaning an estate held of a superior lord - see above); *mesuagium*, 'messuage', a plot of land with a house and other buildings on it.

## The Case of Sir William Septvans, 1366.

### Rotulus Parliamenti de anno Regni Regis Edwardi Tertii quadragesimo.

Queles offices fueront lues en dit Parlement devant touz les Grantz et Communes, et le dit William illoeques veue par mesmes les Grantz, fust avys et agardee par touz les Grantz, qe le dit William estoit deinz age, et qe touz ses Terres et Tenementz mys hors de la possession le Roi par la primere proeve de l'age meins verroi fussoient, ove touz les profits ent sourdantz, en la mein le Roi reseisez, a demurer tan qe a son pleine age.

Et qe touz les Chartres, Escritz, et Obligations, si bien des Estatutz Marchantz et de l'Estaple come autres qeconqes, et aussi Reconissances a qeconqes persones pour le dit William fitz William faites avant cele heure, fussoient cassez et adnulleez, sicome en le Recorde ent fait en dit Parlement, et demurant en Chancellerie plus pleinement appiert, la copie de quele Recorde est cosue a cestes.

Dominus Rex mandavit Breve suum in hec verba: Edwardus, Dei gratia, Rex Anglorum, Dominus Hiberiae et Aquitaniae, dilectis et fidelibus suis Johanni de Cobham de Kent, Thome de Lodelowe, et Willelmo Waure, Salutem. Quia datum est Nobis intelligi quod Willelmus filius et heres Willelmi de Septvans, Chivaler, defuncti, qui de Nobis ut de Corona tenuit in capite, et cujus terre et tenementa cum pertinentibus in Comitatu Kanc', Sussex, Essex, ratione minoris etatis heredis predicti capta fuerunt in manum nostram, etatem suam coram Escaetore nostro in dicto Comitatu Kanc' inde minus rite informato, ad procurationem, imaginationem, et informationem quorundam suggerentium ipsum Willelmum filium Willelmi plene etatis esse, minus sufficienter probavit; Et quod nos in probatione decepti eramus, eo quod predictus heres adhuc infra etatem existit, et per magnum tempus erit, et quod terre et tenementa predicta cum pertinentibus eidem heredi, in nostri deceptionem et amissionem juris et proficui nostri ad Nos in hac parte pertinentes, per dictam Inquisitionem sic falso informatam extra manus nostras liberata fuerunt:

Nos volentes indempnitati nostre prospicere in hac parte prout decet, Assignavimus vos et duos vestrum, quorum vos prefate Thoma alterum esse volumus, ad inquirendum per sacramentum tam Militum quam aliorum proborum et legalium hominum de dicto Comitatu Kanc', per quos rei veritas melius sciri poterit, de etate heredis predicti, et si per Inquisitionem predictam inveniri contigerit ipsum Willelmus filius Willelmi infra etatem adhuc existere, tunc per quos vel per quem probatio etatis sue predicte facta fuit, et ad quorum vel cujus procuracionem, imaginacionem, seu informacionem, et quis vel qui terras et tenementa predicta a tempore probationis etatis predicte occuparunt, et exitus et proficua inde perceperunt, et quo titulo, et qualiter, et quomodo et ubi et in cujus comitiva dictus heres a tempore predicto extitit, et per quem vel per quos consiliatus et deductus fuit. Et si terre et tenementa predicta in Domibus seu Boscis vastata et destructa existant, necne; et si sic, tunc per quem vel per quos, et ad quod dampnum nostrum seu heredis predicti; et quantum terre et tenementa illa valeant per annum in omnibus exitibus juxta verum valorem eandem; et quantum proficuum Nos pretextu probationis etatis predicte sic minus rite capte amisimus, et qualiter, et quomodo, et de omnibus aliis articulis et circumstantiis premissa tangentibus plenius veritatem.

Et ideo vobis mandamus, quod ad certos die et loca quos vos vel duo vestrum, quorum vos prefate Thoma alterum esse volumus, ad hoc provideritis, diligentem super premissis omnibus et singulis faciatis Inquisicionem, et eam distincte et apte factam Nobis in Cancellariam nostram sub Sigillis vestris et Sigillis eorum per quos facta fuit sine dilatione mittatis, et hoc Breve.

Mandavimus enim Vicecomitem nostrum dicti Comitatus Kanc', quod ad certos dies et loca quos vos vel duo vestrum, quorum vos prefate

Thoma alterum esse volumus, ei scire feceritis venire faciat coram vobis vel duobus vestrum, quorum vos prefate Thoma alterum esse volumus, tot et tales tam Milites quam alios probos et legales homines de Balliva sua, per quos rei veritas in premissis melius sciri poterit et inquiri. In cujus rei testimonium has Literas nostras fieri fecimus Patentes. Teste Meipso apud Russhyndon in Insula de Shepeye, xiiio die Aprilis, anno Regni nostri quadragesimo. Per literam de Sigillo vocato le Signet.

Cujus Brevis pretextu predicti Johannes, Thomas, et Willelmus, ad inquirendum super premissis processerunt, et quandam Inquisicionem, et diversas Evidencias super veritate etatis heredis predicti scienda ceperunt, quarum Inquisicionis et Evidenciarum tenores sequuntur in hec verba:

Inquisicio capta coram Johanne Cobeham de Kent, Thoma de Lodelowe, et Willelmo Waure, per Commissionem Domini Regis assignantis ad inquirendum de etate Willelmi filii et heredis Willelmi de Septvans, Chivaler, defuncti, qui de ipso Rege ut de Corona tenuit in capite, et ad quedam alia in Commissione Domini Regis contenta faciendum et explendum, apud Cantuar', die Martis proximo ante Festum Sancti Georgii, anno Regni ejusdem Domini Regis quadragesimo, per Sacramentum Johannis de Northwode, Chivaler, Thome Apuldrefeld, Chivaler, Thome Chuche, Chivaler, Ricardi Atte lèsé, Chivaler, Johannis de Brokhull, Chivaler, Johannis Barry, Willelmi Apuldrefeld Senioris, Henricus Auger, Fulconis Payforer, et Galfridi Colpepir: Qui dicunt super Sacramentum suum, quod predictus Willelmus filius et heres predicti Willelmi in Festo Sancti Augustini Doctoris proximo futurus erit etatis viginti annorum et non plus. Et dicunt, quod duodecim homines, quorum nomina huic Inquisicioni consuta sunt, summoniti fuerunt coram Johanne de Tye, Escaetore Domini Regis in Comitatu Kanc' apud Cantuar' ad certum diem jam preteritum ad etatem ipsius heredis probandam, quorum hominum tres, videlicet Alexander Raven, Johannes Pykeryng, and Thomas Ropere, coram prefato Escaetore jurati non extiterunt, et sic dicunt quod probacio predicta rite [irrite?] nec legitime facta extitit, prout intelligunt. Dicunt etiam, quod Willelmus de Churchelhull, Clericus, fuit primus procurator, imaginator, et informator predicto Willelmo filio Willelmi apud Cantuar' ad prosecucionem suam faciendum per terris et tenementis suis extra manus Domini Regis habendis et ad etatem suam probandam, et post Inquisicionem de etate probanda retornatam dictus Willelmus de Chirchehull, et Lucas de Whetynden, prosecuti fuerunt pro terris et tenementis predictis extra manus Domini Regis habendis, eo quod dictus Lucas fuit retentus de consilio dicti Willelmi filii Willelmi. Et dicunt quod idem Willelmus filius Willelmi habuit medietatem manerii de Aldyngton in Comitatu Kanc' que valet per annum decem libras, et quosdam Mariscos vocatos Lokelyng et Hersyng in Ywade qui valent per annum quadraginta solidos; in qua quidem medietate est quidam Boscus qui valet centum libras ad vendendum, quos idem Willelmus filius Willelmi occupavit a tempore quo Dominus Rex manum suam inde amovit usque Festum natalis Domini, anno Regni dicti Domini Regis tricesimo-octavo, quo tempore idem Willelmus filius Willelmi quendam Johannem Gower de tenementis illis feoffavit, tenendum sibi et heredibus suis imperpetuum, pro quibus quidem Medietate, Bosco, et Marisco dedit quater-viginti marcas, et non plus. Virtute cujus feoffamenti idem Johannes Gower eadem tenementa occupavit a dicto Festo Natalis Domini usque nunc, et adhuc occupat, et exitus et profiscua inde continue percepit.

Item dicunt, quod predictus Willelmus de Chirchehull fuit procurator ut prius imaginator et informator apud Cantuar' ad prosequendum extra manus Domini Regis Manerium de Melton cum pertinentibus in dicto Comitatu Kanc', quod valet per annum viginti libras, et unum Mesuagium in Civitate Cantuar', quod valet per annum viginti solidos. Et post Inquisicionem de etate probanda retornatam predicti Willelmus de Chirchehull et Lucas de Wheyngden prosecuti fuerunt pro Manerio illo et Mesuagio predicto extra manus Domini Regis habendo, et eodem modo prosecuti fuerunt pro decem libratis redditus in Littlebourne et Welle. Et dicunt, quod postea ad Festum Sancti Michelis, anno Regni ejusdem Domini Regis trecesimo nono, ad Ordinacionem Domini Nicholi de Loveyne predictus Willelmus filius Willelmi feoffavit de predicto Manerio de Melton, et redditu predicto in Littlebourne et Welle, virtute convencionis inter ipsum Nicolum et eundem Willelmum filium Willelmi facte, Walterum de Multon, et Ricardum de Sugworth, Capellanos, et Ricardum Manse, Servientes ejusdem Nicholi, ad opus ipsius Nicoli. Virtute cujus feoffamenti iidem Walterus, Ricardus, et Richardus eundem Manerium a tempore predicto usque nunc occuparunt, et adhuc occupant, et exitus et proficua inde perceperunt ad opus ejusdem Nicoli, et dictus Willelmus filius Willelmi decem annuum redditum decem librarum continue occupavit et adhuc occupat.

Item dicunt, quod Willelmus filius Willelmi habuit in dicto Comitatu Kanc' Manerium de Promhull, ex dono et feoffamento Ricardi de Aleste Rectoris Ecclesie de Heriettesham, quod valet per annum triginta et quinque libras, quod quidem Manerium oneratur Johanni Septvans in quodam annuo redditu dictum librarum ad terminum vite sue, et quod quidem Manerium tenetur de Archiepiscopo Cantuar', quod quidem Manerium alienavit predictis Waltero, Ricardo Sugworth, et Ricardo Manse, ad opus dicti Nicoli.

Et dicunt, quod post predictum feoffamentum factum predicto Johanni Gower, dictus Willemus filius Willelmi continue morabatur in comitiva Ricardi de Hurst et eiusdem Iohannis Gower apud Cantuar' et alibi usque ad festum Sancti Michaelis ultimo preteritum, et per totum tempus predictum idem Willelmus filius Willelmi ibidem per ipsos deductus fuit et consiliatus ad alienationem de terris et tenementis suis faciendam; et ab eodem Festo Sancti Michaelis usque Festum Sancti Gregorii ultimo preteritum morabatur cum predicto Nicholo Loveyne apud Penesherst, et alibi, et per ipsum Nicolum, et prefatos Walterum,

Ricardum de Sugworth, et Ricardum Manse, toto tempore predicto idem Willelmus filius Willelmi ibidem deductus fuit, et consiliatus ad alienationem de terris et tenementis suis faciendam. Et dicunt, quod non est aliquod vastum seu destructio in terris et tenementis predictis. Et similiter dicunt, quod Simon de Burgh ad prosecutionem suam propriam fecit se retineri cum predicto Willelmo filio Willelmi essendi de consilio suo, et fecit dictum Willelmum filium Willelmi concedere sibi quendam annuum redditum decem librar' sibi et heredibus suis per scriptum suum percipiendum de dicto Manerio de Melton, quod quidem scriptum liberatum fuit dicto Ricardo de Hurst, custodiendum ad voluntatem ejusdem Willelmi; et postea idem Ricardus liberavit scriptum illud dicto Simoni contra voluntatem ejusdem Willelmi. In cujus rei testimonium huic Inquisicioni Juratores predicti Sigilla sua apposuerunt. Dat apud Cantaur' dicto die Martis, anno quadragesimo supradicto.

Evidencie per quas dicti Juratores scienter cognoscunt de etate predicti heredis patent in quadam Cedula huic consuta.

Les causes pur qoi ils dient et scievent qe l'Enfaunt est deinz age sont tieles; c'est assavoir.

Adeprimes, il est conue chose a plusours Chivalers et Esquiers de las dit Enqueste, q'ils essoient ovesqe le Counte de Huntyngdon quant notre tres doute Seign' le Roi estoit a Caine, et le dit Counte de Huntyndon ovesqe lui en sa compaignie; a quele houre qe le Conte de Ew et le Chauberleyn Tankervill fuent pris et maundez en Engleterre, et adonqes le dit Conte de Huntyngdon retourna en Engleterre pur estre garri d'une maladie quel il avoit, et Monsieur Willelm Septvans, pier l'enfaunt, q'estoit de la compaignie, et retenu le dit Conte, retourna en Engleterre ovesqe lui; a quel temps ils troverent la femme le dit Monsieur Willelm meere l'enfaunt grosse enceinte de meisme l'enfaunt, et le Counte de Huntyngdon s'en ala a Popeler pur sojourner illoqes pur aver ses medicines prest de Londres, et fist la Countesse demorir a

Preston pur estre Commeere a l'enfount quant il fu nee. Et l'enfant fu nee le jour Seint Austyn le Doctour prechain apres, et l'Abbe de Seint Austyn, predecessour l'Abbe qe ore est, et Monsieur Thomas Daldon le eisnee qi mort est, furent Commpiers al dit enfaunt, et la Countesse Commere. Et bien tost apres qant le Counte fu garri il retrourna dela la meer et vient a Siege de Caleys, et Monsieur William de Septvans ovesqe lui; et le dit Monsieur William counta a ses compaignons Chivalers et Esquiers qe pre estoient jurrez en ceste enqueste, Coment puis son departier de eux Dieux lui avoit de sa grace issi visite q'il lui avoit mande un Fitz: et qe ceste chose soit verray ils sont prest de faire quan qe attient a nulles gentz homme de faire: et combien il est passe qe le Siege de Caleys estoit ce n'est pas desconu chose.

Une autre Evidence ils ount, l'Abbe William de Seint Austyn, predecessour l'Abbe qe ore est, Compiere l'enfaunt, bien tost apres ce q'il lui avoit leve de souns morust dedeyns une moys apres. Et meyntenant l'Abbe qe ore est, et les moignes, pursuierent a notre tres doute Seigneur le Roi, pur avoir congie de lui d'aler a novel Election, et notre tres doute Seigneur le Roi les graunta license par sa Patente quele est de Record, et laquele feust monstree ore a Canterbirs, portant date de l'an vintisme le roi qe ore est. Et qe ceste chose soit verray l'Abbe qe ore est, et le Priour de meisme le Maison, et un Doctour de Decrees, et autres Moignes assex de meisme la Maison, sont prest a prover pour lour Serement quant il plerra au Roi.

La tierce Evidence ils ount, il y ad une Sire Johan Frebody, Parsone de l'Eglise de Bocton, qe estoit Tresorer a Monsieur Thomas Daldon qi feust l'autre Compier l'enfaunt, en qi acompte il appiert, q'il livera au dit Monsieur Thomas Daldon, son Signeur et Mestre, une Coupe et un Ewer d'argent pur doner a meisme l'enfaunt, lesqueles il dona a l'enfaunt lendemayn de le Feste Seint Austyn avant dit, l'an vintisme le Roi qe ore est . . .

prout per Recordum et Processum inde habitum et in cancellario Domini Regis retornum plenius poterit apparere. Et quia Dominus Rex informatus, quod predictus Willelmus postquam terre et tenementa que sunt de hereditate sua, et racione minoris etatis sue in manum Regis extiterunt, eidem Willelmo pretextu probationis predicte extra manus Regis liberata fuerunt, magnam partem terrarum et tenementorum eorundem diversis personis alienavit, et se in diversis pecuniariis sumtis et annuis redditibus, tam per Literas de Statuto Mercatorio quam per alia facta diversa in Rotulis Cancellarium Regis irrotulata, pluribus personis obligavit; Recordum et Processum predicta, tam pro Indempnitate ipsius Regis ne custodiam terrarum et tenementorum predictorum per hujusmodi decepcionem amitteret, quam predicti Willelmi ne durante minori etate sua exheredaretur, in Parliamento suo apud Westm' die Lunae in crastino Inventionis Sancte Crucis, anno Regni dicti Domini Regis quadragesimo tento, venire fecit. Quibus Recordo et Processu ac Inquisicione et Evidentiis predictis coram ipso Domino Rege, Prelatis, Magnatibus, et comitate Regni Anglorum in eodem Parliamento ostensis, lectis, et examinatis, dicto Willelmo Filio Willelmi Septvans ibidem personaliter existente, visum est toti Parliamento, Quod idem Willelmus filius Willelmi non erat plene etatis, sicut in probatione predicta continetur. Per quod consideratum est in dicto Parliamento quod probatio illa nullius sit valoris vel effectus; et quod omnia terre et tenementa cum pertinentibus que fuerunt predicti Willelmi de Septvans, patris predicti Willelmi filii Willelmi, et que ratione minoris etatis ipsius Willelmus filius Willelmi heredis dicti Willelmi de Septvans in manu Regis capta, et eidem heredi ut plene etatis pretextu probacionis predicte sic minus sufficienter facte extra manus regis liberata, in manum Regis ad quorumcumque manus devenerint, una cum exitibus inde a tempore probacionis predicte facte perceptis, reseisiantur, et in manu Regis remaneant usque ad legitimam etatem heredis predicti. Et quod omnia Carte, Scripta, et Obligaciones tam de Statutis Mercatoriis et de Stapulis quam alia quecumque ac etiam Recogniciones per ipsum quibuscumque personis ante hec tempora facta revocentur, cassentur, et omnino adnullentur: Et quod Processus fiant per Breve de Scire factum versus omnes illos quibus aliqua terre seu tenementa de hereditate predicti Willelmi filii Willelmi, post probacionem etatis predicte et liberacionem terrarum et tenementorum de hereditate sua extra manus nostras factas, per ipsum Willemus filius Willelmi sunt alienata; et etiam versus illos quibus idem Willelmus filius Willelmi aliquos redditus annuos concessit; necnon versus omnes illos quibus idem Willelmus filius Willelmi in aliquibus debitis per Statuta Mercatoria vel de Stapula, vel per Recogniciones seu Cartas, Scripta aut alia Facta obligatur, ad venire faciendum eos in Cancellarium Regis, ad ostendendum si quid pro se habeant vel dicere sciant quare terre, tenementa, et redditus predicta sic alienata in manum Regis reseisiri; Et Carte, Scripta, Statuta, Recogniciones, Obligaciones, et alia Facta que per dictum Willelmum filium Willelmi fiebant, tanquam irrita et erronea cassari et adnullari non debeant; et ad faciendum et recipiendum quod justum fuerit in hac parte.

The Roll of Parliament from the 40th Year of King Edward III.

### [Summary of the Parliament's decision, in French]

Which verdicts were read in the said Parliament before all the Lords and Commons, and the said William, then present among the same Lords, was advised and judged by all the Lords that the said William was a minor, and that all his lands and tenements, which had been put outside the possession of the king by the first incorrect proof of age, were, with all the revenues arising from them, reseised into the king's possession, to remain there until his full majority.

And that all the deeds, documents, and obligations, those of the Statute of Merchants as well as those of the Staple and others whatever, and also Recognizances made to any person by the said William son of

William before this time shall be null and void, as the record made in the said Parliament and preserved in the Chancery shows plainly. The copy of this record is attached[1] to this.

### [The King's Writ, in Latin]

The Lord King ordered his writ in the following words:

Edward, by Grace of God King of England, Lord of Ireland and Aquitaine, to his beloved and loyal subjects John de Cobham of Kent,[2] Thomas de Lodelowe, and William Waure, Greetings.

Because it has been given to us to understand that William, son and heir of William de Septvans, Knight, deceased, (who held land of us in capite as of the Crown, and whose lands and tenements with appurtenances in the County of Kent, Sussex, and Essex had been taken into our hands because the aforesaid heir was not of age) has insufficiently proven his age before our escheator[3] in the said County of Kent who was not correctly informed of this matter at the instigation, contrivance, and influence of certain men who suggested that this William son of William was of full age; and because we had been deceived in this proof, in that the aforesaid heir was not yet of age and will not be for some time; and because the aforesaid lands and tenements with appurtenances of the same heir were transferred out of our hands by the said inquiry with false testimony, with our deception

---

1 The word translated "attached" literally means "sewed on"; the accompanying documents were in fact sewn onto the main record to make a roll. The French is *consue,* the Latin *consuta*.

2 John de Cobham (died 1355), the 2nd Baron Cobham, was a distinguished nobleman. He was constable of Dover Castle and Rochester Castle. Thomas de Lodelowe was appointed to several royal commissions. All three were members of Parliament.

3 An escheator (one per county) supervised the king's rights as feudal lord, in this case dealing with the reversion of property left by a tenant *in capite,* i.e. a tenant-in-chief, like Sir William Septvans, who held his property directly from the king.

and the loss of our rights and revenues which pertain to us in this matter.

We, wishing to see to our indemnity in this matter as is right, appoint you, two of you, of whom we wish the aforementioned Thomas to be one, to make an inquiry under oath of the knights as well as other respectable men of legal standing in the said County of Kent through whom the truth of this matter can be better known, viz. the age of the aforesaid heir. If in this aforesaid inquiry it comes to be known that this William son of William is still of minor age, then [ascertain] those by whom the proof of the aforesaid age was made, and at whose instigation, contrivance or influence; and who received the aforesaid lands and tenements at the time of the proof of the aforesaid age and who gained the income and revenues from these; and under what title, how, in what way, where, and in whose company the said heir was at the aforesaid time, and by whom he was counseled and misled. [Ascertain] if the aforesaid lands and tenements in buildings or woods have been wasted or destroyed or not; and if they have, by whom and what is the damage to us and to the aforesaid heir; and how much the total income from the aforesaid lands and the tenements is worth per annum according to its true valuation; and how much revenue we have lost as a result of this aforesaid proof of age which was not correctly done; and [to ascertain] the whole truth of what nature and in what manner and in all other aspects and circumstances which are relevant to the aforementioned matter.

We therefore order you that at certain days and places which you or two of you, of whom we wish the aforementioned Thomas to be one, should see to it that you make a diligent inquiry about each and every one of the aforementioned matters, and after you have clearly and correctly done this, that you send it without delay to us in our Chancery under your seal and the seal of those by whom it was done, and with it this writ.

We also order our sheriff of the said County of Kent that at certain days and places which you or two of you, of whom we wish the aforementioned Thomas to be one, shall make known to him, that he should summon to appear before you or two of you, of whom we wish the aforementioned Thomas to be one, all those knights as well as respectable men of legal age from his bailiwick, through whom the truth of the aforementioned matter can be known and investigated.

In certification of this matter we have give these our Letters Patent, with me as witness at Rushendon on the Island of Sheppey, 13 April, the 40th year of our reign.[1] By letter of the seal called "le Signet."

### [Record of the Inquiry, Latin]

On the basis of this writ, the aforesaid John, Thomas, and William proceeded to an inquiry on the aforementioned matters, and made an inquiry and took various evidences to learn the truth of the aforesaid heir's age. The results of this inquiry and these evidences follow in these words:

Inquiry made in the presence of John Cobeham of Kent, Thomas de Lodelowe, and William Waure, by commission of the Lord King who appointed us to inquire about the age of William son and heir of William de Septvans, Knight, deceased, who held lands of the king in capite, as of the crown, and to do and discover certain other matters included in the commission of the Lord King, at Canterbury, the Tuesday immediately before the Feast of St. George,[2] in the 40th year of the reign of the same Lord King, with the following under oath: John de Northwode, knight; Thomas Apuldrefeld, knight; Thomas Chuche, knight; Richard atte lèsé, knight; John de Brokhull, knight; John Barry, William Apuldrefeld senior, Henry Auger, Fulco Payforer, and Geoffrey

---

1 1366.
2 April 23.

Colpepir.[1] All say on their oath that the aforesaid William son and heir of William on the Feast of St. Augustine the Doctor next will be 20 years of age and no more. And they say that 12 men, whose names are attached to this inquiry, were summoned before John de Tye, escheator of the Lord King in the County of Kent in Canterbury at a certain day now past to prove the age of this same heir. Three of these, Alexander Raven, John Pykeryng, and Thomas Ropere, were not sworn before the aforementioned escheator, and thus they say that the aforesaid proof was not duly and lawfully made, as far as they understand.

They also say that William de Churchelhull, clerk, was the first instigator, contriver, and influencer of the aforesaid William son of William at Canterbury that he should make a suit for taking his lands and tenements out of the Lord King's hands and for proving his age, and after the return[2] of the inquiry on proving his age, the said William de Chirchehull and Lucas de Whetynden sued to have the aforesaid lands and tenements out of the Lord King's hands, on the grounds that the said Lucas had been retained as counsel for the said William son of William.

And they say that the said William, son of William, had the moiety [half] of the Manor of Aldyngton, in the county of Kent, which is worth £10 per annum, and some marshes called Lokelyng and Hersyng, in Iwade which are worth 40 shillings per annum, and in this moiety there is a wood which is worth £100 for sale [of wood], which this same William son of William possessed from the time when the Lord King removed his hand from them up to the Feast of the Nativity of our Lord,[3] in the 38th year of the reign of the said Lord King, at which time the said William, son of William, enfeoffed the said tenements to John

1 The spelling of several of these names vary in the sources, and even within a document. For example the spellings Churchehull and Chirchehull are both in the original.

2 i.e. submission of the results.

3 Christmas.

Gower, to hold for himself and his heirs forever, for which moiety, wood, and marsh [John Gower] gave 80 marks[1] and no more. By virtue of which foeffment the said John Gower has occupied the said tenements from the said Feast of the Nativity of our Lord until now, and still occupies them, and continually receives the income and profits therefrom.

Likewise they say that the aforesaid William de Chirchehull instigated, as he previously contrived and instructed at Canterbury, the suing out of the Lord King's hand the Manor of Milton with its appurtenances in the said County of Kent, which is worth £20 per annum, and one messuage in the City of Canterbury, which is worth 20 shillings per annum. And after the inquiry held on proving the age of the aforesaid, William de Chirchehull and Lucas de Wheyngden sued for the aforesaid manor and messuage to be held out of the King's hand, and in the same way sued for the £10 rent in Littlebourne and Welle.

And they say that after the Feast of St. Michael,[2] in the 39th year of the reign of the same Lord King, at the order of Sir Nicholas de Loveyne,[3] the aforesaid William son of William enfoeffed Walter de Multon, Richard de Sugworth, chaplains, and Richard Manse, all servants of Nicholas, for the use of Nicholas himself, of the aforesaid Manor of Melton and the aforesaid rent in Littlebourne and Welle, by virtue of a covenant made between Nicholas himself and the same William son of William. By virtue of this enfeoffment the same Walter, Richard, and Richard have possessed the same manor from the aforesaid time until now, and still possess it, and have taken the income and profits from it for the use of the same Nicholas, and the said William son of William has continuously possessed and still possessed the said annual rent of £10.

1 Lat. *quater-viginti*, which literally is 4 x 20, i.e. fourscore. Some scholars have taken this as a mistake for *quattuor viginti,* 24.

2 Michaelmas, Sept. 29.

3 The lord of Penshurst Manor, hence wealthy and powerful.

Likewise they say that William son of William has in the said County of Kent the Manor of Promhull by gift and feoffment of Richard de Aleste, Rector of the church at Harriettsham, which is worth £35 per annum, and this manor is charged with an annual rent to John Septvans of £10 until the end of his life, and this Manor is held of the Archbishop of Canterbury. [William] alienated this Manor to the aforesaid Walter, Richard Sugworth, and Richard Manse for the use of the said Nicholas.

And they say that after the aforesaid feoffment made to the aforesaid John Gower, the said William son of William was continuously abiding in the company of Richard Hurst and the same John Gower at Canterbury and elsewhere, until the Feast of St. Michael last past, and throughout the whole of that time the said William son of William was there led astray by them and counseled to alienate his lands and tenements, and from the same Feast of St. Michael until the Feast of St. Gregory[1] last past he was staying with the said Nicholas Loveyne at Penshurst and elsewhere, and by this same Nicholas and by the aforesaid Walter, Richard of Sugworth, and Richard Manse, during the entire said time the same William son of William was misled and counselled to alienate his lands and tenements.

And they say that has been no waste or destruction of these aforesaid lands and tenements.

They likewise say that Simon de Burgh, at his own suit, caused himself to be retained by the said William son of William to be of counsel to him, and caused the said William son of William to grant an annual rent of of £10 to him and his heirs out of the said Manor of Melton by a written document. The document was delivered to the said Richard of Hurst, to be kept at the wish of the same William, and that writing was afterwards delivered by the same Richard to the said Simon against the wish of the same William.

---

1 Sept. 3.

In proof of this matter the aforesaid jurors in this inquiry have place their seal. Given at Canterbury the said day of March, in the aforesaid $40^{th}$ year.

### [Evidence heard by the Inquiry from the knights and respectable men of legal standing]

[Latin] Evidences by which the said jurors knew about the age of the aforesaid heir are presented in the schedule attached here.

[French] The evidences by which the jurors know that the child is under age, to wit:

In the first place, many of the knights and esquires of the jury were with the Earl of Huntyngton when our dread Lord King was at Caen and the earl with him in his company,[1] at the time when the Count of Eu and the Chamberlain Tankervill were taken and sent to England, and at the time the said Earl of Huntyngton returned to England to be cured of an illness, and Sir William de Septvans, the child's father, who was part of the earl's company, returned to England with him. They found Sir William's wife, the child's mother, great with the same child. The Earl of Huntyngton went away to Poplar[2] to stay there and to have his medicines near London, and made the countess remain at Preston to be godmother to the child when it was born. And the child was born on the day of St. Augustine the Doctor next following,[3] and the Abbot of St. Augustine, predecessor of the present abbot, and Sir Thomas Daldon the Elder, now deceased, were the said child's godfathers, the countess being godmother. And soon afterwards the earl was cured and returned beyond the sea to the siege of Calais, and Sir William of Septvans with him. And the said Sir William told his companion knights and esquires

1 July 1346. In this campaign the Count of Eu et Guisnes and the Count de Tancarville were captured by the English. The account of this episode is in Froissart Bk. 1.

2 Now part of the London Borough of Tower Hamlets.

3 28 Aug. 1346.

who are on the jury in this inquiry how since his departure from them, God had given him the favor of granting him a son. That this thing is true they are prepared to do what it becomes any gentleman to do,[1] and that he was at the Siege of Calais is not an unknown matter.

There is another evidence: William, Abbot of St. Augustine, predecessor of the present abbot, the child's godfather, very soon after he baptized the child, died within a month later.[2] Soon the present abbot and the monks applied to our dread Lord King to allow them to have a new election, and our Lord King granted a license by patent which is on the record, and which was sent to Canterbury, bearing the date of the 20th year of the present king. That this thing is true the present abbot, the prior of the same house, and a doctor of decrees, and other monks of the same house are ready to swear under oath when the king wishes.

There is a third evidence: there is a certain Sir John Frebody, parson of the church at Bocton, who was treasurer for Sir Thomas Daldon, the child's second godfather, and in his account it appears that he delivered to the said Sir Thomas Daldon, his lord and master, a cup and ewer of silver to be given to the same child, and that the gift was made on the morrow of the aforesaid Feast of St. Augustine, in the 20th year of the present king.

## [The Decision of Parliament, Latin]

So that the report and process held on this matter and returned in the Chancery of the Lord King can more plainly appear.

The Lord King was informed that the aforesaid William—after the lands and tenements which were his inheritance and because of his minority were in the king's hand, and to this same William on the pretext of the aforesaid proof had been transferred out of the king's hand—had alienated a great part of these lands and tenements to

1 i.e. swear to the truth of this matter.
2 on 11 Sept. 1346.

various persons, and in various sums of money and annual income he had obligated himself to several persons by Letters of the Statute of Merchants as well as various actions recorded in the Rolls of the king's Chancery; [the king] caused this record and process to come in his Parliament at Westminster held on the Monday after the Finding of the Holy Cross, in the 40th year of the reign of the said king, both for the indemnity of the king himself, lest he lose the aforesaid lands and tenements by this kind of deception, and for the indemnity of the aforesaid William, lest he be disinherited during the period of his minor age.

The aforesaid record, process, inquiry, and evidences being shown, read, and examined before the Lord King, the prelates, magnates, and commonality of the Kingdom of England in the same Parliament, with the said William son of William Septvans being himself present, it seemed to the Parliament that the same William son of William was not of full age as was stated in the aforesaid proof. It was resolved in the said Parliament: that the proof was of no value and effect; that all the lands and tenements with appurtenances which belonged to the aforesaid William de Septvans, father of the aforesaid William son of William, and which had been taken into the king's hands because by reason of the minority of the same William son of William, the heir of the said William de Septvans, and which were transferred out of the king's hands to the same heir on the grounds that he was of age according to the aforesaid proof (which was not sufficiently done), should be reseised into the king's hands, to whoever's hands they might have come, along with the income received from the time of the aforesaid proof, and should remain in the king's hands until the full legal age of the aforesaid heir. All deeds, documents, and obligations, both of the Statute of Merchants and of the Staple, as well as any and all other recognizances made by him with any persons before this time, should be revoked and made altogether null and void; that the proceedings be done through a writ of *Scire Facias*[1] against all those to whom any lands or tenements from the inheritance of the aforesaid William son of William have been alienated after the proof of the aforesaid age and the transfer of lands and tenements of the inheritance out of our hands by this William son of William; and also against those to whom the same William son of William granted any annual revenues; in addition against all those[2] to whom the same William son of William is obligated through any debts by the Statute of Merchants or before the Staple or through recognizances, deeds, documents, or other contracts; to have them come before Chancery to show if they have or know anything that they can say for themselves, why the aforesaid lands, tenements, and revenues so alienated should not be reseised into the king's hands, and that all his deeds, documents, statutes, recognizances, obligations and other contracts which were made by the said William son of William should not be made null and void as being invalid and erroneous; and to do and receive what is just in this matter.

Additional Reading:

The original documents are in the National Archives: TNA SC 8/247/12329; C 81/1335/50; also see *Calendar of Close Rolls, Edw III*, vol. XII, 1364-1368, p. 33 and p. 279.

L. B. L., 1858 124-136. The bulk of this article is a translation of the Latin and French documents presented here.

John Strachey et al., *Rotuli Parliamentorum* vol. 2 pp. 291-3. This is a printed version of the original handwritten parchment, which was heavily abbreviated. The spelling, punctuation, and capitalization of the 1767 printed text has been retained.

Matthew Giancarlo 2005 pp. 435-464.

John Fisher 1964 Appendix C, pp. 313-318 contain translations of other documents relating to this case.

---

1 A writ ordering a defendant to appear and show cause why a judgment against him should not be entered.

2 The Gower scholar John Fisher mistranslated the phrase *necnon versus omnes* as "not toward those . . ." rather than "against all those..." (Fischer 1964 52), thus wrongly claiming that Gower was exempt from this writ of *Scire facias*. How Gower handled the situation is unknown.

## Two Cases Concerning Geoffrey Chaucer the Poet

A. Deeds of Release To Chaucer in respect of the *Raptus* of Cecily Chaumpaigne, 1380.

On 1 May 1380 a document was entered in Chancery in which Cecily Chaumpaigne (also spelled Champain) agreed to release Geoffrey Chaucer from all actions concerning *raptus* or any other charge. Cecily herself came to the court on 4 May to acknowledge the document, which was witnessed by some of Chaucer's most influential friends: Sir William Beauchamp, the chamberlain of the king's household, for whom Chaucer had performed some service in 1378; Sir John Clanvowe and Sir William Nevill, two knights of the king's chamber; John Philipot, collector of customs (1377-83) during Chaucer's controllership; and Richard Morel, a modestly well-off London grocer and member of the Grocers' Company.

What does *raptus* mean? In legal documents of the time, *raptus* and the verb *rapere* can mean either "rape" or "abduction," the latter usually being the seizure and retention of a young person against his or her will with the purpose of gaining some financial advantage. Chaucer's own father, John Chaucer, was abducted by his aunt in 1324 when she was trying to force the boy into a marriage with her daughter, and Chaucer himself was a member of a commission investigating a similar case in 1387. In both these cases, however, the nature of the offense is made clear by the use of the two words *rapuerunt et abduxerunt* (Crow and Olsen 1966 p. 3, p. 375). When *raptus* or forms of the verb *rapere* are used alone, they seem to mean "rape," for which no other word is used in law without qualification. Furthermore, "abduction" would normally refer to the forcible appropriation of the powers of guardianship over a minor, and Cecily was not a minor in 1380, her father William, a baker, having died in 1360 (hence the *quondam* in the text below). The fact that she acknowledges the release in her own recognizance would argue, too, that there was no parent, husband, or other legal guardian to do it for her, and that she was a woman of at least 21.

The circumstances of this *raptus* are completely unknown: the nature of the offense, whether Chaucer was the principal offender, what the others named here (Goodchild and Grove) had to do with the case, why it was settled with a release. One might guess that Grove was the principal, since he actually paid Cecily £10 (as damages?). Chaucer scholars have busied themselves in discussing this case. For a recent discussion of the entire issue see Cannon 1993. Mr. Cannon found a hitherto unknown document referring to the same case (KB 27/477 membrane 58d - a *coram rege* roll, Easter term in 3 Richard II) which is verbally almost identical to #1 below, but omits the phrase *de raptu meo* and substitutes the generic *tam de feloniis, transgressionibus, compotis, debitis, quam aliis accionibus* . . . "both concerning felonies, trespasses, accounts, debts, and any other actions.." The author suggests that Chaucer had the specific, disgraceful charge deleted. Without further evidence, the matter will never be decided.

Cecily's father William Chaumpaigne was a baker whose will survives and is dated 26 June 1360. Richard Goodchild, cutler, died in 1389. John Grove is mentioned several times in London records; he was commissioned to sell arms and artillery from the Tower of London to raise money for the king.[1] See Crow and Olson 1996 343-7 for these documents and a discussion of *raptus*.

### A Release to Chaucer by Cecily Chaumpaigne.

De scripto irrotulato.

Noverint universi me Ceciliam Chaumpaigne filiam quondam Willelmi Chaumpaigne et Agnetis uxoris eius remisisse, relaxasse, et omnino pro me et heredibus meis imperpetuum quietum clamasse Galfrido Chaucer armigero omnimodas acciones tam de raptu meo tam de aliqua alia re

1 Crow and Olson 346.

vel causa cuiuscumque condicionis fuerint quas unquam habui, habeo, seu habere potero a principio mundi usque in diem confeccionis presencium. In cuius rei testimonium presentibus sigillum meum apposui. Hiis testibus domino Willelmo de Beauchamp tunc camerario domini regis, domino Johanne de Clanebowe, domino Willelmo de Nevylle militibus, Johanne Philippott, et Ricardo Morel. Datum Londonie primo die Maii anno regni Regis Ricardi secundi post conquestum tercio.

Et memorandum quod predicta Cecilia venit in cancellaria regis apud Westmonasterium quarto die Maii anno presenti et recognovit scriptum predictum et omnia contenta in eodem in forma predicta.

(Close Rolls, 219, 3 Ric. II, membrane 9d; calendared in *Calendar of Close Rolls, Richard II.* vol. 1, p. 374).

From the Rolls.

Let it be known to all that I, Cecily Chaumpaigne, the daughter of the late William Chaumpaigne and his wife Agnes, absolve, release, and discharge in perpetuity for myself and my heirs Geoffrey Chaucer, esquire, from all manner of actions either concerning my raptus or concerning any other matter or case of any kind whatsoever which I ever have brought, am bringing or can bring from the beginning of the world up to the day of composing these presents [i.e. documents]. In testimony of this matter I have placed my seal to these presents. These are the witnesses: Sir William Beauchamp, then chamberlain of the Lord King, Sir John de Clanevow, Sir William Nevylle, knights, John Philippott, and Richard Morel. Given at London the first day of May in the third year of King Richard, the second [of that name] since the conquest.

It should be noted that the aforesaid Cecily came into the chancellery of the king at Westminster on the fourth day of May in the current year and acknowledged the aforesaid document and all the contents in it in the aforesaid form.

## 2. A Release to Richard Goodchild and John Grove by Cecily Chaumpaigne.

Noverint universi me Ceciliam Chaumpaigne filiam quondam Willelmi Chaumpaigne et Agnetis uxoris eius remisisse, relaxasse, et omnino pro me heredibus et executoribus meis imperpetuum quietum clamasse Ricard Goodchild coteler et Johanni Grove armurer civibus Londonie omnimodas acciones, querelas, et demandas tam reales quam personales quas versus dictos Ricardum et Johannem vel eorum alterum unquam habui, habeo, seu quovismodo in futurum habere potero racione cuiuscumque cause a principio mundi usque in diem confeccionis presencium. In cuius rei testimonium presentibus sigillum meum apposui. Datum Londonie vicesimo octavo die Junii anno regni Regis Ricardi secundi post conquestum quarto.

(City of London, Plea and Memo. R., A 23, membrane 5d).

Let it be known to all that I, Cecily Chaumpaigne, the daughter of the late William Chaumpaigne and his wife Agnes, absolve, release, and discharge for myself and my heirs in perpetuity Richard Goodchild, cutler, and John Grove, armourer, citizens of London from all manner of actions, suits, and claims, both real and personal, which I have ever brought, am bringing or can bring against the said Richard and John or either one of them for reason of any case from the beginning of the world up to the day of composing the presents. As certification of this matter I have placed my seal to these presents. Given at London on the 28th day of June in the fourth year of King Richard, the second [of that name] since the conquest.

## 3. Recognizance by John Grove that he owes £10 to Cecily Chaumpaigne

Chaumpaigne. Vacat quia solvit.

Secundo die Julii anno regni Regis Ricardi secundi quarto Johannes Grove armurer venit hic coram maiore et aldermannis et recognovit se debere Cecilie Chaumpaigne filie quondam Willelmi Chaumpaigne et Agnetis uxoris eius decem libras sterlingorum solvendas ad festum Sancti Michaelis proximo futurum etc. Et nisi fecerit concedit etc.

(City of London, Plea and Memo. R., A 23, membrane 5d).

Chaumpaigne. Vacated because he paid.[1]

On the second day of July in the fourth year of King Richard the Second, John Grove, armourer, comes here before the mayor and the aldermen and acknowledged that he owes Cecily Chaumpaigne, the daughter of the late William Chaumpaigne and his wife Agnes £10 sterling to be paid at the next-to-come Feast of Saint Michael. And if he does not do this, he grants that etc.

B. A Plea on Debt against Geoffrey Chaucer in the Court of Common Pleas 1388-9

At some time in or before 1388 the poet Geoffrey Chaucer incurred a debt to Henry Atwood, an innkeeper of London, who had to sue for payment in the Court of Common Pleas. Atwood's attorney, Thomas West, presented a petition against several debtors in court during Michaelmas Term (which began in October) 1388. There is no connection between these debtors other than their creditor Atwood. Chaucer and the others were ordered to appear 15 days (the quindene) after the Feast of St. Martin, i.e. 25 November.[2] The complaint and the court order is #1 below. Chaucer did not appear. Atwood made a second complaint, and Chaucer was ordered to appear at the octave of the Hilary term (which began in January), i.e. 20 January 1389. The order is given #2 below. Chaucer did not appear. Atwood appeared in person several times during Hilary Term 1389 to make his plea (#3 below) and

---

1 This note was added after Grove paid. This is a rare case where we know the outcome.

2 The Feast of St. Martin is Nov. 11. Note that the counting of the *quindene* (15 days after the start of the Term) and the *octave* (8 days after the start) is inclusive; the 11th to the 25th is 15 days if the 11th is counted as 1.

during Michaelmas term, at which time Chaucer was again ordered to appear at the octave of Hilary Term (20 January). As usual, there is no record of a final judgment, so it is assumed that Chaucer eventually settled with Atwood.

These documents, as well as a discussion of Chaucer's debts, can be found in Crow and Olson 1966 388-391. The originals are in the British National Archives, Court of Common Pleas, Plea Rolls CP 40. Many of these are available on line at the Anglo-American Legal Tradition webpage hosted by the University of Houston (http://aalt.law.uh.edu/).

**1.** Placita apud Westmonasterium coram Roberto de Cherlton et sociis suis justiciis domini regis de Banco termino Sancti Michaelis anno regnorum Ricardi regis Anglie et Francie duodecimo.

Londonia.

Henricus atte Wode civis et hostelere Londonie per Thomam West attornatum suum optulit se iiii die versus Johannem Pomeray de comitatu Devonie militem de placito quod reddat ei quindecim libras et duodecim denarios. Et versus Galfridum Chaucer armigerum de placito quod reddat ei septem libras tresdecem solidos et quatuor denarios. Et versus Johannem Grede de Westdeen in comitatu Sussexie clericum de placito quod reddat ei octo marcas et decem solidos. Et versus Willelmum Farley de comitatu Suthamtonie armigerum de placito quod reddat ei quinquaginta et tres solidos et quatuor denarios. Et versus Thomam Symon capellanum de placito quod reddat ei quinquaginta et duos solidos quos ei debent et injuste detinent etc. Et ipsi non venerunt. Et preceptum fuit vicecomitibus quod summonerent eos etc.

Et vicecomites modo mandant quod nichil habent etc. Ideo preceptum est vicecomitibus quod capiant eos si etc. Ita quod habeant corpora eorum hic a die Sancti Martini in xv dies per justicias etc.

Pleas at Westminster before Robert Cherlton and his fellow judges of the lord king in session during the Term of St. Michael [= Michaelmas] in the 12th year of Richard, King of England and France.

London

Henry Atwood, citizen of London and innkeeper presents himself through Thomas West his attorney on the 4th day [of the term] against John Pomeray, knight, from the County of Devon, on a plea that he repay £15 12p. And against Geoffrey Chaucer, esquire, on a plea that he repay £7 13s 4p. And against John Grede of Westdeen, cleric, in the County of Sussex, on a plea that he repay 8 Marks 10s. And against William Farley, esquire, from the County of Southampton, on a plea that he repay 53s 4p. And against Thomas Symon, chaplain, on a plea that he repay 52s which he owes and unlawfully retains, etc. And they have not appeared. And the sheriffs were ordered to summon them, etc.

And the sheriffs have stated that they have no etc. Therefore the sheriffs were ordered to seize them if etc. So that they [the court] should have their presence here on the quindene of the Feast of St. Martin for a determination etc.

**2.** Londonia.

Henricus atte Wode . . .[1] Et preceptum fuit vicecomitibus quod caperent eos etc.

Et vicecomites modo mandant quod non sunt inventi. Ideo sicut prius preceptum est vicecomitibus quod capiant eos etc. Ita quod habeant corpora eorum hic in octabis Sancti Hilarii per justicias etc.

Henry Atwood . . . And the sheriffs were ordered to seize them etc.[2]

And the sheriffs declare that they have not been found. Therefore, as previously, the sheriffs were ordered to seize them etc. So that they

1 The order is worded exactly as #1 above.

2 London had two sheriffs, one for the City and one for Middlesex County.

should have their presence here on the octave of St. Hilary for a determination etc.

**3.** Henricus atte Wode civis et hostelere Londonie in propria persona sua optulit se iiii die versus Galfridum Chaucer armigerum de placito quod reddat ei septem libras et tres decem solidos quos ei debet et injuste detinet. Et ipse non venit. Et sicut pluries preceptum fuit vicecomitibus quod caperent etc.

Henry Atwood, citizen of London and innkeeper, presented himself in his own person on the 4$^{th}$ day [of the term] against Geoffrey Chaucer, esquire, on a plea that he repay £7 10s which he owes him and unlawfully retains etc. And he did not appear. And, as many times previously, the sheriffs were ordered to seize etc.

Additional Reading:
*Calendar of Close Rolls, Richard II.* vol. 1, p. 374.
Cannon 1993 74-94.
Crow and Olson 1966.

## A Civil Case of Nuisance

A suit under the assize[1] of nuisance was available for citizens who alleged some damage to their property. Many, if not most, of these suits involve drainage, like the example given here, but others concerned windows that intruded upon the privacy of neighbors, noxious industries (forges, butcher shops) located next door, and the like. These cases were heard in the Guild Hall before the mayor, acting as judge, and a jury of (at least) six aldermen and the recorder, who was often an alderman. The records of these are in Latin with many French certificates quoted in the case files. A calendar (i.e. an index with detailed descriptions, but not a complete translation) of these cases, including an enlightening description of this assize, has been published (Helena M. Chew and William Kellaway, *London Assize of Nuisance, 1301-1431,* London 1973) and is available on-line.

A fairly typical example of a nuisance suit is given here in the original Latin and in translation. A closely related case is discussed in our appendix, Reading Law Records. A summary: In October 1377 (the first year of King Richard II's reign) in the parish of St. Nicholas Shambles (an area for butchers) John Norhampton (also spelled Northampton in modern studies) and his wife Petronilla state that William Newe, the guardian (manager) of the nearby Franciscan monastery, the Greyfriars, in Pentecost Lane has blocked up the drainage ditch which ran from the Northampton's seven properties down the lane, across the monastery grounds to an aperture in the city wall into the Houndsditch, right outside the city walls. (This is now the NE part of the City of London, the financial center.) As a result the run-off from the lane has backed up, harming the tenants of these properties

1 As mentioned elsewhere, 'assize' may mean a decree, law, or regulation; a writ or action which may prompt a trial; the trial itself; or (the modern use) a session of court held periodically in English counties. The assize of nuisance (Lat. *nocumentum*, damage) is the action which leads to a trial.

and rotting the timbers. (Many of these suits allege exactly this type of damage.) John Northampton and his wife Petronilla ask the court to order William Newe to correct the problem at his own expense. After several delays a trial takes place in July 1378 and judgment is given on August 2, 1378, that William shall restore the channel as it was.

Drainage in Pentecost Lane seems to have been difficult. A suit from February 1370, brought by William Newe's predecessor, may give us an idea of the problems he faced:

> Brother Robert de Madyngton, guardian of the Friars Minor, complains by Robert de Watlyngton, his attorney, that Richard Bayser, 'bocher', and Emma his wife have built a 'skaldynghous' in their tenement in Pentecostlane in the par. of St. Nicholas Shambles, in which they slaughter pigs and many other animals, and the water mixed with the blood and hair of the slaughtered animals, and with other filth from the washing (*lotura*) [of the carcasses], flows into the ditch or kennel in the street, through which it is carried into the friars' garden, causing a stench in many places there. The defs. come, but show no cause why the assize should be delayed. The mayor and aldermen, having viewed the premises, give the parties a day to hear judgment.[1]

The Latin document is not a transcript of the hearings, but a summary report of the pleadings during the hearings and the court's decisions. Hence the frequent 'etc.' in the Latin and English texts. For example, when the plaintiffs ask that 'they be treated according to the practices which must lawfully be done by the City of London, etc.' the record is abbreviating their plea, which undoubtedly included much legal boilerplate, by 'etc.'

As far as is known, this particular case created no special stir in London, but the plaintiff, the presiding mayor, and some of the

1 Quoted from 'Misc. Roll. FF: 16 Feb 1369 - 5 May 1374 (no. 569)', in Helena M Chew and William Kellaway 1973 139-154.

aldermen are well-known figures in London politics. John Northampton (or Norhampton) was a wealthy man, largely through his marriage (his second) to the heiress Petronilla (or Parnel). A successful member of the mistery (trades, Lat. *ministerium*) of the drapers, makers or dealers in cloth, he owned many lots, shops, and houses throughout London, including these messuages[1] in the parish of St. Nicholas Shambles, which were rental properties. He also owned land in the suburbs of the City of London.[2] He was alderman in 1375-7 and again in 1381-2. He became Lord Mayor of London in October 1381 (mayors were elected in October) and served until Oct. 1383. He was condemned for sedition the following year and exiled, but was pardoned in 1390. He died in 1398. In politics, he was supported by the smaller, less wealthy misteries of the City and was opposed by the wealthy merchant class, especially those who supplied food to London. The champion of the latter class was Nicholas Brembre, the mayor who presided over this lawsuit. Much wealthier than Northampton, Brembre was Lord Mayor in 1377-8 and 1383-6, succeeding Northampton. An ally of King Richard II, Brembre was condemned for treason in 1387 and hanged in 1388. For a detailed description of London politics and information about the careers of these individuals during the reign of King Richard II, see Ruth Bird 1949. Many documents survive recording the rise and fall of both Brembre and Northampton. The hostility between the two may have been one cause for the long delay in settling this case.

Other known figures mentioned in this case include:

William Chene, an ally of Brembre, was Recorder from at least 1376 to 1389.

Adam Karlille was a member of Parliament for London during the 1370's and 80's.

1 A *messuage* is a piece of property, a lot, with its house and all outbuildings included.

2 A detailed list of his properties in Ruth Bird 1949 9-10.

William Baret was a member of Parliament during the 1380's. A Thomas Baret was an apprentice to Northampton.

Walter Sibyla (or Sibil) was member of parliament in 1378. He was minister to Prussia in 1388 when the Grand Master of the Teutonic Knights complained of his behavior to King Richard II.

Nicholas Twyford, an opponent of Brembre, was elected Lord Mayor in October 1388 and served one term. Note that he was sheriff when this case was first heard in 1377, but alderman when the case returned in 1378.

John Haddele (or Hadle or Hadley), an ally of Northampton, was a member of Parliament during the 1370's and 80's.

As for the outcome of the case: the order to correct the nuisance in 40 days is standard, as is the fine of 40 shillings. We have no information about when or to what extent William Newe actually restored the channel for run-off to the Houndsditch.

### Assisa nocumenti 1377[1]

Placitum assise nocumenti tenementi super tertiam die veneris proximo post finem St. Michaelis Archangeli anno regni regis Ricardi Secundi a conquesto Anglie primo in presentia Nicole Brembre Maioris, Willelmi Chene, Recordatoris, Willelmi Neuport, Adam Karlill, Willelmi Baret, Roberti Boxford, Roberti Lucas, Walteri Sibyla, et Thome atte Noket, Aldrorum, Nicholi Twyford et Andre Pykeman, Vicecomitum.

Willelmus Newe, gardianus domus Fratrum minorum Londonii, summonitus fuit ad respondendum Johanni Northampton Draper et Petronille uxori eius de placito assise nocumenti etc. Et unde iidem Johannes et Petronilla queruntur quod cum ipsi habeant quinque mesuagia constructa et erecta ex parte occidentali cuiusdam venelle vocate Pentecostlane in parochia St. Nicole ad Macellum London' et duo mesuagia constructa et erecta [illegible, perhaps *supra*] ex parte

1 All abbreviations have been expanded and punctuation has been added.

orientali venelle predicte ex quibus tenementis omnes aque temporibus pluviosis, grandinum, et nivium a stillicidiis et gutteris eorundem mesuagiorum stillantes currentes sive cadentes in canello eiusdem venelle a tempore quo non extat memoria stillare, currere, et cadere solebant una cum aquis ab illis mesuagiis eiectis et cursum suum usque ad fossatum de Houndesdych habere per medium ^gardini eorundem[?] guardiani et sic per medium^[1] cuiusdam foraminis in muro lapideo civitatis Londoniarum existente sine impedimento aut nocumento. Idem quod Willelmus quendam murum lapideum construi et erigi fecit ex transverso venelle predicte prope gardinum suum domus predicte et prope mesuagia ipsorum Johannis et Petronelle in quo muro per ipsum gardinum sic constructo habetur unum foramen nimis artum et per ferrimenta aliqualiter obtrusum ^et etiam canellus eiusdem venelle per quem aqua ut predictum currere solebat obstructus est^[2] ita quod aque decurrentes de predictis mesuagiis in canello venelle predicte ut profertur ad locum suum debitum et aptum usque fossatum de Houndesdych supradictum currere nequeant set in mesuagiis predictis temporibus pluviosis grandinum et nivium refluunt et ingrediuntur ut omnes habitantes in eisdem mesuagiis una cum pueris tenentium eorundem, bonis, et catallis suis sepius emergere, consumere, et adnichilare videntur et maeremium et parietes eorundem mesuagiorum putrefactos et corruere faciunt. Per quod iidem Johannes et Petronilla proficuum mesuagiorum suorum predictorum facere non possunt, nec est congrue sustentare ad grande nocumentum liberi tenementi eorundem Johannes et Petronilla et contra consuetudinem civitatis predicte etc. Unde petunt quod facto inde visu per Maiorem et Alderos prout moris est quod canellus venelle supradicte de novo construatur et reparetur sumptibus ipsius Willelmi tam in gardino predictorum fratrum quam in venella supradicta. Ita quod aque stillantes et eiecte de mesuagiis predictis usque ad fossatum de Houndesdych ut predictum

1 section between ^ ^ was inserted between the lines.
2 section between ^ ^ was inserted between the lines.

est cursum suum prout solebant habere possint et ulterius fiat eis quod secundum consuetudinem civitatis Londoniarum de iure fuerit faciendum etc.

Et vicecomites Londoniarum alias testati fuerunt his [hic?] quod predictus Willelmus summonitus fuit per Simonem Mazerer et Nicholas Thame etc. Et predictus Willelmus in propria persona sua venit super terram in presentia dictorum Maioris, Recordatoris, et Aldrorum die veneris supradicto. Et dicit quod ipse habet diversa scripta et munimenta liberum tenamentum domus predicte in quo nocumentum predictum esse supponitur tangentia, que non habet hic ad presens. Et petit diem ad ea habendum etc. secundum consuetudinem civitatis etc. Et datus est ei dies ad ea habendum apud Gyhale Londoniarum in xv^um [1] tunc proximo sequens videlicet die Veneris proximo ante finem St. Luce Evangeliste ^tunc proximo sequens^[2] etc. Idem dies datus est predictis Johanni et Petronille etc. Ad quem diem quia cure pro diversis et arduis negociis curia placitum predictum vacare non potuit, dies datus est partibus usque diem Veneris in xv^um tunc proximo sequens. Et sic continuato inde processu inter partes predictas usque diem Veneris proximum post festum St. Marie Magdalene anno proximo predicti secundo, quo die quia gardianus super terram in presentia Predictorum Maioris et Recordatoris, Johannis Pyel, Adam Stable, Joannis Haddele, Johannis Organ, Roberti Launde, Willelmi Knyghtcote, Johannis Eston, Johannis Vyne, Johannis Hoo, Nichole Twyford, Thome Reynham, Johannis Kirketon, Willelmi Badeby, Johannis Clivele, Johannes Rote, et Adam de St. Ivone, Aldrorum ex proprio cognomento quod talis cursus aque currentis per canellum dicte venelle cursum suum tenere consuevit per medium gardini predicti per quendam gutteram subterraneam a vico predicto usque fossatum de Houndesdych cuius guttere cognovit partem abradicasse et partem inde obstruxisse et per

---

1 I.e. *quindenum*; also several lines below.

2 section between ^ ^ was inserted between the lines.

ferrimentum artasse. Et quia dictus cursus aque sic currentis in fossatum civitatis tangit communitatem etc.

Et sic dubitatur de fraude et cautela inter partes predictas prolocutis ad habendum cursum eiusdem aque in [undeciphered] fossatum predictum ad proficuum et aisiamentum tam dictorum Johannis et Petronille quam gardiani et ad dampnum communitatis etc. Ideo ut veritas inde legitime sciri possit precatus est Johannes Baldok, serviens Maioris quod venire faciat tunc coram dictis Maiore et Aldr' xii etc. de probioribus et senioribus viris parochie qui partibus predictis nulla affinitas attingit ad inquirendum per eorum sacramentum quomodo aque cadentes stillantes et eiecte de domibus predictis currere solebant et debent de iure etc. Qui quidem jurati videlicet Elias de Weston, Willelmus Horwode, Nicholas Jurdon, Johannes Thurkild, Johannes Dorsete senior, Thomas Soneman, Nicholas Thane, Robertus atte Greene, Johannes atte Shoppe, Thomas Martyn, Johannes Curson, et Henry Asshelyn, veniunt et de premissis onerantur. Dicunt super sacramentum suum quod omnes aque tam cadentes et stillantes de domibus predictis de eisdem per tenementum predictum eiecte quam promanentia[?] de pluviis nimbribus et grandinibus a tempore cuius contrarii memoria non existit usque diem quo dictus gardianus predictum murum lapideum ex transverso venelle ut predictum construi fecit et per ferramentum quoddam foramen, per quod aqua predicta cursum suum tenere consuevit, artavit et in partem obstruxit et petras predicte guttere in parte abradicavit et eandem gutteram in parte obstruxit. Currere consueverunt et cursum suum tenere solebant per eandem gutteram petream subterraneam sic per dictum gardianum in partem obtrusit et in parte abradicavit incipientem in fine boreali dicte venelle st sic per medium gardini gardiani et finium predictorum et sic per quoddam foramen in muro civitatis ad hoc factum usque fossatum de Houndesdych prout iidem Johannes et Petronilla superius supponunt etc. Super quo dies datus est partibus predictis de judicio suo audiendo apud Gyhale secundo die Augusti tunc proximo futuro etc. Ad quem diem venerunt partes predicte. Et in presentia Maioris et Aldrorum condictum est quod idem gardianus aperiet et emendari faciat obstructionem per eum in dicta guttera factam, et etiam de novo construi et reparari faciat abradicationem eiusdem guttere per eum similiter factam in forma qua prius fuit ante obstructionem et abradicationem predictas etc. Et hoc infra xl dies proxiore futuro. Alioquin vicecomites hoc fieri fac'[1] Sumptibus ipsius gardiani. Et nichilominus tunc ab eo capiantur xl [solidi] per contemptum etc.

### Assize of nuisance

Plea of the assize of nuisance to a tenement; the third Friday next after the end of the festival of St Michael Archangel, in the first year of the reign of King Richard, the second of that name after the conquest of England [2 Oct. 1377]. Those present were Nicholas Brembre, Mayor, William Chene, Recorder, William Neuport, Adam Karlill, William Baret, Robert Boxford, Robert Lucas, Walter Sibyla, and Thomas atte Noket, Aldermen, Nicholas Twyford and Andrew Pykeman, Sheriffs.

William Newe, guardian of the house of the Minorite Brothers [Franciscan Greyfriars] in London, has been summoned to respond to a case of assize of nuisance brought by John Northampton, draper, and his wife Petronilla, etc. The same John and Petronilla complain that they have five messuages built and constructed on the west side of a lane called Pentecost Lane in the parish of St. Nicholas Shambles in London, and two messuages built and constructed on the east side of the aforesaid lane. From these tenements in times of rain, sleet, and snow the waters from the gutters and downspouts of these same messuages drip, run, or fall into a channel in the same lane from time beyond all memory.[2] Waters usually drip, run, or fall along with the waters ejected from these messuages and take their course to the ditch

1 illegible.
2 Usually considered four generations. In law these are the "degrees" (see glossary).

called Houndsditch through the middle of the garden of this guardian and then through the middle of a certain hole which exists in the stone wall of the City of London without any impediment or damage. Likewise [they complain] that William had a stone wall constructed and built across the aforesaid lane near the garden of the aforesaid house and near the messuages of John and Petronilla themselves. Through this wall constructed by this guardian a hole was built too narrow and in some extent blocked by an iron grating to such a degree that the channel of this same lane (through which the water usually ran) was obstructed, and the waters running down from the aforesaid messuages in the channel of the same lane (as mentioned) are not able to run in their proper and suitable place as far as the Houndsditch mentioned above, but in times of rain, sleet, and snow [the waters] flow back and enter, so that all the tenants in these messuages along with their children, goods, and chattels are seen to be sunk, wasted, and annihilated, and the timbers and walls of these same messuages are caused to rot and fall down. For this reason the same John and Petronilla cannot make any profit from their aforesaid messuages nor is it reasonable that John and Petronilla endure the great damages caused to their buildings contrary to the practices of the aforesaid city, etc. As a result they ask that the Mayor and the Aldermen look into this, as the custom is, and that the channel in the above-mentioned lane be reconstructed anew and repaired both in the garden of the aforesaid Brothers as well as in the above-mentioned lane at the expense of William himself, so that the waters dripping and ejected from the aforesaid messuages might be able to take the course that they usually had to the Houndsditch, as previously said, and that furthermore they be treated according to the practices which must lawfully be done by the City of London, etc.

The London sheriffs have testified elsewhere that the aforesaid William had been summoned by Simon Mazerer and Nicholas Thame, etc. The aforesaid William in person came upon the land in the presence of the said Mayor, Recorder, and Aldermen on the above-mentioned Friday. And he says that he has various documents and writings bearing on the aforesaid House in which the aforesaid damages were alleged, documents which he does not have presently at hand. And he asks for a day, etc. according to the practices of the City. And he was given a day to settle these matters at the Guildhall in London in the quindene 15th day next following, to wit the next Friday before the end of the festival of St. Luke the Evangelist the next following [16 Oct. 1377]. Likewise the same day was given to the aforesaid John and Petronilla, etc.

On which day, because of various laborious concerns the court was not able to be free to hear the aforesaid plea, and a day was given to the parties for the Friday in the quindene next following [30 Oct.]. Thus the case between the aforesaid parties was continued to the next Friday after the festival of St. Mary Magdalene in the next year after the former [23 July 1378]. On this day the guardian came on the land in the presence of the aforesaid Mayor and Recorder, John Pyel, Adam Stable, John Haddele, John Organ, Robert Launde, William Knyghtcote, John Eston, John Vyne, John Hoo, Nicholas Twyford, Thomas Reynham, John Kirketon, William Badeby, John Clivele, John Rote, and Adam de St. Ives, Aldermen. [He testifies] from his own knowledge that the course of waters running through the channel of the said lane was accustomed to take its course through the middle of the aforesaid garden through an underground gutter from the said street to the Houndsditch. He acknowledged that he had uprooted part of the gutter and blocked part of it and narrowed it by an iron grating. And because the said course of water running into the ditch touches the community of the City, etc. And there is suspicion of fraud and deceit between the parties in the statements about the course of the waters into the aforesaid ditch to the profit and easement both of the said John and Petronilla and of the guardian to the harm of the community, etc. Therefore, so that the truth can be known, John Baldok, the sergeant of the Mayor is requested that he should summon a venire before the said

Mayor and Aldermen of 12 etc. of the more honorable and older men of the parish who have no relationship with the aforesaid parties to inquire under oath how the waters falling, dripping and ejected from the aforesaid houses usually and ought to run by law, to wit Elias de Weston, William Horwode, Nicholas Jurdon, John Thurkild, John Dorsete senior, Thomas Soneman, Nicholas Thane, Robert atte Greene, John atte Shoppe, Thomas Martyn, John Curson, and Henry Asshelyn who come and are instructed about the previous matters. On oath they say that all the waters, not only those falling and dripping from the aforesaid houses and ejected from the same through the aforesaid properties but also flowing during rainstorms and sleet from the time when memory does not run to the contrary up to the day when the said guardian had the aforesaid stone wall across the lane built (as previously said) and narrowed and in part obstructed by an iron grating the hole through which the aforesaid water used to take its course, and uprooted the stones of the aforesaid gutter and obstructed part of it - these waters were accustomed to run and usually took their course through the same stone underground gutter, of which part was obstructed by the said guardian and part was uprooted, beginning in the north side of the said lane and then through the middle of the garden and the property of the aforesaid parties, and then through a hole in the city wall made for this up to the ditch of Houndsditch, just as alleged by John and Petronilla above. A day was given concerning these matters to the aforesaid parties to hear their lawsuit at the Guildhall, the second day of August future next [2 Aug. 1378]. On which day the aforesaid parties came and in the presence of the Mayor and Aldermen it was determined that the same guardian will open and will have corrected the obstruction made by him in the said gutter and he shall have the part of the same gutter, which was uprooted by him in a like manner, reconstructed and repaired anew in the shape it was before the aforesaid obstruction and destruction. This to be done within the next 40 days in the future. Otherwise the sheriffs will have this done at the expense of the guardian himself. And nevertheless let 40 shillings be taken from him for contempt, etc.

A scan of this document was supplied courtesy of the London Metropolitan Archives; the file number is CLA 040/02/002/040, i.e. page 40 of the bundle CLA 040/02/002. The older identification (found in Chew and Kellaway below) is Roll FF #618. These documents are roughly 8 ½" by 28" and have been fastened together along the top margin. This particular document is somewhat worn at the right edge, making it rather difficult to read. The interested student may find many more reports from the assize of nuisance on-line at the London Metropolitan Archives website: Go to Search Archive and enter CLA/040/02/003, which is the roll following CLA 040/02/002. See the appendix in this textbook "Reading Law Records."

Additional Reading:

Helena M. Chew and William Kellaway 1973. Available on line.

Ruth Bird 1949.

## A Case of Nonpayment: A Writ of *Cessavit*; Action of *Nisi Prius*.

In May of 1341, Margaret, the widow of John de Roos and landholder in the village of Gedney, Lincolnshire, brought suit against the Abbot of Creake Abbey, about 30 miles east of Gedney in Norfolk.[1] She filed a writ of *cessavit* ("he has ceased"), alleging that the abbot held land of her in return for services: three shillings rent plus two duties, first to supply a canon to conduct divine service at the Chapel of St. Thomas the Martyr, and second to support five poor people. She alleged that he had ceased to provide these services two years previously. After hearing from both parties, the court gave judgment for Margaret.

The writ of *cessavit* was used in various situations. A landlord could bring this writ against a tenant who had not paid his rent or performed required services, and did not have sufficient goods to be distrained (i.e. have his chattels and land confiscated, the landlord's usual resort). After two years of such default the landlord can bring a *cessavit*. There were separate writs of *cessavit* in the case of unpaid rent, in the case of unperformed services by a religious establishment (both being issues here), and in many other circumstances. The details may be found in such old legal textbooks like *The New Natura Brevium* 478-84.

This case also illustrates the action of *nisi prius,* originally a device by which jurors could avoid a trip to Westminster, the location of the king's court. Cases could be pleaded at Westminster, where the inevitable fact-finding and jury deliberations would be expected to occur *Nisi prius justiciarii venissent* . . ., "unless the justices have

---

1 The Ros, Roos, de Roos family was prominent in Lincolnshire. Creake Abbey was founded in 1206 as a house of Austin Canons. In 1341 its abbot was John de Harpole. All the monks and the last abbot died in 1506 and the house reverted to the crown. Its ruins can be seen one mile north of the village of North Creake. See Page, *A History of the County of Norfolk,* 2:370-2.

previously come . . ." to the actual town in which the case arose. This allowed a case to be decided without travel to Westminster, always difficult in medieval times, and probably impossible for many jurymen. In Margaret's case, the jury could make its decision in Lincoln. In later legal language *nisi prius* came to refer to any action tried before judges of the King's Bench.

The entire record of this case in Latin and translation is given below.[1] In addition, since this case is also cited in the Year Book of 15 Edward III, some discussion of the Year Books and of this case's treatment in them is included in the next section. First the Latin.

In margin: Linc. primo die Maii Ro. [= Regno] xv

§ Margareta que fuit uxor Johannis de Roos per Adam de Lymbergh attornatum suum petit versus Abbatem de Creyk unum mesuagium triginta et quinque acras terre et quindecim acras prata cum pertinentia in Gedeneye que idem Abbas de ea tenet per certa servicia et que ad ipsam Margaretam reverti debent per formam statutam de communi consilio regni Regis Anglie inde provisi, eo quod predictus Abbas in faciendo predicta servitia per biennium iam cessavit etc. Et unde dicit quod predictus Abbas tenet de ea predicta tenementa cum pertinentia per fidelitatem et servicium trium solidorum per annum ad festa Sancti Michaelis et Pasche per equales porciones annuatim solvendo et per servicium inveniendo unum canonicum capellanum cotidie in capella Sancti Thome Martiris sita in quodam mesuagio, quod quondam fuit

1 In the older literature this record is cataloged as *Placita de Banco* (= Common Pleas Rolls) Michaelmas term, 15 Edward III, Ro. 457 *dorso* (= back). Today in The National Archives it is catalogued as a membrane (= page) in CP 40/328, a roll which contains several hundred documents. Our document can be studied on line at the Anglo-American Legal Tradition website (http://aalt.law.uh.edu/). On the index page, find 15 Edw. III (1341) and click on CP40/328. Select 328 *dorses*, since our record is on the back of the membrane. Scroll through several pages of thumbnails to 0919. The case in question is at the top of the page. You will see *Linc*[o]. in the margin, indicating a case from Lincolnshire.

Johannis Dory, divina videlicet matutinas horas missam vesperas completorum placebo et dirige et alias orationes celebraturum, et sustentando ibidem cotidie quinque pauperes videlicet inveniendo cuilibet eorum per diem unum panem ponderantem quinquaginta solidos et potagium et cervisiam, et inter duos eorum unum ferculum carnium vel piscium vel alterius cibi secundum quod dies exigunt, et alteri eorundem pauperum medietatem unius ferculi in forma predicta et quolibet altero anno cuilibet eorum unam tunicam de panno pro eis competenti. De quibus servitiis eadem Margareta fuit seisita per manus predicti Abbatis ut per manus veri tenentis sui tempore pacis tempore domini Regis nunc, videlicet de fidelitate divinis servitiis et sustentacionem pauperum ut de feodo et iure et de predicto redditu in domenico suo ut de feodo et iure etc. Predictus Abbatus in faciendo predicta servitia per biennium ante diem impetracionis brevis, videlicet ante primum diem Maii anno regni Domini Regis nunc quintodecimo cessavit etc. Per quod actio accreivit ei petendi tenementa predicta in domenico etc. Et inde producit sectam etc. Et Abbas per Johannem Grace attornatum suum venit. Et dicit quod ipse non potest predicta tenementa predicte Margarete reddere, quia dicit quod ipse non tenet tenementa predicta nec tenuit die impetracionis brevis etc. Et hoc paratus est verificare. Unde petit iudicium etc. Et Margareta dicit quod diem impetracionis brevis sui, scilicet predicto primo die Maii anno regni domini Regis nunc Anglie quintodecimo, predictus Abbas tenuit predicta tenementa cum pertinentia. Margareta per breve suum supponit. Et hoc petit quod inquiratur per patriam. Et Abbas similiter. Ideo perceptum est vicecomiti quod venire faciat hic a die pascha in tres septimanas xii etc. Per quos etc. Et qui nec etc. Ad recognoscendum etc. Quia tam etc. Postea continuato inde inter eos processu per juratas positas in respectum hic usque ad hunc diem, scilicet a die Sancti Hillarii in xv dies anno regni domini Regis nunc Anglie decimo septimo nisi justiciarii ad assisas capiendas assignati in comitatu predicto per formam statutam die sabati proximum ante festum Natalis domini proximo preterito apud Lincoln prius venissent etc. Et modo venit predicta Margareta per predictum attornatum suum et justiciarii ad assisas in predicto comitatu capiendas assignita miserunt hic veredictum jurate predicte in hec verba. Postea apud Lincoln predicto die sabati proximo ante festum Natalis domini coram prefatis justiciariis ad assisas veniunt tam predicta Margareta quam Abbas de Creyke per attornatos suos infra scriptos. Et similiter juratores veniunt qui de consensu parcium electi et jurati dicunt super sacramentum suum quod predictus Abbas predicto die impetracionis brevis Regis fuit tenens de tenementis predictis. Ideo consideratum est quod predicta Margareta recuperet inde seisinam suam versus eum et predictus Abbas in misericordia etc.

**In margin: Lincolnshire. 1 May, Year 15 of the Reign.**

§ Margaret, who was the wife of [the late] John de Roos, through her attorney Adam de Lymbergh petitions against the Abbot of Creake for one messuage of 35 acres of [farm] land and 15 acres of meadow with appurtenances in Gedney, land which the same abbot holds of her in return for certain services and which ought to revert to the same Margaret according to the usual counsel of the reign of the King of England heretofore stipulated, on the grounds that the aforesaid abbot has now ceased to perform the aforesaid services for two years.

And she goes on to state that the aforesaid abbot holds of her the aforesaid tenements with appurtenances in return for fealty and the payment of three shilling per year at the feast of St. Michael and Easter, paid annually in equal installments; and by the service of finding an ordained canon to celebrate daily in the chapel of St. Thomas the Martyr (located in the messuage which once belonged to John Dory) the divine services, i. e. matins, the hours, the mass, vespers, compline, and *placebo et dirige*,[1] as well as other prayers; and by supporting daily at the same place five paupers, i.e. by finding for each of them per day

1 Prayers for the dead.

one loaf of bread weighing 3 lbs.[1] as well as porridge and ale, and between two of them one plate of meat or fish or other food (according to the requirements of the day) and for one of them one-half of a plate in the manner aforesaid, and for each of them in alternate years one coat of cloth suitable for them.

Of these services the same Margaret was seised at the hands of the aforesaid abbot as at the hands of a true tenant of hers in a time of peace during the reign of our present Lord King, i. e. of the fealty [= promise, pledge] of the divine services and the support of the poor men as of fee and right, and of the aforesaid rent in her demesne, as of fee and right, etc. The aforesaid abbot has ceased performing the aforesaid services for two years before the acquisition of the writ, i.e. before the first day of May of the 15th year of our present Lord King, etc. Because of this, an action is available to her of petitioning for the aforesaid holding in her demesne, etc. And therefore she brings suit, etc.

And the abbot through John Grace his attorney comes and states that he is not able to restore the aforesaid holdings to the aforesaid Margaret, because, as he states, he does not hold the aforesaid holdings nor did he hold them on the day of the acquisition of the writ, etc. And he is prepared to prove this. And so he seeks judgment, etc.

And Margaret states that on the day of the acquisition of the writ, i.e. the aforesaid first day of May of the 15th year of the reign of the present Lord King of England, the aforesaid abbot held the aforesaid holding with appurtenances. Margaret submits this in her writ. And she petitions that it be investigated in the neighborhood.[2] And the abbot likewise.

---

1 Lat. '60 shillings' using 'shilling' as a unit of weight; there are 20 shillings to the pound, money or weight.

2 Lat. *per patriam. Patria* in such contexts means district, neighborhood, or a jury.

As so the sheriff was ordered to hold a venire of twelve here three weeks after Easter day, etc. By them, etc. And those who do not, etc. To determine, etc. Because in this way, etc.[1]

Afterwards the proceedings between them being postponed by a respite of the jury until this day, i.e. the 15th day after the feast of St. Hilary in the 17th year of the reign of the present Lord King of England,[2] unless the justices appointed to hear the assizes in the aforesaid county in the established form in Lincoln had come on the Sabbath next before the most recent past feast of our Lord's Nativity, etc. And the aforesaid Margaret soon came with her aforesaid attorney, and the justices appointed to hear the assizes in the aforesaid county gave the verdict of the aforesaid jury in these words. Afterwards in Lincoln on the aforesaid Sabbath day next before the feast of our Lord's Nativity, not only the aforesaid Margaret but also the Abbot of Creake through their attorneys (written below) come to the assizes before the aforesaid justices. And likewise the jurymen come, those who were selected and sworn with the consent of the parties, and state on oath that the aforesaid abbot on the day of the acquisition of the king's writ did hold the aforesaid holdings. And so it was decided that the aforesaid Margaret would recover her seisin against him, and that the aforesaid abbot should be amerced [= fined].

---

1 The last sentences condense the standard phrasing for summoning jurymen.

2 The Hilary term started 14 January; this date is late January 1343, two years after the suit began.

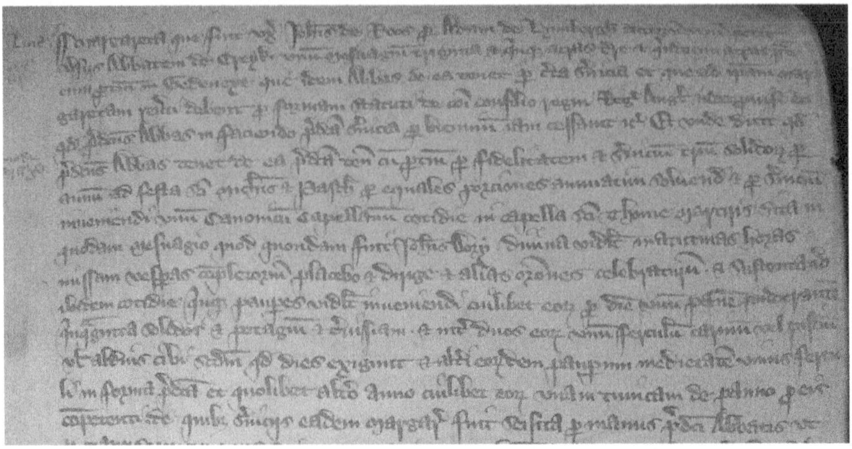

**Margaret's Case**

## The Year Books.

The previous section described the legal record from 1341-3. This same case also appears as a report in the Year Book of 15 Edward III (Pike 1891 448-51). So what are the Year Books? These fascinating sources for our knowledge of English law are courtroom reports roughly analogous to our modern trial transcripts; "roughly" because the Year Books are not verbatim transcripts, but summaries of the lawyers' arguments, either successful or otherwise, accompanied by significant, useful quotations. These Year Books were not official documents like the case record quoted above, but were notes taken down perhaps by junior clerks present in the courtroom and shortly thereafter published in manuscript copies to be used by law students or practicing lawyers as guides to which arguments succeeded, which failed, how to approach each type of case or writ, and other practical hints. There is a continuous series of these reports in manuscript from 1268 to 1535, when individual lawyers began to publish their own reports. (An example of the latter can be found in our section "An Oxford Murder Case.") Most of these were printed in the standard "Black-Letter" edition published in London in 1679 and reprinted in 2007. That edition's text is usually far worse than the text of the many manuscripts, since there was no thought of proofreading. Fortunately, many of the Year Books have received modern editions during the 19th and 20th centuries.

Year Book reports are not included in this anthology because they are written almost entirely in French, the language of court pleading until the 17th century.[1] (Occasionally Latin from the statutes is quoted, as

1 This version of French is called either Law French or Norman-French in the literature. Originally the dialect of the Norman conquerers and of the early English court, by the 17th century it had become a specialized jargon from which most of our legal terms derive. See our section on "The Languages of the Law."

well as a few English quips or proverbs.) These Year Book reports supplement the Latin legal records in several ways. In general the official records give the parties involved, the charges or writs, and the final judgment. The French reports give the arguments used by the lawyers and the reactions of the justices. The reports frequently omit the names of the parties (or get them wrong) and even the final judgment, as in our case here. These facts were not important for the Year Book readers, who were focused on improving their legal acumen.

Our case, a writ of *cessavit* ("he has ceased") brought by Margaret against the Abbot of Creake, is one of those which can be found both in the legal rolls and in the Year Books, and will illustrate the differences between the record (the rolls) and the report (the Year Books). The Year Book report omits much that is in the record translated above, most notably the name of the plaintiff Margaret and the final judgment of the court that Margaret recover possession. On the other hand the report gives the arguments used in court. It begins (in Pike's English translation), "*Cessavit* against the Abbot of Creake," then briefly summarizes the charges, i. e. failure on the part of the abbot to deliver promised services, and the lawyers' arguments. The abbot's lawyer, Pole, arguing a technicality, says that the complaint is not warranted, because the plaintiff has included in the *cessavit* two different kinds of service; on the one hand the abbot's tenancy of the land can be saved by paying the back rent, but on the other hand it cannot be saved because the abbot cannot retroactively perform two years' worth of divine services for the plaintiff. Hence she should have brought two writs, one for each situation. Plaintiff's counsel replies that the objection applies only to a writ of common form. The abbot's counsel accepts this, but states again that the plaintiff should have had two writs. Plaintiff's counsel cites precedent for having one common writ. The abbot's counsel refuses to debate this point and repeats that according to the statutes (Gloucester chap. 4 and Westminster II chap. 41) two writs are required. The chief justice rules for the plaintiff, saying that there cannot be two writs in this case. Issue is now joined on whether the abbot did in fact have the freehold (Fr. *frank tenement*, Lat. *liberum tenementum*) at the time the writ was purchased. The abbot's counsel says: "Will you accept my averment [affirmation] that the abbot is not tenant of the freehold?" The plaintiff is ready to deny it ("Ready, etc. that you are . . ."), and they argue this point, on which the case must have turned, since the report ends here without revealing the judgment for the plaintiff.

Owen Pike (Pike 1893) has discussed other cases which can be found both in the rolls and in the Year Books. Each report evinces the same interest in argument and procedure, and each record an emphasis on the facts. The reports occasionally quote some piece of courtroom wit or humor, one of which is too good to omit. In the 15th year of King Edward I (1286-7; the regnal year began in November) Chief Justice Metingham was hearing a case in which the paternity of one of the parties was challenged. Everyone admitted that the man had been born in wedlock, but it was alleged that his father was not his mother's husband. The Chief Justice refused to consider the objection, saying in English, "Hwo so boleth myn kyn, ewere is the calf myn" (Whoso bulleth my cow, the calf is always mine). The rhyme hints that this is a proverb otherwise unattested (Bolland 1921 76).

Additional Reading:
Bolland 1921.
Fitzherbert 1730. In 1514, Fitzherbert made the first abridgment of the Year Books, the first attempt to provide a summary of English law. His Natura Brevium (1st ed. 1534) was in French. Nutt and Gosling's version (available on archive.org) is in English.
Pike 1893 pp. 266-280.
Pike, *Year Books of the Reign of King Edward the Third. Year XV* 1891. A volume of the Rolls Series. The case transcribed here is #71, pp. 448-51.

## The Negligence of the Humber Ferryman.

Another case which can be found in both the legal records and the Year Book reports is the Humber Ferry case, well known for establishing a precedent for the modern law of contract. In mid-November, 1348, John de Bukton paid Nicholas atte Tounesende of Hessle, a ferryman, to carry his mare across the Humber river.[1] The ferryman overloaded his boat and the plaintiff's mare was lost in some unspecified way. Perhaps the boat capsized or the mare fell overboard. In any event, John brought a bill alleging trespass against the king's peace.[2] In the common law of the time, one could sue for breach of contract using the action of covenant, but the covenant had to be written and under seal. John and Nicholas had no such covenant. John could have sued in a local court, which had few ways of enforcing a judgment. By chance the King's Bench was sitting in York, and the royal courts had developed an action of trespass for wrongfully inflicted injury to persons, goods, or land. However, the plaintiff in such an action had to prove a breach of "the king's peace," i.e. a violation of law and order (trespass was generally thought to happen *vi et armis*), which would certainly not apply in this case of a lost mare.

Nevertheless John brought this action before the King's Bench, alleging trespass, and surprisingly, the court allowed it and found for John. In the years following, the action for trespass began to be applied generally to ill-performance and then non-performance of undertakings. The action was now called *assumpsit* ("he has undertaken") and

1 The one-mile ferry crossing from Hessle to Barton upon Humber is mentioned in the Domesday Book.

2 In medieval courts proceedings could be brought by bill against anyone within the jurisdiction of the courts. In this case the King's Bench would hear this bill since it happened to be sitting in York at the time. The meaning of trespass has changed greatly over the centuries. The earliest examples are cases of undoubted violence with strong criminal elements, hence *vi et armis* "by force of arms." See Plucknett 1956 p. 386, p. 465.

became the basis for the modern law of contract. In addition, although the loss of the mare was not directly or intentionally caused by Nicholas, but simply by negligence, the court allowed this negligence to be chargeable in a trespass action, thus paving the way for our modern law of tort.

> Here is our transcription of the Latin original, which is on King's Bench roll 27, number 354, (This case is second on the membrane. All abbreviations are expanded. In line 3 the usual *se* "themselves" was omitted.)

[in margin] Eboracum § Convictum est per juratam patrie in quam Johannes de Bukton de cane querens et Nicholas atte Tounesende de Hesel ferriman [se] posuerunt quod idem Nicholas die lune proximo post festum sancti Martini anno regni regis nunc vicesimo recipit de ipso Johanne quoddam jumentum apud hesel ad salvo cariandum ultra aquam de homber in navi ipsius Nicholi et idem Nicholas navem illam sic oneravit contra voluntatem ipsius Johannis ita quod amisit iumentum predictum ob defectum ipsius Nicholi prout idem Johannes per billam suam queritur ad dampnum ipsius Johannis quadraginta solidorum, et quod idem Johannes nulla bona seu catalla ibidem amisit sicut ipse per eandem billam queritur. Ideo consideratum est quod idem Johannes recuperet versus prefatum Nicholam dampna sua predicta. et idem Nicholas capiatur etc. Et idem Johannes in misericordia pro falso clamio quo ad catalla predicta etc. --- postea isto termino venit coram domino rege predictus Johannes de Bukton in propria persona sua et cognovit quod predictus Nicholas satisfecit ei de predictis quadraginta solidis etc. Et super hoc venit predictus Nicholas et reddidit se prisone marescalli Regis et petit se admitti ad finem faciendum cum domino Rege occasione predicta et admittitur prout patet per rotulos finium istius termini etc.

Dampna xl s. unde Clericis xl d. Friseby ii s. York. § It was found by jury of the country upon whom John de Bukton of Cave, plaintiff, and Nicholas atte Tounesende of Hessle, ferryman, put themselves, that the said Nicholas, on the Monday next after the Feast of St. Martin, in the twentieth year of the reign of the current king, received from the said John a mare at Hessle for safe carriage across the water of the Humber in the said Nicholas' boat, and that the said Nicholas so overloaded the boat, against the wishes of the said John, that he lost the said mare by the fault of that same Nicholas, as John by his bill complains, to the damage of the same John of 40 shillings, and that the same John lost no [other] goods or chattels at the same time, just as he complains by his bill. Therefore it is decided that the same John should recover against the aforesaid Nicholas the said damages. And let the same Nicholas be taken, etc. And the same John is amerced for a false charge as to the aforesaid chattels, etc.

Afterwards in this term the aforesaid John Bukton in his own person came into the presence of the Lord King and acknowledged that the aforesaid Nicholas had satisfied him in the matter of the aforesaid 40 shillings, etc. And on this matter the aforesaid Nicholas came and surrendered himself as prisoner to the marshal of the king and prays that he be allowed to compound with the Lord King on the aforesaid occasion, and he is allowed, as is clear from the rolls of fines of this term, etc.

[At bottom of entry, strikethrough indicating payment]

*Damages 40 shillings, of which 40 d. to clerks, 2 shillings to Friseby*[1]

**Fine for the Humber Ferryman**

1 Richard Friseby, chief clerk. See the illustration "Fine for the Humber Ferryman."

## The Negligence of the Humber Ferryman.

**The French report with abbreviations expanded[1]:**

I. de B. se plaint per bille, q' G. de F. certain jour et an a B. sur Humbre, avoit empris a carier sa jument pris, etc. en son bateau oustre l'eau de Humbre safe et sain, la ou fist le dit G surcharge son bateau dauters chivals, perquel surcharge le jument perist a tort et damages etc.

*Richmond.* judgment de le bill, que ne suppose en nous nul tort, eins prove q'il averoit accion per breve per voye de Covenenat, plus tost que[2] per voye de Trans'. Par qui etc.

*Bankwell.* Il semble que vous lui fistes trans' quant vos surcharges le bateau, par que sa jument perist, etc. Par que respondez.

*Richmond.* De rien culpable.

[Plaintiff] Prest d'averrer nostre bille, etc. [at alii econtra etc.]

I. of B. complains by bill that G. of F. on a certain day and year at B. on the Humber undertook to carry his mare etc. in his boat safe and sound across the Humber, and that the said G. overloaded his boat with other horses, as a result of which overloading the mare perished unlawfully and harmfully.

Richmond: "[We pray] judgment on the bill, which does not support any unlawfulness on our part, but rather proves that he has an action by way of a writ of Covenant rather than[3] by way of Trespass," etc.

Bankwell: "It seems that you did him a trespass when you overloaded the boat so that the mare perished, etc. Therefore respond."

1 Text from Hastings 1935 p. 35, from *Liber Assisarum*, 22 Edward III (printed 1679), plea 41 (no modern edition). Bankwell is the judge, Richmond the lawyer for the defendant Nicholas.

2 Significant variant readings in the mss. are reported in Kiralfy 1953 424: instead of *ou*, "or," printed in the Black Letter edition of 1679, the mss. have *et nemye per voie* "and not at all by way of trespass"; *plus qe per voie de* "rather than by way of trespass"; and other readings. The old Black Letter Year Books are rife with misprints and errors. There was apparently no thought of proofreading.

3 See previous footnote.

Richmond: “Guilty of nothing.”

[Plaintiff]. “Ready to answer our bill,” etc. [And others to the contrary.]

As usual the Year Book report shows little concern for actual names of the parties or the results (I. de B. is clearly Johannes de Bukton, but it is hard to see Nicholas in G. de F.). Richmond's statement as printed in 1679, that the plaintiff has an action by way of Covenant or Trespass, makes no sense. His point must be that the action must be by way of Covenant rather than by Trespass, and the manuscripts show that he did in fact make such an argument, but the judge did not buy it.

Additional Readings:
Hastings 1936 pp. 35-38.
Kiralfy 1953 pp. 421-4.
Plucknett 1956.

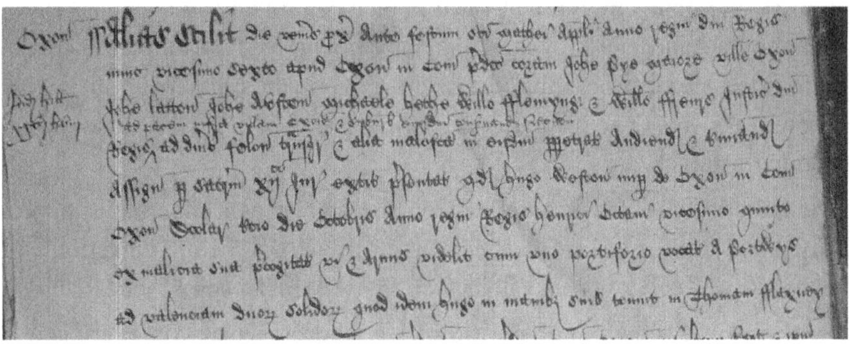

**Hugh Weston's Case**

## An Indictment for Assault, 1535.

During the reign of King Henry VIII in 1535, Hugh Weston,[1] a scholar of Oxford, was indicted for an October 1533 assault on Thomas Flaxney, from the effects of which the said Thomas died the following May, 1534. During the hearing the judges decided that the indictment was flawed and Weston was dismissed *sine die.* He later went on to have a career at the University. Here is the Latin indictment and the decision thereon (last paragraph). This is a summary of the case, not a transcription of what was said at each hearing. The original record of the case can be seen at The King's Bench Roll, KB27/1099 m.3 and 4, available at the Anglo-American Legal Tradition website. A comparison of the handwriting seen in the web pages linked just above and the transcription below will give the observant student some ability to read original legal documents. Some common abbreviations are listed here. The student who wishes to read more of these original texts should study the appendix "Reading Law Records" in this anthology. Here are some of the common abbreviations in the first few lines of the text:

The 5th word in the 1st line, *px, proximo*. The Latin prefixes *per, pro* are p with a stroke through the descender; the curved line over the x means that the word has been shortened.

The 13th word, 1st line, *dm, domini*. "lord'.

The 7th word, 3rd line, *com, comitatu*, 'county'.

The 8th word, 3rd line, *pdto, praedicto*, 'the aforesaid', very common in all these legal texts. Note that the Latin prefix *prae* is p with a curved line over it.

1 Probably Hugh Weston, M.A. (Oxon.), 1532, Rector of Lincoln College 1538-1555, Margaret Professor of Divinity 1540-1558 and reputedly of a lewd disposition: A. à Wood, *Athenae Oxonienses* (1813 ed.) I, 295-297.

*Etc.* is very common in all these case summaries. By using it the scribe avoids having to repeat all the legal boilerplate which any lawyer could supply for himself.

The Latin transcription and translation are from *The Reports of Sir John Spelman,* vol. 2, pp. 297-8.

KB 27/1099 (King's Bench roll, Easter 1536), Rex m.3.

*Oxon'* Alias scilicet die veneris proximo ante festum sancti Mathei appostoli anno regni domini Regis nunc vicesimo sexto apud Oxoniam in Comitatu predicto coram Iohanne Pye maiore ville Oxonie Iohanne Latton Iohanne Austen Michaele Hethe Willelmo Flemyng et Willelmo Freurs Iusticiariis domini Regis ^ad pacem infra villam Oxonie et suburbia eiusdem conseruandam Necnon^[1] ad diuersa felonia transgressiones et alia malefacta in eisdem perpetrata audienda et terminanda assignatis per sacramentum xii Iuratorum extitit presentatum quod Hugo Weston nuper de Oxonia in Comitatu Oxonie scolar tercio die Octobris anno regni Regis Henrici octaui vicesimo quinto ex malicia sua precogitata vi et armis videlicet cum uno portiforio vocato 'a Portwys' ad valenciam duorum solidorum quod idem Hugo in manibus suis tenuit in Thomam Flaxney filium Ricardi Flaxney apud Oxoniam predictam in predicto Comitatu Oxonie insultum fecit et ipsum Thomam cum portiforio predicto super ventrem eiusdem Thome felonice percussit. Et postea eundem Thomam cum Portiforio predicto super caput suum felonice ac diuersimodi percussit et portiforium illud super caput eiusdem Thome fregit dando eidem Thome diuersos ictus super ventrem et caput sua quorum quidem ictuum violencia idem Thomas ad tunc et ibidem super ligna focalia cecidit ac Postquam idem Thomas sic super predicta ligna focalia prostratus fuit predictus Hugo ipsum Thomam ad tunc et ibidem super predicta ligna focalia prostratum iacentem eundem Thomam ad tunc et ibidem tam violenter et fortiter cum cubito et brachiis suis super cor et

1 The passage between ^ ^ was inserted between the lines as an addition.

pectus eiusdem Thome percussit et pungebat quod idem Thomas a predicto Hugone nullo modo euadere seu refugere potuit qui quidem Thomas ex ictibus verberacione et pungione predictis a predicto tercio die Octobris usque quintum diem Maii anno regni dicti domini Regis nunc vicesimo sexto apud Oxoniam predictam languebat quoquidem quinto die Maii predictus Thomas Flaxney ex ictibus et verberacione predictis apud Oxoniam predictam obiit. Et sic predictus Hugo prefatum Thomam apud Oxoniam predictam in Comitatu predicto felonice interfecit et murdrauit contra pacem dicti domini Regis coronam et dignitatem suas etc.—Quod quidem Indictamentum Dominus Rex nunc coram eo Postea certis de causis venire fecit terminandum—Per quod Preceptum fuit vicecomiti quod non omitteret etc. quin caperet eum si etc.—Et modo scilicet die mercurie proxime post mensem Pasche isto eodem termino coram domino Rege apud Westm' venit predictus Hugo Weston in propria persona sua Et reddidit se prisone marescalcie domini Regis coram ipso Rege occasione predicta qui committitur marescalli etc. Et statim de premissis sibi superius impositis allocutus qualiter se velit inde acquietare dicit quod indictamentum predictum minus sufficiens in lege existit ad ponendum ipsum Hugonem eidem Indictamento responsurum. Et pro insufficiencia eiusdem Petit quod ipse de premissis per Curiam hic dimittatur etc. Super quo viso indictamento predicto et per Curiam hic intellectis omnibus et singulis premissis seruientibus domini Regis ad legem ac eiusdem Regis attornato ad hoc conuocatis et presentibus pro eo quod videtur Curie hic quod indictamentum predictum non est sufficiens in lege modo et forma prout idem Hugo pro exoneracione sua premissorum placitando allegauit Consideratum est quod predictus Hugo Weston eat inde Sine die etc.

Sine Die

## The Latin indictment Rex v. Hugh Weston

Oxford. Before now, namely on the Friday[1] [24 February 1535] next before the feast of St Matthew the Apostle in the twenty-sixth year of the reign of the present lord king, at Oxford in the aforesaid county, before John Pye, mayor of the vill of Oxford, John Latton, John Austen, Michael Hethe, William Flemyng, and William Freurs, the lord king's justices assigned to keep the peace within the vill of Oxford and the suburbs of the same and also to hear and determine the divers felonies, trespasses and other misdeeds perpetrated in the same, it was presented by the oath of twelve jurors that Hugh Weston, late of Oxford in the county of Oxford, scholar, on the third day of October in the twenty-fifth year of the reign of King Henry VIII [1533], of his malice aforethought [and] with force and arms (that is to say, with a portes[2] called 'a portwys' valued at 2s. which the same Hugh held in his hands), did assault Thomas Flaxney the son of Richard Flaxney at Oxford aforesaid in the aforesaid county of Oxford, and feloniously did strike him the said Thomas with the aforesaid portes upon the belly of the same Thomas; and afterwards he feloniously and in various ways did strike the same Thomas with the aforesaid portes upon his head, and did break the portes upon the head of the same Thomas, giving the same Thomas various blows upon his belly and head, through the violence of which blows the same Thomas then and there fell down on sticks of firewood, and after the same Thomas was thus laid out on the aforesaid sticks of firewood the aforesaid Hugh then and there with his elbow and arms so violently and forcibly did strike and punch the same Thomas, who was then and there lying prostrate on the aforesaid sticks of firewood, upon the heart and breast of the same Thomas, that the

---

1 Friday (*die veneris*) seems to have been the usual day for hearing cases. Cp. the London assize of nuisance above. Dates are always given as so many days before or after a saint's feast day in such-and-such a year of the king's reign.

2 A portable breviary: OED under portas, portes.

same Thomas could in no way escape or flee from the aforesaid Hugh; which Thomas languished from the blows, beating and punching aforesaid from the aforesaid third day of October until the fifth day of May in the twenty-sixth year of the reign of the said present lord king [1534] at Oxford aforesaid, on which fifth day of May the aforesaid Thomas Flaxney died at Oxford aforesaid from the aforesaid blows and beating; and thus the aforesaid Hugh feloniously did kill and murder the said Thomas at Oxford aforesaid in the aforesaid county, against the peace of the said lord king, his crown and dignity etc.

Which indictment the present lord king afterwards, for certain causes, caused to come before him to be determined.

Therefore the sheriff was commanded that he should not fail etc. to take him if etc.

And now, namely on the Wednesday [17 May 1536] next after one month from Easter this same term, the aforesaid Hugh Weston came in his own person before the lord king at Westminster, and surrendered himself to the lord king's Marshalsea Prison before the king himself, for the aforesaid cause. And he is committed to the marshal etc. And, being forthwith asked how he wished to acquit himself in respect of the foregoing matters charged against him above, he says that the aforesaid indictment is not sufficient in law to compel him the said Hugh to answer the same indictment. And, on account of the insufficiency of the same, he prays that he may be dismissed from the foregoing by the court here etc.

Whereupon, the aforesaid indictment having been seen, and all and singular the foregoing matters having been understood by the court here, after calling together the lord king's serjeants-at-law[1] and the same king's attorney, and they being present: since it appears to the court here that the aforesaid indictment is not sufficient in law, in

1 These were the only men licensed to practice in the King's Bench, where this case landed.

manner and form as the same Hugh has in pleading alleged to discharge himself from the foregoing, it is decided that the aforesaid Hugh do go thereof without day etc.

Without a day [i.e. set to meet again].

Sir John Spelman (ca. 1480-1546) studied law at Gray's Inn, following in the footsteps of his father, Henry Spelman, who was Recorder at Norwich, England. In 1521 John became a serjeant-at-law (*servientes ad legem*), one of the elite group of lawyers who performed much of the work in the royal common law courts. In 1530 he was appointed judge of King's Bench, to fill the vacancy created by the death of Sir John More, Sir Thomas More's father. (Sir Thomas was at the time Lord Chancellor.) Spelman served as judge for about 15 years until his death in January 1546. He is best known as one of the judges in the treason trial of Sir Thomas More. During his career Spelman made a collection of reports on interesting cases which he heard or which he judged himself. As mentioned above, the common law knew a long tradition of reporting pleas in common law cases in publications called the Year Books. A continuous series of such Year Book reports runs from 1268 to 1535; they were printed in the 17th century. (On the Year Books see the section "The Year Books" in this anthology.) Individual lawyers and judges also made their own collections of pleas, but Spelman's is the only surviving collection made by a judge during the reign of Henry VIII. By chance the above case of Rex vs. Hugh Weston is recorded in Spelman's *Reports*.[1] It is in French (as are almost all reports), but he quotes parts of the indictment in Latin.

### Enditement.

H.W. fut indite en Oxon' per nome de H. W. nuper de Oxon' en comitatu oxon' scoler 3 die Octobris anno [domini regis] H. 8. 26 ex malicia sua precogitata vi et armis etc., videlicet cum uno portifero

1 *Spelman's Reports,* vol. 1 p. 103.

vocato 'a portes' ad valenciam ii s., in T. F. insultum fecit et ipsum T. cum portifero predicto super ventrem suum felonice percussit et post ea eundem T. cum portifero predicto super caput suum felonice ac diversimodi percussit qui quidem T. ex ictibus predictis a predicto 3 die usque 5 diem Iunii proxime sequentem languebat, quo die predictus T. ex ictibus predictis apud Oxon' predictam obiit et sic predictus H. prefatum T. apud O. predictam felonice interfecit et murderavit contra pacem etc. et pur ceo que cest parol *postea* ne lymitte certenment a quel iour, mez post estre a auter iour apres le iour de assaut, et sic incerten quaunt le murdre fuit fait. Pur ceo H. W. fuit discharge, mez la court fuit de opinion que le addicion scilicet 'scoler' fuit bon addicion.

## Indictement

H[ugh] W[eston] was indicted in Oxford by the name of H[ugh] W[eston] late of Oxford in the county of Oxford, scholar, that he on the third day of October in the twenty-sixth[1] year of Henry VIII, of his malice aforethought, with force and arms etc. (that is to say, with *uno portifero* called a 'portes' to the value of 2s.) assaulted T[homas] F[laxney] and feloniously struck him, the said T[homas] F[laxney] with the portes aforesaid upon the belly; and *postea* he feloniously and in various ways struck the same T[homas] with the portes aforesaid upon his head; which T[homas] languished from the blows aforesaid from the aforesaid third day [of October] until the fifth day of June next following, on which day the aforesaid T[homas] at Oxford aforesaid died from the blows aforesaid; and thus the aforesaid H[ugh] feloniously killed and murdered the said T[homas] at Oxford aforesaid, against the peace [etc.]

And because the word *postea* does not certainly indicate what day, since it might be at another day after the day of the assault and then it would be uncertain when the murder was done, therefore H[ugh] W[eston] was discharged.

---

1 25th year in the Latin record. The indictment was in the 26th year.

But the court was of opinion that the addition, to wit, 'scholar', was a good addition.

Additional Reading: J. H. Baker, *The Reports of Sir John Spelman*. Volume one contains Spelman's law-French reports and a facing-page translation; volume two contains a valuable 350-page introduction to the state of the law during the reign of Henry VIII and a transcription and translation of the documents relating to cases recorded by Spelman.

## The Languages of the Law. How We plead.

One characteristic of English law that may puzzle us moderns is the fact that it was not in English until a relatively late date. First Latin, then French was the language of the law for several centuries. The reason is not obvious.

The traditional view of the Normans' attitude towards the English language is expressed in Ingulf's *History,* a pseudonymous work probably composed in the 13th or 14th centuries:

> [Normanni] ipsum etiam idioma tantum abhorrebant, quod leges terrae, statutaque Anglicorum regum lingua Gallica tractarentur; et pueris etiam in scholis principia literarum grammatica Gallice, ac non Anglice traderentur; modus etiam scribendi Anglicus omitteretur, et modus Gallicus in chartis, et in libris omnibus admitteretur. Sed de istis satis. (Ingulph, Abbot of Croyland/Crowland, *Historiarum Liber I*)
>
> "The Normans so hated even the English language that the laws of the land and the statutes of the English kings were composed in the French language, and boys even while at school were taught the fundamentals of literacy in French, not in English. The English manner of writing was abolished and the French manner in all documents and books was employed. But enough about this."

This view is not accepted today and the true situation is well described in Pollock and Maitland, *The History of the English Law,* vol. I, pp. 80-88, excerpted here.

"It would hardly be too much to say that at the present day almost all our words that have a definite legal import are in a certain sense French words . . . On many a theme an English man of letters may, by way of exploit, write a paragraph or a page and use no word that is not in every sense a genuinely English word; but an English or American lawyer who attempted this puritanical feat would find himself doomed to silence . . . Common transactions of daily life can be described by English verbs. A man may give, sell, buy, let, hire, borrow, bequeath, make a deed, a will, a bond, and even be guilty of manslaughter or of theft, and all this in English . . . But let us look elsewhere and observe how widely and deeply the French influence has worked. Contract, agreement, covenant, obligation, debt, condition, bill, note, master, servant, partner, guarantee, tort, trespass, assault, battery, slander, damage, crime, treason, felony, misdemeanor, arson, robbery, burglary, larceny, property, possession, pledge, lien, payment, money, grant, purchase, devise, descent, heir, easement, marriage, guardian, infant, ward, all are French . . .

"But all this is the outcome of a gradual process; we can not say that it is the necessary result of the conquest of England by French-speaking men. Indeed for some time after the conquest the English language seems to have a fair chance of holding its own in legal affairs. In the first place, the combat between English and French, if it must begin sooner or later, can for a while be postponed or concealed, for there is a third and a powerful rival in the field. Latin becomes the written language of the law. It was a language understood and written by the learned men of both races: it was the language of such legal documents as the Normans knew, and, though it was not the language of the English dooms or the English courts, still it was the language of the English charters or land-books. In the second place, English had long been a written language, and a written language which could be used for legal and governmental purposes, while French was as yet hardly better than a vulgar dialect of Latin:—French would become Latin if you tried to write it at its best. And so the two languages which William used for his laws, his charters and his writs were Latin and English. Again there good reasons why the technical terms of the old English law should be preserved if the king could preserve them. They were the terms that defined his royal rights. On the whole he was well satisfied with the goodly heritage which had come to him from his cousin King

Edward. If only he could maintain against his followers the rights of the old English kingship, he would have done almost as much as he could hope to do. And so his rights and their rights must be registered in the old English terms. His clerks must still write, if not of *sacu and socne*, still of *saca et soca.* Many foreign words have made their way into Domesday Book, but many old English words which had definite legal meanings were preserved.

"During the century that follows, Latin keeps its preeminence, and when, under Henry II and his sons, the time comes for the regular enrolment of all the king's acts and of all the judgments of his court, Latin becomes the language of our voluminous official and judicial records, From this position it is not dislodged until the year 1731, when it gives place to English [Statute 4 Geo. II c. 26] . . .

"But, though throughout the middle ages some Latin could be written by most men who could write at all, and the lord of a manor would still have his accounts as well as his court rolls made up in Latin, still only the learned could speak Latin readily, and it could not become the language of oral pleading or of debate. Here was a field in which French and English might strive for the mastery. There could for a long while be no doubt as to which of these two tongues would be spoken in and about the king's court. The king spoke French, his barons French, his prelates French, and even when barons and prelates were beginning to think of themselves as Englishmen, some new wave of foreign influence would break over the court; the new French queen brings with her a new swarm for Frenchmen. And 'the king's court' was not then a term with several meanings; the language of courtiers and courtliness was of necessity the language of business, discussion, pleading. All this might well have happened, however, and yet the English language, which was in the future to be the language even of courtiers, might have retained its stock of old and its power of engendering new legal terms . . . [But] slowly but surely justice done in the king's name by men who are the king's servants becomes the most important kind of justice, reaches into the remotest corners of the land, grasps the small affairs of small fold as well as the great affairs of earls and barons. This is no immediate and no necessary effect of the Norman Conquest. It would never have, William himself can hardly have dared to hope for it. The destiny of our legal language was not irrevocably determined until Henry of Anjou was king.

"If we must choose one moment of time as fatal, we ought to choose 1166 rather than 1066, the year of the assize of *novel desseisin* rather than the year of the battle of Hastings. The it was that the decree went forth which gave to every man dispossessed of his freehold a remedy to be sought in a royal court, a French-speaking court. Thenceforward the ultimate triumph of French law terms was secure . . .The things of the law which have English names are things that are obsolete or obsolescent, *sake* and *soke*, *wer* and *wite*: already men hardly knew what these words meant. It is difficult for us to believe that in the local courts, the suitors, who were for the most part peasants, pleaded their causes and rendered their judgments in French; still from the thirteenth century we get books of precedents for pleading in manorial court which are written in French, while we look in vain for any similar books written in English. We may suspect that if the villagers themselves did not use French when they assailed each other in the village courts, their pleaders used it for them, and before the end of the thirteenth century the professional pleader might already be found practicing before a petty tribunal and speaking the language of Westminster Hall. Then in 1362 a statute, itself written in French, declared that as the French tongue was but little understood, all pleas should be 'pleaded, shown, defended, answered, debated and judged; in the English tongue . . .'

"[I]n the thirteenth century French slowly supplanted Latin as the literary language of the law. It is very possible that the learned Bracton thought about law in Latin; he wrote in Latin, and the matter that he was using, whether he took in from the *Summa Azonis* [Azo of Bologna, *Summa Codicis*, a commentary on Roman law] or from the plea rolls of the king's court, was written in Latin. But the need for French text-books was already felt, and before the end of the century this need was being met by the book that we call Britton, by other tracts, and by those reports of decided cases which know as Year Books . . . We must wait for the last half of the fifteenth century if we would see English law written about in the English tongue, for the sixteenth if we would read a technical law-book that was written in English."

Here is the statute making English the language of pleading.

Statutes made at Westminster, Anno tricesimo sexto Edwardi III, Anno Dom. 1362[1]

Cap. XV

Pleas shall be pleaded in the English Tongue, and enrolled in Latin.

**French**

Item pur ce qe monstre est soventsoitz au Roi par Prelatz Dues Counts Barons et tout la communalte les grantz meschiefs qe sont advenuz as plusours du realme de ce qe les leyes custumes et estatutz du dit realme ne sont pas conuz communement en mesme le realme par cause qils sont pledez monstrez et juggez en la lange Franceis qest trop desconue en le dit realme issint qe les gentz qe piedent ou sont empledez en les courtz le Roi et les courtz dautres nont entendement ne conissance de ce qest dit pur eulx ne contre eulx par lour Sergeantz et autres pledours et qe resonablement les dites leyes et custumes serront le plus tost apris et conuz et mieultz entenduz en la lange usee en le dit realme et par tant chescun du dit realme se purroit mieultz governer sanz faire offense a la leye et le mieultz garder sauver et defendre ses heritages et possessions et en diverses regions et paiis ou le Roi les nobles et autres

1 Text and translation from Owen Ruffhead 1763 pp. 311-2.

du dit realme ont este est bon governement et plein droit fait a chescun par cause qe lour leyes et custumes font apris et usez en la lange du paiis le Roi defirant le bon governement et tranquillite de son poeple et de ouster et eschure les maulx et meschiefs qe font advenuz et purront avenir en ceste partie ad pur les caufes susdites ordeigne et eftabli del asent avantdit qe toutes plees qe serront a pleder en ses courtz queconqes devant ses Juftices queconqes ou en ses autres places ou derant ses autres ministres queconqes ou en les courtz et places des autres Seignurs qeconqes deinz le Realme soient pledez monstretz defenduz responduz debatuz et juggez en la lange Engleife et qils soient entreez et enroullez en Latin et qe les leyes et custumes du dit Realme termes et processes soient tenuz et gardez come ils font etonteste avant ces heures et qe per les aunciens termes et formes de counter nul homme soit perdant isint qe la matiere del action soit pleinement monstre en la demonstrance et en le brief. Et est acorde de lassent avantdit qe cestes ordeignances et estatutz de pleder comenceent et tiegnent lieu al quinzeine Seint Hiller prochein avenir.

Item, Because it is often shewed to the King by the Prelates, Dukes, Earls, Barons, and all the Commonalty, of the great Mischiefs which have happened to divers of the Realm, because the Laws, Customs, and Statutes of this Realm be not commonly holden and kept in the same Realm, for that they be pleaded, shewed, and judged in the French Tongue, which is much unknown in the said Realm, so that the People which do implead, or be impleaded, in the King's Court, and in the Courts of other, have no Knowledge nor Understanding of that which is said for them or against them by their Serjeants and other Pleaders; (2) and that reasonably the said Laws and Customs the rather shall be perceived and known, and better understood in the Tongue used in the said Realm, and by so much every Man of the said Realm may the better govern himself without offending of the Law, and the better keep, save, and defend his Heritage and Possessions; (3) And in divers Regions and Countries, where the King, the Nobles, and other of the said Realm have been, good Governance and full Right is done to every Person, because that their Laws and Customs be learned and used in the Tongue of the Country; (4) The King, desiring the good Governance and Tranquillity of his People, and to put out and eschew the Harms and Mischiefs which do or may happen in this Behalf by the Occasions aforesaid, hath ordained and stablished by the Assent aforesaid, that: all Pleas which shall be pleaded in any Courts whatsoever, before any of his Justices whatsoever, or in his other Places, or before any of his other Ministers whatsoever, or in the Courts and Places of any other Lords whatsoever within the Realm, shall be pleaded, shewed, defended, answered, debated, and judged in the English Tongue, and that they be entered and enrolled in Latin; (5) and that the Laws and Customs of the same Realm, Terms, and Processes, be holden and kept as they be and have been before this Time; (6) and that by the ancient Terms and Forms of the Declarations no Man be prejudiced, so that the Matter of the Action be fully shewed in the Declaration and in the Writ. (7) And it is accorded by the Assent aforesaid, that this Ordinance and Statute of Pleading begin and hold Place at the Fifteenth of St. Hillary [= early February] next coming.

This statute was obeyed very tardily, and in fact was attempting the impossible, at least at that time. French continued to be used for oral pleadings, at least by the lawyers, Latin continued to be used to record legal decisions, and (we can presume) most testimony by witnesses was in English. As a result the linguistic skill of a jury foreman or a serjeant collecting testimony for a hearing must have been demanding. In the 12th, 13th, and 14th centuries, such a man would have had to speak English and French, and be able to read Latin, French, and English. Nobility and gentry switched languages without much fuss. The practice of writing documents in one language (here Latin or French) does not mean that the business was done entirely in Latin or French.[1]

1 Clanchy 331. Even the English kings were instructed in Latin, Clanchy 235.

Let's take an example. In his Selden Society volume of Spelman's Reports, J. H. Baker reports the court procedure from the reign of Henry VIII.[2]

1. The court proceeding would begin as follows: Johannes at Style in propria persona sua [*or* per attornatum suum] optulit se quarto die versus Robertum Downe de X. in comitatu predicto husbondman de placito transgressionis. Et ipse non venit. Et preceptum fuit vicecomiti quod capiat eum etc. (John at Style in his own person [*or* through his attorney] has presented himself on the fourth day [i.e. after the return of the original writ] against Robert Downe of X, a husbandman in the aforesaid county, on a plea of X offense. And he has not appeared. And the sheriff has been ordered to seize him, etc.)

2. In court the defendant, here Robert Downe (= John Doe), might orally plead (through his lawyer): "Vous avez cy le dit Robert Downe que defend tort et force ou et quand il devera et dit que . . ."

(You have here the aforesaid R. D. who denies the injury and violence when and where he ought, and says that . . .).

2a. This was entered in the written record as: Et predictus Robertus per L. M. attornatum suum venit et defendit vim et injuriam quando etc. et dicit quod . . . (And the aforesaid Robert through his attorney L. M. came and denies the force and injury, when etc. and says that . . .)

3. If there was a demurrer to the pleading, the lawyer would say: "Que al count fait per le maner nul ley lui mette a responder . . ." (To the count/plea made in this manner no law requires him to respond).

3a. This was entered in the written record as: Quod narracio predicti Johannis at Style [i.e. the plaintiff] in forma predicta facta minus sufficiens in lege exsistit ad accionem predictam versus ipsum Robertum habendam seu manutenendam quodque ipse ad narracionem

2 *The Reports of Sir John Spelman*, vol. 2, pp. 93-94. For more on Sir John Spelman (1495(?)-1544) see the section "An Indictment for Assault, 1535" in this anthology.

illam modo et forma predictis superius factam necesse non habet nec per legem terre tenetur respondere. (That the account of the aforesaid John at Style, made in the aforesaid manner, being insufficient in law in the aforesaid action against Robert to hold or detain Robert, and that to the account previously given in the aforesaid manner and form he sees no necessity nor is he bound in the nation's law to respond.)

4. The plaintiff might respond to the demurrer by saying: "Vous avez cy le dit John at Style que dit que per le plea en barr il ne doit estre bar de son accion quar il dit que . . ." (You have here John at Style who says that according to the plea at the bar he should not be barred from his action, because he says . . .).

4a. This was entered as: Quod ipse per placitum predictum in barram placitatum ab accione sua predicta habenda precludi non debet quia dicit quod . . . (In the aforesaid plea which was pled at the bar, he should not be precluded from his aforesaid action, because he says . . .).

Latin fought a rear-guard action. Richard Morison (1514-1556), secretary to Thomas Cromwell, in his *Persuasion to the King*, lamented that many lawyers knew only French, and that their clerks were responsible for turning the French into Latin for deeds and the like. He proposed that English law should be codified in Latin. [*Spelman* 25] Nothing came of this, neither the codification nor the change of language, despite the prestige of Latin. Indeed a successful law book from the reign of Henry VIII displays a Latin title, *Perutilis tractatus magistri Johannis Parkins interioris Templi socii* (1528), but is in fact written in law-French. Anyone familiar with the common law of the time could see that its terminology could not be put into classical Latin, no matter how deeply the lawyers had read the classics.[1] French-English glossaries were made for training students; one, *The Law-*

1 Sir Thomas More's famous 'witticism' quoted in our introduction illustrates that any translation of the common law into Latin would have been pointless.

*French Dictionary Alphabetically Digested* . . . (1718), is today available online. English finally replaced law-French in the 17th and 18th centuries.

Additional Reading:

J. H. Baker, *The Reports of Sir John Spelman,* 1978.
P. Brand, "The Latin of the Early English Common Law" in Ashdowne and White, *Latin in Medieval Britain* 133-146.
M. T. Clanchy, 1993, especially chap. 6 "Languages of Record" 197-223.
Ingulph, Abbot of Croyland/Crowland, *Historiarum Liber 1*, in *Rerum Anglicarum Scriptores post Bedam Praecipui* p. 512b line 38ff. (London; G. Bishop, R. Nuberie, et R. Barker Typographi Regii Deputati, 1596). Available on-line.
Frederick Pollock, Frederic William Maitland, *The History of the English Law*.
Owen Ruffhead, *Statutes at Large: from Magna Charta to the End of the Reign of King Henry the Sixth*, vol. 1, pp. 311-2. This is volume 1 of Ruffhead's *The Statutes at Large: from Magna Charta to the End of the Last Parliament, 1761* in 8 volumes.

## Reading Law Records

How can a student learn to read the original law records? Several skills are required: a basic knowledge of Medieval Latin, the official language of English legal documents until 1733; an ability to read the handwriting of these legal documents, millions of which survive in the archives, and to decipher the all too frequent abbreviations; and some familiarity with the archives and the different types of legal documents therein, e.g. Pipe Rolls,[1] Rotuli ("Rolls") Parliamenti, Chancery Rolls, Rotuli Curiae Regis, and so on.

1. The knowledge of Latin required is not extensive. The grammar used is basic: simple sentences, often in English word order, with no elaborate subordinate clauses; and a limited vocabulary which can be found in R. E. Latham, *Revised Medieval Latin Word-list*, (London 1973). A dictionary of Classical Latin will not suffice. For example *cimitirium/cemeterium* (various spellings), 'churchyard', seen below, will not be found in standard Latin dictionaries. The British National Archives has posted a useful review of Latin online which every student should study. This very anthology hopes to improve the student's Latin skills.

2. Also on the British National Archives site is an indispensable online tutorial which will train the student to read the handwriting and decipher many of the abbreviations in these legal documents: search for the paleography page at The National Archives. Each of the ten lessons is devoted to a particular document from 1086 to 1422. The student who finishes this tutorial will have a fighting chance of reading any legal document from the period. In addition the student should have on hand one of the textbooks written in the 19th century to help students of that era learn how to read old documents, a skill which was then a

1 Financial records of the Exchequer, so called because they were rolled up so tightly that they looked like pipes.

requirement for law clerks. We recommend Andrew Wright, *Court-Hand Restored*. This useful text contains samples of the typical letterforms, an explanation of the rationale behind many of the abbreviations (they are not random) with a list of the common abbreviations, many examples of old documents which are transcribed into modern print, and a list of the Latin forms of the geographical and proper names found in English documents.

3. Several online sources are available if the student wishes to find a particular document. Most of the documents themselves are at The National Archives, only a few of which are available in digital form on The National Archives website; an example will be studied below. For online access to many legal documents, see the website of the Anglo-American Legal Tradition, sponsored by the University of Houston (http://aalt.law.uh.edu/). This site has almost ten million frames of scanned documents dating from 1176 down to the reign of Queen Victoria. (After 1733 the language is English.) It can be difficult to find the specific document which you are seeking.

The student will also find many books entitled *Calendar of. . .* (e.g. *Calendar of Charter Rolls, Calendar of State Papers, Calendar of Patent Rolls*). These are useful, indeed essential, indexes of the documents which reside in a given archive, often with a description of the contents of the document. An example will be found below.

Since there is no substitute for actually transcribing and translating an unknown text, after some initial study of the handwriting the student must work with an actual text. As an introduction we will examine a specific case from the series of documents called the assize of nuisance, the complaint of Robert Sprotburgh, rector of St. Margaret de Briggestrete, against Arnold Ingelbright, his neighbor, heard 20 April 1380. (For the meaning here of *assize* and a discussion of nuisance in general, see "A Civil Case of Nuisance" in this textbook.) The documentation of this case happens to be available online at The

National Archives website. As mentioned, The National Archives in England has a wealth of material (millions of pages), some on line. Let's take this assize of nuisance as an example. CLA/040 is the code for City of London law court records. CLA/040/02 are London civil court records. CLA/040/02/003 is a particular roll of records dating between 1378-1431, all of which are civil trials of nuisance, like the civil case of nuisance between John Northampton and William Newe elsewhere in this anthology. This roll happens to be available on line. A Calendar (i.e. a detailed index and description) of this roll is also available on line at the British History Online website. The particular case which we want to examine is #623, Friday, 20 April 1380. To quote the first part of the calendar: "Robert Sprotburgh, rector of St. Margaret de Briggestrete, complains that Arnold Ingelbright, 'armurer', has a tenement adjoining his churchyard in the wall of which is a door in the form of a window (*ad modum fenestre*) less than 16 ft. from the ground, and barred with iron, the bars hanging on hooks (*gumphos*) and hinges (*vertivellas*), so that it can be opened and closed at will by the def. and others living or coming there, both men and women, who enter the churchyard and see his private business, and trample the churchyard down and defile it (*sordidant*) . . ." Note that the calendar helpfully gives some of the unusual Latin words in the text.

The original document can be found at the London Metropolitan Archives Collections Catalog (part of The National Archives) at this web address: https://search.lma.gov.uk/

Enter CLA/040/02/003 in the search box and you will be taken to the digital file. On the left you will see thumbnails of all the pages (called membranes, records written on vellum) in this roll. (Not really a roll, this is a collection of vellum membranes sewn together at the top margin, like our legal pads.) Each membrane is about 8 1/2" wide by 28" long. On the right is page 1 of the roll. Click on the thumbnail of page 2 (actually the back side of page 1; pages were not originally numbered). We will describe the first (uppermost) document, which is #623 of the calendar, and begin to transcribe and read some of it. (You will have to go to full-screen and enlarge the text before you have any hope of reading the document.) At the top of the page, written the full width of the page, is the general heading, which specifies the type of case (here an assize of nuisance) and the persons who were in charge of the city's government: the mayor, the recorder, and the aldermen. The first line reads as follows:

1. plita assie noc ten sup tram coram Johe Hadle maiors Willa Cheyne recordj.

Since standard Latin boilerplate (standard expressions found in all documents of this type) are almost always abbreviated, we must expand the abbreviations:

1. placita assise nocumenti tenementi super terram coram Johannes Hadle maioris William Cheyne recordoris

1. Pleas of the assize of nuisance of a holding on the land [heard] before John Hadle, Mayor, William Cheyne, Recorder . . .

Note that a line over a word or letter indicates some abbreviation. The first two words have such lines and are always abbreviated thus. The squiggle (sometimes called a tittle, *Matt.* 5:18, the Spanish tilde) over the last letters of the 3rd and 4th words indicate a longer abbreviation. The very similar squiggle over the -r- in *tram* stands for -er or -re, hence *terram*. The -p- with a line through the descender indicates *per*, hence *super*. A study of the first few pages of *Court-Hand Restored* will make most abbreviations clear. Experience will do the rest.

The next few lines are mostly the names of the aldermen; first names are abbreviated, but not last names. They are:

2. Ad Stable Nicho Brembre Willo Neuport Hohe Eston Johe Bryan Robto Launde Andr

2. Adam Stable Nicholas Brembre William Neuport Johannes Eston Johannes Bryan Robert Launde Andrew

3. Pykeman Wille Badby Johe Horn et Wlte Doget Andrō et Johe Heylesdon vno vic London

3. Pykeman William Badby Johannes Horn and Walter Doget Aldermen and Johannes Heylesdon uno vicecomitis Londinii.

Then comes the date and the regnal year, Friday before the Feast of St. George (on 23 April) in the third year of King Richard II (1380).

4. die veñis px an fine sti Georgii Martyr anno rro Rici scdi tt'io

4. die veneris proximo ante finem sancti Georgii Martyr anno regno Regis Ricardi secundi tertio.

4. the Friday immediately before the end [of the feast] of St. George the Martyr in the third year of the reign of King Richard II.

At lines 5 and 6 the complaint itself begins:

5. Arnaldus Ingelbright armurer sumo fuit ad respondj Robto Sprotburgh rectori oratio

5. Arnaldus Ingebright armurer summonitus fuit ad respondendum Roberto Sprotburgh rectori orationis

5. Arnold Ingebright, armourer, was summoned to respond to Robert Sprotburgh, rector of the chapel

6. Ste Margarete de Briggestrete Londoñ ad plice assie noc etc. Et inde idem Robtus

6. Sancte Margarete de Briggestrete Londonii ad placitum assise nocumenti etc. Et inde idem Robertus

6. of St. Margarete of Briggestreet in London on a plea of the assize of nuisance, etc. And in consequence the same Robert

7. quer qd p'dictus Arnaldus heat unū tēt contiguū solo cimitij eiusdem rectoris

7. queritur quod predictus Arnaldus habeat unum tenementum contiguum solo cimitirii eiusdem rectoris

7. complains that the aforesaid Arnaldus has one holding/house adjoining the land of the churchyard of the same rector...

Note that in line 6 the *etc.* ends a sentence. The rest of the charge is boilerplate and need not be repeated. With close attention to the calendar entry #623, the student should work through the rest of this document. After doing so, the reading of other such documents will be much easier. Practice makes perfect. The student may also practice reading the original membrane which we have transcribed in the section "A Case of Nonpayment" or the King's Bench records in "An Indictment for Assault" in this anthology.

Additional Reading:

Cappelli, Adriano, Lexicon Abbreviaturarum, Leipzig: J.J. Weber, 1928; available on line.

Latham, R. E., *Revised Medieval Latin Word-List from British and Irish Sources.*

Wright, Andrew and Martin, Charles Trice, *Court-Hand Restored or, The Student's Assistant in Reading Old Deeds, Charters, Records, etc.* (London: Reeves & Turner, 1879). The book also contains sample of handwriting from various samples.

# Appendix I (*Latin section titles*)

## GLANVILL

### *Liber I*

*Distinctio causarum secularium.*

*Capitula.*

*1. Distinctio causarum ciuilium.*

*2.,3.Capitula.*

*4. Placita ciuilia ad uicecomites pertinentia.*

*5. Placitorum initia.*

*6. Breve de prima summonitione facienda.*

*7. Quid iuris sit ad primam summonitionem quando summonitus neque uenit neque essonium mittit.*

*8. Breue de saluando die per regem warantum.*

*33. De absentia utriusque partis.*

### *Liber VI*

*1. Placitum de dotibus.*

*2.,3.,4. De amplianda dote ratione questus.*

*5.,6. Breue de recto de pertinentia dotis.*

*7. Breue de transferendo placito a comitayu in curiam.*

### *Liber VII*

*1. De maritagiis.*

*7. Breve de faciendo stare rationabilem diuisam.*

### *Liber XIII.*

*1.,2 De diuersis recognitionibus.*

*3. Breve de morte antecessoris.*

*4. Breue de eodem.*

*7. Quo ordine perueniatur ad hanc assisam.*

*8. Breve de facienda saisina post recognitionem.*

*18. De recognitione de ultimis presentationibus ecclesiarum.*

*19. Breve de summonende recognitione de ultimis presentationibus ecclesiarum.*

*32. De recognitione noue desaisine.*

*33. Breve de noua desaisina.*

*38. Quod nullum essonium in hac recognitione admittitur.*

*39. Breve de catallis reddendis*

*6. Placitum de crimine raptus.*

**BRACTON**

***INTRODUCTIO***

*Quae sunt regi necessaria*

*Si insipiens et indoctus cathedram iudicandi ascenderit.*

*Prohemium auctoris*

*Quae sit materia.*

*Quae intentio.*

*Quae utilitas.*

*Quis finis.*

*Leges iubent et vetant.*

*Sapiens esse debet qui iudicat.*

*Quae sit poena male iudicantis.*

*Quid sit lex et quid consuetudo.*

*Quid sit iustitia.*

*Quid sit ius.*

***DE PERSONIS.***

*Quod omne ius pertinet vel ad personas, vel ad res, vel ad actiones.*

*De prima divisione personarum.*

*Quid sit libertas.*

*Quod nulla acceptio personarum apud deum est, tamen apud homines, quia quidam principantur in terris in rebus spiritualibus, et quidam in temporalibus.*

# Appendix I (Latin section titles)

*Rex non habet parem.*

***DE REBUS.***

*De rebus et rerum divisione: prima divisio.*

*Divisio secunda.*

*Divisio tertia.*

*Quaedam res sunt communes.*

*Quaedam publicae.*

*Quaedam universitatis.*

*Quaedam singulorum.*

*Quaedam sacrae et religiosae quae sunt deo consecratae.*

*Quaedam nullius.*

***RERUM DOMINIO.***

*Qualiter dominia rerum adquiruntur de iure naturali vel gentium.*

*De rerum dominio adquirendo ex causa donationis inter vivos.*

*Quid sit donatio.*

*De distinctione cartarum.*

*Quod de cartis regiis non debent iustitiarii disputare nec eas iudicare.*

*Quid sit possessio.*

*Quid est traditio.*

*Quibus modis amittatur possessio.*

*Qualiter quis uti debeat servitute in communa pastura.*

*De adquirendo rerum dominio ex causa successionis et qualiter heredes succedunt parentibus.*

*[Quid sit hereditas.]*

*Quis dici debeat heres legitimus.*

*De heredibus instituendis.*

*Quid sit homagium et qualiter contrahatur.*

*De sacramento fidelitatis.*

*Quis effectus homagii.*

*De releviis dandis.*

*De donationibus propter nuptias ob causam dotis et de constitutione dotis.*

*Quid sit dos.*

*Quid sit rationabilis dos.*

*Quis possit dotem constituere.*

*Item quando et ubi.*

***DE ACTIONIBUS.***

*De actionibus et quid sit actio.*

*Unde actio oriatur.*

*Quis non possit stipulari.*

*De prima divisione actionum.*

*De possessoria hereditatis petitione, quae dici poterit assisa novae disseisinae.*

*De generibus poenarum quibus homines afficiuntur propter eorum iniquitates.*

*Ubi terminandae sunt actiones civiles.*

***Ubi et coram quibus personis proponendae sunt actiones et probandae.***

*Quid sit iudicium, et in quibus consistit officium iudicis, scilicet in tribus.*

*De sacramento quod rex facere debet in coronatione sua.*

*Ad quid creatus sit rex, et ordinaria iurisdictione.*

*Item ad quid iustitiarii, et iurisdictione delegata.*

*De differentia iustitiariorum.*

*De sacramento quod iustitiarii facient cum iustitiariam receperint.*

*In adventu iustitiariorum de ordine proponendi actiones et eorum officio.*

***DE PLACITIS CORONAE.***

*Qualiter iustitiarii procedere debent in itinere suo et quo ordine.*

*De sacramento duodecim militum electorum ad dicendum veredictum in placito coroner.*

*Capitula de quibus duodecim respondebunt.*

*De crimine laesae maiestatis.*

*De crimine homicidii et qualiter dividitur.*

# Appendix I (Latin section titles)

*De officio coronatorum.*

*De inquisitionibus ubi occisus fuerit.*

*Si raptus virginum.*

*Ad visum de franco plegio.*

*Item quis utlagari possit et debeat.*

*Minor non.*

*Quid utlagatus forisfaciat per utlagationem.*

*Qualiter utlagati post utlagationem ex causa admittuntur ad pacem.*

*De homicidio quod palam et pluribus astantibus perpetratum est, et postea de homicidio quod nullo praesente perpetratum est, et quod dicitur murdrum.*

*Quae causa inventionis murdrorum.*

*Quid dicitur murdrum.*

*Qualiter debeat murdrum praesentari secundum consuetudinem diversorum comitatuum. In quibus vero comitatibus praesentatur sic.*

*Si malefactores fugiant ad ecclesiam, qualiter debeant regnum abiurare si cognoscant latrocinium et feloniam.*

*Si malefactores fugiant ad ecclesiam, qualiter debeant regnum abiurare si cognoscant latrocinium et feloniam.*

*De sacramento qualiter debent regnum abiurare.*

*Quod non debet morari in ecclesia per quadraginta dies, et si velit quid tunc agendum sit.*

*De divisione exiliorum.*

*Qualiter captus produci debeat coram iustitiariis.*

*Si sit aliquis eum appellet.*

*Habet potestatem eligendi quod ponat se super patriam, vel se defendat per corpus suum.*

*Quod in duello iungendo iustitiarius debet omnia diligenter examinare.*

*Vadiatio duelli, et si appellatus victus fuerit vel appellans.*

*In casu non est necesse probare per corpus neque per patriam, ubi praesumptio violenta facit contra appellatum.*

*Prima exceptio et generalis in omni appello de secta, si bene et secundum legem terrae facta sit.*

*Forma sacramenti talis est.*

*Sacramentum faciendum in campo.*

*Fiat bannus regis.*

*Si appellatus victus fuerit.*

*Si primo appellans de facto mortuus fuerit vel defaltam fecerit.*

*Rex potest procedere ex officio suo.*

*Debet a iustitiariis dici ei qui suspectus habetur, quod omnes a iurata amoveat quos aliqua sufficienti ratione suspectos habuerit.*

*Sed quid dicetur de eo qui virilia abscidit alicuius?*

*Quid dici debeat mahemium.*

*Item si deformitas et non mahemium.*

*Appellum de raptu virginum.*

*De verbis appelli mulieris querentis de raptu*

*Si appellatus per patriam fuerit convictus, quae poena sequatur*

*Addicio.*

*Si quis fecerit feloniam de se ipso.*

*Quid sit furtum.*

*De furto manifesto et probatore cognoscente.*

*Quod nemo potest curiam suam habere de probatore vel latrone cognoscente. Et quae placita pertinent ad curiam et quae ad comitatum, et de libertatibus singulorum.*

*Ad vicecomites pertinet huiusmodi placita.*

*De minoribus et levioribus criminibus quae civiliter intentantur.*

*Qualiter quis patitur iniuriam per suos.*

*In quibus casibus servi habent personam standi in iudicio contra dominos suos.*

*Quod atrox iniuria aestimatur multis modis.*

*Quod iniuria per dissimulationem aboletur.*

*De officio vicecomitis.*

# APPENDIX II (*ENGLISH SECTION TITLES*)

## GLANVILL

*Book I*

*1. The division of secular cases.*

*2.,3. The headings.*

*Division of vivil cases.*

*The headings.*

*4. Civil pleas belonging to the sheriffs.*

*5. The beginning of pleas.*

*6. The writ for making the first summons.*

*7. What the law is when the party summoned neither comes nor sends an essoiner in response to the first summons.*

*8. The writ for saving a return day by royal warrant.*

*Book VI*

*1. Pleas of dower.*

*2.3.,4,. Increase in dower as a result of later acquisitions.*

*5.6., The writ of right for land belonging to dower.*

*7. The writ for transferring a plea from the county court to the curia.*

*Book VII*

*1. Marriage portions.*

*7. The writ for upholding a reasonable division*

*Book XIII*

*1. The various kinds of recognitions.*

*3.4., The writ of mort d'ancestor.*

*7. The procedure leading to this assize.*

*8. The writ for delivering seisin after the recognition.*

## Appendix II (English section titles)

*That God is no respecter of persons though men are, since some rule over lands in spiritual matters, some in temporal.*

*The king has no equal.*

*Of Things.*

*Things and the classification of things: the first division.*

*A second division.*

*A third division.*

*Some things are common.*

*Some things are public.*

*Some things belong to the universitas.*

*Some things belong to individuals.*

*Some things are sacred and holy, those consecrated to God.*

*Some things belong to no one.*

*Of Acquiring The Dominion Of Things.*

*How the dominion of things is acquired by the jus naturale or the jus gentium.*

*Of acquiring the dominion of things by gift inter vivos.*

*What a gift is.*

Of the kinds of charters.

*That the justices must not question royal charters nor pass upon them.*

*What possession is.*

*What livery is..*

*In what ways possession may be lost.*

*How one ought to use his servitude in common of pasture*

*Of acquiring the dominion of things by succession and how heirs succeed ancestors.*

*[What inheritance is.]*

*Who ought to be called a lawful heir.*

*The institution of heirs.*

*What homage is.*

*The oath of fealty.*

*What the effect of homage is.*

*Of the giving of reliefs.*

*Of gifts propter nuptias by way of dower and the constitution of dower.*

*What dower is.*

*What rightful dower is.*

*Who can constitute dower*

*When and where.*

*Of Actions.*

*Of actions and what an action is.*

*Whence an action arises.*

*Who cannot stipulate.*

*The first division of actions.*

*Of the possessory action for an inheritance, which may be called the assize of novel disseisin.*

*Of the kinds of punishments set upon men because of their iniquities.*

*Where civil actions are to be determined.*

*Where and before what persons [civil] actions are to be instituted and proved.*

*What a judicial proceeding is [and how civil actions are to be instituted.].*

*Of the oath the king must swear at his coronation.*

*For what purpose a king is created; of ordinary jurisdiction.*

*Why there are justices and of delegated jurisdiction.*

*Of the kinds of justices.*

*Of the oath the justices shall swear when they have received the office of judge.*

*On the arrival of the justices [ad omnia placita]; their duty. Of the order of bringing actions.*

*Pleas of the crown.*

*How the justices ought to proceed ion their eyre and in what order.*

*The oath of the twelve knights chosen to speak the truth in a plea of the crown.*

*The chapters to which the juries shall answer.*

*Of the crime of lèse-majesté.*

*The crime of homicide and the divisions into which it falls.*

*Of the office of coroners.*

*Of inquests: where he was slain.*

*Where there is rape of virgins.*

*At the view of frankpledge.*

*Who may and ought to be outlawed.*

*A minor cannot be outlawed.*

*What an outlaw forfeits by outlawry.*

*[inlawry]: how outlaws after outlawry are admitted for good reason to the peace.*

*Of homicide committed openly and in the presence of many bystanders; and of homicide committed in the absence of witnesses, which is called murder.*

*The reason for devising murder-fines.*

*What is called murder.*

*How Englishry ought to be presented according to the custom of divers counties; in some counties it is presented thus:*

*Of the oath: how he ought to abjure the realm.*

*That [a wrongdoer] ought not to atay in a church for forty days, and if he attempts to do so what is then to be done.*

*Of the kinds of exile.*

*How an arrested man ought to be brought before the justices.*

*When there is one [who] appeals him.*

*He has the power of choosing whether to place himself on a jury or defend himself by his body.*

*That in waging the duel the justice must investigate everything with care.*

*The wager of the duel: if the appellee or the appellor is vanquished.*

*Occasionally neither proof by judicial combat nor the country is necessary: where an overwhelming presumption lies against the appellee.*

*The first exception and a general one in every appeal of a suit, whether it was well made and according to the law of the land.*

*The form of the oath is as follows.*

*The oath to be taken on the field.*

*Let the king's ban be proclaimed.*

*If the appellee is vanquished.*

*If the first appellor against the principle dies or defaults.*

*The king may proceed ex officio.*

*The justices must inform the man under suspicion that he may remove from the jury all those whom he holds suspect for some sufficient reason.*

*But what is to be said of one who castrates another?*

*What ought to be termed mayhem.*

*Where there is disfigurement and not mayhem.*

## Appendix II (English section titles)

*An appeal concerning the rape of virgins.*

*The words of the appeal of a woman complaining of rape*

*If the appellee is convicted by the country, what penalty follows. Addition.*

*Where a man commits felony upon his own person*

*What theft is.*

*How many kinds of theft there are.*

*Manifest theft and the confessing approver.*

*That no one may hold his court on an approver or confessing thief; the pleas that belong to a seignorial court and to the county court; and concerning the liberties of individuals.*

*These pleas belong to the sheriffs..*

*Of minor and lesser crimes brought by civil action*

*How one may suffer an iniuria through his dependents.*

*In which cases servants have personam standi in court against their lords.*

*A grievous iniuria is assessed in many ways.*

*An iniuria may be annulled by dissimulation.*

*The sheriff's duty.*

## GLOSSARY:

**Abate.** To quash (a writ). To enter upon the lands of a deceased freeholder before the heir. To eliminate (a nuisance).

**Abjuration of the realm**. Exile voluntarily elected by individuals, especially those who had sought sanctuary that had expired, in order to avoid trial. It required forfeiture of all property to the crown.

**Admeasurement of pasture.** A writ for the proper division of rights of common, often employed when someone overgrazed common pasture.

**Advowson.** The right to present a candidate for a benefice.

**Aiel.** A writ and action for recovery of land held by a grandfather.

**Alienate (alien).** To transfer ownership of property to another.

**Amercement.** A financial penalty, a fine. Sometimes simply mercy, as to be in the king's mercy, i.e. subject to his penalty.

**Appeal.** To accuse or an accusation.

**Ancient demesne**. Land that could be documented from Domesday Book to have been crown land under Edward the Confessor or William the Conqueror.

**Approver.** One who proves another guilty, hence an accuser or informer.

**Assize.** The session of a council or its published conclusions. A district royal court or its verdict.

**Attach**. To arrest or to secure by means of sureties for future attendance at court.

**Avow**. To make a claim.

**Beaupleader.** A fine for amending an incorrect or defective plea.

**Besaiel.** A writ and action for recovery of lands held by a great-grandfather.

**Blanching**. A blanch (also blank) payment had to be made by assay so as to compensate for deterioration, alteration, or alloying of coinage. The rent on a blanched farm accordingly had to be paid in smelted coins, typically silver that had been alloyed with lead.

**Bookland.** Land held by written title (typically a royal diploma) as opposed to folkland, land held under custom.

**Burgage.** A borough tenement held *in socage*.

***Capias.*** A writ directing a sheriff to arrest someone and produce him before a court.

## Glossary:

***Certiorari.*** A writ directing that written records of some matter be produced.

***Cessavit.*** A writ for recovery of land upon a tenant's failure to return services.

**Cosinage.** A writ in the form *praecipe quod reddat* used for recovery of land held by any blood relationship other than grandfather or great-grandfather.

**Chirograph.** A document produced in triplicate. A copy went to each of the signatories and a third, the so-called foot, was held by a third party.

**Common of pasture.** The right to pasture animals on common land.

**Compurgator**. A character witness, also called an oath-helper, who swears that he believes the oath taken by another. The procedure is called wager of law.

**Count or *conte*.** The account of an action given by the plaintiff or his attorney at the outset of a case. Also called *narratio.* The one delivering the count is a counter or narrator.

***Darrein Presentment***. A writ and an action to determine who has the right to present a benefice.

**De odis et atia (for hatred and ill will)**. A writ directing a sheriff to determine that proper cause existed for imprisonment.

**Deforce**. To keep a rightful owner from possession.

**Deforciant.** One who deforces.

**Degrees**. The steps in a chain to establish hereditary title. Writs of entry were initially limited in their scope by the degrees and could specify no more than two steps in a chain set out as a defective title. Later thinking held that bequests became absolute in the fourth degree, i.e. the third descent to an heir. The extent of the four degrees (father, grandfather,or great-grandfather) matches the extent of living memory since hearsay was permitted in the fourth degree.

**Demandant.** Plaintiff.

**Demesne.** A lord's manorial land not held by tenants.

**Demise**. To convey or grant property by will or lease.

**Deodand.** An object forfeited when it occasioned or was the instrument of someone's death.

**Deraign**. To refute by proof, especially on threat of judicial combat.

**Despite of the king.** Disrespect for the monarchy.

**Disseisin.** Dispossession.

**Distress or distrain**. To seize property, typically chattels, to force payment of rent, debt, or services. A grand distress seized both land and chattels.

***Distringas*.** A writ ordering distraint, the seizure of chattels or lands to satisfy or compel payment of debts and services or court appearances.

**Draw the plea or count**. Present a case before a court.

**Eloign**. To take to a distant place in order to conceal.

**Enfeoffed by charter**. Holding a fee by written document.

**Escheat.** Reversion of lands and goods to the king as forfeitures or feudal incidents.

**Escheator**. A royal official responsible for escheats.

**Essoin.** A legitimate excuse, such as illness, royal service, or pilgrimage, for non-appearance before a court.

**Estreat.** A portion of an original record ordering payment of a fine, made to aid in its collection.

**Exception.** An objection to the presentation of a suit (the count) for such reasons as insufficiency, variance from the writ, or want of capacity to sue.

**Exigent.** The process of securing someone's attendance in court by publishing a series of exactions (public demands). Failure to appear after the fourth exaction was punishable by outlawry.

**Eyre.** A circuit of justices commissioned to hear and judge pleas. An extension of the royal courts in Westminster.

**Farm**. Revenue collected by an authorized agent (often a sheriff) in return for payment of a fixed sum to the king by the agent.

**Fee, feoff, feoffment**. A fief, an estate held on condition of feudal service. Also called a tenement or a freehold.

**Ferling men**. Small landowners.

**Fee farm**. Land held of another in return for a fixed rent without homage or service.

**Fee tail (*feodum talliatum*).** An entailed gift of land (typically as *maritagium*) with the condition that collateral heirs were excluded from inheritance and that the land would revert to the donor on the failure of lineal heirs.

**Fisc**. The treasury or exchequer.

**Formedon** (Latin, *per formam doni*). A writ available to a tenant with rights to land by virtue of a gift in tail. Westminster II, chapter 1 calls formedon his writ of right, although the writ of right per se is limited to tenants in fee simple. There were three forms of formedon: in the descender, in the remainder, and in the reverter.

**Frank marriage (free marriage)**. Tenure of an estate by a man and wife, granted by a blood relative of the wife (typically her father) on condition of their marriage, to be held by the issue of the marriage to at least the fourth generation (the third heir) free of all feudal service.

***Frank-almoin.*** Tenure by which a religious corporation held land in perpetuity in exchange for prayers.

**Frankpledge.** See tithing.

**Free bench**. A manorial custom whereby a woman could retain tenure of her husband's lands after his death until she remarried.

**Grand Assize (Assize of Windsor)**. Trial by a jury of knights to determine possessory rights to a land tenure, introduced by Henry II in 1179 as a royal alternative to trial by judicial combat in a seignorial court.

**Gules (Lammas).** The commemoration of St. Peter's deliverance from prison and the blessing of the first harvest wheat, held on August 1.

**Heriot**. A levy upon the estate of a dead man by his feudal lord, originally in the form of the horse, weapons, and armor that had been lent the man to fight in the lord's defense.

**Hundred.** A subdivision of a county having its own court. Depending on size, a county could be divided into several dozens or several hundreds of these units, which were perhaps originally combinations of tithings.

**Hustings.** A city court equivalent to a county court. The highest court of London.

**Implead**. To sue.

***In capite.*** Land held directly from the king.

***Infangenetheof.*** Jurisdiction by a lord over his own men taken as thieves on his land.

**Inquest or inquisition**. A judicial investigation.

***In socage***. Land held by a tenant in return for rent or specified non-military services.

**Irrepleviable.** Not subject to replevin. Not capable of being replevied.

**Law-worthy men**. Men of good standing in the community.

**Lay fee.** A secular as opposed to an ecclesiastical estate.

**Mancuse**. Unit of coinage equal to thirty silver pennies.

***Mainour***. Stolen goods found in a thief's possession upon his arrest.

**Mainpast**. In effect a tithing comprised of a household's appropriate servants.

**Mainprise**. Sureties responsible for a man's good behavior or court appearance. Also called manucaption.

**Marshalsea**. The court of the king's household marshal. Also called the Verge and presided over by the High Steward.

**Mesne lord.** A lord, not a tenant-in-chief, who holds land from a superior lord and has his own tenants.

**Mesne tenant**. The tenant of a mesne lord.

**Messuage**. A dwelling with outbuildings and land.

***Mort d'ancestor***. A writ to recover an heir's lands that had been entered upon by a stranger.

**Murdrum**. A clandestine killing. The fine paid to the king by the hundred when it failed to produce the perpetrator.

**Neifty**. Villeinage. A writ pertaining to the status of a villein or serf.

***Novel disseisin***. A writ to recover lands of which the holder had been dispossessed.

**Oath helpers**. See compurgators.

**Parcener.** Co-heir.

**Pleas of *vee de naam*** (Latin, *de vetito namio*). Disputes concerning distraints which were settled in special courts (also *withernam*).

***Pone.*** A writ removing a case from a lesser court to a royal court in Westminster.

**Pontage**. A levy paid for the building and maintenance of bridges.

**Quarantine.** A forty day period, following a man's death, during which his widow could continue to occupy his chief messuage while awaiting the assignment of her dower.

***Quare impedit***. A writ claiming improper presentation of a benefice.

**Quindene**. The fourteenth day after a festival counted inclusively.

***Quod permittat***. A writ ordering a defendant to allow a plaintiff to correct a problem, typically to abate a nuisance.

***Quo warranto***. A writ or inquiry to determine by what right or whose authority land was held.

***Recordari facias***. A writ ordering a record of a case to be sent from a county court to Westminster for review.

**Reeve.** Manager of an estate and supervisor of the peasantry.

**Relevium**. Payment due a lord by a tenant upon inheriting an estate. One of the feudal incidents.

**Replevy.** To recover distrained property.

**Rerecounty**. Rear county court. A session of a county court held immediately after a full session. Sheriff's tourns were commonly rerecounty sessions.

**Scutage.** A tax paid in lieu of military service.

**Seisin**. Possession of land as a freehold by a feudal tenant.

**Sergeant-verger**. Sergeant-at-arms.

**Serjeanty tenure (serjeanties)**. Land held in return for designated service.

**Several right of pasture**. Sole and exclusive right to pasture.

**Servitude.** A right in someone's land, such as an easement or the right to take hay.

**Soke (sac and soke).** Suit or jurisdiction. The right to hold a court.

**Subinfeudation**. The practice by which tenants who held land from the king or a chief lord admitted someone to hold a portion of that land as their tenant, thereby creating a chain of tenures from the king down to those who actually occupied the land.

***Supersedeas.*** A writ ordering a stay in proceedings.

**Tenant**. One who occupies an estate in return for payments and services.

**Tenant in demesne**. One who actually occupied the land. Also called terre-tenant.

**Tenement**. An estate or freehold held from another.

**Tithing.** A group, originally comprised of ten men, obligated for the good behavior of one another. Also called frankpledge.

**Tithingman.** The head of a tithing and a petty constable by virtue of the position.

**Toll (toll and team).** A landowner's right to exact a payment for the sale or passage of goods and cattle on his land.

**Tourn.** A sheriff's bi-annual hundredal court. Also called view of frankpledge because the sheriff was obligated at the tourn to ensure that all males over the age of twelve were enrolled in a tithing (frankpledge) or mainpast.

**Tronage**. A duty paid for weighing coarse materials, such as wool, at the public *trona* (weighing beam).

**Turbary**. The right to cut turf or peat from the common land. The land from which the turf or peat is cut.

***Unde nihil habet***. A writ in an action for dower.

***Utfangenetheof***. The right to hold court on thieves subject to another's court taken on one's land.

***Veredictum.*** Verdict.

**Verge.** The area extending twelve miles in all directions from the king's court.

**Verger**. A caretaker.

**View of frankpledge**. The sheriff's review of each tithing in his county, conducted during the bi-annual sheriff's tourn, to ensure that it was fully enrolled with all appropriate males over the age of twelve.

**View of land**. An inquest held upon the site of a property dispute.

**Villein.** A serf.

**Vouch to warranty**. Claim seisin under a certain lord.

**Vouch to warranty by roll or record.** Claim seisin by referencing documentation.

**Vouchee**. A person vouched to warrant a title.

**Wage peace**. To secure persons who would stand surety that someone would keep the peace.

**Waive.** To declare a woman outside the law. Because women did not belong to tithings they did not take an oath to uphold the law and accordingly could not be outlawed.

**Wapentake.** Name given the hundred in some northern and midlands counties.

**Warranty**. A lord's guarantee of his men's tenancies against adverse claims.

**Waste**. Damage to or depletion of an estate by a guardian or tenant who held for life or a limited number of years.

**Writ of Entry.** A writ to recover land unlawfully occupied.

**Writ of indicavit**. A writ prohibiting an action in an ecclesiastical court when it belongs elsewhere.

**Writ of mesne**. A writ directed by an under-tenant against the mesne (intermediate) lord for restitution of restraints made against the under-tenant by a chief lord when the mesne lord had failed to perform his obligated services.

**Writ of Right**. The prototypical writ that initiated a process that at first led to judicial combat but then to jury trial after the institution of the grand assize.

## *Bibliography*

Many of the older books which contain the texts of statutes (*Curia Regis Rolls, The Statutes of the Realm,* many of the *Year Books*) are available on line at archive.org. The original documents themselves are in The National Archives (http://www.nationalarchives.gov.uk/), the London Metropolitan Archives (search under www.cityoflondon.gov.uk/), or available to view at the Anglo-American Legal Tradition website (http://aalt.law.uh.edu/).

Adams, Jenny. *Power Play: The Literature and Politics of Chess in the Late Middle Ages.* Philadelphia: University of Pennsylvania Press, 2006.

Alberigo, J. *et al.*, eds. *Conciliorum Oecumenicorum Decreta, editio altera.* Rome: Herder, 1962.

Amt, Emily, *Dialogus de Scaccario: The Dialogue of the Exchequer.* (Oxford Medieval Texts). Oxford: Oxford University Press, 2007.

Ashdowne, Richard and White, Carolinne, *Latin in Medieval Britain*, Oxford: Oxford University Press, 2017.

Baildon, William Paley. *Select Civil Pleas.* London: Bernard Quaritch for The Selden Society, 1890.

Baker, J. H. *An Introduction to English Legal History*, 4th edition New York: Oxford University Press, 2002.

Baker, J. H. *The Reports of Sir John Spelman,* 2 vols. London: The Selden Society, 1977.

Baker, Sir John, and Milsom, S. F. C., *Sources of English Legal History: Private Law to 1750.* 2nd edition. Oxford: Oxford University Press, 2010.

Bird, Ruth. *The Turbulent London of Richard II.* London: Longmans, Green and Co, 1949.

Bolland, William Craddock. *The Year Books, Lectures Delivered in the University of London at the Request of the Faculty of Laws*. Cambridge: Cambridge University Press, 1921.

## Bibliography


Brand, Paul. "Ireland and the Literature of the Early Common Law." *The Irish Jurist* n.s. (1981): 95-113, rpt. in Paul Brand, *The Making of the Common Law* (London: Hambledon, 1991), 445-64.

Brand, Paul. *The Origins of the English Legal Profession.* Oxford: Blackwell, 1992.

*Calendar of Close Rolls, Richard II.* London: His Majesty's Stationery Office, 1914.

Cannon, Christopher. "Raptus in the Chaumpaigne Release and a Newly Discovered Document Concerning the Life of Geoffrey Chaucer." *Speculum* 68 (Jan 1993), 74-94.

Chew, Helena M. and William Kellaway, eds. *London Assize of Nuisance, 1301-1431: A Calendar.* London: London Record Society, 1973.

Clanchy, M. T. *From Memory to Written Record: England 1066-1307.* Second Edition. London: Blackwell, 1993.

Crow, Martin M. and Clair C. Olson. *Chaucer Life-Records*. Oxford: The Clarendon Press, 1966.

*Curia Regis Rolls of the Reigns of Richard I and John, Preserved in the Public Records Office.* London: His Majesty's Stationery Office, 1922.

Douglas, David C. and George W. Greenaway, eds. and trans. English Historical Documents: 1042-1189.. London: Eyre and Spottiswoode, 1953.

Downer, L. J., ed. and trans., *Leges Henrici Primi.* Oxford: Clarendon Press, 1972.

Fisher, John. *John Gower: Moral Philosopher and Friend of Chaucer.* New York: New York University Press, 1964.

Fitzherbert, Anthony. *The New Natura Brevium of the Most Reverend Judge Mr. Anthony Fitz-Herbert.* London: R. Nutt and R. Gosling, 1730.

fitzNigel, Richard. *De Necessariis Observantiis Scaccarii Dialogus, Commonly called Dialogus de Scaccario,* ed. Arthur Hughes, C. G. Crump, and C. Johnson. Oxford: Clarendon Press, 1902.

fitzNigel, Richard; *Dialogus de Scaccario: the Course of the Exchequer,* ed. and trans. by Charles Johnson, with corrections by F. E. L. Carter and D. E. Greenway. Oxford: Clarendon Press, 1983.

Giancarlo, Matthew. "The Septvauns Affair, Purchase, and Parliament in John Gower's *Mirour de l'Omme.*" *Viator* 36 (2005), 435-464.

Hall, G. D. G. (ed. and trans.), *Tractatus de Legibus et Consuetudinibus regni Anglie qui Glanvilla vocatur (The treatise on the laws and customs of the realm of England commonly called Glanvill.* Oxford: Clarendon Press, 1985.

Hanna, Ralph. *London Literature, 1300-1380.* Cambridge: Cambridge University Press, 2005.

Hastings, Margaret; "Select Documents XXIX" in *Bulletin of the Institute of Historical Research,* 13 1936.

Hillaby, Alexander *et al.*, eds. *The Statutes of the Realm.* 10 vols. London: Dawsons of Pall Mall, 1810-28.

Hillaby, Joe and Caroline. *The Palgrave Dictionary of Medieval Anglo-Jewish History.* New York: Palgrave Macmillan, 2013.

Hunnisett, R. F. *The Medieval Coroner.* Cambridge: Cambridge University Press, 1961.

Ingulph, Abbot of Croyland/Crowland. *Historiarum Liber 1*, in *Rerum Anglicarum Scriptores post Bedam Praecipui*. London: G. Bishop, R. Nuberie, et R. Barker Typographi Regii Deputati, 1596.

Kantorowicz, Hermann. *Bractonian Problems.* Glasgow: Jackson and Son, 1941.

Kiralfy, Albert; "The Humber Ferryman and the Action on the Case" *The Cambridge Law Journal,* II no. 3 (1953), 421-4.

Kiralfy, A. K.; *The Action on the Case*. London: Sweet & Maxwell, 1951.

Luders, Alexander *et al.*, eds. *The Statutes of the Realm*, 10 vols. London: Dawsons of Pall Mall, 1810-28.

LBL; "'Probatio Aetatis of William de Septvans." *Archaeologia Cantiana* I (1858), 124-136.

Langbein, John H.; R. L. Lerner, and B. P. Smith. *History of the Common Law: The Development of Anglo-American Legal Institutions.* New York: Aspen Publishers, 2009.

Latham, R. E. *Revised Medieval Latin Word-List from British and Irish Sources, with Supplement.* Oxford: Oxford University Press, 1980. There is an on-line edition.

Liebermann, Felix. *Die Gesetze der Angelsachsen*. 2 vols. Halle: Niemayer, 1906.

Liebermann, Felix. *Einleitung in den Dialogus de Scaccario.* Göttingen: Peppmüller, 1875.

Madox, Thomas. *History and Antiquities of the Exchequer of the Kings of England.* London: J. Matthews, 1711.

Manley, J. M.; "Lok-Sounday." *Harvard Studies and Notes in Philology and Literature* I (1892), 88-108.

Milsom, S. F. C. *Historical Foundations of the Common Law.* London: Butterworth, 1969.

Milsom, S. F. C. *The Legal Framework of English Feudalism.* Cambridge: Cambridge University Press, 1976.

Page, William, ed. *A History of the County of Norfolk.* 2 vols. London: A. Constable, 1906.

Palgrave, Sir Francis. *Rotuli Curiae Regis: Rolls and Records of the Court held before the King's Justiciars or Justices.* 2 vols. London; Commissioners on the Public Records of the Kingdom, 1835.

Pickering, Danby, et al., eds. *The Statutes at Large.* 46 vols. Cambridge: J. Bentham, 1762-1807.

Pike, L. Owen. "An Action at Law in the Reign of Edward III: The Report and the Record." *Harvard Law Review* 7 (Dec. 25, 1893), 266-80.

Pike, Luke Owen. *Year Books of the Reign of King Edward the Third. Year XV*. London: Her Majesty's Stationery Office, 1891.

Plucknett, T. F. T. *Early English Legal Literature*. Cambridge: Cambridge University Press, 1958.

Plucknett, T. F. T. *Legislation of Edward I.* Oxford: Clarendon Press, 1949; rept. Oxford: Oxford University Press, 1962.

Plucknett, Theodore F. T. *Statutes & Their Interpretation in the First Half of the Fourteenth Century.* Cambridge: Cambridge University Press, 1922; rept. Clark, NJ: Lawbook Exchange, 2010.

Plucknett, Theodore F. T. *A Concise History of the Common Law*. Fifth Edition. New York: Little, Brown, and Co., 1956; rept. Indianapolis, IN: Liberty Fund, 2010.

Plucknett, Theodore F. T."Case and the Statute of Westminster II." *Columbia Law Review* 31 (May 1931), 778-99.

Pollock, Frederick and Frederic William Maitland. *The History of the English Law.* 2 vols. Cambridge: University Press, 1898.

Poole, Reginald Lane. *The Exchequer in the Twelfth Century.* Oxford: Clarendon Press, 1912.

Richardson, H. G. "Glanville Continued." *The Law Quarterly Review* 54 (1938), 381-99.

Richardson, H. G. and G. O. Sayles *The Governance of Mediaeval England from the Conquest to Magna Carta.* Edinburgh: Edinburgh University Press, 1963.

Richardson, H. G. and George Sayles. "The Early Statutes." *The Law Quarterly Review* (1934), 201-3, 540-71.

Rothwell, Harry, ed. *English Historical Documents 1189-1327.* New York: Oxford University Press, 1975.

Ruffhead, Owen. *Statutes at Large: from Magna Charta to the End of the Reign of King Henry the Sixth.* 9 vols. London: M. Baskett, 1763-65.

Schroeder, H. J. *Disciplinary Decrees of the General Councils.* St. Louis and London: B. Herder Book Co., 1937.

Strachey, John, et al. *Rotuli Parliamentorum ut et Petitiones et Placita in Parliamento Tempore Edwardi R. III.* 2 vols. London. 1832.

Stubbs, William. *Select Charters and Other Illustrations of English Constitutional History*. Ninth edition, ed. H. W. C. Davis. Oxford:

Clarendon Press, 1913; paperback reprint, Cambridge: Cambridge University Press, 2012.

Sutherland, Donald W. *The Assize of Novel Disseisin.* Oxford: Clarendon Press, 1973.

Thorne, Samuel E., trans., and George Woodbine, ed., *Bracton on the Laws and Customs of England*. 4 vols. Cambridge, MA: Belknap Press, 1968-77.

Turner, Ralph V. *The English Judiciary in the Age of Glanvill and Bracton, c. 1176-1239.* Cambridge: Cambridge University Press, 1985.

Van Caenegem, R. C. *The Birth of the English Common Law.* Second Edition. Cambridge: Cambridge University Press, 1988.

Woodbine, George E. *Four Thirteenth Century Law Tracts: A Thesis.* New Haven, CT: Yale University Press, 1910.

Wright, Andrew and Charles Trice Martin. *Court-Hand Restored or, The Student's Assistant in Reading Old Deeds, Charters, Records, etc.* London: Reeves & Turner, 1879.

# SOPHRON EDITOR

## *CATALOGUE 2018*

**Caesar's Commentaries: The Complete Gallic War. Revised.** 8vo., xxiv,507 pp.; Introduction, Latin text of all eight Books, Notes, Companion, Grammar, Exercises, Vocabularies, 17 Maps, illus., all based on Francis W. Kelsey.
ISBN 978-0-985081119 *$19.95*

**Virgil's Aeneid Complete, Books I-XII.** With Introduction, Latin text and Notes by W. D. Williams. 8vo., xxviii, 739 pp., 2 maps, Glossary, Index.
ISBN 978-0-985081164 *$27.95*

***Praxis Grammatica.* A New Edition.** John Harmer. 12 mo., xviii,116 pp.; Introduction by Mark Riley. ISBN 978-0-985081126 *$3.95*

**The *Other* Trojan War. Dictys & Dares.** 12 mo., xxii,397 pp.; Latin/English Parallel Texts; Frazer's Introduction & Notes, Index ISBN 978-0-98508115 $14.95

**The Stoic's Bible: *a Florilegium for the Good Life.*** *Third Edition.* Giles Laurén. 8vo., xxxiv,694 pp., 3 illus., Introduction, Tables, Bibliography.ISBN 978-0-985081-0-2. $24.95

**Why Don't We Learn from History?** B. H. Liddell Hart. 12 mo., 126 pp.
ISBN 978-0-985081133 $4.95

**Quintilian. Institutionis Oratoriae. Liber Decimus.** Text, Notes & Introductory Essays by W. Peterson. Foreword by James J. Murphy. 8vo., cvi,291 pp., Harleian MS facsimile, Indexes. ISBN 978-0-985081-8-8 *$19.95*

**Schools of Hellas.** Kenneth Freeman. 12 mo., xxi,279 pp., illus., Indexes.

ISBN 978-0-985081-9-5 *$14.95*

**Cornelius Nepos Vitae.** 12 mo., xviii,424 pp., 3 maps, illus., notes, exercises, & vocabulary by John Rolfe. ISBN 978-0-985081-7-1 *$14.95*

**Greek Reader.** Mark Riley. Based on the selection of Wilamowitz-Moellendorff, with additions, notes and a vocabulary. 12 mo., ix,368 pp., maps & illus.
ISBN 978-0-9897836-0-6 *$12.95*

**Quintilian: *A Roman Educator and his Quest for the Perfect Orator.*** *Revised Edition.* George A. Kennedy. 12 mo., xviii,184 pp. biblio., Index.
SBN 978-0-9897836-1-3 *$9.95*

**Diodorus Siculus. I.** The Library of History in Forty Books. Vol. I. (books I-XIV). 8vo., xxxiii, 701 pp., illus. ISBN 978-0-9897836-2-0 *$25.00*

**Diodorus Siculus. II.** The Library of History in Forty Books. Vol. II. (books XV-XL). 8vo., xviii,610 pp., illus. ISBN 978-0-9897836-3-7 *$25.00*

***La Dialectique.*** Paul Foulquié, in-8,. 160 pp.
ISBN 978-1-4954688-3-4 *$6.95*

**Horace. The Complete Horace.** 8vo., xli,620 pp, 2 illus., introduction & notes after Bennett & Rolfe. ISBN 978-0-9897836-4-4 *$19.95*

**Grote's Legendary Greece. The Pre-history.** Being Chapters 1-XXI of A History of Greece, Part I., 4th. Edit. Complete, ***without footnotes***, frontis. port., 5 maps, lvii,454 pp edited by G. Laurén. ISBN 978-0-9897836-6-8 *$17.50*

**Grote's History of Greece I.** Being Chapters I-XL of A History of Greece, Part II., 4th Ed. Complete ***without footnotes***, port., 9 illus., xii,705 pp. edited by G. Laurén.
ISBN 978-0-9897836-7-5 *$25.00*

**Grote's History of Greece II.** Being Chapters XLI-LXII of A History of Greece, Part II., 4th Ed. Complete ***without footnotes***, 8 illus., vii,802 pp. edited by G. Laurén.
ISBN 978-0-9897836-7-5 *$25.00*

**Grote's History of Greece III.** Being Chapters LXIII-LXXXI of A History of Greece, Part II., 4th Ed. Complete ***without footnotes***, 8 illus., vii,794 pp. edited by G. Laurén.
ISBN 978-0-9897836-7-5 *$25.00*

**Grote's History of Greece IV.** Being Chapters LXXXII-XCVIII of A History of Greece, Part II., 4th Ed. Complete ***without footnotes***, 5 illus., vii,674 pp. edited by G. Laurén.
ISBN 978-0-9897836-7-5 *$25.00*

**Jebb's Isocrates.** Edited with Intro. by Edward Schiappa, David Timmerman, G. Laurén; 12 mo., cxxv, 430 pp., 3 illus., notes, Greek Selections, biblio.
ISBN 978-0-9897836-5-1 *$17.50*

**The Neo-Latin Reader.** *Selections from Petrarch to Rimbaud.* Mark Riley. illus., intro., notes, refs., 12 mo., xvii, 381 pp. ISBN 978-0-9897836-8-2 *$12.95*

**The Mathematical Theory of Bridge.** 134 Probability tables, their uses, simple formulas, applications & about 4000 probabilities. Émile Borel & André Chéron. Trans. by Alec Traub. Revised & corrected by G. Laurén. 8vo., xxviii,474 pp., illus., tables, notes. (**Masterpoint Press**) ISBN 978-1-77140-181-4 *$60.00*

**Emma the Porter.** [Imma Portatrix] by Frederic Herman Flayder. Newly edited and translated by Mark Riley. 8vo., xxx,185 pp., intro., illus., notes.
ISBN 978-0-9991401-0-9 *$12.00*

**Justin. Epitome of the Philippic Histories**. Trans. J. S. Watson. Ed. G. Laurén. 12 mo., 500 pp., chron., illus., map, notes. ISBN 978-0-9991-1-6 $17.50

**Dionysius of Halicarnassus. *The Roman Antiquites* I.** Books 1-6.54. Trans. Earn. Cary. Ed. G. Laurén. 8vo., xxx,588 pp., frontis., Intro., notes.
ISBN 978-0-9991401-2-3 $25.00

**Dionysius of Halicarnassus. *The Roman Antiquites* II.** Books 6.55-13. Trans. Earn. Cary. Ed. G. Laurén. 8vo., vi, 630 pp., frontis., Intro., notes.
ISBN 978-0-9991401-3-0 $25.00

**A Latin Reader for the Study of Early English Law**. (***Parallel texts***) Robert J. Meindl & Mark T. Riley. 8vo., x, 661 pp., frontis., 10 illus, Intro., notes, biblio., glossary
ISBN 978-0-9991401-5-4 $25.00

**STRABO The Geography in Two Volumes, I.** Books I - IX ch2. Trans. by Jones & Sterrett; 8vo., xxxv,564 pp., 9 maps, 5 figs., notes, biblio.
ISBN 978-0-9991401-6-1 $25.00

**STRABO The Geography in Two Volumes, II.** Books IX ch3 - XVII. Trans. by Jones & Sterrett; 8vo., 522 pp., 6 maps, notes. ISBN 978-0-9991401-7-8 $25.00

Available from SOPHRON EDITOR (Amazon worldwide)

In preparation:

**Roman de Troie.** Benoît de Sainte Maure. Trans. by George Kennedy.

**Jordannes**. *The Gothic History*. Mierow trans.

**Origins of Western Institutions**: A Source Book.

Giles Laurén, 4020 Grande Vista Blvd. #114, St. Augustine, FL 32084
enasophron@gmail.com

Made in the USA
Monee, IL
19 October 2026

66039186R00380